BARRY

EICHENGREEN

Hall of Mirrors

The Great Depression, the

Great Recession, and the

Uses—and Misuses—of

History

OXFORD
UNIVERSITY PRESS

OXFORD
UNIVERSITY PRESS

Oxford University Press is a department of the University of
Oxford. It furthers the University's objective of excellence in research,
scholarship, and education by publishing worldwide.

Oxford   New York
Auckland   Cape Town   Dar es Salaam   Hong Kong   Karachi
Kuala Lumpur   Madrid   Melbourne   Mexico City   Nairobi
New Delhi   Shanghai   Taipei   Toronto

With offices in
Argentina   Austria   Brazil   Chile   Czech Republic   France   Greece
Guatemala   Hungary   Italy   Japan   Poland   Portugal   Singapore
South Korea   Switzerland   Thailand   Turkey   Ukraine   Vietnam

Oxford is a registered trademark of Oxford University Press
in the UK and certain other countries.

Published in the United States of America by
Oxford University Press
198 Madison Avenue, New York, NY 10016

Library of Congress Cataloging-in-Publication Data
Eichengreen, Barry J.
Hall of mirrors : the Great Depression, the great recession, and the uses—and misuses—of history /
Barry Eichengreen.
     pages cm
Summary: "A brilliantly conceived dual-track account of the two greatest economic crises of the last
century and their consequences"— Provided by publisher.
ISBN 978–0–19–939200–1 (hardback)
  1. Depressions—1929.   2. Economic policy—History—20th century.   3. Global Financial Crisis,
2008–2009.   4. Economic policy—History—21st century.   I. Title.
HB3717.1929 .E37 2015
330.9'043—dc23
2014012098

9 8 7 6 5 4 3 2
Printed in the United States of America
on acid-free paper

Hall of Mirrors

CONTENTS

Introduction

THIS IS A book about financial crises. It is about the events that bring them about. It is about why governments and markets respond as they do. And it is about the consequences.

It is about the Great Recession of 2008–09 and the Great Depression of 1929–1933, the two great financial crises of our age. That there are parallels between these episodes is well known, not least in policy circles. Many commentators have noted how conventional wisdom about the earlier episode, what is referred to as "the lessons of the Great Depression," shaped the response to the events of 2008–09. Because those events so conspicuously resembled the 1930s, that earlier episode provided an obvious lens through which to view them. The tendency to view the crisis from the perspective of the 1930s was all the greater for the fact that key policy makers, from Ben Bernanke, chairman of the Board of Governors of the Federal Reserve System, to Christina Romer, head of President Barack Obama's Council of Economic Advisors, had studied that history in their earlier academic incarnations.

As a result of the lessons policy makers drew, they prevented the worst. After the failure of Lehman Brothers pushed the global financial system to the brink, they asserted that no additional systemically significant financial institution would be allowed to fail and then delivered on that promise. They resisted the beggar-thy-neighbor tariffs and controls that caused the collapse of international transactions in the 1930s. Governments ramped up public spending and cut taxes. Central banks flooded financial markets with liquidity and extended credit to one another in an unprecedented display of solidarity.

In doing so, their decisions were powerfully informed by received wisdom about the mistakes of their predecessors. Governments in the 1930s succumbed to the protectionist temptation. Guided by outdated economic dogma, they cut public expenditure at the worst possible time and perversely sought to balance budgets when stimulus spending was needed. It made no difference whether the officials in question spoke English, like Herbert Hoover, or German, like Heinrich Brüning. Not only did their measures worsen the slump, but they failed even to restore confidence in the public finances.

Central bankers, for their part, were in thrall to the real bills doctrine, the idea that they should provide only as much credit as was required for the legitimate needs of business. They supplied more credit when business was expanding and less when it slumped, accentuating booms and busts. Neglecting their responsibility for financial stability, they failed to intervene as lenders of last resort. The result was cascading bank failures, starving business of credit. Prices were allowed to collapse, rendering debts unmanageable. In their influential monetary history, Milton Friedman and Anna Schwartz laid the blame for this disaster squarely on the doorstep of central banks. Inept central bank policy more than any other factor, they concluded, was responsible for the economic catastrophe of the 1930s.

In 2008, heeding the lessons of this earlier episode, policy makers vowed to do better. If the failure of their predecessors to cut interest rates and flood financial markets with liquidity had consigned the world to deflation and depression, then they would respond this time with expansionary monetary and financial policies. If the failure of their predecessors to stem banking panics had precipitated a financial collapse, then they would deal decisively with the banks. If efforts to balance budgets had worsened the earlier slump, then they would apply fiscal stimulus. If the collapse of international cooperation had aggravated the world's problems, then they would use personal contacts and multilateral institutions to ensure that policy was adequately coordinated this time.

As a result of this very different response, unemployment in the United States peaked at 10 percent in 2010. Though this was still disturbingly high, it was far below the catastrophic 25 percent scaled in the Great Depression. Failed banks numbered in the hundreds, not the thousands. Financial dislocations were widespread, but the complete and utter collapse of financial markets seen in the 1930s was successfully averted.

And what was true of the United States was true also of other countries. Every unhappy country is unhappy in its own way, and there were varying degrees of economic unhappiness starting in 2008. But, a few ill-starred European countries notwithstanding, that unhappiness did not rise to the level of the 1930s. Because policy was better, the decline in output and employment, the social dislocations, and the pain and suffering were less.

Or so it is said.

Unfortunately, this happy narrative is too easy. It is hard to square with the failure to anticipate the risks. Queen Elizabeth II famously posed the question on a visit to the London School of Economics in 2008: "Why did no one see it coming?" she asked the assembled experts. Six months later a group of eminent economists sent the queen a letter apologizing for their "failure of collective imagination."

It is not as if parallels were lacking. The 1920s saw a real estate boom in Florida and in the commercial property markets of the Northeast and North Central regions of the United States to which early-twenty-first-century property booms in the United States, Ireland, and Spain bore a strong family resemblance. There was the sharp increase in stock valuations, reflecting heady expectations of the future profitability of trendy information-technology companies, Radio Company of America (RCA) in the 1920s, Apple and Google eighty years later. There was the explosive growth of credit fueling property and asset-market booms. There was the development of a growing range of what might politely be called dubious practices in the banking and financial system. There was the role of the gold standard after 1925 and the euro system after 1999 in amplifying and transmitting disturbances.

Above all, there was the naïve belief that policy had tamed the cycle. In the 1920s it was said that the world had entered a "New Era" of economic stability with the establishment of the Federal Reserve System and independent central banks in other countries. The period leading up to the Great Recession was similarly thought to constitute a "Great Moderation" in which business cycle volatility was diminished by advances in central banking. Encouraged by the belief that sharp swings in economic activity were no more, commercial banks used more leverage. Investors took more risk.

One might think that anyone passingly familiar with the Great Depression would have seen the parallels and their implications. Some warnings there indeed were, but they were few and less than fully accurate. Robert Shiller of Yale, who had studied 1920s property markets, pointed now to the development of what looked to all appearances like a full-blown housing bubble. But not even Shiller anticipated the catastrophic consequences of its collapse. Nouriel Roubini, who had taken at least one course on the history of the Great Depression in his graduate student days at Harvard, pointed to the risks posed by a gaping US current account deficit and the accumulation of US dollar debts abroad. But the crisis of which Roubini warned, namely a dollar crash, was not the crisis that followed.

Specialists in the history and economics of the Great Depression, it should be acknowledged, did no better. And the economics profession as a whole issued only muted warnings that disaster lay ahead. It bought into the gospel of the Great Moderation. Policy makers lulled into complacency by self-satisfaction and positive reinforcement by the markets did nothing to prepare for the impending calamity.

It may be asking too much to expect analysts to forecast financial crises. Crises result not just from credit booms, asset bubbles, and the wrongheaded belief that financial-market participants have learned to safely manage risk, but also from contingencies no one can predict, whether the failure of a consortium of German banks to rescue Danatbank, a German financial institution, in 1931; or the refusal of the UK Financial Services Authority to allow Barclays to bid for Lehman Brothers over a fateful weekend in 2008. Financial crises, like World War I, can arise from the unanticipated repercussions of idiosyncratic decisions taken without full awareness of their ramifications. They result not just from systemic factors but from human agency—from the vaulting ambition and questionable scruples of a Rogers Caldwell, who in the 1920s fashioned himself the J. P. Morgan of the South; or an Adam Applegarth, the sporty, hypercon-fident young banker who launched Northern Rock, a formerly obscure British building society, onto an unsustainable expansion path. Their actions not only brought down the firms they headed but undercut the very foundations of the financial system. Similarly, had Benjamin Strong, the über-competent gover-nor of the Federal Reserve Bank of New York, not passed away in 1928, or Jean-Claude Trichet not become president of the European Central Bank as the result of a Franco-German bargain in 1999, the conduct of monetary policy might have been different. Specifically, it might have been better.

It is similarly disturbing in light of the progressive narrative that policy was not more successful at limiting financial distress, containing the rise in unem-ployment, and supporting a vigorous recovery. The subprime mortgage market collapsed in mid-2007, and the US recession commenced in December of that year. Yet few if any observers anticipated how severely the financial system would be disrupted. They did not foresee how badly output and employment would be affected. The Great Depression was first and foremost a banking and financial crisis, but memories of that experience did not sufficiently inform and invigorate policy for officials to prevent another banking and financial crisis.

It may be that the very belief that bank failures were the key event trans-forming a garden-variety recession into the Great Depression caused policy makers to mistakenly focus on commercial banks at the expense of the so-called shadow banking system of hedge funds, money market funds, and commercial paper issuers. The Basel Accord setting capital standards for internationally active financial institutions focused on commercial banks.[1] Regulation gener-ally focused on commercial banks.

Moreover, deposit insurance was limited to commercial banks. Because the runs by retail depositors that destabilized banks in the 1930s led to creation of federal deposit insurance, there was the belief that depositor flight was no longer a threat. Everyone had seen *It's a Wonderful Life* and assumed that a modern-day banker would never find himself in George Bailey's position. But $100,000 of deposit insurance was cold comfort for businesses whose balances were many times that large. It did nothing to stabilize banks that did not rely on deposits but instead borrowed large sums from other banks.

Nor did deposit insurance create confidence in hedge funds, money market funds, and special purpose investment vehicles. It did nothing to prevent a 1930s-like panic in these new and novel parts of the financial system. Insofar as the history of the Great Depression was the frame through which policy makers viewed events, it caused them to overlook how profoundly the financial system had changed. At the same time that it pointed them to real and present dangers, it allowed them to overlook others.

Specifically, it allowed them to miss the consequences of permitting Lehman Brothers to fail. Lehman was not a commercial bank; it did not take deposits. It was thus possible to imagine that its failure might not precipitate a run on other banks like the runs triggered by the failure of Henry Ford's Guardian Group of banks in 1933.

But this misunderstood the nature of the shadow banking system. Money market mutual funds held Lehman's short-term notes. When Lehman failed, those money funds suffered runs by frightened shareholders. This in turn precipitated runs by large investors on the money funds' investment-bank parents. And this then led to the collapse of already teetering securitization markets.

Officials from US Treasury Secretary Henry Paulson on down would insist that they had lacked the authority to lend to an insolvent institution like Lehman Brothers, as well as a mechanism to smoothly shut it down. Uncontrolled bankruptcy was the only option. But it is not as if Lehman's troubles were a surprise. Regulators had been watching it ever since the rescue of Bear Stearns, another important member of the investment-banking fraternity, six months earlier. The failure to endow Treasury and the Fed with the authority to deal with the insolvency of a nonbank financial institution was the single most important policy failure of the crisis. In 1932 the Reconstruction Finance Corporation, created to resolve the country's banking problems, similarly lacked the authority to inject capital into an insolvent financial institution, a constraint that was relaxed only when the 1933 crisis hit and Congress passed the Emergency Banking Act. Chairman Bernanke and others may have been aware of this history, but any such awareness did not now change the course of events.

In part, this policy failure was informed by the belief, shaped and distorted equally by the lessons of history, that the consequences of a Lehman Brothers failure could be contained. But it also reflected officials' concern with moral hazard—with the idea that more rescues would encourage more risk taking.[2] Owing to their rescue of Bear Stearns, policy makers were already being raked over the coals for creating moral hazard. Allowing Lehman Brothers to fail was a way of acknowledging that criticism. Liquidationism—the idea, in the words of President Hoover's Treasury Secretary Andrew Mellon, that failure was necessary to "purge the rottenness out of the system"—may have fallen out of favor owing to its disastrous consequences in the 1930s, but in this subtler incarnation it was not entirely absent.

Finally, policy makers were aware that any effort to endow Treasury and the Fed with additional powers would be resisted by a Congress weary of bailouts. It would be opposed by a Republican Party hostile to government intervention. Ultimately, a full-blown banking and financial crisis would be needed, as in 1933, for the politicians to act.

It was at this point, after Lehman Brothers, that policy makers realized they were on the verge of another depression. The leaders of the advanced industrial countries issued their joint statement that no systematically significant financial institution would be allowed to fail. A reluctant US Congress passed the Troubled Asset Relief Program to aid the banking and financial system. One after another, governments took steps to provide capital and liquidity to distressed financial institutions. Massive programs of fiscal stimulus were unveiled. Central banks flooded financial markets with liquidity.

Yet the results of these policy initiatives were decidedly less than triumphal. Postcrisis recovery in the United States was lethargic; it disappointed by any measure. Europe did even worse, experiencing a double-dip recession and renewed crisis starting in 2010. This was not the successful stabilization and vigorous recovery promised by those who had learned the lessons of history.

Some argued that recovery from a downturn caused by a financial crisis is necessarily slower than recovery from a garden-variety recession.[3] Growth is slowed by the damage to the financial system. Banks, anxious to repair their balance sheets, hesitate to lend. Households and firms, having accumulated unsustainably heavy debts, restrain their spending as they attempt to reduce that debt to a manageable level.

But working in the other direction is the fact that government can step up. It can lend when banks don't. It can substitute its spending for that of households and firms. It can provide liquidity without risking inflation given the slack in the economy. It can run budget deficits without creating debt problems, given the low interest rates prevailing in subdued economic conditions.

And it can keep doing so until households, banks, and firms are ready to resume business as usual. Between 1933 and 1937, real GDP in the United States grew at an annual rate of 8 percent, even though government did only passably well at these tasks. Between 2010 and 2013, by comparison, GDP growth averaged just 2 percent. This is not to suggest that growth after 2009 could have been four times as fast. How fast you can rise depends also on how far you fall in the preceding period. Still, the US and world economies could have done better.

Why they didn't is no mystery. Starting in 2010 the United States and Europe took a hard right turn toward austerity. Spending under the American Recovery and Reinvestment Act, Obama's stimulus program, peaked in fiscal year 2010 before heading steadily downward. In the summer of 2011 the Obama administration and Congress then agreed to $1.2 trillion of spending cuts.[4] In 2013 came expiry of the Bush tax cuts for top incomes, the end of the reduction in employee contributions to the Social Security Trust Fund, and the Sequester, the across-the-board 8½ percent cut in federal government spending. All this took a big bite out of aggregate demand and economic growth.

In Europe the turn toward austerity was even more dramatic. In Greece, where spending was out of control, a major dose of austerity was clearly required. But the adjustment program on which the country embarked starting in 2010 under the watchful eyes of the European Commission, the European Central Bank, and the International Monetary Fund was unprecedented in scope and severity. It required the Greek government to reduce spending and raise taxes by an extraordinary 11 percent of GDP over three years—in effect, to eliminate more than a tenth of all spending in the Greek economy. The euro area as a whole cut budget deficits modestly in 2011 and then sharply in 2012, despite the fact that it was back in recession and other forms of spending were stagnant. Even the United Kingdom, which had the flexibility afforded by a national currency and a national central bank, embarked on an ambitious program of fiscal consolidation, cutting government spending and raising taxes by a cumulative 5 percent of GDP.

Central banks, having taken a variety of exceptional steps in the crisis, were similarly anxious to resume business as usual. The Fed undertook three rounds of quantitative easing—multimonth purchases of treasury bonds and mortgage-backed securities—but hesitated to ramp up those purchases further despite an inflation rate that repeatedly undershot its 2 percent target and growth that continued to disappoint. Talk of tapering those purchases in the spring and summer of 2013 led to sharply higher interest rates. This was not medicine one would prescribe for an economy struggling to grow by 2 percent.

And if the Fed was reluctant to do more, the ECB was anxious to do less. In 2010 it prematurely concluded that recovery was at hand and started phasing out its nonstandard measures. In the spring and summer of 2011 it raised interest rates twice. Anyone seeking to understand why the European economy failed to recover and instead dipped a second time need look no further.

What lessons, historical or otherwise, informed this extraordinary turn of events? For central banks there was, as always, deeply ingrained fear of inflation. The fear was nowhere deeper than in Germany, given memories of hyperinflation in 1923. German fear now translated into European policy, given the Bundesbank-like structure of the ECB and the desire of its French president, Jean-Claude Trichet, to demonstrate that he was as dedicated an inflation fighter as any German.

The United States did not experience hyperinflation in the 1920s, nor at any other time, but this did not prevent overwrought commentators from warning that Weimar was right around the corner. The lessons of the 1930s—that when the economy is in near-depression conditions with interest rates at zero and ample excess capacity, the central bank can expand its balance sheet without igniting inflation—were lost from view. Sophisticated central bankers, like Chairman Bernanke and at least some of his colleagues on the Federal Open Market Committee, knew better. But there is no doubt they were influenced by the criticism. The more hysterical the commentary, the more loudly Congress accused the Fed of debasing the currency, and the more Fed governors then feared for their independence. This rendered them anxious to start shrinking the Fed's balance sheet toward a normal level before there was anything resembling a normal economy.

This criticism was more intense to the extent that unconventional policies had gotten central bankers into places they didn't belong, such as the market for mortgage-backed securities. The longer the Fed continued to purchase mortgage-backed securities—and it continued into 2014—the more the institution's critics complained that policy was setting the stage for another housing bubble, and ultimately another crash. This fear became a totem for the worry that low interest rates were encouraging excessive risk taking. This, of course, was precisely the same concern over moral hazard that contributed to the disastrous decision not to rescue Lehman Brothers.

In the case of the ECB, the moral-hazard worry centered not on markets but on politicians. For the central bank to do more to support growth would just relieve the pressure on governments, allowing excesses to persist, reforms to lag, and risks to accumulate. The ECB permitted itself to be backed into a corner where it was the enforcer of fiscal consolidation and structural reform. In its role as enforcer, economic growth became the enemy.

In the case of fiscal policy, the argument for continued stimulus was weakened by its failure to deliver everything promised, whether because politicians were prone to overpromising or because the shock to the economy was even worse than was understood at the time. There was the failure to distinguish how bad conditions were from how much worse they would have been without the policy. There was the failure to distinguish the need for medium-term consolidation from the need to support demand in the short run. There was the failure to distinguish the case for fiscal consolidation in countries with gaping deficits and debts, like Greece, from the situation of countries with the space to do more, like Germany and the United States. Thus a range of factors came together. The one thing they had in common was failure.

Much may have been learned about the case for fiscal stimulus from John Maynard Keynes and other scholars whose work was stimulated by the Great Depression, but equally much was forgotten. Where Keynes relied mainly on narrative methods, his followers used mathematics to verify their intuitions. Eventually those mathematics took on a life of their own. Latter-day academics embraced models of representative, rational, forward-looking agents in part for their tractability, in part for their elegance. In models of rational agents efficiently maximizing everything, little can go wrong unless government makes it go wrong. This modeling mind-set pointed to government meddling as the cause of the crisis and slow recovery alike. Interference by the government-sponsored entities Freddie Mac and Fannie Mae had been responsible for the excesses in the mortgage market that precipitated the crisis, just as uncertainty about government policy was the explanation for the slow recovery.

It must similarly be, the intuition followed, that fiscal stimulus, as yet another form of government meddling, could do no good. Economists advancing these ideas invoked models in which households, knowing that additional deficit spending now would have to be paid for by higher taxes later, reduce their spending accordingly.[5] This logic suggested that the effects of temporary fiscal stimulus might be less than promised by their Keynesian proponents. But not even these models implied that temporary stimulus would have no effects.[6] Still, freshwater economists (so called because of their tendency to cluster around the Great Lakes) were quick to leap to this conclusion. George Bernard Shaw's aphorism that you can lay all the economists end to end and they still can't reach a conclusion was nowhere more apposite. This inability to agree on even the most basic tenets of economic policy undermined the intellectual case for an effective response.

In much of Europe, in any case, Keynesian theorizing never took hold. The out-of-control budgets and inflation of Weimar left German economists skeptical of deficit spending and led them to argue instead that government should focus on strengthening contract enforcement and fostering competition.[7] This was a more sophisticated position than the "government bad, private sector good" message that bubbled up from the Great Lakes. But it too sat uneasily with the case for stimulus spending and encouraged an early shift to austerity.

If theory of dubious relevance played a role in this policy shift, then so did empirical analysis of dubious generality. Two American economists presented evidence that growth tends to slow when public debt reaches 90 percent of GDP.[8] No one disputed that heavy debts weigh on economic growth, but the idea that 90 percent was a trip wire where performance deteriorates sharply was quickly challenged. Yet the fact that US and British public debts were approaching this red line and that the Eurozone's debt/GDP ratio exceeded it made it expedient to cite the assertion in support of a quick turn to austerity. What he mischaracterized as the "90 percent rule" was invoked by European Commissioner for Economic and Monetary Affairs Olli Rehn, for example, when justifying the policies of the European Union.

Two Italian economists meanwhile presented evidence that austerity, especially if resulting from public spending cuts rather than tax increases, could have contra-Keynesian expansionary effects.[9] Such results were plausible for an economy like Italy in the 1980s and 1990s, with enormous debts, high interest rates, and heavy taxes. In these circumstances, public spending cuts could bolster confidence, and those confidence effects could boost investment. But however plausible such predictions for Italy, they were not plausible for countries with lower debts. They were not plausible when interest rates were near zero. They were not plausible when the country in question, as a member of the Eurozone, lacked a national currency to devalue and could not readily substitute exports for domestic demand. And they were not plausible when the entire collection of advanced economies was depressed, leaving no one to export to.

This did not, however, prevent the doctrine of expansionary fiscal consolidation from being embraced in all its spurious generality by Congressman Paul Ryan, the self-appointed deficit expert in the US House of Representatives. It did not prevent it from being invoked by EU finance ministers in their post-summit press conferences and communiqués. The idea that fiscal consolidation could be expansionary allowed politicians to argue that austerity could be all gain and no pain. That the reality turned out to be different was a rude shock except for those for whom the pain and gain were not the issue but austerity in and of itself was the objective.

The most powerful factor of all in this turn to austerity was surely that policy makers prevented the worst. They avoided another Great Depression.

They could declare the emergency over. They could therefore heed the call for an early return to normal policies. There is no little irony in how their very success in preventing a 1930s-like economic collapse led to their failure to support a more vigorous recovery.

And what was true of macroeconomic policy was true equally of financial reform. In the United States, the Great Depression led to the Glass-Steagall Act, separating commercial banking from investment banking. It led to the creation of a Securities and Exchange Commission to rein in financial excesses. There were calls now for a new Glass-Steagall, the earlier act having been laid to rest in 1999, but there was nothing remotely resembling such far-reaching regulatory reform. The Dodd-Frank Wall Street Reform and Consumer Protection Act of 2010 contained some modestly useful measures, from limits on speculative trading by financial institutions to creation of a Consumer Financial Protection Bureau. But the big banks were not broken up. Rhetoric to the contrary, little was done about the problem of too-big-to-fail. There was nothing approaching the fundamental redrawing of the financial landscape that resulted from Glass-Steagall's sharp separation of commercial banking, securities underwriting, and insurance services.

The fundamental explanation for the difference is again the success of policy makers in preventing the worst. In the 1930s, the depth of the Depression and the collapse of banks and securities markets wholly discredited the prevailing financial regime. Now, in contrast, depression and financial collapse were avoided, if barely. This fostered the belief that the flaws of the prevailing system were less. It weakened the argument for radical action. It took the wind out of the reformers' sails. And it allowed petty disagreements among politicians to slow the reform effort. Success thus became the mother of failure.

But whatever challenges America faced in getting its political parties to agree on regulatory reform paled in comparison with the challenge in Europe. Where reform in the United States required a modicum of agreement between the two parties, progress in the EU required agreement among twenty-seven governments. To be sure, though all governments were equal, some, like Germany's, were more equal than others. But even in this Orwellian Europe, small countries could cause trouble if they refused to go along, as Finland did when asked to aid Spain through EU's rescue fund, the European Stability Mechanism. Reform might require agreement by countries both inside and outside the Eurozone, as in the case of measures to limit bankers' bonuses, which were stymied when the UK took the EU to the European Court of Justice over pay and bonus regulation.

Nothing more epitomized these difficulties than the fight over banking union. With the creation of the euro, banks throughout Europe became even more tightly connected. But those banks and their national regulators failed to take into account the impact of their actions on neighboring banks and countries. The lesson of the crisis was that a single currency and single financial market but twenty-seven separate national bank regulators was madness. The solution was a single supervisor, a single deposit insurance scheme, and a single resolution mechanism for bad banks. Banking union in its fullness was seen as critical for restoring confidence in EU institutions.

In the summer of 2012, at the height of the crisis, European leaders agreed to establish this banking union. They agreed to create a single supervisor to monitor the banks. But then the process bogged down. Countries with strong banking systems hesitated to delegate supervision to a centralized authority. Others complained that their banks and depositors would be paying into a common insurance fund to bail out countries with poorly run financial institutions. Still others objected that their taxpayers would be on the hook when it came to funding the common resolution authority. The one thing these three groups had in common was, well, Germany, whose chancellor, Angela Merkel, demanded revisions of the EU's treaties to specify how these mechanisms would work, and how they would be financed. But treaty revision was somewhere other governments hesitated to go, since it required the assent of parliaments, and in some cases public referenda, in the course of which the EU's most basic understandings could be cast into doubt.

European leaders therefore agreed to half a loaf. They would proceed with the single supervisor but limit its oversight to Europe's 130 biggest banks, while leaving the single deposit insurance scheme and resolution mechanism to later.[10]

This reflected the difficulty of decision making in a European Union of twenty-seven countries. But it also reflected that the EU did just enough to hold its monetary union together. Through emergency loans and creation of an ECB facility to buy the bonds of troubled governments, it did just enough to prevent the euro system from falling apart. This success in turn limited the urgency of proceeding with banking union. This success too became the mother of failure.

That Europe did just enough to hold its monetary union together and that the euro did not go the way of the gold standard in the 1930s were, for many, among the great surprises of the crisis. In the late 1920s, the gold standard was seen as the guarantor of economic and financial stability, because the decade when it was in abeyance, from 1914 through 1924, had been marked by anything but. It turned out, however, that the gold standard as reconstructed after World War I was neither durable nor stable. Rather than preventing the 1931 financial crisis, it contributed to its development, first by creating a misapprehension of stability that encouraged large amounts of credit to flow toward countries ill equipped to handle it, and then by hamstringing the ability of governments to respond. The results were bank runs and balance-of-payments crises, as investors came to doubt the capacity of the authorities to defend their banks and currencies. Freeing themselves from the gold standard then enabled countries to regain control of their economic destinies. It allowed them to print money where money was scarce. It allowed them to support their banking systems. It allowed them to take other steps to end the Depression.

The architects of the euro were aware of this history. It resonated even more powerfully given that they experienced something similar in 1992–93 with the collapse of the Exchange Rate Mechanism through which European currencies were tied together like a string of mountain climbers. They therefore set out to make their new monetary arrangement stronger. It would be based on a single currency, not on pegged rates between separate national currencies. Devaluation of national currencies would not be possible because countries would no longer have national currencies to devalue. This euro system would be regulated not by national central banks but by a supranational authority, the ECB.

Importantly, the treaty establishing the monetary union would make no provision for exit. It was possible in the 1930s for a country to abandon the gold standard by a unilateral act of its national legislature or parliament. Abandoning the euro, in contrast, would abrogate a treaty obligation and jeopardize a country's good standing with its EU partners.

But while avoiding some of the problems of the gold standard, the euro's architects courted others. By creating the mirage of stability, the euro system set in motion large capital flows toward Southern European countries ill equipped to handle them, like those of the 1920s. When those flows reversed direction, the inability of national central banks to print money and national governments to borrow it consigned economies to deep recession, as in the 1930s. Pressure mounted to do something. Support for governments that failed to do so began to dissolve. Increasingly it was predicted that the euro would go the way of the gold standard; governments in distressed countries would abandon it. And if they hesitated, they would be replaced by other governments and leaders prepared to act. In the worst case, democracy itself might be placed at risk.

This, it turned out, was a misreading of the lessons of history. In the 1930s, when governments abandoned the gold standard, international trade and lending had already collapsed. This time European countries did just enough to avoid that fate. Hence the euro had to be defended in order to preserve the Single Market and intra-European trade and payments. In the 1930s, political solidarity was another early casualty of the Depression. Notwithstanding the strains of the crisis, governments this time continued to consult and collaborate, with help from international institutions stronger and better developed than those of the 1930s. EU countries in a strong economic and financial position provided loans to their weak European partners. Those loans could have been larger, but they were still large by the standards of the 1930s.

Finally, the crisis of democracy forecast by those anticipating the euro's collapse failed to materialize. There were demonstrations, including violent demonstrations. Governments fell. But democracy survived, unlike the 1930s. Here the Cassandras of collapse failed to reckon with the welfare states and social safety nets constructed in response to the Depression. Even where unemployment exceeded 25 percent, as it did in the worst-affected parts of Europe, overt distress was less. This weakened the political backlash. It limited the pressure to abandon the prevailing system.

That the experience of the Great Depression importantly shaped perceptions and reactions to the Great Recession is a commonplace. But understanding just how that history was used—and misused—requires one to look more closely not just at the Depression but also at the developments leading up to it. This in turn means starting at the start, namely, in 1920.

PART I | The Best of Times

CHAPTER 1 | New Age Economics

A T FIVE FOOT four and with a round face, Charles Ponzi hardly cut an imposing figure. Having arrived in the United States at the age of twenty-one from Parma, Italy, he did not speak English with the authority of a patrician American financier. But if small in stature, Ponzi would loom large in the literature on financial crises. In time, "Ponzi scheme" would become an indelible part of the lexicon of financial instability, surpassing even the likes of "Greenspan put" and "Lehman Brothers moment."

Ponzi made his name, as it were, with a scheme to arbitrage the market in international postal reply coupons. These instruments were introduced in 1906 by agreement at the Universal Postal Union Congress, held, auspiciously, in Italy. They were intended as a vehicle for sending funds abroad, enabling the recipient to buy stamps and post a reply.

The 1906 congress was convened in the gold standard era, when exchange rates were locked. Delegates thus had no way of anticipating the complications that suspension of the gold standard could create for their agreement. But with the outbreak of the World War, governments embargoed gold exports. Buying gold where it was cheap and selling it where it was dear had been the mechanism through which exchange rates were held stable. With the embargoes, which effectively suspended gold market transactions, currencies began fluctuating against one another.

Among the unanticipated consequences were those for the postal coupon agreement. The United States was the only belligerent whose currency maintained its value against gold during and after the war. European currencies depreciated against the dollar as governments printed money to finance military outlays, a trend only partially reversed with the armistice. As a result, postal reply coupons purchased abroad using European currencies could buy more than their cost in stamps in the United States. In 1919, sensing an opportunity, Ponzi borrowed money from business associates, which he sent to Italian contacts with instructions to purchase postal reply coupons and forward them to him in Boston.

Why Ponzi was uniquely able to detect this opportunity is, to put it mildly, unclear. Not surprisingly, the appearance of substantial profits was an illusion. Ponzi's contacts could assemble only a limited number of coupons, and even then, completing the transaction took time, during which funds devoted to the project were tied up.

And time was not something Ponzi possessed in abundance, since he had promised to double his investors' money in ninety days. To pay those dividends, he was forced to employ the capital obtained from new subscriptions, leaving no funds for the postal coupon arbitrage motivating the scheme. This in turn made it essential to attract additional investors, which Ponzi did by incorporating as the impressive-sounding Securities Exchange Company and hiring a phalanx of salesmen. The scheme collapsed in August 1920 with publication of a *Boston Post* exposé penned by William McMasters—a journalist Ponzi had hired to generate publicity for his operation.[1]

That Ponzi's promise to double his investors' money in ninety days had not raised red flags says something about the readiness of investors to suspend disbelief in the intoxicating financial atmosphere of the 1920s. One can't help but think of the inability of investors in the equally heady 2000s to see through the ability of Bernie Madoff to generate supernormal profits with barely a fluctuation year after year after year.

Indicted for mail fraud, Ponzi pled guilty and was sentenced to three and a half years in federal prison. The investing public of New England, however, was not so easily assuaged. While still in prison, Ponzi was indicted by the State of Massachusetts on twenty-two charges of larceny. The now impecunious defendant served as his own attorney, more than capably at first. But as one trial followed another, he grew fatigued. Where the first jury acquitted, the second deadlocked, and the third found the defendant guilty. Freed on bail, Ponzi fled to the remote backwaters of Florida, where he began doing business under an assumed name.

In 1925, doing business in Florida meant transacting in real estate. Ponzi transformed himself into the promoter of a subdivision near Jacksonville. "Near" in this case meant sixty-five miles west of the city, where Ponzi set about developing (if one is permitted elastic use of the word) an expanse of scrubland covered with palmetto, weeds, and the occasional oak. Subdividing meant driving stakes into the ground to help owners identify their homestead.

Once lots were staked, at an ambitious twenty-three per acre, they were offered at $10 apiece.

The capital needed to purchase, survey, and subdivide the land was provided by investors in Ponzi's Charpon (*Char*les *Pon*zi) Land Corporation. Subscribers were promised $30 for each $10 investment in sixty days, an even more impressive return than in the earlier postal coupon operation. This of course was nothing but another pyramid scheme in which early investors were paid with cash obtained from the proceeds of selling shares to new investors. It didn't take long for the fraud to be detected or for the perpetrator's identity to be revealed. Ponzi was indicted for violating Florida statutes regarding trusts, tried, and again found guilty by a jury of his peers.[2]

———

That Ponzi, on reaching Florida, found a home in the real estate business was no coincidence, Florida being in the midst of a property boom the likes of which the United States had never seen.

The country had experienced real estate booms and busts before, but these had centered on farmland. This was its first urban, or more precisely suburban, real estate boom, driven by the automobile. As more Americans acquired cheap and reliable cars, epitomized by Henry Ford's Model T, suburban living became possible. And as Florida grew accessible to motorized visitors, its temperate climate and cheap land proved a powerful lure. The influx of Northerners who arrived in the winter of 1920–21 were known as "Tin Can Tourists" for their less-than-elegant mode of transport, which sometimes also served as a temporary abode.[3]

Real estate promoters, not a few of whom were also automobile enthusiasts, were quick to recognize the connection. Carl Fisher, who with his brothers founded the Prest-O-Lite Corporation and then Fisher Body to provide acetylene headlamps and bodies to the fledgling motor-vehicle industry, was a case in point. Fisher first encountered the peninsula that came to be known as Miami Beach in 1910 on a honeymoon yacht trip with his fifteen-year-old bride. In the final stages of negotiating the sale of Prest-O-Lite to Union Carbide, he was in a position to buy an elegant vacation and retirement home across the peninsula on Biscayne Bay.

But retirement bored Fisher, who was still only in his thirties. By 1913 he was in the real estate business; by 1915 he was the region's leading property developer. And if there was not enough property to develop, Fisher created more. He moved dredging equipment into Biscayne Bay, pumping up sand to elongate the beach. Will Rogers, as usual, put it best: "Carl discovered that sand could hold up a Real Estate sign, and that was all he wanted it for. Carl rowed the customers out in the ocean and let them pick out some nice smooth water where they would like to build, and then he would replace the water with an island, and you would be a little Robinson Crusoe of your own."[4]

To strengthen the connections between the automobile and Florida real estate, Fisher promoted construction of the Dixie Highway, linking the state with the Upper Midwest. He founded the Dixie Highway Association. He seeded newspapers with articles celebrating the project. He subdued conflicts between rival cities seeking to sit astride the route by laying out both eastern and western branches. No sacrifice was too great in order to deliver the desired flow of traffic.

To be sure, other factors also nourished the Florida property boom, including the strong recovery of the American economy from the postwar recession and expectations that there would now be a permanent acceleration of growth. The 1920s saw a revolution in factory design, as production was reorganized to capitalize on electric power. Factories had traditionally used steam power distributed through a network of overhead drive shafts and brackets. Electrification permitted removal of this steam-related apparatus, making it possible to install overhead cranes to move subassemblies. Electricity also allowed workers to use portable power tools and move freely along the line. This increased their productivity relative to their predecessors, who were figuratively bolted to the shop floor, much like the steam-powered machinery with which they worked. In this way electrification allowed employers to adopt scientific management practices designed to optimize the efficiency of labor input, notably through the time and motion studies of the management consultant Frederick Winslow Taylor.

The full potential of the assembly line, symbolized by Henry Ford's massive River Rouge Complex in Dearborn, Michigan, whose construction began in 1917, could now be realized. This in turn held out the promise of productivity gains at a rate never experienced previously. The fact that real GDP rose by nearly 5 percent per annum between 1922 and 1929, faster than anything the United States had experienced over a comparable period, seemingly confirmed this optimistic view.

Faster productivity growth would mean not just higher incomes but also higher prices for financial assets, or so investors were led to believe. What was true of real estate, in other words, was true also of other investments. The leading corporations added to the Dow Jones Industrial Average in the 1920s, the likes of American Telephone and Telegraph, Western Union, International Harvester, and Allied Chemical, were exemplars of this technological revolution. There is an obvious parallel with the run-up to the 2008–09 crisis, when it was argued that productivity growth would accelerate as firms learned to commercialize new information technologies. The transformative general-purpose technology in the 1920s may have been electricity rather than the computer, but the impact on investor psychology was the same.

———

Monetary policy then poured fuel on the fire. Creation of the Federal Reserve System in 1913 encouraged the belief that the business cycle instability that traditionally plagued the country had been tamed. The Fed was charged with preventing the swings in interest rates that had perturbed financial markets and economic activity in earlier years (with providing an "elastic currency," in the words of the Federal Reserve Act). Insofar as it was likely to succeed, investment would be safer, encouraging the plungers. The 1920s were known as the "New Era," capturing the idea that the country had entered a new age not only of faster productivity growth but also of greater economic and financial stability. Shades of the "Great Moderation," the supposed diminution of the business cycle in the lead-up to the 2008–09 crisis.

Although the Fed was quick to make use of its new policy instruments, it did not deploy them in the anticipated way. The expectation of the founders was that the new central bank would adjust credit conditions to the needs of domestic business. Somewhat unexpectedly, now instead it adjusted them with foreign circumstances in mind. In mid-1924, the Federal Reserve banks cut the interest rates they charged when advancing credit to commercial banks (their "discount rates") from 4.5 to 3 percent, with an eye toward helping Great Britain back onto the gold standard.[5] (The main way central banks injected credit into the economy in this era was by discounting promissory notes held by banks and firms—that is to say, by purchasing them at a discount relative to their face value in return for cash. Hence the term "discount rate.") Britain had experienced more inflation than the United States during the World War, damaging its competitiveness. It consequently lacked the capacity to peg the sterling price of gold or to restore the traditional exchange rate between sterling and the dollar once wartime controls were lifted. The UK therefore abandoned convertibility in March 1919, allowing the sterling-dollar exchange rate to fluctuate and, not incidentally, suggesting opportunities to the likes of Ponzi.

Very Serious People in Britain and America saw reconstruction of the prewar gold standard as a priority. Prominent among them was Benjamin Strong, the influential governor of the Federal Reserve Bank of New York. Strong was firmly of the view that exchange rate instability and the uncertainty to which it gave rise had a withering effect on trade.[6] And the state of trade, foreign as well as domestic, mattered importantly for an America that had assumed Britain's mantle as the world's leading exporter. "Well-balanced prosperity" required absorption by foreign markets of America's "surplus production," in the words of the annual report of the Federal Reserve Board for 1925, a document significantly shaped by Strong.[7] And augmenting that absorption capacity depended in turn on the financial normalization that only the gold standard could provide. In his capacity as secretary, vice president, and then president of Bankers Trust Company and confidant of John Pierpont Morgan, whose firm, J. P. Morgan & Co., possessed its own sister organization in London, Strong appreciated the importance of these international connections. As founding governor of a public agency that saw its mandate as transforming New York into a leading international financial center, he regarded reestablishment of a stable international monetary system as central to that goal.

Under the prewar gold standard, the pound sterling was the sun around which other currencies orbited. Much of the world's trade was financed and settled in sterling, and London was the leading international financial center. Even though the war years and 1920s saw a considerable expansion of international financial business in New York and hence the dollar's acquisition of an international role, Britain's resumption of gold convertibility—permitting sterling to once again be converted into gold at a fixed domestic-currency price—was still seen as a precondition for resumption by other countries. Hence the exchange rate at which sterling was stabilized would in turn determine the rate, in both senses of the word, at which other countries restored gold convertibility.

Britain thus came under pressure from US officials to take this momentous step. Strong, in particular, emphasized the importance of Britain restoring not just gold convertibility but also the prewar exchange rate of $4.86 to the pound. The prewar exchange rate was important for sterling's prestige and, Strong believed, the Bank of England's credibility. The adverse consequences for the international system of failing to restore it, he warned, were "too serious really to contemplate."[8]

Montagu Norman, governor of the Bank of England since 1920, shared his American friend's perspective. In letters to Strong, he emphasized the desirability of returning to a gold standard of the pre–World War I variety. But unlike a modern central banker, Norman made little effort to explain his reasoning. His public utterances were famously inarticulate, something that lent an air of mystery, if not confusion, to his policy decisions. In *The Shape of Things to Come*, the futurist fantasy published in 1933 at the depths of the Depression, H. G. Wells found Norman an irresistible target. "Instead of the clear knowledge of economic pressures and movements that we have today," wrote Wells, looking back from an imaginary future, "strange Mystery Men were dimly visible through a fog of battling evasions and misstatements, manipulating prices and exchanges. Prominent among these Mystery Men was a certain Mr. Montagu Norman, Governor of the

Bank of England from 1920 to 1935. He is among the least credible figures in all history, and a great incrustation of legends has accumulated about him. In truth the only mystery about him was that he was mysterious."

Wells got many things right, including the importance that modern central bankers attach to transparency and communication.[9] The one thing he got wrong was Norman's retirement. In fact, the strange Mystery Man did not step down from the governorship of the Bank of England until 1944.

———

Whether or not his incoherence was purposeful, Norman was the father of constructive ambiguity, the central banker's art, perfected by Alan Greenspan, of leaving things hanging. But one issue about which he was unambiguous was the desirability of restoring gold convertibility at the prewar rate against the dollar. A precondition for achieving this was for the Bank of England to acquire adequate stocks of gold, or equally, assets convertible into gold. And if acquiring adequate stocks required the assistance of the Federal Reserve System, then this was something Strong was ready to provide.

Thus, the low-interest-rate policy advocated by Strong starting in 1924 was designed to help the Bank of England acquire the reserves needed to return to gold. Low interest rates in New York encouraged funds to flow toward London, where rates were higher. Much of this funding ended up in the big London banks. Some ended up in the bankers' bank; in other words, it ended up in the coffers of the Bank of England.

And if market forces did not convey an adequate flow of gold toward London, they could always be supplemented. With this in mind, the New York Fed purchased US treasury bonds, pushing down yields and encouraging additional finance to flow across the Atlantic.[10]

But these financial operations, by themselves, might not be enough to put Britain firmly back on the gold standard. In addition there would have to be a rebalancing of competitive positions. Although British prices had risen more than US prices since the outbreak of the World War, there had been no corresponding rise in British labor productivity. Britain would lack export competitiveness if sterling was stabilized at its former level against the dollar. It would run a chronic trade deficit, and the gold the Bank of England had so laboriously acquired would just leak back out. Avoiding this outcome required reducing prices in the UK or raising them in the United States. Since before the war, British production costs had risen relative to those in the United States, Strong estimated, by 10 percent. Other observers reached similar conclusions. John Maynard Keynes, who had a reputation for expertise in such matters, put the differential at 9 percent.[11]

Strong's hope was that keeping interest rates low would encourage spending, putting upward pressure on US prices and helping to correct the competitiveness gap.[12] In the event, manipulating price levels turned out to be more difficult than anticipated. American prices rose between mid-1924 and mid-1925, but not by enough to erase the cost differential. When Britain returned to the gold standard in April 1925, the problem of inadequate competitiveness remained. Norman would battle it for the better part of six years.

———

The effect of Strong's low-interest-rate policy was therefore less to rebalance the world economy than to unbalance the economy of the United States. The effects manifested themselves in the housing bubble centered on Florida and, before long, Chicago, Detroit, and New York. Neither was the Wall Street boom that dominated the last part of the decade unrelated.

Strong was vehemently criticized by Adolph Miller for subordinating domestic financial-stability considerations to international objectives. A founding governor of the Federal Reserve System, Miller had graduated from the University of California, Berkeley, in 1887 before going on to study in Cambridge, Paris, and Munich. He then taught at Cornell and Chicago (two universities that figure further in this story) before returning to Berkeley to establish the College of Commerce, and finally moving to Washington, D.C., to serve as assistant secretary of the interior, and then as a member of the Board of Governors upon being appointed by his fellow academician Woodrow Wilson in 1914.

Miller regaled in the didactic manner and ample vocabulary of the professor. As described by George Norris, governor of the Federal Reserve Bank of Philadelphia, Miller was intoxicated by his verbal skills, which he displayed in all their glory in the meetings of the Federal Reserve Board and the Open Market Investment Committee.[13] Miller used his verbal powers specifically to propound the "real bills doctrine," which dictated that the central bank should provide just as much credit as was required for the legitimate needs of business and no more.[14] That doctrine, developed in the early eighteenth century by, among others, the Scottish monetary theorist John Law, was intended as a guide to credit creation by the Bank of England, established in 1694. Not satisfied by his role in shaping the Bank of England, Law would go on to found a quasi-central bank for France, the Banque Générale, and play a role in the Mississippi Bubble and crash before retiring in disgrace, but no matter. His real bills doctrine informed the conduct of central bank policy for two centuries and more thereafter.

In particular, the doctrine informed the Federal Reserve Act of 1914, which spoke of the need for an "elastic currency," a system in which supplies of currency and credit expanded and contracted to meet the legitimate needs of business. The failure of supplies of dollar currency and credit to respond in this way had led to sharp interest rate spikes and chronic financial instability throughout US history. This was the problem that creation of the Fed in 1914 was designed to correct.

As an adherent to the real bills doctrine, Miller was quick to conclude that directing Federal Reserve policy to the problems of the British economy, as Strong had done, rather than being guided by the legitimate needs of business was the height of irresponsibility. The professor was acerbic in his criticism of the governor of the Federal Reserve Bank of New York. His unhappiness was deepened, no doubt, by the failure of other members of the Board of Governors and directors of the Reserve banks, typically men of affairs unversed in rigorous monetary analysis, to defer to academics like himself who had been properly schooled in theory and were therefore better qualified to advise on technical matters.

Miller's voice was the loudest, but he was not alone. His criticisms were echoed by, among others, Charles Hamlin, the former assistant treasury secretary and unsuccessful candidate for governor of Massachusetts who now served as chairman of the Federal Reserve Board, and by Herbert Hoover, Strong's onetime ally, President Calvin Coolidge's commerce secretary, and Miller's Georgetown neighbor. Hoover, like Strong, was an internationalist by inclination, but even for him Strong's 1924–25 initiative went too far. It paid too little attention to the domestic repercussions of the policy. Strong, Hoover concluded, had been seduced by his friend Norman; the head of the New York Fed was now a mere "mental annex to Europe."[15] Strong's policy threatened to unleash inflation and fan financial excesses. If it was desirable to help Britain back onto the gold standard, then this should be done by other means, Hoover concluded, not by reducing US interest rates, something which could have undesirable side effects.

Miller and Hoover's instinctual embrace of the real bills doctrine was a manifestation of the power of historical experience in shaping the outlook and actions of officials. Sharp spikes in interest rates resulting in widespread business distress, and in the worst case financial crisis, had been a feature of the US monetary and financial landscape since the country's independence. Hence a doctrine that counseled tailoring supplies of money and credit to the legitimate needs of business, and looking to the level of interest rates to verify that those needs were being met, informed the outlook of many of the founding governors of the Federal Reserve System. Insofar as that doctrine warned against artificially reducing interest rates to help other countries, as Strong had done, following it more strictly would have prevented dangerous imbalances in US property and stock markets from building up. But that same doctrine would also suggest that there was no need for the Federal Reserve to act when interest rates fell from their high levels after 1929—lower interest rates indicating that US business had all the credit and the economy had all the monetary support they required.

The clear implication is that there is no single monetary doctrine for all seasons. This was a lesson Federal Reserve officials and the country would eventually learn at great expense.

———

For the time being, the criticisms of these men had little effect. Strong was the dominant personality in the Federal Reserve System. With his background as J. P. Morgan's right-hand man and his work on the front lines of the 1907 financial crisis, he spoke with authority on matters of financial policy, notwithstanding his lack of formal academic training. His was the voice of experience. If Strong attached more importance to events in London than Miami, then so be it.

And even though Fed policy contributed to the financial excesses of the period, it was not the only factor at work. In addition, there was the enabling role of a financial system that was only loosely regulated. There were governmental efforts to boost real estate and construction activity. There was the fact that housing starts had been depressed in the war years, making for pent-up demand now straining to be released.

Ambitious Florida promoters, liking nothing less than pent-up demand, did their best to liberate it. None was more ambitious than George Merrick, scion of a Congregationalist minister and grapefruit plantation owner. Merrick's avocation was poetry. In 1920, celebrating his Florida environs, he published a volume of verse entitled *Song of the Wind on a Southern Shore.*

> There's a Shore I know—that draws me
> And that warms me all the more!—
> Where the gumbo-limbo grows:—
> And the little lizards doze—
> Where the trade-wind blows
> Through the palm-tufted curvings
> Of the Biscayne shore[16]

Clearly Merrick's principal talent lay in real estate development. Appointed Dade County commissioner in 1915, his main achievement was a network of roads connecting Miami with its future suburbs, and not least with his own planned community of Coral Gables, centered on what had been the family plantation. Pushing his poetic license to the hilt, Merrick pitched Coral Gables as a Spanish-style city where "your 'Castles in Spain' are made real." The pit from which he mined the limestone and coral rock that was used to construct the homes was transformed into a Venetian lagoon complete with bridges, grottoes, and loggias. Merrick advertised in national magazines and out-of-state newspapers, writing much of the copy himself. He lured clients to his still largely undeveloped suburb with free performances of Mabel Cody's Flying Circus, a popular air show. Customers buying lots were rewarded with the opportunity of going aloft and seeing their property from the air.[17] He opened opulent sales offices in New York and Chicago. Purchasing buses to transport potential buyers, he organized excursions from New York, Philadelphia, and Washington, D.C.

Not least, Merrick hired William Jennings Bryan, the former presidential candidate, secretary of state, and famed orator, to deliver the pitch. Bryan had moved to Florida to make life easier for his arthritic wife and immediately became Miami's most famous resident. Having run for president in 1896 on a platform fighting for the small man and against the gold standard, Bryan was now paid by Merrick to stand on a platform of another kind, erected over the water, and speak not of the gold standard but of the Gold Coast. He was paid $100,000 for his year's work, half in cash and half in land.

Coral Gables was successful from the start. More than five thousand customers attended the inaugural auction of home sites in 1921. After barely a year, Merrick was buying additional land in order to expand his vision and his development. Between November 1924 and March 1925, the height of the tourist season, Merrick recorded a remarkable $4 million a month in land sales.

State government officials responded enthusiastically to the boom. This was no surprise, since a substantial number of property developers, like Merrick, not to mention their bankers, graciously agreed to serve in public office. They used soaring real estate taxes to finance local road building and expand public services, creating the appearance of even greater prosperity. In 1923, with the boom in full swing, the Florida legislature placed on the ballot an amendment to the state constitution abolishing income and inheritance taxes with the goal of encouraging migration from the north.[18] Grateful voters overwhelmingly approved the measure. They chose John Wellborn Martin, previously the mayor of Jacksonville, as governor at the conclusion of a campaign centering on his promise to complete an ambitious statewide road-building project. This was one of the things Ponzi was counting on, presumably, when marketing his fictitious development on the outer reaches of Martin's hometown.

Increasingly, the Florida real estate market displayed all the signs of an unsustainable boom in its late stages. Landowners hired binder boys to stand in the hot sun and entice prospective buyers. These young men in white suits, not a few of whom moonlighted as tennis and golf pros, encouraged potential purchasers to commit to a nonrefundable 10 percent down payment known as a binder.[19] At the height of the boom, binder receipts circulated like currency, with hotels, nightclubs, and bordellos all accepting them in payment for services.

Binder boys received a fixed fee when the aspiring purchaser's money arrived at the developer's bank. Like mortgage brokers in the run-up to the 2006–07 real estate crash, they had little interest in whether a purchaser understood the contract to which he or she was committing or, for that matter, was capable of completing the transaction. The typical financial institution provided a mortgage loan only if the purchaser made a down payment of 50 percent.[20] The 10 percent binder therefore implied a commitment to come up with another 40 percent, which for many aspiring property owners was easier said than done.

Coming up with more money would not be necessary, of course, if the binder, which represented first right of refusal on a desirable plot of land, was first sold off to another investor. The faster prices rose, the more prevalent this practice of flipping binders became. Successful binder boys graduated to real estate speculation, trading binders themselves. They put down 10 percent to purchase what was essentially an option on an undeveloped lot with the intention of immediately selling it at a higher price. In the summer of 1925, at the height of the boom, binders were bought and sold as often as eight times a day.[21] Clearly, Floridians in the 1920s had nothing to learn from, and could have taught a few tricks to, property speculators in the run-up to the subprime crisis of 2007–08.

———

This frenzied activity would not have been possible, of course, without the enabling role of the banks. "All the financial resources of existing banking and financial institutions were utilized to the full in financing this speculative movement," as Herbert Simpson, a contemporary expert on the Florida housing boom, put it in an article tellingly entitled "Real Estate Speculation and the Depression," published in the *American Economic Review* in 1933.[22]

> Insurance companies bought what were considered the choicer mortgages; conservative banks loaned freely on real estate mortgages; and less conservative banks and financial houses loaned on almost everything.

Real estate interests dominated the policies of many banks, and thousands of new banks were organized and chartered for the specific purpose of providing the credit facilities for proposed real estate promotions. The greater proportion were state banks and trust companies, many of them located in the outlying sections of the larger cities or in suburban regions not fully occupied by older and more established banking institutions. In the extent to which their deposits and resources were devoted to the exploitation of real estate promotions being carried on by controlling or associated interests, these banks commonly stopped short of nothing but the criminal law—and sometimes not short of that.

Among the worst offenders were the building and loan associations, or B&Ls. In principle, these institutions, like mutual savings banks, were in the business of lending to their members.[23] One can't help but be reminded of the role in the 2008–09 crisis of Northern Rock, which similarly originated as a building society, the British equivalent of a B&L, though this is to get ahead of the story.

Building and loan associations were subject to a patchwork of variable and often lightly enforced state regulation.[24] Lack of more stringent regulation reflected, in part, the belief that their funding was secure. Members held shares rather than deposits, which they were not able to liquidate at their pleasure. This freed B&Ls of the bank-run problem. Loans were collateralized, it was supposed, by rock-solid real estate. B&Ls used minimal leverage; they did not issue debt to supplement their shareholders' equity. Unfortunately, these reassuring observations ignored the fact that those to whom they lent were themselves highly leveraged. They ignored the fact that not all real estate investments were rock-solid.[25]

The building and loan model had worked well in the nineteenth century. Now, however, it was enlisted by property developers to feed their ambitions and advance their narrow ends. B&Ls being easier to incorporate than depository institutions, real estate professionals established them for the purpose of financing residential development projects.[26] A captive board of directors there might be, but it exercised little oversight. Out the window went the notion that B&Ls should extend mortgage credit only to reliable borrowers so as to return income to their members. B&Ls became leaders in extending low-down-payment loans. They issued second mortgages for 30 percent of a property's value after the borrower secured a conventional first loan, typically for 50 percent, from a bank or insurance company, reducing the down payment to 20 percent.[27]

Another increasingly important source of finance for property development was securitization. Developers issued some $10 billion of real estate bonds in the course of the 1920s. A third were backed by residential mortgage interest payments, the remainder by future lease income from commercial real estate projects. Most of the latter were "single property bonds" issued to finance individual high-rise office buildings, apartments, and theaters, although there were also more complex instruments known as "guaranteed mortgage participation certificates"—what we would now call mortgage pass-through securities. Issued by title and mortgage guarantee companies and backed by commercial real estate projects, these more complex bonds were not easily traded. To entice investors to buy them, the issuer guaranteed the holder a rate of interest on the bond of 5 percent. This of course meant that the title or insurance company was on the hook if returns on the underlying investments fell short.[28]

In practice, insurance companies not only guaranteed the bonds but held them in their portfolios. Given the low interest rates on Treasury debt produced by Governor Strong's internationally minded policies, real estate bonds were an attractive alternative. Between 1920 and 1930, the share of life insurance company assets backed by real estate and urban mortgages rose from 35 to 45 percent. The securities in question were also marketed to the public by the bond houses that originated and distributed them. Investors relied on the good name, such as it was, of the originator. There is little evidence that they discriminated among these bonds, demanding higher yields as a function of the riskiness of the mortgage pool.[29] In this way large amounts of finance were channeled from individual investors into commercial and residential property development. In the event, the bonds in question, particularly those issued at the height of the boom, did not fare well in the 1930s.

This market in single-property bonds is a reminder that, along with the residential building boom in Florida, there was a commercial real estate boom centering on Chicago, New York, and Detroit.[30] The 1920s were the decade of the skyscraper. More ground was broken for the construction of tall buildings than in any other decade of the twentieth century. The skyscraper boom reflected advances in construction, including more durable steel-frame structures, improved elevator motors, and application of Tayloresque time-and-motion methods to construction labor. But it also reflected a new financial model in which buildings were erected not simply as company headquarters but as financial investments, in the expectation that space could be leased to rent-paying tenants. New York City's iconic Chrysler Building, for which ground was broken in 1928, served as the headquarters for the Chrysler Corporation but also had a variety of other tenants, from Pan American Airways to Adams Hats.

The commercial real estate market peaked later than the residential real estate market. But it too was inflated beyond all reason. And it too caused major dislocations when it came crashing down.

———

Still, nothing matched the extremes of the Florida property market. Miami saw the most frenzied speculation. The boom was more subdued in Orlando, and it did not reach Jacksonville until late, a fact that may have contributed to Ponzi's downfall. The population of Dade County tripled between 1920 and 1925. The assessed value of property in Miami rose even faster, from $63 million in 1922 to $421 million in 1926. At this point, one in three residents of what was by now a city of eighty thousand was employed in property development in one way or another. At the height of the boom, "[r]ealtors passed slowly through large crowds along Flagler Street. . . barking out their offerings to the accompaniment of music from bands hired by the major developers. . . . At times the sidewalks. . . were impassable due to the great number of realtors transacting their business."[31] Agents buttonholed prospects at the railway terminal as they stepped off the train. Newspapers were weighed down by real estate advertisements. By late 1925, daily editions of the *Miami Herald*, which previously ran to no more than twenty pages, had ballooned to eighty-eight.

Labor grew scarce despite the influx of construction workers, many of whom were reduced to living in tents. George Merrick, displaying his gift for promotion, built an encampment of 375 tents on the outskirts of his development, which he dubbed the "Cool Canvas Cottages at Coral Gables." The labor shortage was compounded by a building-material shortage aggravated by the decision of the Florida East Coast Railway to place a moratorium on shipments. Not only was the Miami rail yard jammed with twenty-two hundred freight cars, but the movement of freight was disrupted by the desperate efforts of the overtaxed railway to double-track its lines. With rail shipments at a standstill, steamships and sailboats were enlisted to move building material. Soon the Miami and Miami Beach docks were so jammed that unloading cargo became impossible. In September the steamship companies followed the railroad by embargoing shipments of furniture, construction machinery, and building materials.

All this was indicative of a bubble in its late stages. What caused it to burst is disputed, as is always the case with bubbles. A stock market correction was one possible trigger: the S&P Composite fell by 11 percent between February and May 1926. An unusually cold winter followed by a hot summer did not reassure homebuyers of Florida's temperate climate. A tropical cyclone came ashore in December 1925, eroding the state's pristine northeast beaches and dealing the market literally another blow. This was followed by a category 4 hurricane, described by the US Weather Bureau as "probably the most destructive hurricane ever to strike the United States," that hit Miami on September 18, 1926. Three Miami Beach residents died in the flooding, a hundred more in Miami proper.[32] The roof was torn off Carl Fisher's vacation home. The Congregational Church in Coral Gables became a relief center—not exactly the purpose for which Merrick had intended it.

Meanwhile, concerns with what was happening in Florida did not stay in Florida. Twenty thousand residents of Savannah, Georgia, up and moved to the Sunshine State, lured by the attractions of the property boom, alarming the city fathers. Investors attracted to Florida real estate withdrew some $20 million from savings banks in Massachusetts. Bankers throughout the Northeast and Midwest grew anxious about the loss of deposits and earning assets.

Concerned as much with the loss of population and deposits as the welfare of residents, officials inveighed against these excesses. Ohio bankers placed newspaper ads warning against doing business with Florida real estate developers. State Commerce Director Cyrus Locher and the chief of the Securities Division, Norman Beck, selflessly traveled to Florida to investigate the market firsthand. In the interest of protecting the small investor, they recommended that companies selling securities backed by Florida real estate should not be permitted to do business in their state. The Ohio state legislature obediently passed a blue-sky law forbidding the practice.[33] Anti-Florida propaganda included the assertion that good meat was unavailable in the state and dangerous reptiles were a threat in the major population centers.[34] The Better Business Bureau, investigating practices in Florida, detected widespread fraud and moved to publish its findings. Ponzi's arrest and prosecution were yet another unwelcome source of publicity.

As is typical of property markets, the volume of transactions fell first, followed after a time by prices. Local government revenues collapsed, and ambitious municipal development projects were abandoned. Bank clearings in Miami fell by two-thirds.[35] One hundred fifty banks failed in Florida and neighboring Georgia, most of them members of the Manley-Anthony chain, so called because the banks in question were all owned or controlled by a pair of bankers, James R. Anthony and Wesley D. Manley, heavily implicated in property speculation, not least in the form of investments in Merrick's Coral Gables development.[36] Depositors suffered some $30 million in losses. Manley himself was arrested for engaging in fraudulent transactions to shelter his remaining assets from bankruptcy proceedings. In his defense, attorneys invoked an insanity plea.

The financial repercussions did not extend beyond Florida and Georgia; still, the episode soured bankers and homebuyers on the residential real estate market. Residential housing starts nationally fell from 850,000 in 1926 to 810,000 in 1927, 750,000 in 1928, and 500,000 in 1929, despite the economy displaying no comparable weakness.

———

With hindsight, some argued that the Federal Reserve should have done more to restrain the property boom. Doing so would have limited the excesses in the financial system and prevented disruptive bank failures in the South. It would have moderated an important source of downward pressure on economic activity that was starting to be felt at the worst possible time, toward the end of the 1920s.

But targeting a specific sector, housing, would have created many of the same dilemmas as targeting the sterling-dollar exchange rate. Fed officials would have been diverting their attention from their fundamental task of providing an elastic currency, with adverse consequences for economic stability. Using monetary policy to damp down financial imbalances might have ended up only bludgeoning the economy.

In a couple of years, with the boom on Wall Street, the same dilemma would reappear. The question then was whether the Fed should raise interest rates in response to the rise in the stock market, in order to prevent development of even more serious financial imbalances and risks. Alternatively, it could continue to direct monetary policy to the needs of the real economy and address financial imbalances through other means. It could rely on what today we would call "macroprudential policy," and what contemporaries called "direct pressure," that is, attempting to limit bank lending to financial markets directly.[37]

Ultimately, the Fed chose the first alternative, raising rates. The consequences would be far-reaching.

CHAPTER 2 | Golden Globe

I T DID NOT take long for financial excesses to migrate from Flagler Street to Wall Street. The same low interest rates and expectations of rapid growth that fueled speculation in property encouraged investment in stocks and bonds. Enthusiasm for stocks was further stoked by exaggerated expectations of the profitability of what might be referred to as, if an anachronism is permitted, a new generation of information technology companies. Much as the Internet was used in the 1990s to trumpet the wisdom of investing in Internet-related companies, radio was used in the 1920s to encourage investing in radio. Radio Corporation of America was one of the most widely traded stocks on Wall Street from the time of its initial listing in 1924.

RCA and the other highflyers were helped along by Wall Street insiders like Walter Chrysler and the Fisher Brothers, of Fisher Auto Body fame. These individuals, auto industry veterans more often than not, were led by the mercurial founder of General Motors turned financial speculator Billy Durant. Under Durant's direction they formed syndicates to purchase RCA stock. They made the soaring price of RCA shares front-page news, attracting small investors and driving up prices still further. At this point the syndicate sold out, taking its profits and in so doing erasing earlier gains.[1]

But even these manipulations did not interrupt the upward trend in the market's favorite. From 1925 to the peak in 1929, the price of RCA shares rose more than tenfold adjusted for splits. The first true growth stock, RCA's price-earnings multiple ultimately exceeded 70. In the event, the company did not pay a dividend until 1937.

What was true of RCA stock was true generally. From early 1926 through mid-1929, the Dow Jones Industrial Average rose without significant interruption. Whether and at what point this should be regarded as a bubble continues to be disputed. It is suggestive that the Dow and corporate dividends rose in lockstep through 1927, as if the run-up in stock prices was a reflection of improved corporate earnings. But in 1928, share prices decoupled from dividends. From this point the Great Wall Street boom—some would say the bubble—was on.[2]

There were as many explanations for the rise in share prices as there were pundits. Expert commentators pointed to expectations of accelerating dividend growth, reflecting the installation of electric motors and adoption of assembly line methods. General Motors was a leader in realizing the potential of these innovations under the direction of the MIT-trained engineer Alfred P. Sloan, who had assumed control when the overleveraged Durant was forced out in 1920.[3] GM reported exceptionally strong profits in 1928, encouraging the belief that the same would be true of other technologically progressive firms. If so, investors overlooked the possibility that GM's strong profitability reflected the fact that Henry Ford had closed down his Highland Park factory in May 1927 in order to retool from the Model T to the Model A, diverting purchases toward his competitor. If savvy investors didn't understand the point, it was because GM's management under Sloan—who was a pioneer not just in scientific management but also in investor relations—did its best to convince them that the surge in profitability was GM's doing.[4]

The other obvious suspect was, as usual, the Fed. In 1927 the Reserve banks once more cut their policy rates to relieve the pressure on the Bank of England. Britain was still struggling to reduce the high labor costs with which it was saddled as a result of the return to gold in 1925. It had been hit in 1926 by a strike by coal miners protesting demands from their employers that they accept wage cuts of 25 percent. In addition, the Dawes Plan, which rescheduled Germany's post–World War I reparations in 1924, permitted the country to make those payments by exporting coal.[5] Germany's reentry into the international coal market now depressed prices, further ratcheting up the pressure for the British industry to cut costs by any and all means.

————

The coal strike lasted six weeks, during which production and exports were disrupted. The result was a deteriorating British balance of payments and gold losses for the Bank of England. Nor were the coal miners Montagu Norman's only problem; he also had the German and French central banks to contend with. First the Reichsbank and then the Bank of France began withdrawing gold from London. The French and German central banks were not reassured by Britain's contentious industrial relations. Not without reason, they saw gold as a better bet than sterling.

The resulting gold losses forced Norman to keep interest rates high, making for more stringent financial conditions. That in turn made things even more difficult for a British economy struggling to regain its footing.

Understanding how these tensions came about requires us to step back and consider the problem confronting the monetary experts who sought to reconstruct Europe's trade and payments after World War I. Like Benjamin Strong, they were convinced that the gold standard was the only durable foundation on which to build. They worried, however, that there might not be enough gold to firmly sink the pilings. Wages and prices had risen sharply during World War I, but gold supplies, reflecting the foibles of the mining industry, failed to follow. The traditional way of squaring this circle was by pushing wages and prices back down. But doing so was no longer palatable politically, in the wake of the war. The electoral franchise was now broader; men who had so valiantly fought in the trenches could no longer be denied the vote. Labor movements grew more militant, as underlined by the British coal strike.

For all these reasons, a policy of wage and price reductions was no longer easy to implement. Nor could more gold for backing money supplies, commensurate with higher prices, be conjured out of thin air, or from under the ground. The only solution was to find a substitute that central banks could use to supplement their existing gold reserves—that they could use to back their issuance of money and credit. Here the obvious supplements were the bonds issued by the US and British treasuries, which in principle were as good as gold—that would, in other words, be readily exchangeable into the yellow metal once the international gold standard was restored.

The idea that central banks should supplement their gold reserves by holding the securities of governments like Britain's was enthusiastically tabled by the British delegation to the international conference convened in Genoa in 1922. It was received with mixed feelings by other European countries anticipating that their securities would not enjoy the same privileged status. Moreover, anything that smacked of a relaxation of gold-standard disciplines raised a red flag in countries that suffered runaway inflation in the first half of the 1920s, Germany of course being the classic case in point. The hyperinflation that reached its chaotic climax in Germany in 1923 came to be seared, seemingly forever, in the country's collective consciousness. It took place when the gold standard was in abeyance; indeed, it is inconceivable that such high inflation could have occurred were the money stock tied to supplies of gold. In France, inflation never quite reached hyperinflationary levels but nonetheless had the same socially corrosive effects. The French inflation similarly took place when the gold standard was suspended. There, too, inflation stabilization coincided with the gold standard's restoration. French and German officials, rendered highly inflation-averse, therefore subscribed to a particularly rigid form of gold standard doctrine subsequently. The policies flowing from that doctrine ultimately created intractable problems not just for Germany and France but ultimately for the United Kingdom, the United States, and the world as a whole.

Inflation may be always and everywhere a monetary phenomenon, but in Germany and France it was more fundamentally a political phenomenon. At its root were the tangle between the two countries over reparations and the division between business and labor as to who would bear the cost not just of those transfers but also of basic social services. Following the signing of the Treaty of Versailles in that other famous Hall of Mirrors, the Inter-Allied Reparations Commission had set Germany's reparations bill at 269 billion gold marks, nearly 200 percent of GDP.[6] This immense sum was unrealistic and unattainable, as John Maynard Keynes, the lead treasury representative to the Paris peace conference, argued in *The Economic Consequences of the Peace*, the December 1919 broadsheet that made him a public figure. Economically, forcing the country to export a multiple of what it imported in order to make large transfers to foreigners threatened to turn Germany's terms of trade (the price of what it exported relative to the price of what it imported) against it, rendering those transfers still harder and, in the limit, impossible to achieve.[7] Politically, reparations fanned international tensions, to put an understated gloss on the point.

Not only were the Allies' reparation demands enormous, but payments were scheduled to continue for forty-two years. Imposing this heavy burden on future generations kept alive the question of who was responsible for starting the war, and then for losing it. This in turn inflamed the debate over who should now bear the cost of repairing the damage. Socialists insisted that business should pay through a one-time levy on business assets, or "seizure of real values." In the spring of 1921 the German Social Democratic economics minister Robert Schmidt proposed that the wealthy should be required to turn over 20 percent of their stocks and bonds and that a 5 percent tax should be paid on the value of landed property. Business and property owners were aghast. As an alternative they constructively suggested raising sales and excise taxes, which conveniently fell on workers.

Equally predictably, the fact that a substantial fraction of tax revenues would be devoted to funding transfers to foreigners reinforced the opposition of both sides to any increase in rates. In the end, the decision taken was to rely on sales and excise taxes, though not heavily enough to close the fiscal gap.

———

Notwithstanding these constraints, the German government initially pursued a policy of fulfillment. This meant making an effort to meet the terms of the reparations agreement, in the hope that good behavior would be rewarded. But rewards were not much on the minds of the French, who had problems of their own, which they blamed on the Germans. The French right wing, in particular, saw economic and financial concessions as a sign of weakness that would only encourage nationalist tendencies in Germany. It followed that the political strength of the center-right Bloc national, in power from 1919, made compromise unlikely.

In January 1923 the French communicated their response to German requests for concessions in no uncertain terms. Under instructions from the prime minister and minister of foreign affairs Raymond Poincaré, the French army reentered the Ruhr Valley, Germany's western industrial flank, with the goal of extracting reparations by force. Railway and mine workers sat down on the job, and the Reichsbank, at government instruction, printed the paper marks that businesses paid their workers.

Poincaré's role in these events, as in the subsequent French inflation and stabilization, was controversial. The French leader was born in 1860 in Bar-le-Duc, not far from France's eastern border. As a child he was prudent and politic; one story has him always carrying an umbrella to school, whatever the weather. He was just a week short of his tenth birthday, in 1871, when, with the defeat of the French Imperial Army, Prussian troops occupied his native Lorraine. Young Raymond's bedroom was taken over by a Prussian officer, and the family was forced to remain in the upper floor of its house for the better part of three years.

From this, one imagines, flowed the mature Poincaré's unbending attitude toward Germany, his refusal to offer concessions on the reparations issue, and his readiness to use military means to extract them. In the words of the British prime minister, David Lloyd George, "M. Poincaré was a Lorrainer born in a province repeatedly overrun and ravaged by Teutonic hosts . . . he himself twice witnessed the occupation of his own cherished home by German troops [the second time being in World War I]. . . . M. Poincaré is cold, reserved, rigid, with a mind of unimaginative and ungovernable legalism. He has neither humor nor good humor."[8]

This evaluation was harsh and condescending, as was not infrequently the case with Lloyd George's appraisals of his political rivals.[9] Still, it conveys a sense of the broader context causing French leaders to frame the reparations issue as they did.

———

Among the casualties of the Ruhr occupation were Weimar's fragile finances. Although the cost of goods and services purchased by the government rose in step with the price level, taxes were paid on earlier incomes and lagged behind. The 10 percent tax on wages, deducted at the source, remained in the hands of employers for two weeks, at the end of which it was paid to the government. With prices doubling every fortnight, the consequences for the public finances were dire.

On March 23 Berlin imposed an additional penalty on anyone who delayed payment of taxes. But the new measure did not begin to correct the problem. The government's finances deteriorated further, forcing still greater reliance on the printing press. Firms, banks, and individuals devoted more and more time to minimizing the impact of the inflation on their personal and corporate finances and less and less to productive activity.

Something had to give. That something, in the end, was French public opinion and German business. For German coal and steel magnates like Hugo Stinnes with investments in the Ruhr, the passive resistance was a disaster. Much like the Scottish-American industrialist Andrew Carnegie, Stinnes had worked his way up from modest means, acquiring a constellation of businesses centering on the coal, steel, and shipbuilding industries and enhancing their efficiency by placing them under one managerial roof. The scale of his business empire meant that Stinnes stood to take large losses if coal mining was immobilized for an extended period.

In September 1923, Stinnes and other leading industrialists therefore agreed to pay back taxes and make coal deliveries directly to France. Berlin agreed to call off the passive resistance. Paris signaled a willingness to reconsider the reparations bill. This renegotiation then followed with the formation of the Dawes Commission at the end of November.

Rudolph Havenstein, the lawyer and civil servant who had served as president of the Reichsbank since 1908, long denied the existence of a connection between his policies of providing cash in return for government and private paper on the one hand and inflation on the other, preferring to blame the price increases on foreign speculators. Havenstein's hand was strong, in that his appointment was for life. But the evidence against his position was, by now, overwhelming. The passive resistance having collapsed, his board turned against him. It announced that the Reichsbank would no longer provide cash and credit in return for the emergency notes issued by German business.[10] And to ensure that the central bank would not abandon its newfound firmness, the government established the office of the Currency Commissioner and authorized its occupant to issue a parallel and hopefully stable currency, the rentenmark. To this office it appointed a well-known banker with political connections, Hjalmar Schacht. Schacht took up the position on November 13.

This marked the death of the hyperinflation and, as it turned out, of Havenstein himself, who suffered a fatal heart attack on November 20, the same day Germany's currency was stabilized against the dollar. The government now moved to have Schacht head the Reichsbank as well. Never one reluctant to engage in self-promotion, Schacht went on to claim that he had engineered the stabilization. The fact of the matter was that he was fortunate enough to assume his position as central banker just as the problem was solved.

As the printing presses slowed, the government's accounts strengthened of their own accord. The hyperinflation was history. But it was not history that was quickly forgotten. This background explains how the Reichsbank became wedded to an unvarnished version of the gold standard. It explains why its successor, the Deutsche Bundesbank, continued to view the world through the lens of the 1920s, not just after World War II but, amazingly, into the twenty-first century—and even after it was absorbed into the European System of Central Banks.

———

France too suffered from chronic budget deficits. The coalition government formed by the Bloc national of conservative parties, which held power from 1919 through 1924, succeeded periodically in balancing the "ordinary" budget of current expenditures but couldn't agree on how to finance the "recoverable" budget of postwar reconstruction costs, so called because there was the expectation, or at least the hope, that these might be recovered from the Germans. At some level, budget deficits were not entirely undesirable, since they indicated that France was incapable of financing its reconstruction on its own. As the British treasury expert Ralph Hawtrey put it, for a French government to balance the recoverable budget "would have been an unpatriotic act, an expression of doubt as to the recovery of reparations in full."[11]

Leaving aside reparations, the obvious solution to the fiscal problem would have been for the Left to agree to an increase in consumption taxes and the Right to concede modest levies on income and wealth. With a bit of shared sacrifice, the problem could have been solved. But there was little inclination to share sacrifice under the circumstances. It was not unlike the German situation except that the reparations shoe was on the other foot.

Meanwhile, the French treasury had to pay the bills. Borrowing long term was not an option. By 1923 the public debt exceeded 170 percent of GDP, given obligations incurred during the war and a deficit on the recoverable budget that now added 7 percent of GDP to the debt every year. Investors were willing to take only short-dated securities that would mature before potential problems of default and inflation materialized. Accordingly, the treasury issued short-term bills, known as national defense bonds to accentuate their connection with World War I. And whenever investors demonstrated a reluctance to purchase them, it asked the Bank of France to step in as purchaser of last resort.

Short-term debt poses risks to financial stability, as a long list of twentieth- and twenty-first-century emerging markets have learned to their chagrin. Because short-term bills mature continuously, the government has to be able to roll them over—to issue new ones to replace those it pays off. If investors worry that inflation is poised to accelerate and therefore hesitate to purchase the new bills issued to replace those that have recently matured, the government will experience a funding crisis. It will be forced to turn to the central bank for cash. That cash, which the central bank provides by purchasing the government's newly issued bills, will increase the money supply and in turn worsen inflation, validating investors' fears. Thus, in the same way that a run on a bank by panicked depositors can be self-fulfilling, so too can be a run on a government's short-term debt.

The result of this dependence on short-term borrowing and advances from the Bank of France was, predictably, repeated bursts of inflation, each more serious than the last. Again, a bit of inflation was not entirely undesirable from the standpoint of the diplomats, since it testified to the country's inability to finance its reconstruction costs. But this was not the view of the French public, which, like all publics, felt inflation in the pocketbook. By the first quarter of 1924, at the height of the Ruhr occupation, retail price inflation had reached an alarming 36 percent.[12] Share prices reacted badly: the index of 300 French securities fell sharply in March. More than a year into the Ruhr occupation, it was apparent that France would not be able to extract more blood from the German stone.

Forced to choose between compromise and hyperinflation, the French Parliament, still dominated by the Poincaré-led Bloc national, opted for compromise, though just barely. After a contentious debate lasting two months, legislators agreed to raise taxes by 20 percent across the board in a measure known as the *double decime*. Since it would take time for the additional tax revenues to materialize, J. P. Morgan, the French government's banker, agreed to provide a $100 million credit conditional on the Parliament first passing the tax increase. Another £4 million (roughly $19 million at the prevailing exchange rate) was then extended by the investment bank Lazard Frères.

This was enough to stabilize the franc for the moment.[13] But it was not enough to prevent inflation from resuming, since the underlying conflict was not resolved. It was not clear whether the *double decime* would be enough to balance the budget inclusive of reconstruction costs; the answer would depend on, among other things, taxpayer compliance. And it was not clear whether the middle classes, on whom the new taxes fell, would be prepared to accept them. The dispute over who would bear the burden heated up again as soon as it became evident, with the failure of the Ruhr invasion, that the answer was "not Germany."

––––––

In elections in May 1924, the Bloc national lost its majority in the Chamber of Deputies, as the unhappy middle-class voters who bore the brunt of Poincaré's taxes turned out in large numbers. The Radicals (essentially, reformist bourgeois liberals), with support from the Socialists, then formed a left-of-center government, the Cartel des Gauches, headed by the longtime Radical politician Édouard Herriot, and sought to reopen the fiscal question. With the 1924 compromise in the balance, there was renewed uncertainty about whether the budget would be balanced. Herriot was sympathetic to the Bolshevik experiment, having visited the Soviet Union in 1922.[14] Though not a Communist himself, his selection as prime minister alarmed the Right. Worried that his government might seek to close the deficit by imposing a levy on wealth, investors rushed to sell their government bonds. The franc plummeted on the foreign exchange market as bondholders scrambled to get their money out of the country. Inflation accelerated again, and tax revenues failed to keep pace with the rising cost of public-sector outlays, as in Germany in 1923. With the government now unable to market even short-term bills and reluctant to raise the rate of interest they offered for fear that this would validate expectations of inflation and worsen the budgetary situation, this left only the Bank of France as bond purchaser of last resort.

The central bank thus faced a dilemma. Parliament had placed a ceiling in 1920 on how many currency notes the bank could issue precisely in order to limit the recourse of governments to inflationary finance. Purchasing government bonds in substantial amounts might now cause those limits to be breached. In an extraordinary turn of events, the Bank of France chose to falsify its published statements, disguising the fact that it had breached the legal ceiling on note issuance. The deception was elegant in its simplicity: the excess was simply placed under the heading "various" (*divers*) on the two sides of the Bank's balance sheet.

In fact, this violation had begun already the previous March, under the earlier Poincaré-led Center-Right government. Secretary General Albert Aupetit, Bank of France Governor Georges Robineau's headstrong second in command, took the initiative in an effort to avoid torpedoing the Poincaré government's stabilization program.[15] To not finance the government's transitional deficits would have precipitated a funding crisis, putting an abrupt end to Poincaré's stabilization effort. For Aupetit, who saw Poincaré's stabilization as the country's best remaining hope and who was anxious to give it time to work, breaking the law was a lesser evil.

With the temporary success of Poincaré's stabilization, the note circulation fell safely below the legal maximum. But Aupetit continued to falsify the bank's weekly statement, understating the note issuance in an effort to convince speculators that the stabilization was a success. In October, as the stabilization lost traction following the change in government, the note issue then rose above the legal ceiling a second time, a fact that the central bank, under Aupetit's leadership, once again hid from wider view.

At this point, Bank of France officials informed Prime Minister Herriot and his finance minister, Etienne Clémentel, of the troubling state of affairs. But they conveniently neglected to mention that the problem had first arisen under the Bloc national government, so as to impress upon Cartel leaders that their own budgetary policies were to blame. This may help to explain why Herriot, though now aware of the deception, hesitated to go public.

The longer the status quo persisted, the larger the gap became between the central bank's published balance sheet and the actual monetary circulation. And the larger the discrepancy, the more difficult it was to hide. By early 1925 its existence was common knowledge among members of the finance committees of the Chamber and Senate.[16] The situation created considerable tension within the Bank of France, to the point where François de Wendel, a leading member of the central bank's governing board, threatened to resign over the matter.

De Wendel's threat tipped the balance toward the faction that favored coming clean. When on April 9 the falsification of the bank's balance sheet was finally revealed, Herriot placed the blame on the bank. He insisted that the actions of his government were no different from those of its predecessors, but no matter. He was forced to resign, following a vote of no confidence in the Senate.

Specialists will recognize here what economists refer to as "fiscal dominance."[17] When fiscal policy makers decide, in their wisdom, to run a budget deficit, and there is nothing the central bank can do about it, the central bank will then have no choice but to buy the government's bonds and tolerate a higher rate of inflation than it would prefer, if it is otherwise impossible to finance the deficit and the alternative is default and financial chaos. In the French case, the central bank went so far as to disregard the law.

There is a parallel with the provision in the statute of the European Central Bank prohibiting it from buying the newly issued bonds of governments. That provision is designed to protect the ECB from fiscal dominance and the European public from inflation. There is also a parallel in how the ECB felt compelled to parse, if not exactly disregard, the provision in 2012 when, in the face of a bond-market crisis, it announced its program of Outright Monetary Transactions to buy government bonds on the secondary market.[18] Sometimes, even central bankers are forced to conclude, there are worse things than a bit of inflation.

————

The problem in France was that the resulting inflation was more than a bit. It persisted for the better part of two years, as one prime minister after another—there were seven in all from June 1924 to July 1926—grappled with the unwillingness of the Left and Right to compromise over the budget. The Left would propose a special levy on capital, and the wealthy would shift their savings abroad. The Right would then propose new taxes on consumption, and workers would take to the streets.

The resulting inflation was ruinous for small savers, rentiers, and military pensioners, the members of society least able to protect themselves. July 1926 saw protests by more than twenty thousand former servicemen and their sympathizers outside the Chamber of Deputies. Blaming foreigners for manipulating the franc and fomenting the inflation, the mob vented its anger by attacking Paris-by-night buses, the preferred vehicle of American tourists. Wealthy French families, fearing social unrest, sent not just their savings but now also their families abroad.

At this point the inflation was seriously disruptive; in some circles it was seen as a threat to French democracy itself. The Left-dominated Chamber of Deputies, in desperation, agreed on July 22 to allow Poincaré to return at the head of a government of national union.

Notwithstanding his harsh policies toward Germany, Poincaré held a reputation for prudence and caution. He was "the man of stability," having made his name by helping to organize the nation's finances during World War I. He had engineered the temporarily successful 1924 stabilization, after all. By raising taxes prior to a parliamentary election, he put the nation's finances before political gain and paid the price.

Poincaré was also a man of stability in that he was not closely identified with either the Right or the Left. In the Chamber of Deputies he was associated with the Moderates. The Bloc national may have been center-right, but Poincaré also had friends and allies among the Socialists, not least Léon Blum, the future premier. As the product of a middle-class family, he identified with the small savers least well positioned to protect themselves from the effects of inflation. Moderation was what the circumstances required. When it came to domestic policies, as opposed to his dealings with Germany, it was what Poincaré offered.

Poincaré was asked to form a union government combining his Center-Right constituency with elements of the Left. There was now a consensus that the politicization of fiscal policy had gone too far. Poincaré's appointment and his formation of a national unity government acknowledged this fact. The politicians, evidently, had learned the hard way that budgetary solutions needed to be agreed by consensus, not forced on the Right by the Left, or vice versa.

Fostering that consensus was now Poincaré's task. Procedures for monitoring incomes and collecting taxes were upgraded with the goal of raising revenues. There was some streamlining of the public administration, with the closure of local law courts and other administrative offices. Funds from the state tobacco monopoly were earmarked for servicing and retiring public debt. This confirmed that there would be no expropriation of the rich, something that the formation of a union government had already, in fact, made clear. Finally, Poincaré proposed to convert the short-term national defense bonds that had been the immediate source of financial vulnerability into stabler long-term obligations.

The desire to shift the burden of stabilization, whether from capital to labor, from the middle classes to the wealthy, or from France to Germany, had burned itself out in the fires of inflation. As a result, Poincaré's limited measures sufficed to cement the 1926 stabilization, which took hold in August. Prices stopped rising; the exchange rate, having depreciated previously, now began to appreciate, to the discomfort of French exporters, who enjoyed their newfound competitive advantage, leading the Bank of France to buy foreign currencies in exchange for francs to slow the currency's rise. The franc was then pegged to sterling and the dollar at the end of 1926, and gold convertibility was restored in 1928.

France's gold standard statutes, like Germany's, were rigid. They prohibited the central bank from purchasing government securities on the market (engaging in "open market operations") and otherwise providing direct financing to the government. As in Germany, a long shadow was cast by the inflation and the social divisions it laid bare.

———

Halting inflation, first in Germany and then in France, encouraged flight capital to return. Inflation having been subdued, there was more confidence that investments would hold their value. The commitment to return to the gold standard, in order to endure, required governments to balance their budgets. Investors thus had new reason to hope that the long succession of deficits and conflict over the incidence of taxes had finally come to an end. In time, this idea that stabilizing the currency somehow guaranteed responsible fiscal behavior and relieved investors of the risk of sovereign default would be revealed as mistaken. This was of course the same mistake committed by those who purchased the bonds of Southern European nations following the advent of the euro in 1999. It had the same consequences.

The influx of foreign money was a mixed blessing for the French and German economies, since it placed upward pressure on their currencies. To prevent the exchange rate from shooting through the roof, to the detriment of exporters, the Reichsbank and Bank of France bought up those foreign funds, in return for marks and francs. But the foreign securities, and sterling securities in particular, acquired in this way were not obviously as good as the gold for which they could be exchanged.

Hence Norman's problem. In the second half of 1926 the Reichsbank began cashing in its sterling balances, taking gold from the Bank of England in return. In the six months ending in February 1927, British gold exports to Germany approached $60 million, a considerable sum. Schacht, now firmly installed as head of the German central bank, was conscious of the constructive role Norman played in the negotiation of the Dawes Plan, under which reparations were reduced and a stabilization loan was secured. But, any such gratitude notwithstanding, Schacht's first responsibility was for his portfolio. His belief in the importance of following the gold standard rules was not tempered by emotion. Schacht therefore presented the sterling he acquired through his sterilization operations to the Bank of England for conversion into gold.

Norman had not been as helpful to the Bank of France when it was grappling ineffectually with debt and currency crises in 1923, 1925, and 1926. He saw France as having been particularly obstructionist in negotiating a reparations settlement. There was also the fact that the Bank of England and Bank of France were vying for influence in Central and Eastern Europe, whose financial business they sought to attract to London and Paris. Although Émile Moreau, successor to Robineau as governor of the Bank of France from 1926 to 1930, characterized his English counterpart as "aimable et charmant," Norman had rebuffed France's efforts to obtain concrete assistance for financial stabilization.[19]

Now, as capital flowed from Britain to France, the tables turned. The foreign assets acquired by the Bank of France were denominated in sterling and issued in London. Responding to the same uncertainties as the Reichsbank, Moreau took the first opportunity to cash them in. He was aware that his request, by draining gold from the Bank of England, would force Norman to raise "Bank rate," the rate the Bank of England charged when discounting bills for other financial institutions. But this was not an undesirable side effect. If the result was tighter conditions in London, the source of a significant fraction of the short-term capital flooding into France, then the policy had corollary benefits from the French point of view. If it created difficulties for the Bank of England, then so be it.

Britain's one source of leverage was the World War I debt that France owed Britain. Norman therefore suggested to Winston Churchill, the Chancellor of the Exchequer, that he ask for its repayment to be accelerated. This threat, thinly veiled, led Moreau to negotiate a compromise in June 1927 in which the Bank of France limited its further conversion of sterling into gold to £30 million. Norman's aggressive diplomacy solved, or at least put off, the immediate problem. But it did not enhance the prospects for friendly monetary relations going forward.

Strong monitored these Franco-British negotiations from his perch in New York. Excepting a hiatus in late 1926 spent in Biltmore, North Carolina, while recovering from pneumonia, he was in almost continuous contact with his friend Norman by cable and letter. Knowing that the opinions of the American central banker carried weight, Moreau forwarded Strong his own account of the Bank of France–Bank of England negotiations in an effort to ensure that Strong formed a balanced view.

The net effect was to impress on Strong the tenuousness of the British position. The continued stability of sterling hinged on the cooperation of the Reichsbank and the Bank of France, but this was not something to be taken for granted. At the same time, these sensible men understood that they were in it together. Strong had held friendly bilateral discussions with Norman, Schacht, and various Bank of France officials. In the case of Norman and Strong, there were more than just friendly bilateral discussions. The two men had met already during World War I on the occasion of Strong's inaugural trip to Europe as governor of the New York Fed and formed a personal bond. They became pen pals and vacationed together twice a year for much of the 1920s, health permitting. If Norman had been able to develop such a fruitful relationship with Strong, why then couldn't these other central bankers reach a similarly harmonious understanding in face-to-face meetings?

Norman therefore suggested that he and Strong meet together with Schacht and Moreau. Strong issued the invitation—he was still recovering from his bout of pneumonia, dictating that the meeting take place in the United States.

Moreau, possessing no English, even then the universal language of central banking, passed the invitation to Charles Rist, his number two.

Strong, Norman, Schacht, and Rist assembled in the first week of July in Woodbury, on Long Island, at the home of US Treasury Undersecretary Ogden Mills. This monumental county seat, designed by John Russell Pope, was one of the most lavish on Long Island, with views in all directions and a central portion that "rises through two stories, with its cornice and parapet of somewhat Italian feeling . . . flanked and carefully held by the well-proportioned blocklike wings whose flat fretted cornices carry the line of the first story order around the entire building."[20]

This was opulent architecture more than befitting a meeting of the world's leading central bankers. Whether the international financial architecture was up to the task was another matter. For five days the central bankers conferred. It was like herding cats; Strong failed even to get all three of his colleagues into a room at the same time. Norman emphasized the delicacy of his position and his limited gold reserves. Schacht and Rist reiterated the importance of adhering to the rules of the gold standard as strictly as possible.

Process of elimination left one central bank to take the initiative. The result was another attempt by Strong to convince the Federal Reserve banks to agree to cut interest rates to support sterling. There was no little irony in the outcome. Strong had agreed to convene the meeting in an effort to encourage adjustments by the European bankers, but it was he who ended up doing the adjusting.

To make the case, Strong saw to it that Norman, Schacht, and Rist continued on to Washington and New York to meet with the board of governors and with Daniel Crissinger, chairman of the New York Fed. These officers of the Fed, evidently, were convinced. By the end of August, eight Reserve banks had voted to cut interest rates by half a point. Adolph Miller would have dissented, but he was summering in California. Later he criticized the decision as giving "a further great and dangerous impetus to an already over-expanded credit situation, notably to the volume of credit used on the stock exchanges."[21]

The majority decision was then imposed on the dissenting Reserve banks, starting with the Federal Reserve Bank of Chicago. This was the first time in the history of the Federal Reserve System that the board of governors imposed its will on dissenting Reserve banks. Strong was pleased, no doubt, to see the board force the other Reserve banks into line. Higher rates in the Midwest than the East had allowed banks in the interior to borrow more cheaply in New York in order to lend to their own customers, resulting in a drain of reserves and gold from the New York Fed. This assertion of authority by the board was an important step toward an integrated Federal Reserve policy, in which decisions were not made by individual Reserve banks following their parochial concerns but instead coordinated across districts with the needs of the national economy in mind.

Unfortunately, it was only a step. When the crunch came, in 1929, coordination would be lacking. And the consequences would not be pretty.

| Competing on a Violent Scale

T HE MOTIVATION FOR the Fed's 1927 interest rate cut may have been to encourage gold to flow to London, but there were other effects. Another immediate consequence was to encourage investors to search for yield abroad. In a period when US treasury bonds returned 3½ percent, bonds issued by foreign governments yielded two and three times as much. Restoration of the gold standard created the impression that there would no longer be exchange rate changes to disturb the returns. One is reminded of the response to the euro, when large amounts of capital flowed from Northern Europe, where interest rates were low, to Southern Europe, where they were two or three times as high. In neither case did the story end happily.

Foreign bonds were not an asset class traditionally favored by American investors. US banks had been prohibited from branching abroad prior to the Federal Reserve Act. They consequently lacked the connections to originate and underwrite foreign loans. There was only limited issuance of foreign dollar bonds in New York before the turn of the century, mainly on behalf of Canadian and Mexican borrowers. Montreal placed a $3 million bond issue in the United States in 1899, and the Hamilton Electric Light and Cataract Power Company sold $750,000 of bonds later the same year. In 1898–99 the Mexican state of Jalisco and the city of Saltillo sold $1.7 million of dollar bonds in New York for construction of sewers and waterworks.

There were also scattered US holdings of European debt securities denominated in the borrowers' own currencies that had been issued in London or another European financial center and resold to American investors. But investing in such securities required financial acumen and knowledge of foreign exchange markets, attributes that were not widespread in the United

States. Consequently the amounts involved were small. By one estimate, foreign-currency securities held by US investors came to just $15 million at the end of 1899.[1] This can be placed in perspective by noting that the U.S. Steel Corporation, on its establishment in 1901, immediately issued $300 million of bonds.

Between 1900 and 1913 foreign loan placements in New York picked up. American investors purchased bonds issued by the London Underground. They purchased securities floated by the Japanese government for financing its war with Russia. But the balance of asset trade was in the other direction.

With the outbreak of World War I, the belligerents sought to access the New York market. This elicited mixed reactions from American officials. The newly elected president, Woodrow Wilson, appointed fellow Democrat and longtime party favorite William Jennings Bryan as his secretary of state. The position was largely honorific, given that the State Department had just 150 employees in Washington, D.C. Still, Bryan could use his bully pulpit and rhetorical skills to advance his views. Ever the moralist (except perhaps in his incarnation as a shill for Florida real estate), Bryan was horrified by events in Europe and convinced that America should remain neutral at all cost. Specifically, he opposed bond sales on behalf of the belligerents as inconsistent with US neutrality. To circumvent his opposition, investment houses like J. P. Morgan & Co. were forced to portray their loans as no more than temporary credits, despite the fact that they were quickly securitized and sold on to the public.

With the sinking of the American liner *Lusitania* by a German U-boat in May 1915, an incident in which 128 American lives were lost, Bryan's position became untenable. He speculated that the passenger liner may have been carrying munitions, arguing that this could justify the German action. Nearly a century later, in 2008, divers were finally able to confirm that Bryan was right.[2] But this was not something that could be verified at the time. Seeing Wilson's cabinet turning against him, Bryan resigned his post.

His resignation opened the floodgates. Between mid-1915 and early 1917, dollar loans to foreign governments, mainly those of France and Britain, exceeded $2 billion. This was a large amount of bond issuance even by the standards of U.S. Steel. Among other things, it had the effect of accustoming American investors to holding foreign bonds.

Following the US declaration of war in April 1917, the country's foreign lending was channeled through governments, including loans by the American government to its European allies. American investors bought the Liberty Bonds of the US Treasury, receipts from which were used to fund war loans. In the late nineteenth and early twentieth centuries, there had been a shortage of US government bonds for private purchase. Now, as a result of the war, the opposite was true. Propaganda was enlisted to create a demand commensurate with the new supply. The Liberty Loan campaign equated investment in government debt securities with patriotism and support for American boys in the trenches. Charlie Chaplin directed a ten-minute film entitled "The Bond" to advance the drive. It portrayed six kinds of bonds, including not just the financial but also those of friendship and sexual attraction. Nine million posters were printed and distributed in support of the campaign. Small savers were induced to invest in debt securities for the first time and became accustomed to the practice. The repercussions would be far-reaching.

———

International capital flows were slow to recover following the armistice, understandably given the still-chaotic state of affairs. But starting in 1923, reconstruction and stabilization loans on behalf of foreign governments were offered to the American investing public in growing numbers. Chief among these were loans to Europe's cash-strapped governments negotiated by the League of Nations. The first such loan was extended to the Austrian government in 1923, followed by loans to Hungary and Greece in 1924.

The US was not a member of the League, an isolationist Congress refusing to grant authorization. But the semi-official status of its loans, and their resemblance to Liberty Bonds, enhanced the appeal to American investors. Much like the presumption today that a country will not default on its obligations to the International Monetary Fund, there was a presumption that a country would not default on its League loans. Admittedly, there was the uncomfortable fact that the League itself committed no capital to the venture. But for investors less than reassured by the association with the League, there was also the fact that the League loans offered an interest rate more than twice that on US treasury bonds.

The signal financial event of 1924 was the Dawes Loan to Germany. This was negotiated not through the League, given US interest in the outcome, but by an ad hoc committee of experts, two from each of the creditor countries. The committee was chaired by the garrulous American banker Charles Dawes. Dawes came from a well-connected Midwestern family; his father, who built the Dawes Lumber Company into a thriving concern, served in Congress together with the young William McKinley. McKinley had enlisted Charles and his verbal powers of persuasion as a fund-raiser in the 1896 presidential campaign in which McKinley defeated Bryan. McKinley rewarded Dawes with appointment, at the age of thirty-one, as Comptroller of the Currency. Dawes later founded the Central Trust Company of Illinois, served as founding director of the Bureau of the Budget, returned to banking, and later served as first head of the Reconstruction Finance Corporation, making full use of the revolving door between public and private sectors. These connections would come in handy when Dawes' bank came to the brink of insolvency in 1932.[3]

Second in command of the US delegation was another, more junior, banker, the laconic Owen D. Young, whom Dawes appreciated for his acuity but also for his brevity, which left the loquacious chairman more time to talk. In 1911, as a young lawyer, Young had bested a General Electric subsidiary in a suit over territorial rights. Recognizing talent, GE hired him as chief counsel, from where he quickly ascended to company president. Young helped establish the National Broadcasting Company (NBC), a leading player in the radio boom of the 1920s. With the experience of the Dawes Plan under his belt, he led the second restructuring of German reparations in 1929 and was a director of the Federal Reserve Bank of New York during the crises of 1930–31. In 1932 he was prime mover in the adoption of the Veterans' Bonus, which would provide useful stimulus to an otherwise moribund economy. He would play a role in the rescue of Dawes' Central Republic Bank and Trust Company, also in 1932. He was cited as receiving special favors from J. P. Morgan and was cross-examined in the Pecora Commission hearings on financial fraud and misbehavior in 1933. If not quite the Forrest Gump of financial crises, Young was to figure in virtually every key financial event of the 1920s and 1930s.

Dawes, Young, and team formulated their strategy while en route to France. The captain of the liner *America* designated the children's playroom for their conferences, Dawes later observing that "the significance of this choice was not wholly lost on us."[4] The delegation worked smoothly. In addition to being a good listener, Young had an ability to provide simple solutions to complex problems.

The Americans, with guidance from Young, agreed to press for back-loading Germany's debt burden. Acknowledging that any proposal for reducing the overall obligation was likely to be a no-go in France, they sought instead to limit the short-term transfer while allowing payments to rise with the growth of the German economy.[5]

This was the proposal that Dawes, upon landing, presented to his European interlocutors. The European delegates were unenthusiastic, but he overcame their resistance by keeping them in continuous session until, exhausted, they gave in.[6] This presumably accounts for the fact that the final report of the committee was unanimous, which in turn explains how its recommendations were then accepted by a conference of leaders in London.

Stabilizing the German currency required not merely adjusting the reparations burden, however, but also arranging an emergency loan, since the Reichsbank was out of funds. The conditions attached to this foreign assistance were daunting even by the standards of early-twenty-first-century Greece. Not only was the government required to balance its budget, inclusive of reparations, but a foreign agent general with far-reaching powers was appointed to enforce the requirement. The Reichsbank was prohibited from extending advances to the state, and investors in the Dawes Loan were given first lien on the revenues of the German state railways.

These measures were intended to reassure foreign investors, which in practice meant American investors. The French and British governments funded their shares of the Dawes Loan by allocating tax revenues for the purpose. The United States, market-oriented as always, relied instead on J. P. Morgan to sell the bonds to the public. The bankers worried that skeptical retail investors, who had not previously bought the bonds of foreign governments, would hesitate to purchase the obligations of what was recently an enemy power now saddled with reparations obligations extending decades into the future.

Such fears were unfounded. By 10:15 on the morning the bonds were issued, Morgan had received twice the number of purchase offers it required. The American public was clearly developing a healthy appetite for foreign debt securities.[7]

For his efforts, Dawes was awarded the Nobel Peace Prize for 1925, along with Sir Austin Chamberlain, the British foreign secretary who had engineered the Locarno Agreements that contemporaries saw as making another European war inconceivable. By this time Dawes had been elected vice president of the United States, a position in which he was singularly ineffective even by the modest standards of that office. Dawes' more enduring legacy was as a musician. His compositions included "Melody in A Major," which became his signature anthem and was played in his honor at official functions. Lyrics were added by Carl Sigman in 1951, and the resulting composition was renamed "It's All in the Game." Tommy Edwards' recording became a number-one hit in 1957, rendering Dawes the only US vice president and Nobel Prize winner to also be credited with a chart-topping song.

———

Like the peace prize awarded Barack Obama, Dawes' commendation was based more on hope than achievement. Even the hope was disappointed. As economic recovery got underway, German politicians and their public grew increasingly restive with the increase in payments required by the plan. The German debt load mounted, raising questions of sustainability.[8] By 1929, even prior to the onset of depression, support for the Dawes Plan had collapsed. It was replaced by the Young Plan, devised by Dawes' sidekick from 1924, which further scaled back Germany's obligation.

But all this was for the future. For the moment, the demand for German bonds was strong. The New York Fed's 1924 interest-rate reduction, taken with the goal of helping Britain back onto the gold standard, whetted the appetite of investors for the high-yielding bonds issued to fund the Dawes Loan. It boosted the demand of American investors for foreign bonds generally. New dollar loans to foreign countries, funded almost entirely by placing bonds in the United States, ran at an annual average of $600 million between 1921 and 1923. In 1924 and again in 1925, with encouragement from the Dawes Plan and then the Fed, they rose to twice that level. In the second half of 1927 and the first half of 1928, following Strong's second internationally motivated interest-rate cut, they rose further still.[9]

Initially, the US market in foreign bonds was the preserve of the same handful of investment banks that dipped a toe in this water before World War I, well-known names like J. P. Morgan & Co. and Kuhn, Loeb & Co. These august institutions knew the market and had contacts with foreign customers. They expected aspiring borrowers to come to them. But the atmosphere grew less cozy after 1924 with the entrance into the underwriting business of additional investment banks. The new entrants included old-line Boston and New York houses run now by an ambitious younger generation, as well as new financial firms. Deposit-taking commercial banks joined the fray, creating securities affiliates to underwrite bond issues on their behalf.

A company like J. P. Morgan had a reputation to preserve. Underwriting an issue with significant risk of default might jeopardize its ability, cultivated over the years, to get other banks to join the syndicate underwriting the issue and to foster confidence among investors. Newcomers to the underwriting business, in contrast, had little reputation to preserve. Their concern was the commission, which could amount to as much as 4½ percent of the value of the bonds. The commission was earned on placing the issue. It could not be clawed back if a bond lapsed into default.[10]

Nor did aspiring underwriters wait for borrowers to come to them. Instead they now ventured into the offices and homes of foreign government officials, including not a few to whom it had not occurred previously that they needed to borrow. Max Winkler, the self-appointed chronicler of this adventurous period, describes the case of a Bavarian town that sought to raise $125,000 for improvements to its power plant but was encouraged by its American underwriter to borrow $3 million to finance, in addition, a swimming pool, a bath house, and a gymnasium.[11] A witness before the Senate Committee on Finance, investigating in 1932 why so many of these loans went bad, described how "at one time . . . there were 29 representatives of American financial houses in Colombia alone trying to negotiate loans for the national government, for the departments, and for other possible borrowers."[12] Borrowers were plied with food, wine, and other less licit pleasures, financed by the expense accounts of visiting bankers. The politically connected were offered finder's fees for their influence. The Senate was told how those same expense accounts were used for "fixing" presidents and officials. Old-line bankers, like Thomas Lamont, a leading Morgan partner, warned of "American bankers and firms competing on almost a violent scale for the purposes of obtaining loans in various foreign money markets," competition of a sort that "tends to insecurity and unsound practice."[13] But old-line bankers were increasingly outnumbered by their younger, less experienced, and more aggressive competitors.

Having secured the borrower's business, the underwriter still had to interest the retail investor. Banks that had built bond departments to place Liberty Bonds now repurposed them to market foreign issues. Using their securities affiliates to circumvent laws prohibiting them from transacting across state lines, they sold bonds nationally. They placed articles in *Harper's* and *The Atlantic Monthly* extolling the virtues of the new instruments. They opened store-front offices to encourage walk-in business. They hired salesmen schooled in high-pressure sales tactics.[14]

Finally, the promoters formed investment trusts, early-twentieth-century forerunners of mutual funds, to sell shares to small investors who would have otherwise found it difficult to obtain the benefits of a diversified portfolio of foreign bonds and to offer the services, however dubious, of professional management. A few investment trusts, a recent British import, had been established prior to the 1920s, but they were now founded in large numbers. There was also a tendency for investment trusts to be "closely intertwined," as Eugene White politely puts it, with the banks sponsoring them, which encouraged bank clients to invest in securities through the affiliated trust.[15] Whereas early investment trusts had tended to hold a fixed portfolio of securities, their more recently established competitors were actively managed—that is, they churned the portfolio. Investment trusts invested in other investment trusts, doubling the fees paid by their customers.[16]

The promotional push, together with the high interest rates on offer, was effective. In the words of Paul Einzig, the prolific British financial journalist, writing in 1931, "During the last seven years or so, bond-selling houses spared no effort to educate the American investor to appreciate the advantages of investing in foreign bonds. Through applying every device of their highly developed art of salesmanship they succeeded, between 1923 and 1928, in placing a formidable amount of foreign bonds of every description with the American public."[17]

Formidable is the word. American investors provided fully 80 percent of the money borrowed by German public credit institutions between 1925 and

1928. They furnished 75 percent of that borrowed by the country's local governments and 50 percent of loans to its large corporations.[18] A loan to Austria financed the construction of a hydroelectric works. A loan to Belgium underwrote investments in roads and ports in the Congo. In all, European governments and corporations were the recipients of nearly half of all US foreign lending in the 1920s.

An additional one-quarter of foreign securities issued in the United States went to Latin America. In Argentina alone, US investors supplied long-term funding to permit the government to repay a short-term loan from the British government. Dollar bonds were floated to enable the Argentine authorities to acquire gold to back the national currency. Dollar bonds funded the construction and improvement of public works, including the railways, and extended the duration of their existing short-term debts. Dollar loans were made to provincial governments to replace expiring sterling credits and in anticipation of tax receipts. Local governments borrowed to build roads, bridges, schools, waterworks, sewage systems, and, critically for a meat-exporting country, cold-storage plants. Argentine municipalities borrowed to build and improve hospitals, power plants, parks, and streets.

———

This was risky business, although it could be argued that it was not without logic. With the American economy growing rapidly, the US savings rate was high. As in early-twenty-first-century China, which similarly saw a high savings rate, prime-age workers at the saving stage of the life cycle had higher incomes than older individuals, now in retirement and dissaving. In Europe, where incomes were depressed by the war and postwar disruptions, savings rates were low. There was a shortage of capital to repair roads, bridges, and factories. That interest rates were higher in Europe than in the United States, which is what worked to attract US investors to foreign securities, flowed directly from this confluence of facts.

Making the case for investment in Latin America was harder. But Latin countries that had expanded their production and exports of agricultural commodities and raw materials during the war could claim that they were enhancing their capacity to earn foreign exchange and hence to service loans. With so much money on offer, it was not hard to make the case.

But even a process with an underlying logic can be pushed too far—a tendency that is not unknown in finance. Foreign loans to underwrite the reconstruction of war-damaged railways and ports or to build cold-storage facilities for Argentine beef exports were one thing; borrowing to build municipal swimming pools and bathhouses was another. With finance so easy, governments were tempted to engage in additional spending. Already in 1926 Schacht worried that all the capital flowing into Germany was encouraging excesses on the part of state and local governments.[19] In May 1927 he instructed the banks to curtail their loans to the stock market in an effort to damp down the boom. But even though this led to a sharp fall in the stock market, it did nothing to discourage borrowing by German municipalities. And the higher interest rates induced by Schacht's policy only made it more attractive for foreign investors to lend.

S. Parker Gilbert, the former US treasury undersecretary appointed as agent generation for reparations to carry out the Dawes Plan, warned of the risks posed by the torrent of foreign capital. German governments, he warned, were "overspending and overborrowing." The economy was at risk of "overstimulation and overexpansion." Sooner or later, doubts would develop about the sustainability of the process. At that point, the inflow of foreign capital would come to a sudden stop, resulting in "severe economic reaction and depression."[20]

The parallels with the recent crisis are almost too obvious. Starting in 2004, a swelling chorus of voices cautioned about the ongoing flow of capital to the United States from China, Germany, and the oil-exporting countries. This was encouraging the profligacy of the US government, they warned, by enabling it to borrow at artificially low rates. The flow of cheap foreign finance would not continue indefinitely, and when it stopped the consequences would be challenging. As it happened, the crisis of which they warned was superseded by another, the collapse of US real estate prices and the market in subprime mortgages in 2006–07. Still, they had a point.

There were also differences. One is that global imbalances in the 1920s were tilted in the other direction: capital flowed from the United States, not toward it. The other is that the Cassandras who warned the process could not continue indefinitely and it was setting the stage for a crisis were right on both counts. When in 1928 the outflow came to a sudden stop, it plunged first Germany, then Latin America, and finally the world into precisely the "severe economic reaction and depression" of which Parker Gilbert, two years earlier, had warned.

———

However frothy the market in foreign bonds, Wall Street was frothier still. On three of the first seven trading days of 1928, the number of shares traded on the New York Stock Exchange exceeded three million, a level that had been reached just eight times over the previous decade. From there, activity rose still higher.

Evidently, the large investors clubbed together in pools organized by the likes of Billy Durant were being joined by a growing number of small savers. Individuals who had relied on professionals employed by investment trusts to manage their portfolios took to buying and selling securities directly. Brokerage firms opened branch offices featuring customers' rooms fitted out with plush carpets and overstuffed chairs designed to create an ambience of comfort and security. Six hundred new customers' offices were opened in 1928 and 1929.[21] Additional rooms were created for female investors, in another sign of the times.[22]

The nature of the attraction is no mystery. Stocks yielded 38 percent in 1927, an extraordinarily high rate by historical standards. They yielded an even more impressive 44 percent in 1928. Credit was available for anyone seeking to share in these heady returns.[23] The process was perversely self-financing, as credit booms are. The higher share prices rose, the more attractive it became for corporations seeking to finance their operations to issue additional equity rather than borrow from banks. This forced the banks to look for other lending opportunities, which they found in the stock market. As share prices then rose further, the collateral on which securities lending occurred became more valuable, justifying still more lending.[24]

The Fed's detractors, both internal and external, criticized it for fanning the flames. By November 1927 James McDougal of the Chicago Fed (whose bank, recall, had resisted Strong's proposal for an interest rate cut earlier in the year but was overruled), together with George Norris of Philadelphia, was advocating higher interest rates to stem the flow of credit into the stock market. Brokers' loans had increased by more than $300 million in the previous five months. In December and January they then rose by an additional $500 million.

For the Open Market Investment Committee, this was finally too much. It agreed, starting in January 1928, to sell securities for cash in order to drain liquidity from the market. The next step was to make borrowing more expensive, with the goal of making it more costly to use credit to buy stocks on margin. Starting on January 25 and extending through the end of February, one Federal Reserve bank after another raised its discount rate. A second round of increases followed in April. The Federal Reserve Bank of New York then raised its discount rate for a third time in May.

———

Although the rise in policy rates was designed to cool an overheated stock market, its effects were most pronounced in Europe. By now, warnings of unsustainable foreign borrowing were rife. With the Fed's action boosting yields on short-term investments at home, foreign bond issuance fell off a cliff. US capital exports dropped from $530 million in the second quarter of 1928 to $120 million in the third. US lending to Germany, after running at more than $150 million in the second quarter, fell essentially to nil in the third. These events anticipated those of the summer of 2013, when the Federal Reserve mooted the possibility of "tapering" its purchases of US Treasury securities, leading investors to expect higher US interest rates, and emerging markets on the receiving end of capital inflows from the United States saw those flows stop and then reverse direction. The shock was uncomfortable, but it didn't begin to approach the severity of that experienced by Europe and Latin America in 1928.

This now was the sudden stop of which Schacht, Gilbert, and others had warned. German industry, by this point all but wholly dependent on foreign finance, was caught in the vise. Producers were unable to borrow the funds needed to pay for materials and labor, while their customers were unable to obtain the credit needed to finance their purchases. Industrial production, hit from both sides, fell by nearly 10 percent in the second half of the year. Freight carried by the German state railways fell even faster. The number of unemployed more than doubled.

A normal central bank would have cut interest rates and made credit available to a weakening economy. But the Reichsbank was not a normal central bank. Maintenance of gold convertibility, as a bulwark against inflation, was its priority. To limit the loss of reserves, it kept the discount rate steady at 7 percent, much higher than the levels prevailing in other European financial centers.

In January 1929, Schacht finally acknowledged deteriorating economic conditions and reduced the Reichsbank's policy rate by half a percentage point, to 6.5 percent. When, as a result, gold started flowing out, he then reversed course, raising the discount rate by 100 basis points (meaning one full percentage point), to 7.5 percent. Not only did this deal an additional blow to an already weakening economy but, with confidence visibly deteriorating, the interest-rate hike did not even succeed in stemming the outflow of capital from Germany or the Reichsbank's loss of gold.

Other European countries dependent on US lending were affected similarly. By the end of 1928 not just Germany but also much of Central Europe was in recession. Only Britain was different; the British economy, having begun to recover the momentum lost in the 1926 coal strike, was still in the expansion phase of the cycle. But starting in September 1928, the Bank of England, like its Central European counterparts, began losing gold to the United States as a result of tighter credit conditions in New York. Sooner or later, it was clear, Norman would be forced to raise interest rates.[25] And it was increasingly questionable, in this light, whether and if so for how much longer the British economy would continue to expand.

———

This money repatriated from Europe was now deposited in US banks, which lent it to brokers and dealers, adding more fuel to the Wall Street fire. The Fed might have attempted to discourage this use of credit with further increases in interest rates. But with the approach of the fall crop-moving season and then the 1928 presidential election, doing so was problematic. The demand for credit tended to spike during the crop-moving season that followed the harvest; with agricultural prices already weak, any attempt to raise rates further was certain to provoke protests in the South and Midwest. And like any central bank, the Fed hesitated to do anything that might excite the public in the run-up to an election.

The device to which the Fed instead turned in 1929 was to directly rein in bank lending to brokers and dealers. This was the policy of "direct pressure," in which it arm-twisted member banks to limit lending for speculative purposes. New York City banks making loans to stockbrokers were warned that they would be cut off from the discount window. This was the board's attempt to surgically deflate the bubble without also damaging the economy. The brain behind it was the much-maligned Adolph Miller, who, as a faithful believer in the real bills doctrine, emphasized the importance of keeping interest rates at a level suitable for the needs of commercial activity. Thus, direct pressure was a way of dealing with the threat posed by an overexcitable stock market—by "optimism gone wild and cupidity gone drunk," in Miller's words—without raising interest rates to a level inconsistent with the legitimate needs of business.[26]

A number of the Federal Reserve banks, led by the Federal Reserve Bank of New York, favored further increases in discount rates. The directors of the New York bank, many of them Wall Street veterans, were especially concerned about what was going on down the street. They understood better than their colleagues in Washington, D.C., that money was fungible. Thus, they appreciated that any reduction in lending by member banks in New York would be offset, at least to an extent, by lending on the part of nonmember banks, member banks elsewhere in the country, and insurance companies, corporate treasuries, investment trusts, and even foreign banks and individuals.[27]

Just as they predicted, this shadow banking system was quick to step into the breach. In the first quarter of 1928, nonbank sources funded nearly half of all broker's loans. In the first half of 1929, as the growth of lending by money center banks was restrained by pressure from the Fed, nonbank sources accounted for fully 72 percent of the total. All the while, the volume of broker's loans moved up. That said, it moved up less quickly than it would have if the New York City banks had not felt the Fed's official pressure, and it moved up less quickly than needed to satisfy demand. Indicative of this fact is how interest rates on call loans continued to rise, pushing up other short-term interest rates in sympathy.

But those higher rates also made life more difficult for business. Reflecting tighter money and credit, the economy showed signs of decelerating in mid-1929. Building activity softened. State and local governments postponed construction projects owing to higher borrowing costs. Weak conditions abroad, reflecting the stop in US lending, showed up in weak American exports.

There has been much debate about who was right and who was wrong in this contest between the proponents of direct pressure and higher interest rates. In the light of recent experience, the answer is clear. We now understand that the best response for a central bank confronted with this kind of dilemma is to assign monetary policy, in this case its lending rate, to the needs of the economy while using regulatory tools like ceilings on loan-to-value ratios for home mortgages and limits on lending to particular sectors (what we would now call macroprudential policy) to address financial risks. This was precisely the intuition of those who advocated direct pressure in 1929: leave interest rates at a level appropriate for the economy and use other tools to limit lending to the stock market.

We now better appreciate the value of that intuition, because this is precisely what the Fed and other US agencies neglected to do in 2005–06, when they failed to use macroprudential policy to clamp down on the flow of credit into US housing markets. Here is a clear case where the events of 2007–08 change how we think about 1929. Real bills may be a discredited doctrine, but the macroprudential policies espoused by Adolph Miller look considerably more sage and sensible in this light.

The problem in 1929 was implementation. It was that the central bank's macroprudential tools were weak. The Fed could apply direct pressure only to member banks, leading to the substitution of nonmember and nonbank credit for bank credit to the stock market. This is a problem for modern macroprudential policy as well: when the authorities attempt to limit bank lending to a particular market, the property market for example, they see some substitution of nonbank credit for bank credit.[28] The solution is to give the macroprudential policy maker regulatory authority over nonbank providers of credit—over insurance companies and the like—as well as over banks. It is to set the "regulatory perimeter" as wide as possible.

This was similarly the problem for the proponents of direct pressure in 1929. But given the country's ramshackle regulatory system—where member banks were overseen by the Fed, state banks that were not members were overseen by state regulators, foreign banks were overseen by foreign regulators, and insurance companies were overseen by state insurance departments and agencies, if at all—it was a problem they were unable to solve. With credit continuing to flow into the stock market in what officials saw as dangerous amounts, the Fed felt compelled to supplement its policy of direct pressure by raising rates in the summer of 1929, compromising the prospects for economic growth.

Fed Governor Ben Bernanke gave a speech in 2002 in which he warned against using monetary policy to prick a bubble, pointing to the catastrophic implications of the Fed's attempt to do so in 1929. But he then went on, curiously, to also dismiss the 1920s policy of direct pressure as ineffectual.[29] A better approach, he implied, was for the central bank not to attempt to lean against a bubble but rather to flood the markets with liquidity if it bursts. We now know that flooding the market with liquidity, or at least flooding the part of the market the Fed is capable of flooding, may not be enough to avert the worst. Better is to strengthen tools like direct pressure rather than to dismiss them because their effects are weak. But this was a lesson that the Bernanke Fed would have to learn the hard way.

COUNTRYWIDE CREDIT WAS the lender at the epicenter of the housing boom, and Angelo Mozilo was the public face of Countrywide. The Bronx-born son of first-generation Italian Americans, Mozilo had gone to work in his father's butcher shop at the age of twelve and then as a messenger for a Manhattan mortgage lender. By the time he was sixteen he had worked his way up from ferrying paperwork to processing loans, progress testifying either to his exceptional ambition or to the straightforward nature of underwriting in the era of plain-vanilla mortgages.

Mozilo stayed with the same firm through his high school and college years and until it merged with Lomax Realty Securities, headed by industry veteran David Loeb. In the mid-1960s Loeb sent Mozilo to Central Florida, which was in the grips of a real estate boom not unlike that of the 1920s. Observing that the boom was being driven by the influx of space engineers to Cape Canaveral, Mozilo recommended taking a stake in a Brevard County subdevelopment. When the bet paid off, Loeb made Mozilo his sidekick.

When Lomax Securities was bought out in 1968, Loeb and Mozilo set out to create their own mortgage company, which they dubbed Countrywide Credit Industries. Initially the name was indicative more of the partners' ambition than the reality. The duo worked out of a single office in Anaheim, California, the Inland Empire to the east beckoning as the final frontier. Loeb served as the firm's strategist, Mozilo as its sales force of one.[1]

Although the business gained traction, costs showed a troubling tendency to escalate. Recruiting and retaining salesmen required paying generous commissions. Turnover was high, in part because Mozilo was a demanding boss—"a son of a bitch," as he proudly put it. Loeb therefore proposed eliminating the sales force and using direct advertising to solicit applications, something that had not previously been tried in the mortgage-banking industry. Mozilo, a salesman himself, resisted but eventually agreed to take the plunge.

Attracting business by advertising meant competing on price, which in turn required keeping costs down. The company's retail offices were standardized, situated in strip malls, and permitted no more than two full-time employees. Gradually the strategy began paying dividends. In the course of the 1970s Countrywide Credit opened four additional offices in California. By 1980 it had forty offices in nine states, no mean feat in a period when mortgage and housing markets were buffeted by interest rates of 20 percent. By the mid-1980s, the 40 offices had grown to 104 and the nine states to twenty-six. By 1992, with nearly 400 branches, Countrywide was the largest mortgage banker in the country and, for that matter, the world.

Reflecting its emphasis on low costs and standardization, Countrywide came to be known as the McDonald's of mortgage banking. The label reflected the extent to which it successfully reduced the home mortgage to a commodity, the financial equivalent of a hamburger, and the loan officer to the white-collar equivalent of a hamburger flipper. Countrywide was an early adopter of information technology to process applications. By the mid-1990s, fully 70 percent of loans passing through its automated underwriting system required no human intervention. Standardization and the commitment to information technology, together with reliance on temporary employees, allowed the company to ramp up when opportunity beckoned and downsize when demand slackened. Countrywide started reselling the mortgages it originated to Freddie Mac and Fannie Mae almost as soon as the two government-sponsored housing agencies were authorized to purchase mortgages not guaranteed by the US government.[2] It diversified into loan servicing, buying the right to service mortgages from other lenders to insulate itself from the ups and downs of loan origination. When interest rates were low, loan origination was big business, but when they were high, prepayments were less common, rendering servicing more profitable. Mozilo referred to this as Countrywide's "macro hedge."

Eventually some of these innovations came to be viewed in a less favorable light. That a majority of loan applications were processed without human intervention meant no independent verification of borrowers' claims of income. Aware that their tenure with the firm was likely to be limited, branch managers focused on originating as many mortgages as possible without due attention to their quality. Loan servicing turned out to provide less insulation from the ups and downs of interest rates and the housing market than Mozilo had posited. But these were problems for the future.

By the 1990s, organic expansion had become harder for what was now the largest player in the mortgage banking industry. This led Mozilo to the fateful decision to expand into low-income lending. In 1993 Countrywide launched a program that he ambitiously christened "House America." Mozilo marketed the initiative as bringing the American dream of home ownership to low-income and minority borrowers. Videos promoting it were narrated by the stentorian Hollywood actor James Earl Jones, who commanded the same vocal authority as William Jennings Bryan.

In practice, House America allowed low-income households to assume a heavier burden of mortgage debt. Countrywide adopted "flexible underwriting practices," reprogramming its automated underwriting systems to approve mortgages for individuals and households lacking the well-documented employment and credit histories needed to obtain conventional loans. "Flexible underwriting practices" was code for down payments of as little as 3 percent, offered in return for a higher interest rate.

This was not the birth of subprime lending. Credit for that invention goes to Long Beach Savings & Loan, a small Orange County–based thrift that eventually morphed into Ameriquest Mortgage. But now Countrywide, the leading player in mortgage origination, jumped with both feet onto the bandwagon.

———

Countrywide was emblematic of what came to be known as the shadow banking system of nonbank financial institutions engaged in mortgage underwriting, securitization, and other activities that had once been the preserve of banks and savings and loan associations (S&Ls), the descendants of the building and loans of the 1920s. The growth of shadow banking in turn reflected a process of financial liberalization stretching back to the early 1970s, not incidentally the same point in time when Loeb and Mozilo established their California-based underwriting operation.

The Wall Street crash of 1929 and the banking crises that battered the US economy prompted the adoption of a panoply of new regulations affecting the banking and financial system.[3] The Glass-Steagall Act separated investment and commercial banking and prevented deposit-taking commercial banks from engaging in security and insurance underwriting. Also in 1933, the Federal Reserve Board adopted "Regulation Q," prohibiting banks from paying interest on demand deposits (essentially, checking accounts), while placing ceilings on permissible rates on time and savings accounts.[4] The Securities and Exchange Act created a government commission to oversee stock and bond markets. The Commodity Exchange Act extended regulatory authority to futures markets.

The result appears, from a distance, as a golden age of financial stability. Between the end of World War II and the 1970s, bank failures were rare. Financial institutions specialized in different types of lending. Banks extended corporate and consumer loans. S&Ls engaged in mortgage lending. Each type of institution was overseen by its respective regulator. The stock market rose and fell, as stock markets do. But when it fell, it did not bring down the financial system and the economy with it.

As time passed, the financial establishment grew restive. Memories of the unstable 1930s faded. The thrift industry, enjoying tax and regulatory advantages, gained market share at the expense of the banks. Deposit taking and lending in London—what came to be known as the Eurodollar market—subjected the banks to additional competition.

A further source of competition, whose existence would have profound implications in 2008, came in the form of money market mutual funds. The first of the breed, the Reserve Fund, was created in 1971 by a pair of failed New York financial consultants, Harry Brown and Bruce Bent.[5] Money market funds invested in treasury bills and commercial paper, not corporate, consumer, and mortgage loans in the manner of a bank. Free of Regulation Q ceilings, they were able to offer savers a more attractive combination of liquidity and interest than on bank accounts, but without, it should be noted, the protection of deposit insurance.

The innovation was heralded as a significant step in the direction of financial democracy, given the miserly returns available on bank accounts. The MIT economist Paul Samuelson, himself a Nobel Laureate, proclaimed that Bent and Brown similarly deserved a Nobel Prize for their innovation. The founders characterized their achievement more modestly. "I wish I could say that our 'invention' resulted from any brilliance on our part," Brown later remarked, "but it was actually a combination of the threat of starvation and pure greed that drove us to it."[6]

The absence of deposit insurance and of any requirement for money market funds to hold reserves as a buffer against risk was justified on the grounds that fund managers invested only in safe assets and managed their shareholders' money conservatively. One dollar invested in a money market fund would always be worth $1, or so the argument ran. The presumption did not anticipate the tendency for fund managers to move into riskier investments as Regulation Q was relaxed and competition created pressure to boost yields, something that regulators first failed to notice and then were reluctant to address, given an increasingly powerful mutual fund lobby. The presumption that shares in money market funds would never fall below par did not anticipate the failure of Lehman Brothers, Lehman being a consequential issuer of the kind of high-yielding short-term notes that the managers of money funds found irresistible.

———

Commercial banks, concerned about the erosion of their deposit base, had been lobbying for the removal of Regulation Q for years. Their calls gained urgency with this new competition and even more when inflation rose, undermining their ability to compete for savings. Regulation Q ceilings were finally phased out by the ironically entitled Depository Institutions Deregulatory and Monetary Control Act of 1980—ironic since its passage resulted from the Fed's loss of monetary control.

The abolition of Regulation Q unleashed a cascade of unintended consequences. A first consequence was to intensify the pressure on S&Ls, which had previously been permitted to offer higher deposit rates than other financial institutions.[7] To limit the damage, the Garn–St. Germain Act of 1982 allowed S&Ls to engage in a range of commercial banking activities, those related to consumer lending, for example, above and beyond their traditional remit of taking deposits and extending mortgage loans. Among its other provisions was one authorizing the extension of adjustable rate mortgage loans. President Reagan, on signing the bill, called it the first step in a "comprehensive program of financial deregulation."[8] Little did he know.

Garn–St. Germain helped set the stage for the S&L crisis of the 1980s by allowing thrifts to take on additional risk without at the same time doing anything to restrain them. But equally important was how the provision of additional financial services by the thrifts intensified the pressure on the banks.[9] Commercial banks had long been frustrated by their inability to underwrite corporate and municipal bonds. Securities markets now having recovered from the 1930s and World War II, big corporate borrowers took to issuing commercial paper and junk bonds. With these instruments offering corporate borrowers new ways of financing themselves, reducing their dependence on bank credit, bank profits were squeezed.[10] The big banks that were the big companies' traditional interlocutors were hurt the most.

At first, money-center banks, with Citibank (the rebranded National City Bank of Chapter 3) in the vanguard, found a new market in syndicated loans to governments in Latin America and Eastern Europe, in an echo of the foreign lending boom of the 1920s. But by the early 1980s these loans had gone bad. For the regulators to insist that the banks acknowledge their losses was not an option, however; doing so would have bankrupted the Federal Deposit Insurance Corporation. Instead the banks were allowed to earn their way back to health, and regulation was loosened to facilitate their efforts.

In December 1986, in response to a petition from J. P. Morgan, Bankers Trust, and Citicorp (the holding company parent of Citibank), the Fed creatively reinterpreted the Glass-Steagall Act to allow commercial banks to derive up to 5 percent of their income from investment banking activities. The investment banking activities in question included underwriting municipal bonds, commercial paper and, fatefully, mortgage-backed securities. In 1987, over the opposition of its deregulation-skeptical, soon-to-be-former chairman, Paul Volcker, the Federal Reserve Board authorized several large banks to further expand their underwriting businesses. If ever there was an illustration of how lame-duck status can weaken a Fed chair, this was it. Under Volcker's successor, the liberalization-minded Alan Greenspan, the Fed then allowed bank holding companies to derive as much as 25 percent of their revenues from investment banking operations.

By the 1990s, then, Glass-Steagall was already weakened. The fatal blow was struck by the merger wave that swept investment banking and brokerage toward the end of the decade. Morgan Stanley, an investment bank, merged with Dean, Witter, Discover & Co., a brokerage and credit card company, in 1997, while the trust company and derivatives house Bankers Trust acquired Alex. Brown & Sons, an investment and brokerage firm. This consolidation of investment houses, brokers, and insurance companies threatened to further disadvantage the banks, which responded by lobbying even more intensely for the removal of remaining restrictions on their operations.

And if lobbying was not enough, there were other ways of forcing the issue. Citicorp moved in 1998 to purchase Travelers Insurance Group, notwithstanding Glass-Steagall provisions requiring it to sell off Travelers' insurance business within two years. The merger would allow Travelers to market to Citicorp's retail customers not just insurance but also its in-house money market funds while giving Citicorp access to an expanded clientele of investors and insurance policyholders. Its main shortcoming was its incompatibility with Glass-Steagall.

The chairmen and co-CEOs of the merged company, John Reed and Sanford Weill, mounted a furious campaign to remove Glass-Steagall's nettlesome restrictions before the two-year window closed. Weill formed an alliance with David Komansky of Merrill Lynch and Phil Purcell of Morgan Stanley to lobby for change. Their arguments received a sympathetic hearing from the Greenspan Fed and also from the White House, in the person of President Clinton's advisor for financial reform, Gene Sperling, and from the Treasury Department, especially when Lawrence Summers succeeded Robert Rubin as secretary in mid-1999.[11] (Rubin left for an advisory position with none other than Citigroup; he started in October.) They were warmly received in the halls of Congress, where bank lobbyists freely roamed.

The main opposition came from Phil Gramm, who complained that no big banks or insurance companies made their headquarters in Texas. Weill lobbied Gramm incessantly; in his 2006 autobiography, Weill reports running into Gramm at a dinner party in 2004 where Gramm remarked, "Congress made a mistake. It should have called the new law the 'Weill-Gramm-Leach-Bliley Act!'"[12]

Glass-Steagall was finally euthanized by Gramm-Leach-Bliley, which repealed residual restrictions on combining commercial banking, investment banking, and insurance underwriting, in November 1999. Weill proudly mounted a four-foot slab of wood on his office wall, etched with his portrait and the words "The Shatterer of Glass Steagall." Much later, in 2012, reflecting on the crisis, he acknowledged that removal of the Glass-Steagall restrictions had been a terrible mistake.[13]

The abolition of Glass-Steagall closed a chapter in US financial history. But it was also indicative of a broader deregulatory trend. Other manifestations included the Riegle-Neal Interstate Banking and Branch Efficiency Act of 1994, which repealed prohibitions on cross-state branching and opened the door to mega-banks. Likewise, the Commodity Futures Modernization Act (CFMA) of 2000 eliminated federal and state regulatory oversight of financial derivatives. CFMA relieved issuers of credit default swaps from having to hold reserves against the possibility that they would actually have to make payments to purchasers of those instruments. Credit default swaps (CDS) had been designed to allow investors in mortgage-backed securities to insure themselves against default on the mortgages in the underlying pool. Now, however, CDS were purchased by buyers who did not also purchase the asset against whose default the insurance was written but simply wished to bet against the housing market. The decision in 2000 to relieve issuers of the obligation to hold reserves against liabilities associated with these contracts would have momentous implications for what followed.

And where deregulation could not be achieved by legislation, it proceeded by fiat. The activist chair of the Commodity Futures Trading Commission, Brooksley Born, was forced out in 1999 by a hostile Fed chairman and treasury secretary after recommending against further deregulation of derivatives. The Securities and Exchange Commission (SEC), under the more accommodating Harvey Pitt and William Donaldson, then loosened its rules for the financial reserves that had to be held by the brokerage units of banks.

Nor was deregulation limited to the United States. For many years European countries had assiduously regulated their banks and securities markets. In 1986,

British Prime Minister Margaret Thatcher, already famous for her commitment to deregulation, then turned her attention to financial markets. Having previously reduced top tax rates, liberalized labor markets, and sold off much of the public housing stock, Thatcher launched her "big bang" financial reform, reducing regulatory restrictions with the goal of enhancing London's position as an international financial center.

Meanwhile the European Union moved to create a single, integrated market in merchandise, labor services, and financial capital. Overregulation, according to the widely accepted diagnosis, was to blame for the slow growth and high unemployment plaguing the continent, and the single market, by prying open the door to cross-border competition, was the pivotal reform that might force European states to lighten that crushing regulatory load. The diagnosis that other sectors and activities were suffering from excessive regulation was extended, for better or worse, to financial services. As a result, the Single European Act, with its goal of establishing a continentwide market by 1992, permitted big European banks to expand into neighboring countries.

At first the banks were slow to respond, and regulators were reluctant to let them. This changed, however, with the establishment of the euro in 1999, which removed exchange-rate risk as a deterrent to cross-border business. As the competition to provide financial services intensified, European banks levered up their bets. Banks in Northern Europe, where interest rates were low, found it impossible to resist the higher yields on loans to Southern European banks and investments in Southern European bonds. Southern European banks, for their part, welcomed the cheap finance provided by their Northern European counterparts, using it to make speculative real estate loans and buy the bonds of their sovereigns.

The result was explosive growth of banking in Ireland and across Southern Europe. In some countries, the assets and liabilities of the banking system grew to large multiples of gross domestic product. In Ireland, claims on the banking system, at their peak in 2007–08, reached 400 percent of GDP.[14] In Cyprus, the liabilities of the banking system peaked out at an extraordinary eight times national income.[15]

———

Thus, no one factor explains the deregulation of banking and financial services. Memories of how banks had collapsed in the 1930s faded with time. Foreign competition created pressure to eliminate restrictions on the range of permissible bank activities. Financial innovation, from development of new lending instruments to establishment of money market mutual funds, undermined the effectiveness of existing regulation.

The dilemma for policy makers was whether to extend existing regulation to these new entities and markets or to relax restrictions on banks and other incumbents complaining that the playing field was tilted against them. A range of arguments militated in favor of the latter. Banks pointed to advances in technology making it easier to use data from one business to benefit another. Computers made it possible to share information and products across activities in the manner of Citibank and Travelers Insurance, rendering the regulatory walls separating banking from insurance more irritating and, arguably, less efficient.[16] Automated credit-scoring techniques like those pioneered by Countrywide Credit encouraged not just routinization of bank lending but also securitization of mortgages, loans, and credits, creating another argument for allowing lenders to branch into underwriting. Commercial banks could cite the experience of the 1990s, when their limited forays into investment banking enhanced profitability without causing noticeable problems.[17]

Academics like the aforementioned Paul Samuelson, together with Eugene Fama of Chicago and Robert Merton of Harvard, meanwhile provided theoretical models of the efficiency of freely functioning financial markets. In reality, their models were only an intellectual point of departure. They identified the restrictive conditions under which asset prices incorporate all the information needed for market efficiency. It was not long before researchers had built up a catalog of empirical anomalies that were hard to square with the efficient-markets view. The fathers of this efficient-markets theory may have understood its limitations, but this was not universally true of policy makers and others who made use of it to justify their positions. In particular, the efficient-markets view found a ready reception from the likes of Chairman Greenspan.

But the role of ideology extended beyond the halls of the Fed and the person of its chairman. In 1992, the Democratic Party moved in a business-friendly direction in an effort to regain the political middle ground. Responding to twelve years of Republican control of the White House, a party traditionally opposed to financial deregulation now embraced Bill Clinton's "third way" of balanced budgets, private-public partnerships, and finance for growth. Political scientists Sandra Suarez and Robin Kolodny emphasize the role of this ideological convergence between Left and Right in setting the stage for financial deregulation. Where the 1992 Democratic Party platform might have been expected to at least express reservations about the concessions extended to financial institutions, it was notably silent on the question of deregulation.[18] The Riegle-Neal, Gramm-Leach-Bliley, and Commodity Futures Modernization Acts were all signed into law by a president affiliated with a party that had once, but no longer, opposed deregulation of the financial sector—the same party that was responsible during the presidency of Franklin Delano Roosevelt for putting in place the elements of modern financial regulation.

———

The result of these measures was a massive increase in the size, complexity, and leverage of US financial institutions. After having remained stable for more than two decades, the share of the financial-services industry in GDP more than doubled from 4 percent in the early 1970s to 8.3 percent in 2006.[19] Some of this growth was natural recovery from the turbulent 1930s and post–World War II years. It can be seen as the financial sector reasserting its role in helping to allocate resources in a complex modern economy. But the remainder, and especially the breakneck financialization of the years leading up to the crisis, is not adequately explained by standard models of the efficiency advantages of a well-functioning financial sector.

Moreover, the growth of the sector was financed to a considerable extent not with equity—not by banks raising more capital—but with debt. The debt in question was incurred by borrowing for a fixed, typically short term from corporations, mutual funds, state and municipal governments, government agencies, and not least other banks. Large banks had the best access to this so-called wholesale money market.[20] Having diversified their business and invested in internal controls, they could argue that they were in the best position to manage the risk of relying on borrowed funds.

Large banks were also in the best position to create the special purpose vehicles used to shift risky assets off balance sheet, minimizing the amount of capital the parent institution had to raise. They were further incentivized to reduce their capital ratios and increase their leverage by the knowledge that they were systemically significant. Because they were too big to fail, they were apt to be bailed out in the event of trouble. This in turn encouraged them to take on additional leverage and risk.

And what was true of banks in the United States was similarly true of banks elsewhere, notably in Europe. Although regulatory preferences and subsidies were also extended to small banks specializing in activities like mortgage lending, in country after country it was the large institutions that expanded their balance sheets and raised their leverage most dramatically.

The extreme cases were broker-dealers like Bear Stearns and Lehman Brothers, whose traditional business was trading securities on behalf of their customers. Historically, these firms had maintained large reserves and limited the riskiness of their investment portfolios. Under pressure from commercial bank competitors, they now moved from one extreme to the other.

In 2007 the typical US commercial bank had a leverage ratio on the order of 12 to 1, measured as the unadorned ratio of assets to shareholders' equity. Lehman Brothers, by comparison, had a leverage ratio of 30, Bear Stearns 33.[21] A leverage ratio of 33 meant that a decline in asset values of just 3 percent could wipe out shareholders' equity and therefore the firm itself if it was forced to acknowledge those losses.[22] As subsequent events would reveal, this was a tenuous position for any financial institution.

How this extraordinary situation was allowed to develop became a key question in the wake of subsequent events. The answer starts with the decline of the private partnership model of investment banking. Traditionally, the New York Stock Exchange had banned public listing of investment banks as too risky. Instead, investment houses were organized as private partnerships or closely held corporations owned and operated by a handful of partners whose interests were not easily bought and sold. The partners thus had a stake in the long-term survival of the institution. By tradition, they sat together around a table in the "partners' room," literally keeping an eye on one another. Peer pressure and close oversight thus served as deterrents to excessive risk taking.

Over time, technological change—development of expensive new computer technology to process transactions, for example—heightened the advantages of scale and made the private partnership model, where the size of the bank was limited by the capital resources of the partners, problematic. It doesn't take much effort to imagine whose lobbying caused the ban on public listing to be removed in 1970. (Answer: the investment banks.) Merrill Lynch was the first big broker-dealer to go public in 1971, followed by Bear Stearns, Morgan Stanley, Lehman Brothers, and Goldman Sachs, the four other members of what collectively came to be known as "the Big Five."

Now the CEO, as head of a public company, and those who worked for him, answered (if at all) to the chief risk officer. Management's interest in the firm was neither illiquid nor long-term. If their risky bets paid off, they earned enormous bonuses. And if big payoffs today were followed by big losses tomorrow, there was no provision for clawing back yesterday's bonuses (a practice that regulators and shareholders sought to change only after 2008). In principle, the board of directors, representing the shareholders, was supposed to push back against excessive risk taking. But outside directors had limited information and, in many cases, limited ability to assess it. In practice, no one was watching the store.

Regulators, for their part, were no better positioned to restrain risk taking and leverage. They took their cue from the banks rather than the other way around. The SEC loosened capital requirements for broker-dealers in 2004 in response to similar action by the European Union and lobbying by the Big

Five, whose members feared losing ground to their foreign rivals. For thirty years, US broker-dealers had been required to apply what was known as the "net capital rule," which obliged them, like their commercial bank brethren, to limit their leverage to 12 to 1. The SEC's 2004 decision now allowed them to use their internal models to estimate, or in practice underestimate, the riskiness of their investments. The broker-dealers reduced their capital cushions accordingly.

The Big Five were also leaders in using special purpose vehicles (SPVs) to shift assets off balance sheet, where they would be free of capital requirements. SPVs were robot firms with no employees or physical location. They existed solely to securitize a bank's mortgage claims, credit card interest due, and other receivables and to sell the resulting instruments on to other investors. If an SPV was unable to pay interest on its securities because of defaults on the underlying pool of residential mortgages, then that was the security holders' problem, or so it was argued. The sponsoring bank was not legally obliged to provide additional resources so that the SPV could meet its commitments. This was the rationale for exempting the banks from having to hold capital to back the obligations of their SPVs.

But everyone knew who was at fault when a special purpose vehicle ran off the road. The blame rested not with the vehicle but with its driver, in this case the parent bank. Failure to lend support could therefore damage the parent's reputation and impair its access to capital markets.[23] In the event of defaults on the pool of underlying mortgages, responsibility for making good the difference reverted to the sponsoring financial institution. The off-balance-sheet liability migrated back onto the sponsor's balance sheet.[24] Just why regulators should have allowed a parent firm transferring pools of mortgages to an SPV to hold less capital in this light is, to put it mildly, unclear.[25]

———

The growth of SPVs was just one manifestation of the larger process of asset securitization. Rather than holding mortgage loans, student loans, auto loans, and corporate loans on their balance sheets, where they had to be funded, banks pooled their loans and transformed them into securities to be sold on to other investors. The pool was split into tranches, with the senior tranche receiving first claim on the cash flow from the underlying loans. The junior tranches received payment only after the senior tranche was serviced. The resulting securities were known as collateralized debt obligations, or CDOs. The sequential payments were referred to, more prosaically, as the "cash-flow waterfall." The presumption was that the senior tranche was safe in the absence of extraordinary events. This façade of security allowed the senior tranche to obtain an AAA rating and be sold off to pension funds and insurance companies, whose mandates allowed them to invest only in high-rated paper.

Mortgage securitization was no new phenomenon. As we saw in Chapter 1, the "guaranteed mortgage participation certificates" of the 1920s, where the title or insurance company issuing the mortgage-backed security guaranteed the purchaser a specified return, bore more than a passing resemblance to the senior tranche of the mortgage securitizations of the early 2000s. But now the process achieved a scale and complexity not seen before. CDOs were tranched a second time and transformed into securities known as "CDOs squared." "CDOs cubed" were not long in following.

CDOs backed by pools of loans then gave way to "synthetic CDOs," whose payment streams were backed not by actual mortgage loans but by portfolios of credit default swaps. Credit default swaps, recall, are insurance contracts that pay out in case of a specified credit event, like a default on a mortgage bond. In practice they were issued by many of the same investment banks active in the securitization business. And they were backed by nothing more than the promise of the issuer to pay in the event that the default in question occurred.

By 2005, the face value of CDOs exceeded $1.5 trillion by one estimate.[26] The "one estimate" qualification is important, since in truth no one really knew the value of CDOs outstanding, much less who held them. Similarly for credit default swaps. One survey conducted by the International Swaps and Derivatives Association suggested that there were $17 trillion of CDS outstanding in 2005. But no one knew for sure.

———

The result was an enormous increase in the flow of credit into US financial markets, and into the housing market in particular. Mortgage and nonmortgage debt had risen in lockstep for three decades.[27] Starting in 2000–01, however, nonmortgage debt as a share of GDP leveled off, while the growth of mortgage debt rose explosively. At the peak in 2006, private mortgage debt was more than half again as high as private nonmortgage debt. Something peculiar was evidently happening in mortgage and financial markets.

Associated with this tsunami of finance was a run-up in home prices unlike anything seen since Florida in the 1920s. Housing prices nationwide, adjusted for inflation, had been essentially trendless from the 1950s through the 1990s. Starting in 1999 they shot up, rising by two-thirds in real terms in just seven years.[28] As in the 1920s, the increase was strongest in certain frenzied pockets, Florida and this time Arizona and California.[29]

The bubble then fed on itself, as bubbles do. More home purchases meant higher property prices, which encouraged bank and nonbank lenders to lend against the collateral of more highly valued homes. This meant additional purchases, still-higher prices, and more collateral against which to borrow. Subprime borrowers, with unprecedented access to credit, purchased homes they could afford only if the property appreciated, allowing them to refinance and extract equity from the investment.

A growing number of homes were purchased with little down payment if any, given a fresh coat of paint, and put back on the market. Tales of individuals of modest means buying multiple properties, the hallmark of a speculative market, became widespread. The Discovery Home Channel began broadcasting a program called "Flip That House." Each episode told the story of an individual or group that purchased a run-down property for little or no money down, gave it a fresh coat of paint, and sold it for a substantial profit. The typical episode glossed over details like closing costs and the need to purchase title insurance, much less the consequences for highly leveraged real estate speculators of a decline in housing prices. Their omission reflected more than the intrinsic limitations of the thirty-minute format.

CHAPTER 5 | Where Credit Is Due

EXTRAORDINARY FINANCIAL EVENTS like the housing boom in the United States rarely have single causes. Among the causes of this one were incentive problems all along the mortgage origination-extension-securitization chain. Mortgage brokers, who were licensed not by the federal government but by the states if at all, had limited interest in the ability of aspiring purchasers to meet their obligations. Like the binder boys of the 1920s, they were in it for the commission. Mortgage lenders who earned closing costs and other fees when extending a loan were similarly inclined to disregard problems insofar as loans were securitized and sold on to other investors.

That declining lending standards accompanied the flow of credit into the housing market and its subprime segment in particular is indisputable. Neighborhoods with an unusually large share of subprime borrowers prior to the boom experienced the most rapid growth of mortgage debt between 2002 and 2005. Similarly, the increase in the share of mortgages that were securitized or sold to financial institutions unaffiliated with the originator was strongest in neighborhoods where there were already a large number of subprime mortgages at the start of the period. All this occurred despite the stagnant growth of income in the neighborhoods in question.[1]

The rating agencies that were the putative gatekeepers of the securitization process earned generous fees for advising lenders on how to structure CDOs so as to secure AAA ratings. As a result they hesitated to confer a low grade on a security to which they lent their imprimatur. Lenders could shop the prospectus around competing rating agencies and publish only the rating that placed their issue in the most favorable light.[2]

Much later, in 2013, the Justice Department filed a $5 billion civil suit against Standard & Poor's for inflating its ratings on residential mortgage-backed securities and CDOs. Already at the beginning of 2007, the complaint alleged, the agency was aware that a deteriorating housing market was undermining the performance of residential mortgage-backed securities but hesitated to cut its ratings for fear of driving business to competing firms. The Justice Department cited an internal email by an S&P analyst parodying the Talking Heads song "Burning Down the House" as evidence that those farther down the corporate food chain understood full well what was happening.[3] It described how, in response to an article in *Fortune* magazine questioning whether the rating agencies were behind the curve, S&P contemplated hiring a public-relations firm rather than reviewing its internal models.[4]

Investors should have known better than to rely on gatekeepers with such dubious incentives. But the complexity of the securities in question made it difficult to independently evaluate the risks. As in any boom period, the rising share of naïve investors in the market, including sleepy regional banks in Germany, made it even less likely that the rating agencies would be caught out.[5]

Or one might think that lenders would have been discouraged from engaging in questionable practices by the risk of damaging their reputation. But new entrants into the mortgage lending business, typically nonbank lenders regulated by state rather than federal authorities, had little reputation to preserve.[6] The boom in subprime lending and securitization in the years leading up to 2007 thus suffered from the same "reputation deficit" as foreign lending in the 1920s. And even where there was franchise value to protect, management had other incentives. Angelo Mozilo was able to reap more than $400 million from selling shares in Countrywide Credit that were part of his compensation package.[7]

Brokers, meanwhile, were encouraged to steer borrowers toward loans carrying high interest rates by a structure known as the "yield spread premium." This paid the broker a fraction of the gain to the lender from putting a borrower into a more expensive loan. This structure was most prevalent in the subprime segment of the market, where consumers were least well informed. A 2008 study by the Center for Responsible Lending concluded that a subprime borrower going through a broker paid $5,222 more in interest over the first four years of a loan on average than if he or she had borrowed from a bank or other financial institution directly.[8]

This is not to say that the banks were less culpable. Elizabeth Jacobson, who worked for Wells Fargo in Baltimore, described in an affidavit how loan officers in poor, predominantly black neighborhoods steered customers toward high-interest subprime mortgages even when the borrower qualified for a better rate.[9] Customers were discouraged from providing income documents and down payments, so they would end up with a more expensive loan. Countrywide Credit, the industry leader and pioneer in automated underwriting, programmed its systems not to list subprime borrowers' cash reserves, which resulted in their being steered away from lower-cost loans.[10] Where Countrywide's profit on conventional mortgages averaged 1–2 percent of the value of the loan, margins on subprime loans were said to approach 15 percent.[11] Many of these more costly loans featured a low teaser rate for an introductory period, after which they reset, together with prohibitive prepayment penalties that made refinancing impossibly costly. If this implied a high likelihood of default, that was someone else's problem, since the mortgage was part of a pool that was securitized, tranched, and transferred to other investors.

In 2009, closing the barn door after the horse had bolted, the Federal Reserve Board issued a regulatory decision prohibiting payments to mortgage brokers and loan officers that were based on the interest rate charged the borrower.[12] In 2012 Wells Fargo settled a Justice Department suit alleging that it had overcharged thirty thousand minority buyers. It agreed to pay $125 million to compensate the borrowers and donate $50 million to a program assisting individuals in making down payments and improving their homes.

———

No aspect of the crisis is more controversial than the role of the government-sponsored mortgage agencies Freddie Mac and Fannie Mae. Fannie, formally the Federal National Mortgage Association, was created in 1938 to purchase mortgages from banks, freeing up resources to permit them to extend new loans. Freddie, formally the Federal Home Loan Mortgage Corporation, was established in 1970 to provide competition for Fannie and to work more closely with S&Ls, Fannie having worked with mortgage banks.[13]

In the early 1980s, at more or less the same time the S&L industry descended into crisis, the two government-sponsored entities expanded their operations. They installed Countrywide-style automated mortgage approval and purchase systems. They securitized mortgages, guaranteed the resulting instruments, and passed them on to other investors. They purchased mortgage-backed securities from other financial institutions, adding them to their portfolios of mortgage-related investments.

The fraction of all mortgages securitized by Fannie and Freddie or held on their balance sheets had remained stable over the course of the 1970s at roughly 10 percent. But in the 1980s, in response to these initiatives, that share took off like a rocket. When it leveled off in the mid-1990s, Fannie and Freddie accounted for nearly 40 percent of the mortgage market.

In and of itself, this growth is not proof of anything. The expansion of Fannie and Freddie's mortgage-purchase and asset-securitization activities was concentrated in 1981–1994. In other words, it long preceded the housing bubble. But the two government-sponsored entities, or GSEs, were still there, their critics allege, blithely providing additional mortgage credit after the housing market lost its moorings in the late 1990s. Though the GSEs were formally private—Freddie was a private corporation from the start, while Fannie was converted in 1968 from a mixed-ownership corporation in which the federal government held shares to a fully private corporation—it was understood that the government stood behind them. If Fannie and Freddie ran into trouble, Congress could be expected to bail them out, since the two institutions were carrying out a public mission.

Because the government was there to lend a hand, Freddie and Fannie were permitted to hold less capital than conventional financial institutions. They were not required to register their debt securities with the Securities and Exchange Commission. This reinforced the perception of a government backstop, such treatment normally being associated with a public agency as opposed to a private corporation. The perception of a public backstop also allowed Fannie and Freddie to fund their activities more cheaply. This in turn made mortgage credit more freely available.

The Housing and Community Development Act of 1992, signed by President George H. W. Bush on the eve of a hotly contested election, then amended Fannie and Freddie's charters to require them to "facilitate the financing of affordable housing." Thirty percent of mortgages acquired or guaranteed by the GSEs were now to originate with individuals in neighborhoods with "low and moderate incomes." In 1999, with another presidential term drawing to a close, the Clinton administration encouraged Fannie to ramp up its purchases of loans to low- and moderate-income homeowners in distressed inner-city districts. In 2000, just a week before the November election, the 30 percent guideline for low- to moderate-income mortgages was raised to 50 percent.

The government's "affordable housing goals" dovetailed with the aspirations of Fannie's ambitious new CEO, Franklin Delano Raines. Having grown up in modest means, in a home that his father built by hand, Raines graduated from Harvard College and then Harvard Law School and studied as a Rhodes Scholar. After working in both the Nixon and Carter White Houses (no mean feat, that) and at the Office of Management and Budget, Raines became a general partner of the investment firm Lazard Frères. As CEO of Fannie Mae, he was the first African American to head a Fortune 500 company. Anxious to make his mark, Raines set a goal of doubling Fannie's earnings in five years. The main way he planned to accomplish this, given the razor-thin margins of the underwriting business, was by using cheap funding to finance expansion of Fannie's mortgage portfolio.

From 1995 through 2003, the share of mortgages accounted for by Fannie and Freddie rose further, from just under 40 percent to 50 percent of the total outstanding. Enterprising companies like Countrywide set up dedicated subsidiaries with the express purpose of selling mortgages to the GSEs. By 2003, Fannie Mae was buying more than 70 percent of all the mortgages that Countrywide issued. When Wall Street then offered to purchase and securitize Countrywide's nonconforming mortgages (subprime and other mortgages that did not meet the GSE's underwriting standards), Fannie lowered its standards to avoid losing market share. Fannie and Freddie may have followed Wall Street rather than leading it, as Phil Angelides, chair of the Financial Crisis Inquiry Commission, later put it.[14] But their actions were no less important for the fact. The two government-sponsored entities, in this view, were key enablers of the mortgage boom.

Other evidence is less supportive of the indictment. Between 2003 and 2006, the share of mortgages purchased by Freddie Mac and Fannie Mae fell back from 50 to 30 percent.[15] In 2003, Freddie Mac revealed that it had misstated its earnings by nearly $5 billion. Similar accounting problems then came to light at Fannie Mae. The scandal forced Raines to resign in December 2004.[16] In response to these scandals, regulators imposed tighter limits on the GSEs' lending activities. The share of mortgages held in the form of the asset-backed securities of entities other than Fannie and Freddie then tripled in the three years from 2003, as other financial institutions stepped into the breach. In the late stages of the boom, it was not the GSEs but other financial institutions that were driving the process.

What was true of the market in general was true of its subprime segment in particular. The share of subprime and near-subprime (Alternative A or Alt-A) mortgages originated and securitized by financial institutions other than Fannie Mae and Freddie Mac quadrupled over the period. Between 2004 and 2006, Fannie and Freddie went from holding nearly half of subprime mortgages securitized and sold into the market to holding less than a quarter. At the height of the housing boom, in other words, a growing share of mortgage credit, in general and to the subprime segment in particular, was being drawn from other sources—that is, from hedge funds, investment banks, and foreign banks that loaded up on mortgage-linked CDOs.

If one wishes to blame Fannie and Freddie for the housing boom, then a more convoluted logic is required. It could be that the private sector, squeezed out of the conventional mortgage market by the GSEs, responded by moving into riskier mortgages. Alternatively, it might be argued that Fannie and Freddie's portfolios had grown so large that their collapse would have destabilized the housing market and the economy, something that the George W. Bush administration, its free-market coloration notwithstanding, was anxious to avoid. The Fed, as the administration's agent, could therefore be expected to do whatever it took to prevent a significant decline in housing prices. This encouraged investors, aware of the situation, to dive headfirst into the deep end of the mortgage securitization pool.

But if the idea was that the "Greenspan-Bernanke put" would place a floor under not just the stock market but also housing prices, then this expectation would prove dreadfully wrong.

———

Perverse incentives to relax lending standards may have been ample, but the lending still had to be financed. Here is where Federal Reserve policy came into play.

The Fed's contribution traces back to the end of the tech bubble in 2000 and Al Qaeda's attack on the Twin Towers. Fearing that these shocks to confidence would mean a weak economy, the Federal Open Market Committee cut the federal funds rate (the rate at which banks lend reserves to one another, which the Fed uses as its interest rate target) from more than 6 percent to less than 2 percent.[17]

Moreover, with inflation already low, FOMC members worried that, if the economy weakened further, the United States might slip into a Japan-style deflation from which it would be impossible to escape. In June 2002, Federal Reserve Board staff published an analysis of how Japan had fallen prey to deflation, highlighting the Bank of Japan's halfhearted policy response. Ben Bernanke, newly appointed to the board of governors, gave a widely cited speech on the dangers of deflation. In his incarnation as a professor at Princeton, Bernanke had authored a series of papers in which he criticized the Bank of Japan for not having done more to head off the problem.[18] Citing the staff's analysis, Bernanke now argued that "when inflation is already low and the fundamentals of the economy suddenly deteriorate, the central bank should act more preemptively and aggressively than usual in cutting rates."[19] He lobbied for preemptive action in the meetings of the FOMC, gaining the support of Chairman Greenspan, who cautioned the committee that it was dealing with a "latent deflationary type of economy." This was a "pretty scary prospect," Greenspan warned his colleagues, "and one that we certainly want to avoid."[20]

But the Fed's policy rate was already at a relatively low 2 percent. Responding "preemptively and aggressively," as the Bernanke Doctrine dictated, therefore required cutting rates and keeping them at a rock-bottom level until the risk of deflation passed. Accordingly, the Fed funds rate was kept at a scant 1 percent on a monthly average basis until May 2004.

Eventually, the National Bureau of Economic Research, the official arbiter of such matters, determined that the trough of the business cycle had been reached ten quarters earlier, in November 2001.[21] In fairness, one should note that the National Bureau's Business Cycle Dating Committee waits for the arrival of definitive data before dating a business cycle peak or trough. This is in contrast to the FOMC, which makes policy in real time. With benefit of hindsight, we can say that the Fed overestimated the risk of deflation and responded *too* preemptively and aggressively. As a student of Japan and of the Great Depression, Bernanke may have been overly sensitive to the danger of deflation at this point in time. In other words, history may be useful for informing the views of policy makers of how to respond to certain risks, but it may also shape and inform outlooks in ways that heighten other risks (something that Federal Reserve historians, looking back at the central bank's experience with the real bills doctrine in the 1930s, should have known perfectly well).

Distorted data may have also contributed to the Fed's exaggerated concern with deflation. Contemporaneous data showed the personal consumer expenditure deflator, cleansed of volatile food and fuel prices, falling to less than 1 percent in 2003, dangerously close to negative territory. Subsequent revisions revealed that inflation in fact had already bottomed out at 1.5 percent and was now safely on the rise.[22] As it happened, the real danger of deflation would develop later, in 2009 after the housing bubble burst. At this point, it can be argued, Bernanke's heightened aversion to deflation came in handy.

———

By the second half of 2004, fears of deflation had subsided. The FOMC moved to normalize the policy rate. But how quickly it could move was limited by the wish to avoid choking off the recovery. 2004 was yet another presidential election year. Raising rates at a pace that posed even a mild threat to recovery might be seen, justifiably or not, as influencing political outcomes.

Consequently, through 2004 and into 2005 interest rates remained significantly below the level normally targeted by the Fed. Specifically, they remained below the level pointed to by the Taylor Rule, so called for having been developed by Stanford University economist John Taylor. Taylor's rule of thumb captured the historical relationship between the Fed's policy target, the federal funds rate, on the one hand and inflation and the shortfall of output from potential on the other. This rule of thumb for what had worked reasonably well in the past quickly became a guidepost for appropriate policy going forward. By Taylor's reckoning, the federal funds rate was as much as three full percentage points below normal in early 2004, and it took the Fed more than two additional years to eliminate the discrepancy.[23]

Unlike 1925–1927, another period when US interest rates were unusually low, the motivation this time was domestic rather than international. It was to avoid deflation, not to help other countries with their balance-of-payments problems. But if the motivation differed, the financial implications were the same. Faced with low yields on treasury bills and other short-term investments, investors stretched for yield. They purchased longer-term securities, not just treasury bonds but also instruments backed by residential mortgages, pushing down long-term rates—including mortgage rates. The interest-rate sensitivity of housing prices and new home starts is notorious; hence the argument, popular after the fact, that the Fed bore heavy responsibility for the construction boom and housing bubble.[24]

The architects of the policy were convinced that they had fended off a catastrophic deflation while contributing only marginally to housing market excesses. Analysis by Federal Reserve staff suggested that low interest rates had a limited impact on the housing market. More important were what central bank researchers called "housing-specific shocks," code for movements in house prices that were not otherwise explicable.[25] It appeared that households were committing to long-term obligations in the form of thirty-year mortgages, and that investors were committing to risky investments in the form of mortgage-backed securities, to a greater extent than could be explained by the historical behavior of interest rates, growth rates, and inflation rates alone.

The explanation, officials like Donald Kohn, Fed vice chairman under Bernanke, concluded after the fact, was not so much that interest rates were lower as that the economy had become stabler, incomes more predictable.[26] The fact, or at least the belief, that output and employment had become less volatile encouraged risk taking. Thinking their incomes were now stabler, households became more comfortable with assuming debt. Investors became more comfortable with stretching for yield. The parallels with the 1920s, when it was similarly thought that the business cycle had been tamed, would have been clear to see, had anyone been inclined to look.

Statisticians date the Great Moderation, as this diminution in the volatility of business cycle fluctuations was known, to the late 1980s. That the shift followed the adoption of a new operating framework at the Fed, which made the pursuit of low and stable inflation a priority, encouraged the belief that improvements in the conduct of monetary policy were responsible for the increase in stability. Again, the parallels with the false stability of the 1920s and the availability of innovations in central banking to explain it are apparent.

Whether changes in Federal Reserve operating procedures were, in fact, mainly responsible for the Great Moderation continues to be debated. One view is that they were, but another is that the decline in the amplitude of the business cycle owed more to good luck—to the absence of oil shocks in particular.[27] Once the Great Moderation came to be seen as part of the problem, policy makers were happy to deny all credit.

———

But even if low long-term rates were part of the problem, those rates were lower than could be explained by Federal Reserve policy alone. This was the bond-market "conundrum" of which Chairman Greenspan spoke in his February 2005 testimony to Congress and to which he returned repeatedly thereafter. Ten-year treasury yields had shown no tendency to rise from mid-2004 through mid-2005 despite the fact that the Fed was raising short-term rates. To the contrary, the rate on ten-year treasuries actually fell, from 4.7 to 4.0 percent.[28] And the interest rate on conventional mortgages fell with it.[29]

The explanation, Greenspan argued, lay in the "tectonic shift" in China and other parts of the developing world from central planning to market-led growth.[30] These fast-growing economies were high-savings economies, since workers now had higher incomes out of which to save. In China's case, this was not the only source of the problem (insofar as an excess of thrift can be said to constitute a problem). In addition, state-owned enterprises contributed to high domestic savings by hoarding their earnings. Those enterprises benefited from privileged access to domestic markets. Officials applied little pressure for them to distribute their profits or to transfer them to the general government budget. Management was mainly interested in empire building, which it could pursue by reinvesting earnings. Combine the quarter of Chinese national income saved by households with the quarter retained by firms, and China was saving and investing, at the peak in 2006, an extraordinary 50 percent of GDP.

Sensibly investing this embarrassment of riches was not easy. Other countries experiencing "economic miracles," like Thailand and South Korea, had sought to do so but learned a painful lesson in the dangers of unproductive investment. Their mid-1990s booms, underwritten by banks that financed the questionable investment projects of commercial property developers and corporate conglomerates, had come crashing down in the Asian financial crisis of 1997–98. The lesson drawn was that it is safer to invest moderately and concentrate on high-quality projects. If doing so meant slower growth, then this was a price worth paying, especially if it meant not having to crawl for help to the International Monetary Fund.

But investing less required finding other outlets for Asia's abundant savings. One conceivable outlet was the government bond market, but there were few government bonds in Asia itself. Asian governments ran surpluses rather than deficits. The limited supply of bonds was snapped up by pension funds and insurance companies, which held them to maturity, rendering such Asian bond markets as existed relatively illiquid.

The opposite was true, of course, of the United States. The US treasury bond market was the single largest and most liquid financial market in the world. The federal government was pumping out treasuries to finance the deficits that flowed from the 2001 recession, the Bush tax cuts, and the Iraq and Afghanistan wars. And if this was not enough to meet demand, there were always the high-yielding securities of Fannie Mae and Freddie Mac.

Thus, Asian countries piled into US treasury bonds and into the securities of Fannie and Freddie. Insofar as purchasing US debt securities pushed the dollar up and local currencies down, this kept the Asian export machine humming. For China in particular, the practice helped sustain the export industries that were the engine of growth.[31]

Estimates of the impact on long-term interest rates of this "global savings glut," as Governor Bernanke dubbed it, ranged as high as two full percentage points.[32] And two percentage points on long-term rates were more than enough to exert a first-order impact on the housing market. This was Greenspan and Bernanke's defense. China, not they, had unleashed the tsunami of credit flowing into the housing market. With China and other emerging markets investing less than they saved, someone else had to invest more. In the event, that someone else was the United States, where the additional investment took the form of residential construction.

The Fed might have attempted to offset these effects by raising rates, but the sustainability of the recovery was uncertain. In 2003, when US central bankers and others began drawing attention to the impact of Chinese treasury bond purchases, GDP growth was running below 3 percent, considerably slower than is typical of recovery from an economic downturn. Against this backdrop, strong construction activity was welcome. Although the run-up in housing prices posed risks, monetary policy was a blunt instrument with which to address them, especially if doing so threatened to add to unemployment and heightened the risk of deflation. Memories of the last time the Fed had used interest rates to deflate an asset bubble, in 1929, served as a cautionary tale.

Above all, there was a reluctance, deeply grounded in ideology, to second-guess the markets. To the contrary, it could be argued that this was a happy outcome all around. Drawing on ample foreign savings, the United States could finance its budget deficits and construction activity more cheaply. Its low domestic savings were less of a constraint on government spending and home building alike. If US households were ramping up their spending, this reflected the prospective acceleration in productivity growth, it was suggested, and the higher future incomes promised by the country's singular facility in applying new information technologies. All this was disturbingly reminiscent of the 1920s, when it was argued that electrification and the assembly line augured a permanent acceleration in productivity and income growth, but no matter. China, for its part, could export its way to a higher level of output and keep its savings in liquid form. The United States imported Chinese manufactures and exported safe and liquid assets, while China did the reverse. This was the best of all worlds.

A few observers raised questions about the sustainability of the process. There were limits to how much Beijing would lend, they warned, to enable the United States to purchase Chinese goods. Sooner or later, China would want to translate its prowess at production into more consumption, at which point the flow of finance into US markets would dry up.

But there was no agreement on when. Those of skeptical temperament observed that the United States had limited capacity to pump out safe assets; pump out too many and they would no longer be safe, leading China to pull the plug. This gave grounds for worrying about what would happen when, as Chuck Prince, in his days as chairman and chief executive of Citigroup, put it, the music stopped.

Unfortunately, almost everyone making the connection between Chinese saving and US interest rates focused on what would happen if China's willingness to finance US current account deficits evaporated abruptly, much as US willingness to finance German deficits had evaporated in 1928. US interest rates would shoot up. Cheap foreign finance no longer being available, the US current account deficit would have to be eliminated at a stroke. The dollar, no longer receiving foreign support, would collapse on the foreign exchange market.

We know from subsequent events that the critics were right to worry. But they were wrong to focus on risks to exchange rates and the balance of payments. It was in housing and securitization, and not the foreign-exchange market, that the critical imbalances built up. Unfortunately, few of those who raised questions about sustainability focused their attention there.

CHAPTER 6 | Castles in Spain

IT WAS NOT just the United States that experienced a housing boom at the turn of the century. Ireland and Spain took a backseat to no one when it came to housing market excesses. Residential real estate prices in the United States rose by 125 percent between 1997 and 2006, but this was child's play compared to Spain, where they rose by 175 percent, and Ireland, where they increased by an extraordinary 260 percent.[1] In the decade ending in 2005, 550,000 homes were built in Ireland, a country of just 4.5 million residents, permanently scarring the pastoral countryside so eloquently celebrated by William Butler Yeats.

If the consequences were the same, the causes differed. Neither Spain nor Ireland saw mortgage securitization on a significant scale.[2] Neither possessed government-sponsored mortgage underwriting entities like Freddie Mac and Fannie Mae. In Ireland the housing boom was, instead, an unplanned step-child of economic success. As late as the mid-1980s, the Republic was regarded as one of Europe's economic sick men, suffering from low productivity and anemic growth. Starting in 1986 the Irish government then balanced its budget, cut taxes, and devalued the exchange rate, enhancing the competitiveness of exports. Foreign companies were attracted by the opportunity to offshore technical manufacturing and services to a low-wage economy populated by native English speakers, not to mention by favorable tax treatment of corporate profits. Income and economic growth accelerated in the 1990s in response to this surge of inward foreign investment. Whether this rapid growth and rise in incomes justified an increase in the demand for housing on the scale subsequently observed is a separate question.

In Spain, the boom in residential construction was driven partly by Northern Europeans buying holiday homes in sunnier climes, not unlike the New Englanders attracted to Florida in the 1920s. This, however, does not explain the construction of multi-unit projects targeted at domestic households in the suburbs of the country's large cities; some, like Ciudad Valdeluz just north of Madrid, became ghost towns when the bubble burst. For this, enthusiastic lending by Spanish banks, notably the regional savings banks or *cajas*, deserves the credit.

The role of bank lending points to the main thing Ireland and Spain shared with the United States, namely an enormous credit boom that pumped large amounts of cheap finance into the property sector. The difference was the source of the credit. In the United States the credit boom was driven by deregulation and securitization, aided and abetted by loose monetary policy and global imbalances. In Ireland, in Spain, and across much of Southern Europe, it was driven instead by the euro.

———

That the impact of the euro would be felt most powerfully in property markets and at the periphery of the European economy was not something that had been anticipated by the currency's founders. The euro project, like the larger process of European integration, had always focused on Germany and France. For France, integrating Europe's national economies was a way of shackling German economic might. This was something French leaders prioritized after World War II. It was something to which they paid renewed attention following German reunification, which by expanding the Federal Republic threatened to destroy any semblance of parity between the French and German economies.

French leaders understood that anything that encouraged intra-European trade would give German firms a stake in peaceful coexistence. Building institutions of economic governance at the European level, they argued, would subject German policies to international oversight.[3] They quickly identified a common currency as a key part of the apparatus deepening economic integration to the point where it became irreversible. As Jacques Rueff, the monetary expert who in his later years was economic advisor to Charles de Gaulle, put it, "Europe will be made of money, or it will not be made." Or in the strikingly similar words of François Mitterrand, the French president in 1992–93, when the decision to move to monetary union was taken, "Without a common monetary system, there is no Europe."[4]

With the passage of time, these statements have taken on an ironic coloration. Monetary integration has come to seem rather less than irreversible.

A process designed to force Europe, and Germany in particular, toward deeper integration later threatened to tear the continent apart. But this was not the view at the time. The commitment of French leaders to economic and monetary integration was sincere. It was rooted in very real memories of more than a century of Franco-German conflict.

German politicians, for their part, saw Europe as a vehicle through which the post–World War II Bundesrepublik, stripped of the prerogatives of sovereignty, could pursue its foreign policy ambitions without threatening its neighbors. A European foreign policy, foreign minister, and army would provide cover behind which the country could advance its foreign policy goals. This had been Germany's strategy for regaining first its sovereignty and then its place on the global stage ever since the approach was formulated by the country's founding post–World War II chancellor, Konrad Adenauer. In the 1960s an equally wily German leader, Willy Brandt, then highlighted monetary union as part of the package of integrationist measures to be offered to Paris in return for France acceding to Germany's foreign policy ambitions. This made monetary union a logical concession when Helmut Kohl, Germany's longest-serving postwar chancellor and a disciple of Adenauer, sought to obtain French approval for German reunification.

Any capsule description of a process as complex as European integration is, necessarily, oversimplified. The relevant oversimplification here is that France sought economic integration, Germany sought political integration, and together these elements were the basis for a deal. To be sure, there were also those in Germany, notably officials of the central bank, the Deutsche Bundesbank, who opposed monetary integration in advance of political integration, and those in France, leading technocrats among them, who embraced political as well as economic integration. Still, that was the essence of the deal. The French achieved quick results with the creation of the European Economic Community in 1957, the Single Market free of barriers to the movement of merchandise, capital, and labor in 1992, and the euro in 1999. The Germans made slower progress but remained no less committed to their goal.

German politicians understood, of course, that it was easier to engage in a bit of economic engineering than to forge a political union. The design of a free-trade area, a single market, and even a common currency could be delegated to technocrats. If there were national sensitivities, protections could be added. To avoid antagonizing powerful special interests, French and German farmers could be extended special treatment when Europe created its free-trade area. Although a single market might require a powerful European commissioner to apply the common competition policy, sensitive areas like bank regulation could be left to national authorities. To reassure Germany that the euro would not be an engine of inflation, member states could be required to make their central banks independent in the manner of the Bundesbank, as Kohl insisted.

Political union, as predicted, was a harder nut to crack. Transferring sovereignty to the European Union was sensitive even in Germany, despite championship of the idea by successive political leaders. Although nationalism was not an honorable German instinct in the second half of the twentieth century, neither was it absent. French leaders were prepared to pursue political integration only on the assumption that they would occupy high positions and set the rules. Everyone therefore understood that, compared to the transition to monetary union, which took seven years from when the Maastricht Treaty was signed in 1992 to when the euro came into being in 1999, the transition to political union would take longer.

The problem was that Germany had not signed up for economic and monetary union without political union. And what was problematic politically was problematic economically. A smoothly functioning monetary union requires an interstate system of taxes and transfers like that in the United States. A single currency and single financial market require a single regulator, a common deposit insurance scheme, and a bad-bank resolution fund—what subsequently came to be known as banking union.[5] But if fiscal policy decisions were going to be made at the European level, this would be tolerable only if there also existed a European Parliament with voice and authority sufficient to hold decision makers accountable for their actions. If there were going to be fiscal transfers to troubled member states, then there would have to be stronger rules for national fiscal policies, along with adequate oversight of those enforcing them. If there was going to be banking union, there would have to be political institutions capable of holding the continent's supranational bank regulators accountable for their actions.

European leaders thought they could force the pace by creating the euro. Once monetary union was a fact, even nationalistic politicians would have to concede that political union was needed to make it work. As Joschka Fischer, the charismatic Green Party politician serving as Germany's vice chancellor and foreign minister, put the point in a 1999 speech to the European Parliament, "with the introduction of the euro . . . an important part of national sovereignty, to wit monetary sovereignty, was passed over to a European institution. . . . The introduction of a common currency is not primarily an economic, but rather a sovereign and thus eminently political act . . . political union must be our lodestar from now on; it is the logical follow-on from Economic and Monetary Union."[6]

This was by no means exclusively a German view. Romano Prodi, the Italian politician serving as president of the European Commission when the euro was established, minced no words in an interview with the *Financial Times* in 1999, saying "[My] real goal is [to draw on] the consequences of the single currency and create a political Europe." Or, in the still-blunter language of Jean-Luc Dehaene, the French-born prime minister of Belgium, "Monetary union is the engine of political union."

An engine is prone to backfiring when its fuel is ignited prematurely. The blind faith of European policy makers in the euro was not unlike the faith invested in the gold standard in the 1920s: put monetary institutions in place, and the political adaptations required for their smooth operation will follow. These were the functionalist arguments that economists supplied to receptive officials.

Specialists in European politics, better attuned perhaps to the realities, were skeptical of this functionalist logic. Just because a certain set of political institutions is required to support a certain set of economic arrangements is no guarantee that they will be produced.[7] Politics, rather than responding to economic logic, has a life of its own.

The founding fathers of the euro had assumed that Europe would have several decades to complete its banking, fiscal, and political union. Unfortunately, the euro area was sideswiped by the financial crisis and the Great Recession, which laid bare the still-incomplete nature of their construct. The idea that monetary union could proceed without political union turned out to be a fatal mistake.

———

That Ireland, Spain, and other countries at the periphery of the European Union were among the founding members of the euro area was another surprise to the architects of the single currency. Study after study had shown that a core of strong and stable Northern European countries—Germany, France, Belgium, the Netherlands, Luxembourg, and perhaps Denmark—would find it easiest to cope with a one-size-fits-all monetary policy. Ireland, Spain, Portugal, Italy, and Greece, where conditions were different, would find the consequences of a common monetary policy less comfortable. It was therefore assumed that monetary union would be limited to that core of strong and stable Northern European countries.

But Ireland was already in the process of moving to Europe's core from its periphery. With an average growth rate of more than 6½ percent between 1990 and 1998, it had already attained one of the continent's highest per capita incomes. Spain, in contrast, was growing only half as fast, making the country's argument, that it was similarly prepared to adopt the euro, more problematic.[8]

Here, however, procedure trumped prudence. The decision to proceed with monetary union, like most EU decisions, was taken by consensus. And if unanimity was required, then countries like Spain, if denied membership, could block the process. Procedurally, there was no way to move forward without their participation.[9]

Even Greece, whose budget deficit was far too large to be driven through the generous loopholes of the Maastricht Treaty, could extract a promise that it would be permitted to join after a couple of years if it made at least cosmetic progress on the fiscal front. It had aid with the optics from Goldman Sachs, which helped the Greek government create the appearance that it had a manageable debt by arranging a deal whereby it got immediate cash, obviating the need to issue additional bonds, in return for pledging future revenues first from its national lottery and then from landing fees collected at its airports. The deals in question were booked as currency trades rather than loans, hiding them in plain sight, or at least hiding them from the European Commission.[10]

And so the euro came to the periphery. It stimulated housing markets by reducing interest rates, which in turn cheapened the cost for households, construction companies, and property developers of borrowing to speculate in real estate. In the 1990s, Spain, Portugal, and Italy had been forced to pay interest on ten-year government bonds at twice the rates demanded of Germany and the rest of Northern Europe.[11] These double-digit interest rates now came down with the approach of monetary union. Investors reasoned that members of the euro area would no longer be able to inflate their way out of trouble now that they had Germanic hard money, in quantities determined by a Germanic central bank. European rules, not to mention the absence of a central bank at the national level to provide money finance for budget deficits, would require governments to follow disciplined fiscal policies. Stability having been enhanced, growth would accelerate. Per capita incomes would converge toward the European norm. Faster growth and stronger budgets would ensure the sustainability of public debts.[12] These assumptions were the basis for the popular strategy of purchasing the bonds of Southern European governments in the expectation that their prices would rise as yields fell. This strategy acquired its own name, as fashionable investment strategies do. It was the "convergence play."[13]

The result was a massive flow of capital into the bond markets and banking systems of Spain, Portugal, Greece, and Ireland from the rest of Europe and the rest of the world.[14] Between 2004 and 2007 those inflows far exceeded the 4 percent of GDP guideline used by the International Monetary Fund as a caution light of risks to stability. That the IMF did not issue warnings of any consequence, despite this violation of historical norms, is itself indicative of the presumption that the situation in Europe was different. Monetary union was a fact. It was irreversible. There was no more reason to worry about current account imbalances and capital flows between euro-area member states than there was about current account imbalances and capital flows between the fifty US states. The bulk of the foreign capital imported by Southern European countries was used to finance private investment, not government budget deficits, the Greek exception notwithstanding. This private investment promised to make the recipient economies more productive, enabling them to repay what they borrowed.

Hence the fact that capital was flowing from high-income countries like Germany to lower-income countries like Spain, Portugal, and Greece could be justified as a good thing. Low-income countries with the capacity to grow fast had the most scope for putting additional capital to work. And with the advent of the euro, the presumption was that the formerly backward economies of Southern Europe now possessed this capacity in abundance. It was not unlike the manner in which the flow of capital from China to the United States was regarded. It too was justified as signifying the best of all possible worlds.

———

The German Federal Republic, in contrast, entered the euro as a poor performer. It was still digesting the former East Germany. Unemployment was high, especially in the eastern *Länder*. Its labor markets were inflexible. All the more reason, it was argued, to invest in the small countries of the European periphery rather than the large, moribund German economy.

Soon thereafter Germany would adopt the "Agenda 2010" reforms of Gerhard Schröder's coalition of Social Democrats and Greens. Schröder was an unlikely candidate to push through radical reforms of the German labor market. His father having died fighting on the eastern front during World War II, he worked as principal breadwinner for his family from the age of fourteen as a building laborer, embracing the militant pro-union politics of his workmates. Schröder then put himself through law school before becoming active with the Young Socialists and serving as defense attorney for Horst Mahler, founder of the notorious Baader-Meinhof Gang, the group of radical anti-capitalist students-cum-terrorists. When elected to the Bundestag, he flaunted his man-of-the-people credentials by wearing a sweater rather than the customary suit.

Over time Schröder moved to the center, as politicians with national ambitions often do. By the time he succeeded to the chancellorship in 1998, the German public, having suffered through years of high unemployment, was ready for something different. Shunning class warfare, the now conservatively suited chancellor cast himself as modernizer, embracing a strategy that combined social justice with economic efficiency in the manner of Bill Clinton and Tony Blair. Just as only Nixon could have gone to China, only Schröder could have convinced Germany's powerful unions that wage moderation, decentralized bargaining, and a reformed welfare state were in their interest. Moving to the center also made political sense: Schröder's Social Democrats faced relatively little political competition from farther left; thus, they had an incentive to move to the middle in order to compete, electorally, with the more conservative Christian Democrats and liberal Free Democrats.

But in the early years of the euro, Schröder's reforms had not yet been adopted, much less had time to work.[15] Productivity was growing faster in Southern Europe than in a still-moribund Germany. All this fed expectations of convergence between Europe's north and south, which made the south the obvious destination for footloose finance.

Juxtaposed against this reassuring backdrop, however, was a trio of disquieting facts.[16] First, saving declined in Southern Europe in the period of strong capital inflows. Evidently, the region was becoming increasingly dependent on foreign finance. This was the opposite of the pattern in China and other fast-growing Asian economies, where savings rates were not just high but rising. It was worrisome insofar as the capital inflows, and therefore the investment they financed, could stop at any time.

A second disturbing trend was the deterioration in competitiveness across Europe's southern tier. Following the 2003 Schröder reforms, unit labor costs in German manufacturing stopped rising, reflecting strong productivity growth and the unions' newfound acceptance of wage moderation. In countries like Spain, in contrast, wage increases far outstripped productivity. The euro promised faster growth, Spanish trade unionists were told. If their future incomes were going to be higher, they reasoned, they might as well partake of the benefits now. The reality, of course, was that faster growth was not guaranteed. Unit labor costs in Spanish manufacturing rose between 1999 and 2008 by a startling 40 percent relative to those in Germany. There was no way Spanish firms could compete.

Conditions in Greece, Portugal, and Italy were no better. Costs of production rose precisely when Germany, implementing its Agenda 2010 reforms, was pushing them down. Once upon a time, the impact of lower labor costs and improved cost competitiveness in Germany would have been offset by a stronger deutschmark. But this was no longer the case now that Germany had the euro.

And the problem was not just German competition. In addition, there was China. This was when Chinese exporters of garments, footwear, and other manufactures moved up-market, invading the product space of Greek, Portuguese, and Italian firms.[17] It was too much to ask of European leaders, when laying plans for the euro, that they should have anticipated the intensification of Chinese competition. In the event, China's incursion into Europe was another surprise that upset the euro applecart.

The third disturbing trend was that the flow of capital into peripheral Europe encouraged residential construction, not fixed investment.[18] Residential construction does little to enhance productivity. The surge in construction activity should have been a warning sign.

———

Even more than in the United States, banks were the conduits for these capital flows. Though US banks were highly leveraged, European banks were more highly leveraged still. US banks were levered by a factor of twelve, according to the conventional metric of bank assets to capital.[19] European banks, by the same measure, were levered by a factor of twenty.[20] In effect, European banks maintained a capital cushion of just 5 percent as protection against losses. This twenty-times leverage, moreover, was only the industry average. Some of the largest banks, like the German giant Deutsche Bank, outdid themselves by boosting their leverage to 40:1.

This was more borrowing and faster expansion of loan and investment books than could be financed simply by accepting retail deposits. Even more than in the United States, European banks supplemented their deposit liabilities by tapping the wholesale money market. They issued short-term debt. They borrowed from other bank and nonbank financial institutions, renewing those borrowings every night. In the first quarter of 2007, the loan-to-deposit ratio of European banks was close to 175 percent, far in excess of that in the United States. That this was true for Europe as a whole meant the phenomenon was not merely banks in Southern Europe borrowing from banks in Northern Europe. European banks as a group were also borrowing from other parts of the world, including the United States, and using the proceeds to fund speculative investments.

This process had several important implications. First, it rendered banks financing illiquid investments in real estate vulnerable to liquidity crises. Although demand deposits are liquid—as their name implies, they can be withdrawn on demand—the individuals holding those deposits can be slow to respond to events. Not so the wholesale money lent by banks to one another, which is not covered by deposit insurance. News about problems with a bank's loans and investments might make it impossible to roll over what it had borrowed. Even if the news was exaggerated—even if the bank was in fact solvent—it might nonetheless experience a liquidity crisis, forcing it to engage in a fire sale of assets or appeal for official assistance.

A second implication was that banking systems, and indeed individual banks, were allowed to grow very large. In 2007, when the crisis first lapped up on Europe's shores, the liabilities of BNP Paribas and Deutsche Bank exceeded 80 percent of the gross domestic products of France and Germany, respectively. The liabilities of the Belgian-Luxembourg bank Dexia and the Dutch bank Fortis exceeded, by a wide margin, the GDPs of their respective home countries. Not surprisingly, these were all banks that would play leading roles in the crisis that followed.

Third, the dramatic expansion of bank balance sheets allowed even more credit to flow into the booming housing markets of the Eurozone periphery. This lent still more impetus to the run-up in housing prices and the construction boom. It rendered Spain's regional savings banks more heavily exposed to the housing market. And for especially voracious banks for which even this exposure was not enough, more could be obtained by loading up on the mortgage-related securities of US banks. The result was the bizarre situation in which European banks borrowed dollars from US financial institutions in order to buy derivative securities issued off balance sheet by those same US financial institutions. This was vendor finance with a vengeance.[21]

In the run-up to the crisis, American officials like Governor Bernanke focused on the connections between the country's trade and budget deficits. They pointed to a single factor, namely the net flow of capital from the "savings glut countries" of Asia and the Middle East, as financing both the US trade and budget deficits, and raised troubling questions about what would happen if for any reason the savings glut countries suddenly turned reluctant to finance those deficits. But in focusing on the trade and budget deficits and on the net capital flow, they missed what turned out to be more important, namely the gross flow of finance from Europe into the increasingly risky securities that underwrote investment in the US housing market. There was no net capital flow between the United States and Europe. Trade between the two regions was broadly balanced. But there was an immense flow of European funds into US mortgage-backed securities and their derivatives, matched by an equal and offsetting flow of bank lending from the United States to Europe.

It was this "banking glut" and not Mr. Bernanke's "savings glut," and its implications for the housing market and not for the budget deficit, that mattered for what followed.[22] But the United States had an extensive recent history of budget deficits and trade deficits; hence there was no deficit of attention to these imbalances. In contrast, there was no precedent, historical or otherwise, for the kind of housing-market boom that developed after the turn of the century, and no precedent for the vendor finance fueling it. Their historical perspective thus informed the risks that policy makers perceived and, equally, the risks they missed.

———

How were these extraordinary financial circumstances allowed to arise? Why did so many supposedly shrewd observers fail to appreciate the risks posed by this overgrown financial system?

Answers to these questions start with the observation that Europe's financial system had always been more bank-based than that in the United States. In the US, banks provided just 30 percent of mortgage lending and 30 percent of corporate funding. In Europe they provided 80 percent of mortgages and nearly 90 percent of corporate loans. If there was going to be an expansion of financial activity in Europe, then the banks, which dominated the financial system, were bound to be in the vanguard.

In addition, big European banks were universal. Unencumbered by the equivalent of Glass-Steagall restrictions, they offered their clients the entire range, or "universe," of financial services. Regulators had traditionally gauged the adequacy of bank capital by placing investments into buckets distinguished by risk, and attached a simple leverage ratio to each. The regulator would then compute the share of the bank's assets in each bucket and determine the maximum amount of leverage permitted for the portfolio as a whole. This was the approach taken in the agreement on capital adequacy negotiated by the Basel Committee on Banking Supervision in 1988.

But big European banks complained that these rules of thumb failed to take into account the diversified nature of their business. If at the same time losses on assets in one bucket went up, losses on assets in another bucket went down, then the portfolio as a whole would be little affected. In a recession, when interest rates and corporate profits both declined, the banks might enjoy capital gains on their holdings of government bonds (the prices of which rose when interest rates fell) at the same time they suffered losses on corporate loans. Europe's large, widely diversified banks argued that they could therefore hold less capital as a cushion against losses. They could compute the riskiness of the portfolio using their internal models, and regulators could use the results to set capital requirements accordingly.

The Basel Committee on Banking Supervision bought into these arguments when it issued its revised capital accord, known as Basel II, in 2004. In 2005 the European Parliament endorsed a capital requirements directive authorizing the adoption of Basel II, and EU regulators moved to implement it in 2007. US regulators were slower to embrace Basel II in what, in hindsight, looks to have been an exceptional fit of prudence.

More generally, the European authorities claimed with no little pride that they were the most sophisticated regulators on the planet. Spanish regulators trumpeted the virtues of their system of dynamic provisioning under which banks were required to put aside reserves in good times to cover losses in bad times.[23] In the event, it turned out that this system did too little to restrain the boom and afforded an inadequate cushion for the losses incurred subsequently. It gave officials and bankers a false sense of security. In bank regulation, it would appear, sophistication is no virtue.

But at the root of the problem was the euro. Relieved of currency risk, banks felt free to borrow and lend abroad. Cross-border competition intensified. Formerly sleepy regional banks, their profits squeezed, took more risk in the gamble to survive. Quasi-public entities like the German bank IKB, perceiving inadequate opportunity in industrial and infrastructure lending, loaded up on high-yielding American CDOs. They understood that their governments, even though espousing the rhetoric of the single market and the level playing field, were invested in the survival of their national champions. Confident that the official sector would come to the rescue if their risky bets failed, they rolled the dice.

In the United States, the 2007–08 crisis originated in the shadow banking system—in the hedge funds, special purpose vehicles, and derivatives markets operating largely outside the regulatory net, before migrating to the commercial banks. In Europe, in contrast, the crisis originated in financial institutions firmly inside the regulatory perimeter. Europe's crisis was a banking crisis from the start.

———

This buildup of vulnerabilities bore more than a passing resemblance to the 1920s. There was the rapid expansion of credit in an American financial system freed of regulatory restrictions. The credit boom in the United States was mirrored by equally dramatic credit expansion in Europe. There was growing competition between bank and nonbank financial institutions and risk taking by financial firms gambling to survive. The length of the lending chain, which connected mortgage brokers and banks to security originators and foreign investors, encouraged opportunism up and down the line.

The credit boom was fueled by lax monetary policy in the United States, again similar to the situation in the 1920s. It was accentuated by the cross-border capital flows spawned by the chronic imbalances between the United States and China. Europe replicated those imbalances at the regional level, shipping large amounts of finance from the continent's north to the south. Much as the restoration of the gold standard encouraged reckless lending in the 1920s by convincing naïve investors that currency risk was a thing of the past, the advent of the euro allowed policy makers to argue, contrary to logic, that not just currency risk but also credit risk had disappeared. Investors swallowed the bait hook, line, and sinker.

As in the 1920s, housing was again the main beneficiary of the credit boom. But where the housing boom of the 1920s had been concentrated in the sparsely populated state of Florida, this one infected not just the United States but also Spain, Ireland, and other European countries. As a result, the boom and bust threatened the stability not only of individual bank and non-bank financial firms but the system as a whole, more so in that those financial institutions were more highly leveraged and thinly capitalized than eighty years before.

Careful students of the 1920s may have been aware of the parallels. But not even they were ready for what came next.

PART II | The Worst of Times

| Spent Bullets

B Y THE SPRING of 1929, the Fed's interest rate increases, reinforced now by the policy of direct pressure, were being felt by the stock market. Brokers' loans, though still available, were getting expensive. Billy Durant, more conscious than most of the importance of cheap credit for Wall Street, grew alarmed and took his concerns to the highest level. Durant arrived at the White House after dinner one evening in early April, by taxi rather than chauffeured limousine to avoid attracting attention. In an audience with President Hoover, he argued that "the Federal Reserve in its tightening of security loans was killing the goose that laid the golden egg."[1] Hoover, critical of the Fed's earlier low-interest-rate policies for fueling speculation, was unmoved.

Having failed to convert the president, Durant next tried to go over the head of the White House by mobilizing public opinion. He purchased fifteen minutes of time on the CBS radio network for an address highlighted by a demand that the "autocrats" on the Federal Reserve Board keep their hands off business.[2] Although the broadcast made a splash, it had no impact on Fed policy.

Unable to influence the central bank, Durant began quietly getting out of the market. The question was how many other investors would follow. Over the summer, the answer appeared to be "not many." Between June and August the Dow Jones industrials advanced by a further 16 percent. The mania for stocks spread from Wall Street to Main Street. Coverage of the markets moved from the business section to the front page of the dailies.

On September 5, Roger Babson, goateed investment guru, amateur business cycle theorist, and prominent prohibitionist, then gave his annual address to the National Business Conference, the punch line of which was "Sooner or later a crash is coming, and it may be terrific." Babson was a devotee of Sir Isaac Newton. His wife, Grace, on a trip to London, had gone so far as to purchase a parlor room salvaged from Newton's house and have it shipped to the Babson Institute, Roger's nascent business school in Wellesley, Massachusetts. Babson believed that Newton's third law of physics applied to financial markets: to every action there is a reaction, and therefore what goes up must come down. Babson had been predicting a decline in stock valuations since the market took off in 1927. He was the first to acknowledge that his pessimism was hardly news. As he put it on September 5 in introducing his remarks, "I am about to repeat what I said at this time last year and the year before." Even a stopped clock is right twice a day. Babson's time was about to come.

The Yale University economist Irving Fisher, like Babson, was both a prohibitionist and partial to the goatee. But where Babson was a student of physics, Fisher had been inspired by scenes of water cascading into mountain pools on a summer trip to Switzerland and now sought to apply the principles of hydraulics to the economy. The fact that liquidity was still ample, Durant's warnings about the future notwithstanding, constituted the basis for Fisher's soon-to-be-notorious proclamation on October 17 that "Stock prices have reached what looks like a permanently high plateau." On Monday, October 21, Fisher doubled down, insisting that any correction was "only shaking out the lunatic fringe."

———————

The Dow Jones average peaked on Tuesday, September 3, at a level that would not be matched for twenty-five years. Share prices fell modestly on September 4 and then sharply on September 5. Thursday the fifth was when Babson gave his speech comparing Wall Street to Florida real estate and predicting the worst. The "Babson Break," as the 5 percent drop that day came to be known, was a reminder that, as Babson's hero Newton might have put it, what went up could come down.

For seven weeks, stock prices drifted downward. There were periodic up days and also sharp sell-offs, as on Thursday, October 3, when the Dow fell by 4½ percent. Traders who bought stocks on margin were hit. "Mortality among speculative Stock Exchange accounts was tremendous," wrote the *New York Times* the following weekend. "Numerous accounts that ran into six figures at the first of the week were entirely extinguished by Friday night."[3]

Still, investors were unprepared for what came next. On October 24, "Black Thursday," the Dow Jones Industrial Average fell 11 percent at the opening bell. In the first thirty minutes, 1.6 million shares changed hands, exceeding typical turnover for an entire trading day. The quotation machinery and transcontinental wire system were overwhelmed.

A market in this panicked state could not be left to its own devices. Taking a leaf from the book of J. P. Morgan the elder, Thomas Lamont, the leading Morgan partner, summoned Charles Mitchell, chairman of National City Bank; Albert Wiggin, chairman of Chase National Bank; William Potter, president of Guarantee Trust Company; and Seward Prosser, chairman of Bankers Trust. (Jack Morgan himself was in Europe, having been more concerned with conditions there.) After a midday meeting of just twenty minutes, Lamont emerged to address the assembled financial press. The economic and financial situation was "fundamentally sound," he affirmed, invoking the standard trope to which bankers and politicians resort whenever markets show signs of distress. Using a term made current by the advent of commercial air travel, he dismissed the morning's drop as the market just hitting an air pocket.

Prices stabilized in the afternoon, whether owing to Lamont's remarks or to hopes that the bankers were ready to back his words with deeds. Then, however, the market was hit by a wave of sell orders from the West Coast, which was only now absorbing news of the morning's carnage. Trading volume, at nearly 13 million shares, was more than double the previous daily high. It took the ticker three hours following the close of business to finish spitting out its record of the day's transactions.

Prices fluctuated uneasily on Friday and again in Saturday's abbreviated trading, buoyed by rumors of support by a pool of bankers organized by Lamont. Volume remained heavy. On Sunday a normally deserted Wall Street was a hive of activity as clerks toted up the damage and hustling messengers relayed the news. Sightseers "picked up from the street a vagrant piece of ticker tape, as visitors seize upon spent bullets on a battlefield as souvenirs."[4]

The Dow Jones industrials lost another 12 percent on "Black Monday," October 28, and 9 percent the following day, "Black Tuesday," as the hoped-for bankers' support failed to materialize. The 16 million shares that changed hands on Tuesday set a record that stood for four decades. Again, traders and bookkeepers were overwhelmed. The Wall Street Bowling League announced that it was postponing further contests owing to the absence of many members.

For margin traders who had lost everything, the New Era was over. "Wall Street was a street of vanished hopes, of curiously silent apprehension and of a sort of paralyzed hypnosis," the *New York Times* wrote in its lead story on October 30. For Will Rogers, flying west from New York on October 24, however, it was much sound and fury signifying nothing.

All day just looking down on beautiful lands and prosperous towns, then you read all this sensational collapse on Wall Street. What does it mean? Nothing. Why, if the cows of this country failed to come up and get milked one night it would be more of a panic than if Morgan and Lamont had never held a meeting. Why, an old sow and a litter of pigs make more people a living than all the steel and General Motors stock combined. Why, the whole 120,000,000 of us are more dependent on the cackling of a hen than if the stock exchange was turned into a night club.[5]

Not everyone was able to view the landscape with such equanimity. Still, there was a considerable body of opinion agreeing with Rogers. Retailers continued to plan for a strong Christmas shopping season. The only hint of what was to come was a report from a Wall Street financier who found himself sitting in a bar alongside his milkman. When the banker remarked that the milk business must have been one of the few activities to have come through the Crash unscathed, the milkman retorted "Unscathed nothing. Do you know that in the past three weeks I have had enough cancellations and reductions in cream order to reduce my business by over $400 a month? People still order the same amount of milk, but they have apparently decided that they can get along without the buying of cream."[6]

———

Leverage has long been cited as a factor in the Crash. When prices fell, brokers who had extended credit to investors called for additional margin, forcing their customers to sell into a falling market. The resulting fire sales then fed on themselves. Contemporary accounts are replete with tales of margin accounts "ripped wide open" and investors being wiped out. This was not the first time that markets would be laid low by this combustible mix of leverage and volatility; nor would it be the last.

Lack of information also played a role. This was not simply an East Coast–West Coast phenomenon or the fact that the ticker ran late. On the worst days, accurate price quotations were unavailable on the trading floor itself. In his classic account of Black Thursday, Maury Klein describes a panicked telephone clerk who, when asked for price quotations by a broker, shouted in desperation "I can't get them. I can't get any information. The whole place is falling apart."[7] This kind of chaotic environment is a fertile incubator of panic. When prices are a matter of speculation, as it were, investors will be tempted to infer them from the actions of other investors. When they hear investors shouting "sell," they will conclude that the only prudent course is to do likewise. At that point, the herd will be off and running.

Investor mood swings can be self-reinforcing, but they are more likely when they have some basis in fact. Thus, a more systematic way of understanding the investor response is in terms of the softening economy. August marked the business cycle peak, according to the subsequent calculations of the National Bureau of Economic Research. Commerce and Treasury officials may have been unaware, but managers knew that firms, if only their own firms, were cutting back. Automobile production was down to 500,000 units in August from more than 600,000 in April and May.[8] In their classic business cycle chronology, Arthur Burns and Wesley Mitchell place the peaks in employment in the iron, lumber, and machinery industries in August, basing their estimates on statistics available at the time.[9] Building permits and construction contracts were off sharply. Although some of this may have been the late summer lull, the drop was more pronounced than in prior years.

Such observations would have created doubts about the New Age presumption that recession was no longer a threat to profitability or a factor in stock-market valuations. So would the behavior of the Federal Reserve. The advent of the Fed, charged with providing an elastic currency, was what had supposedly consigned this kind of recession to the dustbin of history. But in fact, it was the Federal Reserve System, and its lower Manhattan branch in particular, that sought to limit credit availability. On August 9, responding to the rise in share prices, the New York Fed raised its discount rate from 5 to 6 percent. The board's approval of the action was, in effect, a tacit acknowledgment that the earlier policy of direct pressure was not enough. Although 6 percent was still below call money rates, it left the banks little room for error. George Harrison, the Harvard Law School alumnus and longtime Fed staffer who had succeeded to the governorship of the New York Reserve Bank on Benjamin Strong's death in 1928, argued that the increase would be seen as "a warning against the excessive use of credit."[10] One is reminded how the European Central Bank, similarly unaware that an economic and financial storm was brewing, raised its policy rate in April 2008.

Tighter credit in New York meant tighter credit abroad. European central banks, seeing their currencies weakening and gold stocks dwindling as their residents joined Wall Street's festivities, met the Fed tit-for-tat. The central banks of Italy, the Netherlands, Germany, Austria, and Hungary raised their policy rates in the first half of 1929, this despite the fact that their economies were slowing, or in some cases already in recession. Denmark, Sweden, and Norway then tightened in August in response to the New York Fed's rate hike.

The Bank of England had last raised its discount rate in February. Somewhat surprisingly, it now remained on hold through the summer of 1929. Between June and mid-September the Bank of England's gold reserves declined by a further $133 million, but still Norman did not move. The British economy was weak, and an increase in interest rates would only aggravate an already difficult economic situation.[11] Norman understood that an increase would not be warmly received by Britain's newly elected Labour government. With the Hague Conference that led to the Young Plan restructuring of German reparations still underway, he was reluctant to take a step that, by drawing gold from Paris, might antagonize the French.

Norman's hand was then forced by the Hatry Scandal. Clarence Hatry was an odd duck to dictate the course of British monetary policy. The son of a trader in silk and velvet for use in top hats, Hatry was short in stature, like his contemporary Charles Ponzi, whom he vaguely resembled. He also shared with Ponzi a certain entrepreneurial flair and the ability to raise money for dubious projects. And, like Ponzi, he had a miraculous capacity to rehabilitate himself once his earlier business initiatives foundered.

In 1910 the twenty-two-year-old Hatry inherited control of the family silk company from his mother. Within months the business failed and, having put up his personal credit to obtain £8,000 of supplies, Hatry was declared insolvent. Not easily discouraged, he turned next to selling insurance to Austrian immigrants transiting England in order to sail from Liverpool to the United States. Hatry formed the Austrian Immigrants Insurance Association, offering policies that provided for return passage and a resettlement fee if the policyholder was denied entry into the Promised Land. He transferred the risk by reselling the policy to an established carrier, taking as his commission the difference between what the immigrant paid and the cost of the reinsurance.

World War I interrupted the migration of Central Europeans to the United States, putting an end to this business opportunity but creating others. In 1914 Hatry combined the modest profits from his Austrian-immigrant policies with £30,000 of borrowed funds to purchase City Equitable, a reinsurance company. The reinsurance business, then as now, was dominated by German and Austrian firms, so the war created an opening. Hatry reorganized City Equitable to capitalize on the opportunity and within six months sold a controlling interest for £250,000 to Gerard Lee Bevan, a flamboyant British financier, and Bevan's associate, Peter Haig-Thomas.[12] Bevan's forebears had been founders of Barclays; their descendant, known as Jerry, was a high-living stockbroker with a taste for women and Chinese porcelain. City Equitable collapsed in February 1922 when it was discovered that it had issued false balance sheets understating loans to other Bevan-affiliated companies, disguised its speculative investments, and omitted to report that some of its assets were pledged as security against borrowed funds. Bevan was held personally responsible, having kept his handpicked board of directors ignorant of the machinations. He fled to France and then to Vienna, where he lived in disguise before being discovered and arrested. Extradited to Britain, he was convicted of fraud and sentenced to seven years' hard labor at Wormwood Scrubs.[13]

With profits from the sale of City Equitable, Hatry next acquired the Commercial Bank of London, which he used to finance further acquisitions. The result was Amalgamated Industrials, a business empire encompassing shipbuilding, cotton spinning, coal, iron, and pig farming. Hatry's firms were overcapitalized; he issued more shares than needed for their operation as a way of funding additional acquisitions. Doing so unfortunately made it more difficult to offer investors in the early companies a respectable return. Pig farming, in any case, was the most profitable of those activities; the shipbuilding, cotton spinning, coal, and steel industries all suffered from overcapacity and low prices in the 1920s. Hatry avoided the worst by selling off much of Amalgamated Industrials not long after the war.

Hatry next deployed the Commercial Bank, rebranded as the Commercial Corporation in honor of his extrabanking ambitions, to buy up and consolidate firms in the glass and jute industries. The demand for the products of both had been strong during World War I: glass has myriad wartime uses, and jute fiber was used in making the sandbags so essential for trench warfare. The jute industry was dominated by seven family-owned firms in Dundee, Scotland, where some 90 percent of British production was located, jute manufacturing having used whale oil to soften the fibers before weaving and Dundee having been a major whaling center. The industry was already suffering from chronic overcapacity when the wartime demand for burlap sacking declined. Hatry amalgamated the seven firms, eliminated their excess capacity, and took them public in order to enable the founding families to get their capital out. Unfortunately, demand for jute and glass was weaker in the 1920s than during World War I. Hatry and his directors "failed to appreciate the artificiality of the post-Armistice boom" and "the severity of the reaction which was to follow," in the words of the liquidator appointed to wind up the Commercial Bank in 1923.[14]

Not easily discouraged, by 1926 Hatry was back in business, having founded Corporation and General Securities Ltd. Just how he regained the confidence of investors is something of a mystery. He appears to have made some effort to pay off his earlier creditors. He was known for his mental acuity and charm and maintained the lavish lifestyle of a successful entrepreneur, acquiring a racing stable, the largest yacht on British waters, and an elegant home. Two homes, actually. The first, at an address that had once been the abode of the British political economist David Ricardo, featured a rooftop swimming pool where Hatry threw lavish parties.[15] Its successor was in the prestigious Mayfair district, where Hatry installed a cocktail bar in the basement and another swimming pool, this one on the second floor.

Corporation and General Securities provided underwriting services to middle-sized businesses and municipalities, competing on price with the established firms that dominated the market. In the manner of Angelo Mozilo and Countrywide Credit, it used direct marketing to attract clients. Before long, Hatry was taking stakes in the companies whose issues he underwrote. His holdings expanded beyond Corporation and General Securities, which now featured Lord Henry Paulet, the Sixteenth Marquess of Winchester, as figurehead, to include also the Drapery Trust, which specialized in amalgamating department stores, and the Photomaton Corporation, which placed coin-in-the-slot photography machines in railway stations and amusement parks.

––––––

By 1929 Hatry was setting his sights still higher, seeking to acquire United Steel Companies, an enterprise valued at £7 million. United Steel was formed in 1917 as a combination of several steel companies under the leadership of the eponymous Harry Steel. The conglomerate was heavily indebted and therefore vulnerable to soft demand. Demand being soft in the 1920s, Steel was receptive when Hatry proposed to purchase United Steel and its subsidiaries using borrowed funds, sell off their redundant assets, and float the resulting concern on the London Stock Exchange. The strategy was not unlike the one he had employed when forming Jute Industries. It was also not unlike that of a modern private equity firm such as Bain Capital.

The main challenge was borrowing the £8 million. Unfortunately, Norman's decision back in February to increase the Bank of England's discount rate made raising cash more difficult than Hatry anticipated when launching the buyout. The banks demanded collateral, something that Hatry, lavish lifestyle notwithstanding, did not possess in abundance.

Finding himself £900,000 short and with the deadline for completing the transaction approaching, Hatry resorted to desperate measures. Corporate and General Securities having underwritten a number of municipal loans, Hatry still held copies of the bonds of the cities in question. He now printed unauthorized loan certificates for Gloucester, Swindon, and Wakefield as security for additional loans. He raised cash by informing the municipalities for which Corporate and General had provided underwriting services that only some of their bonds had been successfully placed, where in truth the placement was complete, and kept the difference in subscriptions for himself. In addition, Hatry made duplicate copies of securities issued by one of his companies, Associated Automatic Machines, and held by another, the Austin Friars Trust. The same stock certificates securing advances from Barclays Bank were used to secure a loan from Parsons and Co., and then another from Lloyds Bank.[16]

Desperation breeding recklessness, Hatry did not even bother to pledge different securities to various branches of the same bank. While the head office of Lloyds took 100,000 shares in Associated Automatic Machines as collateral, the St. James branch was offered duplicates as collateral for another loan. It did not take long for a clerk to discover the problem and for Lloyds to hire a chartered accountant, Sir Gilbert Garnsey, to investigate its extent. Nor did it take long for word of Garnsey's engagement to spread, and shares in Hatry's companies to collapse.

In the meantime, Hatry borrowed more money to purchase shares in his companies, ward off insolvency, and buy time to gamble for redemption, but in so doing he only dug himself a deeper hole. This pattern became commonplace as the crisis worsened: individuals and institutions experiencing financial distress, operating in an environment of lax regulation, purchased shares in their own enterprises in order to suppress evidence of their insolvency and buy time to gamble for redemption, but in so doing only made for themselves—and society—even larger losses. This was the same practice in which the Bank of United States engaged in 1929 when other investors began to sell its shares in response to worries about solvency, and in which Albert Oustric engaged to ward off failure of his Banque Adam in 1930. It was a practice that would be taken to new heights by management of the big Icelandic banks in 2008.[17]

On September 20, 1929, the Marquess of Winchester issued a statement acknowledging that an investigation of Hatry's affairs was underway. Norman, who had long been suspicious of the flamboyant financier, so informed the London Stock Exchange, which suspended trading in the Hatry Group the same morning. By the close of business, Hatry was arrested and jailed. He was quickly indicted and brought to trial shortly after the New Year. Counsel suggested that the scheme that had brought him down was hatched not by Hatry himself by his voluble Italian colleague, John Gialdini, who properly deserved the blame. Gialdini had threatened to blow his brains out if the United Steel acquisition fell through, before conveniently fleeing the country. No matter; Hatry was convicted and sentenced to the white-collar maximum of fourteen years.[18] Eventually Gialdini was also arrested, found guilty at the conclusion of a trial in Milan, and sentenced to five years and ten months of imprisonment. The contrast with the treatment of white-collar criminals in the wake of the 2008–09 crisis is too obvious to warrant comment.

Inevitably, Hatry's shareholders were wiped out. In addition, some £12.5 million of unsecured liabilities were frozen as a result of the suspension of his companies.[19] A number of London stockbrokers failed, and several banks, including Barclays, announced that their profits would take a hit.[20] One of the few beneficiaries of the episode was, ironically, United Steel, which was able to write down its financial obligations as a result of the subsequent bankruptcy and emerged from reorganization in a stronger financial position.[21]

But in the short run, these events precipitated a sharp fall in the London Stock Exchange and gold losses for the Bank of England. On September 26 Norman bowed to the inevitable, announcing a one-point increase in the discount rate.

The result, a higher cost of credit, was unhelpful for a struggling British economy. But defense of the pound's gold standard parity was paramount. Gold losses, whatever their cause—including Hatry—demanded a reaction. The situation would be different after September 1931, when there was no longer a gold standard to defend. It would be different in the global crisis of 2008–09, when, unconstrained by an exchange rate commitment, the Bank of England, like the Fed, could cut interest rates to a rock-bottom level. For the moment, however, the Bank's priority remained defense of the sterling exchange rate. And that required Norman to tighten the screws.

———

The US Federal Reserve, unlike the Bank of England, still had ample gold reserves. But although free to act, it had to display the will. Following a tumultuous October 28, Black Monday, the New York Fed quickly stepped into the breach. Harrison assembled his board for an exceptional 3:00 a.m. meeting. Before the markets opened the next morning and without prior approval from the board of governors in Washington, D.C., he announced that the New York bank would purchase $100 million of short-term treasury securities. The new purchases were made for the New York bank's own account, separate from the account of the Open Market Investment Committee.

The New York Fed went on to purchase $150 million of government securities. It kept its "discount window wide open," as Harrison put it, giving banks cash in return for commercial paper.[22] (Commercial paper, recall, means promissory notes documenting payments that the banks would eventually receive from their corporate clients.) These steps prevented a spike in interest rates like those in earlier financial crises—prevention of such spikes being the main rationale for the creation of the Federal Reserve System in 1914. By limiting distress among brokers and dealers, the New York Fed averted a more serious meltdown. The *New York Times* praised it for having "insured the soundness of the business situation when the speculative markets went on the rocks."[23]

This was impressively fast action even by the standards of Ben Bernanke. It is hard to see how the Federal Reserve Bank of New York could have done more. Milton Friedman and Anna Schwartz, in their monetary history of the United States, blame the Fed for the depth and duration of the Great Depression. They attribute its inaction to the death of Benjamin Strong, the dominant personality within the system and the individual who best understood how to respond to a crisis. The events of October suggest a more nuanced interpretation. The New York Fed may have been unaware of the havoc that would be wreaked by earlier moves to tighten credit conditions. But once that havoc broke out, Harrison and his colleagues were quick to act. Their actions informed by the real bills doctrine, they knew how to respond to signs of credit stringency and distress. Harrison, in particular, understood the urgency. It was not beyond his capacity to formulate a response and secure the backing of his board. He was capable of decisive action and took it.

One might think that a board of governors similarly beholden to the real bills doctrine would have been reassured. In fact, however, more concerned about prerogatives than policy, its members were furious about not having been consulted. Led by Adolph Miller, the board immediately took steps to limit Harrison's ability to respond in this fashion. The precedent had been set in 1927 when the board overrode the directors of the Chicago Fed, forcing the bank to change its discount rate. Now the board held the New York rate hostage, denying Harrison's request for a reduction to help distressed banks and brokers until New York's directors agreed that further purchases of government securities would be made only with the prior approval of the board. Friedman and Schwartz suggest that the problem was with Harrison—that, had Strong been there instead, he would have been able to face down the board. The fact that the terms of engagement between the board and the Reserve banks had already been changed by the events of 1927 suggests otherwise. The problem was structural, not one of personalities.

But if Harrison and his colleagues understood the need to respond quickly to the financial distress caused by the stock market crash, they understood less well how to respond to subsequent events. So long as the problem was financial distress, they understood it was their responsibility to provide emergency liquidity, in contemporary parlance an elastic currency. That the stock market crash placed New York banks at risk was something the directors of the New York Fed readily grasped.

But once the problem became deflation and depression, there was less agreement on what to do, if anything. The Federal Reserve System had been created to prevent spikes in interest rates. Its officials knew how to respond when, as a result of financial dislocations, credit temporarily grew scarce relative to the needs of business. There was no consensus, however, about what to do if the price level showed a tendency to fall for a period of time. The US price level had trended downward before, in the 1870s and 1880s and again in the aftermath of World War I, without producing a full-blown financial crisis. For Federal Reserve governors, their views informed by this historical experience, it was not obvious that the downward movement in prices was a problem now.

As stringency in the money market ebbed and interest rates normalized, action therefore was perceived as less urgent. The views of Harrison and his directors now aligned with those of the board of governors. The New York bank no longer resisted the instructions of Washington, D.C. To the contrary, it became entirely willing to cease and desist from open market purchases.[24] The economy would quickly pay the price.

CHAPTER 8

The Next Leg Down

THE CONTRACTION ACCELERATED following the crash. Petroleum, pig iron, and steel production all fell in the fourth quarter of 1929. Motor vehicle production declined further. Industrial production fell by 9 percent between early October and the end of the year—that is to say, at a 30 percent annual rate.[1] In 2008, by comparison, US industrial production fell only two-thirds as fast in the three months following the failure of Lehman Brothers.

As bad as things were, this was still no Great Depression. Much as when the Subprime Crisis erupted in 2007, the worst was limited to the United States, and it was still possible to argue that the worst would soon be over. The decline in foreign stock markets was limited. Other countries, not hit by the same massive shock to confidence, saw little fall in industrial production in the fourth quarter of 1929. Canada, though closely tied to the United States, saw no decline in industrial production until December. In France, where stabilization and then recovery had begun late, the economy continued to expand.

Latin America and other regions that relied on commodity exports felt the fallout from the US slowdown most strongly. US firms cut back on purchases of coffee, cocoa, rubber, and silk. With consumer and industrial demand weakening, they saw less need for supplies. Financial problems made it more difficult to obtain trade credit.[2] Whatever the reason, the result was that the United States imported less.

But commodity production follows its own rhythm, with planting and harvest decisions occurring far in advance. The fall now was in prices, not production. Coffee prices fell by 30 percent in the fourth quarter of 1929, corn prices by 15 percent.[3] Commodity prices had already been weak for the better part of a decade, but this now was "an acute attack, supervening upon a chronic form of the same disease."[4] As yet it did not precipitate widespread debt defaults by Latin American countries that had borrowed extensively in the 1920s and now had heavy debts to service. But these would come.

In the final months of 1929 it was still possible to argue that damage from the Crash would be limited—in the language favored by officials in 2007, that the consequences would be "contained." The Fed had prevented the market's sharp correction from infecting the banking system; at least it had prevented serious bank failures. A number of small banks failed in the wake of the stock market crash, to be sure, but then small banks failed all through the 1920s.

By early 1930, however, evidence that the economy was weakening was unmistakable. The 1929 Christmas shopping season was disappointing, and department store sales continued to fall at a 10 percent annual rate in the first half of 1930. There was no question that this was now a recession.

Central banks responded accordingly. The Open Market Investment Committee authorized the New York Fed to reduce its discount rate in half-point increments in February and March.[5] The Bank of England and German Reichsbank cut their interest rates in sympathy. Even the Bank of France, which maintained immensely large reserves and rarely adjusted policy, cut its discount rate by half a point at the end of January, in the first such change in two years.

Initially, financial markets responded favorably. Share prices in New York rose by 16 percent in the first four months of 1930. More than $100 million of foreign government bonds were floated in the United States between January and March. This was just a fraction of 1927–28 levels, but it was still higher than in any quarter of 1929. In the United States, Canada, and the principal European countries, industrial production held steady through the first three months of 1930.

But even if firms were maintaining production, prices were continuing to fall, signaling that demand was not keeping up. By May it was clear that unemployment was weighing on spending in the United States, Britain, and Germany. Demand for the products of French industry was "poor." Economic conditions in Belgium were "unsatisfactory." Japanese business was "inactive."[6]

At this point, the drop in industrial production accelerated dramatically. In the United States, the fall from December 1929 to December 1930 was 21 percent. In Germany it was 23 percent.[7] Conditions in other countries were not much better.

———

This, clearly, was the turning point where a garden-variety recession became something more. Charles Kindleberger, in his classic account, considers four explanations for the break: inadequate US monetary support, trade restrictions, weak commodity prices, and events abroad.[8] It is worth considering them in turn.

On the monetary front, it is again not accurate to say that the Federal Reserve did nothing. Twice, in May and June 1930, the board of governors approved further cuts in the discount rate of the Federal Reserve Bank of New York. By midyear, the rate charged by the New York bank had fallen to less than half the 6 percent level of the previous August. This was at least a step in the right direction. But at this point the board concluded that its work was done. Since the cost of credit was low, its members agreed, credit availability did not now pose an obstacle to stabilization and recovery.

The reality, of course, was that the cost of credit was not so low. Although interest rates had declined, prices were also falling, raising the cost of repayment (what economists refer to as the real interest rate). By June, wholesale prices were fully 7 percent below the late-1929 level.[9]

Perhaps the fall in prices was not yet widely anticipated; if so, it could not have created a hesitancy to borrow. Commodity futures prices, one indicator of expected future price levels, were above actual prices in the first half of 1930, consistent with the notion that the fall in prices was not fully anticipated. But even though futures remained above actual prices, they were also falling. James Hamilton has analyzed the link between commodity futures prices and the overall price level, concluding that market participants expected prices to fall in the first and second trimesters of 1930, albeit by somewhat less than turned out to be the case.[10]

And although yields on three- to six-month treasury notes and certificates had come down to less than 2 percent by midyear, the long-term rates relevant to fixed-investment decisions remained stubbornly high.[11] What more might the Fed have done? To start, it could have reduced its lending rates further. With the discount rate at 2½ percent, there was more room to cut. This was true by the standards of the 1930s, given how the New York Fed had brought the discount rate down to 1 percent by the end of the decade. It was similarly true by the standards of the 2000s, given how the Bernanke Fed brought rates down to 0.25 percent in the wake of the 2008–09 crisis.

But contemporary monetary doctrine held that financial institutions should borrow from the central bank only as a last resort and that the Fed should lend only at a penalty rate. Otherwise, banks would use cheap funding for speculative investments. Firms would engage in overproduction. Or so it was believed by Federal Reserve governors who viewed the future through the lens of the past. In fact, although rash behavior had been a problem in the past, it was not obviously a problem in 1930, the bubble having so recently burst. Be that as it may, the members of the Federal Reserve Board were slow to acknowledge that circumstances had changed.

Some members of the board, Adolph Miller prominent among them, were convinced in any case that lowering rates would be pushing on a string. Miller, recall, was a believer in the real bills doctrine. Central bank credit was useful, in this view, for financing the legitimate needs of business but could do nothing to encourage it when firms were cutting back. Monetary operations could "stimulate the flow of money into use" when business was picking up, but they would do little to encourage borrowing and activity when firms were retrenching.[12] Under these circumstances, there was no alternative to relying on the self-equilibrating tendencies of the market. Stabilization of business conditions would have to come about through "reduced production, reduced inventories, the gradual reduction of consumer credit, the liquidation of security loans, and the accumulation of savings through the exercise of thrift," in the words of George Norris, the former director of the Department of Wharves, Docks, and Ferries of the City of Philadelphia, who now served as governor of that city's Federal Reserve bank.

The Open Market Investment Committee authorized a modest $50 million of securities purchases in March 1930 but then signaled its reluctance to do more.[13] In June the executive committee of the Open Market Policy Conference (the new name of the recently reorganized Open Market Investment Committee) permitted the Federal Reserve Bank of New York to purchase an additional $25 million of treasury securities for two weeks. But that decision was taken mainly for technical reasons, and even then the vote was closely split, indicating that further authorizations were unlikely. After two weeks Harrison proposed extending the program, but the executive committee rejected the request by four to one (Harrison himself providing the dissenting vote). Harrison could have insisted on a more ambitious program; he could have threatened to undertake the purchases for the New York bank's own account, as before. Benjamin Strong would have been bolder, the implication follows. We will never know.

———

The other headline economic event of 1930, the textbooks tell us, was the Smoot-Hawley tariff act. The tariff, those textbooks tell us, had a sharp negative impact on the economy. Unfortunately, the textbooks are wrong.

The tariff was an issue in the 1928 presidential campaign. The Republicans were the party of protectionism, and Hoover courted the Midwest farm vote with promises to tax commodity imports. The House Ways and Means Committee opened its hearings on January 7, 1929, two months and a day after the election. The committee was chaired by Willis Hawley, a long-serving representative from Oregon. Hawley had worked his way up from farm boy to private school principal, professor of history and economics, and president of Willamette College before entering politics; his sponsorship of the tariff was less successful. After serving in Congress for thirteen terms, he would fail to secure the nomination of his own party in 1932.[14] Reed Smoot, after having served five terms in the Senate, similarly was defeated by Democrat Elbert Thomas in his 1932 campaign for reelection.

The tariff legislation that came to be forever associated with Smoot and Hawley took nearly a year and a half to wend its way through the Congress. On June 17, 1930, it was signed into law by President Hoover, ceremonially wielding six solid-gold pens. Smoot-Hawley raised the tariff on dutiable imports from 38 to 45 percent.[15] Creating a congressional coalition had required reaching out to additional constituencies, including eastern manufacturing. The tariff schedule that resulted was a hodgepodge that gave even more generous protection to industry than agriculture.

The question is to what effect. Raising the prices of dutiable imports diverted some spending toward their American-produced substitutes, which domestic producers welcomed under the circumstances. Working in the other direction was the fact that a higher tariff also meant less purchasing power for consumers. But this effect was small, since imports were only 5 percent of US gross national product in 1929 and two-thirds of imports were subject to no duty at all. Putting this all together, Douglas Irwin calculates that Smoot-Hawley reduced US incomes by at most $116 million, or 0.1 percent of 1929 US GDP. This was small potatoes by the standards of the Great Depression.[16]

The tariff has also been blamed for creating uncertainty that discouraged investment. This is not unlike the argument that the Obama stimulus and health care reform in 2009 created uncertainty that discouraged business investment. Robert Edgerton, president of the National Association of Manufacturers, complained in November 1929 that industry and commerce were "in many instances unable to conclude their plans and many programs of development are waiting or threatened with abandonment, while party politics, bloc politics, personal politics, and sectional politics are maneuvering for this or that advantage or to avenge this or that default or embarrassing this or that political personality."[17]

But even if true, the uncertainty of which Edgerton warned was resolved by mid-1930. Robert Archibald and David Feldman analyzed the uncertainty hypothesis by relating investment in fifteen industries to their exposure to foreign trade.[18] Their findings suggest that investment was, in fact, weaker than expected in 1929, when the outcome of congressional deliberations was least clear. But there was no analogous evidence for 1930, in whose first half the outlines of the legislation were being clarified and by the middle of which uncertainty about the tariff had been resolved. Again, the conclusion must be that any negative effects were small and transient.

And if Smoot-Hawley did not have a large impact on the US economy, then it could not have had a large impact on the rest of the world. This is not to deny the existence of negative impacts on particular producers. Italy objected to higher tariffs on its exports of straw hats and olive oil. Swiss watchmakers were up in arms. Spanish exporters of grapes, oranges, and onions were hit by the American measure. Across Latin America, exporters complained of the protection afforded the American farmer. There and elsewhere, the tariff reinforced the problem of weak commodity prices. Smoot-Hawley thus made it harder for commodity producers to earn dollars, in turn making it harder to service their debt.

The question is how much harder. Kevin Carey has looked for this effect in the reaction of the prices of government bonds in June 1930, the month the tariff bill was signed.[19] If the tariff in fact created major problems for commodity exporters, raising the likelihood that they would be forced to default on their debts, then the prices of their bonds should have fallen. Although there is some evidence of this, the effect is again small.

Where Smoot-Hawley mattered was in undermining international comity. It elicited protests from thirty foreign governments. It "intensified nationalism all over the world," in the words of Morgan partner Thomas Lamont.[20] It provoked retaliation and led to the collapse of a conference convened by the League of Nations with the goal of negotiating a coordinated reduction in tariffs. The Depression was a global phenomenon, and containing it required a global response. Any effort to coordinate a response, whether in the form of synchronized interest rate reductions, a debt moratorium, or an emergency loan, was that much harder when governments were at one another's throat over Smoot-Hawley.

Thus, the textbook assertion that Smoot-Hawley worsened the Depression in the United States is bad history in the service of good policy. Although there is no evidence that the tariff had a significant negative impact on the American economy, its ritual invocation helped policy makers resist the protectionist temptation in 2009. That in turn made it easier to mount an internationally coordinated response.

———

Herbert Hoover is a controversial figure in any account of the Depression. He entered the period riding the triumph of his victorious 1928 campaign, admired equally for his personal traits, which included honesty, industriousness, and self-reliance, and his accomplishments, having come from modest background, working his way through Stanford University, using his skills as a mining engineer and entrepreneur to become independently wealthy, and making his name as a humanitarian by heading the Committee for Relief of Belgium and then the U.S. Food Administration during World War I. Prior to his election as president, he was a highly successful commerce secretary.

Four years later he was a defeated man—or, more accurately, a defeated presidential candidate and bitter man. He was bitter over being blamed for a Depression whose roots had taken hold on his predecessor Calvin Coolidge's watch, and which Hoover himself blamed on others, like Benjamin Strong. He was disappointed by his own failure to meet the challenge of the crisis. That failure reflected a mismatch between the president's worldview on the one hand and what was required in the extraordinary circumstances of the 1930s on the other. Hoover was a steadfast believer in monetary and fiscal orthodoxy in a period when the challenges for economic policy were anything but orthodox. He had a Quaker's faith in self-help, associationalism, and a limited role of the state but was confronted by a crisis whose very nature underscored the limits of self-help and need for government intervention. Far from an inspirational leader, he was aloof and sensitive to criticism—the temperamental opposite of Franklin Delano Roosevelt.

Hoover's strategy for bolstering confidence was to preserve the prevailing level of wages. As the *New York Times* summarized the president's arguments, maintaining prevailing wage rates would ensure labor peace. Doing so was desirable on humanitarian grounds. And avoiding wage cuts would preserve "the consuming power of the country."[21] Hoover convened a series of meetings with prominent businessmen, including Henry Ford and Owen D. Young, the latter in his capacity as president and chairman of General Electric. Labor leaders agreed to avoid calling strikes and agitating for wage increases as a quid pro quo.

During World War I, when the imperative was to keep production going at all cost, President Wilson had resorted to this kind of proto-corporatist compact. Wilson pressed employers to offer high wages in return for unions promising labor peace. Hoover, recall, had worked as head of Wilson's Food Administration, when his was a voice for sacrifice and cooperation. He now instinctively reached for a Wilsonian response to the crisis.

But the kind of corporatist compact that was appropriate during World War I was less obviously appropriate in the current downturn. The threat of strikes and walkouts was less, given weak economic conditions. In any case, the policy's impact on spending was uncertain. Although laborers spared wage cuts would spend more, firms forced to pay higher wages saw their profits squeezed, causing them to prune costs by laying off workers and reducing hours. The policy was important for preventing demand from falling faster. At the same time, however, it inhibited the necessary adjustment of costs and discouraged supply. Given how supply- and demand-side effects pulled in opposite directions, the overall effect was limited.

———

With policy doing little to attenuate it, the slump in industrial production continued to deepen. The liabilities of failed nonfinancial businesses reached a record $84 million in December 1930. Other businesses that avoided failure similarly found it difficult to repay what they borrowed. Small rural banks had failed throughout the 1920s. Now in 1930 came a drought in which fifteen states from the Mid-Atlantic to the Ohio and Mississippi River Valleys received only 57 percent of normal rainfall.[22] Agricultural incomes fell by half. The deposits of failed banks rose from an earlier level of $20 million a month to $180 million in November and $370 million in December.

This was the first of several instances when the Fed failed to stave off financial crisis. At least that is how the episode is characterized by Friedman and Schwartz. Other analysts, in contrast, dismiss the events of late 1930 as not rising to the level of a crisis. They point to the fact that fully half of the deposits of failed banks stemmed from just two cases: the Bank of United States and a chain of Southern banks controlled by Caldwell and Company.[23]

Rogers Caldwell was the flamboyant son of a staid Nashville banker. (As will become evident, there is a pattern here.) The younger Caldwell dropped out of Vanderbilt University in 1910 to run his father's insurance business. That Clarence Hatry similarly started out running his parents' business in the same year and similarly graduated to insurance is presumably a coincidence. So is the fact that both men acquired racing stables, though this says something about the personality type.

From selling general insurance, Caldwell moved into selling surety bonds for construction projects. Surety bonds were guarantees of repayment, not unlike today's credit default swaps. From there Caldwell graduated to underwriting the bonds themselves. As in Hatry's case, these tended to be the bonds of municipalities and local government agencies with which the underwriter had developed personal and political connections. Caldwell specialized in the bonds of drainage districts that dug ditches and built levies, that borrowed to finance the work, and that serviced their bonds with taxes. By the late 1920s Caldwell was also underwriting single property bonds to finance hotels, hospitals, and office buildings. Most of these predictably lapsed into default when the commercial real estate boom collapsed in 1929.

In 1919, four years after Hatry acquired the Commercial Bank, Caldwell launched the Bank of Tennessee, which he used to warehouse funds raised by his bond sales. Rather than immediately passing them on to the drainage district or hotelier doing the borrowing, he put them to personal use.[24] Caldwell acquired insurance companies, textile mills, an asphalt supply company, dairies, laundries, a chain of department stores, and a minor-league baseball team, a diverse collection of businesses even by Hatry's standards. In some cases the businesses he acquired were the same ones with which he had contracted to underwrite bond issues. It was easier to secure a steady stream of underwriting business, evidently, if the underwriter also owned the company doing the borrowing. Owning insurance companies had the further advantage that if it turned out to be difficult to sell a bond to other investors, then it could be sold in a related-party transaction to the captive insurer. Also valuable in this stable of companies was Kentucky Rock and Concrete, which supplied asphalt for highway construction projects, often the same ones financed by Caldwell's underwriting business.

At the center of this business group was a chain of banks. A set of separately chartered banks are said to constitute a chain when they are controlled by the same ownership group (recall how chain banking was also the basis for the Manley-Anthony group of banks that failed in 1926 when the Florida land bubble burst).[25] The advantage of chain banking is that it permits the owner to do business in multiple states even when there are prohibitions on cross-state branching. The corresponding problem is that regulators may fail to take into account the liabilities of one bank to another. Banks in a number of states may be supervised by regulators not habituated to sharing information.

Caldwell now took advantage of the fact. His chain extended from Tennessee into Kentucky, Arkansas, and North Carolina. When in 1930 he acquired an interest in the Louisville-based BancoKentucky Company (formally the National Bank of Kentucky), his empire encompassed banks with deposits of $225 million and insurance companies with $216 million of reported assets. For a fleeting moment his conglomerate was the largest investment banking firm in the region. Caldwell built himself a lavish estate patterned after the Hermitage, the home of his hero Andrew Jackson, and furnished it with European mirrors and fireplaces. More precisely, the Bank of Tennessee built it for him: construction was paid for by $350,000 of the bank's funds, and the home was listed as an asset on its balance sheet before being transferred on June 1, 1930, under mysterious circumstances, to Caldwell's personal account.

By this time, many of the investments of the Caldwell empire had gone bad. Caldwell and Company's portfolio of real estate bonds was performing poorly, and its industrial investments were rendered unprofitable by the economic downturn. To stay afloat, the company increasingly relied on the revenues from bond sales on behalf of drainage districts and municipalities temporarily held on deposit at the Bank of Tennessee, and on the ability of the Caldwell banks to attract deposits from unsuspecting households, firms, and, not least, the State of Tennessee. In addition, acquiring BancoKentucky in mid-1930 allowed Caldwell to temporarily replenish the coffers by borrowing $2.4 million from the newly affiliated bank.

The event that exposed the cracks in this façade was closure of the Bank of Tennessee on November 7, 1930. State examiners had already concluded that the bank was undercapitalized and instructed it to make available an additional $4 million of securities to protect depositors. They subsequently discovered that securities of lesser value had been substituted, leading to their November action.

The timing pointed to the importance of political connections for Caldwell's operation. November 7, 1930, was the first Friday after a Tennessee gubernatorial election in which voters returned Governor Henry Hollis Horton for a second two-year term. Horton, previously the speaker of the Tennessee Senate, had ascended to the governorship in 1927 when the preceding governor, Austin Peay, died in office. Already during Horton's first run for a full two-year term as governor in 1928, the close connections between the Horton administration and Caldwell's Kentucky Rock and Concrete, which received state contracts without competitive bids, had been raised as an issue. Caldwell could ascribe his good fortune to another Tennessee power broker, the newspaper publisher and property developer Colonel Luke Lea.[26] Lea advised Governor Horton, and his newspapers, the *Nashville Tennessean* and *Knoxville Journal*, gave the candidate their enthusiastic endorsement. But the colonel was also a business partner of Caldwell's; together the two men purchased a controlling interest in Holston National Bank in Knoxville. Lea, conveniently, was also a director of the Federal Reserve Bank of Atlanta.

Now in 1930 it was alleged that Lea had used the promise of an endorsement to encourage Horton to grant Caldwell further contracts to supply asphalt for state construction projects. Whatever the merits of the accusation, it is clear that Lea and Caldwell were closely connected and that their connections led directly to the governor's office.

Thus, the delay in closing Caldwell's Bank of Tennessee until the Friday after the 1930 gubernatorial election was no coincidence. (To limit panic and give depositors time to gather their wits, regulators have learned to time bank closures to coincide with the weekend.) Failure of the Bank of Tennessee created understandable fears that, once the weekend was over, the Holston National Bank might follow. It was rumored that Holston National had large loans outstanding to Caldwell and Company, which it had funded by borrowing from other banks. Depositors queued up in large numbers to withdraw their balances the following Monday.

Given evidence of mismanagement at the Bank of Tennessee and Holston National's connections to Caldwell, investors had good reason to worry about the solvency of the Knoxville bank. Beyond that, it was unclear what other banks might be implicated. Better safe than sorry, so depositors scrambled to withdraw their money from other banks in Knoxville and neighboring cities. At this point, events showed every sign of degenerating into a full-blown crisis.

———

This placed the ball squarely in the court of the Fed's local branch, the Federal Reserve Bank of Atlanta. Its officers appear to have been fully aware of a central bank's lender-of-last-resort responsibilities. (Lea resigned his directorship on November 15, citing an inability to attend meetings.) The Atlanta Fed had long been one of the more activist branches of the Federal Reserve System.[27] It had early experience with financial distress as a result of the cotton boom and bust that infected its district in the immediate aftermath of World War I. It was also responsible, through a Jacksonville, Florida, branch, for the currency circulation of Cuba, that country having adopted the US dollar following the Spanish-American War. When in April 1926 rumors of the insolvency of a Canadian bank operating on the island sparked a panic and liquidity crisis, the Atlanta Fed boatlifted forty-two pouches of currency to Havana. This allowed other banks to pay out cash to depositors, successfully stemming the run.[28]

Given this experience, the Federal Reserve Bank of Atlanta, like the Federal Reserve Bank of New York, understood the value of full cash drawers for confidence. Its response was thus to make arrangements to ship several million dollars of currency to Knoxville. Tuesday, November 11, being Armistice Day, the banks were closed, providing time to get the cash on the move.

When the Holston-Union failed to reopen on Wednesday, two of its Knoxville-based competitors, the East Tennessee National Bank and National City Bank, experienced panicked runs. These banks had no business connections with the Caldwell-Lea chain, but no matter. More than $1 million was withdrawn by depositors by 2:00 p.m. Fortunately, the Atlanta Fed's "huge stacks of cash and currency" now having arrived, it was possible to pay out cash to depositors; word of this "reassured the most timid."[29] By the end of business on Thursday, most of the individuals who withdrew their money on previous days had redeposited it. A. P. Frierson, president of the Knoxville Clearing House Association (the association through which local banks cleared checks and other payments drawn on one another), was able to conclude with evident relief that "excitement on the part of the depositing public . . . has subsided."[30]

This did not prevent problems in Tennessee from spreading to neighboring states and to non-Caldwell-affiliated banks. But the most prominent failures were of Caldwell-affiliated institutions. Just as ten of the Tennessee banks that failed in this period were Caldwell affiliates, the same was true of forty-five failed banks in Arkansas, fifteen in Kentucky, and fifteen in North Carolina.

Among the casualties was the American Exchange Trust Company, the largest bank in Arkansas. Not only had the American Exchange Trust invested in Caldwell & Company, but Caldwell & Company, together with its partner A. B. Banks & Co., controlled 70 percent of its shares. That a third of its loans were to the bank's own officers and directors was a further indication that this was no normal financial institution. On November 16, responding to $4 million of panicked withdrawals, American Exchange Trust suspended payments.[31] The next day the Comptroller of the Currency closed the National Bank of Kentucky.

The State of Tennessee had $5 million of highway money in the Bank of Tennessee and the Holston-Union Bank, and Caldwell had personally guaranteed the state's deposits. The authorities therefore moved to seize his racing stable of sixty-four thoroughbreds and one stud. To the disappointment of officials, their sale netted only $85,000, a fraction of the value of the bonds Caldwell had guaranteed. The state next attempted to seize his estate, Brentwood Hall, but the title having been transferred to his name, Caldwell was able to invoke the homestead exemption.

Governor Horton did not survive the scandal. He chose not to run for a third term in 1932 and died shortly thereafter. Caldwell and Lea, together with J. Basil Ramsey, president of Holston-Union National Bank and Holston Trust Company, were indicted for using state highway funds to pay off other debts. Lea was convicted, imprisoned in 1934, and paroled in 1936. Caldwell fared better. His conviction was thrown out by the Tennessee State Supreme Court, and he was never retried. State officials did not succeed in evicting him from Brentwood Hall until 1954.

The 1930 banking crisis centered on Tennessee, Arkansas, Kentucky, and North Carolina can be dismissed as the product of a handful of colorful personalities. The crisis was limited to the South and largely, though not entirely, to Caldwell's chain. Not a few financial historians have sought to minimize the events of 1930 in this way.

But in fact, what prevented the crisis from spreading further, both to additional non-Caldwell banks in the South and beyond the region, was the rapid response of the Atlanta Fed. The limited extent of the 1930 crisis reflected not so much its idiosyncratic nature as the quick reaction of the Atlanta Reserve bank. This prevented the insolvency of a limited number of banks from exciting a panic and liquidity crisis that could have engulfed the banking system. That the events of 1930 are not always viewed as rising to the level of a banking crisis, in the true sense of the term, does not indicate an absence of serious problems capable of igniting a major crisis, but rather the ability of a powerful central bank response to prevent the worst.

All this is evidence that Federal Reserve officials, at least some of them, understood how to respond to a panic. The question was whether they would do so again when they next had the opportunity.

———

That opportunity came later in 1930 with the failure of the Bank of United States. This was not the Bank of *the* United States, the proto-central bank that operated from 1791 to 1836. But the name was no coincidence. Like the portrait of the Capitol that adorned the bank's main branch, the name was designed to inspire confidence. A 1926 law prohibited banks from using the words "Federal," "United States," and "Reserve" in their names but was not retroactive. The Bank of United States having been founded in 1913 by Joseph Marcus, a garment manufacturer, the name was grandfathered in.

On Marcus' death in 1928, the bank was taken over by his son Bernard, who immediately became one of the youngest bank presidents in the country. Both Marcuses, but especially the son, pursued policies of aggressive expansion. They increased the bank's capitalization to $25 million, its branches to sixty-one, and its customers to 400,000, the most of any bank in the country. They created affiliates for underwriting and trading securities. They established an investment trust company to sell securities to depositors. Prominent among those securities, it would turn out, were shares in the bank itself.

They also lent for commercial real estate projects, including several large Manhattan apartment blocks. As many as 40 percent of the bank's loans were property-related, compared to the average for New York City banks of just 12 percent. The Bank of United States adopted Florida-like practices, providing second and third mortgages. It lent to developers and, like Caldwell & Company, invested in single-property bonds. It created affiliated companies to purchase land and develop apartment complexes directly.

Other investors were aware that this was not an ideal time to commit to the commercial real estate market. Bank of United States stock began falling in April 1929, this despite the fact that other bank stocks were still rising and the stock market generally was booming. Operating through affiliated companies, Marcus and his executive vice president, Saul Singer, previously head of the Cloak, Suit, and Shift Manufacturers' Protective Association, bought time by purchasing their own stock, in the same way that Clarence Hatry used borrowed funds to buy up shares in his companies. Branch managers were coached to sell shares to unsuspecting depositors.[32]

And what informed investors evidently knew, the regulators knew as well. In the summer of 1929, Federal Reserve and state bank examiners cited Marcus and Singer for running a "sloppy bank."[33] Risk management practices were lax, and the bank's asset portfolio was concentrated in illiquid real estate investments. Prompt corrective action was required.

New York State Superintendent of Banking Joseph A. Broderick worked through the summer of 1929 to merge the Bank of United States with a stronger partner.[34] A prospective partner was found in the private bank J. and W. Seligman, along with a suitable chairman in the person of a vice president of National City Bank, S. Sloan Colt. Negotiations appeared to reach a successful conclusion in the second half of October. But then the market's crash put paid to the merger scheme, as it did to other well-laid plans.

Broderick next sought to interest other banks in acquiring the Bank of United States. There were hopes in early 1930 that it might be acquired by Irving Trust, but when Bank of United States stock rose on rumors of the purchase, the transaction became too expensive, given the uncertainties surrounding the Bank of United States' portfolio of dubious real estate loans. A buyer with deeper pockets was required.

Broderick therefore turned to Manufacturers Trust Company, one of New York's largest banks. Unfortunately, Manufacturers Trust had many of the same weaknesses as the Bank of United States, notably heavy exposure to real estate. Singer didn't make things easier by demanding that his son, like Marcus', be given a position at Manufacturers Trust. Discussions dragged on. That they were underway became public knowledge in October.

The announcement on Monday, December 8, 1930, that merger negotiations had broken down was the spark that ignited the run. In the next two days more than $2 million was withdrawn from the Bank of United States by twenty-five hundred panicked depositors. Customers queued for hours to empty their accounts. Mounted police were summoned to handle the crowds.

This now threatened to become the largest bank failure in US history. An emergency meeting was convened on the premises of the Federal Reserve Bank of New York. It is not clear whether it took place in the same first-floor conference room used for the emergency meeting to discuss the rescue of Lehman Brothers on September 12, 2008, but the building was the same, namely the

Fed's imposing fortress at 15 Liberty Street, which dated from 1924. The all-night meeting on December 10 was attended by a familiar cast of characters: Governor Harrison, J. P. Morgan partner Thomas Lamont, Owen Young in his capacity as a director of the New York Fed, and New York State Lieutenant Governor Herbert Lehman.

Following an unsuccessful attempt to resuscitate the Manufacturers Trust merger, efforts centered on identifying another suitable marriage partner. (One can't help but be reminded how, following the collapse of merger talks between Bank of America and Lehman Brothers, officials in their desperation sought out another partner in the form of Barclays.[35]) But consummating a marriage would take time, especially if the courtship had to start from scratch. In the meanwhile it would be necessary for the Clearing Banks, the association of New York banks overseeing the clearing and settlements process, to guarantee the deposits and other liabilities of the troubled institution.

At 4:00 a.m. on the morning of December 11, at the end of the all-night session, the Clearing Banks refused. It has been speculated that antipathy for the Jewish owners of the Bank of United States played a role.[36] In addition, the Clearing Banks were uncertain of the magnitude of the liabilities they were asked to assume. The bank's complicated group structure didn't make this easy to estimate. Again, the parallel with Lehman Brothers, and the difficulty that Bank of America and Barclays had in making sense of its books, is direct.[37] Conferees having failed to reach an agreement, the bank did not open on Thursday morning.

———

The refusal of the Federal Reserve Bank of New York to support the Bank of United States presumably reflected its judgment that the bank was insolvent (more shades of Lehman Brothers). But the New York Fed was aware of the risk that the crisis might spread further, perhaps to Manufacturers Trust, with its portfolio of real estate loans, and perhaps to other banks. Depositors uncertain about the condition of their bank were apt to withdraw their funds, and if their bank was unable to supply them with cash, the news might spark a panic. To prevent this from happening, the New York Fed immediately took steps to provide additional cash and liquid assets to other banks in the city, purchasing some $40 million of government securities from the banks in the next three days. In the week following, it discounted and bought an additional $100 million of bills. Its intervention prevented the insolvency of one prominent institution from sparking a panicked run and a liquidity crisis.

The Bank of United States, for its part, was taken over by the New York State Banking Department. The other members of the New York Clearinghouse

Association agreed to loan depositors in the Bank of United States up to 50 percent of the value of their deposits on presentation of their pass book, with the deposit serving as collateral. They admitted Manufacturers Trust to their clearinghouse, short-circuiting normal procedures in a step that anticipated the decision to convert Goldman Sachs and Morgan Stanley into bank holding companies over a weekend in 2008.[38]

Evidently, the role of the Federal Reserve at this juncture—in what we know with hindsight to have been the onset of the Great Depression—was more complex than sometimes supposed. Contrary to common assertion, officials within the Federal Reserve System understood the central bank's responsibility as lender and liquidity provider of last resort. Just as they had flooded the markets with liquidity, lending freely against eligible collateral when the stock market crashed in 1929, they now furnished those huge stacks of cash and currency to prevent the problems of Caldwell & Company from spreading and lent freely against eligible collateral to prevent the liquidity problems caused by failure of the Bank of United States from infecting other banks. Their quick reaction explains why the Great Crash did not result in more financial dislocations and why the banking crisis of 1930 was not more severe.

But there was also good luck in that the 1930 crisis centered on Nashville, Knoxville, and New York. The New York Fed, located at the epicenter of the US financial system, and the Atlanta Fed, for reasons of geography having been designated the steward of Cuba's financial system, understood how to respond to a crisis. It was far from clear that other Reserve banks were comparably experienced and well informed, or that their response, when the time came, would be equally adequate.

In 1930, in addition, the Reserve banks were unconstrained. They still had ample gold reserves, obviating any conflict between the obligation to maintain gold convertibility and the provision of emergency liquidity. There was plenty of high-quality commercial paper for the Federal Reserve banks to discount, since business had been in decline only for a matter of months. Things would be different in 1931 and, especially, in 1933.

Moreover, although officials in Atlanta and New York understood how to respond to such financial disturbances, they did not obviously understand the distinction between nominal and real interest rates (the latter, recall, being quoted interest rates adjusted for inflation). They did not understand that low interest rates could signal that the demand for credit, and with it the economy, was weak, not that credit was ample and that the central bank had done its job. Beholden to the real bills doctrine, they did not appreciate their responsibility for managing supplies of money and credit so as to prevent a disastrous decline in the price level, spending, and economic activity. Among the consequences of that decline in spending and activity were gold losses for the Fed, as investors began to ask questions about the prospects for the dollar, and a further decline in commercial paper eligible to be discounted at the central bank.

Thus the central bank would be in a decidedly less favorable position when financial problems returned.

| On Europe's Shores

A LITTLE OVER a year passed between the eruption of the subprime crisis in the United States and its reaching Europe's shores. Similarly, it took barely more than a year from the Wall Street Crash in 1929 for the focus to shift to Europe. Much of the continent was already reeling from the sudden stop in capital flows from the United States and the drop in US merchandise imports. This double-barreled shock meant gold losses for central banks, which they sought to limit by keeping interest rates high. But even though high rates provided an incentive for Europeans to keep their funds at home, they did nothing to encourage firms to invest or households to spend. Where the New York Fed cut its discount rate to 2 percent in December 1930 following the failure of the Bank of United States, the Bank of England was forced to keep its discount rate at 3 percent, and the Reichsbank at an even more painful 5 percent.

The Bank of France was the one European bank in a position to emulate the New York Fed's low interest rate policy, which it did by cutting the discount rate to 2 percent at the beginning of 1931. Having stabilized late, France was not a big foreign borrower and relied little on capital imports. The country's export prices were competitive owing to the franc's depreciation in the first half of the 1920s. As a result, industrial production held steady through much of 1930, excepting only luxury trades hit by the stock market crash (less claret for the bankers).

Moreover, France experienced just one bank failure of consequence, that of Banque Adam, a Calais-based lender brought down by the dubious investments of its principal shareholder, Albert Oustric. Oustric was yet another of those outsized 1920s characters in the manner of Clarence Hatry and Rogers

Caldwell. He started as a waiter in a Carcassonne café. He then worked for a French armaments manufacturer, rising through the ranks during World War I, and made his fortune helping a politically connected Italian financier, Ricardo Gualino, list the shares of his textile manufacturing firm, Snia Viscosa, on the Paris Bourse. Snia had been founded as a trading company before being reorganized in 1922 to produce rayon, like radio, another of the growth industries of the 1920s. (Better rayon than jute.) By 1925 Snia Viscosa accounted for 60 percent of Italian rayon production and was the second-largest producer globally. Gualino had help in growing his business from Mussolini and the Bank of Italy, or at least until he wrote a letter to the prime minister protesting the high level at which the lira was stabilized in 1926. Gualino was understandably sensitive to the matter, if not to Mussolini's reaction to his letter, because his firm exported 80 percent of its production. But for Mussolini, a high and stable lira was a measure of Italy's national prestige and of its leader's accomplishment. When Gualino's heavily indebted industrial empire collapsed in the Depression, he was arrested and sentenced to five years of confinement "for having done serious damage to the national economy."

In the meantime, Oustric made hay while the sun shone, using his profits from Snia to acquire other firms. Companies producing boots and shoes, silk, woolens, leather goods, and sewing machines were his specialty, paralleling Hatry's Drapery Trust. Oustric reorganized the firms in question and issued more stock than necessary, again in the manner of Hatry. This strained the finances of the resulting companies but gave Oustric cash with which to pursue further acquisitions.

And, again like Hatry, Oustric advanced his scheme by acquiring a captive financial institution. He founded the Oustric Bank and expanded its capital from 60 million to 100 million francs, with Gualino subscribing a quarter of the shares. Oustric then gained control of the venerable Banque Adam, a Pas-de-Calais bank that could trace its lineage back to 1784.

In contrast to Montagu Norman's suspicion of Hatry, Bank of France officials seem to have been supportive of Oustric. But Gualino's falling-out with Mussolini, which depressed the value of Oustric's Snia Viscosa shares, and then the decline in the stock market in 1929 undermined his business model. Oustric drew funds from Banque Adam to buy shares in his companies and support their prices, another Hatry-like tactic, but to no avail. When those other ventures went bad, they took Banque Adam down with them. Oustric was arrested for fraud, embezzlement, and engaging in financial irregularities related to Banque Adam. Found guilty, he served thirty-eight months and paid a fine of 31,000 francs.[1]

The political Left and Right both sought to capitalize on the affair. The Right pointed to the involvement of René Besnard, former French ambassador to Italy, in the Snia Viscosa transaction, while the Left emphasized the fact that a number of current and former ministers were on Oustric's payroll. In particular, Raoul Péret, who authorized the Snia Viscosa listing when serving as minister of finance in 1926, subsequently accepted a retainer to serve as Oustric's legal advisor. The revelation so embarrassed the Center-Right government of André Tardieu as to force its resignation.

The political fallout was dramatic, but the only immediate economic impact of the Calais bank's failure was to prevent the fishing fleet of Boulogne from obtaining the advances needed to put out to sea. However unfortunate for the fishermen, this was nothing compared to the turbulent seas buffeting other countries. The Bank of France still had ample gold reserves, and it could acquire more by liquidating the sterling balances accumulated in the wake of the Poincaré stabilization. The question in the aftermath of *l'affaire Oustric* was when economic and financial conditions did deteriorate, not whether the government would have the resources to address them but if it would have the will.

———

In the meantime, the flow of gold toward France meant losses for other central banks, which they attempted to offset by keeping interest rates high. In addition, the Bank of France's ongoing conversion of sterling into gold put pressure on the Bank of England. The Bank of France was criticized by British economists for ignoring the impact of its policies on other countries, not that French officials were inclined to take heed.[2] With the French economy still doing well, they did not feel the urgency that informed contemporary British commentary. It is tempting to draw an analogy with German *Sorglosigkeit* (insouciance) when the euro crisis broke, what with the German economy doing well. If the French balance of payments was strong while the British balance of payments was weak, this was simply a reflection of the hard work the French people had undertaken to strengthen their economy and of Britain's failure to put its economic and financial house in order. If France enjoyed a balance-of-payments surplus, then this reflected the innate frugality of the French, who preferred saving over spending. Will Rogers, ever the trenchant observer, attributed France's seeming prosperity to national character and a penchant for "hard work and watching the pennies."[3] If the British found it hard to honor requests to convert sterling into gold, then this was a problem of their own making. Here again it is tempting again to draw an analogy with the euro crisis and with Germans' scorn for their profligate Southern European neighbors. One can't help but be reminded of Germany's failure to see that one country's surpluses are necessarily another's deficits.

Even if Bank of France officials had wanted to do something, which they didn't, their options were limited. Having endured a chaotic inflation, France now operated a gold standard of the most inflexible sort. The Bank of France was prohibited from purchasing domestic securities, so as to prevent it from directly financing the government, as it famously had in the 1920s. Securities purchases and sales (open market operations) as an instrument for shaping financial market conditions and thereby influencing the direction of gold flows were unavailable. There is an obvious parallel with Article 123 of the statute of the European Central Bank, which prohibits purchasing newly issued government bonds, a restriction that made it hard for the ECB to intervene to stabilize the bond market in 2011–12. A clever ECB eventually found ways around these restrictions, and the Bank of France might have done the same.[4] It could have exploited a loophole allowing it to purchase the bonds of the government's debt management agency, the Caisse d'Amortissement. It could have purchased dollars and sterling, injecting francs into circulation through these transactions on the foreign exchange market.

But its directors were not so inclined, and they were not much influenced by the arguments of foreigners. The Bank of France continued to accumulate gold, intensifying the pressure on other countries. It would not be long before those other countries, and France itself, would pay the piper.

———

Events in Germany brought matters to a head. Having relied more than any other country on capital imports, Germany was hit hardest when these came to a stop. With memories of inflation still fresh, private citizens and officials alike saw gold convertibility as paramount. The question now was whether convertibility could be successfully defended and, if not, what consequences would follow.

In 1930 Hjalmar Schacht was succeeded as head of the Reichsbank by the hardworking, ambitious Hans Luther. Luther was a lifetime politician who had served as town councilor in Magdeburg, as mayor of Essen, and then briefly as chancellor in 1925–26. He had been minister of food and agriculture during the hyperinflation, when he urged restaurants to reduce the size of portions as a way of limiting price increases. Now, as prices and production began to fall, his advice was even less trenchant.

Luther understood at least one thing: the Reichsbank would have little leeway if it became necessary to intervene in support of the banking system.

This possibility was hardly remote. Big German banks had lent extensively to industry, exposing them to the economic downturn. Bank capital was wiped out by inflation in 1922–23, and subsequent recapitalization efforts were wanting. Capital and reserves as a share of bank assets were now just 7 percent, barely a third of earlier levels.[5] This was not as high as the leverage of the big German banks in 2009–10, whose capital ratios were as little as 2½ percent, but it was an extraordinary high level of leverage by interwar standards.

For their part, small German savers burned by the inflation were slow to return. To fund their operations, the banks therefore turned to foreign deposits, which they sought to attract with high interest rates. Big banks with internationally recognized names were in the best position to do so; by 1929 foreign accounts accounted for fully 40 percent of their deposit liabilities. The situation was not unlike that of the three big Icelandic banks in 2008. But, as in Iceland in 2008, the strategy laid the banks open to liquidity problems if foreign depositors chose to repatriate their funds. Worse still, the big banks, their profits weak, could ill afford to keep extra liquidity on hand.[6]

Given the fragility of the financial system, policies of budgetary austerity were, to put it mildly, problematic. Fiscal consolidation that reduced spending threatened to so weaken the banks that the economy would be launched on a downward spiral from which it would be impossible to recover.

Yet balance the budget, it was argued, the authorities must. State and municipal governments binged on cheap credit, just as Parker Gilbert had once warned, incurring heavy debts that now made it impossible for them, and the Reich government, to borrow.[7] Germany's creditors, and specifically the French, were in no mood to contemplate a reparations moratorium. Tampering with the gold parity, given recent inflationary history, was beyond the pale. Given this lack of alternatives, only the option of balancing the budget remained.

Agreeing on how to balance it was another matter. Social Democrats in the Reichstag objected to cuts in unemployment benefits, while the Bavarian People's Party revolted over the government's proposed tax on beer. The Grand Coalition, which was Germany's last democratic gasp, collapsed in 1930 over its inability to square this circle.

The fall of the coalition led to the formation of a technocratic government under Heinrich Brüning. Brüning hailed from the city of Münster, the center of Kulturkampf, the struggle between the Catholic Church and Protestant Prussia. With the end of that conflict, it is said, the Catholic residents of Münster became "more Lutheran than thou." A member of the Reichstag since 1924, Brüning had made his name as a financial expert, in the manner of Paul Ryan, and now set out to balance the budget by any means necessary. Lacking a coherent majority in the Reichstag, he resorted to the emergency powers provided for by Article 48 of the Weimar constitution. Those decree powers did not give the chancellor unchecked freedom of action—he still had to submit his decrees to the Reichstag for ex post approval—but they allowed him to set the budgetary agenda.

Seeing the deficit in the unemployment insurance fund as a major problem, Brüning issued decrees tightening eligibility requirements and reducing payments. He cut the salaries of public servants and reduced state and local government transfers. He decreed a range of new taxes, including one on mineral water, avoiding the need to tax beer.

But radical cuts in public spending in a period when private spending was collapsing had the predictable effect of worsening the slump. The other predictable effect was to weaken support for the government. A freakish alliance of Social Democrats and Nazis now refused to approve the chancellor's decrees.

But Brüning was not one for changing his mind. He responded by dissolving the Reichstag and calling for new elections. To his surprise, voters repudiated his policies. The government took only a third of the seats in the new parliament, while the Communists, National Socialists, and other anti-system parties all gained. The Nazis alone saw a ninefold increase in representation. This was not the first time austerity and depression bred political extremism. Nor would it be the last.

This political backlash, according to Thomas Ferguson and Peter Temin, was what precipitated the German crisis.[8] Brüning's unrelenting austerity, by plunging the economy deeper into recession, increased political polarization. This unsettled investors, who, justifiably worried about what was next, fled in growing numbers.

The Reichsbank's reserves fell sharply in September, with the approach of the election, and again in October, in its wake. The Reichsbank was forced to raise the discount rate by a full percentage point to defend the gold parity. This doing nothing to resolve the political crisis, investors were not reassured. Bank deposits continued to fall as money was spirited out of the country. The only surprise under the circumstances is that this was still just a bank jog rather than an all-out run.

The question, asked also of Southern European countries starting in 2010, was whether other options were available, and specifically if less austerity would have been better. The German historian Knut Borchardt argued that reckless borrowing had locked Germany out of the capital market, leaving no alternative to austerity.[9] Ferguson and Temin conclude differently, saying that had Germany not been forced to endure such severe austerity, the political center could have held. The recession would have been milder, and reform might have proceeded. The government would have been able to regain market access and finance its deficits.

This seems naïve. In fact, market access was never an option for a Germany riven by political conflicts, burdened with crushing debts, and confronting a hostile France. The only way of financing budget deficits would have been by imposing exchange controls and requiring the banks to purchase the additional government bonds, as Hitler did in 1933.

———

This volatile mix of economic depression, political polarization, weak finances, and a paralytic central bank was clearly poised to explode. The spark was the failure of the Creditanstalt, Austria's largest bank.

Formally the Oesterreichische Credit-Anstalt für Handel und Gewerbe, or Austrian Credit Institution for Trade and Industry, the Creditanstalt had been founded by the Rothschilds in the 1860s. The majority of limited-liability companies in Austria did business with the bank. It accounted for more than 50 percent of all bank assets in the country and had a balance sheet of nearly 10 percent of GDP.[10] In 1929 the Creditanstalt acquired its only consequential competitor, the Bodencreditanstalt, with extensive commitments to the textile industry.

This was not an asset portfolio likely to perform well in depressed conditions. Moreover, the Creditanstalt had little capacity to absorb losses. Management was extravagant in spending on premises. Like the big German banks, its buffer of capital was eroded by the inflation that followed World War I.[11]

And, like the big German banks, the Creditanstalt now relied for funding on foreigners. Attracted by high interest rates that the bank could ill afford, foreign individuals and institutions provided 35–40 percent of deposits and other credits. The obvious danger was that this form of finance would move out of the bank and out of the country at the first sign of trouble.

The Austrian government pressed for the Bodencreditanstalt merger, worried as much about the state of the textile industry as the stability of the Bodencreditanstalt itself. Having done the official sector's bidding, the Creditanstalt's top management now apparently believed they could count on government support.[12] As the bank's balance sheet deteriorated, their strategy was therefore to gamble for resurrection. Under the circumstances this meant making more loans to money-losing textile firms desperate to borrow to stay alive. It isn't much of a stretch to see parallels with Lehman Brothers in 2008, from undercapitalization and reliance on risky funding sources to the bank's desperate search for yield and the belief that it would be saved by the authorities if things went wrong.

Nor is it a stretch to see parallels in what happened when the Creditanstalt's difficulties became public knowledge on May 11, 1931, as the bank published its balance sheet for 1930. The bank lost 16 percent of its deposits in the next two days and fully 30 percent in the subsequent two weeks.[13]

The Austrian government understood that the Creditanstalt was too big to fail. Unfortunately, it was also too big to save, with liabilities to foreigners only slightly less than the gold and foreign currency reserves of the central bank. If the Creditanstalt's foreign depositors now sought to repatriate their money, the National Bank would be forced to pay out gold to satisfy their demands. It then would have no way of paying off the foreign liabilities of other banks also seeing panicked withdrawals, a phenomenon that started almost immediately on announcement of the Creditanstalt's losses.

This liquidity problem could be solved only with help from a country having ample gold reserves. This meant France. But Austria had just signaled its intention of entering into a customs union agreement with Germany, in violation of the Versailles Treaty. The proposal was a brainchild of the German Foreign Office, which apparently saw an aggressive foreign policy as distracting the German public from mounting economic problems. It was not an offer that Austria, a small country on Germany's flank, could easily refuse.[14]

In fact, the Creditanstalt crisis was more than a liquidity crisis, as Austrian officials preferred to characterize it. It reflected more than the central bank's lack of the gold and foreign exchange to pay off foreign depositors. The Creditanstalt also had a solvency problem, having taken big losses on its loans to industry. Official denials to the contrary, it quickly became clear that the bank now needed not just temporary access to liquidity but an injection of share capital.

Aware of the importance of the bank to the Austrian economy, the government, headed by Chancellor Otto Ender, agreed to inject 100 million schillings (roughly $14 million), taking a 33 percent ownership stake in return.[15] The problem was that it was not clear where it would come up with the money. The Depression had already reduced tax revenues and raised outlays on unemployment relief. The government had no financial reserves and no ability to borrow. Immediately on announcement of the capital injection, the price of government bonds collapsed. This was the "diabolic loop," evident also in Greece, Spain, and Ireland starting in 2010, when problems for the banks created problems for the public finances, which in turn deepened worries over the banks.

After three weeks of difficult negotiations spanning much of the month of May, the Austrian government was able to arrange a 100-million-schilling loan from eleven countries. Funds were channeled through the Bank for International Settlements, the latter just having been established, with impeccable timing, to handle reparations transfers. But the loan was only half of what had been requested by the Austrian government. It was enough to finance the injection of capital into the Creditanstalt but left no margin for further losses.

Meanwhile, reserves continued to drain from the National Bank, as anxious foreign investors sought to get their money out of schillings and out of the country. The main impact of the loan was thus to finance capital flight, as the additional resources injected into the Creditanstalt were withdrawn first by foreign financial institutions and next by Austrian depositors, who then asked the central bank to convert their schillings into gold.[16]

The Austrian authorities responded in the only way they knew how, by requesting another foreign loan. The lenders, having learned their lesson, this time demanded as a condition that the Creditanstalt's creditors in Berlin, Paris, London, and New York first agree to maintain their balances in Vienna, so that the official money injected into Austria didn't just leak back out. As a further condition, they demanded that the Austrian government guarantee the loan, the earlier loan having technically been to the central bank, not the state. Least reasonably from the Austrian point of view, the French government demanded that Austria abandon the customs union proposal, submit its finances to League of Nations control, and renounce "any steps which might modify the existing political and economic relations of Austria."

In effect, the country was being asked to surrender its sovereignty. The National Bank was scheduled to release new figures for its foreign reserves on Wednesday, June 17. When tabling these demands the preceding day, French officials evidently believed that they had the Austrian government over a barrel.

These French demands were more than the Ender government could bear. It resigned on June 16 on receiving the French government's note. The Bank of England stepped in with a temporary credit, but it was too late. At this point the only alternative to closing the bank was to negotiate an agreement with its London-based creditors, now organized as the Austrian Credit-Anstalt International Committee, committing the latter to not make further withdrawals. The price was steep. In return for a two-year standstill on withdrawals, the successor to the Ender government, led by Karl Buresch, was required to guarantee the banks' liabilities in full. A federal government with a budget of only 1,800 million schillings ($250 million) was on the hook for 1,200 million schillings of bank liabilities.[17] Shades of Ireland in 2008.

The guarantee did nothing to restore confidence in the financial system; it was just the diabolic loop all over again. And the standstill agreement cast a pall over the position of financial institutions in still other countries whose assets in Austria were frozen. If policy makers had been seeking to spread the crisis to other countries, they couldn't have done a better job.

———

German investors, their Austrian balances frozen, scrambled for liquidity, drawing down their deposits in other banks and liquidating other investments. The process was aptly described by the financial journalist Harry Hodson in terms that could be applied equally to the Lehman Brothers crisis: "An individual bank, or the banking system of a country or of the world as a whole, has to remain liquid or perish. If one item among its assets, which had been regarded as liquid, becomes unrealizable for the time being, it must improve its position of liquidity by realizing other assets."[18] In this way the crisis spread to Germany.

Moreover, there was the close family resemblance between the Creditanstalt and the third-largest German bank, Danatbank (formally, Darmstädter und Nationalbank). Like the Creditanstalt, Danatbank was known for its large commitments to industry. Its general partner, Jakob Goldschmidt, was widely viewed as a risk taker. Hjalmar Schacht, in a passage in his memoirs not entirely free of ethnic stereotyping, describes Goldschmidt as competitive "verg[ing] on the ruthless."[19] As Schacht put it, Goldschmidt's aggressive pursuit of business did not exactly endear him to his colleagues.

Among Goldschmidt's favorite tactics was to instigate and execute amalgamations of firms in sectors with excess capacity, in the style of Charles Hatry. His Danatbank had extensive commitments to the textile sector. Now there were unsettling rumors that one of Danatbank's textile-industry clients, the Bremen-based Nordwalle (formally the Norddeutsche Wollkämmerei und Kammgarnspinnerei), had inexplicably gambled on a rise in wool prices and was in perilous shape.

Goldschmidt learned of Nordwalle's problems on May 11, the same day the Creditanstalt's difficulties were announced. And what Goldschmidt knew quickly became public knowledge. Sentiment deteriorated further when it was learned that Nordwalle's speculation in wool had been conducted through a Dutch subsidiary, Ultra Mare, whose existence was unknown even to outside members of Nordwalle's board, which for better or worse included representatives of the banks. The Lahusen brothers, Karl and Heinz, Nordwalle's co-CEOs, repeatedly doubled down on their disastrous bets, borrowing additional funds from Danatbank and other sources to finance their gamble to survive. Observers quickly began to ask whether the same problems hiding in the ledgers of Danatbank might also be lurking in those of other banks with extensive commitments to industry.

This, moreover, was not the only weakness afflicting the banking system. Had the problem just been bad loans to industry, German investors would have been first to withdraw their funds. Residents were presumably best informed about the condition of German industry and thus of the banks. In fact, however, it was foreign investors who were first to run. There was no noticeable increase in currency in circulation—no sign that residents were shifting to currency from deposits. There was, however, a marked decline in the Reichsbank's gold and foreign exchange reserves in the final week in May. This then accelerated in the first half of June, suggesting that foreigners were actively repatriating their funds.

The foreigners in question were unsettled by Chancellor Brüning's not very lightly veiled threats about halting reparations payments.[20] The onset of the Depression did not make the reparations burden any more tolerable. Brüning's truculence was designed to compensate for the unpopularity of his economic policies. He pushed ahead with rearmament, building pocket battleships in violation of the Versailles Treaty. In March 1931 he embraced the ill-fated Foreign Office proposal for customs union with Austria. On June 6, in conjunction with a second round of decrees cutting public-sector salaries and unemployment benefits, he warned that the economy was on the verge of collapse. The implication was that if conditions deteriorated further there might be no alternative to a reparations moratorium.

A reparations moratorium would almost certainly presage a wider moratorium, extending also to private debts. Realizing this, foreign investors rushed to withdraw their remaining funds. On June 13 the Reichsbank responded by raising the discount rate by a bazookalike two hundred basis points. But this did little to reassure foreign investors worried that they might lose all access to their German deposits. Nor could it have reassured anyone aware of the perilous state of the German economy.

———

Brüning was not the only one contemplating a reparations moratorium. President Hoover, seeing conditions in Germany as a threat to the US economy and aware that the election determining whether he served a second term was only eighteen months away, had been toying with the idea since May.[21] In June he set about campaigning for the support of Secretary Mellon, Governor Harrison, and Eugene Meyer, who chaired the Board of Directors of the Federal Reserve System. Meyer, an ambitious, blunt-spoken Californian, had attended the University of California, Berkeley and Yale. He made his fortune as a speculator in railway shares, leveraging the $100 "nonsmoking fund" that his father offered him if he agreed not to smoke until he was eighteen and then the additional $500 if he agreed not to smoke until he was twenty-one. During World War I he directed the War Finance Corporation (WFC), created to finance essential industries, including banks and railroads jeopardized by wartime dislocations. He then went on to head the Reconstruction Finance Corporation (essentially a repurposed version of the WFC) and, eventually, to purchase the *Washington Post* and serve as the first president of the World Bank.[22] Meyer later claimed that he and not the president had originated the idea of a reparations moratorium, although Hoover claimed the credit in his autobiography, to the chagrin of Meyer, who was later to remark that Hoover's memoirs should have been entitled "Alone in Washington."[23]

Hoover announced his one-year moratorium proposal on June 20. The initiative was received unhappily in Paris, the State Department having failed to alert the French in advance. Pierre Laval, newly installed as prime minister, summoned the American ambassador to complain about the president's "shock tactics." Hoover was not pleased; in his view the French were all too complacent. "Our French friends need to get a stronger taste of Depression," he is reported to have remarked. Unlike in 1923, however, France was in no position to send troops to enforce its claims.[24]

In contrast to the politicians in Paris, investors reacted positively. Stock and commodity markets rallied on announcement of the moratorium proposal. Unfortunately, the three-week delay in finalizing the agreement largely neutralized those confidence-enhancing effects. Investors realized that a moratorium on reparations payments, by itself, would not be enough to relieve the pressure on the Reichsbank, whose gold reserves had already fallen to the legal minimum. Luther and the board of the central bank could defend the gold standard by restricting credit, or they could support the banks by discounting freely. They could not do both, at least not without help from a foreign loan.

On the same day Hoover announced his moratorium, Luther obtained a modest $100 million credit from the Bank of England, the Bank of France, the Federal Reserve, and the Bank for International Settlements. The loan was just enough to balance the Reichsbank's books and make it look as if its gold reserves were still adequate. But this was not the shock and awe needed to restore confidence. Gold losses resumed within days. On June 22, again to prevent the Reichsbank's gold reserve from falling below the legal minimum, Luther was forced to announce fresh restrictions on its discounts of private paper. With the central bank now limiting the availability of credit, industrial production fell further.

On July 2 news of the crisis at Nordwalle and Danatbank hit the stands. The Reichsbank announced its intention of supporting Danatbank, but limited reserves prevented it from following through. On July 5, with the central bank's gold cover ratio below the statutory minimum of 40 percent, it withdrew support. Luther justified the action by citing the inadequacy of Danatbank's collateral, anticipating language to which central bankers would again resort three-quarters of a century later in connection with Lehman Brothers.

On Thursday, July 9, a desperate Luther flew off to London, Paris, and Basel, the latter being the home of the Bank for International Settlements. Luther can be criticized for many things, notably his role in the hyperinflation and support for Hitler, but he was a pioneer of shuttle diplomacy. Not even an airplane, however, could win this war. Luther's meeting with Norman, at Victoria Station, where the English central banker was preparing to board a train to Dover, was tense. Norman was not on such friendly terms with Luther as he had been with Schacht. Personalities aside, Norman worried that the Reichsbank would be in no position to pay back what it borrowed. He was not prepared to move without guarantees from the German government and the participation of France.

But pocket battleships and the Austro-German customs union left the French unsympathetic. They demanded that Germany drop its customs union proposal, commit to full resumption of reparations payments, and renounce rearmament spending as a precondition for assistance. For Brüning, who had staked himself to an aggressive foreign policy, this was impossible.[25] The chancellor now dismissed Luther's trip as a "fiasco." The exhausted central banker flew home empty-handed.

In Luther's absence, representatives of the major German financial institutions continued to meet at the offices of Deutsche Bank und Disconto-Gesellschaft, the country's biggest bank. The government organized the parlay in the hope that other banks might be induced to inject funds into Danatbank in return for some of its remaining assets. But the banks refused to be corralled. It did not help that Danatbank's books were opaque. Like those of the Bank of United States, they could not be sorted out over a weekend. Moreover, there was good reason to fear that Danatbank's losses might turn out to be greater than acknowledged previously. Nor did it help that Danatbank, like the Bank of United States, was run by a Jewish senior partner for whom his fellow bankers felt less than full sympathy.

Luther cabled George Harrison in New York, pleading for a credit. Though sympathetic, Harrison was not prepared to move without the participation of the Bank of England and Bank of France. In 2008, the Federal Reserve offered to provide loans of dollars to the European Central Bank and the Swiss National Bank. Technically, it swapped them US dollars in exchange for commensurate amounts of their respective currencies, enabling these other central banks to supply their own banks and firms dollars with which to repay their borrowings. The Bernanke Fed provided a quartet of $30 billion loans to the central banks of Mexico, Brazil, South Korea, and Singapore. The course of the 1931 financial crisis might have been quite different had the New York Fed, likewise, acted on Luther's request. But the Reichsbank's capacity to repay what it borrowed was uncertain. Harrison had been stung by the criticism directed at the New York Fed when Strong tailored policy to foreign needs in 1924 and 1927. And it is not clear that Harrison would have now had the full support of the Federal Reserve Board. Better, under the circumstances, to share the burden with the Bank of England and Bank of France. Unfortunately, burden sharing was easier to imagine than to arrange.

Emergency meetings at the Reichsbank continued fruitlessly through the weekend. At 3:00 a.m. Monday morning, July 13, the sleepless Luther again left for the airport and a breakfast meeting with Norman, who had now arrived in Basel, and Clement Moret of the Bank of France. The three central bankers having failed to reach an agreement by 9:00 a.m., Danatbank did not open its doors.

Other German banks immediately suffered heavy withdrawals. On Monday night, seeing no alternative, the Reich government declared a two-day bank holiday. Officials again asked the other big banks to guarantee Danatbank's liabilities, and again they refused. This forced the authorities to extend a public guarantee, which only deepened concern with the government's finances. This was the diabolic loop yet again, as the need for governments to guarantee the liabilities of the banks so damaged confidence in the official sector's own balance sheet that the security of the guarantee was cast into doubt.[26]

When the banks reopened on Thursday, withdrawals were limited to half of the account holder's balance or ten thousand marks (the equivalent of $2,350), whichever was less. Funds could be transferred between German banks, but not abroad. The Reichsbank limited the availability of foreign exchange to "cases of vital necessity," reserving the right of defining vital necessity for itself.[27] The worst fear of investors, that their formerly liquid funds in Germany would be rendered unavailable as a result of government action, came to pass. Having failed to organize collective support by other banks and equally to obtain adequate support from its foreign counterparts, the Reichsbank was left with no choice. In an atmosphere poisoned by mutual distrust, banks and governments sleepwalked together into disaster.

CHAPTER 10 | Will America Topple Too?

THROUGH MAY AND June, Germany insisted it was not Austria. Britain and the United States now insisted they were not Germany. This, however, did not stop the crisis from leapfrogging first the channel and then the Atlantic. Where the German crisis developed over the better part of two years, it took just weeks to reach London, and only days after that to infect New York.

Harrison, having experienced the failure of the Bank of United States, understood the urgency of offering Germany assistance to keep the crisis from spreading. Norman, in contrast, not having experienced a major bank failure on his watch, adopted a harder line. With hindsight, we know that Norman should have been more concerned about the condition of British banks that had extended credit to German exporters and about the attrition of his reserves. But having been under pressure for months, he was on the verge of exhaustion. On July 28 he collapsed, remaining confined to bed for a week. On August 15, in the company of his sister, Mrs. Agnes Chalmers, he boarded a liner for Canada. There he remained through much of September, in only limited telegraphic and wireless contact with London.[1]

Norman's condition may help to explain why the Bank of England failed to act decisively as its reserves drained away.[2] In his absence, policy was made by committee, and committees take time to agree. Another factor was that the Bank of England faced the same dilemma as the Reichsbank, namely whether to defend the exchange rate or support the economy, but not having suffered through the same debilitating inflation it made the other choice. Joblessness was a concern, with 22 percent of individuals who were covered by the unemployment insurance scheme out of work. A Labour government committed to restoration of full employment had been in power since 1929. To raise rates under these circumstances threatened to antagonize that government and undermine public support for the central bank. Ralph Hawtrey, probably the economist with the subtlest mind in H.M. Treasury, understood. "To raise the rate when unemployment among insured work people had risen to 22 per cent, was surely to gild the lily," he later explained. "If, in the language of 1848, the price of the convertibility of the note was to be a further disemployment of labour, the position had become untenable. And in fact it had."[3]

Then there was the weakness of the banks. London's privately held investment banks, or merchant banks as they were known for their practice of lending to merchants engaged in overseas trade, had guaranteed bills issued by German firms anticipating export receipts. Once bills were so guaranteed, they could be sold on to other investors. In normal circumstances this was easy money; the bank made a commission, and instances when it was necessary to deliver on the guarantee were rare. The resemblance to the credit default swaps issued as insurance by banks eighty years later is more than skin-deep.

But circumstances in 1931 were hardly normal. An unsettled foreign exchange market made it hard to sell German bills to other investors, forcing the banks to warehouse them on their own balance sheets. And in the summer, following the Creditanstalt and Danatbank crises, payments by Austrian and German firms to their foreign creditors were frozen. The fact that the banks possessed little liquidity to spare had just been highlighted by the Macmillan Committee, the group of bankers, economists, and other experts, including Keynes, set up in 1929 to investigate the connections between trade and industry.[4] In some cases, moreover, the problem was more than just liquidity. The credits that the three largest investment banks in London, Kleinworts, Schroeders, and Hambros, had extended to German firms engaged in import and export trade exceeded their paid-in capital, or partners' equity, which was the only way of absorbing losses. If their loans to Austrian and German firms were not repaid, these banks were effectively broke.[5]

Norman himself was a onetime merchant banker, having helped to lead the firm Brown Shipley, where his maternal grandfather had been a partner. So were a number of other Bank of England directors. These men understood the banks' problems. They knew that the joint-stock banks (commercial banks to Americans, clearing banks in British parlance) had made large short-term loans to merchant banks desperate for liquidity. The problem, they realized, affected the entire British financial system.

The condition of the banks helps to explain why the Bank of England made no further changes in its discount rate after July, despite gold continuing to drain away. Instead it made an exception to the practice of lending only against good collateral, agreeing to discount bills backed by frozen German debts.[6]

This was not unlike what the Federal Reserve and the ECB did in 2008 when they loosened their collateral requirements to support the financial system. But it was the opposite of what a central bank that was committed to halting gold losses would have done.

For currency speculators, there was no question of what bet to make in this light. It was to borrow sterling and present it to the Bank of England for conversion into gold. The central bank might raise interest rates to make borrowing more costly. But if it hesitated, more speculators would join the queue. It would consequently be forced to suspend convertibility and allow the pound to depreciate against gold and foreign currencies. Speculators could then buy back at a lower price the sterling they had previously sold.[7]

Unwilling to raise the discount rate given the weakness of the banks and the economy, the Bank of England's only recourse was to sell francs and dollars in an effort to inflict losses on traders who had done the opposite. If those traders, who had borrowed the sterling they used to buy francs and dollars, suffered losses as the bank now sought to drive sterling up and the franc and dollar down, their lenders might hit them with margin calls, or demand early repayment. By "squeezing" the bears in this way, the central bank hoped to drive them out of the market.

The Bank of France used the same tactic, with some success, when the franc was under attack in the 1920s. But interest rates then were relatively high. Borrowing was expensive, and those who borrowed money to speculate in currencies had to show results quickly. Now, in contrast, interest rates were low, and speculators could afford to finance their positions. If their lenders demanded more cash, they could find it. As a result, they could afford to wait out the central bank.

In the meantime, selling francs and dollars only accelerated the depletion of the central bank's reserves. The Bank of England first reported gold losses on July 13, the day of Danatbank's failure. Over the subsequent two and a half weeks it lost some £30 million of reserves, amounting to roughly 25 percent of what it still possessed.

————

Britain had not entered the crisis with a budget deficit (shades of Spain in 2007). The Labour government sought to establish that it was a responsible fiscal steward by toeing a cautious fiscal line. However, revenues fell off as the slump deepened, while spending on unemployment compensation rose. Already debt servicing costs were heavy: the debt-to-GDP ratio approached 200 percent in 1931 as a result of obligations incurred during World War I and then deflation in the 1920s.

Although the government's debt was heavy, it was not unmanageable. The situation was not unlike that of Japan in the early twenty-first century. If debt service costs could be brought down in line with lower global interest rates, and if the growth rate of national income could be pushed up, then the debt-to-GDP ratio could be held at a sustainable level. But with a high exchange rate and restrictive financial policy, the outlook for GDP growth was dim.

This left only austerity as a way of squaring the circle and, it was hoped, restoring confidence in the government's finances and the economy. A six-person "supercommittee" to investigate the problem was set up under the chairmanship of Sir George May, the recently retired secretary of the Prudential Assurance Company, whose reputation as Britain's leading actuary evidently qualified him for the role. The committee's two Conservative and two Liberal members agreed that balancing the budget was essential for restoring confidence. The only feasible way of doing so, given the "unduly large" burden of taxation, they concluded, was by reducing public spending.

Their conclusion was not entirely unexpected. The Conservative motion in the House of Commons calling for establishment of the committee had tasked it with making recommendations for "effecting forthwith all practicable and legitimate reductions in the national expenditure." The majority's recommendations thus focused on reducing unemployment benefits and the salaries of constables, teachers, and members of the armed forces. The committee's two Labour members dissented but did not offer a concrete alternative.

The Labour cabinet was unable to endorse the majority report, foundering on the committee's recommendation to cut unemployment benefits. But neither was it able to agree on other measures. The government was therefore dissolved on August 24 in favor of a government of national unity dominated by Conservatives but headed, awkwardly, by the Labour prime minister, Ramsay MacDonald. (For his efforts, MacDonald was expelled from the Labour Party.) The new government agreed on budgetary economies and, by so doing, was able to secure an £80 million loan from a foreign bank syndicate headed by J. P. Morgan.

But the failure of these measures, introduced on September 10, to restore confidence and stem the Bank of England's gold losses indicates that the budget was not the fundamental problem. The deficit was as much a consequence as a cause of the crisis. The problem was rather the weakness of the economy and the banks, which prevented the Bank of England from prioritizing defense of the sterling parity. This was not a problem that balancing the budget, in and of itself, could solve. To the contrary, austerity only served to aggravate it.

The contradiction surfaced when the May Committee's recommendation to reduce salaries for the armed forces provoked unrest in the ranks.

On September 15 sailors on the Royal Navy's Atlantic Fleet anchored in Cromarty Firth near the Scottish port of Invergordon refused to fall in for duty, and four ships were unable to leave harbor. This was passive resistance rather than mutiny on the high seas, but the headline writers did not make such careful distinctions. Investors were quick to imagine wider civil disobedience. When ministers then indicated during Parliamentary question time willingness to compromise with the "mutineers," they did not reassure investors of their commitment to stay the budgetary course.

All this had the predictable effect of accelerating the run on the pound. The contradictions of British economic policy, which emphasized austerity in an unprecedented slump, made the outcome unavoidable.

After the drama of the summer, the final chapter was anticlimactic. On the evening of September 20, its reserves approaching the legal minimum, the Bank of England announced that it was suspending the convertibility of sterling into gold. On Monday, Parliament passed the Gold Standard (Amendment) Act, validating this fait accompli. But there was little sense of impending calamity. Investors, and more broadly British society, heaved a collective sigh of relief. The exchange rate against the dollar fell by 20 percent, where it stabilized. That was it in terms of immediate repercussions. From London's standpoint, the outcome was surprisingly benign.

———

Not so from New York's. Britain's suspension of gold convertibility challenged the belief that there was such a thing as a safe haven. If one of the world's two financial powers could abandon the gold standard, then it was not inconceivable that the other might do the same. "Everywhere men asked," in the words of Lawrence Sullivan in his contemporary account of the crisis, " 'Will America topple too?"[8]

Uncertain of the answer, currency speculators trained their sights on the dollar. They were joined by central banks rushing to liquidate the deposits they held in New York. The Bank of England had reassured its fellow central banks that sterling would not be allowed to depreciate. Gérard Vissering, the head of the Netherlands Bank, had phoned the Bank of England on Friday, September 18, to sound out his British colleagues, two days prior to the suspension and resulting depreciation. Reassured that its holdings of sterling were safe, the Dutch central bank maintained its position. The devaluation cost the Netherlands Bank dearly, and it cost Dr. Vissering his job.

Having been fooled once, central banks were not willing to be fooled again. The Federal Reserve Bank of New York described the subsequent rush for the exits as "the most rapid outflow of gold experienced by this country and probably by any country."[9] Especially egregious was the conversion of dollars into gold by the Bank of France, the European bank with the largest foreign currency reserves. Hoover was furious, suspecting French payback for his reparations moratorium. He was hard-pressed to contain his anger when hosting French Premier Laval at a White House dinner in October. According to Henry Stimson, Hoover's secretary of state, Hoover held the French premier personally responsible. Not that Laval's humor was much better, given the earlier spat over the president's reparations plan.

Unlike the UK, the United States had not suspended the gold standard during or after World War I, and it was not prepared to suspend it now. On October 8, the directors of the Federal Reserve Bank of New York voted to raise the discount rate from 1½ to 2½ percent, and the board approved. A week later New York raised its rate again, this time to 3½ percent. The other Reserve banks quickly followed.[10] Doing so made borrowing to speculate against the dollar more expensive. But by making credit more costly, it also aggravated banking-sector problems.

The most immediate problems now centered on Chicago.[11] The preceding decade had seen explosive growth in the city's outer suburbs, known as the Bungalow Belt. The growth of these new neighborhoods of low-rise homes on wide lots with space for garages reflected the same factors feeding the Florida property boom, namely cheap credit and the automobile. But in contrast to Florida, Illinois law made no reference to branch banking. Long before, in 1843, the state had experienced a disruptive crisis with the failure of the State Bank of Illinois and its half-dozen branches. The law's silence was interpreted subsequently as prohibiting branching. New suburbs therefore relied on new banks for financial services. Not a few of those new banks were chartered by the same real estate moguls who developed the suburbs they now served. They lent aggressively for property development and, in 1920s fashion, repackaged and sold their loans as mortgage bonds.

The longer-established banks of the Loop felt compelled to compete, which they did by lending for commercial real estate development and issuing single-property bonds. Moreover, they offered, in the manner of the Bank of United States, to repurchase those bonds from unsatisfied investors. As mortgage defaults piled up, bondholders sought to collect on the promise. In June 1931 several banks announced that, due to unforeseen circumstances, they were unable to keep it. Those announcements raising obvious concerns, their depositors began to run. June 8 saw a run on the Foreman Group of banks. (If Illinois law was interpreted as prohibiting branch banking, it did not prevent group or chain banking in the manner of Tennessee.) Runs quickly engulfed other banks downtown and in the suburbs. Newspaper reports ignited sympathetic panics in Toledo and elsewhere.

Against this backdrop, Britain's abandonment of the gold standard and the Fed's discount rate increases exacted a toll. Bank closures followed not just in Chicago but in Philadelphia, Pittsburgh, Youngstown, and other cities. Aside from standing ready to discount eligible paper, the Philadelphia, Chicago, and Cleveland Reserve banks did little to help the distressed institutions. Instead the imperative of defending the gold standard carried the day. Virtually the only figure within the Federal Reserve System to push for more aggressive action to help the banks was Owen D. Young in his capacity as director of the Federal Reserve Bank of New York.[12]

———

These financial problems were another blow to American companies struggling to keep their heads above water. Interest rates paid on prime commercial paper, which reputable firms relied on to finance themselves, now rose by an additional 2 percentage points. The spread between AAA and Baa bonds, which measures the premium riskier corporations have to pay in order to borrow, widened further. Wholesale prices fell by an additional 5 percent between July and December. Unable to borrow, firms and households cut back. Industrial production fell by 10 percent over the second half of the year. This was a repeat of the disastrous experience of the second half of 1930, imposed now on an economy even less able to bear it.

Moreover, whereas in 1930 acute distress had been limited to the United States and Germany, it was felt virtually everywhere in the final months of 1931. Everywhere prices were falling. There were failures of systemically significant banks not just in the United States but across Central and Eastern Europe and, significantly, now even in Europe's once-strong economy, France.

Governments came under pressure to do something, anything. For members of the British Commonwealth and Scandinavian countries with close economic ties to the UK, this meant following Britain off gold. No longer obliged to defend a particular level for the exchange rate, their central banks could cut interest rates to support their struggling economies.

The newfound flexibility similarly allowed them to better support their banks. Of the two dozen countries going off gold in 1931, only one, Sweden, suffered a banking crisis subsequently. The Swedish exception reflected the death, apparently by suicide, of the colorful industrialist Ivar Kreuger and the collapse of his financial empire. Even then, the failure of Kreuger's lender, the Skandinaviska Kreditaktiebolaget, did not spark a general panic since the Swedish state now had the wherewithal to sort out the mess.[13]

Eastern Europe opted to follow Germany and Austria, declaring debt moratoria and imposing exchange controls. Latin America, not knowing which example to emulate, abandoned the gold standard and suspended debt-service payments both, at the same time.

———

In the United States, in contrast, balanced-budget doctrine and gold-standard ideology still carried the day. Andrew Mellon, who swore by the banker's canon as faithfully as anyone, was by now President Hoover's longest-serving cabinet member. Mellon continued to insist that by embracing fiscal and financial rectitude and limiting government intervention, confidence could be restored. But this approach, embraced by his president, did nothing to break the diabolic loop between declining spending and banking problems. For this failure as much as anything, Hoover's term came to be seen as a failed presidency.

Notwithstanding the scorn heaped on him subsequently, Hoover did not entirely fail to grasp the problem. He understood that if banks did not lend, farmers would not plant, firms would not invest, and households would not spend. Without measures restoring confidence in the banks, in other words, recovery was unlikely.

Unfortunately, the banking crisis in the second half of 1931 indicated that the Reserve banks were not capable of such measures. Many troubled banks were not members of the Federal Reserve System, and many member banks lacked eligible commercial bills to pledge to the Fed. In any case, most directors of the twelve Federal Reserve banks did not see the resolution of banking problems as their responsibility.

Hoover, on the other hand, may have understood what needed to be done, but this didn't mean he wanted government to do it. He preferred self-help to intervention by the Federal Reserve, or for that matter by any agency of government. Having been raised a Quaker, he subscribed to the doctrine of neighborly self-reliance. The crisis was best addressed, in his view, by organizations like the National Association of Manufacturers and the American Association of Bankers. This had been the president's response to the stock market crash, when he exhorted business organizations to maintain the prevailing level of wages and labor unions to forgo strikes. It was similarly his response now.

Hoover's plan for dealing with the banking crisis was thus to solicit contributions to a voluntary pool known as the National Credit Corporation (NCC). Participating banks would contribute an amount equal to 2 percent of their deposits and in return qualify for assistance. The corporation's loan decisions would be made not by the government but by committees of local bankers.

With more liquid banks aiding their less liquid brethren, the latter would regain the capacity to lend.

This would not be unlike the interbank cooperation organized during the 1907 crisis, with leadership from J. Pierpont Morgan and help from Benjamin Strong. On that occasion, the failure of the Knickerbocker Trust Company had undermined confidence in other New York City banks, causing banks in the rest of the country, which customarily placed deposits of their own in New York, to withdraw those funds. While the insolvent Knickerbocker Trust was allowed to go under, the stronger New York banks pooled their resources and lent them to their weaker but solvent peers. They also issued clearing-house certificates—essentially, promissory notes they agreed to accept from one another in payment—to ensure that solvent banks would have adequate liquidity.[14] In this way the 1907 crisis was resolved. Indeed, this was not the first time this approach to stemming a banking panic was tried. In fact this kind of cooperation was commonplace before 1913, as President Hoover himself was now quick to observe.[15]

The meeting on Sunday, October 9, where Hoover presented his plan was secret to avoid raising even greater alarm about the condition of the banks. It was held not at the White House but at the apartment of Secretary Mellon. The familiar cast of characters included Thomas Lamont from J. P. Morgan, Albert Wiggin from Chase National Bank, and Charles Mitchell from National City Bank, along with Hoover, Mellon, and Treasury Undersecretary Ogden Mills.

The bankers were not enthused. Weak banks, they observed, were in no position to contribute 2 percent of their assets to a common pool. Strong ones would be subsidizing their weaker brethren. In other words, the bankers understood that the problem was not just one of liquidity; many distressed banks were insolvent. For the solvent to lend to their insolvent brethren would be throwing good money after bad. Bankers in a position to contribute wanted the association's loans to be collateralized but recognized that distressed banks lacked good collateral.[16] In effect, good collateral was something that only the government possessed. George Harrison had brought these problems to Hoover's attention already on Friday, October 7, but Hoover's belief in the power of self-help was too strong for him to modify his plan.

Friedman and Schwartz attribute the absence of mutual support on the part of the banks to the existence of the Federal Reserve. Rather than providing mutual support as they had before 1914, the bankers now expected the central bank to bail them out. This analysis suggests otherwise. The events of 1931 were both different from and more serious than the liquidity crises that had occurred prior to 1914. 1931 was a crisis of solvency in which outside help was essential. These were not circumstances under which voluntarism could carry the day.

In the event, Hoover's National Credit Corporation made only $10 million of loans through the end of the year, reflecting lack of adequate collateral and the big bankers' lack of sympathy for their smaller, more troubled counterparts. One is reminded of the Public-Private Partnership Investment Program for Legacy Assets of 2009, under which the government sought to get private investors to buy the toxic paper on bank balance sheets, though here too little came of it.[17]

———

At this point, not even Hoover could deny that government intervention was required. The next election was less than a year away, which was enough to convince even an incumbent committed to voluntarism that this was no time to stand on principle.

Conveniently, a model was at hand in the form of the War Finance Corporation (WFC), created by Congress in 1918 to make loans to industries and banks finding it difficult to borrow in wartime. The WFC was repurposed as an emergency finance corporation for making loans to banks, industries, and local credit agencies during the recession of 1920–21, and then to help farmers struggling with low crop prices. Although it had been dissolved in 1929, there was now a powerful argument for resurrecting it.

The case was made by Eugene Meyer, the same banker who previously ran the WFC, worked on Hoover's debt moratorium, and now served as chairman of the Federal Reserve Board. Extraordinarily for a central banker, Meyer himself drafted the enabling legislation. The agency as he designed it would lend not just to banks but to railroads, whose bonds weighed on the portfolios of the banks, and to farmers, whose pleas resounded on Capitol Hill. Meyer had made his fortune buying and selling railway securities, something that may have been more than incidentally connected with the plan's favorable treatment of the latter.

The bill establishing what came to be known as the Reconstruction Finance Corporation (RFC) was introduced into the Congress on December 7 and signed into law on January 22, 1932. By February 2, with a skeletal staff of former employees of the WFC, the RFC was up and running. The Treasury supplied $500 million of capital and was prepared to issue an additional $1.5 billion of bonds on the corporation's behalf.[18]

Hoover picked Meyer to chair the RFC's bipartisan board and Charles Dawes, of Dawes Plan fame, as president of the corporation. This was only the latest turn in the Dawes revolving door. Dawes had recently resigned, to Washington's surprise, as ambassador to the Court of St. James. (He was succeeded by Andrew Mellon, who was in this way gracefully put out to pasture.) Speculation was rife that Dawes might challenge Hoover for the Republican nomination. Not only did appointing him to the RFC put a prominent banker and public statesman at the helm, but for Hoover it was a way of occupying a potential rival. The fact of the matter was that Dawes had bigger fish to fry. He had reason to be concerned about the survival of his family's Chicago banking empire, something of which Hoover appears to have been unaware. For Dawes, the RFC was an ideal perch from which to gather intelligence on the condition of the banking system and cultivate political contacts.

Unlike the ill-fated NCC, the RFC made extensive loans, conflicts between big and small bankers not inhibiting it. But like the NCC, the RFC required good collateral. As a result, only banks possessing it were able to borrow. The RFC thus did little to address solvency problems.

———

If the banks and the economy were going to receive significant help, it would have to come from elsewhere, namely from the Federal Reserve. Congress helped by giving the central bank more room for maneuver. The Fed was constrained by the shortage of eligible securities—good collateral—against which to provide credit. The Federal Reserve Act required it to hold collateral, or back its note issue, with either gold or commercial paper generated in the course of business transactions, consonant with the real bills doctrine. Economic activity having been in decline for more than two years, partly because of the Fed's earlier reluctance to do more about it, there was now a shortage of business transactions to produce commercial paper eligible to be held as backing for Federal Reserve notes. This might force the central bank to contract the note issue or, even worse in the eyes of officials, abandon the gold standard.

In February 1932, Mellon's successor as treasury secretary, Ogden Mills, warned Hoover that the country was within weeks of being forced off the gold standard owing to the shortage of eligible securities. Hoover convened an emergency meeting of Harrison, Meyer, and Dawes, who agreed that the solution was legislation, which the president invited Senator Carter Glass and Representative Henry Steagall, chairmen of their respective chambers' banking committees, to draft. Their bill modifying the supposedly sacrosanct gold standard, allowing the Fed to discount a wider range of securities, passed on February 27 without debate.[19] Crises have a way of concentrating the mind.

The Fed was now free to take proactive steps to make credit more freely available. More than that, it was compelled to do so. Senator Elmer Thomas,

Democrat of Oklahoma, was advancing legislation to require the Fed to print $2.4 billion of banknotes. Under the Thomas Plan, the government would sell bonds in that amount to the Reserve banks, and the Reserve banks would issue a corresponding amount of new currency notes. Thomas was a disciple of William Jennings Bryan, for whom he had campaigned in 1896. Concerned for the farmers and ranchers whom he saw as being crucified on a latter-day cross of gold, Thomas pressed for a "stabilized" or "honest" dollar. He was able to make common cause with another group of congressmen seeking immediate payment of the bonus previously prom-ised World War I veterans, who figured that the new bank notes could be used to fund bonus payments. Not for the last time did politics shape monetary policy.

These domestic politics notwithstanding, Federal Reserve officials worried that such inflationary measures would be poorly received abroad. The French, in particular, would be quick to grasp the incompatibility of inflation with the dollar-franc exchange rate, prompting them to liquidate their dollar balances. Harrison warned his colleagues of the danger. Better than courting it, he sug-gested, was to initiate a modest program of monetary expansion using the room provided by Glass-Steagall and thereby head off congressional insistence to do more. Limited measures might alleviate the pressure applied by the likes of Senator Thomas without at the same time exciting the French.

This the Fed now set out to do, with New York's leadership, purchasing treasury securities on the open market, first at the modest rate of $25 mil-lion a week and from April at a more ambitious $100 million weekly, pro-viding the markets with a corresponding amount of cash. The New York Fed might have done more but for its gold problem. Each Reserve bank held its own gold reserves. Each conducted its own open market purchases, sub-ject now to approval by the Board. But the New York Fed was the branch to which foreigners turned when they demanded gold. The New York bank therefore saw its gold-cover ratio (essentially, the ratio of gold in its vaults to its notes and other liabilities in circulation) fall in June to less than 50 per-cent. This was already dangerously close, in the view of Harrison and his colleagues, to the 40 percent minimum permitted by the Federal Reserve Act. The directors of the New York bank therefore were compelled to limit the rate of purchase.

Securities purchases continued at this moderate pace through the first half of the summer. In August, the House and Senate then recessed for the summer holiday and fall election. The pressure on the Fed was off. Open market pur-chases were halted. But they had not been without effect in the interim. Prices had stabilized, and certain lines of production, motor vehicles for example, had actually risen. But these now fell back. And banking problems returned with a vengeance.

———

The Federal Reserve Bank of Chicago, unlike the Federal Reserve Bank of New York, still had ample gold reserves. By transferring some of the excess to New York, it might have allowed the New York bank and the system to ramp up their securities purchases. But the Chicago bank under James McDougal had long been critical of New York's activism. McDougal, recall, had objected to Benjamin Strong's internationally motivated interest-rate reductions in 1927. He now rebuffed requests to transfer his excess gold to New York. The board could have compelled him to do so, but it was aware that McDougal had other problems. June saw runs on some three dozen banks in Greater Chicago. These were mainly neighborhood banks in the Bungalow Belt, as in 1931. But there was an important exception: Central Republic Trust, a big Loop bank headed by none other than Charles Dawes.

Dawes tendered his resignation as the RFC head just days before Central Republic's problems broke into the open. He was aware that his family bank was in trouble and would almost certainly need help. Dawes himself, as a sometime government official, owned only a few shares in the bank, but his family firm, Dawes Brothers, Inc., was its single largest shareholder; Central Republic Trust was known as "the Dawes Bank." Along with its investments in real estate, Central Republic had lent heavily to a group of companies controlled by Samuel Insull, who monopolized the provision of electricity and gas to the households, manufacturing firms, and urban railways of Greater Chicago. Insull got his start as secretary to Thomas Edison's agent in London and then worked as Edison's private secretary in New York. In the 1880s, while still in his twenties, he helped to arrange financing for Edison's pioneering electrical utility franchises. Insull became a vice president of Edison General Electric when it was formed in 1889, second vice president of the General Electric Company in 1892, and then president of the Chicago Edison Company shortly thereafter. Chicago Edison was a small company at the time, but one with significant growth potential, since residents of Greater Chicago were still almost entirely unserved by electricity.

After twenty years of growing Chicago Edison, Insull formed the Middle West Utilities Company to buy up utility providers in neighboring communities and states. Middle West Utilities was a major beneficiary of the electrification boom of the 1920s, when manufacturing production, not to mention urban life, was revolutionized by the new power source. The low interest rates and easy credit of the period made it easy for Insull to finance his acquisitions. By 1932, Middle West Utilities controlled more than a hundred companies providing electricity to five thousand towns. Insull financed some of his acquisitions by issuing equity, but even more by borrowing, notably in the form of short-term loans from banks. Prominent among them was Central Republic, run by the Dawes family, which like Insull had an interest in promoting the growth of Chicago. It did not hurt that Dawes and Insull socialized together or that Insull contributed to the campaigns of Republican politicians on Dawes' recommendation.[20]

The Depression had a predictable negative impact on Insull's highly leveraged operation. The demand for electricity and utility company revenues declined. By April 1932, Insull's companies were filing for bankruptcy, creating problems for their bankers. Because Insull had organized his holdings as a collection of separate companies rather than one integrated unit, banks were able to disregard provisions of the state banking code intended to limit their exposure to any one borrower to 15 percent of its share capital (the amount of money the owners committed to the bank's operation).[21] When Insull's companies filed for bankruptcy protection, Central Republic's $12 million of loans to his companies and affiliates in fact amounted to more than 50 percent of its capital.[22] Management was either exceptionally sloppy or too closely connected to Insull for its own good.

Initially the hope was that the bankruptcy receiver would find the resources needed to pay the bankers what they were owed. Insull's companies controlled actual power plants that supplied actual electricity to actual customers. But as the receiver uncovered a growing list of irregularities, it became apparent that any such assets would be dwarfed by Insull's debts. In early June, Insull fled for the safety of Paris. On June 22 the news that he had arrived there, superimposed on the drumbeat of bank failures in the Bungalow Belt, ignited the run on Central Republic.[23]

———

This was the backdrop against which Dawes warned thirty of his fellow bankers, assembled at Central Republic's Chicago headquarters on Friday, June 24, 1932, that his bank would be unable to open its doors the following Monday, absent assistance. By this point there was only one place from which such assistance could come, namely the RFC. The optics were unfortunate, Dawes until recently having headed up that self-same federal agency. He therefore let one of his Chicago banking colleagues, Melvin Traylor of the First National Bank, lead the negotiations.

Traylor cultivated a spic-and-span image. He was born literally in a log cabin, and as president of First National he still lived in a modest frame house near Lincoln Park. But Traylor's bank also had loans to Insull's companies, so he was not exactly disinterested. He was allied with Chicago Mayor Anton Cermak and politically connected at the national level, having served on the American delegation to the conference that established the Bank for International Settlements. Thus, delegating the negotiations to Traylor did not prevent angry members of Congress from crying cronyism.

The decision to extend the loan, taken over a weekend under intense time pressure, was made at the highest level. President Hoover himself helped organize it, the directors of the RFC being on holiday or at the Democratic National Convention, as it happened, in Chicago. Nothing could have embarrassed a sitting president more than to appear to have fomented a crisis in the city where the opposition was holding its nominating convention. In 2008, when the government scrambled to rescue Bear Stearns, not just the president of the New York Fed but the treasury secretary was involved in negotiations.[24] That the President of the United States helped to orchestrate the government rescue of Central Republic was more remarkable still.

The rescue of Central Republic resembled the rescue of Bear Stearns in other ways as well. As in the case of Bear Stearns, the decision to offer assistance was taken in the belief that the bank was too big and connected to fail—that allowing it to collapse would ignite a nationwide panic. As in the case of Bear Stearns, the size of the rescue, $90 million, was unprecedented. Not only was this the single largest loan the RFC had made, but it was three times the size of all the loans the Federal government made to the states in 1932 for relief for the unemployed and homeless. As in the rescue of Bear Stearns, normal procedures were short-circuited. There is no evidence that the officers of Central Republic were even required to complete the standard loan application.

As in the case of Bear Stearns, there was controversy about whether the agency in question had exceeded its authority in extending the loan. The RFC was authorized to lend only if it expected that it would be repaid—that is, only if it believed that the bank it was helping was solvent. The RFC's inspectors had their doubts, just as examiners in 2008 had their doubts about Bear Stearns. Lobbying by Traylor and Jesse Jones, an influential RFC director who, conveniently, was a delegate to the Democratic National Convention and on the scene, convinced Hoover and the RFC to go ahead.

The RFC's bazooka reassured depositors. Although as many as twenty-six other Chicago banks, mainly small ones associated with a local real estate developer by the name of John Bain, had experienced runs and been forced to suspend operations in the week leading up to the RFC rescue of Central Republic, bank runs now quickly came to a halt. Although a few additional banks failed in subsequent months, these were mainly small banks in remote places like Idaho and Nevada. News of their failure was unsettling, but they were too small to be systemically significant. As in Knoxville and New York in 1930, the official response, this time by the RFC rather than the Fed, prevented the crisis from spreading further. Hoover, with an election approaching, was willing to act. With the swift intervention of the RFC, any reluctance on the part of the Chicago Fed was, for the moment, a nonissue.

But the rescue also ignited criticism of bailouts of fat-cat bankers with political connections. Treasury Secretary Mills, Chase National Bank's Winthrop Aldrich, and Michigan Senator Couzens, who chaired the Senate committee overseeing the RFC, all questioned whether the corporation had overstepped its bounds, and the bounds of prudence, by bailing out an insolvent institution. To address complaints that the RFC was giving the well-connected preferential treatment, Congress required the RFC to inform it, starting in August 1932, of the identity of all banks receiving loans, information that was made public. As a result, the banks grew reluctant to apply for RFC assistance for fear that this information would be seen as a sign of weakness.[25] Starting in September, borrowing from the RFC fell off. In October industrial production headed back down.

Government officials accused of cronyism began looking for an opportunity to repair their reputations. They needed to show that they were capable of playing hardball with a troubled bank. In 2008, in the wake of Bear Stearns, they found that opportunity with Lehman Brothers. In the wake of Central Republic, they found it with the Guardian Group of banks.

———

Following the Democratic convention, the news flow was dominated by the contest between Hoover and Roosevelt. As the events of 2008 remind us, crises often occur around elections, when policy uncertainty is highest.

FDR's intentions were obscure; nothing he said in the course of the campaign indicated whether he would abandon the gold standard. But Roosevelt's activist bent and desire to break with Hoover were no secret. With his victory in November and through the four-month interregnum that followed, investors worried that the end of the gold standard was drawing near. The president-elect held meetings with gold-standard skeptics like Professor George Warren of Cornell University. Leading financiers, including Traylor of the First National Bank of Chicago, Chairman Aldrich of Chase National Bank, and Arthur Ballantine, the outgoing US Treasury undersecretary, urged him not to tamper with the monetary standard. But FDR refused to be drawn.

In effect, the president-elect was offering investors a one-way bet. If they sold dollars for gold and the United States did devalue the dollar, their gold would rise in value. If instead the new president adhered to gold-standard orthodoxy, they could repurchase dollars subsequently and lose nothing. This was the same one-way bet taken by investors who questioned the commitment of the Bank of England to defend gold convertibility in 1931.

It now produced the same result. Gold drained out of the Federal Reserve System and out of the country. Whether the central bank, increasingly short of gold, would have the capacity to help in the event of further financial problems was unclear.

The answer came from the banking panic that erupted in Michigan in mid-February, two weeks before FDR took office. At the center of the crisis was the Guardian Group of banks, in one of which, Union Guardian Trust Company, Henry Ford via his son Edsel was the largest investor. In the same way Central Republic was known as the Dawes Bank, the Guardian Group of banks was known as the Ford Group. The Guardian Group had engaged in a range of dubious practices, including building for itself an ornate headquarters of gilded bricks and lending to its officers so they could speculate in stocks. It had made extensive home mortgage loans, and with the auto industry deeply depressed, many of its loans to unemployed autoworkers were in default. This, clearly, was not a bank that could survive much longer, absent the injection of financial resources by either its owners or the government.

On Wednesday, February 8, Edsel Ford briefed Treasury Secretary Mills and RFC President Charles Miller, Dawes' successor, and on the ninth representatives of the Guardian Group traveled to Capitol Hill to brief Michigan's two senators, James Couzens and Arthur Vandenberg. That evening the pair attended a White House meeting together with Mills, Deputy Secretary Ballantine, Commerce Secretary Roy Chapin, and the RFC's Miller.

Michigan's spokesmen made the case for government intervention in no uncertain terms. Within forty-eight hours Ballantine and Chapin had arrived in Detroit with the goal of organizing a loan. Ballantine was an official of the outgoing Hoover administration, but he also had long acquaintance with the incoming president. As an undergraduate he had edited the *Harvard Crimson* when Roosevelt was a staffer. Nor was Ballantine exactly an outsider. An attorney, he represented the Dodge Brothers when their company was acquired by Chrysler, one of Ford's principal rivals. Chapin was a Michigander and, like Ford, a onetime auto executive, having served as chairman of the Hudson Motor Car Company, a forerunner of the American Motors Corporation. Perhaps not incidentally, he had been a founding director of the Guardian Trust Company. It was a little like having a former Goldman Sachs CEO in his position as Treasury secretary help arrange the conversion of Goldman Sachs into a bank holding company in September 2008.

Ford's Union Guardian was as systemically significant as Charles Dawes' Central Republic Trust, which the RFC had bailed out in June. But given criticism of that earlier action, Ballantine and Chapin now demanded that Ford inject $4 million of capital into Union Guardian as security for a loan, and asked in addition that Ford commit not to withdraw the Ford Motor Company's $7.5 million of deposits in the bank. The RFC could offer help only to a solvent bank, the two officials explained. Ford's $4 million capital injection and commitment of deposits were needed for Union Guardian to qualify.[26] The line between solvency and insolvency might be sketchy, but with the firestorm whipped up by the RFC's rescue of Central Republic, there was now intense pressure to draw it.

Ford refused to cooperate. He knew the RFC had supported Central Republic and did not believe it was prepared to let Guardian go under. He understood that the RFC had not exactly stood on principle the previous summer. He believed the Hoover administration would regard the collapse of Michigan's banks as a devastating blow to a staggering economy. He upped the ante by threatening to withdraw $25 million of Ford Motor Company funds on deposit with a second local bank, the First National Bank of Detroit, another one that had already suffered heavy withdrawals.[27] His, he evidently believed, was a clear case of too big to fail.

Ballantine and Chapin were aware that dire consequences might follow from allowing Guardian to go under. But they were also aware that Congress was furious about what it perceived as RFC favoritism toward big business, which Ford symbolized even more than Dawes. That Michigan Senator Couzens, Ford's former business partner and rival, was among the critics—and that Couzens chaired the Senate committee responsible for the RFC—did not make their job any easier. Couzens was sure to make an issue of any concession, and specifically of any loan that did not require Ford to subordinate his deposits.[28]

So too was Father Charles Coughlin, the controversial Roman Catholic priest and inspirational radio broadcaster. Coughlin blamed business for the ills of the American economy and the Depression in particular. Located as he was in nearby Royal Oak, Michigan, he saw no better symbol of business than Henry Ford. Earlier, Coughlin had criticized Ford, who contracted to build tractors in the Soviet Union, of fostering communism and exporting American jobs. Now, using his nationwide radio network, he accused Ford and his bankers of having fomented the crisis to secure a taxpayer bailout.

Although the RFC had previously helped the Guardian Group—its first loans to subsidiaries of Guardian dated to May 1932—with Ford's refusal to commit his deposits it declined to do more. Hoover argued that allowing Guardian to fail would be a disaster. Jesse Jones introduced a motion to give Guardian a loan but was voted down by the RFC board. Just as the US Treasury allowed Lehman Brothers to fail in September 2008 in part to make a political statement and correct the moral hazard created by its earlier bailout of Bear Stearns, the RFC allowed Guardian Trust to go under.[29]

Failure to prop up Union Guardian led to panicked runs on Monday, February 13. At 1:32 a.m. the next morning Michigan Governor William Comstock, in office for only weeks, declared a statewide bank holiday. The auto companies suspended all advertising, and the Ford Company laid off half its employees. Reflecting the extent to which America's industrial center of gravity had shifted to the Midwest and to the auto industry center of Detroit specifically, the crisis quickly spilled over. Michigan companies, their local accounts frozen, scrambled to draw on their deposits in neighboring states. The Michigan holiday thus precipitated runs on banks in Ohio, Indiana, and Illinois. Maryland declared a bank holiday on February 25, five more states on March 1, six on March 2, and five on March 3. Foreigners, seeing this chaos, rushed to cash in their dollars. Gold hemorrhaged out of the Federal Reserve Bank of New York.

On March 3 the Federal Reserve Bank of New York asked the Federal Reserve Bank of Chicago, still with excess gold, to purchase or rediscount $400 million of its securities. Again Chicago refused. Better, the directors of the Chicago bank evidently concluded, to save those resources for an even rainier day.

This was a disaster of miscalculation and obduracy all around. By February 1933 industrial production in the United States had fallen to just 53 percent of its 1929 level. Prices had collapsed. Unemployment was approaching 25 percent. The banking system was allowed to disintegrate over the misplaced priority attached to moral hazard. Among the consequences were the disgrace of a sitting president and the inauguration, on March 4, of a charismatic if yet unproven successor.

The only question was whether the new captain could right the sinking ship. This, of course, was the same question asked of Barack Obama following his inauguration in January 2009.

CHAPTER 11 | Largely Contained

HOME PRICES PEAKED in the United States at the end of 2005 and the beginning of 2006. Having risen for the better part of a decade, they fell by 1 percent in the fourth quarter of 2005 and 3.3 percent in the first quarter of 2006. The 1 percent fall at the end of 2005 could be dismissed as a fluke, the difficulty of identifying comparable sales rendering all indices of property prices less than precise. But two consecutive quarters of declining prices and a cumulative fall of more than 4 percent were harder to ignore.[1]

Already contrarian investors were starting to bet on further declines in the housing market. John Paulson, a merger-arbitrage expert best known for his lavish parties, began buying credit default swaps that would pay out in the event of defaults on subprime mortgage pools. Jeff Greene, a failed Los Angeles real estate speculator, learned of Paulson's strategy and replicated his trade. Andrew Lahde, a freelance hedge fund trader with a background as a Southern California beachcomber, followed a similar strategy on a smaller scale. Michael Burry, a small-time fund manager whose training was as a physician, did the same out of San Jose.[2]

These contrarians were outsiders. That many of them worked not on Wall Street but in California is revealing. They were not part of the Wall Street machinery. They were not prone to having their views shaped by colleagues enjoying big paydays from the securitization business.

But given their status as outsiders, it was easy to dismiss their nettlesome views. The dominant strategy within the investment banking community remained taking on additional mortgage-related risk because other institutions were taking on additional mortgage-related risk. Lehman Brothers, Bear Stearns, Citigroup, and Merrill Lynch all continued to increase their mortgage-related exposures in 2006 because they saw their rivals doing like-wise. This was groupthink at its best. Dissidents suggesting otherwise were banished from the inner sanctum. Such was the fate of Madeline Antoncic, Lehman's chief risk officer, who as recently as 2005 had been singled out as "Risk Manager of the Year" by *Risk Magazine*, the semi-official organ of the risk-management industry.[3]

A few individuals and institutions endowed with exceptional intellec-tual flexibility and not overly burdened by scruples were able to play both sides of the fence. Goldman Sachs continued to distribute collateralized debt obligations backed by pools of mortgages, earning handsome fees. Yet even while it marketed those securities the firm was betting against them in its trading operations. The bank's own positions—that instead of investing in the securities in question, it borrowed and sold them in the expectation that their prices would fall—indicate it did not believe the senior tranches of those CDOs deserved their AAA ratings. But if so, Goldman did not feel obliged as investment advisor to warn its clients, whether they were the German bank IKB, the Australian hedge fund Basis Yield Alpha (Master), or Bear Stearns Asset Management. These counterparties, Goldman argued, were "sophisticated investors." They could take care of themselves. Meanwhile, the truly sophisticated investors like Goldman were reducing their exposure to mortgage-related risk.[4]

———

By the fourth quarter of 2007, the cumulative fall in home prices had reached 9 percent.[5] High loan-to-value mortgages with rates that reset after a grace period were sold to households in the expectation that home values would continue to rise. Not a few borrowers purchased more house than they could afford in anticipation of flipping it before the interest rate recast.[6] This strategy no longer being viable in a falling market, they defaulted in growing numbers.

As new mortgages became harder to originate, brokers also experienced dis-tress. Ameriquest, the single largest subprime lender as recently as 2005, closed all but four of its retail branches and eliminated four thousand jobs. Ownit Mortgage Solutions became the first subprime lender to file for Chapter 11 bankruptcy, in January 2007. American Freedom Mortgage, American Home Mortgage, and then New Century Financial followed in turn.

It was clear by this time that the housing sector was on the cusp of a wrenching adjustment. What was not clear was the powerful negative impact this would have on the economy. Everyone understood that home prices had stopped rising, but there was little awareness of broader consequences. Expert commentary suggested that the impact would be restricted to the housing market, and its subprime segment in particular. The implications for the economy, the financial system, and the labor market would be limited, it was comfortingly asserted. Fed Chairman Bernanke and Treasury Secretary Henry Paulson used strikingly similar language when seeking to characterize the consequences. "The impact on the broader economy and financial markets of the problems in the subprime markets seems likely to be contained," Bernanke testified in March 2007.[7] In a speech to a business group a month later, Paulson reassured his audience that although "we've clearly had a big correction in the housing market . . . I don't see [problems in the subprime mortgage market] imposing a serious problem. I think it's going to be largely contained."[8]

Officials see it as their role to reassure. But the absence in the first half of 2007 of policy action to support the slowing economy suggests that policy makers believed what they said.[9]

———

A confluence of factors lay behind this collective failure of imagination. To start, there was an inability to imagine how fast and far home prices could fall. There might be sharp declines in certain regional markets, as happened in Florida in 1926 and might now occur in the Inland Empire of Southern California, but not in the country as a whole. "We've never had a decline on a nationwide basis," Bernanke observed. "What I think is more likely is that house prices will slow, maybe stabilize, might slow consumption spending a bit. I don't think it's going to drive the economy too far from its full employment path, though."[10] When home prices did start falling nationwide, Secretary Paulson was quick to conclude that they were "at or near the bottom." This kind of nationwide fall was an aberration, at most a one-time adjustment, not an ongoing trend.[11] These statements were not just for public consumption; they were indicative of the consensus in official circles. The March 2007 minutes of the Federal Open Market Committee, for example, spoke of how "accumulating data suggested that the demand for homes was leveling out."[12]

The mistaken belief that home prices could not fall on a nationwide basis was, of course, what a historical perspective like that brought by a scholar of the Great Depression such as Chairman Bernanke should have served to correct. Home prices had dropped by 25 percent in nominal terms between 1929 and 1933, and by fully 30 percent from their peak in 1925. They had dropped nationwide. As an expert on the Great Depression, the chairman was surely aware of the fact.

The assumption behind his "We've never had" statement was that the earlier decline in housing prices, like the decline in the overall price level, was possible only because the recently created central bank had neglected its responsibilities. It was not possible now that seasoned monetary policy makers were on the job. This assumption in turn reflected the intellectual sway of Milton Friedman and Anna Schwartz's interpretation of the Great Depression, according to which an inexperienced Fed was responsible for the collapse of output and prices. It reflected the further belief that modern central bankers had assimilated Friedman and Schwartz's analysis. There is no better expression of the view than the remarks addressed by Governor Bernanke to Professor Friedman in 2002, on the occasion of the latter's ninetieth birthday: "Regarding the Great Depression. You're right, we did it. We're very sorry. But thanks to you, we won't do it again."[13]

This was of course simply the policy community's collective belief in the Great Moderation in another guise. Because central bankers had learned the lessons of history, they would avoid the mistakes that caused sharp drops in housing prices and the economywide price level starting in 1929. Instead they would take proactive steps to ensure that the incipient decline was contained. And if the aggregate price level and economic activity were stabilized, any nationwide fall in housing prices would be limited.

When it became clear in 2007 that a significant decline in home prices was in fact underway, it was still possible to argue that the financial system would not be implicated. When property prices fell in 1926, only a few isolated bank runs and bank failures followed. The impact on the financial system was limited and mild. This was not the case in 1933, admittedly, when nonperforming mortgage loans brought down the Guardian Group of banks and helped precipitate a full-blown panic. But the circumstances then were different. Retail depositors, fearing for their savings, ran at the first sign of trouble. The Federal Deposit Insurance Corporation now guaranteed deposits up to $100,000. The kind of panicked runs affecting the Caldwell chain of banks in 1930, Charles Dawes' Central Republic Trust in 1932, and Henry Ford's Guardian Group in 1933 were no longer possible. Or so it was thought.

By early 1933, moreover, the contraction had been underway for more than three years. Unemployment exceeded 20 percent. Widespread mortgage defaults threatened the stability of any financial institution with exposure to the housing market. In 2007, in contrast, the economy was continuing to expand. Unemployment was still below 5 percent. So long as the expansion persisted, it was possible to argue that the majority of borrowers would be all right, along with the majority of financial institutions. And even when the expansion ended, as all expansions do, there was still that experienced central bank to prevent events from spiraling out of control.

The financial system, moreover, had come a long way since 1933. Banks had strengthened their controls. They possessed a cornucopia of instruments with which to hedge and diversify risk. In an October 2005 speech, Alan Greenspan, who more than anyone epitomized this supposed wisdom, acknowledged that the current expansion, like all expansions, would ultimately end but reassured his audience that the US and world economies, and their financial systems, were more resilient than ever.[14]

What this reassuring, and in retrospect curiously one-eyed, assessment missed was the structure of housing finance. Even limited declines in housing prices could now disrupt the mortgage market because of how lending was structured. And the impact of worsening mortgage-market conditions could have much graver implications for the financial system because of the increase in leverage and the development of a shadow banking system subject to minimal regulation. Those implications would be especially serious for banks that warehoused collateralized debt obligations in the vain hope of selling them, for special purpose vehicles that loaded up on the speculative equity tranche in ignorance of the risk, and for bond insurers and credit default swap specialists like American International Group that sold insurance on those contracts. And if markets in CDOs and CDS were disrupted, the appetite for subprime and even conventional mortgages could dry up, feeding back on the housing market. There would then be spillovers to the commercial paper market, money market mutual funds, the banking system, and ultimately the economy itself.

Unfortunately, this alphabet soup of CDOs, SPVs, and CDS was not part of the staple diet of erstwhile Princeton professors of economics. Nor were these complex financial structures incorporated into the Federal Reserve's model of the economy. Fed staffers were more likely to have graduated from university departments of economics than investment bank trading floors. Only a handful had even heard of collateralized debt obligations. It is thus unsurprising that they failed to sound louder warnings.

———

The shock, as in 1929, came from outside the banking system. In June 2007, Bear Stearns announced that it was halting redemptions from two hedge funds heavily invested in CDOs. By the end of May, the more aggressively managed of the two vehicles, the tongue-twistingly named High Grade Structured Credit Strategies Enhanced Leverage Fund, had received redemption requests from roughly half its account holders. These were not demands that the fund could meet, given that there was now no market for its assets and no other way of raising cash. Bear had marketed the funds as low-risk vehicles invested in AA and AAA securities. The rating agencies that helped to structure those securities had compliantly bestowed the requisite AA and AAA ratings.[15] Thus, the lock-up was a shock not just to investors in the two Bear Stearns funds but also to investors in other funds with positions in what were similarly supposed to be high-grade, low-risk securities but were now revealed as anything but.

Leverage too played a role, as in 1929. The Bear Stearns funds had used their collateral and their parent's good name to borrow from other financial firms. Though the difference between the cost of borrowing and the return on AA and AAA-rated securities was small, multiplied many times it could still promise a healthy return on equity. This made leveraging the portfolio an attractive, and indeed an essential, part of the strategy.

But leverage could pose an existential threat if the investments in question went bad. If big lenders like Merrill Lynch and Goldman Sachs refused to roll over their loans, it was not clear where else the borrowers could turn. If those companies then moved to seize the collateral the borrowers had pledged, it would quickly become apparent that there was not enough to go around. There would be a rush to seize the remaining assets, and the borrowers would be thrust into bankruptcy, creating significant losses for the lenders. Better was to gradually wind down the two Bear Stearns funds. Their assets could be sold off in an orderly fashion to maximize the recovery rate rather than being dumped on the market in a fire sale.[16]

But doing so required patience, something that was in short supply. In addition, there was the uncomfortable fact that Bear Stearns, with a reputation for hard-nosed business practices, was the one Wall Street firm that refused to contribute to the collective rescue of the mega-hedge fund Long-Term Capital Management in 1998. As a consequence, Bear was not now the recipient of much goodwill from the financial community.

On June 20 Merrill Lynch, preoccupied by its own problems, seized $850 million of collateral from Bear Stearns. Learning of Merrill's action, Lehman Brothers quickly followed. Bear put up $1.6 billion of its own funds to keep the two funds afloat but quickly concluded that it was facing a bottomless pit.[17] On July 31 it requested bankruptcy protection for its troubled funds. Bear Stearns was out the $1.6 billion, causing investors to question whether its top officers in fact deserved their reputation for hard-headed, cigar-chomping management.

The lesson was as alarming as it was clear. Deposit insurance may have eliminated runs on commercial banks by retail depositors, but it had not eliminated runs by wholesale lenders on the shadow banking system of which the two Bear Stearns funds were part. Nor, when the time came, would it prevent runs on their parent institutions.

———

As in the 1920s, a shock that originated in the United States quickly infected other countries. In the 1920s US banks lent to European banks and governments, which invested the money in illiquid assets like municipal swimming pools (illiquid in the financial sense of the word). When US lending dried up, the European borrowers were unable to continue funding those projects, much less repay what they borrowed. This time, European banks again funded illiquid investments by borrowing dollars from their American counterparts. As US banks incurred losses on their housing-related investments, their foreign lending again dried up, placing the European borrowers in a 1920s-like bind.

And this was not all. In the 1920s some European borrowers turned around and invested their dollars in an ever wobblier US stock market. This time, again, European banks turned around and invested their borrowed funds in the United States, including in the questionable CDOs distributed by those same US banks.

Banks in the United States, like Goldman Sachs, may have developed reservations about the subprime-linked CDO market by late 2006, but the same was not true of the Düsseldorf-based IKB or France's BNP Paribas. IKB, or the Bank for German Industry Obligations (Bank für deutsche Industrieobligationen), was founded in 1924 to supply funds to cash-strapped German firms in the wake of the hyperinflation. In addition to lending to small and medium-sized enterprises, IKB found its way into real estate lending.[18]

But given its mandate to provide finance to the German economy, it was not at all clear just why the bank now saw fit to invest in securities backed by US subprime mortgages. Why its managers thought they were capable of navigating those treacherous shoals is even less obvious. Actually, it was obvious to IKB's ambitious CEO Stefan Ortseifen, who saw doing so as a way of transforming a medium-sized bank that specialized in lending to medium-sized companies into a global player. To that end, Ortseifen created an off-balance-sheet company, Rhineland Funding, and listed it on a compliant Irish stock market. As a special purpose vehicle, Rhineland didn't have to hold capital against its investments, in turn allowing IKB to lever up its bets. This was a classic 2000s financial play. It now came back to bite the bank.

The biggest single bite came in the form of the Abacus deal that eventually became the subject of congressional hearings and a Justice Department investigation.[19] This brings us back to John Paulson. In late 2006 Paulson decided to place big bets against the housing market. Paulson was a mergers-and-acquisitions specialist at Bear Stearns who went on to found a hedge fund specializing in the debt of troubled companies. He was not a housing specialist, which may have been what enabled him to go against the grain. Nor did Paulson require sophisticated evidence to reach his contrarian conclusions. He saw home prices rising in his Southampton, New York, neighborhood. One of his analysts thought to gather data on home prices going back to 1975, leading to the hallelujah moment when Paulson saw that inflation-adjusted prices nationwide had risen faster after 2000 than before.

These were thin reeds on which to rest big bets. But big bets against subprime-linked securities were what Paulson now placed. He sought to borrow the securities in question and sell them, in the expectation that he could buy them back at lower prices in the not-too-distant future.

One indication of the size of those bets was the difficulty Paulson had in finding toxic securities to borrow in the requisite amounts. Easier, he concluded, was to create them. If those dubious securities could then be successfully sold to other investors, Paulson could borrow and sell them in anticipation of the subsequent price decline.

This was the effort in which he now enlisted Goldman Sachs. With Goldman's help, Paulson selected the mortgage-backed securities to which his tailor-made CDO would be linked. He rejected mortgages originated by well-known banks like Wells Fargo in favor of those of dubious entities like First Franklin Bank of California. Down payments on First Franklin mortgages averaged a paltry 7 percent. Thirty-seven percent of its mortgages were interest-only loans; the homeowner's payments were limited to interest in the initial years but then required balloon payments of principal down the road. Many featured loan-to-value ratios in excess of 100 percent, meaning the loan was more than the price of the property.

These were the mortgages most at risk now that the market had turned down. Hence the CDOs they backed were most likely to decline in price. They were the perfect securities for Paulson to borrow and sell, given his negative outlook on the housing market.

Paulson paid Goldman Sachs a cool $15 million for the privilege of attaching the bank's name to the resulting CDO. Specifically Goldman attached the Abacus name, Abacus being one of the first CDO programs the bank had launched in 2004 and one in which IKB had already invested. An abacus is, of course, a device intended to help the user add and subtract. IKB, it turned out, needed all the help it could get.

The German bank appears to have been aware of the possibility of conflict of interest. It informed Goldman Sachs that it would buy additional mortgage-linked CDOs only if Goldman arranged for a third party to co-manage the deal. Goldman brought in ACA Management, a CDO specialist, to double-check Paulson's arithmetic. It seems unlikely that this particular firm was chosen at random. ACA's parent, the ACA Financial Guaranty

Group, had only a single-A rating from Standard & Poor's, rendering its bond insurance products uncompetitive. ACA, in other words, was desperate for business. And business was what Abacus offered.[20]

ACA met with Paulson & Co. and with Fabrice Tourre, the Goldman vice president in charge, in January 2007. Its analysts approved 55 of 123 mortgage pools submitted by Paulson, took the fees and lent its imprimatur. But it did not obviously understand the deal or Paulson's plan of betting against it, since ACA purchased $42 million of Abacus securities for its own account and issued credit default swaps guaranteeing nearly $1 billion of the senior tranche.[21]

IKB bought $150 million of notes when the deal, known as Abacus 2007-AC1, closed in April 2007. As an employee of Paulson & Co. put it in an internal email, banks like IKB had "neither the analytical tools nor the institutional framework" necessary to dive into the deep end of this particular pool.[22] With subprime mortgage defaults rising, the timing could not have been worse.[23] By early 2008, 100 percent of the bonds selected for Abacus 2007-AC1 had been downgraded, making it the worst-performing synthetic mortgage-related deal in history—a record that will stand forever given the impossibility of a downgrade rate greater than 100 percent. Within two years, half of the 500,000 mortgage loans backing the deal were in default or foreclosure. This testifies to Paulson's efficiency in selecting the mortgage pool. The $15 billion his firm cleared testifies to this even more powerfully.

By July 30, barely three months after Abacus 2007-AC1 closed, IKB was forced to restate its financials. It had financed its investments by issuing commercial paper backed by other assets. In a pattern that would be repeated more than once, it now lost access to this market and had to be bailed out by its creditors and the German government. Two other regional *Landesbanken*, Saxony-based Sachsen LB and the North Rhine–Westphalian state bank West LB, followed it down. In an ironic twist, IKB was eventually sold for pennies on the dollar to the US-based private equity shop Lone Star Funds.

———

Just ten days earlier, in releasing its quarterly financials, IKB had asserted that it would not be affected by mortgage losses in the United States. The obvious question, now that this claim was shown to be false, was whether similar problems lurked in the balance sheets of other banks. The financial crisis featured many misstatements, but few as glaring as Standard & Poor's response to the IKB announcement. On the day the bank restated its financials, Stefan Best, lead analyst of European banks for the rating agency, reassured a reporter that there was little reason to worry about other financial institutions. "So far the banks feel pretty comfortable," Mr. Best observed. "There is a pretty high threshold before they would take a hit."[24]

Anyone inclined to accept Best's prognosis was disabused of the notion when the French megabank BNP Paribas revealed that it too had incurred significant losses on subprime-related investments. Shortly before the markets opened on Monday, August 9, BNP announced it was suspending three in-house hedge funds because of problems with their holdings of US mortgage securities. Observers were startled to learn that the three funds, thought to be invested in euro-denominated money market instruments, were in fact heavily exposed to American subprime risk. BNP sought to calm its clients by blaming the funds' difficulties on exceptional liquidity problems and insisting they would recover when the markets normalized. More than 90 percent of the securities held by the three funds were rated AAA or AA, the firm's CEO, Baudouin Prot, reassuringly noted. It did not go unnoticed that this was the same reassurance Bear Stearns had provided just prior to suspending its two in-house funds.[25]

Not all financial crises have a definitive starting date, but this one clearly did. The 2007 crisis can be said to have erupted on August 9, the day of the BNP Paribas announcement. Realizing that if this land mine could have been hiding in BNP's financials it could be hiding anywhere, banks abruptly stopped lending to one another. The interbank market, on which banks trade liquidity overnight, seized up starting in Europe. Interbank rates tend to track the rate banks pay when borrowing money from the central bank, since central bank loans and interbank loans are close substitutes under normal circumstances.[26] But circumstances now were anything but normal. On August 9 interbank rates soared far above the ECB's target.

As yet, there were still no panicked depositors lining up outside European banks. But the collapse of the interbank market still threatened a crisis of the first order. European banks, recall, were even more leveraged than their American counterparts. They relied less on retail deposits and more on funds borrowed from other banks. Their distress was immediate and severe.

This finally was enough to galvanize a soporific European Central Bank into action. As recently as July 3, oblivious to the risk of a liquidity shortage, the ECB had raised interest rates. Liquidity, according to the presumption in Frankfurt, was an American problem. The BNP Paribas event at least had the salutary effect of shattering this illusion. At 10:26 a.m. Central European Time on August 9, less than ninety minutes after the start of trading, the ECB announced that it was ready to act. Two hours later it released a statement affirming its readiness to provide not just liquidity but *unlimited* amounts of liquidity.[27] The Fed may have provided liquidity to banks lending to distressed brokers and dealers following the Crash in 1929, but it had never made this kind of open-ended commitment. Even in Frankfurt they had evidently read Friedman and Schwartz.

———

This was just the kind of crisis that, as an economic historian, Chairman Bernanke had been studying for years. As the sun rose on Washington, D.C., the Fed injected $24 billion into US financial markets. In a press release issued the next day it affirmed its readiness to supply as many dollars as the markets required. "The Federal Reserve will provide reserves as necessary through open market operations," the central bank averred. "As always, the discount window is available as a source of funding." The Fed lent an additional $38 billion on August 10, coordinating the action with similar steps by the ECB and the central banks of Japan, Canada, Australia, and Hong Kong.

This, it could be argued, was exactly the response recommended by Friedman and Schwartz. The only problem was that this was no longer your mother's, or Friedman and Schwartz's, banking crisis. Central banks are in the business of lending to commercial banks. But this crisis, unlike that of 1930–1933, was not centered on commercial banks. Rather it centered, at least for the moment, on the shadow banking system of hedge funds, money market mutual funds, and commercial paper issuers, which were not the Fed's regular counterparties. This in turn meant that central bank interventions were less effective than supposed.

First to be infected were the hedge funds. Funds thought to be exposed to US mortgage risk suffered massive withdrawals, often by other funds. They were unable to obtain lines of credit, irrespective of whether the Fed provided banks with liquidity, because banks refused to lend. Fund managers dumped mortgage-related securities in response, creating losses for other fund managers. These were not problems that either federal deposit insurance or central bank lending to commercial banks could address.

Next to be infected was the market in asset-backed commercial paper. Large companies extending student loans and car loans and having credit-card and trade receivables customarily bundle them together and borrow against them for 90 to 180 days. Selling the resulting securities, known as asset-backed commercial paper, allows them to meet their expenses without having to wait for collections on the underlying assets. It is hard to overstate the importance of asset-backed commercial paper as a funding source for US banks and firms. As of August 2007, as much as $1.2 trillion worth of asset-backed commercial paper was outstanding. To put the figure in context, this was more than the value of all outstanding US treasury bills.[28]

Revealingly, the stock of asset-backed commercial paper had almost doubled in the preceding eighteen months. Supplies could have risen so rapidly, suddenly risk-conscious investors realized, only at the expense of credit quality. Mortgages and mortgage-related derivatives, they discovered to their horror, figured disproportionately among the assets backing recent commercial paper issues. This shouldn't have been a surprise, of course, since specialized mortgage originators like Countrywide Financial had long been among the principal issuers.[29]

Issuers of asset-backed commercial paper, like banks, were in the business of issuing liquid short-term debt to finance illiquid investments. Consequently, when investors pulled the plug, the result was not unlike a slow-motion bank run. In July 2007 only 5 percent of issuers had been unable to roll over their outstanding commercial paper when it matured. By the end of August this fraction was up to 25 percent. By the end of November it was 40 percent.[30] This run on the commercial paper market, like the run on the hedge funds, was a phenomenon to which the provision of federal deposit insurance was, at best, irrelevant.[31]

The liquidity crisis sparked by the collapse of the commercial paper market quickly infected the corporate and financial sectors. Countrywide Financial, now holding the poisoned chalice as the nation's largest mortgage lender, averted bankruptcy only by arranging a costly $11.5 billion credit line from a consortium of banks. Ameriquest, once the largest US subprime specialist, was forced to wind down its remaining operations.

———

The next domino to fall was the British building society Northern Rock. The Rock, as it liked to be called to indicate its solidity, was an amalgam of two venerable Newcastle building societies, the Northern Counties Permanent Building Society and the Rock Building Society, which dated from the nineteenth century. A building society is the British equivalent of a credit union, a cooperative financial institution owned and operated by its members. The species acquired its name from having been founded by workers in the building trades. Building societies tend to specialize in mortgage lending. Northern Rock was one of the larger and, for many years, more successful examples of the type.

But rapid expansion of the sort to which its executives aspired could not be financed by members' subscriptions alone. Northern Rock first sought to acquire other building societies. This being inadequate to satisfy management's appetite for funding, the society was demutualized. Taking advantage of the freedom conferred by Margaret Thatcher's big-bang financial reforms,

Northern Rock followed the example of building societies like Abbey National and the Halifax, converting itself into a bank and thereby enabling management to float shares on the London Stock Exchange.

No longer having members looking over their shoulders, the management team, led by Adam Applegarth, sought to grow the bank at breakneck speed. Applegarth was a local, born in Sunderland, and a graduate of Durham University. He joined the bank straight out of university and rose quickly through the ranks, being appointed CEO in 2001 at the age of thirty-eight. Applegarth's most prominent attributes, along with his ambition and love of sports, which made him a boon drinking companion and endeared him to his bank colleagues, were supreme confidence and a willingness to take risks. Northern Rock under Applegarth adopted all the trappings of a progressive twenty-first-century mortgage lender. The bank financed its operations not by attracting deposits but by borrowing from other financial institutions; it relied on wholesale funding more heavily than any other UK financial institution. It loosened down-payment requirements for mortgage borrowers to increase its market share. Its signature product, the "Together loan," allowed homeowners to borrow as much as 125 percent of the value of their home.[32] The bank opened branches in shopping centers, à la Countrywide. It offered high interest rates to attract Internet deposits. It outsourced mortgage origination to independent brokers. It securitized and sold off its loans, raising money for yet further operations, through a special purpose vehicle with the solid-sounding name of Granite on the tax-advantaged island of Jersey.

All this allowed Northern Rock to expand at a 20 percent annual rate for the better part of two decades. But, as should have been evident to anyone observing this rapid expansion, it also allowed vulnerabilities to build up. With the development of problems in the US market, Northern Rock found itself unable to securitize and sell off its loans.[33] And in the wake of the August 9 BNP announcement, the wholesale money market collapsed. In effect, the two obvious avenues for raising cash, selling off mortgage-backed securities to investors and borrowing from other banks, dried up simultaneously.

On August 10 Applegarth huddled with his board chairman, Matthew Ridley. Ridley was a onetime journalist and libertarian philosopher turned mass-market author. The celebrity sire of an old Northumberland family, his most successful book, *The Red Queen*, used a character from Lewis Carroll's *Through the Looking-Glass* to illustrate a theory of sexual reproduction. Popular science has its place, but that place is not obviously the boardroom. This background, in other words, did not qualify Ridley to advise on how to cope with a liquidity crisis. Nor did Applegarth have other ready sources of advice.

Aside from Ridley, Northern Rock's board was dominated by local notables like Andrew Fenwick, a member of the department-store family of the same name. These individuals added luster to the masthead, but none was capable of restraining an ambitious CEO, much less managing a funding crisis.

———

To raise liquidity Applegarth was reduced to selling off assets for whatever he could get. What he could get, unfortunately, was not enough, once-liquid securities now fetching only rock bottom prices. At this point, Applegarth had no choice but to appeal to the Bank of England, as he did starting in mid-August. Finally on Thursday, September 13, after a month of lobbying, he obtained his long-sought "liquidity support facility." The plan was to announce it the following Monday, leaving the weekend for a calming publicity campaign. Unfortunately, the decision leaked on Thursday night, leaving no time for preparations. The timing was doubly unfortunate for the fact that the Chancellor of the Exchequer, Alisdair Darling, and the governor of the Bank of England, Mervyn King, were committed to traveling to Portugal on Friday for a regularly scheduled meeting of EU officials. Canceling the trip would have fed the sense of panic, but in the absence of King and Darling it was not clear who was minding the store.

Nor did it help that the UK possessed a limited deposit-insurance scheme that fully covered only the first £2,000 of deposits. Up to £35,000, there was then a partial guarantee, and above that there was none. Britain had not suffered a bank run in 150 years—not even in the Great Depression, when the decision to go off the gold standard had enabled the Bank of England to cut interest rates and provide liquidity support to financial institutions and markets. Given this history, a comprehensive guarantee designed to head off runs seemed superfluous.

But simply because something hadn't happened in 150 years was no guarantee, as it were, that it couldn't happen in the circumstances of 2007. Investors immediately realized that the country's deposit-insurance scheme did not provide much in the way of assurance. On Friday morning panicked depositors swamped Northern Rock's website with requests for withdrawals, causing its servers to crash. Fearing that it was deliberately failing to process their requests, customers lined up outside its branches, attracting camera crews. Overwhelmed tellers barricaded themselves in the bank's offices. King and Darling, in Porto, were reduced to watching these events on TV.

In the course of the day, panicked clients withdrew more than £1 billion, the equivalent of 5 percent of the bank's retail deposits. Queues again formed outside branches in Sheffield and North London the next morning, and the constabulary was called for crowd control. Sunday was an enforced holiday, but withdrawals resumed on Monday. That evening Darling, fearing contagion to other banks, was forced to issue a taxpayer-backed guarantee of Northern Rock's deposits.

No one emerged from this episode with his reputation enhanced. The Financial Services Authority, the lead supervisor, had clearly done too little to discourage Northern Rock from adopting a risky business model. It focused mechanically on whether the bank met the Basel II requirements for capital adequacy while neglecting its breakneck expansion and risky funding. Its stress tests failed to anticipate, much less incorporate, the kind of liquidity problems Northern Rock would experience in 2007. When blame was parceled out, the FSA paid a high price. It was first stripped of all meaningful regulatory authority and then abolished in 2013.

The Bank of England under King similarly underestimated the gravity of the threat. Already in mid-August Northern Rock had approached the bank for assistance but was rebuffed. Bank of England officials made it clear that Northern Rock should find a market solution. On September 12, just days before central bank officials concluded they had no choice but to provide exceptional liquidity support, King wrote the House of Commons affirming his belief that the banking system, of which Northern Rock was part, was capable of handling its own problems. If Northern Rock found it impossible to raise the requisite capital and liquidity, then it should be acquired by a stronger rival.[34]

This was a misreading. It was never realistic to think that another bank might acquire Northern Rock, given the opacity of its balance sheet. This was a lesson that US policy makers would learn when Lehman Brothers faced its existential crisis in 2008. At a minimum, the acquiring institution would have demanded a backstop facility from the Bank of England, something Governor King was reluctant to provide.[35] The idea that Northern Rock might regain access to the wholesale money market was equally fantastic. And management knew it. Receiving the cold shoulder from the Bank of England, they explored using the bank's single branch in the Republic of Ireland to obtain liquidity from the more accommodating ECB, before concluding that this was problematic from a legal standpoint.

The attitude of Bank of England officials is not easy to understand. Part of the explanation may be that Britain had not experienced a bank run on Governor King's watch. Indeed it had not experienced a full-fledged bank run since 1866, as noted above. The absence of a recent bank run to concentrate the mind was similarly part of why Montagu Norman did not feel the same urgency as his American counterpart, George Harrison, to provide emergency assistance to Germany when the 1931 banking crisis showed signs of leapfrog-ging to London. But if memories of the bank-run problem were remote in 1931, they were even more remote in 2008.

Another factor may be that King and others at the Bank of England were imperfectly informed of the situation facing Northern Rock. The central bank had been stripped of many regulatory duties in 1997 when it was granted independence from the Treasury. Central bank independence was a way of depoliticizing monetary policy, something that the newly formed government of Tony Blair sought to do in order to demonstrate its economic bona fides. But if the Bank of England was going to be independent, then it needed to be cut down to size. Responsibility for supervision and regula-tion was therefore shifted to the Financial Services Authority. Officially, the FSA cooperated with the Bank of England and the Treasury. But as in any bureaucracy where information is power, there was a gap between principle and practice.

As a result, Bank of England officials were uncertain about whether they possessed complete, up-to-date information on the condition of the banks. This reinforced their reluctance to become involved in the problems of individ-ual financial institutions. In any case, preventing financial instability was now officially someone else's problem. And bailing out distressed financial institu-tions too freely might only encourage neglect on the part of that someone else, the FSA.

This brings us to the most important factor, namely the preoccupation of King and his colleagues with moral hazard. The governor was critical of the ECB's decision on August 8 following the suspension of the two BNP Paribas funds to provide the markets with unlimited amounts of liquidity. In his September 12 letter to the House of Commons, he warned that provid-ing banks with liquidity against a wider range of collateral would encourage excessive risk taking.[36] "The provision of large liquidity penalizes those finan-cial institutions that sat out the dance," King wrote, echoing Chuck Prince. It "encourages herd behavior and increases the intensity of future crises." The implication was that liquidity would be provided only at a penalty rate after other options were exhausted.

This hard line against moral hazard was quite different from the lend-now-and-ask-questions-later approach of the Bernanke Fed. Again, it is worth recalling that the Bank of England, unlike the Fed, had not experienced a full-blown banking panic in 150 years. As a result, Friedman and Schwartz's narrative leading to the conclusion that the central bank's first responsibility is to head off a panic, after which there would be ample time to deal with moral hazard, was not assimilated to the same extent.

The effort to teach a lesson to the Adam Applegarths of the world came at a high price. The Labour government, seemingly making things up as it went, was compelled to issue a blanket guarantee of Northern Rock's deposits despite the fact that it lacked clear statutory authority to do so. After adopting a hard line on moral hazard, the Bank of England was forced to open the floodgates, providing emergency liquidity. Applegarth resigned in November. Ridley was removed as chairman, and other board members followed him out the door. Failing to find a buyer, the government nationalized the bank the following February. In the five months Northern Rock was left in limbo, losses continued to mount. Eventually, in 2012, the remnants of the Rock were sold to Virgin Money for £820 million, leaving British taxpayers with losses of more than £2 billion. This was a high price tag for the slow and inconsistent response of officials.

And the fact that Britain experienced its first bank run in 150 years did not reassure observers of the condition of its financial system or the competence of its authorities.

CHAPTER 12

Scant Evidence

A T THIS POINT, the third week of September, conditions showed every sign of spiraling out of control. Fire sales by Northern Rock and other banks put downward pressure on asset prices, inflicting losses on investors. A problem that had once seemed confined to hedge funds invested in subprime-linked securities and building societies with extensive commitments to the mortgage market was now creating very serious problems for investors of all types.

Prominent among those other investors were money market mutual funds in the United States. Although money market funds had been around since the 1970s, as explained in Chapter 4, their devotion to commercial paper was new. With the growth of alternative investment vehicles, money funds had found it increasingly challenging to attract and retain investors. An obvious way of doing so, as we also saw in Chapter 4, was by offering higher returns. This they sought to do by replacing the treasury bills in their portfolios with higher-yielding commercial paper.

The most venerable money market fund, Reserve Primary Fund, was a case in point. For many years its managers had followed a conservative strategy, offering their liquidity- and safety-minded investors a return slightly below that on high-quality short-term corporate debt. But as they saw their customers lured away by other investment vehicles offering higher returns, they responded by adding more asset-backed commercial paper, first slowly and then sharply in 2007.[1]

The Securities and Exchange Commission was not unaware of this tendency to stretch for yield. It therefore limited money funds to holding AAA or AA-rated commercial paper.[2] This quaint regulation hailed from the bygone era when defaults on high-grade commercial paper were rare. This would not be the last time the SEC was shown as behind the curve.

Nor did the Fed's injection of liquidity into the banking system afford money funds much relief. It did not relieve the stress on the commercial paper market, given that banks now refused to buy or lend against suddenly illiquid asset-backed paper. Failing to relieve the stress on the commercial paper market, it similarly failed to relieve the pressure on the money funds.

Investors had been told that a dollar in a money market account, like a dollar in a bank, would always be worth a dollar. News to the contrary—that a money market fund had suffered losses and was unable to return one hundred cents on the dollar—could therefore cause them to flee. Indeed this problem of investor panic was even greater for money market mutual funds than for banks. Unlike bank accounts, money market mutual fund accounts were not covered by federal deposit insurance. And unlike banks, money market mutual funds had no capital—no additional resources with which to absorb losses.

The only solution under the circumstances was for money market funds to be rescued by their parents, whether commercial banks or fund families. In the second half of 2007, forty-three money market mutual funds were quietly bailed out this way. These sponsor-based rescues replenished their balance sheets. They prevented investor runs for the time being. But they also created false confidence that runs were unlikely. They encouraged the false belief that there was little risk of even the highest-yielding funds "breaking the buck"—breaking the promise that a dollar in a money market account would always be worth a dollar.[3] That false confidence would come back to haunt investors—and policy makers—a year later when even more severe turmoil put those parent banks and fund families at risk.

———

The hedge-fund run, the collapse of the market in asset-backed commercial paper, and the bailout of money market mutual funds were enough to convince policy makers that they had a situation on their hands. The Fed cut the discount rate by half a percentage point on August 17, eight days after the BNP announcement. To reassure investors that adequate funding would be available, it offered to lend for thirty days rather than just overnight. It then cut rates a second time, by an additional fifty basis points (half a percent), in mid-September. To lubricate the interbank market, it purchased $47 billion of securities from "primary dealers," the big banks with whom it regularly did business. On December 11 it cut policy rates (both the discount rate and the federal funds rate) by an additional twenty-five basis points. On December 12, sparking some controversy, it announced the creation of a Term Auction

Facility through which it would lend to all depository institutions and not just primary dealers. On January 22, acting exceptionally between regularly scheduled FOMC meetings, it cut the federal funds rate by an additional seventy-five basis points. Eight days later, at the next regularly scheduled meeting, it reduced the funds rate by another fifty points.

This was an impressively rapid response, demonstrating that Fed officials understood full well how to respond to signs of financial distress. This was not new knowledge. As we saw in Chapter 7, George Harrison and his colleagues had understood equally how to respond to the financial distress caused by the 1929 crash. But now the lessons of that history were clearly drawn. The response of the Bernanke Fed was even more forceful.

In addition, Bernanke and Co. avoided the mistake of 1931, when Harrison hesitated to aid European banks in distress, allowing the crisis to infect still other countries.[4] The destruction that could be wrought by inadequate international cooperation was another lesson widely drawn from the Great Depression.[5] In response, central banks invested in arrangements for fostering such cooperation, for example repurposing the Bank for International Settlements from a reparations bank to a venue for regular exchange of views on the part of monetary officials. The result was more scope for international cooperation.

One example of this was how, starting on December 12, the Fed made credit available to a Europe desperate for dollar funding by negotiating currency swaps with the European Central Bank and the Swiss National Bank. Trading dollars for euros and francs enabled the ECB and SNB to make dollars available to their banks.[6] In time, these swap agreements would be criticized by, among others, libertarian congressman and perennial presidential candidate Ron Paul for putting the Fed's balance sheet at risk. In fact it was the ECB and SNB, not the Fed, that bore the risk of European banks not being able to repay what they borrowed.

In addition, the Fed lent dollars directly to European commercial banks via the discount window—that is, by taking their paper directly. On August 20 the US subsidiary of Commerzbank borrowed $350 million from the Fed. Deutsche Bank borrowed $2.4 billion on November 8. Calyon, the corporate banking arm of the French bank Crédit Agricole, borrowed $2 billion.

As subsidiaries of foreign banks, these entities were not required to hold capital to back their US operations, the belief being that their European parents stood behind them. Lacking reserves of their own, Calyon and the American subsidiaries of Deutsche Bank and Commerzbank relied on their ability to sell asset-backed commercial paper when the need for dollar liquidity arose. But markets in asset-backed commercial paper were now frozen, and the foreign parents in question had only limited dollars of their own. They were thus forced to turn to the Fed. Although the three foreign bank subsidiaries posted collateral for their loans, this would not have calmed Congressman Paul, who—had he known—would have screamed bloody murder about the Fed bailing out foreign-owned financial institutions.[7] Together with borrowing at the discount window being seen as a sign of weakness, this explains why the transactions in question were kept quiet.

The fiscal policy response was similarly rapid by Washington standards. Negotiations between Congress and the White House began in earnest in January 2008. Although the Democrat-controlled Congress and Republican executive did not agree on the composition of a fiscal stimulus, with the Republicans favoring tax cuts and the Democrats preferring increases in food stamps and unemployment benefits, they agreed to split the difference. A $150 billion stimulus, the equivalent of 1 percent of GDP, comprising $100 billion of tax cuts and $50 billion of spending, was passed after less than a month. The administration agreed not to push for a Bush-style tax policy—it agreed that the tax cuts could be temporary rather than permanent—while the Democrats agreed to additional investment deductions for business. The first rebate checks went out in April. This was an impressive display of bipartisanship to which policy makers found it difficult to rise subsequently.

––––––

Leading to the question: Why did it fail to avert the worst?

A first answer is that, fast as it was, the policy response was inadequate given the powerful negative impulse in the pipeline. By the end of 2007 the economy was already in recession. Yet there was still little awareness of how rapidly the outlook was shifting. As a result, following the policy measures of late 2007 and early 2008 there were no comparably significant policy initiatives to support a weakening economy by the Fed or the Congress in the late spring and summer of 2008.

Consider the Fed. At its October 2007 meeting the Federal Open Market Committee acknowledged only a modest slowing of growth and noted "scant evidence" that the correction in the housing market was spilling over to the rest of the economy. As late as the summer of 2008, real-time data suggested that the economy was continuing to expand. At midyear, forecasts for the second half of 2008 were still for continued growth.[8] As late as the August 2008 meeting of the Federal Open Market Committee, Richmond Reserve Bank president Jeffrey Lacker expressed skepticism "about the magnitude of the drag on consumption and investment spending that credit market conditions are likely to create."[9] At the mid-September 2008 meeting of the committee, members were still anticipating "sluggish growth" in the second half of the year.[10]

Even at this late date, in the aftermath of Lehman Brothers, there was still limited appreciation, then, of how the financial system was amplifying the shock to the housing market. There was still little understanding of the broader implications. The Fed had reduced policy rates sharply between August 2007 and January 2008 in response to signs of slower economic growth. There were a couple of more reductions in rates at the time of the Bear Stearns crisis in March and April 2008, but these were small by comparison. Much like its predecessor in late 1929, at this point the Fed concluded that its work was done.

Later—too much later—the Fed would cut policy rates further, all the way to zero. It would adopt unconventional policies of quantitative easing (large-scale purchases of treasury bonds and mortgage-backed securities) to provide more support for the economy. It would take radical steps to unfreeze financial markets. Hindsight suggests that it should have moved more quickly and aggressively, taking these kinds of steps already in early 2008. But exceptional action could be justified only by the threat of an exceptional slowdown. And, as yet, awareness of this threat was not there.

As a student of the Great Depression, Bernanke was more concerned than many of his colleagues, and many of the regional Reserve bank presidents serving on the Federal Open Market Committee in particular, that mounting financial problems might now lead to a serious recession.[11] Those other members of the Fed's policy-making committee viewed developments not through the lens of the 1920s and 1930s but through that of the post-1970 experience on which they were weaned. The decade of the 1970s had been one of inflation, when the Fed veered seriously off track, and the preoccupation of subsequent monetary policy makers was inflation, not crisis. Even now, with the economy on the brink of the most serious crisis in eighty years, it was those fears of inflation that continued to shape their outlook and guide their thinking.

Their specific worry in the wake of the sharp interest rate cuts taken between August 2007 and January 2008 was that the Fed would be too slow to "take back" the liquidity it had given the markets, leading to a surge of inflation. The fact that food and fuel prices were rising, owing as it happened to strong demands from China, seemed to some to validate those fears. At the FOMC's April 2008 meeting, Philadelphia Fed president Charles Plosser warned of the danger that higher energy and commodity prices would cause producers, facing higher costs, to mark up the prices of other goods (that so-called headline inflation would be passed through into core inflation cleansed of volatile food- and fuel-related components). Richmond's Lacker warned that "persistently high headline numbers could become ingrained in household and business decisionmaking." Kansas City's Thomas Hoenig warned of "significant inflation pressure from goods prices, especially imported goods prices."[12] Bernanke pushed back, suggesting that what these gentlemen were observing was a change in relative prices—higher food and fuel prices accompanied by more slowly rising prices of other goods and services. But policy was made by consensus, and the consensus view was shaped by memories of the inflationary 1970s, not the crisis-ridden 1930s.

Those fears of inflation largely immobilized the Fed's policy-making committee until after the failure of Lehman Brothers in September, and even then some members were strikingly slow to revise their outlook. Chairman Bernanke may have known better, but again policy was made not according to the chair's dictates but by committee. And Bernanke's committee was more consensus-oriented than most. Some previous Fed chairs might have imperiously overridden colleagues' objections, but this was not Bernanke's way. The result was that the Fed failed to do more. With private lending contracting, the result was a de facto contractionary policy and inadequate monetary support for the economy.

Similarly, a fiscal stimulus of 1 percent of GDP was too little to make a difference given the negative impulse in the pipeline. Banks, firms, and households were all deleveraging furiously. The majority of the stimulus, recall, took the form of rebate checks, perhaps only half of which the recipients went out and spent.[13] A stimulus five times as large would be adopted a year later, and some would argue that even this was too small. With hindsight, we can say that a bit of additional stimulus at the beginning of 2008 might have averted the need for very much larger stimulus in 2009. More public spending in 2008 to offset retrenchment by households and firms would have meant a more slowly decelerating economy, fewer bad loans, and stronger financial institutions. Whether it would have significantly altered the course of events, given the already tenuous state of affairs, we will never know.

Whatever the answer, doing more at the beginning of 2008 could be justified only if there was awareness that conditions were deteriorating rapidly. And, again, such awareness was not there. Congress would have to see a much more serious crisis before it was prepared to pass the $800 billion Troubled Asset Relief Program in October 2008 or the $787 billion Obama stimulus in 2009.

What this episode reveals is that better understanding of how policy should respond to changes in economic and financial conditions is not enough when evidence of those changes is incomplete. The evidence at the time did not convince officials that economic conditions were deteriorating rapidly. Though they may have understood better than their predecessors in 1929 how to react to such a deterioration, this alone did not guarantee an adequate response. One reason the Fed did not do more in 1929 was that, in the wake of the Crash, observers believed the economy was continuing to expand.[14] One reason the Fed did not do more in the last months of 2007 was again that observers, even though aware that growth was slowing, believed the economy was continuing to expand. Having themselves now lived through such an episode, modern critics are likely to show more sympathy for 1920s policy makers, who, in the early stages of their crisis, faced significant uncertainty about the state of the economy.

In addition, just as every generation writes its own history, to paraphrase the 1916 comment by the president of the American Historical Association, H. Morse Stephens, every generation remembers its own history.[15] For many members of the FOMC in 2008, the influential history was that of high inflation some thirty years earlier—that is, in their own lifetimes—rather than the more distant echoes of a Depression-era past. For members of Congress, the relevant history was of recent decades characterized by chronic budget deficits, not of a Depression-era crisis when additional government spending could have been part of the solution and not the problem.

The parallel with the 1930s, then, is direct. In the 1930s Federal Reserve officials, looking to the preceding period when sharp increases in interest rates signaled financial distress, took the decline in interest rates following the Great Crash as a sign that there was no need for policy makers to do more. This historically rooted preoccupation caused officials to misinterpret the decline in interest rates—to see it as evidence that policy was accommodating rather than that all demand for credit had evaporated. Policy, as a result, was inadequately supportive of the economy, and the consequences were disastrous.

Now, in 2008, Federal Reserve officials looking back on the 1970s took the rise in headline inflation as evidence that monetary stimulus was excessive and that more would be counterproductive. This historically rooted preoccupation with inflation caused them to misinterpret the rise in food and fuel prices, which was being driven by China and not by their own policies. As a result, policy was again inadequately supportive of the economy. And, again, the consequences were disastrous.

A final reason policy failed to avert the worst was that policy was still targeted at the banks, while many of the most treacherous problems were, in fact, in the shadow banking system. Providing the banks with liquidity, whether through the discount window or the Term Auction Facility, did nothing to relieve the stress on mortgage securitizers, commercial paper issuers, and money market mutual funds, given the banks' reluctance to lend to their shadowy counterparts.

Eventually the Fed would attack this problem by purchasing securitized mortgages, asset-backed commercial paper, and related assets directly. But not in 2007, and not until conditions had deteriorated further. The 1930s crisis centered on the banking system. Influenced by that history, it was to the banking system that the Fed now looked. Lending to banks was the Fed's bread and butter. Extraordinary circumstances would be required before established practice could be discarded. And in the second half of 2007, policy makers were not yet there. There had been resistance within the Fed, on moral hazard grounds, to creating the Term Auction Facility through which the central bank lent to counterparties other than the primary dealers. In addition there would have been external resistance, from Representative Paul and others, had the Fed adopted even more unconventional policies, buying mortgage-related securities for example, while there was still "scant evidence" of a slowdown.

―――――

In the absence of a more forceful response, industrial production declined in January 2008, again in February, and again in March.[16] The Dow Jones average continued to slide, its cumulative fall reaching 20 percent.[17] Still, the markets were unprepared for what came next, next being Bear Stearns. The run on Bear marked a new stage in the crisis. It was a run not on a hedge fund, a money fund, or an issuer of asset-backed commercial paper but on a bank with open trades with five thousand other financial and nonfinancial firms.[18] The run on Bear demonstrated that the banks at the center of the financial system, and not just their shadowy counterparts, were now fundamentally at risk.

That Bear Stearns became a target was no coincidence. It was the smallest of the Big Five investment banks. It had been singled out of the herd by the failure of its two hedge funds the previous summer. Its former CEO and still board chairman Jimmy Cayne had been publicly portrayed as more interested in golf, bridge, and marijuana than the fate of his company.

Bear was also highly leveraged. With little capital of its own, in order to meet obligations it depended entirely on the goodwill and forbearance of its lenders. It had been attempting to raise additional capital, but without success. It was heavily invested in Alt-A mortgages, which were just one step up from subprime. Cayne's successor as CEO, Alan Schwartz, was a onetime professional baseball pitcher turned investment banker who had worked his way up through the ranks. Schwartz was known for being easygoing and even-tempered, in contrast to Cayne, but complex derivative securities were not part of his repertoire.

On learning about the firm's derivatives positions on the fly, Schwartz recognized that Bear Stearns couldn't stay afloat without a cash infusion. The firm had been attempting to obtain it by selling its derivatives holdings to Blackrock, PIMCO, or another stronger financial player. But against the backdrop of the unfolding crisis, those positions were now impossible to dispose of even at a loss. The effort to do so would inevitably become public knowledge, causing investors to conclude that the seller was mortally wounded.

On Monday, March 10, Moody's downgraded the mortgage-backed debt of yet another Bear Stearns fund, fueling rumors about the condition of its parent. Whether the value of Bear's portfolio of securities was in fact sufficient to meet its obligations was unclear, now that markets had seized up, and it was impossible to obtain price quotations from buyers. It could be that Bear was solvent and the situation could be stabilized by an infusion of cash or a takeover by a stronger, deep-pocketed competitor. But there was also the possibility that the fundamental value of its mortgage securities had fallen so far that the bank was broke, in which case its lenders would be wise to get out before it was too late. No one knew for sure.

What followed was essentially a run by the other large financial institutions that had provided Bear Stearns with liquid funds. One after another, lenders refused the firm's collateral, forcing it to meet commitments with cash. Where Bear had started the week with $18 billion of cash and liquid securities, by Thursday night its cash balances had fallen to less than $2 billion.

At this point there was no question that when the firm opened on Friday morning it would be out of cash and out of business. On Thursday night Schwartz communicated the bad news to Federal Reserve Bank of New York President Timothy Geithner. This gave the Fed just hours to put in place emergency assistance sufficient to get Bear to the weekend, over which a more durable solution might be reached.

Schwartz's decision to call Geithner was revealing. The Fed was not Bear Stearns' regulator, that dubious distinction belonging to the Securities and Exchange Commission, Bear formally being a dealer in securities. But the SEC, having been set up to oversee securities brokers, was over its head in seeking to regulate, much less resolve, what was in reality a bank with an exceedingly complex balance sheet. In 2007 its inspectors had meekly signed off on Bear's accounts. When SEC chairman Christopher Cox learned that Schwartz was reaching out to the government, he confidently assured Treasury Secretary Hank Paulson that the firm was sound and would find a buyer in a matter of weeks.[19]

Though the Fed was not in the business of regulating, much less lending to, investment banks, it had something more important, namely the power of the printing press. It was the only government agency able to come up with large amounts of money overnight. The solution agreed to at 8:00 a.m. on the morning of Friday, March 14, an hour before the markets opened, was for the Fed to lend $12.9 billion to JPMorgan Chase, a bank that the Fed did regulate and that not incidentally was the dominant player in the market in which Bear Stearns obtained its short-term funds.[20] JPMorgan would then pass the money on to Bear in a so-called back-to-back transaction.

Significantly, the loan to JPMorgan was nonrecourse. In other words, although Bear Stearns put up collateral in the form of securities notionally valued at some $14 billion, the central bank and not JPMorgan was on the hook if those assets turned out to be worth less than the paper they were written on. This transaction thus exposed the Fed, and indirectly the taxpayer, to the risk of losses, since the Fed regularly turned its profits over to the Treasury. This realization was not received happily on Capitol Hill. It weakened public support for further interventions, the fear being that more liabilities for the taxpayer might be hiding behind the curtain. The financial system survived the Bear Stearns crisis. Faith in the central bank did not.

To justify its exposure to a non-commercial-banking firm, the board of governors invoked a heretofore obscure provision of the Federal Reserve Act permitting the central bank to lend not just to member banks but also to individuals and corporations under "unusual and exigent circumstances."[21] This provision was in fact yet another legacy of the Great Depression. In 1932 Congress had added a Section 13(b) to the Federal Reserve Act in response to business complaints that the banking crisis had interrupted the provision of private bank credit, and to populist concerns that the Federal Reserve was favoring finance over business (sound familiar?). Section 13(b) allowed the Fed to make loans to private business so long as circumstances were "unusual and exigent" and the borrowers were engaged in agricultural, industrial, and commercial transactions.

The provision was rarely used, but it remained on the books. It was broadened in 1991, in response to lobbying by Goldman Sachs, to permit the Fed, under what was now known as Section 13(3), to lend directly to securities firms in emergencies. Current circumstances clearly qualified.

———

That JPMorgan Chase was the middleman in this transaction was a fact freighted with irony. Pierpont Morgan's role in helping to contain the 1907 financial crisis was in a sense the event that had led to the founding of the Federal Reserve, given fears that a private crisis manager could turn rescue operations to his advantage. Morgan partner Thomas Lamont had played a prominent role in 1930, working with the New York Fed and New York State Banking Commission, in seeking to resolve the Bank of United States. JP Morgan Chase CEO Jamie Dimon was Sandy Weill's right-hand man when Weill engineered the Citicorp-Travelers merger that drove the final nail into the coffin of Glass-Steagall. Having moved on to head the Chicago-based Bank One, Dimon had then unsuccessfully attempted to purchase Bear Stearns, the very bank he was now being asked to rescue.

Dimon, like Owen Young before him, served on the board of the Federal Reserve Bank of New York. He was a graduate of Harvard College and a third-generation financier. The Bear Stearns crisis was an opportunity to step into the shoes Pierpont Morgan had worn in 1907. On the morning of Friday, March 14, when Geithner, Bernanke, Paulson, and other government officials considered whether to provide the $12.9 billion loan, Dimon was plugged into the phone call and spoke for the financial community, warning that the consequences of a Bear Stearns failure would be catastrophic. When the policy team convened a conference call with other bank CEOs later that morning, it was Dimon, not Geithner, Paulson, or Bernanke, who took the lead in fielding questions.[22]

The challenge was to find another bank capable of absorbing Bear Stearns. The task was not unlike the attempt to find a marriage partner for the Bank of United States in 1930. It now became apparent, not entirely to the surprise of certain of the principals, that JPMorgan Chase was the only plausible suitor. It had the size and, as clearing bank for Bear's transactions, some knowledge of its positions.

But the more closely Dimon's people scoured Bear Stearns' books, the more illiquid securities they unearthed. Bear had sold off the liquid ones in the struggle to stay alive. Dimon's solution lay in the fact that the government was desperate to find a buyer. He had the authorities over a barrel, and he knew it. On Sunday morning he announced that he was prepared to pursue the purchase only if the authorities took $30 billion of illiquid mortgage-linked securities off his hands.

There being no time for the Congress to approve, once more the Federal Reserve stepped into the breach. But the Fed couldn't purchase the securities of institutions like Bear Stearns, even under unusual and exigent circumstances; it could only lend to such entities. The central bank circumvented this restriction by drawing on one of the same financial-engineering devices that had contributed to the crisis. Instead of purchasing the assets of Bear Stearns, it created a special purpose vehicle, named Maiden Lane LLC after the street running alongside its New York branch, to do so for it. The Fed then "lent" to the SPV, which then turned around and purchased securities from Bear.

This now was a much larger and longer-term commitment than the central bank had taken previously, when lending Bear Stearns, via JPMorgan, $12.9 billion for a couple of days. Geithner and Bernanke therefore obtained a promise from Secretary Paulson that if Maiden Lane took losses on the transaction, Treasury would do its best to compensate the Fed.[23]

JPMorgan's management, from Dimon on down, was pleased by the deal. It allowed Dimon to position himself as savior of the financial system in the manner of Pierpont Morgan before him. It gave JPMorgan Chase a presence in prime brokerage, the business of providing financing to hedge funds, something it had lacked previously. Having initially offered $4 a share, Dimon had lowered the offer price to $2 on the advice of Paulson, who insisted on demonstrating that government assistance came at a heavy price. Ultimately, JPMorgan Chase upped its offer to $10 a share to prevent some of Bear's top talent, themselves investors in the company, from walking away.[24]

JPMorgan Chase ended up paying $1.5 billion for a bank that as recently as January 2007 had been valued at $20 billion and whose headquarters building at 383 Madison Avenue alone was worth close to $1.4 billion.[25] In his March 2009 letter to shareholders, Dimon asserted that he expected the Bear Stearns acquisition to contribute $1 billion of annual earnings to the company.[26] This was nothing if not a healthy annual return on a $1.5 billion investment.

Much later, in 2012, Dimon claimed that JPMorgan Chase made the purchase as a public service. "We did them [the government] a favor," he explained at the Council on Foreign Relations. "We were asked to do it, and we did it at great risk to ourselves."[27] Risk, of course, is not something with which bankers are unfamiliar. One senses an ex post rationalization of the fact that, rather than earning $1 billion a year, as expected, JPMorgan ended up taking losses on the assets it inherited and the lawsuits it incurred as a result of the Bear Stearns acquisition. There was also an undercurrent of resentment in Dimon's remarks, reflecting the fact that Treasury and the Fed did not come to his defense when the New York State attorney general filed a civil suit against JPMorgan Chase, alleging that Bear Stearns had deceived investors in mortgage-linked securities in 2006. To the contrary, the US Justice Department pursued JPMorgan for misrepresentation of the quality of securities sold to Fannie Mae and Freddie Mac, both by its own units and by the Bear Stearns units it now acquired, eventually reaching a settlement in which the bank agreed to pay $13 billion. As Dimon put it, when first acknowledging losses related to Bear Stearns, "And yes, I put it in the unfair category."

Dimon was not the only one with second thoughts. The Fed was criticized for exceeding its mandate. It was accused of encouraging risk taking by other firms that would now similarly expect official help if things went wrong. In fact, the Fed was ultimately (meaning, in 2012) repaid the entirety of its loan, with interest, once the mortgage-related securities acquired by Maiden Lane matured or were successfully sold off. In hindsight, this suggests that Geithner, Paulson, and Co. were right to diagnose Bear's problem as essentially a liquidity crisis and proceed with an emergency loan. Still, the criticism to which the central bank was subjected, and its own discomfort with these unprecedented interventions, would cause it to hesitate when it next faced an analogous problem.

The situation was not unlike 1933, when similar instincts were allowed to prevail. A Reconstruction Finance Corporation stung by criticism of its decision to rescue Charles Dawes' Central Republic chose to make a statement by allowing Henry Ford's Union Guardian to go under.[28] The result was the mother of all banking crises. One might think that this history would have informed decision making now. In the heat of the moment, it did not.

––––––

On Friday, July 11, the FDIC seized Indymac Bank, the S&L arm of the seventh-largest mortgage originator. An analyst from none other than Lehman Brothers warned that the government-sponsored housing companies Freddie Mac and Fannie Mae could be next.

Though it was hardly news that Freddie and Fannie had incurred losses, the Lehman report catalyzed the market's fears. Specifically, it excited the single largest purchaser of Freddie and Fannie's bonds, the Chinese government. To a greater extent than investors closer at hand, the Chinese continued to pay attention to the reports and analyses of the investment banks and rating agencies. As they now curtailed their purchases, shares in Freddie and Fannie cratered. Doubts grew about whether the government-sponsored entities would be able to fund themselves in future debt auctions.

Over the July 12–13 weekend, the Fed stepped once more into the breach, invoking unusual and exigent circumstances in order to add Freddie and Fannie to the list of mendicants with access to the discount window. Secretary Paulson asked the House and Senate for authority to inject capital into the two institutions. After two weeks of politicking, Congress agreed. The administration invoked that authority in September, placing Freddie and Fannie into conservatorship and guaranteeing their obligations. The mortgage giants were effectively nationalized.

Allowing Freddie and Fannie to fail was not an option, however much free-market purists might have wished otherwise. Fannie and Freddie, as holders of some $5 trillion of outstanding mortgage-backed securities, were an order of magnitude larger than Bear Stearns. With the collapse of the subprime market, they were purchasing or guaranteeing fully two-thirds of all new mortgages. The housing market, already reeling, could hardly be expected to absorb the consequences of closing them down.

This didn't mean, however, that Congress and the commentariat were happy about the fact. Paulson pushed hard for the enabling legislation, but his party pushed back. Congressional Republicans were irate about being asked to bail out a pair of GSEs they saw as subverting the free operation of the market. The Fed was dressed down for helping JPMorgan help Bear Stearns. This was nothing, however, compared to the criticism now heaped on Treasury for bailing out Freddie Mac and Fannie Mae. This criticism surely colored views of how to respond to the next crisis.

All this suggests that when the Lehman Brothers crisis erupted eight weeks later, Treasury and the Fed were looking to make a statement. With an election just two months off (notice again the proximity of crises to elections), they wanted to reassure the politicians that they too were weary of bailouts.

As a result, little was done to prepare for what, after the fact, was seen as the inevitable. It was not as if officials were unaware of Lehman's plight. The collapse of Bear Stearns had raised questions about the viability of the investment banking model of which Lehman was a prime exponent. The cost of buying insurance against Lehman's failure shot up once Bear's difficulties became known. The cost of buying protection against the failure of Morgan Stanley also rose, albeit less dramatically, indicating a clear hierarchy of concern. Paulson's telephone log recorded ten calls a month to Lehman CEO Dick Fuld between Bear Stearns' rescue in March and Lehman's failure in September. Paulson emphasized the need for Lehman to raise capital. Fuld emphasized the difficulty of doing so. He indicated in no uncertain terms that a strategic investor like JPMorgan Chase would be needed if his firm were to survive the release of its quarterly financial statement in September.

At the same time, the very fact that Lehman's problems were well known was reason for thinking it could go down without taking the financial system along with it. Investors had time to hedge their exposures and otherwise prepare. Or so it was believed, in particular by Chairman Bernanke, according to his subsequent testimony to the House Financial Services Committee. "The failure of Lehman posed risks," Bernanke acknowledged. "But the troubles at Lehman had been well known for some time, and investors clearly recognized—as evidenced, for example, by the high cost of insuring Lehman's debt in the market for credit default swaps—that the failure of the firm was a significant possibility. Thus, we judged that investors and counterparties had had time to take precautionary measures."[29]

The problem was that some risks are too big to hedge. This was the case of those of American International Group (AIG), which sold copious amounts of insurance against Lehman's failure. And some investors, in their wisdom, thought that the smart thing to do in the circumstances was to avoid incurring the cost of insurance. There may have been a tendency, in other words, to assume that because Bear Stearns was rescued the same treatment would be extended to Lehman Brothers.

———

But Lehman's problems ran deeper. It owned more toxic mortgages. It had more debt than Bear Stearns, in excess of $660 billion.

And Lehman had, if anything, even more dysfunctional management. If Jimmy Cayne's weakness was poker, Dick Fuld's was building his bank, whatever the cost. The grandson of one of Lehman's major clients, Fuld had joined the firm as an intern in 1969. He quickly became a successful bond trader, being endowed with the athleticism, combativeness, and profane mouth of the ilk. Fuld was promoted to head of the fixed income division and became CEO in 1994 when American Express divested itself of the bank. Fuld was conscious that his company lacked the size of JPMorgan Chase and the cachet of Goldman Sachs. For a hypercompetitive CEO, no strategy for correcting this unacceptable situation was too ambitious. And when those strategies went awry, Fuld, unlike Cayne, was not inclined to step aside.

Historians hesitate to hang world-changing events on personalities, exceptions like Friedman and Schwartz's attribution of the Great Depression to Benjamin Strong's untimely death notwithstanding. But Fuld's personality is unquestionably part of the explanation for why Lehman continued to move aggressively into real estate when other investment banks had already concluded that the jig was up. It explains why he refused to entertain an acquisition offer from the Korea Development Bank in the summer of 2008.[30]

And personality explains, if anything can, how Fuld could believe, when he preannounced Lehman's whopping $3.9 billion third-quarter loss in a conference call on September 10, that the markets would be reassured by his having a plan for winding down the bank's exposure to commercial and residential real estate. Fuld's plan, it turned out, was nothing more than placing the firm's real estate assets into an off-balance-sheet vehicle—unfortunately named "SpinCo." Just who would finance SpinCo was unclear, given that Lehman couldn't. Investors were quick to conclude that SpinCo was spin.

It was bad luck, or bad planning, that Fuld's conference call was announced on a Tuesday and not at the end of the week. News of the call was enough to send the company's stock into a tailspin. JPMorgan Chase, always the markets' friend, then demanded that Lehman put up an additional $5 billion in cash in order to maintain its credit line. That was all the cash Fuld had on hand, although he was able to temporarily replenish the piggy bank by borrowing on the repo market. The fact of someone still being confident that Lehman's collateral was good was notable in itself. It is powerful testimony to the enduring belief that the Treasury and Fed would find a way out.

What followed was a reprise of Bear Stearns weekend, with Bank of America CEO Ken Lewis playing the Jamie Dimon role. But Bank of America was already having trouble digesting the troubled mortgage lender Countrywide Financial, whose acquisition in January 2008 was Lewis's signal achievement. (After four years, Bank of America's acquisition of Countrywide came to be seen as "the worst deal in the history of American finance," in the words of Tony Plath, a University of North Carolina professor, a sentiment that was widely shared.[31]) If he was now going to do more, Lewis preferred to acquire Merrill Lynch with its Thundering Herd of sixteen thousand brokers (or "trusted financial advisors," as Merrill preferred to put it) and their three million brokerage accounts, as he did on Sunday, September 14.[32] Lehman's bad real estate investments were larger than Bear's, what with housing and mortgage-market conditions having continued to worsen. Where JPMorgan had succeeded in getting the authorities to take $30 billion of Bear Stearns assets, Lewis indicated on Friday that the comparable number for Lehman would be $40 billion. The following day he upped his estimate to $70 billion.

Treasury indemnification would again be needed for the New York Fed to contemplate buying, indirectly of course, $70 billion of Lehman Brothers' assets. But this is what Paulson now refused to provide. The treasury secretary had felt stinging criticism over earlier bailouts. He was on record as having dismissed Bear Stearns as a special case and insisting that it "was not something that we *ever* intend to repeat."[33] This was not a commitment on which he could easily go back.[34]

Paulson was further hamstrung by the fact that Treasury lacked open-ended authority to purchase mortgage-related assets, something it would acquire only with congressional passage of the Troubled Asset Relief Program in October. Although it was impractical now to sell off the $30 billion of Bear Stearns assets acquired in the spring, given the illiquidity of the markets, there was reason to think they would be worth something eventually (and, as noted above, the government ended up making money once they were sold). Lehman Brothers' assets, in contrast, were a write-off waiting to happen. As treasury secretary, Paulson later argued, he lacked the authority to subject taxpayer funds to this risk.

This may have been the factor that drove the decision to let Lehman go under. If so, it reflected the single most important policy failure of 2008.

Regulators had been watching Lehman at least since the Bear Stearns rescue in March.[35] They knew the firm's mortgage-related losses were mounting and that it was at risk of losing access to market funding.[36] They knew that they lacked the authority to lend to an insolvent institution, but equally that putting it through bankruptcy would be disastrous, since its obligations would be frozen for the duration. Yet nothing was done to endow Treasury with the authority to wind up Lehman in an orderly way in the six months between Bear and Lehman.

In part this was a failure of imagination—an unwillingness to believe that an institution several times the size of Bear could actually run into the wall. In part it was a political problem: given populist opposition to bailouts for big financial firms, Congress was reluctant to give Treasury additional powers until the alternative was for the economy to go off a cliff, as finally happened in October. In 1932 the Reconstruction Finance Corporation similarly lacked the authority to inject capital into insolvent financial institutions, limiting its efforts to contain the spreading crisis. Only when the worst financial crisis in U.S. history struck in 1933 did Congress finally pass the Emergency Banking Act, relaxing this constraint. If Great Depression scholars like Bernanke were aware of the precedent, their awareness did not now alter the course of events.

The decision—or nondecision—to give Treasury and the Fed the powers needed to seize and forcibly recapitalize an insolvent investment bank could be made only by Congress. Not for the first time, political passions rather than cool economic and historical logic shaped the response. Treasury had already gone once to the well, asking Congress for authority to bail out Freddie Mac and Fannie Mae, and Congress was decidedly reluctant to consider another such request. To further complicate matters, the decisions in question were being made in an election year. Against this backdrop, there was no willingness on the part of the administration to go to Congress in the summer of 2008 to request additional powers.[37]

This left only the option of assembling a consortium of banks to take the bad Lehman assets off Bank of America's hands. Staff and officials at the New York Fed scrambled to develop the requisite plan in the days prior to Lehman weekend. But it was never clear why other banks would be willing to play their part, given the toxic nature of Lehman's assets. In 1998 the New York Fed had successfully assembled a consortium of financial institutions to provide emergency liquidity support to the troubled hedge fund Long-Term Capital Management. This was the consortium in which Bear Stearns famously refused to participate. Still, that experience offered a model.

But LTCM, like Bear, had good if illiquid collateral. Lehman was a different story. One interpretation is that by opting for the private-sector solution,

Paulson and his colleagues were implicitly agreeing to let Lehman Brothers go bust, appropriately it can be argued insofar as it is not the role of the government to keep an insolvent institution afloat. A more plausible conclusion is that no one—not Lewis, not Paulson, and certainly not the SEC—knew how bad Lehman's balance sheet was until the weekend. They believed in the viability of the private-sector solution until it was too late. It was like Hoover's attempt to engineer a private-sector solution to the crisis in 1931, not realizing that for many banks the problem was one of solvency, not simply liquidity.

But if this is the explanation for the failure, it was a failure now of due diligence by the bank, its regulators, and its counterparties. It was a failure of the Treasury, Fed, and Congress to prepare for the worst. It was a failure of the system.

In a last-ditch effort, Paulson and his colleagues attempted to broker the sale of Lehman to Barclays, the big British bank having expressed an interest in a deal. But the possibility of consummating it over a weekend was always remote. If Lehman was big by US standards, it was even bigger by the standards of the British financial system. This was sure to give pause to the prospective buyer. Barclays could trace its origins back to goldsmith banking in the seventeenth century. It had not survived for more than three hundred years by taking leaps in the dark. The bank and its regulator, the Financial Services Authority, would need time to parse the books. Uncomfortably, Barclays, like JPMorgan in the case of Bear Stearns, would have to guarantee Lehman's trades even before the sale was consummated by a shareholder vote simply in order to keep the troubled bank afloat. Barclays was aware, in addition, that Bank of America, another potential suitor, had chosen to walk away.

On Sunday the FSA made clear that it had no intention of blessing the union. Lehman's fate was sealed. That the Barclays deal was even pursued testifies to the desperation to which US policy makers were driven.[38]

———

It was no secret that Treasury and the Fed had been working to find a buyer for Lehman Brothers, and the example of Bear Stearns created at least some confidence that they would succeed. Hence Lehman's failure was unexpected. The results were chaotic. With the authorities in denial, Lehman's bankruptcy filing was delayed until 1:45 a.m. on Monday morning. With Asian markets already open, judgment was swift. The market in Singapore slumped by 2.9 percent, Taiwan by 4.1 percent, India by 5.4 percent.[39]

Twelve hours passed before Paulson finally entered the White House press room to reassure the assembled that it was not the end of the world. His audience was not convinced. With $613 billion of debts, Lehman's was the largest bankruptcy in US history. The Dow fell by 504 points, or nearly 5 percent (its largest drop since the first trading day after September 11, 2001). Monday, September 15, 2008, was the worst day ever for the S&P financials, which closed down more than 10 percent.[40]

And if customer accounts at Lehman were not safe, who was to say the same might not be true of Goldman Sachs or Morgan Stanley? Hedge funds, mutual funds, insurance companies, and college endowments all rushed to withdraw their funds from these once-impregnable firms. Not knowing who might be next, all willingness to lend evaporated. The commercial paper market and the interbank overnight market shut down tight.

This was nothing less than a full-fledged run on the shadow banking system. Deposit insurance of $100,000 was irrelevant when the institutions in question were prime brokers rather than commercial banks. Confidence was all there was. It did not survive the mixed signals of US officials and their foreign counterparts.

CHAPTER 13

The Spiral

I T WAS HARD to imagine that things could get worse. But worsen they did with AIG.

The AIG story is one of the more extraordinary chapters in this extraordinary tale. The company, originally known as American Asiatic Underwriters, was founded in 1919 by Cornelius Vander Starr, Northern California native, ice cream salesman, and clandestine operative for the US government. Starr's introduction to Asia came via a job with the Pacific Mail Steamship Company. Developing a taste for the region, he became, at the age of twenty-seven, the first Westerner to sell insurance to the Chinese residents of Shanghai. (Shades of Clarence Hatry selling insurance to Austrian immigrants before 1914.) Starr insured Chinese shipping companies against losses to marauding pirates off what is now the Indonesian coast. He wrote fire insurance for factories in China and the Philippines.

During World War II, Wild Bill Donovan, head of the US Office of Strategic Services (OSS), then used Starr's employees to gather intelligence on the enemy powers' assets in the Far East. Starting in 1942, following US entry into the war, Starr took personal control of the clandestine operation. He helped Donovan use American Asiatic's commercial property insurance records to identify promising bombing targets. Subsequently Starr set up a pair of front companies, Metropolitan Motors Overseas Incorporated and a New York edition of the *Shanghai Evening Post and Mercury*, whose employees acted as agents for the OSS.[1]

Following the occupation of Beijing and Shanghai by Communist forces in 1949, Starr moved his headquarters to New York. Under his successor, the driven, strong-willed Maurice ("Hank") Greenberg, the rebranded American

International Group grew into the largest underwriter of commercial and industrial insurance in the world. It provided travel and life insurance to households and managed the retirement plans of one in ten Americans. Where Lehman Brothers had $600 billion of debts, AIG's obligations ran to the trillions.

But someone inside AIG apparently believed its experience in commercial and industrial insurance qualified it to sell protection against the failure of collateralized debt obligations. The company's trading arm, AIG Financial Products, was one of the first shops to move into writing specialized insurance on CDOs in the 1990s. The insurance contracts in question, credit default swaps or CDS, had been invented at JPMorgan, with which AIG Financial Products did extensive business.[2] Unlike Dr. Frankenstein, the mad scientists at JPMorgan appear to have understood that their creation could run amok, and they wrote CDOs and CDS with a modicum of restraint. Not so AIG Financial Products, which wrote insurance not just on high-grade securities but also on CDOs backed by subprime mortgages. By mid-2008, the unit had written an extraordinary $500 billion worth, enough to put its corporate parent in jeopardy.

AIG Financial Products was run by Joseph Cassano, who had previously worked at Drexel Burnham Lambert, which pioneered the junk bond business. Average annual compensation of Cassano's four hundred employees exceeded $1 million.[3] Salary and bonuses accounted for a third of the unit's total revenues. AIG's dominant position in markets for commercial, industrial, and life insurance gave it a high credit rating, which in turn relieved it of the obligation to hold collateral to back its CDO insurance. Other financial institutions, lacking AIG's AAA rating and having to post more collateral as a result, had higher costs of providing CDO insurance. AIG Financial Product thus became the dominant player in this market.

In effect, Financial Products was taking a highly leveraged long position on the US housing market. How it was that the corporate parent, not to mention the regulator, looked the other way takes some explaining. Part of the explanation is that credit default swaps could be sold to AIG's board as simply another form of insurance of the sort that the company had long been in the business of providing, although the instruments in question were in fact entirely different. Hank Greenberg, whose aversion to risk was sometimes described as "sociopathic," might have understood the difference, but Greenberg was forced to resign in 2005 over an accounting scandal.[4] Having failed at succession planning, he was followed by a series of short-lived, less-than-impressive CEOs. Part of the explanation may also be that AIG Financial Products was a profit center, rendering the corporate parent loath to question its practices. Part of the explanation may be that Cassano was secretive—he refused to share information on his underwriting activities even with his corporate higher-ups—something that he got away with by virtue of his legendary temper and his unit's profits.

AIG Financial Products was headquartered in London, beyond the purview of the New York State Insurance Department, which oversaw AIG's insurance operations, and the Federal Reserve System, the ostensible steward of the American financial system. It booked trades through a French bank and sold derivatives insurance to European banks that loaded up on subprime-related products. CDS protection allowed the European banks to reduce the capital they were required to hold against their subprime-related investments. The banks could then expand their balance sheets and take on additional risk. One of Greenberg's successors as CEO, Edward Liddy, in testimony before the House Financial Services Subcommittee on Capital Markets in 2009, charmingly referred to the practice as "balance sheet rental."[5]

From a European perspective, AIG Financial Products looked less like an insurance company than a highly leveraged bank, which is of course precisely what it was. European officials logically moved to subject it to bank regulation. Unfortunately, they didn't specify whose bank regulation, or where.[6] The AIG unit arranged for the purchase of a savings and loan, American General Bank, thereby subjecting itself to oversight (if loose use of the word is permitted) by the Office of Thrift Supervision.

OTS was a particularly hapless agency created in 1989 in response to the S&L crisis. Thrifts made plain-vanilla mortgage loans; OTS had no particular competence in derivatives. The regulator's responsibility was to AIG's thrift subsidiary, so it viewed the operations of the larger company solely in that light. Visits by examiners were limited to Financial Products' lowly branch office in Connecticut. The fact that Financial Products had enjoyed a fourfold increase in credit-related revenues in just one year, though noted in OTS's 2006 audit, elicited nothing in the way of substantive comment, much less corrective action. If one fact epitomized the consequences of the ramshackle US regulatory system, this was it.

AIG Financial Products suffered mounting losses as the housing market tumbled. But it was not just the falling housing market; in addition, triggers in the insurance contracts sold by Financial Products required its parent to put up additional collateral if AIG's credit was downgraded to single A. The existence of these provisions was not widely known even within the company, given the secretive manner in which Cassano ran his operation. Their presence came to light on the afternoon of Monday, September 15, following the failure of Lehman Brothers, when Moody's and Standard & Poor's, late again to the game, downgraded AIG.

—

There was more alarming news the next day. Reserve Primary Fund, America's most venerable money market mutual fund, had some $785 million of Lehman Brothers paper in its portfolio, a fact proudly trumpeted in its July financial statement. The fund's septuagenarian co-founder and manager, Bruce Bent Sr., now learned of Lehman's bankruptcy courtesy of a headline spied at an airport newsstand while on holiday in Italy celebrating the fiftieth anniversary of meeting his wife.

Within twenty-four hours of Lehman's bankruptcy, nearly half of Bent's shareholders had asked to redeem their shares. These were not demands that the fund could easily meet by selling other investments, given demoralized markets. Back in 2007, recall, other troubled money funds were bailed out by their fund families or investment bank parents.[7] But the $62 billion Primary Fund lacked a deep-pocketed investment-bank patron and had no obvious alternative. Bent was sufficiently alarmed to instruct his son, Bruce Bent II, to contact New York Fed President Geithner. Geithner being otherwise engaged, the junior Bent left a message.

The Bents first attempted, without success, to raise $100 million from the banks with which they booked their trades. Next they sought a buyer for their troubled fund, efforts that were similarly unavailing. The only option remaining was to halt redemptions and allow shares to go to a discount.[8] Reserve Primary Fund duly announced that it was breaking the buck, reducing the value of its $1 shares to 97 cents. It announced further that it would consider additional requests for redemptions only after seven days.

Just months earlier, Bent Sr. had warned his shareholders that "Unfortunately, a number of money funds, and a number of investors that selected them, have lost sight of the purpose of a money fund and the simple rules that guide them in their foolhardy quest for a few extra basis points. The cash entrusted to a money fund is your reserve resource that you expect to be there no matter what."[9] Savers did not react well to news to the contrary and scrambled to get out. The biggest withdrawals were experienced by money market funds run by institutions like Morgan Stanley and Goldman Sachs that had interacted extensively with Lehman. Since money funds had been the main buyers of asset-backed commercial paper from large corporations, the last signs of life now flickered out of the commercial paper market.

Defenders of the mutual fund industry argued later that this was an overreaction. Lehman Brothers paper accounted for only 1 percent of the Reserve Primary Fund's investment portfolio. Shareholders in the fund ultimately recovered more than 99 percent of their investments. But those same shareholders suspected that Primary Fund was not the only money fund with exposure to Lehman and, more important, that Lehman might not be one of a kind. The plight of Primary Fund reminded them that money market funds held no capital and were uninsured. Later it emerged that nearly thirty other money market mutual funds suffered losses large enough to force them to similarly break the buck but avoided doing so because they were again bailed out by their corporate parents, a luxury that Reserve Primary Fund did not enjoy.[10]

Money market funds developed in the early 1970s as an alternative to bank accounts, interest rates on which were limited by the Regulation Q ceilings adopted in 1933.[11] With the elimination of Regulation Q in the mid-1980s, they then lost their raison d'être. But that didn't mean they faded quietly into the night. The failure of the Securities and Exchange Commission to require them to hold banklike capital buffers was an implicit subsidy that had allowed them to outlive their usefulness, with disastrous consequences.

———

This, the third week of September, was when the crisis reached its most dangerous point. Runs by individual investors on money market funds and by institutional investors on their investment-bank parents engulfed the shadow banking system. Consumed by fears of counterparty risk, the banks refused to lend. Even the most reputable companies, like General Electric, were unable to borrow.

Desperate circumstances prompting desperate measures, Treasury announced that it was temporarily guaranteeing the liabilities of the money funds. Guarantees are well and good, but to be credible they have to be backed. To this end Paulson authorized use of the Exchange Stabilization Fund, another legacy of the Great Depression. The ESF was created in 1934, following US departure from the gold standard, with the goal of stabilizing the dollar. Now this $50 billion pot of money was used to reassure investors in money market funds that there would be no more buck breaking—that if their money market fund was unable to give them a hundred cents on the dollar, the ESF would.[12]

The guarantee was a prominent statement, but the fact of the matter was that $50 billion was only a drop in the bucket compared to the $3 trillion of outstanding money market shares. Again, the Fed was the only institution with sufficiently deep pockets to address the problem. But the central bank lacked the authority, even under unusual and exigent circumstances, to purchase asset-backed commercial paper directly from money market funds and provide them with cash in return. The way around this problem was the convoluted and convolutedly named Asset-Backed Commercial Paper Money Market Mutual Fund Liquidity Facility, or AMLF. Through the AMLF, the Fed lent money to State Street and JPMorgan, two of the custodians with whom the money funds held their investments and booked their trades. In turn, State Street and JPMorgan purchased commercial paper from the mutual funds, providing them the cash they needed to meet redemptions. In the end, the Fed financed more than $200 billion of commercial paper purchases by the two banks and a handful of smaller custodians.

Stabilizing money market shares and raising the limit on deposit insurance from $100,000 to $250,000, as the FDIC did subsequently, were popular steps, since they addressed the concerns of small savers. Other measures benefiting large financial institutions were more controversial. The controversy extended to the AMLF, which circumvented statutory limits on the Fed's ability to intervene in securities markets and through which State Street and JPMorgan, it eventually emerged, earned healthy profits.[13]

An immediate case in point was when the Fed stepped in on Tuesday, September 16, to rescue AIG. The Fed initially balked at aiding an insurance company over which it possessed no regulatory authority. Unusual and exigent circumstances might permit it to lend to an investment bank like Bear Stearns, but lending to an insurance company was too exceptional, whatever the exigency. Federal Reserve officials indicated as much to AIG's CEO, the former Citigroup executive Robert Willumstad, and to the company's chief financial officer, Steven Bensinger, in a phone conversation on the morning of Saturday, September 13. New York Fed President Geithner and Treasury Secretary Paulson told Willumstad in no uncertain terms that there would be no government assistance or guarantee for AIG. Echoing the language used by Bank of England officials in their discussions with Northern Rock, they urged the company to find a private-sector solution.[14]

This was a misreading all around, again echoing the case of Northern Rock. The officials in question overestimated the ease of arranging a private-sector solution, while Willumstad et al. underestimated the cost. AIG first attempted to raise additional capital by selling some of its insurance units to Warren Buffett's Berkshire Hathaway and then by selling preferred shares to the private equity shop J. C. Flowers & Co. But Buffett was not interested, and AIG rejected Flowers' price as too high. A few days later Buffett would instead invest $5 billion in Goldman Sachs. Ultimately AIG management would pay an even higher price for assistance.

Fed officials then sought to enlist Goldman Sachs, AIG's principal derivatives trading partner, and JPMorgan Chase, the central bank's now customary private-sector consort, in organizing a line of credit. The banks would issue a bridge loan until AIG was able to sell its insurance units, raising the cash needed to meet commitments. Officials invoked the precedent of Long-Term Capital Management, whose counterparties had collectively provided the liquidity needed to finance that troubled fund's collateral calls.[15] But the liquidity problem in 1998 was LTCM-specific; other financial institutions were flush with funds. Now everyone was potentially short of liquidity, and every bank was happy for other banks to furnish AIG with emergency assistance so long as it could husband its own liquid resources. The banks would have been better off had they acted collectively. But collective action is difficult under duress; it is even more difficult under time pressure. Efforts to assemble a bank syndicate to aid AIG went nowhere.

But if AIG was allowed to collapse, it might bring down the big counterparties, including even Goldman Sachs. Suppressing all qualms—and contradicting denials made to bankers and the insurer in previous days—the Fed, with the support of the Treasury, again declared unusual and exigent circumstances. It provided an $85 billion capital infusion packaged as a Federal Reserve Bank of New York credit line, obtaining 79.9 percent ownership in return.[16] Following the precedent of Bear Stearns, the loan was extended through a pair of special purpose vehicles, Maiden Lane II and III. The capital injection stripped AIG's shareholders of fourth-fifths of their stake. It was contingent on the immediate resignation of Willumstad.

Even though the terms were tough, they were not popular.[17] If Lehman could fail, congressional critics asked, why was it imperative that AIG be saved? To Treasury and Fed officials, the answer was clear. Lehman's failure had caused major disruptions in financial markets, and AIG's balance sheet was many times larger. Because AIG also had retail business—it insured households and firms—failure would be even more destructive of confidence. Helping AIG was uncomfortable, but the alternative of uncontrolled bankruptcy would have been worse.[18] Still, the Fed and Treasury did not cover themselves with glory, having insisted in preceding days that they would not bail out the company under any circumstances.

There was more consternation on Sunday, September 21, when, short-circuiting its usual procedures, the Federal Reserve announced that it was authorizing Goldman Sachs and Morgan Stanley, the only two investment banks still standing, to convert themselves into bank holding companies. As holding companies, Goldman and Morgan Stanley would be able to borrow from the central bank on a permanent basis. As a quid pro quo, the two banks were required to raise additional capital. Still, that the step was taken without the conventional review prompted complaints of the big boys again being accorded special privileges. It was another indication that the crisis was still far from contained.

Paulson and Bernanke made clear by their body language that they were uncomfortable with all this improvisation. Tapping the Exchange Equalization Fund, setting up Maiden Lane II and III, financing State Street and JPMorgan Chase's purchases of asset-backed commercial paper, and allowing Goldman and Morgan Stanley to become bank holding companies overnight were extraordinary steps, taken with the acquiescence of the White House but without congressional authorization. The election was barely a month away, and the Republican candidate for president, Arizona Senator John McCain, was making critical noises about these unprecedented interventions.

There was fear, moreover, that AIG was only the tip of the iceberg. If the crisis spread to Morgan Stanley, Bank of America, and Goldman Sachs, interventions on an even greater scale might be required. With a massive balance sheet and the ability to conjure money out of thin air, the Fed had the capacity to take their toxic assets off the banks' hands. But Bernanke lacked the political cover. And Paulson lacked the authority.

On Friday, September 19, at the end of an historic week, a sleep-deprived Paulson, together with Bernanke and SEC Chairman Christopher Cox, joined President Bush in the Rose Garden. The president announced he was requesting additional powers for Treasury to stabilize the financial system. Just how those powers would be deployed was vague. They would be used, the officials explained, to purchase mortgage-backed securities from financial institutions, but no details were provided. The press described the requested authority as "sweeping" and "expansive."

The emphasis on asset purchases reflected Paulson's belief that the problem was one of liquidity. The United States was experiencing a liquidity crisis centered on mortgage-backed securities, which had spilled over into the market in asset-backed commercial paper and now threatened the banks. Having Treasury buy up those securities at reasonable prices, it followed, would restore liquidity to the markets. The banks would be able to price their assets. They would again become willing to buy and sell, and importantly to lend. The financial system, its pipes unclogged, would begin functioning again.

Elsewhere, there were doubts. It was not obvious why Treasury's operatives would have a better idea than did market participants of what constituted a fair price for the banks' toxic securities. Offer too little and the banks would not sell. Offer too much and they would reap a massive windfall at taxpayers' expense.

There were suspicions, moreover, that the problem was not just one of liquidity. The banks had taken big losses on their subprime-related investments and thus needed to raise capital to resume normal operations. Without capital, they had no buffer against losses. And without a buffer against losses, they would refuse to lend.

But raising capital under stressed financial conditions was not easy. There was the alternative of government money, but Paulson, like many Republicans, opposed using taxpayer funds to inject capital, a step that he referred to, poisonously, as nationalizing the banks.[19] Overpaying for toxic assets was a way of recapitalizing the banks by stealth. But this investment of public money would not come with control rights, something the government had insisted on in the case of AIG. And surreptitious recapitalization lacked legitimacy. It threatened to provoke an even bigger political reaction.

Nor were the skeptics convinced by Treasury's three-page proposal requesting authorization to spend up to $700 billion purchasing mortgage-backed securities. What was in reality only a starting point for discussion was ineptly packaged as draft legislation. Nothing was said about taxpayer protections or congressional oversight. When declaring unusual and exigent circumstances, Chairman Bernanke at least was required to obtain the assent of four other members of the board of governors.[20] Under Treasury's proposal, the secretary would enjoy virtually unchecked powers.

The Troubled Asset Relief Program, or TARP as the plan immediately became known, was wounded on arrival. Within days, reluctance to grant sweeping new powers to the Treasury secretary coalesced with Republican opposition to all further government intervention. On September 29, the bill authorizing Treasury to spend $700 billion on asset purchases was defeated in the House by 228 to 205. That two-thirds of Republicans opposed the bill was embarrassing for the administration and for Paulson especially. The Dow fell by 778 points, or 7 percent, on the news.

But if Congress could speak, then so could the public. In 1929, only 8 percent of Americans had owned traded securities. Now ownership of common equity was ubiquitous, thanks to the creation in 1978 of 401(k) retirement accounts. Unhappy account holders, seeing their retirement nest eggs shatter, lit up congressional switchboards, which quickly got their representatives' attention. On Friday, October 3, on its second try, the House passed the TARP by a vote of 263 to 171. The Senate having already acted, President Bush quickly signed the bill into law.

Congress, still wary about the open-ended powers granted the Treasury, agreed however to release only the first half of the funds. Thus it was unclear whether Treasury would have the resources to repair the financial system. Equally unclear was whether it possessed a coherent strategy for using them. On the Friday the TARP was voted, the Dow Jones Industrial Average plunged by more than 800 points before recovering the majority of its losses.

On Monday, October 6, it then fell by a further 370 points, or nearly 4 percent. This was not a vote of confidence.

Inevitably, the task of triage fell to the Fed. On Tuesday, October 7, it announced an increase in the size of the Term Auction Facility and that it would lend an additional $300 billion to banks with end-of-year cash needs. The next day it announced a more radical step, the creation of a Commercial Paper Funding Facility to lend directly to corporations and nonbank financial institutions. In his most influential research on the Great Depression, Bernanke had in 1983 detailed how the collapse of the commercial paper market on which corporations issue short-term debt disrupted the flow of credit to the corporate sector in the 1930s. The Commercial Paper Funding Facility was designed to prevent a replay of this history. The mechanism was another special purpose vehicle, à la Maiden Lane I, II, and III. Once again, the lessons of the Depression, as distilled by historical scholars, informed the response of policy makers (in this case the two actors being one and the same). As for whether that response would be enough to avert another depression, time would tell.

| Fish or Foul

FOR THE MOMENT, there was an eerie absence of financial accidents else-where. This allowed European leaders to insist that the post-Lehman crisis, like the subprime crisis of 2007, was an American problem demanding an American solution. But there were reasons for questioning whether the calm would last. At the top of the list was the perilous state of Europe's banks. They were even more highly leveraged than their US counterparts.[1] They relied on dollar funding, which the ECB and Bank of England could not provide.[2] Some, like IKB, were heavily invested in subprime-linked securities, while others were heavily exposed to local housing markets and had loaded up on the high-yielding debts of Southern European governments.

Fortis, a Belgium-based financial conglomerate with operations in Luxembourg and the Netherlands, was the poster child for these excesses. It was not just Belgium's biggest bank but also its single largest employer. Half of all Belgian households held accounts there. It had 85,000 employees worldwide and was the twentieth-largest business in the world by revenue. In other words, it was a clear case of too big to fail.

Fortis' chairman since 1990 was Maurice Lippens, whose namesake grandfather had been president of the Belgian Senate and then governor general of the Congo. The grandson, like King Leopold II before him, sought to make his mark with an ambitious program of acquisitions. Fortis first purchased MeesPierson N. V., a three-hundred-year-old Dutch private bank, obtaining a presence in investment banking. Next it acquired American Bankers Insurance Group, expanding its presence in the US market. Seeking to branch into emerging markets, it purchased banks in Poland and Turkey. In 2007, at the worst possible time, it paid handsomely to acquire ABN AMRO's retail businesses. ABN AMRO being the eighth-largest bank in Europe by assets, this was a big bite to swallow.[3]

Fortis was also heavily involved in structuring CDOs, for which it gathered subprime-mortgage-linked securities, holding them on its balance sheet until the securitization deal closed. Epitomizing these operations was the soon-to-be-notorious Timberwolf II deal. Its forerunner, Timberwolf, had closed in 2007 just before the subprime crisis struck. It was a collaboration between Goldman Sachs and Greywolf Capital Management, a Purchase, N.Y., financial firm run by a team of Goldman alumni. Bear Stearns' two ill-fated hedge funds had invested heavily in Timberwolf, which lost more than 80 percent of its value within five months. Timberwolf was later immortalized by Michigan Senator Carl Levin, in a hearing of the Senate Permanent Subcommittee on Investigations on conflicts of interest in the financial sector, as "one shitty deal" (Levin was in fact echoing an unflattering emailed remark by a Goldman executive).

By the time Greywolf Capital proposed Timberwolf II, Goldman had concluded that warehousing subprime-linked securities, as necessary for getting the deal off the ground, was too risky. But in Fortis, Greywolf found a less fastidious partner. Fortis lost more than $400 million on the securities it warehoused in preparation for Timberwolf II, a deal that never came to market.[4] So much for the idea, repeated ad nauseam by European officials, that US banks were to blame for the excesses of the CDO market.

These problems may have been common knowledge among insiders, but the impact of Lehman's failure on derivatives markets gave them additional salience. Shares in Fortis fell by 35 percent in the week ending on September 26, reducing its market valuation to €12 billion, barely half what it had just paid for its chunk of ABN AMRO. Fortis' interim CEO Herman Verwilst then ill-advisedly used the "b word" (bankruptcy) in seeking to reassure investors, prompting withdrawals by business clients. Having fallen victim to foot in mouth disease, Verwilst was quickly put out to pasture, but the damage was done. The three Benelux governments stepped in over the weekend, injecting €11 billion of new share capital to keep Fortis afloat. As a condition, they demanded the resignation of Chairman Lippens. The Dutch government, as a matter of national pride, further required the upstart Belgian firm to sell off its stake in what was originally Dutch ABN AMRO.

There was then more bad news from Ireland the following Monday, when shares in the country's six big banks fell by a third. Deposits were guaranteed up to €100,000, the Irish authorities having raised the limit from €20,000 a week earlier. But this did nothing to restore the banks' access to wholesale money markets. Nor did a €100,000 guarantee reassure business customers with deposits vastly in excess of the ceiling.[5]

And there was yet more bad news from Brussels, where shares in Dexia, the big Franco-Belgian financial conglomerate that was one of Fortis' principal competitors, also fell by a third. Dexia could trace its origins to the 1860s, when its progenitor, the Crédit Communal de Belgique, was founded to lend to municipal governments. (It almost seemed as if the older and more venerable the financial institution, the more risk it now took and the more excitement it created.) After more than a century of quietude, the Crédit Communal merged with its French counterpart, the Crédit Local de France, in 1996. The rebranded company then acquired the American firm Financial Security Assurance (FSA), whose business was providing credit enhancements—insurance policies—to boost the marketability of municipal bonds. What with local governments borrowing heavily on the municipal bond market, FSA quickly became Dexia's most profitable division.

Dexia displayed all the defining financial characteristics of the era. Its assets were forty times core capital. Only 15 percent of its liabilities were customer deposits acquired through its retail banking network. It insured $400 billion of US municipal bonds and asset-backed securities and made a large loan to Depfa Bank, a German bank headquartered in Dublin that underwrote US municipal bonds with contracts containing AIG-style buyback triggers. It had a significant derivatives portfolio, forcing it to post additional collateral as the value of its investments declined. Its FSA unit had announced a $331 million net loss for the second quarter of 2008, and there was every reason to think that the third quarter would be worse.

Shares in Dexia plunged on the Monday after the Belgian, Dutch, and Luxembourg governments intervened in Fortis, and it too lost access to the wholesale money market. The French and Belgian governments responded on Tuesday by injecting €6.4 billion of emergency funding and sending off the firm's management.

———

Last but not least, there was Iceland. This small mid-Atlantic island better known for fish than finance had not registered on the sonar of many investors. There was some awareness that IceSave, the offshore brand of the Icelandic bank Landsbanki, offered high interest rates on Internet savings accounts to customers in the United Kingdom and the Netherlands. Kaupthing (in Icelandic, Kaupþing) Bank, the largest Icelandic bank, similarly offered Internet-based Kaupthing Edge accounts through its overseas subsidiaries and branches to customers in European jurisdictions from Luxembourg to the Isle of Man.[6] Investors were aware that the three big Icelandic banks had embarked on an extraordinary acquisitions binge. But consciousness of what had transpired in Iceland became widespread only when things went dreadfully wrong.

There has been a tendency to ascribe the hyperfinancialization of the Icelandic economy to certain idiosyncrasies of national character.[7] In a speech in London in 2005, Ólafur Ragnar Grímsson, the country's long-serving president, ascribed the audacity of Iceland's financiers and entrepreneurs to the fact that Icelanders were descended from the Vikings. The country had been a society of farmers and fishermen as recently as two decades earlier, when "necessity dictated that the fish catch had to be brought ashore and processed immediately when the boats came into harbour and that they had to be turned and collected when the weather was favorable," bequeathing a strong work ethic.[8] "Icelanders are risk takers," Grímsson, in his celebration, continued. A successful fishing boat captain is self-confident, aggressive, and ready to take risks, these also being the attributes of a successful bond trader.

Turning Iceland into a financial center thus required only a government decision to privatize the fish catch, assign every fisherman a quota, and create a market on which those quotas could be traded. Aggressive Icelanders trading fishing quotas discovered that they apparently possessed a natural aptitude for trading financial claims. Soon the financial services boom was on. By 2008, bank assets were nearly ten times the size of GDP. This all but guaranteed that, sooner or later, the worst would come to pass.

A bit of reflection suggests that this story is too easy. Privatization of the fish catch occurred already in the 1970s, and the trading of quotas already in the 1980s. But as recently as 2003, bank assets as a share of GDP were only marginally higher than in the United States.[9]

From 2004 through the middle of 2008, the balance sheets of the three big Icelandic banks then rose by a cumulative factor of eight. What drove the boom were not quirks of national character but tangible policy decisions, the most important of which were privatizing and deregulating the banks. In 1994 Iceland joined Europe's free-trade area, the European Economic Area, in order to strengthen its bargaining position in negotiations over fishing rights. But as a member of the free-trade area, it had to relax controls on capital flows. Hence it was no longer possible to maintain interest rates on bank deposits lower than those prevailing abroad. This forced deregulation of interest rates, which in turn created momentum for bank deregulation generally.

Ideology also played a role. The 1990s saw the ascendancy of a new generation of libertarian politicians who, reacting against the small island's cozy state-run system, advocated a program of radical liberalization. Among them were Davíð Oddsson, from the conservative Independence Party, who served as prime minister from 1991 to 2004, minister of foreign affairs until late 2005, and then governor of the central bank from 2005 to 2009; and Hannes Hólmsteinn Gissurarson, a University of Iceland professor of political science and Hayek scholar, who, having previously written on fisheries management, in 1992 published a book describing how Iceland could transform itself into a global financial center. If there was a quirk of Icelandic national character, it was how quickly the dominant political ideology could shift between the extremes of statism and libertarianism—just as it shifted back after the crisis.

Support for the libertarian arguments of these young renegades was grounded in the backlash against the overly close connections between Icelandic government and business—in complaints that cronyism, in the sanitized Icelandic version, was rampant, and that the solution was to get the government out of business. Central to their program was privatization of three state banks: Landsbanki; Íslandsbanki, later renamed Glitnir; and Búnaðarbanki, which was subsequently purchased by a small bank, Kaupthing, and henceforth known by that name. Unfortunately, privatization and liberalization by themselves did not guarantee a reduced role for the state, much less that Iceland would miraculously transform itself into a world-class financial center. In a country of fewer than 300,000 residents, the incestuous connections between political elites and business managers that informed the backlash against the state-run economy were not eliminated; to the contrary, they had, if anything, even more scope to operate.

Be this as it may, the belief in light-touch regulation that informed policy toward the banking system in the US and UK found a happy home in Iceland. The speed of the shift meant that the owner-managers of what had until recently been public financial institutions possessed no firsthand experience or institutional memory of how badly things could go wrong. The regulators, meanwhile, were hopelessly understaffed, not unlike the US Securities and Exchange Commission.

Freed to borrow on foreign money markets, the big three Icelandic banks did so with abandon. They used foreign funding to finance a wave of acquisitions, mainly in the Nordic countries and the UK. This by itself did not make the Icelandic case exceptional; banks in other European countries, including not least Germany, similarly relied on wholesale funding, and similarly embarked on an acquisitions binge.[10] Rather, what made the Icelandic case an exception, and exceptionally risky, were a pair of additional features.

First, the banks' balance sheets were inflated by their aggressive pursuit of offshore deposits and the rapid growth of IceSave and Kaupthing Edge accounts in particular. Put those offshore deposits together with the wholesale funding, and the result was an enormous banking system atop a tiny island economy. It was either the politicians' and bankers' dream of Iceland as an international financial center or a nightmare come true.

Second, more than 70 percent of the liabilities of the three big banks, Kaupthing, Landsbanki, and Glitnir, were denominated in foreign currency. The banks claimed that they were prudently managing the risks of borrowing dollars, pounds, and euros by lending to firms and households in those same currencies. This of course neglected the possibility that the country's exchange rate might weaken, in which case Icelandic firms and households with incomes in krona would be unable to repay their foreign currency loans.

It should have been clear that no loan book could grow so prodigiously without compromising quality. The banks were allowed to lend generously against housing collateral whose value had tripled since 2003 and against corporate shares whose prices were up by a factor of five, levels whose sustainability was, to put it mildly, questionable. They kept little in the way of a meaningful capital cushion. Many of their loans were to insiders, who used them to purchase additional shares in their own banks and finance other acquisitions.

As questions were asked—what was a small windswept island off the northwest coast of Europe doing with a banking system eight times GDP, and could balance sheets that had grown at such an extraordinary pace possibly weather the global economic downturn—the banks' shares came under pressure. The banks' owners responded, like Clarence Hatry, Bernard Marcus, and Albert Oustric before them, by purchasing their own shares so as to buy time and ward off evidence of insolvency. Starting in mid-2007, Kaupthing purchased its own shares whenever their prices ticked down and it could do so without being detected. It provided financing to Sheikh Mohammed Bin Khalifa Bin Hamad al-Thani of Qatar to buy a 5 percent stake and gave the Sheikh a guarantee against losses. Glitnir Bank made large loans to its principal owner, the Baugur Group, which used them to double its holdings of bank shares.[11] In 2013 four executives of Kaupthing, including the CEO and board chairman, were convicted of fraud in connection with the Qatari transactions and sentenced to five years in jail. Investigations of other related transactions at Kaupthing and the two other big Icelandic banks are ongoing. Whatever their legality, these transactions were indicative of how desperate the banks' owners, now also their managers, were to buy time in the gamble to stay alive.[12]

Already in 2006, a number of investment banks had issued negative reports on the Icelandic financial system, pointing to a worrisome pattern of cross-ownership between the banks and their big shareholders and clients. In 2007 a planeload of asset managers flown to Reykjavik by Barclays Capital came away worried by the country's highly leveraged financial system. Informed by this experience, a group of fifty macro hedge funds organized by Drobny Global Advisors of Manhattan Beach, California, began shorting the krona and Icelandic financials. In April 2008, late once more to the game, Fitch placed Iceland's big banks on negative watch.

———

Thus, what followed was not wholly unexpected. On Thursday, September 25, 2008, against the background of turmoil in the United States and Europe, Glitnir, the smallest of the three big banks, informed the Central Bank of Iceland that it would be unable to meet payments on loans due on October 15. Glitnir was named after the gold- and silver-encrusted hall of Forseti, the Norse god of law and justice, but no matter. Its balance sheet had been damaged by falling asset prices, and the bank now lost access to the wholesale money market. A big German state bank, Bayerische Landesbank, refused to roll over €150 million of loans, and Glitnir had nowhere else to come up with the money.[13] Over the ensuing weekend, the Central Bank of Iceland considered extending the bank a €600 million loan but concluded that its collateral was inadequate; Glitnir was effectively insolvent. To prevent its collapse, the government announced the intention of injecting, via the central bank, some €600 million of new share capital, effectively nationalizing the institution.[14]

There was only one problem. €600 million was an enormous sum for a small economy. It was not clear, in other words, where the authorities would come up with the money. An analogous proportion of US GDP was $700 billion, equivalent to the entire TARP. In Iceland, this was now allocated to just a single bank, and not the largest one. Not to mention the further problem that the need to replace Glitnir's foreign-currency-denominated borrowings, soon to mature, would exhaust the central bank's reserves of foreign exchange.

If they had not had it before, investors had reason now to question the Icelandic banking model. On Tuesday, September 30, Fitch downgraded the three big Icelandic banks, citing their reliance on wholesale funding, rapid expansion into overseas markets, and the possibility of a hard landing for the Icelandic economy.[15] Doubting the adequacy of the sovereign backstop, depositors rushed to withdraw their funds not just from Glitnir but from Kaupthing and Landsbanki as well.

It did not help that Landsbanki had made loans to finance the purchase of shares in the now-bankrupt Glitnir by the bank's recent owners. Nor did it help that the exchange rate fell sharply on the news of Glitnir's difficulties, raising doubts about Kaupthing and Landsbanki's loan books. The ECB had extended loans to the three banks' Luxembourg subsidiaries against collateral denominated in Icelandic krona; it now demanded additional margin.[16]

The final straw came when the British Financial Services Authority instructed Kaupthing's UK subsidiary to keep liquid funds in London equal to 95 percent of its Edge account liabilities, preventing the subsidiary from helping the parent with its liquidity needs.

Within days, all three big Icelandic banks had collapsed. If it had been unclear before where the government would find the funds to recapitalize Glitnir, it was even less clear now how it could save the big three, whose combined liabilities were more than eight times national income. Printing money was no answer, since this would do nothing to address the fact that the bulk of the banks' liabilities were denominated in dollars, euros, and sterling.

This left only forcing losses on the banks' creditors. On October 6, the day before the Landsbanki bankruptcy, Iceland's Parliament, the Althing, adopted a measure guaranteeing all deposit accounts of residents.[17] But this measure said nothing about the banks' other creditors, be they institutional investors holding the bonds of the banks or Dutch and British households with IceSave and Kaupthing Edge accounts. When the government then split Landsbanki into a new government-owned institution, whose Icelandic assets, acquired in part by earlier foreign borrowing, fully covered its deposit liabilities to residents, and old Landsbanki, whose assets were only a fraction of its liabilities, the implication was clear.

The collapse of the banks was a shock to Iceland's self-image. It was a shock most of all to the banks' creditors, the most visible of whom was the pop star Bubbi Morthens. Known locally as the Icelandic Bruce Springsteen, Morthens was second only to Björk as an Icelandic pop icon. Notwithstanding the fact that one of his bands was called Das Kapital, Morthens had followed the example of David Bowie by securitizing his royalties. But he had the bad luck to securitize them through Glitnir and the bad judgment to invest the proceeds in the bank's securities. The notion that it made sense to turn a stream of songwriting royalties into an unhedged bet on a highly leveraged bank was indicative of the prevalent Icelandic belief that the route to riches ran through finance. Morthens' shares were written down by 85 percent with Glitnir's partial nationalization. When it became clear that the bank was broke, his holdings were wiped out. Morthens played a series of free concerts to dramatize the plight of the bank's creditors. His was a doleful tune.

————

Iceland's insurance fund ostensibly guaranteed deposits, including Landsbanki's IceSave and Kaupthing's Edge accounts, up to €20,877 per customer per bank as required by the European Economic Area legislation that authorized the banks to operate elsewhere in Europe.[18] But this was cold comfort, as Shakespeare would have said, apropos of Iceland, given that the resources to make good on the guarantee were not there. Payments into the guarantee fund had been set on the basis of deposits at the end of the previous year, which hardly sufficed in a period when deposits were growing exponentially. In any case, the architects of the guarantee fund had not foreseen the wholesale collapse of the financial system.

If British households were unmindful of such details, the same was not true of the Bank of England and Financial Services Authority. On Friday, October 3, the FSA effectively seized the UK operations of Landsbanki and Kaupthing, placing their funds into a segregated account at the Bank of England, and instructed their Icelandic parents to come up with more money for these accounts. On the Tuesday morning following, the Icelandic Minister of Finance, Árni M. Mathiesen, informed the UK chancellor, Alisdair Darling, that the Icelandic government, now the de facto owner of the banks, might not be able to come up with this kind of money.

Mathiesen's answer should not have come as a surprise, since British households' $5 billion of IceSave accounts were nearly 50 percent of Icelandic GDP. As Davíð Oddsson observed from his perch at the central bank, so burdening Icelandic citizens' children and grandchildren "would be slavery for other people's fault."[19] The "other people" to whom Oddsson was alluding included not himself, of course, but other Icelandic bankers, British depositors unable to resist the lure of suspiciously high interest rates, and a British regulator that had done nothing to restrain them.

Already the website of the UK IceSave operation was overwhelmed by traffic. It was closed down along with Landsbanki on October 7, leaving depositors in the lurch. This led to one of the more ignominious chapters in the crisis as the British authorities invoked the UK Anti-Terrorism, Crime, and Security Act to seize Landsbanki's UK assets, ostensibly to protect those customers. The Anti-Terrorism Act was passed in the wake of September 11 to help Britain's security apparatus pursue foreigners bent on violent acts. Compensating the holders of Internet bank accounts was presumably not what members of Parliament had in mind. Be this as it may, the act was now used by Gordon Brown to comfort his public.

Placing Iceland on a list with Al Qaeda, the Taliban, Sudan, North Korea, and Iran caused a freeze on banking transactions between Iceland and other countries. The stock market was shut. The foreign exchange market was closed, leaving the Central Bank of Iceland to provide foreign exchange for essential purposes only. To angry Icelanders, it seemed like a replay of the "cod wars," the dispute over fishing rights with the UK in the 1960s and 1970s.

Some 20 percent of Iceland's population signed an online petition decrying the British government's action. Thousands of Icelanders posted self-portraits to the web. Each held a handmade sign reading: "I am not a terrorist, Mr. Brown."[20]

In 2009, when Britain chaired the Group of Twenty, Brown would seek to position himself as the orchestrator of international cooperation. He would have a lot of positioning to do.

| Toward Better Times

| Revival or Reform

FRANKLIN DELANO ROOSEVELT was inaugurated as thirty-second president of the United States on a cold and blustery March 4. The extraordinary circumstances were signified by the presence of automatic-weapon emplacements along the route from the White House to Capitol Hill. It had been three weeks since Roosevelt was the target of an assassination attempt by an unemployed bricklayer in which five bystanders were wounded, including one, Chicago Mayor Anton Cermak, critically. The president-elect was addressing a gathering at Bayfront Park in Miami following a cruise on Vincent Astor's yacht. Cermak was there to apologize for having opposed him at the nominating convention and to lobby for RFC assistance for Chicago's banks. In his confession, the gunman, Giuseppe Zangara, explained, "I kill kings and presidents first, and next all capitalists."[1]

But the placement of the machine-gun nests at the entry of federal buildings indicated they were designed to guard not so much the new president as government property, against occupation by the unemployed masses. The events of 1932 had created grounds for concern, if not necessarily for expecting attacks on federal buildings on inauguration day. Working-class demonstrators, some organized by communist-inspired Unemployed Councils, demanded relief services and a stay on evictions. Mayor Cermak had been forced to rescind cutbacks in city relief programs in response.[2] In December some three thousand unemployed had caravanned to Washington, D.C., for a National Hunger March down Pennsylvania Avenue.

Economic conditions deteriorated further in the months between the election and inauguration. By March 4, banks in thirty-seven states were shut or under state-government-imposed restrictions on withdrawals.[3] With panicked households unwilling to spend and producers unable to borrow, industrial production fell to just two-thirds the 1925–1929 average. Freight car loadings were down 56 percent. Automobile production was barely a quarter of its 1929 level. At 2:30 a.m. on the morning of the inauguration, Herbert Lehman, who had succeeded Roosevelt as governor, closed New York's banks. The Stock Exchange shut its doors for only the third time in history, the previous occasions having been in 1873, due to an earlier financial panic, and with the outbreak of World War I. This, one might say, was Wall Street's first Lehman moment.

———

Such was the situation confronting the new president. There was, of course, the criticism, levied by President Hoover among others, that FDR had brought this dire situation on himself. Hoover had reached out to his successor for help in stabilizing the banking system. Roosevelt's refusal to cooperate robbed the incumbent president, down to his last days in office, of remaining legitimacy, or at least of the will to act.

In particular, Hoover believed that Roosevelt's reluctance to endorse the gold standard inflamed the crisis of confidence. Subsequent events do not support this view. FDR took six additional weeks to clarify his position on the gold standard but only days to restore confidence in the banks. Still, Hoover was convinced of the need to remove this source of uncertainty. He therefore sought to lock the president-elect into a pro-gold-standard position.[4] FDR refused to be pinned down. He may not have yet decided against maintenance of the gold standard, but he wanted to keep his options open.

In addition, FDR and his Brains Trust were aware that they would have had to negotiate the terms of any bank holiday with Hoover and his appointees. And prior to March 4, they would not have had powers of office with which to back their views. The more Machiavellian interpretation is that the worse the situation was on March 4, the more problems could be blamed on Hoover, and the more positive would be the reception of his successor's initiatives.

In his inaugural address, Roosevelt sought to communicate that the day marked the dawn of not just a new administration but also a new era of hope and action. But just what form that action would take was uncertain, in part because it was not obvious who had the president's ear. On the economy, Roosevelt consulted three distinct groups of advisors.[5] The first was a team of progressives led by the Harvard law professor Felix Frankfurter, who had cultivated FDR almost from the moment he appeared on the national stage. Their relationship went back to World War I, when Roosevelt was assistant secretary of the navy and Frankfurter chaired the War Labor Policies Board.

Frankfurter and his students were proponents of an economic and political philosophy developed by Supreme Court Justice Louis Brandeis. Brandeis was concerned to limit the concentrated economic and political power of the robber barons, a problem that gained salience with the development of the assembly line and growth of industrial monoliths like Ford and General Motors.[6] The Brandeisians denied that big firms had efficiency advantages, something they were free to do since they were lawyers rather than economists. Nostalgic for an idealized past of small family firms, the urban equivalent of Jeffersonian democracy, they now sought to restore it by regulating large enterprises.

The Brandeisians were more concerned with reform than recovery and saw the Depression as an opportunity to advance their agenda. Thus, not a few of the regulatory burdens imposed on industry by the New Deal, of which business so vociferously complained, were the products of the febrile minds of Frankfurter and his circle.[7] In December 1933 the English economist John Maynard Keynes published an open letter in which he criticized the Roosevelt administration for emphasizing reform over recovery. Whether he knew it or not, Keynes was really criticizing the Brandeisians and FDR for lending them his ear.[8]

A second group of advisors was made up of professors at Columbia University, including the institutional economist Rexford Tugwell, the corporate law specialist Adolph Berle, and the political scientist Raymond Moley. Founding members of the Brains Trust, they had advised FDR during the campaign. In contrast to Frankfurter's circle, they accepted the inevitability of big business but sought to counter it with big government.[9] More generally, members of this group espoused an expanded role for government in organizing activity, given their conclusion, entirely logical under the circumstances, that the market could not be relied on to do so.

More moderate members of the Brains Trust, believing that the market had broken down only temporarily, therefore called for an expanded role for the government at most on a transitory basis. Some like Tugwell, however, saw the breakdown as symptomatic of deeper problems and justifying a permanent role for government in planning the economy. Again, given the depth of the Depression and extent of dislocations, this conclusion was not illogical. In their view, the urgency of initiating economic recovery combined with the call for far-reaching structural reform to prompt proposals for regulating wages and prices and reducing acreage under cultivation. The National Industrial Recovery Act (NIRA) and the Agricultural Adjustment Act were in large part inventions of this second set of advisors.

A third group was made up of inflationists, led by Cornell University agricultural economist George Warren, with support from gentleman farmer and Roosevelt neighbor Henry Morgenthau. Morgenthau was once the publisher of *American Agriculturalist* magazine; his farm specialized in growing Christmas trees. He became treasury secretary when the president's initial designee, William H. Woodin, was forced to resign for health reasons.[10] In 1929, on becoming governor of New York, FDR created an Agricultural Advisory Commission to advise on farm problems, with Morgenthau as chairman and Warren among its members. As specialists in a sector that saw excess supply already in the 1920s and the prices of whose products fell fastest between 1929 and 1933, Warren and his circle sought to apply the lessons they drew from the farm sector to the economy as a whole. They saw pushing up prices and wages as relieving crushing debt burdens. If abandoning the gold standard was necessary in order to achieve this, then so be it.

Warren's agrocentric views were lent a veneer of respectability by Yale University monetary economists James Harvey Rogers and Irving Fisher. Rogers was an expert on the gold standard and could speak with authority on its deflationary effects. Fisher was precluded from formally advising Roosevelt by his notorious "permanently high plateau" remark, made of the stock market in 1929, not to mention his advocacy of eugenics and support for Prohibition. But his 1933 article on debt deflation, in which he argued that falling wages and incomes could further damage the economy by making existing debts harder to repay, lent intellectual heft to Warren's case for inflation.[11]

The first order of business was resolving the banking crisis. The Brandeisians then, like progressive economists Paul Krugman and Joseph Stiglitz more recently, favored nationalizing the banks.[12] So did progressive senators Bronson Cutting of New Mexico and Robert La Follette, Jr., of Wisconsin. But like Barack Obama in 2009, Roosevelt hesitated. Seizing scores of banks and replacing their management with government administrators would take time, which was in short supply. Injecting public money would have been problematic for a president committed to balancing the budget. At a personal level, FDR socialized with prominent investors and financiers like Vincent Astor; Thomas Lamont, the J. P. Morgan partner, had rented Roosevelt's 12th Street townhouse years before. Notwithstanding his populist rhetoric about banishing the money changers from their "high seats in the temple of our civilization," the new president preferred to work with the bankers rather than against them.[13]

Consequently, Roosevelt's approach to resolving the banking crisis did not differ materially from Hoover's. Already on the Friday night before the inauguration, outgoing Treasury Secretary Mills met with Professor Moley and

Treasury Secretary-designate Woodin.[14] With no set ideas of their own, and having promised the president-elect a bank rehabilitation plan within days, Moley and Woodin simply adopted the plan of their predecessors. The New Deal may have been famously experimental, but there was no experimentation here.

On Sunday, March 5, his first full day in office, FDR invoked the Trading with the Enemy Act to suspend gold transactions and declare a four-day bank holiday, an expedient that would have an echo in Gordon Brown's invoking the UK Anti-Terrorism Act in 2008. This too had been considered by Hoover; the outgoing president even recommended that FDR invoke the Trading with the Enemy Act at a White House meeting on March 3.[15]

Roosevelt next summoned the Congress into emergency session, giving his team three days to finalize their plans. Although the Emergency Banking Act submitted for consideration by the House and Senate—read to the House actually, only one copy being available—was scarcely longer than the three-page memorandum submitted by the Paulson Treasury in September 2008, its reception was different.[16] The House approved the bill by voice vote after just forty minutes and no opportunity for amendment. The Senate passed it three hours later, by an overwhelming 73 to 7. The president signed the bill the same night.

Title I of the act gave legal status to the bank holiday. This had already been recommended to Hoover by a Justice Department uneasy about use of the Trading with the Enemy Act.[17] Title II then empowered the treasury secretary to reopen financially sound institutions while placing unsound banks under the supervision of conservators.[18] A version of this had been prepared for Hoover's use by the Comptroller of the Currency. Title III authorized the Treasury Department to instruct the Reconstruction Finance Corporation to inject capital into financial institutions, taking preferred stock in return. This eliminated the provision in the RFC act permitting the corporation to lend to illiquid financial institutions but not to inject capital, a distinction that had frustrated its efforts to rescue Henry Ford's Guardian Group. This had already been recommended to President Hoover by Franklin Fort, a former Republican member of the House Banking and Currency Committee. Title IV, finally, amended the Federal Reserve Act to loosen collateral requirements for lending to illiquid banks. It allowed the Federal Reserve to issue specially designed Federal Reserve Bank Notes, separate from its normal obligations, against "any notes, drafts, bills of exchange or bankers' acceptances, acquired under the provisions of this act"—against virtually any and all collateral, in other words.

The resulting legislation was not original, but it was comprehensive. Whether it worked would become evident soon enough.

———

Over the weekend the president used his first fireside chat for a simplified exposition of the plan. On Monday, when banks in the twelve Federal Reserve cities reopened, the crisis was over. As the *New York Times* put it, "In contrast with the 'runs' to withdraw funds which preceded the moratorium, there was a general 'run' yesterday to deposit or redeposit money. The banks generally reported heavy deposits and small withdrawals. In all cases, deposits were said to be larger than withdrawals."[19] On Tuesday, when banks in other cities reopened, customers complained of the difficulty of getting through the doors for the number of other depositors crowding their lobbies. Capitalism was saved in eight days, as Raymond Moley modestly put it.[20]

All this happened before any new RFC-backed bank recapitalization. FDR barely had time to install his man Jesse Jones as head of the corporation.[21] Yet the return of confidence in the banks was immediate. What does this tell us about the nature of the 1933 banking crisis? It suggests that the crisis was driven, in substantial part, by panic. In the same way that panic can be self-fulfilling, it can be dispatched by a time-out and a reassuring fireside chat. The time-out, as progressive historians Charles Beard and George Smith put it, performed the same function as "a slap in the face for a person gripped by unreasoning hysteria."[22]

The fireside chat was more reassuring for the fact that the new president was still enjoying a honeymoon with the public. This in turn suggests that FDR was wise to refuse to cooperate with Hoover. An analogous plan advanced by a discredited president would not have received the same benefit of the doubt. And, extenuating circumstances or not, only a president still on his honeymoon could have pushed such a far-reaching bill through Congress in a matter of hours.

The comprehensive audit of which the Emergency Banking Act spoke and of which historians have spoken subsequently was, in fact, less than comprehensive. It was hardly possible to do a comprehensive audit in two weeks. George Norris, looking back on his experience as governor of the Federal Reserve Bank of Philadelphia, describes how, on receiving instructions from Treasury Secretary Woodin on March 10 to take applications from member banks to reopen, he was literally "besieged with visits and telephone calls from bankers all over the district, whom I could not refuse to talk with." Norris immediately recognized the impossibility "in such a short time to make the careful study of the condition of seven or eight hundred banks which alone would justify my passing a sentence of life or death upon them." He appointed the chairman of his board, the chief national bank examiner of the district, and the head of his examination department, a Mr. Hill, as a three-person committee to ostensibly make this determination over the subsequent weekend. "It was a delicate and difficult task, so onerous and responsible, and performed under such a cruel limitation as to time" that it drove Mr. Hill to a nervous breakdown.[23]

If the comprehensive audit was partly smoke and mirrors, the new powers bestowed on the Federal Reserve System were real, and they had very real effects. The Banking Act empowered the Fed to discount notes, drafts, bills, and acceptances as it saw fit, ensuring that the banks would have the liquidity needed to meet the needs of their depositors. This was not yet deposit insurance, but the implicit guarantee had much the same effect.[24] The promise that the Fed would intervene with the emergency provision of liquidity, by calming investors, bought time to conduct a more systematic evaluation of the banks, which proceeded over subsequent months, and then for recapitalization—for the injection of additional funds by private investors and the RFC.

These were lessons that were relearned in 2012 when investors in European sovereign debt panicked but the European Central Bank calmed the markets with its program of Outright Monetary Transactions (OMT).[25] Much as with the Fed's commitment to provide emergency liquidity in 1933, OMT didn't actually have to be activated; its mere announcement was enough to reassure. It at least bought time to conduct additional stress tests and recapitalize the banks.

Finally, the quick return of confidence suggests that the plan as a whole—conservatorship for insolvent banks, a commitment to provide emergency liquidity, and, where necessary, recapitalization with public funds—made a lot of sense. These elements were well known prior to Roosevelt's taking office; they just had to be implemented. Resolving a banking crisis, this experience suggests, is not rocket science.

———

The special session of Congress, conceived to address the banking crisis, proved so successful that Roosevelt quickly broadened its mandate from one "b" to three. The second "b," after banking, was beer. FDR proposed legalizing 3.2 percent beer, providing liquid refreshment for his honeymoon.

More consequential was the third "b." Here the president sought to burnish his conservative credentials by making good on his promise to balance the budget. FDR's modern critics have made much of the growth of federal spending during his first term. Roosevelt's deficits were some of the largest in US history outside of wartime. Public debt rose more quickly than in the Hoover years. Ambitious public works projects, from the Grand Coulee Dam to La Guardia Airport, were funded by the Roosevelt administration. Some have gone so far as to argue that deficit spending was the key measure used by the new president to signal his commitment to ending the Depression.

By challenging prevailing policy dogmas, they indicated that Roosevelt was intent on changing the policy regime.[26]

This is a revealing instance of economists seeing in the historical record what they want to see. In fact, Roosevelt did not view himself as out to challenge prevailing policy dogmas, but to uphold them. He believed in balanced budgets. This was an aspect of prevailing policy dogma to which he subscribed as firmly as Hoover.

The president's goal was to balance the budget immediately, completely, and, if necessary, on the backs of his supporters. His first message to Congress after declaring the bank holiday was on economies in government. "For three long years the Federal Government has been on the road toward bankruptcy," he solemnly intoned.[27] Deficits made for the uncertainty that led to the banking crisis. By undermining confidence, they added to the ranks of the unemployed. To drive home the point, FDR appointed as his budget director Lewis Douglas, a representative from Arizona and the strongest voice in the House for balancing the budget. Douglas had warned more than once of the dire consequences of not doing so. His rhetoric would have warmed the heart of Pete Peterson, the twenty-first-century crusader for a balanced budget.[28] Not balancing the budget, Douglas apocalyptically warned, would "plung[e] the whole world into darkness."[29]

Under the plan drawn up by Douglas, the budget would be balanced entirely through spending cuts.[30] Defense spending would fall by 8 percent from amounts budgeted previously.[31] This testifies to the priority FDR attached to budget balance, given Japan's incursion into China and Hitler's rise. Federal wages and salaries were not just frozen but reduced, saving $20 million and $105 million on the military and civilian sides. The largest single saving came from cuts in military pensions, what today we would call entitlements. These savings would accrue from the elimination of payments to veterans disabled for reasons other than their military service.

This was an extraordinary proposal given that disabled veterans were among those hardest hit by the Depression. If they had voted in 1932, they voted for FDR. Cutting their payments was not something Hoover could have done, given the firestorm whipped up by his decision to allow General Douglas MacArthur, supported by Majors George S. Patton and Dwight D. Eisenhower, to disperse the Bonus Army of World War I veterans encamped in Anacostia.[32] Twelve Democratic senators, including Michigan's James Couzens, opposed the reductions, but the bill passed overwhelmingly.

It is unclear how Roosevelt planned to reconcile this commitment to balanced budgets with his other policy ambitions. The press suggested that he hoped to make greater use of existing resources, using military recruiting offices to reach out to the unemployed, for example, and prior appropriations for the federally owned hydroelectric dam and nitrate plant at Muscle Shoals, Alabama, to expand public works. Others question whether FDR was really committed to budget balance. He was already planning to create an emergency budget, they allege, to be financed by borrowing, alongside a regular budget, which would give the appearance of balance.

The fact of the matter is that Roosevelt was conflicted. He sincerely believed in balancing the budget. But having done so once on the backs of the unemployed, he was not prepared to do so again when economic conditions showed only limited improvement. So, as one New Deal program followed another, the emergency budget expanded.[33]

Still, none of this weakened FDR's belief in the principle of balanced budgets. In his 1935 budget message he insisted that "The Federal Government must and shall quit this business of relief" or else pay for whatever elements were not eliminated.[34] He repeated the call when Congress showed itself willing to pay out a bonus to World War I veterans in 1936.[35]

Thus, if FDR's fiscal policy was a "change in regime," this was a change that would take the advent of World War II to acquire conviction. His deficits were inadvertent. As Keynes had warned in his December 1933 letter, they were too small to make a difference.[36]

———

More important for changing the outlook was monetary policy. This was not yet decided by the gold embargo of March 4, which prohibited banks from paying out gold coin, bullion, or certificates and allowed gold to be exported only under licenses granted by Secretary Woodin. FDR had no choice but to impose the embargo; Hoover would have done so already had he not lost the will to act. The Federal Reserve Bank of New York was out of gold. Had foreigners sought to export it, there was no way the bank could have furnished it.

But the embargo was widely thought to be temporary, just as the bank holiday was temporary, and it could have easily ended up as such. The United States had suspended gold convertibility before, in the exceptional circumstances of the Civil War, but resumed it subsequently. Other countries had suspended and resumed after World War I. Treasury Secretary Woodin's first words on taking office were to reassure everyone within earshot that the United States had not left the gold standard. "It is ridiculous and misleading to say that we have gone off the gold standard, any more than we have gone off the currency standard," he announced. "Gold merely cannot be obtained for several days." Woodin was not being disingenuous; as an avid supporter of the monetary status quo, he believed what he said.[37]

Roosevelt took six weeks to weigh his options. This was long enough to conclude that a functioning banking system and whatever confidence a balanced budget might inspire were not enough to sustain a recovery. Conditions had improved between March and April, but then it is hard to imagine that they could have worsened, given the catastrophic starting point. Not just banks but also shops and factories were closed. With no money in their pockets, people were not buying. Across America the streets were quiet, even deserted. In Akron, Ohio, "The rubber shops closed. Streetcars ran on half schedules. Coal companies shut. Thousands of men still employed despite the Depression were sent home from work 'temporarily laid off.'"[38] Although April was better than March, it was not better than January before the state bank holidays. Industrial production in April barely matched the January level. Employment actually fell by an additional 2.3 percent over the three months from January.[39]

Clearly, more had to be done. Roosevelt's first step was to announce that the embargo on gold exports would continue indefinitely. This opened the door to other measures to push prices up, like those advocated by Senator Elmer Thomas, who proposed a measure mandating government purchases of silver. Thomas, recall, had already been advocating similar measures in 1932, prompting the Fed to take preemptive expansionary action.[40] Which way FDR would now jump became clear when he and Thomas met on April 19. The two men emerged with a compromise that Thomas appended to the bill that became the Agricultural Adjustment Act. The revised Thomas amendment did not set a target for silver purchases but gave the president permission to reduce the gold content of the dollar—equivalently, to push up the dollar price of gold—by as much as 50 percent.

The Dow Jones Average surged by 9 percent on the news. Even today, April 19 remains on the list of the twenty largest daily percentage gains. So much, then, for the belief that abandoning the gold standard would devastate confidence. "The rank and file of the financial district embraced with enthusiasm the prospects of inflation after years of grinding deflation" was the way the *New York Times* put it.[41]

The second step was to make clear that the change was permanent—that the administration had no intention of again subordinating price stability to the imperatives of the gold standard. This Roosevelt accomplished by informing the World Monetary and Economic Conference that stable prices were his priority. The conference had convened in London on June 10. Within three weeks, conferees drew up a declaration calling for a return to the international gold standard.[42] Although their statement was hedged with allowances for countries to return at a time and level of their choosing, there was nonetheless the prospect that it would create pressure for resumption at previously prevailing exchange rates.

That the US delegation had been able to agree on anything was remarkable in itself. Along with Hull, a dyed-in the-wool free trader, Roosevelt sent Key Pittman, an acolyte of William Jennings Bryan. Pittman, the senior senator from the silver-mining state of Nevada and chairman of the Foreign Relations Committee, had inserted into the 1932 Democratic Party platform a plank advocating an international monetary conference; what was left unsaid was his hope that the conference might decide in favor of silver coinage. Now, in London, Pittman left nothing unsaid. He talked nonstop about measures to support silver prices. The exasperated lead German delegate, none other than Hjalmar Schacht, waved his hands in despair on being subjected to yet another Pittman lecture. There is no shortage of tales of Pittman's adventures in London, including his shooting out streetlamps with his revolver and taking a bath in a sink in the pantry at Claridge's.[43]

Another prominent member of the US delegation was Senator William Couzens, the onetime Henry Ford partner whose influence had made it difficult for the RFC to rescue the Guardian Trust Company.[44] FDR may have chosen Couzens for his protectionist views—that is, to neutralize the secretary of state. If so, he was not disappointed. Couzens repeatedly clashed with Hull, speaking out against tariff reductions and refusing to be bound by Hull's instruction that all public statements by US delegates be cleared through him. FDR also sent James Cox, the former governor of Ohio and newspaper publisher, whose hard-money views neutralized those of Pittman. The remaining two delegates were Representative Samuel McReynolds of Tennessee and Ralph Morrison, a wealthy Texan. None of the members of the six-person delegation had prior experience with an international conference.

Roosevelt may have been surprised that, with this kind of leadership from the Americans, the conference made progress, but he was quick to capitalize on the fact. On July 3, in his bombshell message, transmitted to London from Washington, D.C., he rejected the conference declaration, asserting that priority should instead be attached to policies stabilizing the purchasing power of money. He dismissed the gold standard as exemplifying "the old fetishes of international bankers," language that succeeded in antagonizing the bankers and foreign leaders equally. The inflammatory rhetoric was designed to make his priorities unmistakable, not just to the delegates in London but to the American public. Historians continue to ask what convinced investors that the administration was committed to raising prices. What convinced them was that Roosevelt was prepared to antagonize his allies, shoulder blame for the collapse of the conference, and hang his own delegation out to dry.

FDR's bombshell has been criticized for driving a final nail into the coffin of international cooperation. It was invoked in 2008–09 as an example of the kind of nationalistic policies that governments responding to the Great Recession should avoid.[45] By pushing down the dollar, the United States aggravated the competitiveness problems of other countries. By derailing the conference, Roosevelt destroyed the last chance for a coordinated response.

In fact, this supposed "lesson" of history is mistaken. The alternative to monetary nationalism was not a coordinated response to the Depression for the simple reason that governments could not agree on how to respond. European governments saw the priority as stable exchange rates rather than a stable price level. Rather than seeking to vanquish deflation, they saw inflation, by which they were haunted as a result of their 1920s experience, as the real and pressing danger. Not having experienced a slump as long and deep as that of the United States, they continued to prioritize liquidation over recovery. Only if speculators felt sufficient pain, they insisted, would another round of excesses and an even more serious depression be avoided. This was not a view with which Roosevelt could make common cause.

So much, then, for coordinated action. Officials in various countries were unable to agree on a common diagnosis of the economic problem, pointing them to different remedies. Initially, Roosevelt hoped otherwise. As recently as April 19 he had spoken of the desirability of stabilizing currencies, which would be feasible if countries also agreed on coordinated reflationary action. But meetings with other heads of state, notably Édouard Herriot, the former prime minister who chaired the foreign affairs committee in the French Chamber of Deputies, convinced him that it was not to be.[46] The only route to reflation was unilateral. It ran through the bombshell message.[47]

In 2008–09 there would be more scope for coordinated action because the authorities in various countries shared a common diagnosis of the problem. The idea that the collapse of the World Economic Conference in 1933 was regrettable and that anything similar should now be avoided—like the textbook interpretation of the Smoot-Hawley tariff—was an instance of bad history encouraging good policy.

———

Roosevelt's third step was to push up the price of gold, and with it the prices of other commodities. On October 22 he announced he was authorizing the Reconstruction Finance Corporation to purchase newly mined gold. The timing is explained by pressure from Western states to get agricultural prices up. Dissatisfied by the pace of progress, Senator Thomas, ever the instigator, announced a conference of farm and industry leaders on October 24 and threatened to lead a million-man march on Washington.

The president now sought to preempt this movement. Every morning, over his breakfast of orange juice and eggs, he decided in consultation with Henry Morgenthau and Jesse Jones by how many cents to raise the RFC's offer price. On some days he raised it by a couple of cents, on others more. The purpose, as Jones later described it, was to keep the speculators guessing.[48]

The goal of higher commodity prices and the strategy of pursuing it by pushing up the price of a particular commodity, gold, were clear. But the tactics were opaque. No one knew by how much the president would push up the price of gold on a particular day. Critics complained that the administration's capricious approach was discouraging investment. In November, the Federal Advisory Council, a group of bankers advising the Federal Reserve Board, warned that uncertainty was depressing the bond markets. Only when that uncertainty was removed, the council admonished, would there be a lasting improvement in business.

Keynes, in his December letter to the president, agreed. "The recent gyrations of the dollar," he wrote, "have looked to me more like a gold standard on the booze than the ideal managed currency of my dreams." FDR's game of blindman's bluff with currency speculators was creating confusion. Stabilizing the price of gold at a higher level, say $35 an ounce, was one way of removing this uncertainty. But doing so might be inconsistent with the president's goal of boosting commodity prices. Better, Keynes concluded, was for the administration to announce a goal for monetary policy—a price level target, for example—and a modus operandi for achieving it. His preference was for the Treasury to intervene in the foreign exchange market to hold the dollar within a range but push it up or down as needed to keep the price level stable.[49]

Keynes' recommendation, not for the first time, made a lot of sense. FDR's decision in January to instead re-peg the dollar to gold at $35 an ounce could have been a disaster.[50] There could have been gold outflows, putting downward pressure on the money supply, in which case deflation and the negative expectations it engendered would have been back.

As it turned out, economic problems and political tensions in Europe caused gold to flow toward America rather than away. The gold bloc centered on France was still locked in deflation, and investors were looking for a way out. The storm clouds of World War II were already blowing up. In response, European investors shifted toward the dollar, an obvious safe haven. As they did so, they pumped up US supplies of money and credit, helping to stabilize the American price level.[51] Roosevelt's monetary policy may have been less than ideal, but fortunately for him, European policy was worse.

Readers will recognize here the dollar's "exorbitant privilege" as the world's only true safe haven currency.[52] The origins of that status, then, go back to 1934. This was the first in what eventually became a long series of instances when investors rushed into dollars in response to untoward events. This behavior gave the United States, in effect, an automatic insurance policy—that is, a currency that strengthens when things go wrong. This insurance would come in handy in 2008 with the failure of Lehman Brothers.

| Something for Everyone

THE NEW DEAL involved much more than just changes in monetary and fiscal policies. FDR and his Brains Trust quickly realized that they could use the special session of Congress to push through a variety of additional measures before the sense of urgency passed. There was the Civilian Conservation Corps, a favorite of a conservation-minded president who as governor had assigned ten thousand unemployed New Yorkers to reforestation projects. There was the Tennessee Valley Authority to improve navigation, undertake flood-control projects, and supply cheap electricity. There was the Federal Emergency Relief Administration to give the states $500 million for payments to the poor and unemployed.

Above all, there were the Agricultural Adjustment Act and National Industrial Recovery Act, the New Deal's signature programs. George Warren and Rex Tugwell may have belonged to rival advisory factions, but they shared a concern for agriculture. They also shared a diagnosis of its ills centering on overproduction and depressed prices. The growth of production was a fact, if not one limited to the United States. It reflected increases in acreage under cultivation in Canada, Argentina, and Australia during and after World War I. Low prices were also a fact and one for which the Smoot-Hawley Tariff made little difference, as we saw above.

For FDR, these problems were a priority. His first successful campaign was in the rural districts of Dutchess County, New York, and where farmers were a key constituency. His advisors, led by Raymond Moley, noted that many bank failures were in areas where farmers suffered from depressed prices. Moley thus saw addressing the farm problem as important for solving the banking crisis.

But the plan—an agency to make federal payments to farmers limiting production—was less than ideal. Farmers were offered acreage reduction contracts obliging them not to cultivate a portion of their land, and were compensated accordingly. The payment was financed by a tax on millers who ground wheat into flour, along with other commodity processors, in order to create the impression that farmers were not being financed by the taxpayer.

Better would have been to subsidize the adoption of new techniques so farmers could cut costs and live with the reality of abundance. Another bureau, the Farm Credit Administration, went some way in this direction by providing farmers with low-interest loans for mortgages and the purchase of inputs. But the administration could have gone further down this road. Its failure to do so is more striking for the fact that Roosevelt appointed as his agriculture secretary Henry A. Wallace, a farmer with a degree in animal husbandry who founded Hi-Bred Corn, a company that developed and sold high-yielding hybrid seed varieties. Hi-Bred became Pioneer Hi-Bred before eventually being sold to the DuPont Corporation, while Wallace became FDR's vice presidential running mate in 1940, succeeding John Nance Garner. From the vice presidency he went on to serve as commerce secretary, thereby becoming the only former vice president to serve in the cabinet. Wallace then ran as Progressive Party candidate for the presidency in 1948 on a platform advocating an end to the Cold War and to segregation.

As a pioneer in the commercialization of hybrid seed, Wallace appreciated the promise of cost-cutting technology. But even the innovation-minded Wallace also supported crop set-asides. Linking subsidy checks to adoption of new seed or machinery, if more efficient in the long run, would have done little to alleviate the farmers' immediate plight. And relief was urgent, given increasingly violent farm protests. It was urgent given the administration's worry that pressure from farm interests might force adoption of populist monetary policies.[1]

———

However valid the argument that overproduction leading to low prices was a problem for agriculture, it clearly had no relevance to industry. Cost-reducing technological change in manufacturing, as symbolized by electrification and the assembly line, was rapid in the 1920s.[2] Profits were healthy. In contrast to agriculture, increases in the supply of manufactures did not outstrip demand until spending collapsed in the 1930s.

But such observations did not prevent Roosevelt's economists from generalizing their diagnosis of agriculture's ills to the rest of the economy. If prices were low, then this reflected excess supply and ruinous competition. And if the problem was ruinous competition, the solution was to limit output and raise prices. On sending Congress the bill establishing the National Recovery Administration, Roosevelt described his goal as "to prevent unfair competition and disastrous overproduction."[3] Section 3(a) of the National Industrial Recovery Act provided for codes of fair competition under which firms would limit production and raise prices. The act suspended antitrust laws in order to remove legal impediments to collaboration. In the event that firms working together did not achieve the desired result, Section 4(b) allowed the president to intervene to prevent destructive wage and price reductions.

And if excessive competition leading to low prices was a problem in product markets, then why not also in labor markets? The provisions of the NIRA protecting the right of workers to organize can be seen in this light. Encouraging producers to act collectively but not allowing workers to do so would have been politically unbalanced in any case. If employers were going to enjoy higher prices and profits, it followed that they should be compelled to share them with their employees. And to ensure that those benefits were distributed widely, the available work should be spread by limiting hours.

This is the best one can do in attempting to reconstruct a logic for the NIRA. It reflected the tendency for Roosevelt and his advisors, men like George Warren and Henry Wallace, to generalize from the problems of agriculture to the economy as a whole. It drew inspiration from a plan offered already in 1931 by Gerard Swope, president of General Electric, in which he recommended suspension of federal antitrust laws to enable firms to limit excess production and raise prices, together with higher pay and fringe benefits for workers to share the wealth. It was informed by the views of Adolph Berle, a founding member of the Brains Trust, whose work emphasized that the era of the small family firm was over and government had a role in ensuring that large corporations served the public purpose.[4]

The alternative is to acknowledge that there was not, in fact, a coherent logic for the NIRA. It was an effort to demonstrate that the new president and Congress were prepared to do something, anything, to shock the economy out of its torpor. The NIRA offered something for everyone: for planners who believed that industry needed government direction; for associationalists who saw the solution as producers acting together; for progressives who sought collaboration between employers and workers; for labor leaders fighting for the right to organize; for followers of Senator Hugo Black, Democrat from Alabama, who advocated work sharing; and for social reformers seeking to outlaw child labor. That FDR appointed several groups of advisors to draw up language and then combined their recommendations suggests something for everything was just what he wanted.

———

A kickoff campaign of parades and public events in June 1933 encouraged two million employers to sign a provisional blanket code. Signatories agreed to pay a minimum wage and limit weekly hours to thirty-five or forty. The blanket code was then superseded by codes for each individual industry, more than five hundred in number, establishing price floors and allowing workers to bargain collectively. With government approval came the antitrust exemption and permission to display the Blue Eagle symbol.

From a macroeconomic standpoint, the result was a disaster. It was a classic case of prioritizing reform over recovery, as Keynes put it in his open letter. The act did nothing to stimulate demand.[5] But by pushing up costs, it limited supply (limiting supply of course being precisely the goal). Between July and September, hourly wages rose 22 percent, 19 percent adjusted for the rise in prices, something that is otherwise inexplicable in a period of double-digit unemployment. With higher costs came lower output. In the first half of 1933 industrial production rose and fell in step with the price level. After adoption of the blanket code, industrial production dropped sharply even while prices continued to rise.[6]

That the NIRA was destructive of efforts to stimulate recovery is all but unanimously agreed by economists. Michael Weinstein, working in the Keynesian tradition, estimates that the NIRA, by pushing up costs, knocked a cumulative 8 percent off output. Friedman and Schwartz, leading monetarists, conclude that investment was significantly depressed by the profit squeeze. Harold Cole and Lee Ohanian, exponents of the new classical approach to business cycle analysis, assert that unemployment was as much as a quarter higher than in the absence of the NIRA.[7] Who says economists can't agree?

In addition to its direct effect on costs, the NIRA was criticized for creating uncertainty. Codes differed across industries. Enforcement was erratic. By early 1935 state offices charged with monitoring compliance with the law had noted more than thirty thousand "trade practice complaints," only a fraction of which were pursued. Some of this criticism was simply business pushing back against government interference. These problems may also have been exaggerated by the press, which was hostile to the NIRA code promulgated for the newspaper industry.[8] There may be a kernel of truth in business complaints about uncertainty and red tape, but the effects should not be overstated. William Anderson's analysis of the variance of stock prices suggests that the NIRA did not reduce the risks facing firms, but neither did it raise them significantly.[9]

The ultimate uncertainty was whether the Supreme Court would rule the NIRA unconstitutional on the grounds that it delegated prerogatives assigned by the Constitution to Congress instead to the executive branch. The occasion for doing this was an appeal in 1935 by Schechter Poultry Corporation, a Brooklyn-based company that lost its Blue Eagle (irony intended) for selling diseased chickens across state lines. The decision came to be known, for obvious reasons, as the "sick chicken case." The NIRA violated the constitutional separation of powers, the court ruled. By applying codes to Schechter, moreover, Congress had exceeded what was permissible under the Commerce Clause, since the Schechter brothers merely bought chickens in other states; the birds they slaughtered in New York stayed in New York.

Chastened by the court, FDR dropped more than four hundred cases claiming code violations and left for a weekend cruise aboard the presidential yacht. As the *Chicago Tribune* put it, "The cackling of the sacred geese saved Rome from the Barbarians, and clucking of Mr. Schechter's hens has saved the United States from the New Deal."[10]

The Court next invalidated the Railway Pensions Act, which had created a pension scheme for 1½ million railroad workers, for imposing an unfair burden on large railways.[11] It overturned the Agricultural Adjustment Administration for levying an unfair tax on commodity processors.

Roosevelt responded to this setback by replacing the objectionable provisions of the NIRA with more carefully crafted measures. The National Labor Board was replaced by a National Labor Relations Board. The minimum-wage and child-labor provisions of the NIRA were replaced by more clearly drafted measures under the Fair Labor Standards Act. A second Agricultural Adjustment Act addressed the defects of its predecessor, financing payments to farmers out of general revenues rather than a tax on food processors.

In addition, FDR pushed harder for initiatives promising to mobilize public support for the New Deal, like federal pensions (Social Security) and welfare (the Works Progress Administration, created earlier but now expanded). Most famously, he sought to pack the Supreme Court with sympathetic appointees. Though the tactic damaged the president politically, it succeeded in moderating the Court's opposition to government intervention. In particular, the justices, responding to the pressure, adopted a more expansive interpretation of the Commerce Clause.[12]

The effects are clear. The legal framework and doctrines pioneered by the National Labor Board did much to shape the subsequent National Labor Relations Act. For better or worse, the first AAA shaped the provisions of the second. Some New Deal programs, like the Civilian Conservation Corps and Works Progress Administration, were temporary, but others like Social Security, welfare, unemployment insurance, the minimum wage, child labor laws, and the right to organize became indelible features of the American landscape.

———

Inevitably, this observation points to the question of why the progressive response to the Great Recession was so much more limited than its New Deal predecessor. In terms of social programs, the post-2008 response was limited mainly to health care reform, and even that was an uphill fight. Rather than expanding existing programs, there was pressure from the Republican Party for retrenchment—to cut back on the provision of food stamps, for example. There was nothing remotely resembling the earlier expansion of social protections in the wake of the Great Depression.

The contrast is equally stark when we consider financial regulation. The Glass-Steagall Act of June 1933 not only forced commercial banks to divest themselves of securities affiliates but established deposit insurance and the Federal Deposit Insurance Corporation, a government entity with the power to resolve insolvent banks.[13] Glass-Steagall was far-reaching reform, much more far-reaching than the banking reforms of 2010.

What explains the contrast? It is not as if bank and business lobbies were less well organized in the 1930s. State bank associations campaigned intensively against both more liberal branching laws, which exposed their members to new competition, and burdensome regulations, including deposit insurance. The Missouri Bankers Association sent delegations to Washington to impress upon lawmakers the depth of its opposition. The American Bankers Association vehemently opposed deposit insurance. Association president Francis Sisson denounced insurance as "unsound, unscientific, unjust, and dangerous" for forcing careful banks to pay for the mistakes of their reckless competitors. The association flooded the White House with telegrams in a last-ditch effort to get FDR to veto Glass-Steagall.[14]

Nor is it obvious that banks suffered more adverse publicity. To be sure, there were the sensational 1933 hearings of the Senate Committee on Banking and Currency directed by Ferdinand Pecora, the incorruptible, cigar-chewing former assistant district attorney for New York.[15] But Pecora was a financial neophyte. He was better at uncovering bad behavior by individual bankers than laying bare structural flaws in the financial system. And to the extent that Pecora focused on a few bad apples, reflecting his limited knowledge of the workings of Wall Street, the hearings made the case for systemic reform (as opposed to punishing individual malefactors) less compelling. It is hard to argue, anyway, that the public anger he whipped up was so much greater than that greeting Wall Street's titans when they testified to the Financial Crisis Inquiry Commission in 2010.

Prior to the adoption of Glass-Steagall, Pecora in fact examined just one commercial bank, National City. The ten days of hearings, centering on the testimony of its chairman, Charles Mitchell, were gripping, but they focused more on the questionable actions of one individual than on systematic problems. Mitchell was known as "Sunshine Charley" for his perennially positive outlook, and he arrived wearing an Angelo Mozilo–style tan acquired on vacation in the Bahamas. Mitchell, like Mozilo, had started out as a salesman, in his case of Liberty Bonds. He had the smooth manner of the type, which did not serve him well in this context. The most sensational revelation was that Mitchell had sold eighteen thousand National City shares to his wife and bought them back subsequently in order to reduce his tax liability. Mitchell was forced to resign his chairmanship, thus becoming the first victim of New Deal financial reform. But that was it for Pecora's pre-Glass-Steagall interrogation of the commercial banks.

On May 23 Pecora turned to investment banking and specifically to J. P. Morgan & Co. Here the shocking revelation was that the firm had given preferential access to initial public offerings to prominent insiders, including William Woodin, the newly appointed Treasury secretary; Charles Dawes, of RFC and Dawes Bank fame; and Owen D. Young. But again these disclosures did not speak to such substantive issues as the separation of investment and commercial banking, the desirability of branching, or the need for deposit insurance. And the revelations, however damning, were no more embarrassing than the knowledge that Goldman Sachs had aided John Paulson's efforts to construct a toxic asset portfolio for use in shorting the housing market, or that Countrywide Financial had provided mortgages on favorable terms to "friends of Anglo," including Fannie Mae Chief Executive Franklin Raines and Senate Banking Committee member Christopher Dodd.[16]

In some sense, the reformers were simply pushing on an open door. On March 7, well before the adoption of the Glass-Steagall Act, National City Bank announced that it was liquidating its securities affiliate. The next day Chase National Bank declared that it would follow suit. This was a victory for board chairman Winthrop Aldrich over the opposition of former bank president Albert Wiggin, who shared Jimmy Cayne's passion for poker and built Chase National into the financial conglomerate it was.[17] Wiggin had resigned his presidency of the bank in December 1932, shortly before he was revealed by the Pecora Commission to have begun selling his shares in Chase even while using his bank's money to support them. The Securities and Exchange Commission later adopted a provision prohibiting short sales by insiders known as the "anti-Wiggin Section."

But the point is that, new issuance having collapsed, the banks were more than ready to abandon the securities business. The collapse of security markets was so complete that the banks saw no hope of reviving them. The Glass-Steagall separation of commercial and investment banking simply validated a transition that was already underway.[18] There were again significant dislocations in securitization markets starting in 2008, but a 1930s-style collapse was averted by the extensive interventions of the Federal Reserve and others. Looking forward, the banks could foresee the recovery of their underwriting and trading activities. And indeed, within five years many of the activities for which pre-2008 securitization markets were notorious were back. Not only were the big banks seeking to maintain their existing range of activities, but some were attempting to expand them further. All this caused the industry to resist efforts to rein in practices like proprietary trading.

Another explanation sometimes offered for the success of 1930s reform is that members of Congress had already come to a common diagnosis of the problem. Senator Glass pushed for years for more expansive branching laws and centralized supervision of the banking and financial system. More than a hundred bills for establishing a federal system of deposit insurance were introduced in Congress over the preceding fifty years. One such measure, introduced in April 1932 and co-sponsored by Representative Henry Steagall, received majority support in the House, if not yet the Senate. But Steagall opposed centralized supervision and more extensive branching, while Glass opposed deposit insurance. Their followers were similarly divided.

Nor does the explanation lie in the legislative process. On other issues Congress deferred to FDR, "treating him more like a prime minister than a traditional American president."[19] The Emergency Banking Act of March and the National Industrial Recovery Act of April were passed virtually unchanged from the drafts the administration sent to the Hill. But the specifics of banking reform were contested in both chambers. Roosevelt himself was skeptical of deposit insurance. As a former governor, he was aware of the checkered history of earlier state deposit insurance schemes. The official photograph of the president signing the Banking Act creating FDIC insurance does not show him to have been especially happy about the fact. Treasury Secretary Woodin, a manufacturer of railway freight cars and only secondarily a financier, similarly saw no justification for extending special treatment to the banks. What is true of the executive branch was true also of the Federal Reserve System: leading Federal Reserve officials similarly opposed deposit insurance.[20]

Ultimately, the explanation for such far-reaching reform can only be the severity of the crisis. It brought the financial system and the economy to their knees. It robbed the banks of all interest in holding onto their securities business. It created a groundswell of support for reforms like deposit insurance sufficient to overcome the opposition of entrenched interests. Millions of Americans had their life's savings placed at risk by the banking crisis. Their alarm created strong support for deposit insurance, and more generally for far-reaching financial reform.[21] It gave the reformers not just the mandate but the votes.

And what was true of financial reform was true more widely. The depth of the Depression and the hardship and distress it caused were the fundamental factors lending momentum to the push for social reform.

After 2008, in contrast, the success of policy makers in preventing the worst took the wind out of the reformers' sails. Fewer than one thousand banks failed, compared to more than nine thousand in the 1930s. Where the Dow Jones Average fell by nearly 90 percent from its peak in 1929 to its trough in 1933, the Standard and Poor's 500 fell by significantly less, by 56 percent, in the seventeen months from October 2007. This was still an alarming decline in asset values, to be sure, but it pales in comparison with the 1930s.

Similarly, it took only months in 2008–09, not more than three years, to organize a monetary and fiscal response. Unemployment still peaked at a distressing 10 percent in 2009, but this was much lower than the catastrophic 25 percent of 1933. Deprivation and hardship there were. Hunger and homelessness were widespread. But still, distress did not rise to the level of the Hoovervilles and Dust Bowl of the 1930s.

After 2008, business as usual may no longer have been possible, but business near usual still was. The very success with which twenty-first-century policy makers prevented their crisis from causing another Great Depression thus limited support for radical reform. President Obama may not have consciously prioritized recovery over reform, the opposite of FDR. But it turned out that way.

Securities-market regulation was different only insofar as the reformers were writing on a blank slate. There was no meaningful federal regulation of US capital markets before the Securities Act of 1933. Protecting investors from fraudulent practices was left to the states. Kansas passed the first blue-sky law requiring registration of securities brokers in 1911 in response to complaints that itinerant financial peddlers were selling shares in mythical mining companies to unsuspecting investors.[22] Responding to exaggerated claims of what was achieved and then to the financial excesses associated with the Florida land boom, other states followed suit.

Although these blue-sky laws were intended to hold financial salesmen to minimum standards, they were easily circumvented by out-of-state brokers selling securities by mail. Many state agencies in any case lacked the ability to enforce their laws. Only eight states appropriated the resources necessary for operation of a full-time securities commission. Even where such commissions operated full-time, they lacked the capacity to detect and prosecute fraud. This was the case with the New York State attorney general's efforts to enforce the Martin Act, adopted in 1921 to fight financial fraud.[23]

In their defense, securities market professionals pointed to vigorous self-regulation. The New York Stock Exchange claimed to hold aspiring issuers to higher transparency standards than any of the states with blue-sky laws—and certainly New York. The exchange's listing committee required issuers to provide information on balance sheets, profits, and corporate governance. But the information content of these disclosures was less than met the eye. In the absence of generally accepted accounting standards, issuers could choose what information to report and how to report it. A 1929 study of 580 firms listed on the New York Stock Exchange found that barely half reported gross income.[24] And if a firm found even these guidelines too restrictive, it could simply register on the Curb Exchange (subsequently the American Stock Exchange), where still less disclosure was required.

Nor did self-regulation prevent insider trading and market manipulation. To the contrary, members of the New York Exchange's listing committee were among the organizers of the notorious pools that drove stock prices up and down in the 1920s. Such practices alarmed the Brandeisians, the justice's 1914 collection of essays, *Other People's Money*, having focused on how money translated into power. Along with identifying a problem, Brandeis prescribed a solution, namely transparency. "Publicity," he wrote in a passage that President Roosevelt was fond of quoting, "is justly commended as a remedy for social and industrial diseases. Sunlight is said to be the best of disinfectants; electric light the most efficient policeman."[25]

Brandeis' acolytes, in the persons of Felix Frankfurter and his followers, now grasped the opportunity to translate these principles into action. The 1933 Securities Act governing new issues and the 1934 Securities Exchange Act regulating secondary market trading liberally applied Brandeis' disinfectant.

The question was how far to push the public sector's role. It was whether, in addition to requiring disclosure, regulatory agencies should be empowered to assess that information and act on it. The bill the administration sent to Congress proposed creation of a federal commission with the power to evaluate the merits of stock offerings and prohibit them where it judged a filing as inadequate.[26]

For Representative Sam Rayburn, the powerful Commerce Committee chairman and future House speaker, this was a bridge too far. Frankfurter's boys were called back to revise the bill. Under the revision, information on profits, losses, and compensation of corporate officers would be validated not by the government but by independent auditors using standardized accounting procedures. This would make the accountancy profession one of the few beneficiaries of the Great Depression.

But there might be other practices, like the pools of the 1920s, from which more informative listing documents afforded little protection. Thus the 1934 act also outlawed market manipulation and created a government agency, the SEC, with the authority to pursue it. The Securities Exchange Act contained a Section 10(b) authorizing the commission to address abusive practices like insider trading and fraud not covered by other sections.

This was the template that guided regulation of US securities markets for the better part of the twentieth century. While enshrining the principle of caveat emptor, it recognized that there were practices against which the individual emptor could not caveat himself. If left unaddressed, these might discourage future generations from participating in the stock market, just as they discouraged the 1930s generation. Oversight was needed not simply to protect the investor but to allow securities markets and the economy to flourish. The new template rejected self-regulation as a basis for such oversight. What was necessary instead was an SEC with sufficient human and financial resources to root out market manipulation and fraud.

This model served the country well for more than fifty years. But as memories of the 1930s faded, confidence in self-regulation rose from the grave. And even among those willing to acknowledge the possibility of market failure, there was skepticism about the ability of underpaid, overtaxed public employees to detect it.

Ultimately, this skepticism proved self-fulfilling. Funding for the SEC barely kept pace with inflation and lagged behind stock issuance in the 1990s. After September 11, 2001, the perceived need to devote more budgetary resources to another kind of security—national security—combined with the Bush administration's skepticism of regulation to starve the SEC of resources. In the same way that the New York State attorney general lacked the resources to enforce the state's blue-sky law in the 1920s, the SEC lacked the resources to exercise adequate oversight of financial markets now. The result was Charles Ponzi by another name. His name was Bernie Madoff.

———

Mortgage relief is a last area where the response in the 1930s was more far-reaching than anything in recent years. But in this case it is not possible to argue that a more serious crisis led to a more concerted response. The post-2006 slump in home prices and construction was, in fact, every bit as serious as that of the 1930s, reflecting the extent to which the earlier expansion was led by housing. In both cases, sales prices fell by a third from peak to trough. Nonfarm housing starts fell to just 10 percent of 1920s levels in the depths of the Depression, compared to barely 25 percent of the 2005 level in 2010.[27]

If not a more pronounced slump in home prices, what then explains the more concerted response in the 1930s? The answer lies in the structure of housing finance. Lenders, recall, required down payments of as much as half the purchase price. As a result, few homeowners found themselves with mortgages exceeding the value of their homes even when prices fell by a third. This eliminated the need for radical write-downs of principal, which would create large losses for the banks or significant costs to the taxpayer. Bridging measures that kept housing finance flowing and provided help with interest payments could thus go a long way toward resolving the crisis.

Initially, Hoover took a characteristically voluntarist approach to the problem, appointing expert committees to study the housing market and convening a December 1931 conference on home building and ownership. But he also revived an earlier proposal by the Senate Committee on Reconstruction and Production (the Calder Committee, chaired by William M. Calder, the senator from New York) to address the post–World War I housing shortage by creating a Federal Home Loan Bank System. Calder was the son of a builder. He trained as a carpenter and was formerly the building commissioner for the Borough of Brooklyn, all of which heightened his interest in housing.[28] The Home Loan Bank System as he saw it would provide liquidity and oversight to building and loan associations, comparable to the liquidity and oversight that the newly created Federal Reserve System was making available to their commercial bank competitors. This was the proposal Hoover now sought to revive. The December presidential conference endorsed it, and Congress followed with the Federal Home Loan Bank Act of 1932.

But the Federal Home Loan Banks extended loans only to building and loan associations (not surprisingly, since the United States Building & Loan League helped draft the legislation), while ignoring the problems of other housing lenders. And they did nothing to offer borrowers interest-rate relief. More comprehensive and effective measures would have to wait on the change in administration.

These took the form of the Home Owners' Loan Corporation, or HOLC, yet another product of the Hundred Days. The HOLC rolled over mortgages, giving borrowers interest rate relief but leaving principal intact. Its mortgages bore an interest rate of 5 percent, as opposed to rates of 6 to 8 percent on conventional loans, and ran an unprecedented fifteen years to maturity.[29]

The trick was transferring mortgages to the corporation without damaging bank balance sheets or straining the public purse. The HOLC purchased mortgages in exchange for bonds guaranteed by the government. Those bonds paid an interest rate of only 1 to 3.5 percent but were free of default risk. A liquid secondary market in HOLC bonds was quick to develop, allowing banks to convert them into cash. Importantly, banks were free to reject HOLC offers. This meant that mortgage lenders benefited from the program.

The difference between what the HOLC earned and what it paid the bondholders gave it a margin with which to work. The HOLC further limited its exposure by restricting loans to 80 percent of the value of property.[30] Borrowers thus had skin in the game. Further declines in prices would have had to be substantial, in other words, to trigger widespread defaults. The 80 percent threshold was just high enough to permit a borrower who had made a 50 percent down payment but seen his property values fall by a third to stay in his home.[31]

Over its life, the HOLC bought more than a million mortgages. It held mortgages on one in ten nonfarm owner-occupied homes and fully 20 percent of home mortgage debt by 1936.[32] By taking toxic mortgages off bank balance sheets, it helped to resolve the banking crisis. It also helped the housing market. Charles Courtemache and Kenneth Snowden find that counties with HOLC offices, where the corporation's activities were most extensive, had higher home values and home ownership rates at the end of the 1930s. Price Fishback and his coauthors find that the HOLC encouraged construction activity by limiting the incidence of defaults and foreclosures. In particular, its loans increased the supply of housing in smaller cities where problems in a few local banks could have major repercussions for the construction sector and generally.[33]

All this was achieved at limited cost, because down payments were large, obviating the need for reductions in principal. This in turn limited the need to impose losses on the banks, of the sort that principal reductions would have entailed, and losses for the government, which would have resulted if the HOLC paid more for loans.[34]

Someone still had to bear the losses from lower home values. In the event, that someone was the homeowner. Except insofar as it limited downward pressure on home prices by limiting defaults, the HOLC did nothing to change this.[35] But by keeping mortgage credit flowing and reducing interest rates, it was able to keep families in their homes, limiting a major source of distress.

The irony was that the HOLC and other New Deal housing reforms, like the Federal Housing Administration created in 1934 to insure long-term mortgages, reshaped the market in ways that set the stage for the 2008–09 crisis. Mortgages were now federally guaranteed, encouraging financial institutions to accept smaller down payments. The 20 percent norm established by the HOLC remained the standard for down payments even after the corporation was wound up. Depression-era policies also helped to create national appraisal and construction standards that encouraged funds to flow more copiously into regions with booming housing markets. Most controversially, there was the creation of Fannie Mae in 1938 to encourage new lending by purchasing Federal Housing Administration–insured home mortgages from local banks.

It is not right to argue that these 1930s changes were responsible for the housing boom and bust after the turn of the century. But without them, the housing boom and subprime crisis could not have taken the form they did.

CHAPTER 17 | Takahashi's Revenge

T HE GREAT DEPRESSION was a crisis not just for the United States but for the world. It was the most serious global crisis in memory. For most countries it was the most serious crisis since World War I.

One might think that a crisis of this magnitude would have shocked governments and central banks into action. But officials hesitated to resort to the kind of exceptional measures to which they had turned in wartime. Balanced budgets remained the order of the day, or the aspiration of balanced budgets anyway, since achievement of the same remained elusive. This was very different from the response in 1914, when orthodoxy quickly gave way in the fight for national survival.

Likewise, the gold standard may have collapsed, but central banks and their political masters were reluctant to capitalize on their newfound freedom. Instead they sought to surrender it as quickly as possible by re-pegging the national currency, if no longer to gold then to sterling or the dollar. The instincts that led FDR to re-peg the dollar to gold at $35 an ounce already in January 1934 and to do what he could to restrain the growth of government spending were by no means uniquely Rooseveltian, or for that matter uniquely American.

The specifics were shaped, to be sure, by distinctive aspects of each country's experience. That said, it is possible to identify some common factors affecting the policy response, or lack of response, virtually everywhere. There was belief in the analogy between the household budget and the government budget. Governments should live within their means, and any tendency to do otherwise could only come to grief. Keynesian theories of countercyclical fiscal policy had not yet been developed, for better or worse. (Opinions differ.) Historians of economic thought like to point to contemporaries like Bertil Ohlin in Sweden and Paul Reynaud in France, who were able to intuit the argument for deficit spending in a slump. But even if recovering early proto-Keynesian arguments from contemporary writings is popular sport, it is hard to maintain that such arguments had much of an impact. What mattered more were the imperatives of rearmament, which led governments to increase spending and tolerate deficits as a matter of national survival, as they had in World War I. The bulk of that deficit-financed military spending occurred later, in the second half of the 1930s, by which time the crisis was long in the tooth.

In addition, there was the association of budget deficits and central bank credit creation with inflation, first during World War I and then in the 1920s.[1] In countries like Germany, the public was traumatized by inflation. With that history still vivid, officials were reluctant to contemplate anything that might be seen as courting a recurrence of the experience, however remote and however radically circumstances were now changed. What is more remarkable is how those same fears of inflation, brought alive by this history, informed and inhibited policy in other countries, like the UK, that had experienced the phenomenon only at second hand.

Associated with these fears was an all-but-universal reluctance to abandon the exchange rate as the anchor for monetary policy. The exchange rate against gold had been the basis for central bank decision making for years. The one peacetime exception, the first half of the 1920s, was a disaster of inflation and financial instability. The gold standard had malfunctioned, but there was no coherent alternative for conducting monetary policy. Much later, in the 1990s, central banks developed the conceptual framework known as "flexible inflation targeting."[2] When the crisis hit in 2007–08, they were willing to let their currencies move, if such movement was a corollary of monetary policies directed at stabilizing prices and output. But in the 1930s, the absence of a coherent alternative to the traditional exchange-rate-centered approach to monetary policy left central banks reluctant to abandon it. This in turn limited their ability to stabilize not just prices but also the economy and its financial system.

This reluctance allowed the Depression to deepen and persist. That depth and persistence in turn did much to discredit prevailing economic and financial arrangements. In some cases, as in the United States, this prompted efforts to repair and rehabilitate the market system. It led to regulatory reforms designed to stabilize financial markets, institutional reforms to strengthen the conduct of monetary policy, and social policy reforms to protect those unable to protect themselves. In other cases, as with Germany, the Depression and the failure of policy makers to address it led to less constructive outcomes. The market system was rejected in favor of state direction. This alternative to fixing the broken market economy, it would transpire, was far worse.

———

The exception that proves the rule, demonstrating what was possible when a government took concerted action, was Japan. The country had already endured a difficult decade, growing at less than 1 percent per annum between 1919 and 1929. Activity was disrupted by bank runs and financial panics. Failure of the Osaka-based Masuda Bill Broker Bank in April 1920 provoked runs across the country. In February 1922 the failure of Ishii Corporation, a lumber company speculating in commodities, sparked runs in Osaka, Kyoto, and Kochi Prefecture on banks thought to have ties to Ishii and one another. The Kanto Earthquake of 1923 wrought financial as well as physical damage, destroying the offices of fully 80 percent of all banks in Tokyo, leading to fears of more bank runs, and prompting a moratorium on debt payments. The government encouraged the Bank of Japan to discount commercial paper and other obligations payable in the affected areas and adopted an emergency ordinance promising to indemnify the bank, not unlike how the US Treasury in 2008 offered to indemnify the Fed for any losses it incurred as a result of its rescue of Bear Stearns.[3] There was then a further round of runs in 1927, when in the course of the debate in the Diet over the terms of that compensation officials revealed the existence of financial problems in Suzuki & Co., a large trading house in Kobe, and its financial partner, the Bank of Taiwan.[4]

This litany of woes and the need for central bank intervention on each occasion resulted in delays in returning to gold.[5] Japan finally did so in January 1930, in an act of exquisitely bad timing. The consequences were not unlike those in Britain, only worse. As in Britain, prices had risen sharply during the war. But in Japan, it was not possible to push them back down as rapidly as in Britain in the 1920s. Instead the Bank of Japan was forced to provide credit to keep the banks on life support. Thus, it could not restore the prewar exchange rate against sterling and gold.

Once conditions finally normalized sufficiently for the prewar exchange rate against sterling to be restored in 1930, the yen was significantly overvalued. This made for trade deficits and gold losses. It fed expectations that, when Britain abandoned the gold standard in September 1931, Japan would necessarily follow.

The Minseitō Party campaigned during the 1928 national election on a platform to cut wasteful public spending and restore the gold standard. The prime minister from 1929, Osachi Hamaguchi, appointed Junnosuke Inoue as his finance minister because he thought that Inoue, a fellow believer in gold standard orthodoxy, could successfully execute the policy. The austere, upright Inoue having done so successfully, he had much invested in the policy status quo. Following Britain's departure from gold, he quickly reaffirmed that the monetary standard would be defended. The Bank of Japan raised the discount rate in October and again in November in an effort to carry out his wishes.[6]

The Federal Reserve had responded similarly to the reserve losses precipitated by Britain's departure from gold.[7] But where America's gold peg held, Japan's did not. Japan had a greater recent record of financial instability. Worried about the state of the banking system and doubtful about the capacity of the central bank to continue draining liquidity from financial markets, National City Bank, the Hong Kong and Shanghai Banking Corporation (HSBC), Sumitomo, Mitsui, and Mitsubishi sold yen for dollars. Gold outflows continued unabated.[8] Unable to agree on steps to contain them, the Minseitō-led government was forced to resign on December 12.

This brought to power the opposition Seiyūkai Party, and specifically Finance Minister Korekiyo Takahashi. The elderly Takahashi was an unlikely revolutionary. The illegitimate son of a court painter at Edo Castle, he was born in 1854, a year after the arrival of Commodore Perry's black ships, and as an infant was adopted into the lowest rank of samurai. As a young man he served as an entry-level bureaucrat, first in the Ministry of Education and then in the Ministry of Agriculture and Commerce, before going to work for the Bank of Japan. For having helped to arrange the foreign loans that financed the country's war against Russia, he was awarded a peerage in 1905. In 1913, not yet forty, he was appointed finance minister. By 1931 he was on his fifth tour of the position. This obviously was no financial neophyte.

Takahashi held the further advantage that by 1931 Japan had formulated its monetary policy without support from the gold standard for more than a decade. Making monetary policy without that familiar structure was thus not something with which he or the Japanese public was unfamiliar. The decision to return to gold in 1930 having been taken by his predecessor, a member of the opposition party, Takahashi could reverse it without embarrassment.[9] In addition, there was a sense of rivalry between Inoue and Takahashi. Inoue was an exponent of not just the gold standard but also fiscal austerity; his rival Takahashi was happy to position himself as the opposite.

This decision to follow Britain off gold was not unlike the response of a number of other countries, as we will see below. What was unique was Takahashi's concerted use of policy to jump-start the economy. Immediately on embargoing gold exports, he moved to push down the exchange rate in order to vanquish expectations of deflation and strengthen export competitiveness.

In March 1932 he proposed that the Bank of Japan directly purchase all newly issued government bonds, expanding the money supply. This was actually more than a proposal, since the Bank of Japan was not independent but, in fact, under the supervision of the Ministry of Finance, Article 16 of the Bank of Japan Act providing a legal basis for the finance minister to instruct the central bank to engage in transactions in government bonds. There was little resistance within the bank; to the contrary, Takahashi received intellectual and political support from the deputy governor, Eigo Fukai, a fellow English speaker and friend.[10] Other members of the bank's administrative hierarchy were more skeptical but, the central bank not having exactly covered itself in glory, were in no position to object.[11]

In June Takahashi then submitted a supplementary budget providing for new spending on rural relief and on the army's military operations in Manchuria, where renegade officers, protecting Japan's colonial holdings there, had staged a terrorist incident they blamed on Chinese bandits, allowing them to launch a police action. Takahashi himself was opposed to Japan's military intervention in Manchuria, but he could still use it to advance his economic strategy.[12]

All this, Takahashi now proposed, should be financed by bond issuance. Remaining limits on the ability of the Bank of Japan to purchase those bonds were then removed by a law raising the amount of unbacked currency the bank could issue from ¥120 million to ¥1 billion, and by a second measure placing controls on capital outflows. The expectation, clear in light of Takahashi's actions and statements, was that the Bank of Japan would do its part to help finance his deficits. The government and central bank would be working in harness to actively bring deflation and depression to an end.

This, then, was an aggressively reflationary monetary policy made credible by fiscal expansion. In other words, it was precisely the policy claimed, erroneously, to have been followed in the United States under FDR.[13] But in Japan, unlike the United States, the fiscal expansion was real.

Here at least is one case where economic analysis may have played a role. Takahashi had firsthand knowledge of Western economic literature, having gained fluency in English at the age of eleven, when he was sent to the treaty port of Yokohama to study with American missionaries. (Takahashi was selected for foreign-language studies by a progressive samurai who understood that Japan, to survive, would need to import military technology, notably from the United States and Britain, and that language skills would be needed for the next generation to achieve these ends.[14]) Takahashi was familiar with the *Tract on Monetary Reform*, the 1923 book in which Keynes emphasized the distinction between exchange rate stability and price stability and the need to prioritize the latter. He was up to date on subsequent intellectual developments, being an avid reader of the *Times* of London.[15]

The results of his initiative were dramatic. Rates on short-term money fell from 15 to 1 percent. The money supply stabilized in 1932 before rising sharply in 1933. In the year from December 1931, the yen depreciated by more than 40 percent against the pound sterling and 60 percent against the dollar. Wholesale prices rose by 7 percent in 1932 and 12 percent in 1933, while industrial production rose even faster. Real GDP grew by 7 percent in 1932 and 8 percent in 1933.[16]

This was a happy outcome for the economy, if not also for Takahashi. When Japan returned to full employment in 1935, he cut back on defense spending—resulting in his assassination by disaffected military officers.

———

Japan's experience thus illustrates what concerted monetary expansion, backed by fiscal stimulus, could do. But it is hard to find other similar examples. More typical was the response of the Bank of England. The bank's hand had been forced, as we saw in Chapter 10, by the run on sterling that led to the suspension of convertibility in Montagu Norman's absence. But even then, it was far from clear what would come next. The pound fell to $3.40 in the first week of floating, losing a quarter of its value. After a brief recovery, it then fell further to $3.23 at the beginning of December.

At this point Norman grew worried that any further decline would fatally undermine confidence. He also had to address the concerns of other governors and directors who had stepped into policy roles in his absence. Since assuming the governorship in 1920, Norman had turned the Bank of England virtually into a personal fiefdom. But his incapacity over the summer and absence at the time of the country's most critical financial juncture transformed internal decision-making processes. Committees were set up in his absence; advisors were consulted. Following his return, they continued to meet and to advise. Decisions now were taken collectively, in response to collective hopes and fears.

Specifically, there was the collective fear that if panicked sales of the currency followed, Britain would succumb to the kind of inflation that had infected France and Germany in the 1920s. That inflation was the fear at a time when unemployment was 22 percent—when deflation was the real and present danger—can only be understood in light of collective psychology informed by this recent Continental experience.

Concerned that sterling was on the brink, Norman and his colleagues kept the bank's policy rate at 6 percent through the end of the year and into 1932. The idea that sterling was poised to collapse was far-fetched, of course.

The currency still had faithful followers in the banks and governments of the Commonwealth and Empire, and in other countries with extensive trade relations with Britain. But there was no more powerful conservative impulse than fear of the unknown, the gold standard having been the touchstone of policy for more than a century.

Norman, predictably, made no bones of his desire to return, albeit at a lower parity than before. Even Keynes, famously a critic of Churchill's decision to return to gold in 1925, now encouraged the government to pursue an international agreement to restore gold convertibility and fixed exchange rates, albeit with the higher gold price and lower backing ratios needed for price stability. But agreement on a gold peg remained elusive.[17]

This context makes the cautious reorientation of policy easier to understand. Time was needed for old fears to subside. Only on February 18, nearly five months following the suspension of convertibility, did the Bank of England finally cut interest rates, from 6 to 5 percent. No exchange rate collapse or inflationary outburst materializing, it cut rates to 4 and then 3.5 percent in March, and finally to 2 percent in July. This, then, was the advent of Britain's policy of "cheap money," ten long months after the collapse of the old regime.

In fact, the important policy innovations, as in Japan, were undertaken not by the ever-conservative central bank but by the Treasury. Neville Chamberlain, son of Joseph Chamberlain (the father having been mayor of Birmingham, a member of Parliament, and, in his time, the country's leading protectionist politician), was appointed Chancellor of the Exchequer as a result of the October 1931 general election, which saw decisive rejection of the failed Labour government and election of a Conservative-dominated parliament. Eventually, Chamberlain's name would become synonymous with appeasement. But if as prime minister and geopolitical strategist he was a disaster, he was a singularly effective chancellor by the standards of the time.

Effective by the standards of the time meant balancing the budget, as Chamberlain energetically set out to do with backing from his Conservative majority.[18] His biographer, William Rock, captures well the prevailing ethos: "There was no relief from taxes; that might lead to a premature relaxation of the efforts which were beginning to produce a revival of public confidence. Drastic economies were necessary before the normal expenditures and revenue could be balanced; therefore, drastic economies there would be."[19] The resemblance with the policies of the David Cameron–led Conservative-Liberal government starting in 2010 was more than superficial.

Equally consequential was Chamberlain's decision to set up an Exchange Equalisation Account (EEA) in the Treasury. The stated purpose of the account was to smooth fluctuations in the value of sterling by intervening in the foreign exchange market. In practice, however, the bulk of that intervention took the form of purchasing foreign exchange with sterling in order to keep the currency from rising. As Susan Howson, the unofficial historian of the EEA, judiciously put it, "It is clear that the authorities wished to reduce fluctuations in the exchange value of the pound, particularly upward fluctuations."[20]

Using the EEA, Chamberlain kept sterling at a competitive level and ensured an adequate supply of domestic credit. Although he consulted with the Bank of England, it was the chancellor who made the final decision on the stance of policy. This was another example, in the manner of Takahashi, where a political leader seized the reins from a central bank that hesitated to act. Yet another instance of the same, as we have seen, was in October 1933, when FDR intervened in the gold market to push prices up and the dollar down.

As in the United States, and in contrast to Japan, however, there were no large-scale budget deficits accompanying this monetary expansion and no pressure on the central bank to buy the bonds issued to finance them. Moreover, a central bank discount rate of 2 percent, which was what Britain now enjoyed, was not cheap money by the standards of Mervyn King or Ben Bernanke. Supplies of money and credit increased only as permitted by inflows of foreign currency, which were then absorbed by the EEA in exchange for sterling. These could be fickle: inflows grew large in December 1932, when worries developed about a possible dollar devaluation by the US president-elect, but they could be small and even negative at other times. The British money supply, broadly defined, grew by 10 percent in 1932 but then stagnated in 1933.[21] There was no attempt to push sterling down or to expand the money supply more aggressively. Once FDR completed his gold-buying program, the sterling rate against the dollar essentially returned to its early-1931 level, where it was stabilized.

If this was weak soup by the standards of Japan, the policy was better than nothing. A higher domestic currency price of gold meant a higher price level. Wholesale prices stopped falling in the summer of 1932, coincident with the reorientation of policy. Industrial production bottomed out in the third quarter and started rising in the fourth. The subsequent recovery was driven by interest-rate-sensitive spending, notably housing starts, motor vehicle sales, and, beginning in 1934, industrial investment. Cutting interest rates and preventing further falls in the price level also reduced the cost of servicing the heavy public debts inherited from World War I. Britain was able to maintain debt sustainability without having to endure even more severe public spending cuts.[22] This was not vigorous recovery à la Japan, but it was recovery after a fashion.

———

Members of the Commonwealth and Empire and other countries trading heavily with Britain were uncertain how to proceed. With their partner now off the gold standard, the advantages of adherence to that system were clearly diminished. There was an incentive to allow the currency to depreciate along with sterling in order to limit the loss of competitiveness in the British market. But rather than follow Takahashi in taking aggressive action, they followed Chamberlain, re-pegging to the pound, generally at levels not too different from those prevailing before 1931. In effect, it was the chancellor and the technicians at the Bank of England implementing his policy who determined the price level of the members of the sterling area.

The extent to which the subsequent policies remained exchange-rate-centered is striking.[23] Sweden is regularly held up as one country that developed a coherent alternative in the form of price level targeting. The Riksbank, the country's central bank, set an explicit target for the price level, it is said, and adjusted policy accordingly. Swedish policy was informed by economists like Gustav Cassel and Eli Heckscher, who were skeptical of the efficacy of the gold standard. The country had a long intellectual tradition, pioneered by the great Swedish economist Knut Wicksell, of prioritizing the stability of the price level as the proper aim of central bank policy.[24] And, critically, Sweden had the advantage of not having endured a disruptive German- or French-style inflation, allowing officials to contemplate alternatives.

There was much rhetoric about the desirability of stabilizing the price level. The Banking Committee of the Swedish parliament, or Riksdag, which supervised the central bank, formed a committee to consider alternatives. It warned against the precipitous resumption of gold convertibility and urged avoiding both deflation and inflation. Riksbank researchers constructed a new index of consumer prices to enable the central bank to better monitor price level trends.

But, new index of consumer prices or not, the board of the Riksbank remained preoccupied by the stability of the exchange rate, this still being regarded as the most reliable indicator of inflationary or deflationary tendencies. When the krona then showed signs of strengthening excessively in the spring of 1933, it was pegged to the pound at a level that remained unchanged until the outbreak of World War II. Having depreciated sharply in the Kreuger crisis of 1932, the currency was now competitively valued.[25] But that valuation was more an inadvertent consequence of the crisis than a conscious monetary strategy. So much, then, for price-level targeting as an alternative to exchange-rate-centered policies.[26]

The story in Latin America was again similar. Since the United States rather than the UK was the most important trading partner of many Central and South American countries, they pegged their currencies to the dollar.[27] Their governments having borrowed heavily abroad, currency adjustment was delayed until something was first done about the debt; otherwise, depreciating the currency would have made external obligations denominated in dollars impossible to service. Exchange controls were imposed to limit imports. One Latin American country after another then suspended debt service payments, after which devaluation of the currency could follow. Although antagonizing the creditors by halting interest payments was not ideal, foreign lending had already collapsed; there were worse fates now than having one's bonds de-listed in New York and London. With the collapse of foreign trade, there was similarly less fear of trade retaliation.[28]

Having been cut loose from gold, the currency and balance of payments were now supported by imposing tariffs on imports of manufactured goods. Latin American countries had not seen much in the way of industrial development prior to this period.[29] This now began to change as currency depreciation and tariff protection caused households and firms to substitute the products of domestic manufacturing firms for imported manufactured goods.[30] There were also other less salutary government interventions, like those of the Coffee Stabilization Council in Brazil, which purchased fourteen million bags of coffee, only to burn them and dump them at sea in a futile attempt to support the world market price.

———

Still this was nothing remotely approaching the extent of intervention in Germany and the countries of Central and Eastern Europe soon to come within its orbit. Germany, Austria, and Hungary, as victims of 1920s hyperinflation, were supremely reluctant to contemplate anything that might be construed as monetary manipulation. Even after the 1931 financial crisis, they continued to maintain the pretense, if not the reality, of the gold standard. Rather than allowing their currencies to move, they applied exchange controls to limit capital flight. Hungary was first to do so, in July 1931, when it was infected by the banking crisis in its old imperial partner, Austria. Within months Czechoslovakia, Bulgaria, Romania, and Yugoslavia all followed.

An advantage of exchange restrictions for authoritarian governments was that they provided an additional lever with which to control the economy. By controlling the allocation of foreign exchange, they could determine the source and composition of imports. Exchange control was thus a step toward market socialism and, ultimately, central planning. It was an instrument of foreign policy that governments, notably Germany's, deployed by demanding concessions and negotiating bilateral agreements with trading partners over which they had economic leverage.

Germany, as it did in other contexts, took these destructive tendencies to the extreme. Hitler himself was not especially knowledgeable of economic matters. On being appointed chancellor by President Paul von Hindenburg in January 1933, he turned for guidance and advice to Hjalmar Schacht, the Magician who had supposedly conjured up the 1924 stabilization. As power hungry as ever, Schacht not so secretly cultivated the chancellor-to-be and encouraged a reluctant Hindenburg to appoint him following the Nazis' strong showing in the 1932 election. Thus, among Hitler's first acts was to reappoint Schacht to the presidency of the Reichsbank, replacing Hans Luther.

Power hungry or not, for more than six months Schacht made essentially no use of his monetary powers to reflate the economy. With memories of hyper-inflation omnipresent, he allowed the money supply to keep falling for the balance of 1933.[31]

But in the absence of monetary reflation, it was necessary to resort to less savory methods to stabilize the economy. Strikes were banned and union officials were arrested as the Nazis sought to boost employment by keeping wages low. Prices were controlled, and a price commissioner was appointed to monitor them. The Nazis established marketing boards with the exclusive right to purchase agricultural goods, first to support farm prices and then to keep them down as the economy recovered. They signed long-term contracts with industrial groups to purchase their output at fixed prices, using the threat of nationalization to secure favorable terms. From there it was a small step to establishing the Hermann Göring Works and other government-owned enterprises.

Understanding where the real power lay, Schacht moved in 1934 to the Ministry of Economics while also retaining his central bank presidency. There he enjoyed the kind of decree powers of which central bankers can only dream. Starting in September, when he announced his "New Plan" for overseeing all foreign exchange purchases and sales, with the exchange rate for trade depending on the country, there was a sharp shift in the composition of imports from consumer goods to the materials needed for rearmament. From this point, Schacht's control of the country's international transactions was complete.

However unsavory the means, the government's ends were achieved. Output rose by 25 percent between 1933 and 1935, rescaling the peak reached in 1928. All this was done in the interest of rearmament, and only incidentally recovery, but no matter. Growth was led by capital spending on the military-industrial complex (steel, chemicals, aircraft, and motor vehicles). "Hitler had found a cure against unemployment before Keynes was finished explaining it," was the way the Cambridge economist Joan Robinson put it.[32]

This was an exaggeration. The budget deficit of the Reich rose from essentially zero in 1932 to 3 percent of GDP in 1934, where it remained until 1937. This was a significant fiscal stimulus by the standards of the time, but it was too small to restore full employment in an economy with an unemployment rate above 20 percent and in which output had fallen more than 25 percent below potential.[33] The association between budget deficits and inflation was still too vivid for even Hitler to engage in aggressive fiscal expansion.

And it is not as if whatever employment was created stimulated consumer spending. Wages were controlled. The availability of consumer goods was limited. Farmers were prohibited from borrowing to finance modernization and obtain working capital. "Guns, not butter," the well-known slogan, was in fact coined by the Nazi propaganda ministry in 1935 to impress on the German public the priorities. Hitler could point to the restoration of full employment, but the main mechanisms by which this was achieved were the introduction of compulsory military service in 1935; transformation of the voluntary labor service into the obligatory Reich Labor Service, in which men aged eighteen through twenty-five were required to serve six months; and the Nazis' propaganda campaign against the labor force participation of women—not the Keynesian stimulus of which Joan Robinson admiringly spoke.

———

The Nazis were a peculiarly German aberration, although they had analogs in antisystem parties in other countries experiencing deep depressions, whose mainstream parties showed little ability to cope with the consequences. But even where the result was not political extremism, deflation encouraged an interventionist response.

This was most notably the case in countries that clung to the gold standard—France, Belgium, the Netherlands, Switzerland, and Italy—where deflation and depression were worst. Spending on final goods being in short supply, their governments resorted to tariffs and quotas to bottle it up. The Netherlands, having been faithful to free trade since the sixteenth century, now raised import duties by 25 percent and applied quotas and licensing fees to both imports and exports.[34] France had negotiated commercial treaties with its neighbors in the 1920s under the leadership of the visionary pan-Europeanist foreign minister Aristide Briand; now it applied quotas, product by product and country by country. Belgium, an open economy reluctant to tax foreign goods for fear of retaliation, doubled its tariffs between 1928 and 1935 while, in self-protection, negotiating special bilateral agreements with its powerful French neighbor. Defending the strong lira established by Mussolini in 1927, Italy adopted the largest absolute increase in tariffs of any country save Germany and used comprehensive exchange controls as a lever for negotiating German-style bilateral clearing arrangements with its trading partners.[35]

Governments resorted to these disruptive interventions because existing institutions and policies had not delivered socially acceptable outcomes. If free trade did not deliver the goods, it followed that trade needed to be managed. If foreign lending was associated with instability, then foreign lending needed to be controlled. In fact, what made the Great Depression great were not the problems of trade or even foreign lending, but the flawed monetary and fiscal policies that flowed from a flawed monetary and fiscal regime. But where that regime was too deeply embedded to be uprooted, governments unable to respond by fiscal and monetary means responded in the only way they knew, by controlling trade and capital flows.

The alternative treatment, like chemotherapy administered to a cancer patient, had unfortunate side effects. Tariffs were not raised across the board. Instead, the most generous protection was afforded to the least efficient agricultural and industrial sectors, which were most desperate to attract spending and most at risk of losing sales to foreign competitors. These, naturally, were the sectors that lobbied most intensively for help and got it more often than not. Sectors propped up by protection grew accustomed to public support and adept at lobbying for its extension. The same sectors that benefited from these interventions in the 1930s, like agriculture, were again the recipients of the most generous protection after World War II.[36]

The consequences for international relations were even worse. Germany used its trade-policy levers to increase the dependence of its Eastern European neighbors on its economy.[37] Trade-policy conflicts in turn hindered the efforts of the allies to form a united front against the Reich.

After 2008–09, central banks were criticized for cutting interest rates to zero and expanding their balance sheets in the effort to reflate their economies, on the grounds that those policies distorted financial conditions, threatened an outbreak of inflation, and had other damaging side effects. A close reading of the 1930s suggests that the counterfactual in which central banks sat on their hands would have seen even more damaging consequences.

| Dip Again

I T IS A commonplace that economic recovery from a financial crisis is slower than recovery from a normal recession. If so, US experience starting in 1933 is an exception. Industrial production doubled between the first half of 1933 and the first half of 1937. Real GDP rose by 50 percent.[1] The starting point was low, but recovery at this pace is no less impressive for the fact.

From there, output headed back down. A double-dip recession was of course the last thing America needed. Output in 1937 was still far below late-1920s levels. Unemployment was still 14 percent.[2] Unless one believes that the damage wrought by the Depression somehow reduced the productive potential of the economy, perhaps by rendering the unemployed unemployable, recovery still had room to run.

It thus took a concerted effort by everyone from FDR on down to produce another recession. The president had again become obsessed with balancing the budget. Large deficits, as he saw it, were a sign that the economy was still ill. Balancing the budget, on the other hand, would signal that the emergency was over. Doing so would give a welcome boost to confidence.

Not for the last time in the annals of economic policy, there was also an element of political expediency involved. Having campaigned in 1932 on a promise to balance the budget, FDR became fixated on the idea with the approach of the 1936 election. It was not so much criticism from the Republican Right that the president feared. Rather, he worried about a challenge from the Left in the person of the radio priest Father Charles Coughlin, who would attack him for failing to crack down on the wealthy and for having been too easy on the bankers. Although Coughlin had supported FDR in 1932, he now turned against him on the grounds that the New Deal was insufficiently ambitious;

it marked "two years of surrender, two years of matching the puerile, puny brains of idealists against the virile viciousness of business and finance, two years of economic failure."[3] Coughlin's own program was a mishmash of conservative and radical ideas, ranging from simplification of government and the tax system to the nationalization of essential industries. The radio priest might not be a serious candidate, but his upstart Union Party still had the capacity to siphon off votes.[4]

Thus, balancing the budget and populist tax policies could go hand in hand. This political strategy led FDR to push, and the Democrat-controlled Congress to agree to, higher taxes on individuals with incomes above $100,000. A new tax was also levied on undistributed corporate profits, which the wealthy had been using, the president suggested, to shelter income.

These higher taxes were not helpful, but neither are they the entire explanation for the recession that commenced in 1937. The increase in income taxes affected only a fraction of the 1 percent of highest earners. The undistributed profits tax could have depressed investment spending by encouraging firms to pay out dividends rather than using retained earnings to underwrite capital projects. However, the most detailed study of the tax, by Charles Calomiris and Glenn Hubbard, concludes there was little tendency for firms with attractive investment opportunities to forgo them. Numerous investment projects promising high returns had been deferred during the Depression. Companies were now willing to use their retained earnings to finance them, undistributed profits tax or not. The fact that investment was the most strongly growing component of GDP in the second half of 1936 makes it hard to hang the recession on the undistributed profits tax alone.[5]

———

More important, surely, was the restrictive turn in monetary policy. The prices of raw materials and primary products had begun moving up with the recovery. Mindful of the experience of the 1920s, the Fed was quick to warn that higher prices might spill over to financial markets and into another wave of financial speculation. Almost as if on command, the Dow Jones industrials began rising in July.

Marriner Eccles, the Utah businessman-banker newly installed as governor of the Federal Reserve Board, was less concerned than many of his colleagues. Introduced to FDR by Rexford Tugwell, whom he had met on an earlier trip east, Eccles was involved in drafting the Banking Act of 1935.[6] The act transferred the power to set discount rates and conduct open market operations once and for all from the Reserve banks to the board of governors, and it conferred on the board the power to change reserve requirements for member banks.[7]

Centralizing the power to set discount rates promised to avoid a replay of the disastrous experience of the 1920s, when Reserve banks failed to coordinate their policies. Empowering the board to alter reserve requirements gave it another instrument with which to influence bank lending.

Transferring power from the regions to Washington, D.C., was anathema to Senator Carter Glass, who had contributed to the original legislation that established the central bank's decentralized design. But greater centralization was not uncongenial to FDR. More generally, the central bank's failure to contain the Depression and stem the banking crisis undermined support for Glass' decentralized design. Glass and his allies, the banker Owen Young among them, opposed the reform as subjecting monetary policy decision making to "political control." But political control was no longer patently undesirable, given the manifest incompetence of apolitical decision making.

The Banking Act sailed through Congress, and FDR was quick to draw the logical conclusion and appoint Eccles, his personal monetary reformer, to head the reorganized Fed.[8] Eccles claimed no association with Wall Street, which worked in his favor. His straightforward manner and background as the grandson of a blind covered-wagon pioneer gave him the benefit of the doubt. That he had managed a chain of twenty-eight family banks across three states and virtually invented the chain banking model, which caused so much trouble in other contexts, was conveniently overlooked, as was the fact that his construction company was heavily involved in the public works project later known as Hoover Dam. Eccles is sometimes said to have been the model for the George Bailey character in *It's a Wonderful Life*. In his autobiography he describes how, faced with a bank run, he mounted the counter of the First National Bank in Ogden in 1931 to reassure anxious depositors that the bank had adequate cash.[9]

But installed in his new position, Eccles found to his chagrin that his powers were ineffectual. The now higher dollar price of gold, in conjunction with unsettled conditions in Europe, caused foreign funds to flow toward the United States, where they piled up in the banks. Swimming in cash, banks had no need to borrow from the Fed. As a result, changes in the discount rate, the instrument on which the Federal Reserve relied to fine-tune financial conditions, had no impact on bank behavior.

The decision by the Federal Reserve Board under Eccles to raise reserve requirements from 13 to 19.5 percent in August 1936, 22.5 percent in March 1937, and 26 percent in May was intended to restore the effectiveness of the central bank's conventional policy tools. It was a way for the Fed to reassert its control of financial conditions.[10] But Milton Friedman and Anna Schwartz argue that these higher reserve requirements were the blunt instrument that caused the 1937–38 recession.[11] Bank lending peaked in the first half of 1937, they observe, coincident with the second increase in required reserves and immediately prior to the downturn in industrial production. The increase in reserve requirements must have been the cause.

Modern scholarship has not been kind to their argument. Thomas Cargill and Thomas Mayer compare the response of member banks with that of banks that were not members of the Federal Reserve System and were not subject to the higher reserve requirements. Any differences in subsequent lending behavior were too small, they find, to have contributed significantly to the 1937–38 recession.[12] Charles Calomiris, Joseph Mason, and David Wheelock, focusing exclusively on Federal Reserve member banks, similarly find that the increase in reserve requirements had little impact on bank behavior.[13] These conclusions are consistent with the views of Eccles himself, who believed the increase in reserve requirements had little impact on the current state of the economy but was intended only to restore the effectiveness of the Fed's policy instruments for future use.[14] Thus, if a slowdown in bank lending precipitated the recession, it must have had other sources.

Treasury Secretary Morgenthau was among those preoccupied by the specter of inflation. Morgenthau had no formal training in economics and little experience in business, as his public appearances and cabinet interventions betrayed. He owed his cabinet post to his personal relationship with FDR, his Dutchess County neighbor, and to the untimely death of his predecessor, William Woodin. But this did not now deter him; inflation was an easy enough problem to understand. Benjamin Strong's policies between 1924 and 1928 had allowed excessive amounts of credit to build up in the banking and financial system, ultimately with destabilizing consequences. Or so was the historical recollection of Morgenthau and his circle.

And if excessive money and credit was a threat, Treasury had the upper hand when seeking to address it. Starting in December 1936, the Morgenthau Treasury sought to address this supposed inflationary threat by neutralizing the impact of gold inflows on credit markets. Every ounce of gold that flowed into the country from abroad could still be sold to the Treasury for $35, in principle adding that much more currency and credit to existing supplies and stoking inflation. To neutralize the inflationary threat, the Treasury Department now sold bonds from its portfolio in the same amount, mopping up the additional cash and removing it from circulation.[15]

Several pieces of evidence point to the importance of these operations for the 1937–38 recession. First, the nine months separating their initiation from the downturn is about the amount of time normally required for a monetary shock to be transmitted to the economy. Second, these Treasury operations depressed the money supply by roughly 10 percent, a large amount.[16] Finally, unlike the increase in reserve requirements, Treasury operations can also account for the timing of the recovery. Treasury ended its policy of neutralizing the impact of gold inflows on the economy in February 1938, in response to evidence that a recession was underway. In April it then began reversing earlier operations.[17] As expected, this imparted a sharp positive shock to the money supply and bank lending.

Activity bottomed out in June 1938, and the economy began to recover. Where the post-1929 downturn continued for nearly four years, this one lasted just one. The difference reflected the speed with which monetary conditions were relaxed. It is hard to imagine a more convincing demonstration of the power of policy.

This historical experience was widely cited as a cautionary tale by those who worried, starting in 2009, that the Fed might prematurely abandon its accommodative monetary stance.[18] They invoked the episode to warn that an economy only starting to recover from a financial crisis could require an extended period of monetary support. This historical instance when monetary policy had turned restrictive even while output remained as much as 15 percent below potential was part of what prompted the Bernanke Fed to maintain a relatively accommodative stance for the better part of six years.

———

Another popular explanation for the 1937–38 slump is the president's hostility to business. Kansas Governor Alf Landon, the Republican candidate, emphasized this when opposing Roosevelt in the 1936 presidential campaign. FDR in turn made much of business's opposition to his candidacy, disparaging his business critics as "economic royalists."[19]

In a study that attracted considerable attention following the 2008–09 crisis, Robert Higgs argued that government interference with the economy and uncertainty about regulation were responsible for the 1937–38 double dip.[20] The Social Security Act, the National Labor Relations Act, and the Banking Act all were passed over business opposition. Rapid-fire changes in antitrust law, labor law, securities law, and tax law—rapid-fire changes being the hallmark of the New Deal—unsettled business owners. Businessmen polled by the American Institute of Public Opinion overwhelmingly blamed uncertainty and the president's hostility to business for impeding the recovery.[21]

The main evidence Higgs adduces in favor of his uncertainty hypothesis is that the share of construction in private investment was lower in 1935–36 than in the second half of the 1920s. Construction is the form of investment most likely to be discouraged by uncertainty, since construction projects take time.

But a considerable proportion of construction in the 1920s was of residential and commercial real estate, as we saw in Chapter 1. It is hard to see why the construction of homes and offices a decade earlier should be taken as a metric for the adequacy of investment in industrial plant and equipment in the 1930s. The principal legacy of that earlier real estate boom now was an overhang of unoccupied commercial properties. Entire floors of the Empire State Building, which real estate professionals referred to disparagingly as the "Empty State Building," remained unoccupied in the 1930s. Then there were the glut of residential property and the mortgage crisis, which the HOLC went only partway to resolve.

Higgs' other evidence is the difference between interest rates on short- and long-term corporate bonds. Rates on short-term corporate bonds rose starting in 1934, but long-term rates rose even faster. Higgs ascribes the disproportionate increase in long-term rates to uncertainty about the economic future. "Investors' confidence in their ability to appropriate the longer-term interest payments and principal repayments promised by the country's most secure corporations plummeted between early 1934 and early 1936," he writes.[22] Anxious bondholders, responding to this uncertainty, demanded an additional premium in order to hold long-term claims on those corporations.

But rates on long-term government bonds also rose relative to those on the government's short-term obligations, and no one seriously doubted the government's commitment to servicing its debt. The explanation for these sympathetic movements is simple. Roosevelt had pushed up the price of gold, leading investors to anticipate inflation rather than deflation. With the economy poised to recover, they expected the demand for credit to recover with it. More demand for credit would mean higher interest rates. Higher expected future interest rates thus pushed up long rates starting in 1934. This in fact is the standard behavior of interest rates in recoveries.[23] It is similarly standard for the gap between long-term and short-term interest rates to narrow with the approach of a recession—which is what happened in 1937.

———

If one insists on a supply-side explanation for the 1937–38 recession, then one must look to the labor market. The administration had sought to raise wages and prices as part of its fight against deflation. As we have seen, it was even more successful in pushing up wages, which perversely raised labor costs and discouraged hiring at a time of 25 percent unemployment. The National Labor Relations Act, signed into law in 1935, then encouraged unionization by prohibiting discrimination against workers who belonged to a labor organization and requiring employers to bargain collectively with the workers' designated representative. So fortified, union membership doubled in two years.[24]

Workers quickly sought to determine how far they could push their new labor rights. The big three automobile firms, with their elaborate supply chains, were the obvious place to push. By disrupting production at a plant that was the sole source of a component, an isolated strike could shut down an entire firm. Sit-down strikes began at the Firestone and Goodyear Tire and Rubber Companies in Akron, Ohio, in early 1936. Following Roosevelt's landslide victory, they spread to General Motors' Fisher Body No. 1 in Flint, Michigan, which housed one of only two sets of dies used to produce the bodies of GM's 1937 model cars. (The plant was a descendant of the Fisher Body Corporation, which features in the story of Carl Fisher and Florida real estate in Chapter 1.) GM's weekly output fell from more than fifty thousand units in December 1936 to just fifteen hundred two months later, leaving the company no choice but to quickly reach an agreement with the United Auto Workers. Chrysler followed in weeks. Only Henry Ford, a sworn enemy of unionization, held out until 1941, but even the Ford Motor Company granted generous wage increases to keep the unions out.

Average hourly earnings in the auto industry rose by more than 20 percent between October 1936 and July 1937. For the moment, the auto companies left their prices unchanged, but everyone knew that the cost increase would mean higher prices with the arrival of the new model year in the second half of 1937; the auto companies' advertising anticipated as much. Consumers considering a new car were thus encouraged to purchase it before the price increases hit. As Joshua Hausman shows, sales were far above expectations in the first half of 1937 and then sharply lower in the second half. The timing coincides almost exactly with that of the recession.[25]

The question is whether the Roosevelt Administration was responsible for this eruption of worker militancy. In fact, FDR was no more than a lukewarm supporter of the Wagner Act, whose true champion was New York Senator Robert Wagner, a longtime advocate of labor rights. In any case, more than just legislation was at work. It is not surprising that, having taken wage cuts of as much as 50 percent since the start of the Depression, workers at GM and other auto firms went after increases when the demand for their products began to recover.

As in 1929, the slump had negative repercussions abroad. Although international trade and financial linkages had loosened since the 1920s, the US economy was still too important for it to be otherwise. Imports of manufactured and semi-manufactured goods fell off with the double dip. Raw material prices had risen with recovery, benefiting long-suffering Latin American exporters. They now reversed direction, not just in the United States but globally.

Still, the downturn in the rest of the world was short and shallow compared with 1929–1931. When exports to the United States tailed off, central banks and governments were no longer compelled to raise interest rates to prevent their exchange rates from weakening. They were now free to cut interest rates in order to encourage additional domestic spending to substitute for the US spending that was lost.

But getting to this point was not easy. Well into 1936, a hard core of European countries still clung, perversely, to the gold standard of prior years. In France, Belgium, Italy, and Poland there was a reluctance to open the door to the kind of interest-group infighting that spawned deficits and inflation in the 1920s. There was fear that Anglo-Saxon speculators would destabilize exchange rates and currencies, as they allegedly had a decade earlier. For the Netherlands and Switzerland, clinging to the gold standard was important for cementing the position of Amsterdam and Zurich as financial centers. For Poland, allying monetarily with France was a way of building financial defenses against Germany.

The political reaction against austerity then pulled the plug on this rump gold bloc. France, recall, had run budget deficits for much of the 1920s. When deficits then returned with the collapse of tax revenues in 1931, they brought with them the threat of renewed inflation and crisis, or so French leaders warned. Balancing the budget thus came to be seen as essential for maintaining confidence, fostering investment, and reviving growth. Although some French governments, like the right-wing coalition headed by Pierre Laval, pursued policies of austerity almost gleefully, others like the left-wing coalition led by Édouard Herriot did so reluctantly. Herriot, besides having been the victim of the 1925 Bank of France scandal, was known for being kind-hearted, which was probably a factor in his choice as prime minister again in 1932. But even Herriot was intimidated by the imminent arrival of the bond-market vigilantes.

Nor was it permissible to contemplate abandoning the gold standard. Expert French commentators were aware that cheap money had helped to stabilize the British and US economies, but they warned recovery induced in this way was temporary and unsustainable. Anesthetized from the pain of the Depression, speculators would be quick to resume the kind of reckless behavior that culminated in the 1929 crash.

One of the few to question whether austerity was the route to prosperity was Paul Reynaud, the Sorbonne-trained lawyer, amateur statistician, and early-1930s finance minister who represented a Parisian electoral district encompassing the Bank of France in the Chamber of Deputies. That Reynaud came from the Center-Right made his apostasy particularly compelling. But

Reynaud understood more clearly than most of his parliamentary colleagues that deflation and devaluation were the only available alternatives; there was no other way of squaring the circle. This contrasts with the members of the Socialist Party, whose slogan was the hopelessly unrealistic "Neither deflation nor devaluation."

Reynaud, as a Rightist, preferred deflation. In 1934 he attacked the Conservative National Unity government of Gaston Doumergue and the Radical-led government of Edouard Daladier alike for not implementing more draconian fiscal cuts in the effort to push down wages and costs.[26] But the failure of his increasingly pointed attacks to produce results and the reluctance of successive French governments, notwithstanding their very different political colorations, to pursue deflation more vigorously, especially if this meant antagonizing shopkeepers, public servants, and farmers, led Reynaud to conclude that regaining competitiveness through deflation was infeasible in practice.

What was unique about Reynaud was not his appreciation of the difficulty of deflation but rather his ability to recognize the implication. If deflation was infeasible, then devaluation—abandoning the gold standard—was the necessary alternative. Reynaud was no devaluationist, but he had the intellectual flexibility to change his position when, as Keynes would have said, the facts change. He was among the few able to distinguish the effects of currency depreciation in the 1920s, when demand exceeded supply and inflation resulted, from the effects of currency depreciation now, when deficient demand was the problem.

But Reynaud's style as a renegade—he adopted similarly unconventional positions on diplomatic and military issues—did not endear him to his colleagues. Nor did his temperament. Reynaud was the smartest person in the room, and he knew it. The more his parliamentary colleagues resisted, the more strident, sarcastic, and ineffective his interventions became.[27]

This summary might almost be dismissed as a caricature of the parallels between prevailing views in 1930s France and the policy dogmas of the twenty-first-century Eurozone were it not in fact an entirely accurate portrait of contemporary French opinion. Defense of the gold standard was seen as a moral imperative. Jean Tannery, newly installed governor of the Bank of France in 1935, spoke of it as "not solely a national necessity" but "a duty of far wider scope." The choice was "between certainty and illusion, thrift and speculation, productive work and the profit of the moment."[28] The same moralizing that underlay the commitment to austerity in post-2009 Europe rings through in Tannery's words.

———

It is not entirely obvious why blind faith in the gold standard endured for so much longer in France than in Britain or the United States. Initially French leaders could invoke what seemed like the country's genetic immunity to the Depression. Stabilization of the franc came late, and the extended period of turbulence that preceded it bequeathed a backlog of investment projects whose exploitation kept growth going for a time. The undervalued franc gave French industry a leg up and helped the country accumulate a war chest of gold. This allowed the Bank of France a margin of error. It allowed toleration of gold losses rather than forcing it to raise interest rates when outflows accelerated after 1933.[29]

And even when France felt the brunt of the Great Depression, the rise in unemployment was limited. France was more heavily agricultural than Britain and Germany. Workers who had recently moved to the cities retained connections in the countryside and returned to their villages when manufacturing employment turned down. The result was subsistence rather than prosperity, but subsistence was better than nothing.[30] This de facto safety net limited the political reaction against the policies responsible for the Depression. The result was not unlike Japan in the 1990s, which experienced a growth collapse and deflationary crisis; but the rise in unemployment was similarly limited due to early retirement, work sharing, and political pressure on large employers, and the political reaction was also surprisingly mild.

This is the only way of understanding why the French public continued to tolerate, for as long as it did, the policies of Pierre Laval, who returned for a second term as prime minister in 1935. Laval came from a modest background as the youngest child of a café proprietor and butcher in a village in the Auvergne, although he was a consummate political operator and, by this time, a wealthy man. Starting political life as a Socialist, he made his name as an attorney defending strikers, trade unionists, and left-wing agitators. He was asked in 1911 to stand, unsuccessfully, as Socialist candidate for the Chamber of Deputies in the Neuilly-Boulogne constituency of Paris, before winning a parliamentary seat in 1914 on a second try. In and out of office through the 1920s, Laval made his fortune from investments in two provincial newspapers, Le Moniteur de Puy-de-Dôme and the Lyon Républicain, and in the pioneering Radio-Lyon, acquisitions he financed with the help of banks and an investment trust that apparently appreciated the synergies between politics and media.

With wealth, Laval moved to the Center and then to the Right. In 1931, after the government of André Tardieu was brought down by the Oustric banking scandal, Laval was asked to head a new Center-Right government. This was the government that blocked an emergency loan to Austria during the Creditanstalt crisis and then came to loggerheads with the Hoover administration over reparations. Laval's was not an overwhelmingly positive record, and his government fell over a confidence vote in February 1932. That *Time* magazine chose him as its "Man of the Year" for 1931 reflected more his disarming man-of-the people image, on display during his US trip, than any positive achievement.

The most noteworthy aspect of Laval's year as head of government was the opportunity it afforded him for a tête-à-tête with Heinrich Brüning. His visit to Berlin in September 1931 was the first official visit to the German capital in half a century by a French statesman of comparable stature. Its main effect appears to have been to give Laval an appreciation of Brüning's approach to economic management.

By early 1935 the French Depression was fully underway. Investors increasingly feared that the franc would go the way of sterling, the dollar, and, closer to home, the Belgian franc. The Bank of France lost more than 10 percent of its gold reserves in May 1935 alone. The conservative government of Pierre-Etienne Flandin fell owing to its inability to restore confidence, and in June Laval was returned to power.

Laval now demanded Brüning-like powers of decree to cut the salaries and pensions of civil servants and veterans. He at least attempted to put a more sympathetic face on those policies; taking a leaf from FDR's book, he explained them in a fireside chat.[31] Seeking to capitalize on his image as a humble peasant, Laval used straightforward language and a homespun manner to convey his simple message: like a household in straitened times, the French state needed to tighten its belt, and balancing the budget would entail painful sacrifices all around. Laval's decree laws reduced central and local government expenditures by 10 percent and cut the wages and salaries of public employees by the same amount. Although these sacrifices were painful, there was no alternative. "You don't have to be an expert or a financier," Laval explained in man-of-the-people terms, "to realize that if you want to spend more than you have, you soon end up bankrupt. What is true for individuals," he intoned, invoking classic pre-Keynesian logic, "is also true of the national community."[32]

The predictable result was protest on the Left, which was convinced that Laval's emphasis on expenditure cuts favored the rich. The Communists and Socialists issued a joint manifesto denouncing Laval's "decrees of misery." In an echo of the Invergordon "mutiny," when British sailors threatened with pay cuts failed to fall in for duty, clashes broke out between workers at naval arsenals in Brest and Toulon and the municipal police. Conservative alarm over this left-wing agitation bolstered support for the proto-fascist organization of veterans known as the *Croix de Feu* ("Cross of Fire").

In response Laval, like Brüning before him, doubled down with a second set of decrees. Issued in August, they combined spending cuts with a cosmetic public-works program designed to sway public opinion. Here there again was inadvertent homage to FDR, who had combined budget balancing with measures to limit the increase in the cost of living and obeisance to the idea of stimulating the economy. This is the best one can do in attempting to put a coherent face on Laval's flurry of edicts.

That Parliament was in recess for the remainder of the summer allowed the government to survive into the fall. A third set of austerity measures followed on October 31, the day Laval's decree powers expired. The only thing that kept him in office was the reluctance of the Radicals, the moderate left-of-center party, to support the Socialist-Communist alternative, which they feared would mean devaluation.

————

By early 1936, even the French public had had enough. The Radicals, the Socialists, and the Communists formed a Popular Front for the April and May legislative elections.[33] The result was increased support for the Popular Front, but also for Far Right parties. With the Left commanding a small majority, the Radicals and Socialists, with support from the Communists, duly formed a government headed by Léon Blum.

Blum was the antithesis of Laval, electorates in this period tending to replace failed leaders with their temperamental and political opposites. Born in Paris, not the provinces, to a well-to-do family, Blum attended the prestigious École Normale Supérieure, whereas Laval had spent just a year studying in Lyon. Unlike Laval, who gravitated to the right, Blum remained a Socialist for life. Where Laval went on to collaborate with the Nazis and was tried and executed as a traitor, Blum opposed granting full powers to Marshall Pétain, leading to his arrest and imprisonment in Buchenwald and Dachau.

Blum campaigned in 1936 on a platform that included an end to public spending cuts, a commitment to large-scale public works, and radical reform of the Bank of France.[34] But even he ruled out devaluation as a bridge too far. Like FDR in 1932, Blum insisted that, though he would stabilize the economy by pushing up incomes and encouraging spending, he would not devalue. There would be "no monetary coup d'état," he reassured an anxious Chamber of Deputies.[35]

But just how the new premier proposed to square the circle was unclear. Not a few commentators suspected, as they had of Roosevelt, that Blum had determined to devalue before the election. It seems more likely that Blum, like Roosevelt, was uncertain about how to proceed. When the new government removed Jean Tannery as governor of the Bank of France for his association with deflation, it replaced him not with Pierre Quesnay, a deputy director known to favor devaluation, but with Émile Labeyrie, whose views on the subject were obscure.

After years of falling incomes, French autoworkers, like US autoworkers in 1936, were quick to attempt to collect the higher wages and easier conditions they were promised in the campaign. The initial sit-down strikes erupted when workers at Berliot, a manufacturer of cars, trucks, and buses, celebrated May Day by taking the day off and were fired in response. Strikes then spread to La Havre, where metalworkers in the aviation industry sat down on May 11. From there they spread to the metalworking factories of Paris, to Renault, and to the rest of the economy. The strikers succeeded in shutting not just factories but also bars and bakeries and, indeed, virtually the entire economy, aside from essential police and administrative services.

This was the situation confronting the new government on taking office in June. It responded with the Matignon agreements, named after the Hotel Matignon, the residence of the prime minister. The accord was negotiated between the unions and the employers' confederation, with the government as mediator, rather than legislated as in the United States, but the inspiration from the New Deal was clear. The Matignon agreements recognized the right to strike. They offered a 15 percent rise in private-sector pay. They granted a two-week annual holiday and a forty-hour workweek.

But their main effect, like that of the NIRA, was to raise production costs. Industrial production fell back starting in June, and unemployment began rising immediately. Sharply higher costs and prices depressed exports, leading to gold losses in August.

Blum didn't want to devalue, but he didn't know what else to do. It didn't help that his finance minister, Vincent Auriol, the Socialist party spokesman for financial issues, failed to offer a constructive alternative. Auriol's strategy for reconciling reflation with the gold standard was to predict the imminent return of confidence and, at the same time, to threaten currency speculators with capital controls. These were not exactly compatible—or confidence inspiring—policies.

Further deflation having been ruled out by the election, the only alternatives now remaining were devaluation and exchange control. Labeyrie and others joined Auriol in blaming the speculators and pushed for controls. In the end, Blum chose to follow the Americans rather than the Nazis; alliance politics as much as Socialist economic views carried the day.[36] The gold standard was abandoned on September 25. To save face, Auriol attempted to dress up the event as a "monetary adjustment" rather than devaluation.

About the true nature of the adjustment, however, there was no question. The franc dropped by 25 percent on the news. An exchange equalization fund like that established in the British Treasury was quickly created to manage the floating franc and keep it in a range between 25 and 35 percent below its earlier gold standard levels.

————

On the Saturday following announcement of the French devaluation, it took only a few hours for the Swiss National Bank to be overwhelmed by requests to convert francs into gold and for the Federal Council to acknowledge reality: "Switzerland Regretful" was how the *New York Times* headlined the news. Regret was not, however, the dominant emotion of investors. Swiss government bonds rose by 7 percent, Swiss railway bonds by 10 percent, on the first trading day following the weekend.

The pressure shifted next to Amsterdam; it took just hours for the Dutch government to throw in the towel. At this point the only country still on the gold standard at an unchanged parity was Albania, which continued to receive large loans from its political patron in Rome.[37] The Albanian nation would pay a high price for this financial support when it was occupied and forced into political union with Italy in 1939.

For the countries that now regained their monetary autonomy—or, more accurately, had monetary autonomy thrust on them—the question was how the public would react. In Holland, where workers and employers were well organized along religious as well as economic lines, it was straightforward to bring the social partners together and reach an agreement to trade wage restraint for investment. Prices now rose with depreciation, but costs did not follow. The result was a sharp increase in profitability; share prices rose by nearly 60 percent over the succeeding year. Industrial production was 37 percent higher in the first five months of 1937 than in the comparable period the year before. Rather than undermining confidence and exciting capital outflows, as the advocates of "rigor" had warned, depreciation prompted the repatriation of flight capital, making funds more freely available to industry and stimulating investment.

The Swiss case was similar. Depreciation of the Swiss franc brought about a sharp increase in export competitiveness. The improved profitability of export-oriented firms boosted share prices and investment. Deposits at Swiss banks rose in the wake of devaluation, contrary to the expectations of those who had argued that abandoning the gold standard would destroy Switzerland's status as a safe haven and financial center.

In each case currency depreciation removed the pressure for internal devaluation. It limited the need to reduce wages and costs, firm by firm and industry by industry. Export prices could be pushed up at a stroke. The Netherlands and Switzerland being small countries with institutions of social solidarity that could be used to restrain pressure for increases in wages and public expenditure, it was possible to prevent costs from following.

France, on the other hand, was a large country polarized by five years of deflation. Those who suffered most, members of the working class, now demanded recompense, making it impossible to restrain wages. The budgetary discipline of earlier years having been discredited, little could be done to limit the growth of public spending.

And where the Dutch and Swiss governments could blame devaluation on events beyond their control—they could point the finger at Paris—in France devaluation reflected the contradictions of the government's own policies. Blum's earlier insistence that the franc would not be devalued did not make the medicine go down easier or enhance the credibility of his promises. The right time to devalue would have been June, on taking office, in the manner of Takahashi. Blame for gold losses and problems of inadequate competitiveness could then have been laid on the doorstep of the previous government.

Instead, Blum vacillated. As a result, when devaluation finally came it did little to revitalize the French economy. Initially, some of the financial capital that had fled the country over the summer flowed back in, buoying the Paris Bourse. But the depreciation of the franc was smaller than the depreciation of sterling in 1931 and of the dollar in 1933. The US and UK could threaten to push their currencies down further if the French were too aggressive, forcing the Blum government to negotiate an agreement promising to limit franc depreciation. Together with the increase in costs, this meant there was little improvement in competitiveness.

By November, capital was once more flowing out, and industrial production was heading back down. Having condemned Laval's earlier use of decree powers, Blum now demanded them for himself. When the Senate denied his request, he resigned. For France, devaluation was an opportunity lost.

CHAPTER 19

Preventing the Worst

I N 2011, IN an interview with the *Daily Telegraph*, Bank of England Governor Mervyn King succinctly summarized what had been achieved by the response to the crisis. "We prevented a Great Depression," King baldly stated. Readers may have been inclined to dismiss the comment, coming from a leading central banker, as self-aggrandizing hyperbole, but King's assertion was not inconsistent with the facts. Global GDP dropped by a disastrous 15 percent between the peak in 1929 and the trough in 1932. Between 2008 and 2009, in contrast, it fell by just a fraction of 1 percent, and growth resumed already in 2010.[1] Even in the advanced countries hit hardest, the fall in 2009 was 3.5 percent of GDP, and growth turned positive again the next year. All was not sweetness and light, but this at least was no Great Depression.

There is no question that policy makers deserved much of the credit. Not all of it, of course. Changes in economic structure over the intervening decades also helped to moderate the slump, insofar as the relatively volatile industrial sector became less important in the advanced economies, while the stabler service sector acquired a heavier weight. The growth of government strengthened the effectiveness of automatic fiscal stabilizers, which work mainly by reducing tax payments when incomes fall. Nothing similar happened in the 1930s, since taxes accounted for a much smaller share of GDP and because governments did what they could to prevent deficits from emerging. The institutionalization of the global trading system, culminating in creation of a World Trade Organization with binding dispute-settlement powers, discouraged resort to beggar-thy-neighbor trade restrictions.[2] Central bank cooperation was fostered by regular meetings at the Bank for International Settlements. Solidarity among governments was forged by heads of state and ministers meeting as the G20.

These institutional developments built in turn on the lessons of the 1930s. The growth of government reflected the conviction, seemingly ineluctable in the wake of the Great Depression, that the market left to its own devices was unstable. It reflected the conclusion that if individuals were unable to protect themselves from the vicissitudes of an unstable market, then government would have to protect them, if capitalism was to survive. New Deal programs establishing work relief, unemployment insurance, and Social Security are all to be understood in this light.

Similarly, belief in the importance of fiscal stabilizers was an implication of the theories developed by John Maynard Keynes in response to the Depression. These theories showed that fiscal policy is especially powerful in a depression, when interest rates approach zero. The worst thing governments can do, economists concluded on the basis of this experience, is to raise taxes and cut public spending in a slump. Central banks were reorganized to prevent the monetary mistakes of the 1930s from being repeated. Decision-making power was centralized in the hands of the Federal Reserve Board, as we have seen, to prevent the Reserve banks from working at cross purposes. Efforts to strengthen the institutions of international economic cooperation were likewise animated by the view that they had failed disastrously in the 1930s.

The institutions for the most part survived intact, though the historical lessons inspiring their creation did not. Initially, central banks responded more forcefully than in 1929, making use of their enhanced powers. Governments cut taxes and boosted public spending to offset the fall in private demand. In April 2009, at the London G20 summit that was the high point of international cooperation, they agreed to coordinate their fiscal initiatives and shun beggar-thy-neighbor policies. The US Congress extended the duration of unemployment benefits to ninety-nine weeks. It increased food stamp eligibility and benefits in recognition that the crisis was having a disproportionate impact on the most vulnerable.

Although the specifics varied across countries, the response, qualitatively, was everywhere the same. Given the speed with which the crisis unfolded, there was no alternative to relying on the institutions and instincts developed in response to the Great Depression. And given the challenge of making sense of the unprecedented news flow, there was little resistance to relying on the kind of monetary and fiscal stimulus, financial triage, and extensions of the safety net that post-Depression thinking deemed appropriate for a crisis as serious as that of the 1930s.

Following this initial push, however, the debate and with it the policy response began to shift. Conservative critics had long been concerned by the growth of government and warned against excessive deficits. Now they began pushing back against the budget deficits and government programs associated with fiscal stimulus. Debt sustainability rather than high employment or growth became the priority. At the February 2010 Group of Seven meeting of finance ministers and central bank governors in Iqaluit, remote Northern Canada, the call for austerity was embraced under the Northern Lights. Fiscal consolidation rather than stimulus became the focus, even though economies were still far from fully recovered from the crisis.

In Europe, health care and pensions for retirees were cut in the name of fiscal consolidation. The 2012 presidential campaign in the United States was dominated less by the plight of the unemployed than by the "47 percent" of the population that, in the words of Republican candidate Mitt Romney, was "dependent on the government." Romney may not have triumphed, but his rhetoric and arguments did. Or so it seemed when Congress limited access to food stamps, and North Carolina replaced extensions in unemployment benefits with cuts in relief.

Similarly, the opponents of monetary activism warned that the aggressive expansion of central bank balance sheets portended inflation, and that purchases of mortgage-backed securities by the Federal Reserve and of sovereign bonds by the ECB delayed the necessary consolidation of private and public finances. By keeping interest rates low, they limited the pressure on households and governments to tighten their belts. The critics mounted strident attacks on central bank policies in the pages of the *Wall Street Journal* and elsewhere. The classic example was the open letter to Chairman Bernanke in the *Journal* on November 15, 2010, signed by twenty-three economists, investors, and political strategists, whose money quote read as follows: "We believe the Federal Reserve's large-scale asset purchase plan (so-called 'quantitative easing') should be reconsidered and discontinued. We do not believe such a plan is necessary or advisable under current circumstances. The planned asset purchases risk currency debasement and inflation, and we do not think they will achieve the Fed's objective of promoting employment."[3] The language in Europe may have differed, but the sentiment was the same.

The worry that central banks were prone to debasing the currency was, to be sure, of long standing. In Europe, it was deeply rooted in 1920s experience. The preoccupation was reinforced now by concern that the monetary authorities were interfering with the operation of the market and, by artificially supporting the economy, weakening the pressure to undertake structural reforms.

Increasingly these arguments reshaped policy, even if the dangers to which they pointed were largely illusory. Inflation remained subdued so long as recovery was incomplete, slack was extensive, and interest rates were near zero.

The assumption that structural reform would proceed more quickly if central banks tightened the screws was just that: an assumption.

But, illusory or not, these critiques led central bankers to brood over the negative consequences of their policies. Members of the Federal Open Market Committee were obliged to explain how the Fed would exit from its accommodative policies. Although actual exit remained a matter for the future, talk of exit had a depressing effect. ECB President Mario Draghi was compelled to temper his commitment to "do whatever it takes" to defend the euro with a warning that ECB purchases of government bonds were contingent on pursuit of structural and budgetary reforms.[4] But qualifying the point in this way limited the effectiveness of the commitment to do whatever it took. The pressure on central banks was more intense to the extent that the arguments of the critics received official hearing, whether from Ron Paul and his "Audit the Fed" bill in the US House of Representatives or the German Constitutional Court in its readiness to consider the constitutionality of the ECB's Outright Monetary Transactions. All this helps to explain why central banks hesitated to do more despite the fact that recovery from the recession remained weak.

Thus, after a brief period in 2008–09 when the analogy with the Great Depression was foremost in the minds of policy makers and the priority was to stabilize the economy at all cost, the emphasis shifted. The priority now was to balance budgets. For central banks it was preventing an outbreak of inflation, however chimerical. This shift occurred despite the fact that the recovery continued to disappoint. Rather than avoiding the mistakes of the 1930s, policy makers almost seemed intent on repeating them.

———

Barack Obama's electoral victory on November 4, 2008, was decisive. His opponent, Arizona Senator John McCain, had not been helped by the crisis. McCain represented continuity with the now-discredited policies of George W. Bush. His understanding of complex financial matters was shaky. At a much-reported White House meeting on September 25, convened at the behest of the McCain camp, Obama demonstrated his grasp of the crisis. The Democratic candidate offered a thoughtful analysis while his Republican opponent sat in stony silence and then offered only vague platitudes about protecting the taxpayer.

What was apparent to participants in the White House meeting was apparent to the public as well. Obama better projected the cool demeanor of a capable crisis manager. He was better able to make sense of the crisis and the case for government action to resolve it. On November 4 he won 365 electoral college votes against McCain's 173. Although Obama's victory in 2008 was not as resounding as Roosevelt's in 1932—FDR received 472 electoral college votes to Hoover's 59—the Democrats again took control of both houses of Congress.[5]

The period between election and inauguration was now briefer than in 1932. Support for shortening the interregnum was indeed strengthened by the economic difficulties created by the four-month-long transition from Hoover to Roosevelt, although the effort to amend the Constitution to this effect was already underway. But even though the inauguration was moved from March to January, the awkward interval still lasted ten weeks. In the meantime, the task was to keep the financial system afloat.

Much of the heavy lifting in this period, like others, was done by the Federal Reserve. On November 25, 2008, in response to evidence of distress in securitization markets, the Fed announced it would purchase up to $100 billion of direct obligations of Fannie Mae, Freddie Mac, and the Federal Home Loan Banks and $500 billion of their mortgage-backed securities with the goal of restarting mortgage and housing markets. Purchases of mortgage-backed securities were not, however, something with which Fed staff had experience. The announcement therefore indicated that the central bank would be hiring private fund managers to execute the trades. This inaugurated the first round of what came to be known as quantitative easing.

In a second unprecedented step, the Fed announced creation of the Term Asset-Backed Securities Loan Facility, or TALF, for lending to hedge funds and other private investors to finance their purchases of securitized consumer loans. Lending to consumers had turned prohibitively risky. Those loans, moreover, were impossible to finance. Banks customarily bundled them together and sold them to hedge funds, which borrowed much of the money needed for their purchase. Now, however, the money market had seized up, and banks refused to lend. Who knew whether the kind of problems that brought down the market in mortgage-related securities also implicated the market in securitized consumer loans?

The consequences were alarming. If consumers were unable to finance their purchases, they would be unable to spend. Less spending would make for more unemployment, more defaults, and more problems for the financial system.

This was the vicious cycle the Fed now sought to break. Bernanke and Co. announced their readiness to provide up to $180 billion in loans to hedge funds and others purchasing securitized consumer loans. But offering to lend would not be enough if investors, worried by consumer defaults, hesitated to borrow. The Fed therefore promised to forgive its loans were consumers to default in large numbers. Treasury for its part put up $20 billion of TARP money to partially indemnify the central bank against losses.[6]

This was a clever way of leveraging Treasury's scarce capital. It testified to Paulson's mastery of financial engineering in his Goldman Sachs years. The plan's corresponding shortcoming, as with other financial-engineering schemes, was its complexity. There was the question of which securities would qualify, and how to ensure that the hedge funds would have skin in the game. A solution to the latter problem was found by requiring the hedge funds and others borrowing from the Fed's new facility to put up additional collateral against their loan. The other difficulties were eventually worked out by the government's attorneys. But "eventually" turned out to mean after four months, which was how long it took to get the consumer-lending program up and running.

Nothing better illustrates why the Fed's credit market interventions were so controversial. Lending directly to hedge funds reflected a delayed recognition, following Lehman's failure, of the importance of the shadow banking system. Better late than never. But guaranteeing those loans fanned fears of moral hazard and complaints that the Fed was extending yet another stealth bailout, this time to hedge funds and the banks with which they did business. And $20 billion of Treasury money did not guarantee that the Fed would escape all losses; it certainly did not let the taxpayer off the hook. Complex maneuvers of the kind the Fed employed to help Treasury lever up its TARP funds were leagues away from conventional monetary policy. Extraordinary times demand extraordinary measures, but extraordinary measures invite criticism if they defy easy explanation.

———

The motivation for these unconventional policies was, of course, distress in financial markets. And the reality was that the Fed was the only institution with an infinitely expandable balance sheet and the ability to respond quickly.

An additional motivation was that conventional monetary policy was reaching its limits, forcing the Fed to take unconventional steps. The FOMC had already brought its target for the federal funds rate down to 1.5 percent on October 8, 2008, and then to 1 percent on October 29. It flooded financial markets with liquidity. On December 16 the FOMC reduced its target for the Fed funds rate to between zero and 0.25 percent. The policy rate was as low as it could go. The Fed essentially committed to providing however much credit financial markets required, at zero cost.

Doing so was unprecedented in the history of the Federal Reserve System. Only once before, in the wake of September 11, 2001, had the FOMC pushed the Fed funds rate as low as 1 percent. Never had it been pushed lower. Even in the depths of the Great Depression, the discount rate, the 1930s equivalent of the Fed funds target, never fell below 1½ per cent, a level reached only in the New York district in 1931.[7] Even then, other Reserve banks, concerned to husband their gold reserves, had hesitated to go along. The current policy of providing unlimited access to Federal Reserve credit at essentially zero cost was very different. It was an indication that officials, their views informed by 1930s experience, were prepared to employ all the monetary power at their disposal to stabilize the financial system and prevent the economy from succumbing to deflation.

Bernanke was concerned that the decision should not be perceived as his policy, or the New York Fed's policy, as was the case in the 1930s, but rather as the system's policy. This would prevent the Fed's confidence-inspiring capacity from being diminished by internal divisions of the sort that raised questions about the commitment of the Federal Reserve in the Depression. In the run-up to the December 16 FOMC decision the chairman therefore worked to form a consensus in favor of the step. Agreement to cut to zero was successfully achieved.

Reaching this consensus allowed Federal Reserve officials to speak with one voice and impress the markets with their resolve to prevent the worst. Doing so was important in order to address the immediate threat of financial collapse. But deciding policy by consensus also prevented the Fed from responding even more aggressively to the continued threat of deflation and, soon, the disappointing pace of recovery. Several Reserve bank presidents had reservations about larger securities purchases, open-ended commitments, and numerical targets for policy, all of which might have helped to support a faster recovery. These reservations were grounded in worries that the Fed would be unable to "take back" the stimulus it had applied with sufficient speed, causing inflation and financial excesses to build up. As in the summer of 2008, a less consensus-oriented chairman might have dismissed their objections out of hand. But not Chairman Bernanke.

———

These initiatives—providing unlimited amounts of credit to the banks, financing purchases of commercial paper through the TALF, and purchasing mortgage-backed securities from Freddie Mac and Fannie Mae—all reflected the belief in official circles that the problem was one of liquidity. Trust had dried up. Doubts prompted collateral calls, forcing borrowers to engage in distress sales of assets, in turn requiring more collateral calls. From this diagnosis flowed a prescription: if the authorities stepped in with securities purchases, injecting liquidity into the markets, conditions would normalize.

That the problem was one of liquidity was Paulson's diagnosis in particular. Asset purchases, recall, were the focus of the TARP as proposed to Congress by the Paulson Treasury at the end of September.[8] The notion that the problem was fundamentally one of liquidity resonated with a Treasury secretary exposed to the inner workings of financial markets by his experience at Goldman Sachs. This diagnosis and the policies to which it pointed were politically expedient in that they enabled Treasury to deny that it was providing bailouts to individual financial institutions, plausible deniability being essential in the wake of the AIG rescue if the TARP was to have a snowball's chance of congressional approval. And it could even be argued that, insofar as the Fed and Treasury made their purchases at fire-sale prices, they might end up turning a profit.

There were just two problems. First, it would take weeks or even months to put in place the apparatus for security purchases. The securities in question were complex and varied, which was of course part of what had gotten investors in those same assets into trouble in the first place. Purchasing them would require Treasury to contract with private fund managers knowledgeable of the market, including some of the same financial institutions involved in originating those securities. Compensation schemes and mechanisms for monitoring fund manager performance would have to be arranged. All this would take time. And time was the one thing even scarcer than liquidity.

Second, there was the reluctant realization—reluctant on Paulson's part— that the issue was more than just one of liquidity. Banks that made big bets on real-estate-related investments had taken big losses. They now had inadequate capital as a buffer against losses, rendering them unable to borrow and reluctant to lend. Providing them with additional liquidity by purchasing their securities at something resembling current market prices would do little to solve this problem. As a student of the Great Depression, Bernanke could recall how FDR had used the bank holiday to reassure the public that any bank allowed to reopen would be adequately capitalized. Already in September, prior to final passage of the TARP, the Fed chairman was suggesting to Paulson that capital injections might be required to restore confidence and restart bank lending.[9]

It took ten days following passage of the TARP for Paulson & Co. to acknowledge these facts and agree to use $250 billion of TARP money to recapitalize the banks. On Monday, October 13, Columbus Day, Paulson, Bernanke, New York Fed President Geithner, and Sheila Bair, chair of the FDIC, convened their now-legendary meeting with the CEOs of nine big banks. The officials made clear the importance of those banks present all accepting public capital. If any refused, banks receiving assistance would be singled out as weak links, creating the same problem that had bedeviled the RFC from mid-1932. There was more than a little reluctance on the part of the CEOs and no little chest beating, or so journalistic accounts suggest.[10] Geithner and Paulson made clear that CEOs who resisted were unlikely to have their phone calls returned.

The terms were not onerous. The banks would be required to pay a dividend of 5 percent, significantly less than if they sought to raise capital on the market—assuming of course that they were able to access the market at all. Goldman Sachs, the bank in the strongest position, had just succeeded in raising $5 billion of capital privately, from Warren Buffett's Berkshire Hathaway, but paid handsomely for the privilege. It promised Buffett a 10 percent dividend on his shares, fully twice what was now demanded by the government.[11] Moreover, the government's new capital didn't come with voting rights. Treasury would acquire only nonvoting senior preferred stock, limiting its ability to intervene in future bank operations.[12]

These provisions were precisely what made this use of TARP funds controversial. Cheap capital smelled of subsidies. Preferred shares without voting rights made the taxpayer a silent partner while the banks called the tune. The government would have no way of compelling banks taking public money to use it for lending to corporations and households desperate for funds.

Finally, this shift in use of TARP funding did not enhance Treasury's reputation for policy consistency. It encouraged the view that Paulson was still groping for a response. As David Swensen, manager of Yale University's endowment, put it, policy makers acted "with an extraordinary degree of inconsistency. You almost have to be trying to do things in an incoherent and inconsistent way to have ended up with the huge range of ways that they have come up with to address these problems."[13]

Such suspicions were not entirely wide of the mark. Unlike Robert Rubin, the Clinton-era treasury secretary similarly confronted with crises on his watch, Paulson did not have an overarching worldview to guide his decision making. In his memoirs, Rubin describes his particular view of market dynamics and how this led him to adopt what created at least the appearance of a systematic approach to decision making. Rubin kept a sense of personal detachment, whereas Paulson reacted emotionally to events, swinging from one solution to another. The title of his memoirs, *On the Brink*, almost seems to be referring to his mental state.

As it happened, it would take just days for events to bring the two men together. The occasion would have implications not just for Paulson's reputation but also for Rubin's.

———

Paulson continued to assert that diverting $250 billion of TARP funds to recapitalization was a one-off event and that the balance would still be used for asset purchases. He had promised as much when seeking congressional approval for the TARP, making it problematic to change tack now.[14]

In the event, it took less than a month for the secretary to drop the idea of purchasing toxic assets in its entirety. Market conditions were continuing to worsen, leaving no time for an elaborate purchasing operation. Capital injections promised a bigger bang for the buck.

Not only was there no time for complex financial engineering, but at this point the problem had migrated from the security markets to the banks, the beating heart of the financial system. The banks' capital shortfall was real. Still, the press struggled to make sense of yet another policy shift. Coverage of Paulson's November 12 press conference announcing the new strategy was unsympathetic. That Treasury was changing course yet again disconcerted the markets, which dropped by 5 percent.

The implication of the authorities now concentrating on recapitalizing the banks was that regulators knew something that others, as yet, did not. Investors quickly concluded that Citigroup, the largest US bank still standing, was the weak link. Their worries were rooted in awareness that Citi embodied all the worst features of twenty-first-century banking. With a limited deposit base, it relied on wholesale funding. Having pioneered multinational banking as far back as the 1920s, much of the wholesale funding came from skittish foreign investors. It held extensive positions in consumer loans, questionably underwritten commercial real estate, and collateralized debt obligations tied to subprime mortgages. It had not turned a profit since the second quarter of 2007, although management continued to pay dividends in an effort to convince investors that the reality was otherwise.

Inchoate fears gave way to panic on November 19, when Citi announced it was forced to wind up a structured investment vehicle heavily invested in subprime-related CDOs. Its stock fell by 23 percent, culminating several months of sharp declines.

But even in this wounded state, Citigroup still had more than $3 trillion of assets, counting those hidden away in its SPVs. If any US bank was too big to fail—if any bank had consciously set out to become too big to fail—this was it. Rubin, now in his capacity as chairman of the executive committee of Citigroup's board, reminded Paulson of these facts in a series of characteristically "low key" telephone calls.[15]

The legal niceties that Bernanke, Geithner, and Paulson had cited in connection with the decision to allow Lehman Brothers to go down were set aside in these dire circumstances. Sheila Bair was the one notable dissenter from the decision to go ahead with a bailout. Concerned to husband her agency's $35 billion insurance fund, Bair proposed putting Citibank, Citigroup's insured national bank subsidiary, into receivership. Bernanke,

Geithner, and Paulson all argued that Citibank was not easily disentangled from the larger financial group of which it was part. Not only was Citigroup larger than Lehman, but it was more international. The kind of problems that arose when Lehman failed and its British regulator froze its accounts would be immensely more disruptive. For all these reasons, Treasury and Fed officials insisted there was no alternative to the rescue cobbled together over the weekend of November 22–23.

In the plan as ultimately structured, the government injected $20 billion of share capital, again taking preferred shares in return. Bernanke suggested common stock, but Paulson demurred. Had it received common stock, the government would have ended up "owning a large part of the bank," as Paulson subsequently put it, prompting unwelcome headlines about nationalization.[16] The government did, in fact, end up owning almost half the bank, given how Citigroup's market cap fell to little more than $20 billion following announcement of the bailout. The only difference, again, was that its shares did not come with voting rights.

Officials agreed, in addition, to split the losses on $300 billion of Citigroup's toxic assets. Citi would take the first $29 billion of losses, after which the government would absorb 90 percent, with the TARP, the FDIC, and the Fed taking them in turn. This was another way of leveraging Treasury's limited funds.[17] Providing insurance against losses on mortgage-related investments, moreover, was a less transparent way of providing assistance than injecting more capital or purchasing those assets outright. It was a way to deflect accusations that the authorities were providing another mega-bailout.[18]

The bailout left a sour taste for those who recalled this bank having been a prime mover in the elimination of Glass-Steagall. Citi was now advised by Rubin, who was also once Paulson's colleague at Goldman Sachs. Regulatory oversight of the bank was headed up by the New York Fed, whose president, Timothy Geithner, was Rubin's protégé during the latter's years in the Clinton Treasury and had just been announced by President-Elect Obama as treasury secretary-designate. The conspiracy theories to which this gave rise were over the top, but the optics did not make rescuing the bank, or subsequently its competitors, any easier.[19]

The reality that congressional opposition to bailouts without strict conditions, including replacement of top management and retention of voting rights on behalf of taxpayers, had been circumvented with the help of these financial-engineering devices fed skepticism about even more forceful steps to recapitalize the banking system. Still, the mold was cast. It was used again in January when the government bailed out Bank of America.

President Bush had hoped to leave this task to the new administration. Congress had not yet agreed to release the second half of the TARP funds, and Bush was reluctant to ask for fear that his last significant act might have to be to veto a congressional bill prohibiting its disbursal. In addition to the embarrassment, this visible sign of disapproval by Congress would not reassure financial markets. But indications that Bank of America would shortly be announcing a $2 billion loss for itself and a $22 billion loss for its newly acquired investment banking division Merrill Lynch threatened to spark another panic. Bush proved more willing to act than Hoover in his last days in office. On January 12, 2009, he requested the second tranche of TARP funds, and Congress reluctantly agreed. Three days later a deal was struck to use the TARP to inject $20 billion of new capital into Bank of America. The government and the bank agreed to split the losses on its $118 billion of mortgage-related assets ninety-ten, following the Citigroup formula, after the first $10 billion of losses, which would go to the bank.

And with this official support in place, Bank of America was able to announce its quarterly results the next morning.

| Stressed and Stimulated

Tʜʀᴏᴜɢʜ ᴀʟʟ ᴛʜɪs, the president-elect and his team were watching uneasily. Lawrence Summers, chair-designate of Obama's National Economic Council, and Christina Romer, selected to chair the Council of Economic Advisors, resisted the idea of more stealth bailouts on fairness and moral-hazard grounds.[1] They preferred to find a way of seizing, recapitalizing, and reopening so-called too-big-to-fail institutions—nationalizing and quickly reprivatizing them while breaking them up along the way. Other academics farther from the seat of power argued the case for nationalization even more strongly.[2] For the academics, the approach taken by Sweden to repair its banking system in the 1990s had considerable appeal: the authorities would seize the troubled financial institutions and transfer their toxic assets to a government-run "bad bank," which would sell them off over time. The restructured banks could then be recapitalized and reopened, the shareholders having been wiped out and management unseated along the way.

But Obama's political advisors, from Chief of Staff Rahm Emanuel on down, feared sticker shock were the administration to go back to Congress for more funds to recapitalize the banks. Bank nationalization, even temporary nationalization, was anathema to large segments of the American public, not to mention to the banking lobby. Its academic advocates, unlike Treasury Secretary-Designate Timothy Geithner, had not been involved in the most recent round of bank rescues, allowing them to develop an idealized notion of how seamlessly nationalization and reprivatization would work. White House advisors toyed with the idea of testing out the Swedish approach on a single bank, where still-troubled Citibank was the obvious candidate, but the logistics were daunting.

Geithner, for his part, opposed any intervention that might disrupt business as usual and damage the prospects for recovery. He feared that nationalizing one bank might create expectations that others would follow, causing investors to sell their shares in a self-fulfilling prophecy. He was skeptical that there was such a thing as temporary nationalization. The step would demoralize the markets, rendering the nationalized institutions impossible to sell. About this aspect, at least, he was right, as countries like the UK, which went the nationalization route, would discover in the course of time.

But avoiding nationalization required coming up with an alternative, something that was easier said than done in the early days of a new administration, as Raymond Moley and William Woodin could have explained. Where Paulson's Treasury was chaotic, Geithner's was understaffed. Vetting senior appointees was laborious, and congressional confirmation was far from ensured. Although Treasury under Paulson had a thin bench of economists and finance specialists, the situation under Geithner was worse.

The result was reminiscent of how the Roosevelt administration, lacking ideas, adopted the bank rehabilitation plans of its predecessor. Similarly, Geithner's plan was—wait for it—to use TARP funds, suitably leveraged, to buy toxic loans and assets from the banks. It was essentially an expansion of the TALF, which targeted consumer loans, to mortgage-backed securities, property loans, and CDOs. This was the essence of the Public-Private Investment Program for Legacy Assets, or PPIP, announced on March 23, 2009, for which $22 billion of TARP funds was earmarked.

There were other elements of continuity as well. Buying securities would require partnering with private fund managers, as in Paulson's security purchase scheme.[3] There would have to be a way of ensuring that fund managers had skin in the game, like the hedge funds that were the government's partners in the TALF. In other words, if they bought securities for the government, they would also have to buy securities for themselves, at the same prices, as a way of ensuring they did not overpay. In addition to putting up TARP funds to buy securities directly, the Treasury, the FDIC, and the Federal Reserve would guarantee each pool of securities purchased up to 85 percent of the amount bid by investors, much as they had guaranteed 90 percent of the legacy assets of Citigroup and Bank of America.[4]

PPIP excited much negative commentary for the same reasons that these earlier interventions did so. It was difficult to understand. It relied on mortgage securitization and leverage, the very forms of financial engineering that had given rise to the crisis. It involved another open-ended guarantee, exposing taxpayers to losses. It looked to be overpaying for toxic assets again, since the banks would be reluctant to sell at a loss.

But the most serious problem was the same one that derailed Paulson's original scheme for security purchases, namely the time needed to scale it up. The Fed had taken four full months to get the TALF up and running, and Treasury lacked its experienced staff. PPIP was finally launched in September 2009. Rather than removing $1 trillion of bad loans and assets from the banks' balance sheets, the program ended up eliminating just $40 billion, a veritable drop in the financial bucket.

With nationalization off the table and PPIP on hold, Treasury's backup plan of stress-testing the banks was the only option left standing. Secretary Geithner unveiled the idea at a poorly received press conference on February 10, where attention focused on the asset-purchase program. Now the stress tests became the centerpiece of the strategy. Specialists at the Fed and the FDIC, working with Treasury, would construct scenarios for the performance of the banks' mortgage loans, credit card loans, auto loans, and other assets. Nineteen big banks, together with their supervisors, would then estimate their losses under what was referred to as the adverse scenario, "adverse" being one rung up from "worst-case." If a bank's reserves were too small to plug the hole, it would have to raise more capital. If it had trouble raising capital from investors, it would have to take it from the government. With only needy institutions tapping public funds, the burden on taxpayers would be limited. And with every bank adequately capitalized, investors would be reassured. The banks, possessing the resources and cushion against losses to resume lending, could do their part to encourage recovery.

The exercise was greeted with skepticism on the part of investors, the informed public, and even the White House. Supervisors lacked the expertise to value complex securities, forcing them to defer to the banks and their in-house models. If their scenarios were too optimistic and the amount of new capital was small, the markets might dismiss the process as a charade. But if their scenarios were dire and the amount of capital was large, the banks might be unable to raise it, forcing them into the hands of the government in the nationalization scenario investors and officials both feared. Either way, confidence would be damaged rather than restored.

The stress testers thus had a Goldilocks problem: the porridge had to be neither too cold nor too hot. Not being required to value the banks' assets at current market prices, they could instead tweak their model-based estimates of those prices to produce the desired result. Or they could adjust their assumptions about the banks' future earnings growth.

Not surprisingly, the total ultimately selected—for selected it was—was $75 billion, roughly halfway between the low and high estimates of $35 billion and \$125 billion.[5] It was not so low as to be dismissed as a gift, nor so high as to make it impossible to raise. It was less than the \$125 billion the government had compelled the nine big banks to take a few months earlier. Just in case, it was also less than the Treasury's remaining TARP funds.

Bank stocks jumped when the results were released.[6] With hindsight, it is clear that this marked the beginning of the end of the crisis. But, even now, just why is unclear. Geithner's hunch, like Paulson's before him, was that the banks were not, in fact, insolvent and that, with time and the support of investors, they could earn their way back to health. Not a few other supposed experts had asserted that the banks were insolvent and could be stabilized only by a massive infusion of public funds. In the event, the experts were wrong, while Geithner was right. The banks may not have leapt back into lending with both feet—in fact they dipped their toes in only cautiously—but they were able to steady themselves, raise additional capital, and get back to business.

Doing so required a modicum of investor confidence. Here it helped that the stress tests, unlike the earlier rescues of Bear Stearns, Citigroup, and Bank of America, were not thrown together over a weekend. They were just credible enough to inspire confidence. Appearance, in this case, made for reality. Such is the nature of banking, where confidence is in the eye of the beholder.

In 1933, when declaring the bank holiday, the Roosevelt administration similarly put up a good front. It solemnly declared that only solvent banks would be allowed to reopen. In reality, it was hardly possible in the subsequent two weeks to conduct careful inspections of each and every financial institution, urban legend notwithstanding. Yet the government permitted the vast majority of banks to reopen, providing only verbal reassurance that they were adequately capitalized.

The stress tests were now conducted with comparable solemnity and produced comparable results. Given their effects, it becomes necessary to view the 1933 bank holiday and its aftermath in a somewhat different light and to acknowledge that, like the stress tests, they involved more than a little showmanship.

A less happy interpretation is that the Good Housekeeping Seal of Approval conferred by the tests was tantamount to a colossal government guarantee. The nineteen biggest banks received special attention. Treasury asserted that they were solvent. Nine of them, starting with Goldman Sachs and JPMorgan Chase, required no additional capital. Citigroup, Bank of America, and eight of their less pristine competitors would be adequately capitalized if they raised only an additional \$75 billion of capital, or so the government averred. If they then got into trouble, it stood to reason that this would be due to events not of their own making, and that the authorities, having attested to their soundness, would bail them out.

In this respect as well, the response resembled 1933, when the Emergency Banking Act empowered the Federal Reserve to discount notes, drafts, bills, and acceptances as the central bank saw fit, allowing it to provide the banks the liquidity they needed to meet the needs of their depositors. And as in 1933, the policy response stabilized the banking system, but by opening the door to moral hazard on a massive scale.

Or perhaps, as in 1933, it was not so much the measures addressed at the banking system as other policies that were responsible for the happy outcome.

———

The most contentious responses were the Obama administration's $787 billion fiscal stimulus and three rounds of quantitative easing by the Federal Reserve. The stimulus excited no end of controversy then and continues to do so today. The case was straightforward for those whose views were informed by the experience of the 1930s. The Hoover and Roosevelt administrations had done too little to offset the decline in private spending. Although the New Deal featured prominent public investment projects, from the Grand Coulee Dam to the Triborough Bridge, the increase in spending was too small to make a significant dent in a double-digit unemployment rate. All this was doubly unfortunate in an environment of near-zero interest rates, when there was little danger that an increase in public investment would crowd out a commensurate amount of private spending. The research of Obama's Council of Economic Advisors chair, Christina Romer, pointed to the conclusion that fiscal policy made only a limited contribution to recovery because the fiscal initiatives of the period were small by the scale of the problem.[7]

This was the mistake whose repetition the Obama stimulus was designed to avoid. Moving an eleven-hundred-page bill from first draft to final passage in a bit more than three weeks was a considerable achievement. It was fast action even by the standards of FDR's Hundred Days, which Obama like every subsequent president-elect had studied (and Obama was more studious than most). The act was hailed by House Appropriations Committee Chairman David Obey as "the largest change in domestic policy since the 1930s." The *Washington Post*, de facto arbiter of such inside-the-Beltway matters, concluded that the stimulus bill represented "the start of a new ideological era that places the federal government at the center of the nation's economic recovery."[8]

Given these elevated expectations, it was all but inevitable that disappointment would follow. During the interregnum, Romer, along with Jared Bernstein, soon to be appointed Vice President Biden's economic advisor, used a simple model to calculate how much stimulus was needed to offset the decline in private spending. This involved, first, estimating the decline in spending and hence the gap to be filled. Romer and Bernstein then divided the result by a textbook estimate of the fiscal multiplier.[9] What could be easier?

Several things, it turned out. To start, output was already falling faster than anyone realized, rendering it inevitable that unemployment would rise higher and making the Romer-Bernstein team look too optimistic. Given the exceptional nature of the crisis—how firms, unable to get credit, were cutting back on production and drawing down their inventories at an unprecedented rate—it is not surprising that government surveys did not fully capture how quickly output was falling. Still, the fact that unemployment failed to stabilize at 8 percent as advertised enabled the critics to question the effectiveness of the policy. Their questions provided ammunition for the advocates of an early turn to austerity.

Moreover, the amount of stimulus finally agreed was less than suggested by Romer and Bernstein's own calculations. Their modeling indicated that filling the output gap would require a stimulus of $1.2–1.8 trillion, depending on the magnitude of the contraction in the pipeline and the policies of the Federal Reserve. But numbers above $1 trillion were enough to give heartburn to even congressional Democrats. The Republicans had already labeled their opposition the party of tax-and-spend. They denigrated the legislation by appealing to the American public's instinctive hostility to big government. "This bill is supposed to be about jobs, jobs, jobs, and it's turned into nothing more than spend, spend, spend," as House minority leader John Boehner put it.

An election might have just happened, but this also meant that midterms were a mere two years away. Keeping the Democrats in Congress on board thus required not making the increase in the deficit too large. $1 trillion was the trip wire; the political operatives were unanimous that the stimulus had to come in below this. Arguments were therefore offered for why $800 billion was enough. A larger stimulus would panic the markets. The rise in unemployment was baked in; nothing could be done to prevent it. It is not clear whether anyone believed these rationalizations. This was economic logic enlisted on behalf of political ends.

A few White House strategists imagined that Congress might solve their problem. Once the House and Senate added their bells and whistles, the final bill would be larger than requested by the administration. But this didn't figure with the rise of the Tea Party, the loose populist coalition advocating reducing the size of government by any and all means, or with a refusal to cooperate on the part of House Republicans. It didn't figure with political rancor set in motion by the crisis and the bailouts taken in response.

An administration and a president convinced of the merits of a larger stimulus could have campaigned for it. Obama could have invested the political capital he possessed as a result of his recent electoral victory. He could have appealed to GOP senators from swing states like Maine and Pennsylvania. Going over the heads of Congress, he could have appealed to the public. But Obama's instinct was to weigh the options, not to campaign for his program. It was to compromise, not confront. The economic advisors who might have helped him make the case did not speak with one voice. And the political advisors agreed that an aggressive campaign for a larger stimulus was not the best use of the president's political capital.

Finally, there was the conflict between shovel-ready projects promising an immediate economic impact and the longer-term agenda to renew the country's infrastructure, enhance its energy efficiency, and invest in its people. Focusing on forms of stimulus spending that could be rolled out quickly was critical for containing the crisis. Without an immediate boost to spending, there would be nothing to break the vicious circle of private-sector deleveraging and financial-sector distress. Front-loading the stimulus was also a way of signaling that it was an exceptional measure to which the administration had been driven by exceptional circumstances and that it would be rolled back once the crisis passed. Reflecting these arguments, more than half of total stimulus spending was concentrated in 2009–10.

But insofar as this was the emphasis, it meant that the country's structural problems went unaddressed. Geithner describes how during the transition Obama hoped for an inspiring project like a smart electric grid, but his advisors talked him out of it.[10] The Obama administration would have no Grand Coulee Dam to point to in seeking continued support for its approach. Nine billion dollars for high-speed rail was a limp substitute. That the stimulus left no physical legacy allowed the skeptics to denigrate the effects and advocate quick abandonment.

Rather than a short recession followed by a vigorous recovery, the United States experienced an extended period of high unemployment. That recovery was slow meant the economy would have benefited from infrastructure investment that took years to roll out. The need for additional government spending was an opportunity to develop a coherent plan for spending on not just infrastructure but basic research and education, in order to better position the country to meet the challenges of the twenty-first century.

But this is different from saying it would have made sense to shift more of the $787 billion of stimulus away from transfers to state and local governments in 2009–10 and toward spending on long-term infrastructure projects in subsequent years. Fewer transfers to the states in 2009 would have meant more unemployment and financial distress, a high price to pay for infrastructure renewal. The circle could have been squared by adding appropriations for infrastructure spending without also cutting back on transfers to the states. But an even larger stimulus that would have permitted the government to pursue not-yet-shovel-ready projects without forcing it to cut back short-term spending was not in the political cards. And the throes of a crisis, when policy makers were struggling to prevent the financial system from seizing up, was an awkward time to ponder a national development plan.

———

Evaluations of the stimulus continue to differ. But it is not enough for detractors to point to the fact that unemployment peaked out at 10.1 percent, two full percentage points higher than initially promised. Nor is it enough to observe, à la Mervyn King, that another Great Depression was avoided. The question must be posed as a problem in counterfactual history. How much higher would unemployment have been without the stimulus? Would there have been a Great Depression–like slump in its absence?

Any serious effort to answer these questions requires a model of the economy that can be put through its paces with the stimulus and without. Different models predictably yield different results. Keynesian models with a large fiscal multiplier point to large positive effects. In contrast, classical full-employment models in which interest rates rise with public spending, causing a commensurate amount of private spending to be crowded out, suggest no positive output effects. In the world of evidence-free modeling, anything goes.

But the world of modeling, and more generally the world itself, is not evidence free. Models have implications that can be set against evidence as external tests of validity. The classical model predicts, to pick an example not entirely at random, that the stimulus should have driven up interest rates, whereas the Keynesian model does not. The fact that interest rates remained low thus favors one class of models over the other.

Although government agencies like the Congressional Budget Office typically employ several models for purposes of policy analysis, the models they use are limited to those whose implications are not wildly inconsistent with the facts. Employing a number of data-consistent models, CBO estimated that real GDP was 1.7–4.5 percent higher in the second quarter of 2010 with the stimulus than without, after which the effect diminished.[11] The actual fall in GDP between 2007 and 2009 was 3.4 percent. The midpoint of the CBO's high and low estimates thus suggests that the output loss would have been about twice as large in the absence of the stimulus. The number of full-time-equivalent jobs was 2.0–4.8 million higher, according to its estimates, than in the absence of the stimulus.[12]

The experience of other countries, where policies and economic outcomes differ, is another basis on which to evaluate US experience. If the recession was deeper and longer in countries where circumstances were otherwise similar but stimulus spending was less, then the magnitude of the difference can be used to identify the relevant counterfactual. International organizations like the IMF engage in this kind of counterfactual thinking. The work of the Fund's chief economist, Olivier Blanchard, points to fiscal multipliers above 1 (1.3 is the middle of his estimated range). This suggests that, other things equal, $400 billion of stimulus spending in calendar year 2010 raised GDP by $520 billion, or roughly 4 percent in a $13 trillion economy.[13] The conclusion is consistent with the range suggested by the CBO's modeling.

A related strategy is to compare the change in output and employment across US states and counties receiving differing amounts of federal funding. James Feyrer and Bruce Sacerdote of Dartmouth College adopted this approach, finding substantial effects of aid to low-income individuals and infrastructure spending and sizable impacts of the stimulus overall. The effect is smaller than estimated by the CBO and the IMF but still considerable. A team of Berkeley, Stanford, and MIT economists adopting a similar approach made use of the fact that Medicaid matching funds provided by the stimulus varied widely across states. (On a per capita basis, Washington, D.C., received almost five times the per capita transfers of Utah.) They concluded that $100,000 of additional matching funds increased employment by 3.5 job-years and that an additional $100,000 of federal outlays raised final spending by as much as $200,000.[14] This suggests an even larger impact than other approaches.

Finally, historical experience provides a basis for imagining the counterfactual. Eighty years of scholarship may not have produced universal agreement on the effects of New Deal policies, but it has yielded a broad consensus on what worked and what didn't, on which policies were more and less important, and what should have been tried but wasn't. It suggests that fiscal policy worked where it was tried and didn't where it wasn't. It points to the effectiveness of policies that put money in consumers' pockets, like the 1936 Veterans' Bonus, but also to the case for taking advantage of singularly low borrowing rates to finance infrastructure projects. It suggests that public spending, whether for rearmament or other purposes, had especially large effects in an environment of near-zero interest rates. All this implies that the Obama stimulus helped, but that it would have helped more had policy makers aimed higher.

CHAPTER 21

Unconventional Policy

E VEN MORE CONTROVERSIAL, if that is possible, were the policies of the
Federal Reserve. The Fed was criticized equally for doing too much and
too little. Members of the too-much school warned that its insistence on keeping interest rates low augured an explosion of inflation. When that inflation
failed to materialize, they then dismissed the Fed's credit market interventions
as frustrating the necessary consolidation of the country's finances. The central
bank, they warned, was only setting the stage for more financial excesses like
those that caused the crisis.

Members of the too-little school, for their part, complained that the Fed
had abdicated its responsibility for full employment. Preoccupied by credit
market conditions and intimidated by pugnacious critics, the central bank hesitated to turn to unconventional policies, and when it did a strict upper limit
was specified on what would be done, limiting the effectiveness of its interventions. It allowed inflation to undershoot normal levels. It allowed nominal
income to stagnate.

The Fed started injecting large amounts of credit into the economy, recall,
following the failure of Lehman Brothers. It pushed the Fed funds rate down
toward zero and set a 0.–0.25 percent target for the rate on December 16, 2008.
But even then there was little sign that low interest rates were having the
desired effect. Given heightened risk aversion, there was a visible reluctance to
borrow and spend on the part of households and firms.

The question was what to do next. Here there were three options (first considered at the Fed's two-day policy meeting on December 15–16). One was to
make statements about future policy with the goal of shaping expectations and
through that channel to attempt to influence spending. If the Fed could use

statements of intent to create expectations of higher inflation, then households and firms anticipating higher prices would be more inclined to spend.[1] In 1933 FDR attempted to shape expectations of future prices and policies by loudly rejecting "the old fetishes of so-called international bankers." Perhaps the Fed now could say something less provocative but equally forceful.

The challenge for Fed officials was to make credible statements about future policy. Were inflation to rise above a politically comfortable level of, say, 2 percent, there would be pressure on the Federal Open Market Committee to tighten. Bondholders and others on fixed incomes would make their displeasure known. The Fed would feel the political heat.

Monetary policy makers, moreover, were indoctrinated for generations in the impossibility of being half-pregnant. If inflation was allowed to exceed customary levels, they feared, the central bank could lose control. The credibility of its commitment to maintaining price stability would be damaged, undermining the ability to achieve its goals. Memories of the 1970s, for those who had lived through the decade, and histories of the 1970s for those who had not, strongly informed the outlook of officials, shaping and constraining policy.

For all these reasons, raising inflation above 2 percent and keeping it there would not be easy. Statements to this effect threatened to collide with the central bank's mandate for low and stable inflation. That the responsible policy under the circumstances was to act irresponsibly, allowing inflation to rise temporarily, encapsulated the contradictions of the crisis. Such convoluted arguments did not sit easily with the straightforward demeanor of central bankers.

The FOMC groped for language that was both acceptable and effective, the problem being that what was acceptable was not effective, and what was effective was not likely to be acceptable. Starting in December 2008 it spoke of conditions warranting "exceptionally low levels of the federal funds rate for some time." "For some time" was weaker than "until unemployment falls to 6.5 percent" or "until growth consistently exceeds 3 percent." Stronger statements would have constituted acknowledgment that the FOMC prioritized other factors as much as it did inflation. Doing so would have been appropriate in the circumstances of an exceptional crisis. It would have been the responsibly irresponsible policy. But the contradiction was more than monetary policy makers could bear.

This dilemma prompted consideration of a related option, namely adopting an explicit inflation target. The Fed could endorse a target of, say, 3 percent and declare readiness to pursue whatever policies were required to hit it. Bernanke was a proponent of an inflation target in his earlier academic incarnation.[2] A formal target, he had argued, was easy to communicate. The policies for achieving it were easy to justify and explain. It would then be correspondingly less likely that aggressive moves to support a depressed economy would be misinterpreted as the Fed abandoning its commitment to price stability. The effectiveness of policy would be enhanced.

But for a target to be credible, it would have to be pursued through thick and thin. It would have to be a beacon for policy whether the economy was doing badly or well. It would have to be set at a high level in the short run to give the economy a significant boost. But there might then be pressure to reduce it subsequently. And if it was common knowledge that the target was not set in stone, whether the Fed was committed to achieving it would inevitably be questioned.[3]

Skeptics also questioned whether it was within the capacity of the Fed to raise inflation to 3 percent under depressed conditions. A formal inflation target, they warned, would violate the cardinal rule that policy makers should never target a variable they couldn't control. Much later, in 2012, the Fed moved part way toward an inflation target, issuing a "longer-run goals and policy strategy statement" identifying 2 percent as the inflation rate best aligned with its mandate. A year after that, the FOMC committed to keeping interest rates low until unemployment reached 6.5 percent.

This, finally, was the kind of numerical guidance advocated in 2009 by those who complained that the Fed was too timid. But back in 2009, in the throes of the crisis, the consensus to make such numerical commitments was not there.[4] The institutional apparatus for monetary policy adopted in the course of previous decades, at whose center was the mandate to pursue low inflation, continued to guide and constrain policy. When most of the Reserve bank presidents serving on the FOMC, if not also the chairman, looked back at history, they looked back at the 1970s, when an outburst of inflation damaged the central bank's credibility. Highly unconventional policies such as explicit numerical guidelines suitable for highly unconventional circumstances were not yet in the cards.

––––––

The third and final option was asset purchases. These were a way for the Fed to signal a commitment to avoiding deflation and of shaping market expectations. They could be used to make credit available to specific markets like that for home mortgages. Pushing the Fed funds rate to zero affected the short-term interest rates at which banks lent to one another but had only an oblique impact on rates on mortgages and corporate bonds. But by purchasing asset-backed securities, the Fed could attempt to influence the latter directly.

QE1, the first round of quantitative easing, sailed in November 2008, when the Fed announced it would purchase $600 billion of loans and securities of

Fannie Mae, Freddie Mac, and the Federal Home Loan Banks and created the TALF to buy $180 billion of consumer loans. In March 2009 it then raised the ceiling for purchases of mortgage-related securities and announced it would buy $300 billion of longer-term treasury securities. But as the implications sank in, investors realized the message was ambiguous. Convincing the markets that it would do whatever it took required the Fed to commit to continuing asset purchases until the risk of deflation had passed. But QE1 was limited in size. By tracking the central bank's balance sheet, investors could determine when the program would end. Specifically, they could see that it would end in the second half of 2009.

But Bernanke and his FOMC colleagues hesitated to issue an open-ended commitment. They were anxious to reassure everyone within earshot that, bad as things were, the United States was not at risk of a Japan-like slump, and that the Fed had not been driven, in desperation, to open-ended easing. The Fed's interventions, as they characterized them, were selective and surgical. They were designed to open the financial system's clogged arteries and restore the free flow of credit. Bernanke emphasized that the Fed was engaging in "credit easing" with the goal of restoring the functioning of specific credit markets, not quantitative easing in the manner of Japan.

Unfortunately, this hair splitting limited the effectiveness of the policy. Expected inflation remained perilously close to zero through much of 2009 and 2010. Private employment growth was running below a hundred thousand jobs a month, less than half what was needed to reduce the unemployment rate. The United States was then hit by the debt crisis in Europe, exciting fears of a double-dip recession. There was worry inside and outside the Fed that the US economy was slowing to stall speed. All these were arguments for doing more. Discussions within the FOMC turned from inflation, which had continued to preoccupy many members of the committee in 2008, to the risk of a Japan-style deflation in 2010. Indicative of this was how James Bullard, president of the Federal Reserve Bank of St. Louis—previously a leader among those warning of inflation—shifted into the dangers-of-deflation camp.[5]

This was an impressive display of the ability of a central banker to shed his earlier intellectual skin. It was admirable flexibility and ability to recognize that circumstances had changed—at least by the standards of the 1930s, when the better part of four years and appropriation of monetary control by the executive branch from the central bank had been required for an equally radical reorientation of policy. No doubt histories of 1930s experience, as taught by the likes of Friedman and Schwartz, had something to do with the contrast.

Yet through late 2010 the Fed bought just $30 billion of treasury notes a month, barely enough to keep its balance sheet from shrinking as securities purchased earlier matured.[6] This reluctance to do more reflected the drumbeat of external criticism of the central bank. Warnings that it was setting the stage for an inflationary explosion continued nonstop. Although this argument was made in its most unvarnished form by radio talk-show hosts, for whom it was a way of attracting an audience, members of the Federal Reserve Board and regional Reserve bank presidents hesitated to dismiss it out of hand. One can't help but be reminded of the reluctance of the Bank of England to cut interest in the months following Britain's departure from the gold standard in 1931, until it eventually became clear that no Weimar-style inflation was in the cards.

Other critics questioned the effectiveness of the central bank's securities purchases and argued that they did more to create uncertainty than to resolve it. The Fed, they fretted, would take losses on its portfolio of long-term investments when interest rates recovered. They warned of asset bubbles. Insofar as quantitative easing provided an incentive for businesses and consumers to bring forward spending to today, they worried that it might only reduce spending tomorrow, creating an endless demand for quantitative easing to keep the economy going. They warned that by providing cheap liquidity, the Fed was relieving the pressure for Congress and the president to more forcefully recapitalize still-undercapitalized banks. They argued that the Fed should recognize that the economy was being held back by an oversupply of new homes, by the need to shift resources from construction to other activities, and by the heavy indebtedness of households, problems that could not be solved by monetary action alone.

Indeed, it was argued that insofar as the first round of quantitative easing involved mainly purchases of mortgage-related paper, these only delayed the inevitable adjustment of the housing market. Such structural problems required a congressional response. It followed that Federal Reserve initiatives papering them over merely relieved the pressure on the politicians to act. The critics complained that the Fed had exceeded its mandate to act as a responsible steward of the currency and that, if it wouldn't rein in these efforts on its own, legislators should do so for it.

These criticisms may or may not have been justified. The costs of the Fed's policies may or may not have outweighed the benefits. But whatever one's view, there is no question that these critiques left the members of the FOMC reluctant to do more.

———

Given this political context, the timing of the decision to launch a second round of quantitative easing was not entirely a surprise. This came on November 3, 2010, one day after the midterm congressional elections. QE2 involved the purchase of $600 billion of treasury securities over eight months. The new rate of purchase was about two and a half times what the Fed had been doing the previous year. Markets responded as they had to QE1, which is to say positively. In early 2011 inflation expectations moved up from 1.4 percent, uncomfortably close to deflationary territory, to a healthier 3 percent.

QE2 was attacked by Republicans who had just regained control of the House of Representatives for setting the country up for a burst of inflation. Depressing the interest rate on treasury bonds made it easier for the government to borrow, which they argued reduced the pressure for Congress and the White House to address the country's debt and deficit problems. By fueling financial market excesses, if not now then in the future, the policy set the stage for an even more debilitating crisis.

Finance ministers in Europe, Asia, and Latin America meanwhile denounced QE2 for pushing down the dollar. They portrayed the policy as attempting to solve America's problems at foreign expense. Brazilian finance minister Guido Mantega accused the US central bank of engaging in a currency war. German finance minister Wolfgang Schäuble criticized the Fed for "artificially depress[ing] the dollar exchange rate by printing money."[7] The motives of these foreign critics varied. The European critics worried that the strength of the euro against the dollar aggravated the competitive difficulties of the struggling Eurozone periphery. In Latin America, the strength of local currencies against the dollar similarly created competitiveness problems. Low interest rates in the United States encouraged capital to flow toward emerging markets, where yields were higher, feeding frothy asset markets and excessive bank lending. The effects varied, but one thing these countries had in common was their distaste for US monetary policy.

History would show these criticisms to have been misplaced. Contrary to the predictions of the American critics, inflation continued to run below 2 percent, not just for the life of the program but for several years subsequently. The economy's problem was not budget deficits and structural imbalances as opposed to inadequate demand; it was both. And where it was fully within the capacity of the Fed to address the problem of deficient demand, there was no evidence that doing so reduced the pressure on policy makers to tackle other issues. QE2 did not prevent US policy makers from addressing the budget deficit; it did not deter them from raising taxes on the wealthy or imposing the Sequester to limit the growth of discretionary spending in 2013. And worries that encouraging households and firms to bring spending forward to the present might simply reduce spending in the future, putting the central bank on a treadmill from which it could not escape, reflected the fallacy that there existed a fixed lump of spending that could only be redistributed over time.

Foreign officials, for their part, failed to ask whether they would have been better off had the US central bank failed to act. For the Fed to instead allow the United States to slip back into recession would have been devastating for the rest of the world. But their critical comments, misguided or not, did not make it easier for the Fed to stay the course, much less for it to ramp up its security purchase programs further. They did not make for a happy backdrop to President Obama's appearance at the G20 summit in Seoul, South Korea, in November 2010. Obama had hoped to position himself as a champion of international economic and financial cooperation. Instead, the Fed's "bomb-shell message" announcing QE2 made the Seoul summit come off more like the 1933 World Economic Conference.

Given its reluctance to do more, Fed policy was only a temporary palliative. Inflation expectations, after rising to 3 percent in early 2011, fell back until they were once more hovering at barely 1 percent when the program expired in early summer. In the case of QE2 as with QE1 before it, reluctance to make an open-ended commitment rendered the Fed's policy just a temporary sugar high.

The third time, hopefully, was the charm. In September 2011 the Fed announced plans to purchase ten-year treasury bonds using the proceeds from sales of its existing holdings of shorter-dated treasury securities. The program was designed to reduce ten-year treasury and mortgage rates with the goal of stimulating the housing market and investment generally. It did not entail further expansion of the Fed's balance sheet. Rather, the policy involved shift-ing the composition of the portfolio toward more long-dated paper in order to depress long rates relative to short rates. It was designed to twist the term structure of interest rates, if you will.

The new program was dubbed "Operation Twist" to signify the fact. The advantage of the label was that it was not QE3 and could not be attacked as more of the same. It had a historical precedent, namely an earlier Operation Twist, undertaken in 1961 with the goal of pushing down long rates to encour-age investment while keeping short rates high to support the balance of pay-ments. In 2011, when the Fed was under constant criticism for its unprecedented interventions, a precedent afforded political cover. Avoiding a further expansion of the central bank's balance sheet was also a way of bringing on board FOMC members worried about the inflationary consequences of security purchases.

The initial plan was to purchase $400 billion of long-term treasuries between October 2011 and June 2012. With employment growth still slow in the summer of 2012, the FOMC then extended the program through the end of the year, with one Reserve bank president, Jeffrey Lacker of Richmond, dissenting. In September, with the economy still weak, it added $40 billion of outright purchases of mortgage securities in a move that was unavoidably labeled QE3. At the end of the 2012, with unemployment still at 7.7 percent, the FOMC then announced that the Fed would continue buying treasury securities at the previous rate of $45 billion a month, although now that it was essentially out of short-term securities it would no longer sell these in equivalent amounts. Purchases of mortgage-backed securities would continue as well. Richmond Reserve Bank President Lacker once more voted against.

This, now, was a significant departure from prior policy. For the first time, the Fed made an open-ended commitment to keep interest rates low and continue its security purchases until the economy healed. Accommodative policies would remain in place as long as unemployment exceeded 6.5 percent and inflation remained less than 2.5 percent. This commitment was designed to influence expectations, and it did. Expected inflation, having hovered close to zero and falling alarmingly into negative territory in the second half of 2012, now moved up toward 1 percent.

The problem was that expectations of inflation did not rise higher. They still failed to approach the central bank's 2 percent target. That the Fed committed only to maintaining security purchases at their previous pace and not to increase them further presumably explains why the target continued to be missed.

———

The challenge for evaluating fiscal stimulus is that different models yield different results. In the case of quantitative easing, the problem is worse since there are essentially no models. The macroeconomic models used by central banks have underspecified financial sectors. The inability of those models to effectively capture how changes in financial conditions affect the economy was, after all, one reason the financial imbalances of the pre-2008 period went undetected.

Policy evaluation, like the policy being evaluated, necessarily proceeds by the seat of its pants. A first, obvious place to look is at the change in interest rates. Ten-year treasury bond yields declined from 3.35 percent before the first round of quantitative easing to a little more than 2 percent by the end of 2008. The question is how much of this was due to policy as opposed to a weak economy, fears of deflation, and the flight to safety, all of which similarly put downward pressure on treasury yields. One would want to know how much of the effect was enduring; treasury rates began moving up again in early 2009, leading some critics to suggest that the program had no more than a transient effect. One would also want to know the impact on rates on riskier assets more relevant for private investment decisions. And what is ultimately at stake, of course, is the impact on employment and economic growth.

Policy analysts have no choice but to assemble an answer using separate sources of evidence, like a child building a tower out of Lego bricks. To gauge the impact of Fed purchases on ten-year treasury bonds and mortgage-backed securities, they compare the yields on these securities before and after policy announcements. They then examine the response of corporate bond rates to changes in treasury yields. Finally, to gauge the impact on output and employment, they can feed the change in corporate bond yields into a large-scale model of the economy.

The first step, then, is to examine ten-year treasury rates around the time of policy announcements. If the period is short—just the day before and after the announcement, for example—then it is plausible that this policy announcement and not confounding factors on adjoining days accounts for the observed change in rates. Joseph Gagnon and three Federal Reserve colleagues used this approach to evaluate the first round of quantitative easing, comparing interest rates immediately before and after its announcement.[8] They found that the ten-year treasury yield fell by a little less than 100 basis points.[9] The central bank would have had to reduce the federal funds rate by fully 200 basis points to achieve an effect of this magnitude, had the Fed funds rate not already been cut to zero, of course.

In addition, the ten-year treasury yield fell even more than the two-year yield. This suggests that the announcement operated mainly by indicating that the Fed would be draining long-duration securities from the market. Investors appear to have been skeptical that the FOMC, by announcing its program of security purchases, was committing to keep policy rates low for an extended period. Had they believed this, the announcement would have exerted an equally powerful effect on short-term rates. This is consistent with the view that because QE1 was limited in scope it had only a limited effect in changing expectations of future Fed policy.

Writing subsequent to the four Fed economists, Arvind Krishnamurthy and Anna Vissing-Jorgensen were able to consider QE2 as well as QE1.[10] They looked at interest rates not just on treasury bonds but also on the mortgage-backed securities and corporate bonds that matter for real estate lending and corporate investment. In addition, they compared the minutes and hours immediately before and after the announcement. Considering this shorter time period makes it even less likely that the observed change in interest rates is being contaminated by other factors.[11]

Krishnamurthy and Vissing-Jorgensen found that QE1 and QE2 placed downward pressure on interest rates on ten-year treasuries and also other relatively safe assets. More importantly, QE1, in the course of which the Fed purchased more than $1 trillion of mortgage-related obligations, also had a negative impact on yields on risky mortgage-backed securities, as well as a smaller negative impact on corporate bonds.[12] In contrast, QE2, which was limited to purchases of treasury bonds, had only a small impact on mortgage-backed securities and no impact on corporate bonds. This may explain why, when launching QE3, the Fed again focused on mortgage-backed securities—and why the housing market recovered in 2013.

So when the Fed purchased safe assets, it mainly succeeded in driving down interest rates on safe assets. When it purchased risky assets, something it did only sporadically because doing so was politically contentious, it mainly succeeded in driving down returns on risky assets. In both cases it had little success in using security purchases to signal that it would keep policy rates low for an extended period or to raise expectations of inflation. Krishnamurthy and Vissing-Jorgensen do find some evidence of changes in the prices of Treasury Inflation Protected Securities (TIPS), pointing to a modest positive impact on inflation expectations. They find some sign that QE announcements had a modest negative impact on short-term treasury rates, as if investors took those announcements as a signal that the Fed might keep its policy rate lower for longer. Evidently, the more times the Fed repeated the policy, the more it succeeded in convincing investors it was prepared to stay the course.

Even so, expectations of inflation continued to undershoot the Fed's 2 percent target. With hindsight, larger purchases and bolder statements would have been better. But given the political pressure, this was not to be.

Finally, one can use a model of the economy to rerun history without the Fed's asset purchases. Janet Yellen, who was then vice-chair of the Federal Reserve Board, reported such an exercise using the Federal Reserve's in-house model in early 2011.[13] The results suggested that unemployment would have been 1 to 1 ½ percentage points higher in the absence of QE1 and QE2. Private payroll employment would have been roughly two million jobs lower.

The linkages between financial markets and the economy are not one of the strengths of this class of models, as noted. That said, these are the best estimates we have. Put them together with estimates of the impact of the fiscal stimulus, and it appears that the fall in the unemployment rate from 10 percent in October 2009 to 7.5 percent in early 2013 was largely attributable to policy. As Mervyn King averred, policy makers prevented another Great Depression. They prevented the unemployment rate from persistently exceeding 10 percent.

At the same time, they could have done more. And their failure to do so largely explains why the recovery continued to disappoint.

PART IV | Avoiding the Next Time

| Wall Street and Main Street

L IKE THE ROOSEVELT administration before it, the Obama administration's response to the crisis entailed much more than just the use of fiscal and monetary tools. It included an impressive array of initiatives targeted at specific sectors, from housing and motor vehicles to financial services.[1] Few if any of these, however, began to approach, in ambition or achievement, the initiatives launched under the New Deal.

In particular, the Obama administration's attempts to provide distressed homeowners with mortgage relief were a pale imitation of what was achieved by the Home Owners' Loan Corporation of the 1930s. Changes in the nature of housing finance in the intervening period made it more difficult to restructure mortgages without imposing large losses on either the banks or taxpayers, something that was both a political and an economic nonstarter. The Dodd-Frank Wall Street Reform and Consumer Protection Act of 2010 did not begin to rise to the ambition of the Glass-Steagall Act of 1933 or the Securities Exchange Act of 1934. By more successfully deploying their monetary and fiscal tools, policy makers this time prevented the worst. And by preventing the worst, they allowed the vested interests that benefited from the prevailing financial system to regroup. They relieved the pressure for root-and-branch reform.

———

Residential construction had accounted for 6 percent of US GDP at the peak in 2005; its share now fell to barely 2 percent. Construction activity always falls sharply in a recession, to be sure. But what was worrisome now was how weak residential construction continued to act as a drag once the economy began to recover.

To explain the failure of construction to recover, observers pointed to the outsized building boom prior to 2006 and the exceptional severity of the recession, which drained the pool of potential homebuyers. Problems in the banking system and securitization markets made it hard to finance construction of new subdivisions and apartment buildings. Mortgage underwriters, having embraced lax standards before, swung now to the other extreme. Regulators tightened their scrutiny of lending practices.

Above all, as many as four million of the sixty million American homeowners with mortgages had fallen behind on their payments by early 2009 and were at risk of foreclosure. It took a home builder of unusually sunny disposition to invest in a new subdivision with this massive shadow inventory hanging over the market. A further ten to fifteen million households were encumbered with mortgage debts that now exceeded the value of their homes. For the moment, they were still current on their mortgages, but there was always the risk that they might walk away, adding their homes to the list of bank-owned properties. In addition to the drag on the construction sector, there were the losses for the banks. There was the deterioration of neighborhoods blighted by untended properties. Above all, there were the dislocation and suffering of families losing their homes.

In the 1930s the Home Owners' Loan Corporation helped to mitigate these problems.[2] But there was no HOLC this time. Instead the Obama administration responded with a set of limited initiatives that failed to deliver even on their own modest ambitions. The Home Affordable Modification Program (HAMP) was designed to provide financial incentives for banks and mortgage servicers to reduce interest rates for four million homeowners unable to make their monthly payments. Servicers satisfying program provisions received an up-front fee of $1,000 and further modest payments if the borrower remained current. But as of late 2013, just 1.3 million mortgages had been modified under the program. The government had spent barely a quarter of TARP funds earmarked for the purpose.

The Home Affordable Refinance Program (HARP) was designed to permit an additional five million homeowners not immediately at risk of foreclosure to refinance at lower rates. To qualify, a mortgage must have been acquired by Freddie Mac or Fannie Mae. Conveniently from this point of view, Fannie and Freddie now owned or guaranteed a majority of US home loans. Less conveniently, Freddie and Fannie's independent administrator, Ed DeMarco, who was charged with rehabilitating the GSEs, resisted enlisting them in the cause. By mid-2011 barely a million homeowners had been helped, and by the end of 2013, six full years into the crisis, fewer than 3 million homeowners had availed themselves of this program. There were also initiatives for lending money to unemployed homeowners and transfers to the states for anti-foreclosure programs. But fewer than one in thirty homeowners were helped by these government programs, compared to one in ten in the 1930s.

Policy makers struggled with both ethical and budgetary dilemmas. A program narrowly targeted at delinquent homeowners would reward those who had stopped paying, using the tax dollars of others whose homes were also underwater but who nonetheless continued to make their payments. A program addressing the problems of all twenty million homeowners whose mortgages exceeded the value of their homes would, however, quickly become so expensive as to be politically toxic.

Alternatively, the foreclosure problem could have been addressed through changes in statute. Judges could have been empowered to restructure mortgages in personal bankruptcy proceedings, just as they restructured other debts.[3] Senator Obama had sponsored legislation to this effect, and Candidate Obama endorsed the concept. But for President Obama, this would have meant losses for the banks, which preferred to extend and pretend—to hope that their problem loans would be repaid once the housing market recovered. Some loans might have to be written down, but the banks preferred to realize these losses later, when their condition was stronger.

And, despite the bailouts, the banks remained a powerful lobby. Community banks lobbied against legislation to allow bankruptcy judges to meddle with their mortgage portfolios, just as they had lobbied against deposit insurance in the 1930s.[4] This created doubts that legislation empowering judges to restructure mortgages could attract the necessary supermajority of votes in the Senate. In any case, a policy that implied large losses for the lenders would have undermined Treasury's strategy for rehabilitating the financial system, which was based on the banks' earning their way back to health. Secretary Geithner opposed any form of intervention that meant losses for the banks. The Senate was quietly told that bankruptcy reform was not a priority of Treasury, and legislation aimed at revising the statute died a quick death.

It has been argued that the difference in the 1930s was decisive action to resolve the banking crisis. By declaring a bank holiday, closing down bad banks, and allowing only well-capitalized depository institutions to open, it is said, FDR strengthened the banking system sufficiently so that it could absorb losses from a more ambitious mortgage restructuring initiative.[5] This, as we have seen, is inaccurate. The main thing FDR did was to provide a cooling-off period, some soothing words, and the capacity for the Federal Reserve to act as a lender of last resort through the Emergency Banking Act of 1933. Then as now, the banks were too weak for the government to force them to absorb large losses. The Home Owners' Loan Corporation, recall, bought only mortgages that financial institutions willingly sold.

In fact, the HOLC could help as many as one in ten homeowners without massive budgetary costs and without imposing large losses on banks and other mortgage lenders because its help was limited to interest-rate relief. This was all many homeowners needed, since, given down payments of as much as 50 percent, few of them were underwater even with the sharp fall in house prices. The fact that more homeowners were underwater in 2009 as a result of having made smaller down payments made resolving the foreclosure crisis harder.[6]

Finally, the greater complexity of mortgage finance made restructuring more difficult. Having purchased a mortgage, investors might lose as much as 40 percent if a home was repossessed; such were the costs of evicting the occupant, sprucing up the property, and putting it on the market. They therefore had an incentive to agree to at least some reduction of principal to keep the borrower in his or her residence. Homeowners, however, dealt not with investors but with mortgage servicers, who were set up to collect monthly payments if they were made and to foreclose if they were not. Servicers were not competent to restructure mortgages, as subsequent tales of lost paperwork and serial miscommunication made clear. Nor did the prospect of a $1,000 HAMP payment give them much incentive to acquire the capacity.

In principle, this was a problem that the public sector could solve. The federal government hired twenty thousand specialists to administer the HOLC and oversee mortgage restructuring in the 1930s. This time, in light of the greater complexity of mortgage finance, the commitment of manpower would have had to be greater still. But given pervasive distrust of big government, there was resistance now to doing anything similar.

———

The Great Depression and the banking crisis prompted passage of the Glass-Steagall Act, creation of the Securities and Exchange Commission and the Federal Deposit Insurance Corporation, and measures strengthening the power of the Federal Reserve to act as a lender of last resort. These reforms did not eradicate every trace of the earlier banking and financial system. The United States still had a large number of banks, matched now by a large number of regulators. The shadow of history was too long for it to be otherwise. Still, by creating deposit insurance, establishing a proper lender of last resort, and subjecting banks and securities markets to stricter regulation, policy makers drew the right lessons. By strengthening confidence in the banking and financial system and limiting risk taking, they inaugurated what was, in retrospect, a singular half-century of financial stability.

Financial reform this time was more limited. The most important explanation, alluded to above, was the very success of policy makers in preventing the worst. Building on the lessons of the 1930s, they averted an economic calamity on the scale of the Great Depression. The Depression discredited inherited financial arrangements. The implosion was so complete that there was little left to risk by radical reform. Unquestionably, the rescues of Bear Stearns, AIG, Citigroup, and Bank of America and the failure of Lehman Brothers were a shock. But this shock paled in comparison with the catastrophe that was 1933, when the banking and financial system was shut, the basis for the monetary standard was suspended, and economic activity ground to a halt. With things so bad, it was hard for the opponents to argue that root-and-branch reform would make them worse.[7]

The other factor standing in the way of more fundamental 1930s-style reform was the size and complexity of the financial system. The complexity of megabanks like Citigroup, Bank of America, and Wells Fargo made breaking them up more easily said than done, however much the proponents of breakup asserted otherwise. Not only were the big banks still in business but, as a result of the shotgun marriages presided over by the authorities, they had grown even bigger. There was a wider range of financial institutions and instruments to be brought into the regulatory net, including hedge funds, insurance companies, and money market mutual funds. Because the cogs of the financial system were interlocking, radical reform of the rules governing one might have unintended consequences for others. If money market funds were obliged to hold costly capital, for example, they would have to reduce their returns. Investors would shun them, forcing the money funds to curtail their purchases of commercial paper. Hence reform of the rules governing money market funds might have a negative impact on the commercial paper market and impair the operation of the financial system as a whole.

Similarly, the existence of a wide variety of derivative instruments complicated efforts to drive their trading into clearinghouses and onto exchanges. Although easily standardized securities would survive such requirements, others might not. It was not clear which were which, or whether those that survived would mainly be the instruments used by farmers for hedging risk or speculators for manipulating it.

And derivative securities were traded not just in the United States but internationally. In the 1930s world of controls on capital flows, it was possible for national authorities to proceed unilaterally. But if other countries now failed to follow the United States in tightening regulation, transactions and the institutions undertaking them might simply move offshore, much as AIG Financial Products had moved offshore before the crisis. The $6.2 billion of trading losses incurred by JPMorgan's Chief Investment Office in 2012 similarly occurred offshore. As former Senator Ted Kaufman, onetime chief of staff to Joe Biden and no friend of the financial services industry, put it, Bruno Iksil, the JPMorgan trader immediately responsible, wasn't called the "London Whale" because he worked in Philadelphia.[8]

The regulatory apparatus was similarly more complex. The United States had as many as seven separate bank regulators, each with its turf. Lobbying by regulators as well as the regulated made radical reform such as creation of a single consolidated bank supervisor impossible to achieve. Moreover, there now existed international standards for capital and liquidity, the Basel Accord, with which the United States had to comply. Compared to 1933, there were simply more facts on the ground. Incremental reform was still possible, but radical reform was hemmed in on all sides.

———

There were two estimable congressional leaders in 1933, Carter Glass and Henry Steagall, but there were now two equally effective leaders in Congressman Barney Frank and Senator Christopher Dodd. Frank, the chair of the House Financial Services Committee, had an outsized ego even by congressional standards. Prone to strong statements and bad jokes, and conscious of his reputation as the quickest mind in the House, he did not shy away from denigrating his opponents. But he was able to master complex technical issues and had a knack for shepherding controversial legislation through committee. Dodd, chair of the Senate Banking Committee, ran a disastrous presidential campaign in 2008, and as a "friend of Angelo" he received mortgage loans on his houses in Washington, D.C., and Connecticut from Countrywide Financial. But he was committed to forging a bipartisan consensus, and as a lame-duck senator who announced his decision not to run for reelection in January 2010, he saw successful financial reform legislation as his legacy.

The result was the Dodd-Frank Wall Street Reform and Consumer Protection Act of 2010, which sought to strengthen the system rather than overturn it. At its center were measures to raise capital and liquidity requirements, create a regulatory entity responsible for systemic stability, and protect consumers. Dodd-Frank applied capital requirements at the level of the bank holding company, and not just its commercial banking subsidiary, in order to limit holding-company smoke and mirrors. It specified more demanding capital requirements for banks holding financial derivatives. It required more capital in general.

Following a lengthy comment period, the regulators issued rules implementing these directives. Banks were required to hold equity capital in the amount of 7 percent of their risk-weighted assets.[9] To limit their ability to manipulate their risk weights and shift assets off balance sheet, large internationally active banks were made subject to a simple leverage ratio of 5 percent, including off-balance-sheet exposures (and an even higher 6 percent for the eight largest banking organizations). Large banks were put on notice that, reflecting their systemic importance, they would be subject to capital surcharges to be specified later.[10]

If a step in the right direction, this was still less capital and more leverage than many thought prudent. But in raising capital requirements, the Fed, the FDIC, and the Comptroller of the Currency were limited by the opposition of community banks, which warned that much higher capital requirements could put them out of business. In applying higher capital and liquidity requirements to the largest banks, they were influenced by warnings that heavier requirements would damage the ability of US banks to compete internationally. These questions were all mind-numbingly complex, making it hard for the public to counter the lobbyists.

Creating a regulator responsible for not just the health of individual financial institutions but the stability of the system was similarly more easily said than done. Although the Fed was the obvious entity to assume this function, it was not the most popular agency in town. The issue was taken up in March 2009, just when it was learned that the recently bailed out AIG Financial Products was paying retention bonuses of up to $6.4 million to seventy-three key employees. The Fed had provided the money to bail out AIG. It had known about the bonus payments but had no power to prevent them, or so it claimed. Later it emerged that AIG had been permitted to use the bailout funds to pay off obligations to Goldman Sachs at 100 cents on the dollar. Not only was the Fed aware of the fact, but it instructed AIG's lawyers not to disclose to the SEC internal memos authorizing the payments.

Whatever the merits of the decision, rewarding the Fed with additional power was a political nonstarter under the circumstances. Not that bestowing those powers on the Treasury Department would have been more popular. With encouragement from Sheila Bair, Frank opted for a committee as the path of least resistance. The Financial Stability Oversight Council, as the committee came to be known, included the Fed and eight other regulators, along with the Treasury secretary in the chair.[11]

Committees move slowly and can find it hard to take decisive action. The Oversight Council took nearly three years to designate two nonbank financial companies, AIG and General Electric Capital, as systemically important and therefore subject to consolidated supervision.[12] Opting for a committee rather than a single systemic stability regulator was unfortunate from this point of view. This outcome again illustrated how chance events like the timing of AIG's bonus payments could have long-term consequences.

Chris Dodd was quick to embrace the idea of a consumer financial products safety commission as a political winner. Frank and the White House similarly saw it as a way of doing something, at least symbolically, for Main Street. The creation of what came to be known as the Consumer Financial Protection Bureau was championed by Elizabeth Warren, the tireless Oklahoma-born Harvard law professor specializing in personal bankruptcy law. Warren's campaign was sufficiently effective that her appointment to head the new bureau was blocked by deregulation-minded Republicans. Events took an ironic turn when that denial led Warren to run, successfully, for the Senate as a progressive Democrat in 2012.

The new bureau was charged with rooting out predatory and abusive practices like impenetrable mortgage documentation and up-front fees for debt-relief services that failed to materialize. Again the community banks resisted, on the grounds that they had not engaged in such practices and that the intrusion of a consumer protection bureau would complicate their lives. But the groundswell of support was irresistible. That the financial-services lobby was quick to complain of the bureau's use of enforcement lawyers on examination teams and policy requiring regulated entities to turn over all internal compliance documents, including those protected by attorney-client privilege, is an indication that it got off to a fast start.

Derivatives regulation was the other major item on the agenda. The government was compelled to bail out AIG because of its $446 billion of bilaterally settled credit default swaps, default on which might have caused its counterparties to collapse. Reformers now proposed moving transactions in such instruments onto exchanges where they could be netted and cleared electronically, limiting the open positions of traders. Prominent among the advocates was Gary Gensler. This was the same Gary Gensler who was once the youngest person ever to be made partner at Goldman Sachs and who shepherded the Commodity Futures Trading Act, which deregulated trading in credit default swaps, while serving as undersecretary for domestic finance in the Clinton Treasury. But the crisis had opened his eyes, and as chair of Obama's Commodity Futures Trading Commission he now pushed for moving derivatives trading onto electronic exchanges.

But exchange-based trading would have meant lower fees for the banks. It would have required standardizing derivative instruments and eliminating made-to-order business. The less-than-satisfactory compromise was to move settlement of derivatives transactions not onto exchanges but into clearinghouses. Self-organizing clearinghouses run by financial institutions were the main way banks cleared payments and dealt with failures prior to the advent of the Federal Reserve. Following that model, all institutions buying or selling a derivative security through a clearinghouse could be required to put up a margin payment. Those margin payments could then be used to make other counterparties whole in the event of the failure of one of their number.

The problem was that clearinghouses, by sharing risk in this way, also concentrate it. If several members fail simultaneously, the clearinghouse itself may be rendered insolvent and have to be bailed out. This reform, such as it is, may end up only creating yet more too-big-to-fail institutions. Whether this is a step forward only time will tell.

———

The remaining changes focused on filling the regulatory gaps revealed by the crisis. Dodd-Frank created a Federal Insurance Office in the Treasury to monitor the insurance industry and hopefully head off future AIGs. It created an Office of Credit Ratings in the SEC to oversee the rating agencies.[13] It required the Federal Reserve to conduct annual stress tests of bank holding companies with $50 billion or more of total assets.[14] It expanded the regulatory perimeter by requiring hedge funds to register with the SEC and revoking the exemption enjoyed by investment advisors with fewer than fifteen clients.[15] Though these were useful steps, they were far from revolutionary.

Then there is what Dodd-Frank failed to do. It did not eliminate too-big-to-fail, either by breaking up the banks or by prohibiting them, Glass-Steagall style, from making risky investments.[16] Instead, the six biggest banks—JPMorgan, Goldman Sachs, Bank of America, Citigroup, Wells Fargo, and Morgan Stanley—were allowed to grow 37 percent larger by the end of 2013 than in 2008–09, at the height of the crisis. Although Dodd-Frank gave the FDIC orderly liquidation authority—that is, the power to impose losses on a failed institution's shareholders and creditors—simply bestowing that power doesn't mean that the agency will be prepared to use it, especially if the result will be market disruptions and contagion to other financial institutions. The fact of large financial institutions operating across borders means that orderly resolution will require close cooperation between courts and regulators in a number of countries, in order to avoid a disorderly scramble for assets like what followed the failure of Lehman Brothers. Simply bestowing orderly resolution authority on a US agency does nothing to advance this.

A related provision of Dodd-Frank requires more than one hundred large financial institutions to provide the regulators with "living wills" describing how their affairs will be wound up in the event of failure. In the first such wills submitted in 2012, the banks described hopefully how their various divisions might be smoothly sold off to competitors. But those plans said nothing about who might buy the operations of a failed megabank in a crisis. They gave few grounds for confidence that regulators would be willing to euthanize a big bank given uncertainty about the consequences. Officials talked a good game about ending too big to fail. The reality was different.

The alternative to too-big-to-fail would have been too-safe-to-fail. Deposit-taking banks could have been turned into "narrow banks" permitted to make only safe and liquid investments. A strict version of Glass-Steagall, as advocated by Warren, could have been resurrected. But, again, radical reform was a bridge too far. Instead, the Obama administration settled for what came to be known as the Volcker Rule, championed by former Fed chairman Paul Volcker, which merely sought to ban trading for the bank's own book rather than on behalf of its clients or as a way of hedging risks. This was a way for the administration to look as if it was taking tough action. Scott Brown's surprise victory in the special election to replace Senator Edward Kennedy in January 2010, making him the first Republican to represent the Commonwealth of Massachusetts in the Senate in four decades, was enough for the president to stake out a more populist, antibank position.[17] The Volcker Rule was a means to this end.

But its efficacy, like that of orderly resolution authority and living wills, was doubtful. The Volcker Rule was watered down to meet the objections of the financial services industry and obtain a sixtieth filibuster-proof vote from none other than Senator Brown.[18] Rather than banning proprietary trading, banks were still permitted to invest up to 3 percent of their equity in such trades. In any case, it was unclear where to draw the line between legitimate hedging and market-making trades on the one hand and speculative trading for the bank's own book on the other. The $6.2 billion of losses suffered by JPMorgan from bets placed by the London Whale highlighted the iffy nature of the distinction. JPMorgan described these as "legitimate portfolio hedging operations" compatible with the Volcker Rule, whereas an inspector for its embarrassed regulator, the Comptroller of the Currency, dismissed them as a "make believe voodoo magic 'composite hedge.'"[19]

The experience of the 1930s suggests that radical reform is possible only in the wake of an exceptional crisis. Absent that crisis, business as usual remains the order of the day, and radical reform that threatens to disrupt such business is ruled out. An exceptional crisis halts such business for a time. The problem starting in 2009, if it can be called a problem, was that policy makers managed, just barely, to prevent a 1930s-style crisis. There was still business as usual to conduct. Radical reform that interfered with customary banking practices could be criticized as jeopardizing the recovery then slowly getting underway. This left only strengthening the existing system, as opposed to replacing it. And the incremental nature of the reform process, which unfolded slowly as new rules implementing Dodd-Frank directives were proposed by the regulators, allowed concentrated interests, notably the bank lobby, to re-form and mobilize in opposition.

Radical reform, 1930s style, may have appealed in principle, but it proved impossible in practice.

CHAPTER 23 | Normalization in an Abnormal
Economy

IN 1936 FRANKLIN ROOSEVELT grew anxious about a budget deficit that
had ballooned to an unprecedented $4.3 billion. With pressure from his
administration, Congress agreed to raise taxes on households with incomes
above $100,000 and on corporations with undistributed profits. In 2011
Barack Obama grew concerned about a budget deficit that topped $1.2 tril-
lion for a third successive year. In response Obama negotiated an agreement
with Congress to raise taxes on the 1 percent of earners with incomes above
$400,000, in early 2013. The agreement also allowed earlier cuts in payroll
taxes to expire, causing the rate paid by workers to jump from 4.2 to 6.2 percent and reducing take-home pay by $1,000 for a US family earning $50,000
a year. These steps were coupled with "sequestration," under which the defense
budget and nondefense discretionary spending were cut by 8.5 percent.[1]

Roosevelt's tax increases were not the only, or even the most important,
reason for the economic slowdown that blossomed into a recession in the final
months of 1937. More important, as we saw in Chapter 18, was the failure
of monetary policy makers to offset the contractionary effects. Nor were the
budget measures of the Obama administration and Congress, even conjoined
with the slowdown in federal spending as the 2009–2011 stimulus drew to
a close, the entire explanation for the disappointing recovery from the Great
Recession. Also important was the failure of the Federal Reserve to do more
to offset the negative impulse and instead start talking about tightening monetary policy.

But in both cases the desire to restore normal fiscal and monetary policies before normal economic conditions had returned was heavily responsible for the disappointing state of the economy. US unemployment still

exceeded 17 percent when World War II erupted in Europe. Without the double-dip recession of 1937–38, it would have been 5 percentage points less.[2] Unemployment in 2013, at 7.4 percent, was lower, reflecting the policy initiatives taken in 2009–2011. Even so, on almost any measure the recovery continued to disappoint. Growth averaged barely 2 percent per annum between 2011 and 2013, less than half the pace of the typical post–World War II expansion. The fall in the unemployment rate was driven less by improved labor market conditions than by a falling participation rate, as discouraged workers withdrew from the labor force.

There are good reasons for recovery from a slump caused by a financial crisis to be slower than a normal recovery.[3] Financial crises follow periods when households, in their exuberance, incur heavy debts. The subsequent process of deleveraging, in which those same households, now face-to-face with reality, seek to work down those debts, persists into the recovery, limiting their spending. Banks, still in the process of rebuilding their capital and repairing their balance sheets, are meanwhile limiting their lending.

But the implication is not that the disappointing recovery following the 2008–09 financial crisis was inevitable. If the private sector, intent on deleveraging, spends less, then the public sector can spend more. If commercial banks lend less, then the central bank can lend more. The authorities can continue until the private sector is ready to take up the slack. The presence of unemployed resources in the wake of a crisis means there is space for the economy to bounce back even more vigorously than from the typical recession.

The Roosevelt recovery illustrates the point. Between 1933 and 1937 real GDP rose at an annual average rate of more than 8 percent despite household balance sheets and the financial system being seriously impaired. This is not to suggest that the United States could have matched this impressive rate of economic growth starting in 2009. But it could have done better.

————

FDR understood the need for additional government spending to replace the private spending that had dried up. As he put it with directness in 1936, "No one lightly lays a burden on the income of a Nation. But this vicious tightening circle of our declining national income simply had to be broken. . . . We accepted the final responsibility of Government, after all else had failed, to spend money when no one else had money left to spend."[4]

At the same time, Roosevelt never entirely relinquished his preoccupation with fiscal soundness or his embrace of the analogy between the household budget and the government budget. The Federal debt-to-GDP ratio was only

40 percent in 1936, less than half the 90 percent scaled in 2010, but the size of the government and its tax take, out of which debt service had to be paid, were also less. Failing to address the problem would have jeopardized confidence, in the view of the president and advisors.

Then there were arguments for raising taxes on equity grounds.[5] The rich had not suffered the same excruciating pain as the common man in the Depression. It was only just, as Roosevelt and his fellow Democrats saw it, for the wealthy to now pay their fair share to finance New Deal programs designed to right these wrongs.

Not least, there were political considerations. Roosevelt had campaigned in 1932 on a promise to balance the budget. With the approach of another election, he worried that failure to carry it out might be turned into a political liability by his opponents.[6]

Barack Obama, on assuming the presidency, shared all three motivations. The moral argument was that the top 1 percent had greatly increased their share of the national income in the fifteen years leading up to the Great Recession. The wealthy may have suffered capital losses in the downturn, but in the 2009–2011 recovery the incomes of the top 1 percent again grew faster than incomes overall. In the two decades ending in 2011, the real incomes of the top 1 percent rose by more than 57 percent, those of the bottom 99 percent by less than 6 percent. The top 1 percent effectively captured nearly two-thirds of all income gains.[7] It was only fair and just that they should pay their commensurate share in taxes.

There was also a sense among Obama's advisors that the budget had become a political liability. The midterm gains of the Tea Party underscored the danger. In the view of Rahm Emanuel, Obama's chief of staff, and David Axelrod, his senior political advisor, the president had to be seen as addressing the deficit. Their position played into Obama's own cautious fiscal instincts and his belief that government was bloated and inefficient.[8] It encouraged his inclination to accept cuts in spending if the Republicans in turn agreed to increases in taxes. Unfortunately, the president did not anticipate the Republicans' readiness to accept his offer while refusing to give anything in return, or their willingness, when push came to shove, to allow the economy to fall off the cliff.

Last, there were economic arguments. Large deficits leading to unsustainable debts could undermine business confidence. The June 2010 projection of the studiously nonpartisan Congressional Budget Office showed the deficit widening after 2014 as a result of mounting entitlement spending. It showed publicly held debt as a share of GDP rising sharply. Something had to be done now to address these problems looming in the not-too-distant future. Or so it was argued by the Concord Coalition, the Committee for a Responsible

Federal Budget, and the *Fiscal Times*, all founded by Peter G. Peterson, commerce secretary under Richard Nixon, onetime head of Lehman Brothers, and co-founder of the Blackstone private equity group. A durable solution to these problems required bipartisan support. And getting Republican agreement on a medium-term plan, the president's political advisors argued, would entail addressing the opposition's concerns over the immediate deficit.

But abdicating government's responsibility to "spend money when no one else had money left to spend" risked aborting the recovery and plunging the economy back into recession. Here, however, the possibility of health care and entitlement reform held out hope of squaring the circle. Less public spending and smaller deficits starting in, say, 2014 would mean less government borrowing and lower interest rates at that future date. And downward pressure on interest rates in the future would put downward pressure on interest rates now, insofar as investors look forward. Investors anticipating higher treasury bond prices would start buying today, reducing current yields. Hence any negative impact on the recovery from current spending cuts would be offset, in part, by the positive impact of future spending cuts operating through lower interest rates.

This mechanism was a key factor back in the recovery from the 1991–92 recession. President Clinton's 1993 conversion to fiscal consolidation under the tutelage of his National Economic Council director Robert Rubin unleashed just such a low-interest-rate-led recovery. Consolidation that put downward pressure on interest rates helped to stimulate investment and growth. The Clinton administration alumni who now populated the Obama White House looked back nostalgically on this episode.

The flaw in their logic, it should have been clear, was that interest rates had already been pushed as low as they could go. The recession associated with the 2008–09 crisis was fundamentally different from the recession from which the United States recovered in 1993. The economy had now fallen into a liquidity trap. Interest rates couldn't be depressed further by promises of lower deficits down the road. Even if coupled with a credible commitment to future deficit reduction, deficit reduction now could only hinder recovery.[9]

With hindsight, this fly in the ointment is blindingly clear. The question is why it wasn't discerned at the time.

———

As early as the beginning of 2009—indeed, even while the design of the fiscal stimulus to counter the Great Recession was still being discussed—influential voices within the administration were urging the new president to signal his commitment to closing the deficit. Already during the transition, Treasury

Secretary–designate Geithner advocated putting in place plans for reducing the deficit to 3 percent of GDP by the end of the president's first term, 3 percent being the talismanic threshold for fiscal prudence that the Europeans, in their wisdom, had enshrined in the Maastricht Treaty establishing their economic and monetary union.

But as Geithner grew preoccupied by the banks and their stress tests, the role of fiscal consolidator in chief was assumed by Peter Orszag, the Princeton and London School of Economics–educated economist who had worked with Rubin as an aide in the Clinton White House. In a 2004 paper, Orszag and Rubin, together with the economist Allen Sinai, argued that the adverse impact of budget deficits, and by implication the benefits of future fiscal consolidation, operate mainly through their impact on confidence. In other words, even in an environment of near-zero interest rates, where the promise of future budget cuts could not push rates down still further, there could nevertheless be a positive effect on business investment, as in the Clinton years, insofar as investors were rendered more confident and secure. Orszag, Rubin, and Sinai were writing before the environment of near-zero interest rates materialized, but the implication is clear. "Under the conventional view," they wrote,

> ongoing budget deficits decrease national saving, which reduces domestic investment and increases borrowing from abroad. Interest rates play a key role in how the economy adjusts. The reduction in national saving raises domestic interest rates, which dampens investment and attracts capital from abroad. . . . The adverse consequences of sustained budget deficits may well be far larger and occur more suddenly than traditional analysis suggests, however. Substantial deficits projected far into the future can cause a fundamental shift in market expectations and a related loss of confidence both at home and abroad. The unfavorable dynamic effects that could ensue are largely if not entirely excluded from the conventional analysis of budget deficits.[10]

From his perch at the White House Office of Management and Budget, Orszag now argued that just such a confidence effect was needed to spur investment. The way to secure it was by making a down payment on fiscal consolidation, starting by asking every department to cut $100 million from its operating budget.

This faith in elusive confidence effects would have resonated with Henry Morgenthau, but it was not universally shared by President Obama's economic advisors. In particular, it was not shared by Lawrence Summers, head of Obama's National Economic Council, or Christina Romer, chair of his Council of Economic Advisors. Summers emphasized that investment and growth depended not just on confidence about the future but on conditions now. Romer warned against precipitous fiscal consolidation like what had helped to trigger the recession of 1937–38.[11]

But Orszag's nonpartisan, dispassionate, Rubinesque analysis appealed to Obama, who in May 2009 tasked him with drafting a memo laying out medium-term fiscal options. None of those options was implemented immediately, but the OMB director's advocacy of medium-term consolidation posed an obstacle to a second stimulus when it became evident in the course of the year that unemployment was rising faster than anticipated. And Orszag's emphasis on medium-term consolidation helped lay the groundwork for the ill-fated negotiations between the White House and congressional leadership to narrow the budget deficit in 2011.

Emanuel and Axelrod were similarly concerned already in the spring of 2009 that deficits were a political liability. Their concern deepened in the fall when the Democrats lost control of statehouses in New Jersey and Virginia. Evidently, the Republicans' anti-big-government rhetoric was resonating with independent voters. There was a backlash against the government's anti-crisis measures, including the stimulus, fed by the observation that financial interests were not being made to pay. The banks had been bailed out. Bonuses continued to be paid, and there were as yet few instances of legal action against the miscreants.

Then there was the failure of the stimulus to deliver everything promised. The main reason unemployment rose significantly above the 8 percent peak projected by Romer and Jared Bernstein may have been that the economy was already contracting faster than anyone appreciated in 2008 and not that the stimulus itself was ineffectual, but this distinction was difficult for non-economists to understand and for economists to explain. As unemployment rose higher than Obama's advisors predicted would happen in the absence of the stimulus, the critics could contend that deficit spending was not just ineffectual but counterproductive. This argument may have been bad economics, but it was good politics.

In addition, by 2010 there were signs that the economy was beginning to improve. Although unemployment remained high, in excess of 9 percent, GDP at least was growing. It rose by 3.9 percent in the first quarter, not atypically for the expansion phase of the cycle, making it seem as though the shift to fiscal consolidation could safely proceed. Admittedly, conditions were worsening in Europe, which had done less than the United States to address its banking-sector problems and where the new Greek government of George Papandreou had just revealed that the fiscal and financial situation was even worse than acknowledged previously.[12] But the fact that Greece's structural and political problems manifested themselves in a gaping, previously undisclosed budget hole only strengthened the presumption that the real and present danger was fiscal profligacy. When European and American officials assembled for their summit in Iqaluit in early 2010, their interests in fiscal consolidation were aligned.

Finally, one cannot entirely dismiss the argument that President Obama's inexperience as a tactician hastened the shift to austerity.[13] Obama assumed that he and House leadership could reach an accommodation in which his offer of modest budget cuts would be met with Republican agreement to modest tax increases. On that basis the two sides could then craft a medium-term fiscal plan. But this approach did not figure with the rise of the Tea Party or a Republican leader, John Boehner, who felt obliged to cater to his caucus. In the negotiations in the winter and early spring of 2011 over the continuing resolutions to keep the government operating, not only did Boehner reject all tax increases, but he brought to the table escalating demands for spending cuts, threatening to shut down the government if they were not agreed. In this way the White House permitted the House Republicans to frame the debate as the amount by which spending would be cut.

The capstone was the budget proposal issued in April 2011 by Wisconsin Representative Paul Ryan, chairman of the House Budget Committee. A former speechwriter for Congressman Jack Kemp, Ryan now set out to make his name as the House's preeminent budget specialist. His budget, entitled "The Path to Prosperity," foresaw an additional $6.2 trillion of spending cuts over ten years. The nature of those cuts was largely unspecified, and what *was* specified reduced the federal budget largely by shifting Medicare expenditures onto individuals and the states, an idea that was a nonstarter politically. But this did not prevent Ryan's budget from defining the political contest as who could cut the most.

―――

The stage was thus set for negotiations in the summer of 2011 over the debt ceiling, the cap on the value of the bonds that the Treasury was permitted to issue. In practice, raising the debt ceiling simply authorized Treasury to pay bills that the government had already incurred. But it provided another pressure point for Republican negotiators. Not raising the ceiling would force the government to default on some of its obligations. Treasury would have to decide whom to pay and whom not to pay. It might choose to pay bondholders in preference to, say, government contractors. But doing so was unlikely to reassure even the bondholders. If there was a context in which Orszag-like arguments about the importance of confidence mattered, this was it.

Members of the Tea Party, for their part, were more than happy to force a technical default. Default was a guaranteed way of shrinking public spending, and for the Tea Party this was the only thing that mattered, which gave the Republican leadership additional bargaining leverage. The Republican position was that any increase in the debt ceiling had to be matched dollar for dollar with future spending cuts.

Over a barrel, the White House capitulated. Its capitulation took the form of an agreement, engineered by House and Senate leadership, to cut spending by $1.2 trillion over ten years.[14] It agreed to the creation of a "supercommittee," formally the Joint Select Committee on Deficit Reduction, comprising twelve members of Congress, to propose a further $1.2 trillion of cuts for approval by the full House and Senate. If the supercommittee was unable to reach an agreement by the end of November, across-the-board cuts, exempting only entitlements and military salaries, would kick in starting in 2013.

The idea was to make the cuts so painful and inefficient that there would be irresistible pressure for the supercommittee to agree. But the irresistible turned out to be resistible. Threatening to play Russian roulette with the economy was ineffectual, given a populist wing of the Republican Party more than willing to gamble on an empty chamber. It is not entirely surprising that a committee whose members ranged from Representative Chris Van Hollen of Maryland, a close ally of House Majority leader Nancy Pelosi and steadfast supporter of social programs, to Senator Pat Toomey of Pennsylvania, a former currency swap trader for Morgan, Grenfell & Co., Tea Party spokesman and staunch opponent of raising the debt ceiling, was unable to agree. And so the Sequester, which cut discretionary civilian spending and the military budget alike by 8.5 percent, came into effect starting on March 1, 2013.

This is not to say that the White House, like the Bourbons, learned nothing. At the end of 2012, when the Bush tax cuts were slated to expire, it drew a line when it came to extending them for the top 1 percent of income earners. At the same time, however, it acquiesced to the call for higher payroll taxes from those concerned for the longer-term solvency of the Social Security system.

The structural budget deficit (the deficit with the impact of the business cycle removed) narrowed by 1¾ percent of GDP in 2012 as the stimulus wound down, and then by 2½ percent of GDP in 2013 as a result of tax increases and the Sequester. The International Monetary Fund, not normally an advocate of public spending, criticized the pace of deficit reduction as excessive and warned that it was subtracting between 1⅓ and 1¾ percentage points from US growth in 2013.[15] If recovery from the financial crisis continued to disappoint, this was not because disappointing recovery was inevitable. At least this is the conclusion if one believes that dysfunctional politics and policies are not the inevitable result of financial crises.

———

Ordinarily, one might have expected the Fed, aware of the increasingly contractionary stance of fiscal policy, to take steps to offset or dampen the effects. The Federal Reserve Board was certainly aware of the problem, having highlighted it in the 2013 "Report on Monetary Policy" transmitted to Congress in July.[16]

But the circumstances in 2013 were not ordinary. The federal funds rate, having already been reduced to 0–0.25 percent, was as low as it could go. The FOMC indicated its intention of keeping it there as long as unemployment remained above 6.5 percent and inflation one to two years ahead was not seen as exceeding its 2 percent target by more than half a percentage point. The FOMC also continued its program of large-scale asset purchases, buying mortgage-backed securities at a rate of $40 billion a month and long-term treasuries at $45 billion a month. In addition, it was reinvesting the principal payments on maturing mortgage-backed securities and rolling over maturing treasuries. It signaled that it would continue these policies until the labor market outlook improved. The Fed was already doing a lot. Indeed, it faced criticism from conservative circles for doing too much.

Still, the central bank could have done more. It could have ramped up its purchases of mortgaged-backed securities and treasury bonds. It could have widened the tolerance band around its 2 percent inflation target from half a percentage point. It could have raised the target itself. Doing so would have been a departure from monetary convention, but there was an argument for unconventional action when unemployment was stubbornly high, growth continued to disappoint, and fiscal consolidation placed sharp contractionary pressure on the economy. Larger securities purchases or a 3 percent inflation target were not as radical as Roosevelt's decision to abandon the gold standard and engage in large-scale purchases of gold. Abandoning the gold standard and requiring citizens to exchange their gold for paper currency constituted a revolutionary change in the conduct of monetary policy. Additional securities purchases or even a higher inflation target would have been weak soup by comparison.

Differences in decision-making processes partly explain the contrasting outcomes. In 1933 the decision to suspend the gold standard could be taken by one man, the president, by executive order, since his party controlled both houses of Congress, which were prepared to validate his order. FDR could act decisively. Starting in October, he could use the powers of the Reconstruction

Finance Corporation to buy however much gold he wished, consulting only his trusted advisors Henry Morgenthau and Jesse Jones. Morgenthau, in his wisdom, could manage the money supply as he saw fit through the Treasury's gold sterilization program. Few in Congress complained that the Executive Branch had usurped powers that properly rested with the Federal Reserve. To the contrary, influential voices from Elmer Thomas on down pressed the president to pursue a more expansionary policy by any means necessary. The Fed's catastrophic missteps had not exactly burnished its reputation or buttressed public and political support for its independent conduct of monetary policy. In 2013 influential voices warned that the Fed's unconventional policies—purchases of mortgage-backed securities designed to support the housing market, for example—exceeded its mandate for the preservation of price stability. These critics in turn raised questions about its independence. This episode eighty years earlier is a reminder that failing to pursue the central bank's mandate for high employment, whether explicit or implicit, may jeopardize its independence as well.

In 2013, in contrast to 1933, monetary policy was made by committee, specifically by a committee of seven Federal Reserve governors and five Reserve bank presidents. It is the nature of committees to move slowly, something that is truer of the Federal Open Market Committee than most. The FOMC values consensus. Members may dissent, but they are aware that too many dissents raise questions about the coherence of policy. All this makes compromise the order of the day. Changes in monetary policy, for better or worse, tend to be incremental, not radical.

In the summer of 2013, those incremental changes were in the direction of less accommodation, not more. In May, in addressing Congress' Joint Economic Committee, and then in June, in a post-FOMC press conference, Chairman Bernanke indicated that the central bank might start cutting back on its securities purchases and could conceivably halt them entirely by mid-2014, despite the absence of overt inflationary pressures and continued lackluster growth. Though there was as yet no actual tapering of securities purchases, the contractionary effect of the more restrictive future monetary policy signaled by his statement was felt immediately.[17] Ten-year treasury yields jumped from 2.3 to 2.9 percent over the subsequent two months, pushing up the thirty-year mortgage interest rate from 4 to 4.5 per cent and slowing the recovery of the housing market.

Several factors combined to prompt this shift in the policy outlook. Observers worried that low yields on treasury bonds were encouraging investors to take on additional risk. They worried that purchases of mortgage-backed securities were fueling another round of housing market excesses. These warnings came not only from perennial critics of the central bank but also from Reserve bank presidents who, even though they had their fingers on the pulse of local housing and banking markets, were sometimes less attuned to the economywide effects of monetary policy. But even Chairman Bernanke echoed their concerns in a speech at the Federal Reserve Bank of Chicago in May 2013, when he noted that the central bank was "watching particularly closely for instances of 'reaching for yield' [where investors moved into riskier investments in search of higher returns] and other forms of excessive risk taking."[18]

There were also doubts among FOMC members about the effectiveness of monetary stimulus. Richmond Reserve bank president Jeffrey Lacker argued that an additional 50-basis-point reduction in treasury bond yields and mortgage rates would do little to encourage faster growth in an economy that was being held back by an aging population and burdensome regulation. As he put it in May 2013, although growth had resumed, "it appears as if it's limited, in large part, by structural factors that monetary policy is not capable of offsetting. In this situation, the benefit-cost trade-off associated with further monetary stimulus does not seem promising." The Dallas Fed's Richard Fisher, though not a voting member of the FOMC, made up for his lack of a ballot with an abundance of metaphor, arguing that confidence was apt to be missing in the absence of a credible medium-term fiscal plan and that until then "the Fed is, at best, pushing on a string and, at worst, building up kindling for speculation and, eventually, a massive shipboard fire of inflation."[19] Their diagnoses were dubious, but their noisy dissents made it more difficult for the central bank to stay the course.

Above all, that the Fed, together with other policy makers, had averted another Great Depression discouraged it from doing more. Members of the FOMC could draw solace from the fact that the housing market was doing better. They could feel comfort that state and local government finances were improving. They could point to the fact that there had been no collapse of activity as in 1929–33. This allowed them to give a hearing to the critics of central bank activism and indulge their desire to return to a more conventional monetary policy, conventional economy or not. US policy in 2008–09 prevented the worst, as policy makers proudly noted. But that very result, ironically, now worked to shape policy in less positive directions.

CHAPTER 24 | Making Things as Difficult as
Possible

IF DOMESTIC POLICY created headwinds for US recovery, then events elsewhere, in Europe, did not help. The euro crisis broke into the open in 2010 even before US fiscal and monetary policies shifted in a more austere direction. The consequences were catastrophic first and foremost for the members of the European Union. But they also weighed on the performance of other economies, including a United States still struggling to recover from the worst recession in eighty years.

The Europeans had long been working to make things as difficult as possible. They neglected the problems in their banks. They neglected the deterioration of competitiveness across Southern Europe. They neglected the chronic fiscal problems of Greece, which in their wisdom they admitted to the Eurozone in 2002.

And in creating the euro, they closed off all avenues for resolving these problems. There was no possibility of devaluing the national currency because there was no national currency to devalue. There was no scope for regaining the devaluation option, since there was no provision for exiting the Eurozone. There was no banking union to accompany the monetary union. In the absence of a single bank supervisor and a mechanism for winding up bad banks, there was no way of forcing national regulators to recapitalize or liquidate insolvent financial institutions. There was no procedure for restructuring the debts of troubled governments—no sovereign bankruptcy code. There was no mechanism for providing emergency assistance to governments or consensus on the design of the associated policy conditions. There was not even agreement that the European Central Bank should act as a lender of last resort, injecting credit as needed to stabilize the financial system.

This last fact did not prevent the ECB from actively contributing to the crisis. Oblivious to the brewing storm, it raised its main policy rate by 25 basis points to 4.25 percent in July 2008. This decision was extraordinarily destructive. The United States had been in recession since the end of 2007, and it was implausible that Europe would remain immune from the effects. Problems caused by their speculation in the US subprime market had already surfaced at IKB and BNP Paribas.[1] Property prices in Ireland and Spain were already at a peak. That there would be problems for banks in these countries was predictable, even if it was not predicted by the ECB. The growth of money and credit across the Eurozone was visibly slowing. The rate of growth of the M3 money supply crested at the beginning of 2008 before heading steadily downward, heralding an impending slowdown in bank loans to the private sector and in the growth of the economy.

This was no time for monetary tightening. But there is no doubt about what motivated the ECB. Headline inflation was running at more than 3 percent, uncomfortably above the 2 percent rate ECB officials saw as the permissible ceiling. Their mistake was to focus on the headline. Inflation accelerated in the first half of 2008 owing to sharp increases in commodity and energy prices, fueled by strong demand from China and other energy-hungry, fast-growing emerging markets. But commodity and energy prices are volatile. They can come down as quickly as they go up, as they now did in response to the slowing of the world economy. In the end, core inflation—inflation cleansed of the transitory effects of volatile commodity and energy prices—never once in 2007–08 breached the ECB's 2 percent threshold, measured monthly.

Unlike the Federal Reserve, the ECB had always looked to headline inflation. In 2005 its president, Jean-Claude Trichet, touted the importance of privileging the measure. In the United States, with its flexible, decentralized labor markets, gas prices might go up or down without much of an impact on wage settlements. But in Europe, Trichet explained, higher food and fuel prices were passed through quickly into higher wages in the annual bargaining round, given countries' strong, centralized unions. This made headline inflation the relevant measure for forecasting future price pressures. "Measures of 'core' inflation have, at least in the past, been shown to lag behind, rather than lead, the developments in headline inflation," as Trichet put it in his 2005 remarks. "It would appear inappropriate to exclude energy from the price index," he concluded, "and at the same time retain other items. . . ."[2]

However plausible this argument was in 2005, it was no longer so in 2008. Growth was slowing. Unemployment was poised to head higher. The idea that there was about to be an explosion of wage demands was incredible under the circumstances.

If the distinction between headline and core inflation was too subtle for policy makers, that was because it was too subtle for the public. The public associated the euro with increases in the cost of essentials like bread and coffee. Bakers and baristas were accused of rounding up prices in 2002 when the final changeover from the franc and lira took place. The euro, the public concluded, was an inflation-prone currency. At the very moment Trichet was making his fateful defense of headline inflation, he was being hounded by *Paris Match* about how Europeans "label the euro a factor of inflation after seeing the price of a loaf of bread rise from five French francs to €1, an espresso from five French francs to €1.20, or a scratch card from ten French francs to €2." While insisting that the observation was exaggerated, Trichet nonetheless conceded that "the idea that the euro is inflationary remains rooted in the collective consciousness because, at the time of the changeover to the single currency, a very few prices increased disproportionately."[3] Given this consciousness, those very few prices were too sensitive to ignore.

In Germany, where inflation aversion ran deep, the distinction between headline and core inflation was dismissed out of hand. As the first French president of the ECB, Trichet, a career financial diplomat, was committed to establishing that he was as Teutonic monetarily as any German. His commitment extended to taking German language lessons. More substantively, it extended to embracing the concept of headline inflation and attaching priority to keeping it below 2 percent, regardless of whatever problems might be developing in the banking system or the economy.

After Lehman Brothers, the position changed. Even the ECB, notwithstanding its temperamental opposition to policy activism, felt compelled to act. That headline inflation, under pressure from the crisis, was now falling toward its 2 percent target certainly helped. The ECB Governing Council cut the bank's key interest rate to 3.75 percent, 3.25 percent, and then 2.50 percent in October, November, and December 2008. It expanded the list of assets acceptable as collateral in credit operations. It signaled readiness to supply as much liquidity as financial institutions might require.[4] To be sure, interest rates were still substantially above zero, unlike in the United States. The ECB's initiatives were more modest than the first round of quantitative easing launched by the Fed in November. Still, this was better than nothing.

————

But the damage done by the earlier policy action was not easily repaired. Economists are not able to estimate with precision the lags between money growth and output, but few among them question that it takes several quarters for the full effects of a monetary impulse to be felt.[5] Thus, while Eurozone

GDP turned only mildly negative in the second half of 2008, it then moved sharply lower, shrinking at an annual rate of 2.2 percent in the first half of 2009, reflecting the effects of the tightening of monetary conditions a year earlier. The European recession was now underway, compounding the problems of banks, property developers, and governments, first and foremost in Europe itself but also in other countries like the United States.

With the ECB's failure to move faster, the problem of output stabilization landed squarely in the lap of governments. If central banks weren't going to do more, then governments were going to have to do it for them, where "it" meant fiscal stimulus *à l'amérique*. But stimulus in one country was no more feasible than socialism in one country. The economic effects of tax cuts would spill out to other countries, given the tendency to spend on imports as well as domestic goods. If one country went ahead with fiscal stimulus, it would bear the entire cost, in the form of heavier debts and interest payments, while reaping only a fraction of the benefits. This was a problem everywhere, but it was especially a problem in Europe, where economies were small and, as a result of European integration, highly interdependent.

Awareness of this problem in early 2009 coincided with the United Kingdom assuming the chairmanship of the Group of Twenty, leading to the decision by Gordon Brown to make a concerted fiscal response the centerpiece of the London G20 summit. Brown had made a successful political career by compensating for his lack of charisma with what even his critics acknowledged was a keen analytical mind. He was a student of history, having read the subject at Edinburgh University. He studied the ill-fated London Economic Conference of 1933 and was anxious to cement his legacy—perhaps, more accurately, to repair his legacy, following use of the UK Anti-Terrorism Act against Iceland in 2008 and the Northern Rock fiasco.

Whether owing to this historical background or for other reasons, Brown was the one national leader who clearly saw the full picture of the crisis and the need for an internationally concerted response. From this point of view, his chairmanship of the G20 in early 2009, like the presence of historically literate scholars such as Bernanke at the head of important central banks, was fortuitous. In the run-up to the April 2009 London summit, Brown barnstormed Europe, the United States, and Latin America. Over dinner at Downing Street, he reminded G20 leaders of the failure of the 1933 conference and how "that failure had foreshadowed all the other terrible events of that decade and the one to follow," remarks presumably intended to overcome resistance to fiscal stimulus on the part of German Chancellor Angela Merkel.[6]

The 1933 conference had been held at the Geological Museum, where, it was said, nothing that happened disturbed the fossils; this one was held at the ExCel Center in the London Docklands, an area that had flourished as the City, London's financial district, expanded eastward. But no more: the ExCel Center, in a sign of the times, had just been acquired by the Abu Dhabi National Exhibitions Company. Leaders assembled at this less-than-auspicious venue found it difficult to agree. Nicolas Sarkozy, like Merkel, attached higher priority to financial re-regulation and cracking down on offshore tax havens than to immediate steps to stabilize the economy. Neither the United States nor China appreciated having the Europeans, with financial problems of their own, lecturing them on regulatory reform.

In the end, leaders were able to create at least the impression of a united front. They agreed to provide additional resources to the IMF, positioning it to make larger loans to countries in need. (In time, the countries in need would turn out to be European.) They finessed the controversy over publishing a list of tax havens, as demanded by the French, by removing the item from the G20 communiqué and delegating the task to the Organization for Economic Cooperation and Development, conveniently headquartered in Paris.

Most consequentially, leaders compiled their existing pledges to apply fiscal stimulus and added more. They promised support for the IMF and the World Bank, bringing the total to a headline-grabbing $1 trillion. Brown later referred to this as the "one-trillion-dollar plan," claiming it was the step that decisively broke the fall of the world economy.[7] Colin Bradford and Johannes Linn, writing on the first anniversary of the London summit, echoed this assessment, lauding the London G20 as "the most successful summit in history."[8]

Whether future historians, benefiting from more distance, will share this favorable assessment is questionable. Fiscal stimulus in 2009 was indiscriminate: increases in government spending were initiated by countries with light debt loads and, equally, by countries lacking fiscal space that would pay a heavy price. Stimulus was undertaken by countries with their own currencies, like the UK, whose central banks could backstop the market in government bonds and keep interest rates low, and equally by countries lacking a national currency and national central bank, placing them at the tender mercies of the ECB. The largest stimulus as a share of GDP by a Eurozone country in 2009 was in Spain, a country with big banking and property-market problems coming down the pike. Before long, investors would question the ability of the Spanish sovereign to service its debts, and Madrid would come to regret its fiscal ambition. Greece did not announce a new stimulus package but saw the budget balance decline by a further 5 percent of GDP as a result of tax shortfalls and public-spending increases already in the pipeline. The situation in Portugal was similar.[9] Wiser would have been for countries with fiscal space, like Germany, to do more and for others with debt problems to do less. The need for such nuance is obvious in hindsight.

But the idea that additional spending provided a way out of the crisis sat uneasily with the German public, limiting how much fiscal stimulus Merkel could push through the Bundestag. Southern European governments, on the other hand, were predisposed to spend more. They already had ambitious public-expenditure programs in place. Some like Spain were in denial about the extent of their banking and financial problems and the drain these would place on their treasuries. But in the absence of stronger coordinating mechanisms at the level of the G20 and the European Union, the path of least resistance was to take advantage of the pattern of denial—in effect, to exploit Europe's weaknesses and not its strengths.

The result was more like the 1933 World Economic Conference than officials were prepared to acknowledge. Much as France could insist then that it had not contributed to the breakdown of the international monetary and financial system and therefore should not have to make sacrifices to contribute to its revival, Germany could insist now that it was not responsible for the 2008–09 crisis and therefore should not become more heavily indebted in order to resolve it. The result was less cooperation than met the eye. Those like Prime Minister Brown who saw the bigger picture failed to paint it in the appropriate shades of gray.

———

It was not just officials who were in denial, of course. Investors were equally indiscriminate in allowing governments to proceed as they wished. In every Eurozone country other than Ireland and Greece, ten-year government bond yields remained lower in September 2009 than before the outbreak of the global credit crisis. And even in those two countries, they still barely topped the early-2008 level fully a year and a half later. Earlier, analysts looking forward to the creation of the euro had argued that market discipline in the form of higher bond yields would prevent reckless fiscal behavior in the monetary union.[10] But now, the first time since the advent of the euro that debts and deficits were about to become a serious problem, such discipline was notable by its absence. Southern European governments were allowed to career recklessly ahead.

In particular, the markets continued to accept the fiction that sovereign debt problems were impossible in a monetary union. The creation of hard money, by removing the access of Southern European governments to the printing press, somehow eliminated the risk not just of currency devaluation but also of sovereign default, or so investors were inclined to believe. It is not as if Germany or some broader collection of Eurozone economies was about to assume responsibility for debts of the troubled countries. But it is striking, looking back, how investors remained blissfully unaware of the crisis about to engulf them.

Greece was the wake-up call. That the country had fiscal problems was not news. As recently as March 2009, the Council of the European Union had reprimanded Athens for fiscal slippage. It warned that the government, having recorded a deficit for 2008 in excess of the permissible 3 percent ceiling, and with a deficit target of 3.7 percent of GDP for 2009, was in violation of the Stability and Growth Pact, the EU's fiscal surveillance mechanism. Greece was at risk of being subjected to the Union's Excessive Deficit Procedure and to humiliating oversight by the European Commission.

The fantasy, of course, was that the deficit was just 3.7 percent. The Greek government's accounting arm, the Hellenic Statistical Authority or ELSTAT, had long since been cooking the books. Already in 2004 the European Union's statistical agency, Eurostat, voiced reservations about the quality of the Greek figures. From there the situation only deteriorated further. 2009 being an election year, the parliamentarians, taking full advantage of the low interest rates on offer as a result of the euro, were showering fiscal favors on their constituents in furious competition for votes.

The election in October was a victory for the Panhellenic Socialist Movement (PASOK), bringing the government of George Papandreou to power. Papandreou was the scion of the Greek equivalent of the Kennedy clan of American politicians. His paternal grandfather was prime minister on three separate occasions. His father, Andreas, founded PASOK following the restoration of democracy in 1974. It might seem as if Greece was in comfortable hands.

But Papandreou was an awkward figure to lead the country at this difficult juncture. He was born not in Greece but in St. Paul, Minnesota, where his father was a university professor of economics, and spent his formative years in Berkeley, California, where Andreas served as chair of the department. The son spoke English like a native but Greek like a foreigner, which did not impress the men in the tavernas. It didn't help that, having received bachelor's and master's degrees from Amherst College and the London School of Economics and worked as a researcher, Papandreou projected a clinical air that reminded observers less of a Kennedy than, say, a Jimmy Carter. (The difference was that Papandreou's degree was in sociology, not nuclear engineering.) Papandreou adopted a nontraditional approach to public service, notably a US-style commitment to affirmative action and a rather non-Greek—some would say non-PASOK—belief in rooting out corruption and financial excesses. His main strengths as a politician were a pleasant demeanor and easygoing nature. Decisiveness and the ability to take hard decisions were not his forte.

In September 2009, in advance of the October elections, both Papandreou and his leading rival, Prime Minister Kostas Karamanlis, were visited by Bank of Greece Governor George Provopoulos. Provopoulos warned the politicians that the bank's cash-based fiscal data indicated that the budget deficit was in fact running at a rate of 1 percentage point of GDP per month, or more than 12 percent on an annual basis. Immediately after the elections, Governor Provopoulos then met with both Papandreou and his newly appointed finance minister, the LSE-trained economist George Papaconstantinou, and warned them that the bank's data, which tracked transfers to and from the government's accounts, showed that the deficit for the first nine months was already 10 percentage points of GDP. The implication was that the deficit might amount to a staggering 13 percent of GDP for the calendar year. The following day Provopoulos met again with Papaconstantinou in an effort to underscore the urgency of the situation. The previous government may have been responsible for this unprecedented pre-election spending binge, but it was not as if the new government was not warned.

Had he been more decisive, Papandreou could have acknowledged the problem on assuming the prime minister's office in October. He could have blamed it on the earlier conservative government of Karamanlis and positioned himself as a new broom. But there was a reluctance to come clean and a temptation, in the tradition of earlier Greek governments, to deny reality. PASOK had made its electoral promises, and there was pressure now to keep them. It would have taken an unusually strong-willed and decisive prime minister to tell his constituents that, circumstances having changed, it was not in their interest that those campaign promises now be kept. Papandreou, alas, was not that kind of leader. In temperament and intellect he was not unlike Édouard Herriot, who had been confronted with a similar fiscal deception, initiated by the previous French government, on taking office in 1924. Like Herriot before him, Papandreou hesitated to disown the policy—with what proved to be disastrous consequences.

Thus, the PASOK-led government's fiscal adjustments were consistently too little, too late. Every week saw a new announcement from ELSTAT, as it dug deeper into the books of state hospitals and the like and discovered that the deficit was even larger than previously feared. Starting in early October it acknowledged that the deficit was actually 7.8 percent of GDP, more than twice the 3.7 percent previously announced. In successive revisions it then raised the deficit ratio to 9.8 percent, 11 percent, and finally 12.7 percent of national income, arriving at almost exactly the figure to which the central bank's cash-based accounting had pointed months earlier. Every announcement was then met by a statement from Papandreou about how the government proposed to respond to the news. Every response was too little to address the underlying problem, much less get ahead of it.

Investors drew the obvious conclusion. Adding ELSTAT's new estimates of the deficit to previous figures on accumulated government debt, they could see that the debt was actually more than 110 percent of GDP. All of a sudden the inconceivable—that a Eurozone country could default—was conceivable.[11] Fitch downgraded the Greek government to BBB+ in early December. That the government had previously enjoyed an AAA rating and that it took until December for this adjustment to be made says something about how closely these supposed private-sector experts were paying attention.

In response, yields on ten-year bonds jumped from 4.99 to 5.3 percent. Papandreou and his cabinet insisted that the situation was in hand. "We will reduce the deficit, we will control the debt, and there will be no need for a bailout," Finance Minister Papaconstantinou insisted. "We are not Iceland," he asserted in the first of a series of ignominious country comparisons that would soon come to characterize the crisis.[12]

On Christmas Eve, the Hellenic Parliament passed a so-called austerity budget. In a bow to strong unions with ties to PASOK, this did not provide for cuts in public sector wages. The new budget promised only to bring the deficit down to 9.4 percent of GDP. This was still more than three times the level that the EU, and now suddenly attentive investors, regarded as prudent. And just how Mr. Papaconstantinou proposed to fund the difference was unclear.

At this point, the European Commission belatedly swung into action. Shortly into the New Year it issued a report on Greek government deficit and debt statistics indicating that it was shocked to find out that there had been misreporting going on in here. It conceded that Greece would need a bridge loan, given the obstacles to closing the deficit at even the rate proposed by the government in December. This pointed in turn to the question of who would cough up the funds. Would countries like Germany, with deep pockets, step up, or should the Greeks, having made their bed, be forced to sleep in it and impose losses on their creditors? This issue of who would bail out Greece, and eventually other crisis countries, would come to exert an increasingly corrosive influence on European politics. The bad smell would linger for years.

The hesitancy of the lenders reflected doubts, not entirely without foundation, about the reformist intentions of the Greek government. Necessarily, loans would come with conditions. "No guarantees without control" was how Merkel charmingly put it.[13] Less straightforward was who would be in charge of setting the conditions and exerting the control. The European Commission, on which each country had its anointed commissioner, was not above politics. Creditor-country governments could hardly be asked to assume this sensitive political function. Germany had occupied Greece during World War II, and the application of policy conditionality by Berlin would inevitably be characterized as another German invasion. In early 2010 there were not yet posters in Athens of Merkel in a storm trooper's uniform. These would come.

———

And so the Europeans swallowed their pride and called in the IMF. The Fund had experience in negotiating loan conditions. Its man in Athens, Poul Thomsen, had done similar work elsewhere in the region.[14] The IMF had an ambitious managing director, Dominique Strauss-Kahn, preparing to run for the French presidency and anxious to be seen as helping his fellow Europeans. Not least, the organization's coffers had just been topped up by the G20, conveniently for the budget-conscious Europeans.

Thus the decision was taken in March to outsource negotiation of the conditions to the IMF. At least this was the appearance. The reality was different, since the Europeans didn't hesitate to object to conditions they didn't like and Strauss-Kahn was anxious to please them. The IMF would finance a third of the bailout. The other two-thirds would be provided by a newly established EU rescue fund, the European Financial Stability Facility. (Subsequently, this would be renamed the European Stability Mechanism, or ESM.) Member states would contribute to the facility as a function of their size and strength, meaning Germany would contribute the lion's share. Greece's compliance with the terms of the agreement would be monitored by the IMF, the European Commission, and the European Central Bank, known collectively as the Troika.

The first Troika mission landed in Athens on April 21. Ten-year bond yields continued to rise as investors now openly questioned the government's ability to service its debts. Debt in the amount of €9 billion was set to mature on May 9, and there were doubts about whether Athens could market the bonds needed to replace them. If it failed, the government would run short of cash, something the Bank of Greece, as a member in good standing of the European System of Central Banks, no longer had the capacity to print. The authorities might have to stop servicing the debt. The bond market would collapse. The whole thing, as Mr. Papaconstantinou neatly put it, "could blow up in our face."[15]

If so, the consequences would not be limited to Greece. Someone, after all, had lent it all that money. In particular, German banks, led by the troubled Commerzbank, held some €17 billion of Greek debt.[16] The exposure of the German private sector, including pension funds, insurance companies, and thrifty burghers searching for yield, came to as much as €25 billion, a considerable fraction of what the Greek government owed.[17] What was at stake, in other words, was not just the solvency of the Greek government but the stability of the German financial system.

May 9, when the €9 billion of Greek bonds matured, was also the date of Germany's regional elections. Knowing how her bread was buttered, it took Chancellor Merkel just days to pledge support for a Greek aid package, subject as always to the caveat that "appropriate conditions are met." Those conditions, extending beyond fiscal policy to encompass "labor market reforms, product market reforms, financial sector reforms, [and] statistics," were set out in a report by the Troika. The Eurogroup of finance ministers pitched in, helping to assemble a joint euro area/IMF financing package of €110 billion, with a €20 billion first installment set for disbursal in May.

This was extraordinarily fast action, born of a combination of self-interest and panic. It solved exactly nothing. The May 2010 agreement with the Greek government focused on reversing out pre-electoral increases in spending without dealing with the long-standing excesses of the Greek state. Additional cuts in government spending focused on public investment, excising economic muscle rather than fat. There was excessive reliance on tax increases to finance entitlements and sinecures, making life more difficult for Greek companies struggling in the face of collapsing demand.

And when it came to structural reform, the May program focused on the passage of measures as opposed to their implementation. Since the mid-1990s the Greek parliament had passed as many as five separate laws prohibiting smoking in tavernas and cafes, yet Greeks continued to smoke in such places. Measures mandating structural reform proceeded in the same spirit. By focusing on the adoption of statutes as opposed to their enforcement, the Troika only enabled the Greeks' worst instincts. The Greek government may have done a less-than-adequate job of responding to the crisis, but it had less-than-adequate help.

Moreover, in projecting the impact of the adjustment program, the Troika neglected the fiscal multiplier. It fell to the Greeks to remind the European Commission and the IMF that, because theirs was a relatively closed economy relying minimally on imports and exports, the effects of government spending cuts on domestic producers would be unusually large. In early 2012 Provopoulos, the governor of the Greek central bank, published an article in the *Financial Times* emphasizing the point.[18] The same implication flowed from the fact that the country lacked a national central bank capable of cutting interest rates to offset the impact on aggregate demand of cuts in public spending. Starting in 2011 the Greek authorities repeatedly warned the Troika to this effect. But the foreign authorities, confident in their views, paid these warnings no heed.

As a result, the Troika underestimated how hard Greece would be hit by the budget cuts, the loss of investor confidence, and the deteriorating external environment. The IMF's projections forecast the Greek economy as shrinking by 4 percent in 2010 and by a further 2.6 percent in 2011 before stabilizing and resuming its growth in 2012. The actual contraction was 4.9 percent in 2010 and 7.1 percent in 2011, followed by a further 6.4 percent in 2012 and 4.2 percent in 2013. In all, the economy contracted fully three times as fast as forecast by the Troika, all but matching what the United States had achieved, as it were, in the Great Depression. Unemployment rose to a socially calamitous 27 percent, exceeding even what the United States endured in the 1930s.

Evidence that the Troika's sour medicine wasn't working made it correspondingly harder to marshal support in Athens for additional doses. This further weakened investor confidence, which in turn aggravated the crisis. The Troika report spoke of implementation risk, noting dispassionately how "policies supporting the arrangement are very ambitious and the associated social costs are significant."[19] It had no idea.

This catastrophe was no laughing matter. What was laughable was the Troika forecast that the debt-to-GDP ratio would crest at 150 percent before trending downward. This scenario left no room for undershooting growth targets, for slippage in raising revenues, or for delays in pension reform. The IMF, in applying its plain-vanilla debt-sustainability analysis, failed to acknowledge the depth of Greece's problems. In its last precrisis review, it pointed to half-hearted reform and inadequate policy adjustment but projected a contraction of just 1–2 percent in 2009, owing to the global financial crisis, and then recovery starting in 2010.[20]

Indeed, it almost seemed as if the projections the Troika now produced for the growth of the Greek economy were less an input than an output of its debt-sustainability analysis. IMF rules permitted the institution to extend large loans only if it judged a country's debt to be sustainable "in the medium term."[21] The figures for Greek growth were those needed for the debt to peak out at 150 percent of GDP in 2012–13, as policy makers promised. The alternative would have been debt forgiveness for Athens and a haircut for the bondholders. The slate could have been wiped clean, allowing Greece to start over.

But no one was prepared to go there. Debt restructuring could be messy and disruptive. The IMF had a long history of hesitating to recommend restructuring for crisis countries because of those uncertain implications. The Europeans were even more reluctant, since there was no uncertainty about how German and French banks holding Greek government debt would be affected.

The French finance minister, Christine Lagarde, was particularly adamant in opposing restructuring.[22] Lagarde was aware that French banks were saddled with nearly as much Greek debt as their German competitors were.

And not just German and French banks; in addition, the ECB itself had bought more than €25 billion of Greek government bonds put up for sale by French and other commercial banks by the time the Greek program was announced, making Trichet a steadfast opponent of any debt write-down. In statement after statement, European officials asserted that restructuring was a red line that could not be crossed. On the Friday the Greek program was announced, Josef Pröll, the Austrian finance minister, was trotted out to repeat the refrain. Asked whether Greek debt should be restructured, he asserted, "Most certainty not. We are providing €100 billion in loans. Greece has to plow through."[23]

Eventually, in 2012, privately held Greek government debt was written down by 75 percent, it having become evident that the earlier debt-sustainability arithmetic was chimerical. In 2013, in a melancholy reflection on the Greek program, the IMF acknowledged that "an upfront debt restructuring would have been better for Greece although this was not acceptable to the euro partners."[24] Hindsight is twenty-twenty.

CHAPTER 25 | Men in Black

IN THIS WAY the Troika succeeded in transforming the Greek crisis into an existential crisis for the euro and the European Union. This is giving one blunder a lot of credit—but then, credit where credit is due. Encumbering Greece with debt to the Troika in addition to its debt to private creditors saddled the country with a crushing burden. The imposition of painful conditions was resented, more so as it became apparent that the program would not deliver the rapid resumption of growth. If support for reforms crumbled, the Troika might pull the plug. It was no longer inconceivable that the Greek government would abandon the euro and start printing money. The idea that the euro was irreversible was a casualty of this series of missteps. The damage would take years to repair.

A second casualty was the credibility of a Europe whose crisis-containment plans were shown to be incredible. Having seen the European Commission and the ECB, with IMF acquiescence, commit to an implausible set of policies, investors now questioned their competence. It did not take long for the public more generally to lose faith in the technocrats in Brussels and Frankfurt.

In addition, letting Greece's creditors off scot-free (for such was the implication of eschewing debt restructuring) offended the sensibility of taxpayers already on the hook for costly bank bailouts. And if voters were offended, their leaders had to display suitable indignation. At a bilateral meeting in the French seaside resort of Deauville in October 2010, Chancellor Merkel and President Sarkozy agreed that investors should share the costs of future crises instead of leaving taxpayers liable. In the future, a government experiencing a crisis would be expected to make its bondholders a take-it-or-leave-it offer. They would be asked to exchange their existing bonds for new ones worth, say, fifty cents on the euro as a condition of official assistance. With the full weight of the European Union behind the government in question, the creditors would have no choice but to agree.

Merkel and Sarkozy's statement was a response to the political backlash unleashed by the failure of the Greek program to impose any burden sharing on private interests.[1] But this unqualified declaration that there would be a restructuring whenever a country got into trouble sounded alarm bells for investors. Yields on Irish, Spanish, and Portuguese bonds shot up. As a result of Merkel and Sarkozy's walk on the beach, doubts about European debts were generalized. One troubled country after another lost access to financial markets. Jean-Claude Trichet was apoplectic. Attending a meeting with finance ministers and other high EU officials when news of the Franco-German deal broke, he reportedly shouted, "You're going to destroy the euro!" (In French— so much for those much-vaunted German language lessons.)

Had European leaders purposely set out to create a fiscal and financial crisis, they couldn't have done a better job. In alarm, Merkel and Sarkozy backtracked on their Deauville commitment. Debts were sacrosanct, they declared, and would not be restructured after all. But the damage was done. The taboo over restructuring was broken.

The reality, of course, was that some debt restructuring was inevitable, backtracking or not. Not all debts are sustainable, as Greece would demonstrate soon enough. Whether or not this was so would have to be determined on a case-by-case basis. Saying that restructuring was ruled out made no more sense than saying it was automatically ruled in. By now attempting to reinstate the taboo, European leaders only highlighted their own inconsistency and how out of touch they were with reality.

———

These missteps had a series of further implications, none of them pretty. First, Europe took a hard right turn from fiscal stimulus to austerity even earlier than the United States—even before the Obama stimulus wound down in 2012 and the Sequester commenced in 2013. If debts were not going to be restructured, then they would have to be repaid. And they could be repaid only through some combination of tax increases and public spending reductions. The Greek case, ignoring its special nature—for ignore it is what officials did—lent salience to the idea. In lavishing fourteen monthly salaries on public servants (not just the Christmas bonus but yet another bonus month of pay), Athens was spending too much. By allowing physicians to report taxable incomes that were sometimes as little as €1,000 a month, it failed to crack down on tax cheats or make a credible effort to fund public programs.

Some increase in taxes and reduction in public spending were clearly required, although whether austerity on the scale prescribed by the Troika was called for was another matter.

Other countries running budget deficits were now seen as requiring a dose of the same medicine, especially once they lost market access in the wake of Deauville. It mattered little that their problems were not at all like those of Greece. It made no difference that their budget deficits were largely a consequence of the crisis; Spain and Ireland, for example, were running surpluses until 2008. But if governments were unable to borrow and if the ECB, the one entity in a position to do so, was unwilling to lend, then they had no choice but to cut. The Hellenic motif inspired the belief that Southern European governments were profligate. It played into the German presumption that, whatever the circumstances, belt tightening was appropriate. Keynesian doctrine, whether at the level of formal theory or simply FDR's instinctual understanding that government must "spend money when no one else had money left to spend," never gained traction in Germany. Deficit spending in the 1920s was synonymous with inflation. The country's one real experience with anything resembling Keynesian fiscal policy, in the 1930s, had associations with rearmament, Hitler, and worse. And if German taxpayers understood one thing, they understood that the alternative to budget cuts was more emergency finance, of which they would be asked to provide the largest part.

Hence the shift to austerity, driven by a combination of political self-interest and deep-seated ideology, was general. Tax increases and spending cuts drained nearly 1½ percent of GDP's worth of net public spending from the Eurozone economy in 2011 and another 2 percent in 2012. Olli Rehn, EU commissioner for economic and monetary affairs, spoke in hopeful Orszag-like tones of how budget cuts would "restore confidence" and boost investment, but there was no increase in investment.[2]

Others referred wistfully to how the capacity freed up by the reduction in domestic spending might be redeployed toward exports. But this failed to take into account the fact that the cuts in spending were Eurozone wide. With even Germany in austerity mode, there was nowhere for additional Spanish and Italian exports to go. It did not reckon with the lethargic growth of the advanced-country world in the wake of the financial crisis. And it did not take into account the strength of the euro, reflecting the ECB's reluctance to cut interest rates and expand its balance sheet as aggressively as the Fed.

Work by the IMF's Olivier Blanchard, cited above, implied that these public spending cuts chopped as much as 2 percentage points off Eurozone growth in 2011 and 3 percentage points in 2012.[3] Thus, the slowdown from 2.0 percent in 2010 to 1.5 percent in 2011 and −0.6 per cent in 2012 was entirely man-made. Specifically it was made in Brussels, home of the Commission, and in Europe's national capitals. Europe, unlike the United States, had essentially avoided a double-dip recession in 1937–38. After three years of sharp decline between 1929 and 1932, industrial production began to recover, as we have seen, rising by 1935 to within 10 percent of the previous peak. This time the initial decline lasted only one year and the recovery in 2010 was sharp. But then, with the turn to austerity, industrial production started back down. By 2013 it was *more* than 10 percent below the 2008 peak. In other words, Europe was doing even worse than in the Great Depression.

The consequences were ironic, for those able to see irony through their tears. There was the irony of the IMF, not normally an advocate of deficit spending, recommending that European countries go slower on fiscal consolidation. There was the irony that spending cuts and tax increases did not succeed even in their immediate goal of enhancing debt sustainability. With the Eurozone continuing to contract, the debt-to-GDP ratio continued to rise, reaching 93.4 percent in the second quarter of 2013. If the objective was to restore fiscal solvency, this was not the way to go about it.

A second implication was the loss of European solidarity and damage to the European Union. For more than fifty years, the EU functioned as a trust-building mechanism. It provided a framework through which European countries could collaborate peaceably and in which Germany could flex its economic muscles without intimidating its neighbors. It was a way for the citizens of diverse countries, speaking many languages and with their own national traditions, to cultivate a common European identity. As shared money, the euro was supposed to be the capstone on this process.

As a result of how the euro crisis was handled starting in 2009, it did not turn out this way. Instead of breeding solidarity, management of the crisis by the Commission and the ECB opened up a psychic gulf between Northern and Southern Europe. The German broadsheet *Bilt* wrote how "proud, cheating, profligate Greeks" bent on exploiting the responsible German taxpayer should be ejected from the Eurozone. The Greek press responded with a photo montage of the Victory Column in Berlin topped by a giant swastika, and it disinterred the long-buried issue of Germany's failure to pay post–World War II reparations.

The traditional response to such crises had always been more Europe. If a single currency and a single financial market implied the need for a single bank supervisor at the level of the European Union, then the answer was to create one. If debt problems implied the need for fiscal union, and if fiscal union in turn implied the need for political union, then the answer, again, was to move forward toward fiscal and political union. So it had been, in fits and starts, for more than fifty years.

But there was now a lack of trust in the institutions and individuals charting the course. In a spring 2013 survey, conducted at the behest of the European Commission, no less, pollsters determined that fully 60 percent of respondents did not trust the EU. This was double the share in 2007.[4] The change reflected a sharp increase in those with a negative image of the EU, pessimism about the future of the Union, and skepticism about the efficacy of the single currency. The arguments for complementing monetary union with banking union, fiscal union, and political union were compelling. But the disastrous way in which the crisis was handled made the goal harder to achieve.

Going backward, on the other hand—back to national currencies—promised only chaos. For one country, say Greece, to abandon the euro would immediately excite expectations about the others, causing investors to flee. Seeing depositors run on their banks, governments would be forced to respond with deposit freezes and capital controls. It seemed unlikely that the EU's single financial market, and for that matter the EU itself, could survive these events. Going back was no solution. Europe, it seemed, was stuck.

———

Europe's crisis was first and foremost a banking crisis. Its banks were overleveraged, undercapitalized, and excessively exposed to the property market. Their problems had been brewing for years. But now, with some ingenuity, policy makers succeeded in transforming the banking crisis into a financial crisis, a growth crisis, and a political crisis.

Ireland is the prime case in point. If Greece was uncompetitive and deficit-prone, Ireland was the opposite. Having grown rapidly for two decades, it had shed its image as Europe's sick man and was now the best-performing European economy. Its skilled workforce, efficient business environment, and firm-friendly corporate tax code were magnets for foreign investment. Ireland had been running budget surpluses since 2003. In 2006, shortly before the fall, the surplus reached an impressive 3 percent of GDP. National government debt declined from an already modest 34 percent of GDP in 2000 to just 25 percent in 2007.

The exception to these generalizations was the banks. Though not quite matching Iceland, Ireland had experienced an extraordinary banking and financial boom. ("What's the difference between Iceland and Ireland?" it was subsequently asked. Answer: "One letter and six months.") From the turn of the century, the assets of the banking sector grew at an annual average of 25 percent, five times as fast as the economy and fully twice the Euro-area average. Domestic credit to the nonfinancial private sector rose from 80 percent of GDP at the end of 2002 to nearly 180 percent in September 2008.

Irish banks funded themselves abroad, attracting deposits from yield-hungry German households and large loans from foreign banks and bondholders. Foreign borrowing by the Irish banking system tripled between 2002 and 2008. Loans were nearly twice deposits on the eve of the crisis, indicating how heavily the banks relied on so-called wholesale finance. The resulting funds were then lent to property developers and homebuyers. Where mortgage and real estate loans had accounted for a bit more than a third of all bank lending in 2001, they were nearly 60 percent in 2005.

Still, the banks' massive lending to property developers and the building boom they engendered—by 2006–07 building and construction accounted for fully 9 percent of Irish GDP, half again as much as in the United States— were not enough to dampen the rise in house prices, which quadrupled in the decade ending in 2005.[5] The banks demanded little in the way of money down. Fully a third of all mortgages taken out by first-time homebuyers in 2006 had 100 percent loan-to-value ratios. The banks accommodatingly offered interest-only mortgages to help stretched homebuyers meet their monthly payments.

Still, affordability had its limits. House prices could not rise indefinitely at an annual rate of 15 percent, three times the rate of growth of incomes.[6] There seems to have been awareness that the increase would slow at some point, and perhaps even go into reverse. But as in the United States, where policy makers famously predicted that the fallout from the subprime crisis would be contained, there was no premonition of the consequences. In a perfectly timed financial-sector assessment released in August 2006, an International Monetary Fund team concluded that "the financial system seems well placed to absorb the impact of a downturn in either house prices or growth more generally."[7] You can't make this up.

There is some controversy over the extent to which neglect of these excesses reflected naïveté, as is plausibly the case of the IMF, as opposed to self-dealing by bankers and property developers. Bank managers were encouraged to bor-row from their own banks, allowing not a few to acquire "sizeable property and site portfolios."[8] Banks like Anglo Irish, ultimately number one as a source of taxpayer losses, "catered for a relatively limited number of customers, many of them in the property development sector."[9] Managers granted instant credit approval to friends in the property sector; the loans in question were rubber-stamped by the bank's credit committee after the fact. Not until the late stages of the boom were the minutes of Anglo's credit committee even taken. Many loans were backed not by cash flow or collateral but by simple personal guarantees.[10] These practices were characterized, when corporate strategy was described, as "relationship banking." Anglo's CEO and then chairman Seán

FitzPatrick proudly observed how, when "you deal with Anglo Irish Bank, you don't deal with the bank, you deal with the individual . . . the final decision maker."[11] With hindsight, this was not a positive.

In the case of Anglo, the other main borrower was management itself. Eventually it emerged that FitzPatrick had borrowed more than €150 million from the bank, and as much as €121 million in 2007 alone, using his shares as collateral but warehousing his borrowings at the Irish Nationwide Building Society, an ostensibly unrelated institution, so as to hide them from Anglo's auditor, Ernst & Young, and from readers of Anglo's annual report.[12] In his wisdom, FitzPatrick appears to have invested much of what he borrowed in additional Anglo stock. In 2010, in the wake of Anglo's collapse, he declared bankruptcy. Subsequently he was arrested in connection with an investigation into "financial irregularities at a financial institution." In addition, Anglo extended loans to the wealthy Irish businessman Sean Quinn to finance his purchases of the bank's stock on margin. These loans grew frighteningly large when Anglo stock began falling in the wake of the Bear Stearns rescue, which dragged down Anglo shares and forced Quinn to meet margin calls.[13]

One can't help but wonder where the regulators and their political masters were before the fact. The answer is not hard to find: in addition to intimate relations between bankers and property developers, there were also close connections with the politicians, perhaps inevitably in what was a small economy. On the eve of the crisis, FitzPatrick played an eight-hour round of golf with Taoiseach (Irish head of government) Brian Cowen, followed by an impromptu dinner at the golf resort's hotel. FitzPatrick's successor as Anglo CEO, David Drumm, was repeatedly briefed on government strategy toward the bank when the crisis broke. This banker-developer-politician nexus was a glaring exception to the Irish rule of efficient regulation and aboveboard management.

———

It is not surprising that the turmoil following the failure of Lehman Brothers should have raised questions about the ability of Anglo, and of other Irish banks that took it as their business model, to make good on their obligations. Nor is it surprising that this realization precipitated a sharp fall in bank share prices and anxiety among depositors. What is remarkable is the alacrity with which Irish leaders, with help from Brussels and Frankfurt, transformed this simple banking crisis into a national calamity.

The agent of disaster was the bank guarantee. Ireland had already raised its deposit guarantee to €100,000, as noted earlier. An even more generous guarantee to reassure large depositors would not have been unprecedented; recall that this was when the United States was poised to raise the ceiling on deposit insurance to $250,000. But no one anticipated that Cowen would throw a blanket over all the banks' liabilities, not just their deposits but also their wholesale borrowings from bondholders and others.

How exactly this decision emerged from Cowen's mysterious all-night meeting on September 29 is disputed.[14] In a normal bank failure, to the extent that there is such a thing, small depositors are protected. Other creditors are wiped out or, in the event that the bank has residual value, see their claims converted into equity in the surviving institution. This is the model toward which EU authorities groped somewhat ineptly when winding up Laiki Bank, the troubled Cypriot lender, in 2013. But in Ireland's case, the bondholders, many of whom were sophisticated foreign institutional investors who presumably knew the risks they were taking, were made whole. They were made whole by the Irish taxpayer, with whom the government stuck the bill.

Since the liabilities of the Irish banking system were a multiple of national income, with even a modest loan loss rate the bill would become enormous. The politicians claimed they were misled by Anglo executives who understated how much money was needed to pay off the creditors, but they should have known better. Rather than the €7 billion of temporary assistance initially requested, Anglo ultimately required more than €30 billion, none of which was recovered. Paying off the creditors of all six Irish-owned retail banks eventually cost taxpayers €64 billion, roughly €14,000 for every Irish man, woman, and child. Whether the Irish citizenry would really be prepared to shoulder such a heavy burden in order to make the banks' creditors whole was uncertain. That uncertainty in turn cast a long and disruptive shadow over the Irish economy.

This colossal bill started coming due in 2009 but exploded in 2010, when the deficit soared to more than 30 percent of GDP (you read that right).[15] Public debt, admirably low three years earlier, now rose to 100 percent of national income. The ECB, as the price for its continued provision of liquidity, demanded that the Irish government immediately recapitalize the banks. Swift bank recapitalization has its merits, but not when doing so threatens to bankrupt the sovereign. And it was not just the bank recapitalization costs; in addition, there was the fact that the denominator of the debt/GDP started shrinking as Ireland, reeling from the end of the property boom and seeing the government slam on the fiscal brakes, became the first European country to enter recession.[16] The economy contracted by an alarming 9.8 percent in 2009 and another 3.2 percent in 2010 in nominal terms, those being what are relevant for the capacity of a country to service nominally denominated debts.

Thus, what had been a banking crisis became a fiscal crisis, as investors questioned the capacity of the Irish sovereign to service its debt and worried that their bonds might be restructured. Yields shot up across Southern Europe in the wake of the Deauville declaration, but nowhere as dramatically as in Ireland. (This was when Ireland won its honorary Southern European status.) By early November 2010 the yield difference between ten-year Irish bonds and German *bunds* was 6.65 percent.

These were not rates the Irish sovereign could afford. And so the country was driven into the arms of the Troika. Losing its fiscal sovereignty—for that was what accepting the budgetary demands of the IMF, the Commission, and the ECB effectively entailed—was devastating for a country that had gained its independence only in 1922 at the end of a long, drawn-out bloody battle. Enda Kenny, leader of the center-right opposition Fine Gael party, accused the Cowen government of turning the Republic into a fiscal protectorate. "This is a democracy and people died on the street for it," he railed. "It will not be closed down by incompetence."

———

This, of course, was much sound and fury signifying nothing. Neither Cowen nor Kenny could conjure resources out of thin air. Ireland was desperate for finance, of which the Troika was the only source. But neither the IMF nor the European Union would lend without assurances. Predictably, these took the form of the now-standard program, leavened only by a bit of additional emphasis on downsizing the banking system. As agreed in December 2010, Ireland would receive €67.5 billion, much of which would go to recapitalizing the banks, overhauling their funding structure, and defraying the costs of the National Asset Management Agency, or NAMA, the "bad bank" created to acquire troubled property development loans and sell them off for whatever they would fetch.[17]

Importantly, there was no effort to bail in bank creditors. The two-year blanket guarantee adopted in September 2008 had just expired when the 2010 program was finalized. It would have been possible to write down the value of senior bonds to limit the cost of repairing the banks' balance sheets. But European officials were concerned about the stability of banks in other countries. Revisiting the Irish guarantee would have raised questions about the security of their bonds and unsettled their holders. This rendered the Troika reluctant to renegotiate. The Cowen government had made its bed and now must sleep in it.

The Kenny-led Fine Gael–Labour coalition that succeeded it following the February 2011 general election might be thought to have had other options. Almost immediately, the new finance minister, Michael Noonan, approached the Troika with a proposal to write down obligations to the senior bondholders of Anglo Irish and the Irish Nationwide Building Society. (Irish Nationwide, FitzPatrick's consort, had been almost as enthusiastic a property lender and suffered equally catastrophic losses.) But the ECB was a full partner in the Troika, and its president, Jean-Claude Trichet, was insistent that any attempt to impose losses on bank bondholders would hit confidence and impair the ability of banks to access funding, not just in Ireland but across the Eurozone. In any case, debt to the bank bondholders was being replaced on the Irish national balance sheet by debt to the Troika. If bondholders were no longer sufficiently senior to escape losses, who was to say that the same might not also be true of official creditors? In other words, any change in the program acknowledging that the blanket bank guarantee was a bad idea might ultimately come out of the European Union's hide and pocketbook.[18] Given Ireland's dependence on Troika funding, the new government quickly fell into line.[19]

Since so much of the Troika's rescue funding went to repair the banks and pay off their creditors, the Irish government had no choice but to curtail other spending. The hope was that cuts could be limited as the economy stabilized and recovered. The delusion, which infected Dublin, Brussels, Frankfurt, and Washington alike, was that growth would resume in 2011. "After two years of sharp declines in output," the memorandum of agreement with the European Commission and IMF read, "the Irish economy is expected to broadly stabilize this year before expanding during 2011–14." The Troika went on to detail its logic. "As domestic imbalances from the boom years are being repaired, the recovery will, at least initially, be primarily export driven. We project that GDP growth will increase over time as export performance filters through to investment and consumption, consumer confidence returns, and labour market conditions improve."

What did not filter through, evidently, was that with the general turn to austerity there was no one to export to. Nor did it sink in that, as a result of European policy makers' blunders, other crisis countries saw their spreads explode, were also on the verge of losing market access, and would similarly be forced into the tender clutches of the Troika.[20]

It would take the better part of three years, not three months, for recovery to commence. In the meantime, unemployment soared to 15.1 percent. The residents of Ireland responded as they had to the Great Famine: by emigrating. Between 2008 and mid-2013 nearly 400,000 persons left the Republic, whether for other English-speaking economies or, in the case of recent arrivals, back to their country of origin. Many of the emigrants were the best and the brightest. The damage would not be easily undone.[21]

Every unhappy European country was unhappy in its own way, as noted in the introduction. Portugal, for instance, had neither the heavy public debts of Greece nor the housing and banking problems of Ireland. But its policy makers, the Social Democrats under José Manuel Barroso (who on leaving office was rewarded for his achievements with appointment as president of the European Commission) and then the Socialists under José Sócrates equally, had done little to prepare the country for the challenges of the twenty-first century. What passed for modern manufacturing, the apparel and footwear industries, had long since succumbed to pressure from China. Some Portuguese companies borrowed to expand, but the borrowers were mainly small, low-productivity firms in the service sector, which did nothing to enhance international competitiveness. Between 2000 and 2008, per capita GDP grew, cumulatively, by a dismal 5 percent. By 2010, with recession now underway, per capita income had fallen back to the levels of ten years before.

Rather than investing in skills and training, Lisbon used the saving in interest costs conferred by the euro to build motorways and roundabouts, which became impressively traffic-free with the recession. It raised taxes to make good on promises to increase pension payments to retirees. Raising taxes, on labor in particular, prevented public debt from exploding but only made modernization even more difficult for Portuguese firms.

Thus, Portugal was poorly positioned when the crisis struck. The government's coping strategy amounted to attempting to fly under the radar. The country's small size and absence of high-profile Greek- and Irish-style problems, it hoped, would allow the markets to overlook the weaknesses. But this approach was no longer viable with investors now on high alert. The government lost market access and in the spring of 2011 was forced to negotiate a €78 billion Troika program. Spending cuts, tax increases, a freeze on civil service pay, and a deep recession followed. Unemployment rose to 18 percent, youth unemployment to twice that level.

Spain was not Portugal, as Spanish policy makers went to great lengths to remind anyone within earshot. Its big banks, Banco Bilbao Vizcaya Argentaria (BBVA) and Grupo Santander, derived much of their income from profitable operations in Latin America. National government debt was just 36 percent of GDP.[22] The country boasted a number of internationally competitive companies, from Telefonica in communications to Gamesa in wind turbines, and Inditex, which owned the Zara fashion chain and operated outlets in more than a hundred countries. Spain did not suffer a dramatic loss of export market share in the decade following the advent of the euro as big firms, in particular, boosted their productivity.[23] A large domestic market meant that the country was home to multinationals like Ford and Volkswagen, which could now gear their production toward exports.

But try as they might, Spanish officials could not distract investors from a collapsing property market that threatened to produce a collapsing banking system. Most immediately threatened were the cajas, semipublic savings banks that had lent aggressively to homebuyers and real estate companies. Once upon a time, back in the 1960s, the cajas accounted for barely 10 percent of Spanish financial assets. But deregulation, combined with the belief that the authorities implicitly stood behind them, allowed them to expand their balance sheets. Now they accounted for nearly 50 percent of the financial system.

Investors understood from Ireland's experience that the authorities could not stand by as savings banks, which constituted such a large share of the financial system, drowned in bad loans. But they understood equally that rescuing them could bankrupt the state. As is the case of all banking crises, there was deep uncertainty about the extent of the losses the banks were facing. And so long as that uncertainty lingered, it cast a shadow over the solvency of the Spanish sovereign, and by implication over the future of the euro.

Initially, the government of José Luis Rodríguez Zapatero sought to address the problem with a series of half measures. It created a bank restructuring fund, the Fondo de Reestructuracíon Ordenada Bancaria, or FROB, to recapitalize the banks but hesitated to use it for fear of damaging the public finances. The FROB, though authorized to lend €99 billion, had disbursed only €14 billion by 2012 when the banking crisis peaked.

The government next attempted to strengthen the cajas by brokering a series of mergers, hoping that cutting excess capacity and redundant staff might strengthen their financial position. But this did nothing about the bad property loans contaminating their books other than concentrate them in a smaller number of hands. The most important merger was between heavyweight Caja Madrid and six smaller savings banks. The successor institution, Bankia, assumed the mantle of the single largest holder of real estate assets and was happily listed on the Spanish stock exchange in July 2011. Just ten months later, with Bankia swimming in bad loans, the government was forced to seize it and inject €23.5 billion of share capital, further straining the public finances.[24] The interest rate on the government's ten-year bonds jumped to 7 percent on the news, a level that was clearly unsustainable.

So began the elaborate courtship dance between the Spanish government and its Eurozone partners. The banks needed help, which the government did not obviously have the wherewithal to provide. But a Troika loan to the government to enable it to rescue the banks would only transform the banking crisis into a sovereign debt crisis, as in Ireland. In principle, the European

Stability Mechanism, the EU's rescue fund, could lend directly to the banks, in contrast to what was permissible for the IMF, which was allowed by its Articles of Agreement only to lend to governments. But if it did so the Spanish sovereign would be off the hook, and the shareholders in the ESM, starting with the German government, might end up footing the bill. There was also the desire of the new center-right government of Mariano Rajoy, in office since the end of 2011, to avoid the humiliation of an EU-IMF program. Having insisted during the campaign that Spain shared few of the problems of Greece, Ireland, and Portugal, Rajoy was understandably anxious to avoid visits by the Troika's "Men in Black."

The resulting compromise was purposely ambiguous. On June 9, 2012, the Eurogroup of finance ministers agreed to provide €100 billion to recapitalize the banks. The loan would be extended not to the Spanish government but to the FROB, although the government would be "responsible," in the language of the loan agreement, if the FROB was unable to repay. This furnished a pot of funds, hopefully sufficient to meet the banks' immediate capital needs, and just enough ambiguity about whether it was an obligation of the sovereign or the FROB to hold out hope that, in the worst case where the pot had to be emptied, the government budget might be spared. The monies in question would come entirely from the ESM, not a third from the International Monetary Fund as in the agreements with Greece, Ireland, and Portugal. Rajoy thus avoided having to submit to the embarrassment of an IMF program. The Fund's role was limited to helping monitor banking-sector reforms, while the Commission would use its regular procedures, to which all members were subject, to ensure the government stuck to its commitments. There might be no Men in Black, but there would still be men in gray.

Notwithstanding its other ambiguities, the ESM loan at least created the certainty that there would be €100 billion to recapitalize the banks. The next task was to convince the markets that this was enough. To this end, Rajoy took a leaf from Tim Geithner's playbook, stress-testing the principal financial institutions. As in the United States, the exercise was touted to be rigorous and apolitical. The government delegated it to outside experts from the financial consultancy Oliver Wyman. It was not entirely reassuring that this was the same consultancy that, in its "State of the Financial Industry 2007 Report," selected Anglo Irish as the world's best bank. Rajoy was presumably banking on the fact, as it were, that the markets had short memories. Still, this was better than having the government do the test itself.

The consultants had the same Goldilocks problem as US stress testers in 2009. The estimated capital shortfall could not be so small as to be dismissed as unrealistic, nor so alarming as to heighten fears for the solvency of the banking system and the state. Fortunately, there was a residual item called the "excess capital buffer"—essentially, an assumption about how many of their existing assets the banks would be able to sell—that could be adjusted to affect the bottom line.[25] The estimated capital shortfall reported in September 2012, just under €60 billion, was midway between the much smaller figures Spanish regulators were claiming previously and the €100 billion ceiling set by the ESM loan. The precision was spurious, but the result was not wholly inconsistent with the facts. Spain's EU partners were reassured that they were not lending into a black hole, and investors that the €100 billion credit line would be enough.

There is an obvious parallel with US experience in 1933 and 2009. All three episodes show that the line between illiquidity and insolvency is difficult to draw for a banking system, as for a government. A liquidity crisis born of panic can push a banking system with real but containable problems over the edge into insolvency. This is especially the case when information about the condition of the banks is incomplete, allowing the panic to feed on itself. Conversely, providing additional information on the condition of the banks, even if imperfect, combined with credible lender-of-last-resort facilities may be just enough to fend off the panic. It will prevent a mad scramble for the exits that does even deeper damage to the banks.

In 1933, this was the formula applied by the Bank Holiday and the Emergency Banking Act. In 2009, the combination of Treasury's stress tests and the Fed's standing ready to act as a lender of last resort drew a line under the acute phase of the financial crisis. Now in 2012, the Oliver Wyman report, in combination with €100 billion of ESM funds, similarly took the specter of a full-blown banking crisis off the table.[26] This did not mean that the Spanish recession, much less the European recession, was over. But it bought time for policy makers to contemplate their next steps.

| Euro or Not

T HE UNITED KINGDOM, like the United States, Ireland, and Spain, experienced a phenomenal housing boom that turned to bust.[1] It had an overgrown financial sector that accounted for as much as 10 percent of gross value
added and more than a quarter of all corporate income tax payments but was
now forced to retrench. For an economy with these features, a recession of some
magnitude was baked in.

But not a recession of this magnitude and duration. The UK took until
2014 to regain the 2008 level of GDP, lagging every other Group of Seven
advanced economy with the sole exception of Italy.[2] These aspects of the British
downturn were products of policy. Starting in 2010, the UK's fiscal stance
turned strongly contractionary. The May 2010 general election saw voters
repudiate the Labour government of Gordon Brown and led to the formation
of a Conservative-Liberal coalition headed by David Cameron. The new government was bent on eliminating the deficit by any means necessary. To that
end, Cameron's chancellor, George Osborne, submitted his own version of an
emergency budget in 2010 that featured front-loaded spending cuts and an
increase in value-added tax.

The resulting fiscal consolidation was the most severe undertaken by any
of the large advanced economies, more than 5 percent of GDP between 2009
and 2012. The effects were immediate and severe. The British economy had
initially stopped contracting at the end of 2009, and GDP growth recovered
to ½ percent in the first half of 2010 and then 1 percent in the third quarter.
At that point, however, the effects of Osborne's budget were felt. The fourth
quarter of 2010 saw the economy contracting again by 0.2 percent. 2011 was
then a year of bouncing along the bottom, with limp growth in the first and

third quarters and contraction in the second and fourth. The Office of Budget Responsibility, the UK's independent, nonpartisan advisory body, estimated that economic growth was more than 1 percent lower than otherwise in the 2010–11 fiscal year as a result of these policies. It was then 0.7 percent lower in 2011–12 and 0.3 percent lower in 2012–13 as the initial impact of earlier policies began to fade.[3]

The coalition's response was to stay the course. This led to the exceptional situation where the IMF recommended shifting public spending toward items that would do more to boost demand in the short run. It further recommended that the government consider, in the absence of evidence of recovery, slowing the pace of fiscal tightening.[4]

This turn to austerity was also exceptional in that the UK did not share the constraints of other European countries. Debt may have been too high for comfort, but it was still less than 70 percent of GDP when the coalition took over in 2010. The UK was not Greece, to invoke a familiar phrase; the costs of loans and capital injections into the Royal Bank of Scotland, Lloyds, Northern Rock, and Bradford & Bingley, amounting to roughly 8 percent of GDP, had already been sunk.[5] Nor was it Ireland, in other words.

Most important, the UK was not a member of the Eurozone. It had a central bank with the power to print money and backstop the market in the government's bonds. This gave the government more fiscal space than a comparably indebted Eurozone country. Fiscal consolidation could have been back-loaded. It could have waited until the economy was strong enough to handle it.

All this renders the coalition's obsession with austerity more than a little difficult to understand. Cameron's Chancellor Osborne, like Blair's Chancellor Brown, was a student of history, in his case having taken the subject at Oxford. This, however, did not prevent him from disregarding the history of the 1930s or embracing the "Treasury view" of fiscal policy. In 1929, the view of the Treasury that "any increase in government spending necessarily crowds out an equal amount of private spending or investment, and thus has no net impact on economic activity," in the words of Chancellor Winston Churchill, was invoked in opposition to an increase in the deficit.[6] Chancellor Osborne and others in Treasury were not prepared to go quite this far in arguing that fiscal consolidation was likely to have no net impact on economic growth, but they did argue that the effects were unlikely to be large. They argued further that not proceeding with consolidation would have adverse implications. Failing to narrow the deficit would expose the UK to the kind of confidence crisis already affecting Greece, Ireland, and Spain, depressing investment and growth.

This, of course, confused the situation of a country like the UK, with a debt-to-GDP ratio of 70 percent, with a country like Greece, whose debt-to-GDP ratio was closer to 170 percent. It confused the situation of a set of Eurozone countries that no longer possessed a national central bank capable of backstopping the government bond market with the situation of a country still possessing its own central bank. Having shown the wisdom to stay out of Europe's flawed monetary union, Britain now embraced the flawed logic that it was required to behave like a monetary union member.

Cameron and Osborne, it should be noted, were staunch believers in Conservative doctrine of a limited state. And when better to limit the state than in a supposed crisis of fiscal sustainability, with, absent early action, the debt/GDP ratio poised to cross the red line of 90 percent of GDP?[7] In October 2010, as part of its fiscal consolidation effort, the government released a list of 192 public agencies that would be abolished or have their funding withdrawn. They ranged from the Infrastructure Planning Commission to the Health Protection Agency, which provided information and advice to health professionals and the general public on new and emerging health threats, and the British Educational Communications and Technology Agency, which sought to promote and coordinate the use of information technology in education. Many of these agencies, it will be clear, were involved in mobilizing resources for infrastructure, education, and research.[8] Better, in the Conservative view, to let the market do the mobilizing and get government out of the way. Other agencies that were axed, like the UK Film Council and the Farm Animal Welfare Council, were symbols of government ambition that the Conservative-led coalition now sought to uproot. If a short recession—short being what the Coalition anticipated—was the price for eliminating this wasteful spending and these intrusive government agencies, then it was a price worth paying. As Jeremy Warner of the conservatively oriented *Daily Telegraph* candidly put it, "In the end, you are either a big-state person, or a small-state person, and what big-state people hate about austerity is that its primary purpose is to shrink the size of government spending. . . . The bottom line is that you can only really make serious inroads into the size of the state during an economic crisis. This may be pro-cyclical, but there is never any appetite for it in good times; it can only be done in the bad."[9]

Finally, there is no denying the element of political expediency involved. Like the Obama stimulus, Labour's emergency budget had not delivered everything promised. Thus, when the Conservatives and Liberals campaigned against Labour's failed policies, they campaigned against deficit spending. As in the United States, their arguments resonated with a voting public that instinctively embraced the analogy between the household budget and the government budget and sought an outlet for its anger with the crisis and the government-funded bailouts of financial institutions mounted in response. Proceeding with fiscal consolidation allowed the Coalition to tar Labour as the party of deficits. It took a divided US government several years to agree on tax increases for the 1 percent and the Sequester. In the British system, which did not admit of divided government, the shift to austerity was immediate and severe.

———

If the UK undertook a major fiscal consolidation, on the order of 5 percent of GDP, this was nothing compared to what was asked of Greece. The Troika program specified spending cuts and tax increases of fully 11 percentage points of GDP over three years. This was more than Greek society, and for that matter any society, could sustain, making some slippage unavoidable. Drastic spending cuts made deep recession inevitable, tall tales of expansionary fiscal consolidation notwithstanding. As we saw above, the recession was significantly deeper than forecast by the Troika. And the further the Greek economy sank, the more by which tax revenues undershot projections, and the higher the debt/GDP ratio rose.

The IMF under Dominique Strauss-Kahn was anxious to support the Europeans in their plans. But by May 2011 Strauss-Kahn was out, having been forced to resign following accusations that he sexually assaulted a housekeeper at the Sofitel New York Hotel.[10] The IMF operated under rules permitting it to lend only when it had an expectation of being paid back. It was permitted to grant a country "exceptional access"—that is, to lend more than six times its quota subscription in the institution—only if it judged the debt to be sustainable. Already in May 2010 the Fund's normally pliant staff had felt unable to certify that the Greek government's debt was "sustainable with a high probability," forcing the executive board to provide a waiver on the grounds that not lending would cause terrible contagion to other countries. But the longer the Greek crisis festered, the more difficult it was for the IMF to continue to lend under such circumstances. Special rules for European countries raised the ire of directors representing Latin America, which had not enjoyed such privileges when experiencing debt crises of their own. At the same time, the idea that Greece would be able to return to the markets in 2012, once more selling bonds to private investors, was a pipe dream.

Something had to give. One option would have been for the country's EU partners to shower it with more money. But at this point the Greek bailout was politically toxic, not just in Germany but in the Netherlands, Finland, and other Northern European countries. By process of elimination, officials were led to think the unthinkable: the debt would have to be restructured.

For a year and a half, aside from the walk on the beach at Deauville, European leaders had denied that debt restructuring was feasible. The prospect of restructuring, with significant losses for bondholders, would create chaos in financial markets. Institutional investors would be bankrupted. They would dump the bonds of other troubled Eurozone countries. Greece would be tied up in litigation for years. Jürgen Stark, Germany's man on the ECB executive board, warned that a Greek restructuring would be a "catastrophe." His executive board colleague Lorenzo Bini Smaghi, formerly director general at the Italian Ministry of Finance, warned the Greek government that restructuring was "political suicide" and that any step in this direction would "jeopardize all of Europe."[11]

The reality, of course, was just the opposite. It was possible, events would show, for Greece to restructure its debt and obtain significant relief with a minimum of uncertainty and a maximum of investor participation. Money could be set aside to recapitalize its banks, and banks elsewhere could prepare for the inevitable. With support from the institutions of the European Union, other countries could be sheltered from the fallout. But changing course would be a blow to the credibility of European officials like Stark and Bini Smaghi, who had warned that restructuring would be Armageddon. Before long they would be former European officials.

The result was another year of waffling and delay. German Finance Minister Wolfgang Schäuble first proposed that the IMF and ECB organize a "voluntary" debt exchange in which investors would receive longer-maturity bonds but concede no debt reduction. What advantage this would have for the Greek government was never clear. Next a committee of French banks tabled a proposal that again included no nominal debt reduction. The Institute of International Finance, an association of big institutional investors, proposed exchanging the outstanding bonds for four new bonds with different durations and coupons. The new bonds would help Greece with its immediate financing problem by providing cash flow relief. But the plan required minimal concessions of investors and perversely increased the debt with which the Greek government was encumbered.[12]

It is not surprising that the banks preferred a deal that maximized their returns. But that did not mean it helped with the Greek government's economic and financial problems. This was a clear failure of leadership by the IMF and the EU, which allowed the banks to call the tune and asked Greece to dance to it. If officials had consciously sought to roil the markets, this would have been how to go about it.

After three more months of dithering, European leaders finally acknowledged that the longer they waited, the worse things became. At their summit on

October 26, 2011, they finally "invited" all parties to develop a bond exchange that would cut the value of Greek debt to private investors by 50 percent. After four more months of discussions, the Greek government finally made investors a take-it-or-leave-it offer. It turned out to be an offer they couldn't refuse. When the deal closed in April 2012, more than 97 percent of private investors accepted. The face value of their bonds was reduced by more than half, and the new bonds bore lower interest payments than their predecessors. More than €100 billion of Greek debt was vaporized.

———

This, then, was the orderly restructuring that European officials had dismissed as a mythical beast. It was the first major debt exchange in Europe since World War II. It was the largest debt exchange in history.

What made it possible?

First, 60 percent of Greek bonds were held by banks and other investors susceptible to arm twisting by their governments. Those governments saw a successful restructuring, now that it was underway, as in the public interest and dropped not very thinly veiled hints about the adverse consequences of not going along.

Second, it helped that 86 percent of Greek government bonds were subject to Greek law, so their provisions could be changed by a simple act of the Hellenic Parliament. (The remainder had been issued under English law, making it subject to British courts.) The parliament took advantage of this by passing a measure that authorized the Greek-law bonds to be restructured if a qualified majority of bondholders agreed.[13] Potential holdouts, now subject to majority rule, had no legal recourse, as they were quick to realize. More positively from the point of view of the bondholders, the new bonds were governed by English law, meaning they included protections that the old Greek-law bonds lacked.

This was progress at last. Unfortunately, achieving it took nearly two and a half years, during which the Greek people labored under a crushing burden and the credibility of all parties suffered. Nor was the debt relief that Greece obtained obviously enough. The €42 billion of Greek bonds held by the ECB, together with the €13 billion of bonds in the hands of national central banks, were not restructured. Government debt was still a crushing 150 percent of GDP.

There were no celebrations in Athens. The recession continued to deepen. Increasingly the question was when the next restructuring, this time involving debt held by the official sector, would occur.

———

All along, the ECB was steadfastly opposed to any form of debt restructuring. The idea was resisted, as we have seen, by members of its governing council from Jean-Claude Trichet on down. These worthies were aware that the ECB was a substantial holder of Southern European bonds. They understood that if the logic of restructuring was allowed to play out, the institution's balance sheet would take a hit. They worried that the ECB would have to intervene with further bond purchases to protect governments and banks elsewhere from the fallout.

Preoccupation with its profit-and-loss statement is not what one expects of an institution charged with ensuring the stability of financial markets and the economy. ECB officials were no doubt sensitive to the fact that politicians, notably in Germany, would be displeased if the ECB took losses on its portfolio. But it was properly the responsibility of those officials to frame the discussion and direct attention to the central bank's higher duties. This began to happen after the presidency of the central bank passed from Trichet to the former Italian Treasury and Goldman Sachs economist Mario Draghi, notably when Draghi vowed in the summer of 2012 that the ECB would do what it took to preserve and defend the Eurozone. Better late than never.

In other ways as well, the ECB compounded the Eurozone's plight. In 2010 it erroneously concluded that recovery was underway and began phasing out its nonstandard monetary measures.[14] It remained fixated on headline inflation, raising interest rates in the spring and summer of 2011 in response to a transient spike in food and fuel prices. With the German economy still growing, one can't help but think that the ECB's action was taken more with German than Eurozone-wide concerns in mind. Raising rates at this juncture tightened the screws on financially strapped banks and firms and made life harder for governments. Interest rates on Spanish and Italian bonds shot up, inaugurating the next and more serious phase of the crisis.

ECB officials hesitated to do more to support growth because they feared that doing more would relieve the pressure on Southern European governments to reform. Lower interest rates and more extensive securities purchases that helped European economies to grow would make fiscal consolidation less urgent. They would weaken the pressure to implement politically difficult reforms.

The resulting pattern became predictable. Whenever the situation turned truly dire, the ECB would do just enough to hold things together. It would activate its Securities Market Programme (SMP), purchasing the bonds of Southern European countries facing soaring funding costs and helping European banks seeking to unload them.[15] It would loosen the terms of the Longer-Term Refinancing Operations (LTROs) under which it provided liquidity to the banks.[16] But as soon as the patient stabilized, the medication was curtailed. The SMP was suspended.[17] The conditions attached to LTROs were tightened. The economic situation then predictably deteriorated, raising fears about the survival of the euro. The ECB would respond by reactivating the SMP and liberalizing the conditions attached to its LTROs.

The result was a stop-and-go policy, first under Trichet and then under Draghi, that provided inadequate support for the European economy. The M3 money supply grew by a disastrously low 0.6 percent in 2010 and by just 1.5 percent in 2011. For an economy capable of growing by 1 to 2 percent and a central bank with a 2 percent inflation target, one would have liked to see M3 grow by at least 4 percent. In late 2011, following the ECB's two "proactive" interest-rate hikes, bank lending to the private sector again went into decline. It then fell steadily over the course of 2012.[18] The central bank's inconsistency, repeatedly turning on the tap to prevent the subject from expiring from dehydration but then turning it off with the goal of encouraging it to proceed more quickly to the oasis, greatly compounded the difficulties of the European economy.

The unavoidable conclusion is that the ECB, like the Fed in the 1920s, misunderstood its mission. The Fed's first responsibility then was not to help Britain back onto the gold standard or to deflate the Wall Street bubble but rather to tailor supplies of money and credit to the needs of the US economy. The ECB's first responsibility now was not to ratchet up the pressure for fiscal and structural reform but to use monetary policy to maintain a respectable rate of M3 growth and otherwise support financial stability and growth. The Fed, in the Great Depression, learned its lesson the hard way. The ECB, it should be noted, was only thirteen years old in 2012 when the consequences of these mistakes came to a head—the same age as the Federal Reserve in 1926, when the Florida real estate bubble burst—not that this qualified as an excuse.

By the summer of 2012, the situation was dire. Europe was back in recession. Government bonds had been downgraded once more by the rating agencies. Ten-year Spanish and Italian bonds were trading at interest rates 500 basis points above those on ten-year German *bunds*. Depositors were fleeing Southern European banks. The Dutch and Finnish governments were in revolt against extension of more financial assistance. The intentions of the new Greek government formed in the wake of the May–June legislative elections remained unclear. The possibility that Greece might abandon the euro was widely mooted.[19] This, it was feared, would open the door to a wider Eurozone collapse. If the goal of ECB officials was to keep the pressure on Southern European countries, in this at least they succeeded.

But by putting the survival of the Eurozone at risk, they went too far. This recognition prompted Draghi's statement on July 26, 2012, at an investor conference in London, that "the ECB is ready to do whatever it takes to preserve the euro. And believe me, it will be enough."[20]

Draghi's announcement was followed by the decision of the Governing Council to establish a program of Outright Monetary Transactions. OMT, as it quickly became known, was a mechanism for purchasing the bonds of troubled European countries. It was not unlike the Securities Market Programme that preceded it, with two exceptions. First, it did not come with a ceiling on purchases or a terminal date. Second, ECB purchases of bonds on the secondary market were conditional on the government of the country in question negotiating an adjustment program with the European Stability Mechanism, the EU's rescue fund. With this program in place, the ECB could provide as much support as the government and banks might require. It could do whatever it took.[21]

––––––

The crisis taught the United States some hard lessons about the inadequacies of financial regulation, though acting on those lessons was more easily said than done. It similarly taught Europe some painful lessons about the flaws in its monetary union. Fiscal discipline was inadequate. Surveillance by the European Commission regularly ignored other developments affecting the stability of the union, such as the capital flows that allowed for the deterioration of competitive positions in the south. Europe lacked a single supervisor capable of reining in the banks that were the conduits of those cross-border flows. There was no mechanism for transfers of budgetary resources from high-unemployment regions to low. Europe learned, at considerable cost to itself, the difficulties that resulted from monetary union without banking and fiscal union.

In the United States, it was immensely complicated to get the executive and legislative branches to agree on reforms. This was nothing, however, compared to the difficulty of getting seventeen euro-area governments to agree, much less twenty-seven when the reforms in question involved not just the euro area but the entire European Union. At any point in time there was an election pending in some member state, causing the reform process to be caught up in politics. The German Constitutional Court might rule the latest directive of the Commission or policy of the ECB inconsistent with the country's national constitution.[22] Far-reaching reforms could require revisions of Europe's treaties. But this threatened to open the Pandora's box of Europe's most basic rules and understandings. With some governments obliged to put treaty revisions to a public referendum, the outcome was uncertain. And if there was one thing European leaders had learned, it was that markets do not react well to uncertainty.

Moreover, the dominant narrative, which set abstemious Germans against profligate Greeks and, more generally, thrifty Northern Europeans against spendthrift Southerners, played up distributional aspects of the crisis. It highlighted the conflicting interests of the parties to the reform effort. None of this made progress easy.

So reform proceeded haltingly. Efforts focused initially on strengthening oversight of budgetary policies as a way of assuaging the German public. The response took the form of six new EU regulations and directives known as the "six-pack," perhaps to appeal to beer-loving Germans.[23] These changes were designed to strengthen the Stability and Growth Pact, under which governments committed to targeting budget deficits of no more than 3 percent of GDP and public debts of no more than 60 percent, or at least to making progress toward those goals. The six-pack provided a concrete definition of what constituted a "significant deviation" from such progress. It allowed procedures leading to sanctions and fines to be launched against a country making insufficient headway in reducing its debt ratio toward 60 percent and not just against countries with a deficit above 3 percent. It required countries to target a structural deficit, with cyclical effects removed, of no more than 0.5 percent of GDP.[24]

These new rules were supposed to be made more credible and enforceable by requiring a qualified majority of EU member states to vote to overturn the application of sanctions, rather than requiring a qualified majority to vote to apply them.[25] The new rules were now to be embedded in national law by the member states, each of which was instructed to pass a legislative act or constitutional amendment to that effect. Compliance with this law or constitutional provision was to be monitored by an independent national agency equivalent to the US Congressional Budget Office. The European Court of Justice, for its part, was empowered to impose sanctions or fines on countries failing to adopt those laws and constitutional amendments, or to create those independent councils. For more than ten years European countries had shown great alacrity in ignoring the Stability and Growth Pact; governments sought to tie their hands without much success. Whether this strengthened set of restraints would work better only time would tell.

The second item on the reform agenda was banking union. In principle this meant a single supervisor responsible for overseeing the operation of banks across the Eurozone or the European Union so that the implications of their activities not just domestically but across borders would be properly taken into account. It meant a single deposit insurance scheme to rule out beggar-thy-neighbor changes in deposit insurance policies like Ireland's in 2008. And it meant a mechanism for winding up insolvent banks, backed by a common fund akin to that administered by the FDIC in the United States.

Again, more easily said than done. National supervisors were reluctant to cede their prerogatives. No EU institution possessed the competence to supervise more than six thousand banks spread across seventeen countries, and it was not clear how quickly such competence could be acquired. There was no agreement on where to house the single supervisor, inside the ECB, where information could be shared with the lender of last resort, or in a separate self-standing agency so as to minimize conflicts with the central bank's price stability mandate. A common deposit insurance scheme and single resolution mechanism were resisted in Germany for fear that German banks and taxpayers would end up footing the bill for the mess created by banks in other countries. The realism of such fears was questionable, since German banks were as highly leveraged, poorly governed, and troubled as any. But the dominant narrative, in which frugal Germans were forced to bail out improvident Greeks and Spaniards, continued to shape perceptions and hinder reform efforts.

The result, after a year of delay, was agreement in 2013 to designate the ECB as the single supervisor while building a Chinese wall between its monetary and supervisory functions. Separate boards would oversee the two activities. One hundred thirty large institutions engaged in extensive cross-border activities would be supervised by the ECB, while the rest would continue to be overseen by their respective national supervisors, "subject to the authority" of the ECB, whatever that meant. After six more months of negotiation, there was then agreement on the structure of a common resolution scheme, but one in which the funding would initially come from national authorities, not the Eurozone as a whole. This agreement consequently did nothing to break the diabolic loop between banking and debt crises.[26]

Fiscal transfers between booming and depressed regions were the hardest nut to crack. François Hollande, the Socialist leader elected French president in mid-2012 by voters who expressed in no uncertain terms their displeasure with Nicolas Sarkozy's handling of the crisis, floated a proposal for joint funding of a Europe-wide unemployment insurance fund. This landed with a thud in Berlin. The same was true of schemes for Eurobonds backed by Eurozone countries as a group. For Germany, as for other countries that identified as Northern European, this was a bridge too far.

Thus, the task of completing Europe's monetary house continued to resemble the home renovation project that never ends.

———

In both Europe and the United States, the policy initiatives taken in response to the crisis were just enough to prevent the collapse of monetary arrangements and financial systems. They were just enough to ward off a contraction on the scale of the Great Depression. It may not have felt that way in Athens or in Stockton, California. But the conclusion stands. Central banks, in Mario Draghi's words, were prepared to do what it took. Governments, their views of what constituted an appropriate response likewise informed by the experience of the 1930s, were similarly prepared to use fiscal policy to stabilize demand and avert a contraction as severe as the Great Depression.

But their very success encouraged second thoughts. It was inevitable that some of the assistance provided by central banks and spending ministries would flow to banks and nonbank financial institutions, since credit is the lifeblood of the market system. But as anger swelled against the financial institutions implicated in the crisis, it fueled a backlash against the central banks and fiscal authorities that stepped into help them. Moreover, politicians overpromised, as politicians are prone to do. When a serious recession followed, even if not a recession as serious as the Great Depression, their policies were dismissed as failed. Vast deficits and the unprecedented expansion of central bank balance sheets excited fears of inflation and were hard for politicians to defend. Subtle arguments about the difference between household and government budgets or about the benign implications of monetary expansion when the economy is in a liquidity trap were hard to impress on a public accustomed to sound bites.

Thus, in the first round of elections that followed the crisis, deficits and central bank activism became political liabilities. Office holders seeking to maintain their majorities, knowing which way the wind was blowing, embraced austerity. Central banks limited interventions for fear that doing more might excite critics and jeopardize their independence. If the initial response prevented a contraction on the scale of the Great Depression, the turn to fiscal austerity and monetary restraint now prevented the recovery from matching that of the 1930s.

The same was true of financial reform. Efforts to strengthen regulation were less far-reaching than analogous efforts following the Great Depression. There is no question but that the prevailing system of regulation had failed catastrophically, provoking calls for root-and-branch changes. But this time the economic consequences of that failure were more successfully contained. The same was true of the financial consequences: where the Standard & Poor's index fell by more than 85 percent between its peak in September 1929 and the trough in July, it fell by "just" 57 percent in the seventeen months following its October 9, 2007, peak and then recovered more quickly.[27] As a result, fundamental reform seemed less urgent. The architects of the prevailing system may not have emerged from the crisis with their reputations burnished, but neither were they discredited to the same degree as in the 1930s. Hence they could become the architects of reform.

All this the United States and Europe had in common. What Europe had in addition was an unfinished monetary union that was impossible to dismantle and equally impossible to complete. When in the 1930s reaching international agreement on adoption of reflationary policies proved impossible, countries moved unilaterally, abandoning the gold standard and reflating on their own. Unilateralism had costs. International trade and comity suffered. But unilateralism at least created the policy space needed for depressed economies to recover.

Informed by this experience, the experts were quick to predict that Greece, accompanied perhaps by Europe's other crisis countries, would exit the Eurozone. But the euro proved more resilient than the gold standard. Reintroducing a national currency where one no longer existed was more difficult than devaluing an existing unit. The members of the European Union had even more invested in the euro than did governments in the 1930s in the gold standard. Along with their monetary union, they had a single market and political arrangements fifty years in the making. That these could be imperiled by dismantling the Eurozone was the implication of exit limited initially even to one country.

The Greeks were understandably incensed about being subjected to humiliating inspections by the Troika and by the endless recession to which they were now consigned. The Germans were outraged over being asked to bail out their profligate neighbors and being labeled brutal paymasters for their efforts. But when push came to shove, both sides were prepared to do just enough to hold the Eurozone together. Germany and its European Union partners provided emergency loans, not once but repeatedly. Greece swallowed hard and accepted deep cuts in public-sector salaries and social programs, not once but over a succession of years. In neither case did voters turn to anti-euro parties in numbers as large as in the 1930s. The Greeks had no desire to go down in history as the pariahs who demolished the euro and the European Union. The Germans, as beneficiaries of those arrangements, in the end understood that they had to sacrifice to make them work.

Here, then, the history of the 1930s was an imperfect guide to policy outcomes. Where the earlier crisis led to the collapse of the gold standard, this one did not lead to the collapse of the Eurozone. At least not yet.

Conclusion

THE HISTORICAL PAST is a rich repository of analogies that shape perceptions and guide public policy decisions. Those analogies are especially
influential in crises, when there is no time for reflection. They are particularly
potent when so-called experts are unable to agree on a framework for careful
analytic reasoning. They carry the most weight when there is a close correspondence between current events and an earlier historical episode. And they
resonate most powerfully when an episode is a defining moment for a country
and a society.

For President Harry S. Truman, in deciding whether to intervene in Korea,
that historical moment was Munich. For policy makers confronted in 2008–
09 with the most serious financial crisis in eighty years, that moment was
the Great Depression. Given the close correspondence between the events of
2008–09 and the 1930s, the earlier episode, or more precisely the lessons of the
episode as distilled by economists and historians, powerfully shaped perceptions and reactions.

Policy makers, according to this distillation, should respond swiftly and
forcefully to incipient financial distress. This means injecting liquidity into
financial markets to prevent problems from spreading further. It means sort-
ing out insolvent banks from those that are illiquid, while continuing to
extend emergency liquidity to the latter but closing down or recapitalizing the
former, in this way restoring confidence and allowing the financial system to
start functioning again.

But even though this monetary and financial triage may prevent financial
distress from deepening, it will not undo the damage already done. Given
the disruption to financial markets, it will not be enough to prevent a serious

recession. It will not be enough to get the economy moving again if heightened risk aversion creates a reluctance to borrow and lend. In such circumstances, it will be necessary to increase public spending to offset the decline in private spending. This emergency response should be forceful, but it should also be temporary. It should be wound down when private spending recovers, in order to prevent debts from spiraling out of control.

Help, in the form of extending the duration of unemployment benefits, augmenting provision of food stamps and expanding access to social services, should meanwhile be provided to the unemployed casualties of the crisis. Helping these less fortunate members of society is fair and just insofar as their suffering results from the malfunctioning of a system that operates disproportionately to the benefit of others. But such help is also required to maintain broad support for prevailing economic and political processes.

Last but not least, the flawed monetary, fiscal, financial, and social policies that allowed the crisis to develop in the first place should be fixed through comprehensive reforms put in place before the sense of urgency has passed.

Such were the lessons of the Great Depression as distilled by economic and historical scholars. Milton Friedman and Anna Schwartz made the case for forceful central bank action to prevent banking crises, deflation, and depression in a book hailed as one of the most important works of twentieth-century economic history. John Maynard Keynes made the case for public spending to counter depressed economic conditions in one of the most influential books in all of economics. Karl Polanyi made the case for social and regulatory reform in a book published to great acclaim in 1944.[1] Those making consequential decisions in 2007–08 did not all have firsthand knowledge of these authors. But they were aware of their arguments, given how their conclusions were passed down through the generations and had come to constitute a standard historical narrative.

Policy makers in the United States and other countries, their actions informed by this narrative, responded quickly and forcefully to events. Central banks cut interest rates and flooded financial markets with liquidity. Governments unfurled front-loaded programs of fiscal stimulus. Although efforts to recapitalize the banks were more tentative, they were enough. Collapse of the monetary and financial system was averted. Support for democracy and the market economy did not crumble. This at least was no Great Depression.

The paradox is that we failed to do better. Unemployment in the advanced economies still rose to double-digit levels, not as high as in the Great Depression but higher than in normal recessions, and higher than anticipated by those taught to believe that economic science had cracked the problem of avoiding a Depression-like slump. Financial distress was more acute than expected by those taught to believe that central banks and regulators had learned how to prevent a 1930s-style crisis. Recovery was marred by slow growth, high unemployment, and a falling rate of labor force participation. It remained sluggish for longer than could be explained by the need for firms and households to work down excessive debts and banks to repair damaged balance sheets, alone.

It can be argued that high unemployment and deep recession are unavoidable in the wake of a financial crisis, appropriate policy response or not. But this observation, even if correct, only pushes the problem back another step. The paradox then is that we failed to anticipate, much less prepare for, the possibility of this crisis.

Ironically, the roots of this failure lay in the same progressive narrative of the Great Depression. Entirely correctible flaws of collective decision making, this narrative explained, were responsible for the inability of contemporaries to appreciate the risks to stability in the 1920s, and then for their failure to deal effectively with the consequences in the 1930s. Modern-day policy makers learned from the mistakes of their predecessors. Scientific central banking informed by a rigorous framework of inflation targeting reduced economic and financial volatility and prevented serious imbalances. Advances in supervision and regulation limited financial excesses. Deposit insurance eliminated bank runs and financial panics. The dominant narrative of the Great Depression, that it was caused by avoidable policy failures, was itself conducive to the belief that those failures could be—and had been—corrected. It followed that no comparable crisis was possible now.

This belief, we now know, was dreadfully wrong. The economic and financial instability of the 1920s and 1930s may have been heavily associated with inflation and deflation, problems that inflation targeting, the twenty-first-century version of Friedman and Schwartz's stable money growth rule, could plausibly claim to have solved. But this did not mean other risks to stability were eliminated. To the contrary, the long period of economic stability, the Great Moderation, encouraged investors to take on additional risk. The eighty years since the advanced economies last experienced an equally serious crisis allowed them to ignore the consequences. Time dampened awareness that financial markets are unstable. Market participants are continuously innovating, sometimes in the effort to better serve their customers but other times to evade regulations put in place in response to earlier problems. The regulatory bloodhounds are unable to keep pace with the well-fed private-sector greyhounds. The result is a widening gap between actual regulation and what appears, with hindsight, as best regulatory practice. All this suggests that the longer the period of stability persists, the greater the risks. But this is not the perception while the party is underway.

In addition, a long period of stability born of good policy or good luck empowers those inclined to argue that regulation is too strict. A regulatory response to the Great Depression, which produced a tightly cosseted financial system and an extended period of stability, thus contained the seeds of its own destruction. Financiers could argue that since they had learned to better manage risk, capital and liquidity requirements for financial institutions could be relaxed. Restrictions on cross-selling financial products could be removed. The heavy hand laid on financial markets in the 1930s could give way to light-touch regulation. The instability of financial markets and hence the dangers of light-touch regulation should have been another lesson of the Great Depression as distilled by economic and historical scholars. This view existed as well, but it resided mainly on the fringes of economics.

Why it remained out of the mainstream is worth pondering further. If such powerful lessons for how policy makers should respond to a crisis were remembered, how could other equally powerful lessons about what could cause it be forgotten?

Part of the answer is that historians always did a better job of describing the fateful decisions that transformed the recession of 1929 into the Great Depression of the 1930s than of understanding the origins of the recession itself. Explanations of the onset of the crisis were the least systematic and satisfactory part of the historical narrative. Lessons about what can cause a crisis and how to avoid one were less powerful because the corresponding history was less well developed and less effectively distilled.

In addition, recent experience reminds us that the causes of crises are not so simple and, consequently, not so readily identified and avoided. Flawed conceptual frameworks and wrongheaded policies there were in abundance, but the Great Depression involved more. We now appreciate how policy makers in the 1920s and 1930s were forced to take decisions on the basis of partial information about the state of the economy, just as the Federal Reserve didn't know how rapidly conditions were deteriorating at the end of 2007 and President Obama's economists didn't know how fast the economy was shrinking in 2009. The problem wasn't simply that they didn't know how to react to a certain set of conditions. It is that they didn't know the conditions. A crisis is a time when the pace of events seems to accelerate and when information is especially incomplete. Having lived through such a moment in 2008–09, we better appreciate how a similar moment must have felt in 1929.

This is just one example of how the Great Recession will change how we understand the Great Depression. We now better appreciate the tendency to take credit for an extended period of stability, extrapolate that stability into the future, and let our guard down. We better understand the inclination to offer ex post rationalizations for large and unsustainable lending flows. We better understand the temptation to reduce the art of economic policy making to a simple rule, whether it is that the central bank should focus on a rate of inflation of 2 percent, as recommended by the tenets of inflation targeting, or that it should provide only as much credit as is required by the legitimate needs of business, following the dictates of the real bills doctrine. We better understand the anger spawned by bailouts of fat-cat bankers and how this complicates the extension of public support for troubled banks. We better appreciate how viewing the future through the lens of the past can distort as well as illuminate—how Europeans starting in 2010 could remain fixated on the risk of 1920s-style inflation when deflation was the real and present danger, or how US policy makers could remain preoccupied by excessive risk taking after 1929 when in fact a dearth of risk taking was holding back the economy. We better understand the reluctance of central bankers, sensitive to political criticism, to do more to promote recovery. And we better understand the instincts that led governments in the midst of a crisis to cut spending prematurely.

Finally, we better appreciate that economic analysis and advice are not enough. Policies still have to be implemented. And here deeply held political ideologies and agendas stand in the way. These are by no means new themes in histories of the Great Depression. But recent events will cast them in a more prominent light.

The progressive narrative—that advances in risk management and regulation had eliminated the danger of a 1930s-style financial crisis—similarly rested on a particular, historically informed vision of the risks. The crisis of the 1930s, in the standard narrative, resulted from runs on banks that governments and central banks did too little to prevent and whose effects they did too little to contain. But this focus on the banks caused twenty-first-century policy makers to miss the growing importance of the nonbank financial sector of hedge funds, money market funds, and special purpose vehicles. It caused them to miss the importance of derivative securities and other nonbank financial claims. This neglect was especially consequential in the United States, where, by the early twenty-first century, nonbank sources had come to provide more than two-thirds of credit to the nonfinancial private sector. But it was more general.

This shift had profound if unappreciated consequences. Federal deposit insurance did nothing to enhance confidence in money market mutual funds, whose shareholders were now as prone to run as bank depositors in the 1930s. Capital requirements for banks did nothing to deter excessive risk taking or provide a buffer against losses when the risky assets were held by the offshore arms of insurance companies, like AIG Financial Products. But the bank-focused crisis of the 1930s and the enduring influence of that narrative encouraged policy makers to overlook this change in the locus of risks.

In Europe, where the nonbank financial sector furnished only 30 percent of credit to households and firms, the story was different. There it was still about the banks. The financial system had long been more bank-based in Europe than in the United States. Now, as memories of the banking crises of the 1930s faded and deregulationist forces gained traction, it was the banks that benefited disproportionately in country after country. The Creditanstalt crisis, in which the failure of a bank that supplied half of all credit to the Austrian economy triggered the collapse of Central Europe's financial system, might have served as a cautionary tale. But not all European countries shared such histories. And banking policy, in any case, now was made at the European level. Even in countries that did share such a history, memories of it were lost in the din, overwhelmed by arguments about the efficiency advantages of megabanks and advances in scientific risk management.

In addition, some countries like Britain, fortunate to have been spared a banking crisis in the 1930s, were less than alert to the need for the central bank to act as a lender of last resort. Not having experienced a bank run in 150 years, they provided only limited deposit insurance. The result was the first bank run in 150 years.

The single greatest failure to learn appropriate lessons from this earlier history was surely the decision to adopt the euro. The 1920s and 1930s illustrated nothing better than the dangers of tying a diverse set of countries to a single monetary policy. Experience under the interwar gold standard highlighted the tendency for large amounts of capital to flow from countries where interest rates were low to where they were high, and the destabilizing consequences that would follow when those flows came to a stop. It highlighted the economic pain and political turmoil that would result when the only available response was austerity. That history should have given European leaders pause before moving ahead with the euro.

This failure is a reminder that there does not in general exist a single historical narrative, but several. History is contested. One narrative portrayed the fixed exchange rates of the 1920s gold standard as the problem; another instead indicted the unstable exchange rates of the 1930s as a source of disruptive beggar-thy-neighbor policies.[2] This second interpretation resonated with recent European experience, given how disruptive exchange rate changes, as recently as 1992–93, had thrown a wrench into the gears of European integration. Many will now argue that this was a questionable reading of the 1930s. In the event, it led to the questionable decision to move to the euro, with unquestionably disastrous consequences.

In the end, the Europeans did just enough to prevent the collapse of their monetary system. Like the Americans, they did just enough to avoid another Great Depression. But their very achievement weakened the incentive to do more. The monetary and financial system not having collapsed as completely as in the 1930s and the economic consequences being less dire, the urgency of radical reform was less. Financial interests spared damage on the scale of the 1930s were better able to mobilize in opposition to radical reform. Creditor countries were able to mobilize in opposition to proposals for pooling the debts of the monetary union partners and moving forthwith to banking union. Social policy reform was similarly less far-reaching because social distress was less.

Moreover, this policy success, such as it was, allowed governments and central banks to heed the call to return to normal policies as soon as the emergency passed. Unfortunately, the return to normal policies preceded the return to normal conditions. Under normal conditions the expansion of central bank balance sheets would have ignited inflation. The large budget deficits of the American and British governments would have caused interest rates to spike. That these consequences did not now follow should have made clear that economic conditions were still far from normal. But this did nothing to diminish the intensity of the call for governments to balance their budgets sooner rather than later.

As governments scaled back their spending, central bankers, concerned by the continued weakness of the economy, felt compelled to do more. But if unelected technocrats with narrow mandates were one thing, unelected technocrats with sweeping powers were another. Anxiety over their unprecedented interventions was shared by the central bankers themselves. The policies were unconventional, and central bankers are nothing if not conventional. Inflation aversion, the most deeply held convention of all, rendered moot the idea of raising the inflation target as a way of bringing down the cost of borrowing in this exceptional slump. Historical memories of the 1970s, when inflation had been allowed to run out of control, were more immediate for many of the central bankers on the Federal Open Market Committee than distant memories of deflation in the 1930s. Those more immediate memories caused them to hesitate to turn to unconventional policies even when deflation became the immediate threat.

Moreover, the longer unconventional policies persisted, the more political criticism they invited. Central bankers concerned to protect their independence grew more anxious still to return to conventional policies. The reluctance of twenty-first-century central banks to do more brought to light another lesson of the Great Depression, namely that central banks doing too little to support economic growth can also see their independence compromised and be stripped of their powers. But prior to recent experience, which highlighted this risk, this observation was not part of the conventional narrative.

Then there was the worry that low interest rates were encouraging investors to move into riskier assets. Policy, in this view, was only setting the stage for another bubble and another crash. This was of course the same fear that had prevented the authorities from responding more forcefully in the 1930s. Viewing the world through a historical mirror, they were unable to recognize that the problem in the 1930s was deflation rather than inflation. It was too little risk taking, not too much. Five years after Lehman Brothers, it was not hard to see the same funhouse mirror at work.

The concern with moral hazard was real, albeit more real for some policy makers than others. They worried about the consequences of creating expectations that everyone would be bailed out. But the concern was also political. Bailouts were politically contentious. Criticism fed the desire to find a bank that could be made an example, whether Lehman Brothers in 2008 or Union Guardian Trust in 1933.

The European version of this moral hazard argument was that too much central bank support for the prices of government bonds and even for economic growth would weaken the pressure on governments. Politicians and their constituents had to feel pain in order to appreciate the urgency of structural reform and fiscal consolidation. This problem was one of moral hazard, but also of moralism. The euro crisis, seen from Frankfurt and Berlin, was caused by feckless Southern Europeans. The subprime crisis that rendered Europe so vulnerable was caused by reckless Americans. The miscreants needed to suffer in order to mend their ways. The instincts that informed Andrew Mellon's policies of liquidationism are easy to criticize, and they have come in for much criticism from historical scholars. Our own experience suggests they are universal human instincts. They are not easily suppressed.

This tendency to frame the crisis in moralistic terms did not make cooperation in countering it any easier. The historical narrative that governments and central banks, working at cross purposes, made things worse in the 1930s inspired the effort in 2008–09 to coordinate monetary and fiscal policies and shun protectionist responses. But once the emergency passed, sustaining cooperation became harder. As fatigue set in, coordination gave way to finger pointing. German Finance Minister Wolfgang Schäuble criticized the Federal Reserve for pushing down the dollar, deriding its policies as "clueless." US President Obama cast not-so-veiled aspersions at the Europeans for not moving faster to fix their banks. In this light, the failure of governments and central banks to mount a cooperative response to the European financial crisis in 1931 and then to the global economic crisis in 1933 becomes easier to understand.

Nowhere was the finger pointing worse, this time, than in Europe, where the Northern European narrative that set industrious Germans against spend-thrift Greeks had as its Southern European counterpart an account that set ill-starred Greeks against unsympathetic Germans. This was not a framing that made it easy to extend foreign assistance, or even to accept it. It was not conducive to debt mutualization or debt forgiveness. A balanced analysis would have observed that for every reckless borrower there is a reckless lender. It would have acknowledged that it was easier for one country to export its way out of trouble than for every Southern European country to do so. It was easier to conjure up an export miracle with the support of an accommodating monetary policy and a weak euro, as in Germany in the early 2000s, than now that the opposite conditions prevailed. These same conclusions followed from the contrast between the 1920s, when France, with an undervalued currency, enjoyed an export boom, and the 1930s, when a depressed Europe was unable to collectively export its way out of a slump. But given how the crisis was framed, these implications were now lost on the French government and, more importantly, the German.

This more balanced analysis would have also conceded that no country is prepared to bail out a troubled neighbor without attaching conditions and putting in place mechanisms to ensure it is repaid. But a moralistic framing of the crisis that pitted the virtuous against the unprincipled was not condu-cive to this balanced view. It did not incline the lenders to propose reasonable conditions or borrowers to accept them. Successful countries could not resist the conclusion that their success derived from their virtue and that, to succeed, other countries only had to develop like-minded virtue. Unsuccessful countries were led to believe that their more successful neighbors took satisfaction in their plight.

Finally, that policy makers did just enough to prevent another Great Depression weakened the incentive to think deeply about causes. Having avoided financial collapse, it was still possible to defend America's banking and financial system and Europe's monetary union as the worst alternatives except for all the others (to paraphrase Winston Churchill on democracy). As a result, there was little discussion of executive compensation practices, in the financial sector and generally, and their implications for financial stability. In the wake of the crisis, there was the short-lived Occupy Movement, which questioned the merits of financialization and warned of growing inequality. But there was no sustained discussion of the roots of these phenomena or their consequences.[3] Inequality reflected the failure of society to provide the major-ity of its members with the education and training needed for a world of global competition. It reflected technical change that made it easier to substitute robots for workers. There was little willingness to address these problems or to acknowledge that the disappointing recovery from the crisis reflected not just headwinds from deleveraging but also a long period of underinvestment in infrastructure, basic research, and education.

Addressing these problems would have required not a quick and temporary stimulus but sustained national and international strategies for investing in infrastructure, education, and research. It would have required mobilizing the necessary resources. It would have required hard thinking about how to ensure that the resources so mobilized were deployed productively. It would have meant pondering what kind of financial sector was needed to best support the growth of the nonfinancial economy and how to structure regulation to produce it.

In many cases, addressing these problems would have required more government, not less. This was the response to the Great Depression, but it was not the response now. The irony was that policy makers, by preventing the kind of depression that brought about the New Deal, discouraged hard thinking on the role of government.

Finally, the fact that policy makers did just enough to prevent another Great Depression meant that too little was done to make the world a safer financial place. Although banks are now subject to modestly higher capital and liquidity requirements, *modestly* is the operative word. Big banks are required to write living wills, and the Dodd-Frank Act in the United States includes a procedure for orderly liquidation of large financial institutions. But it is unclear whether those wills and liquidation procedures are actually to be used, given fears of exciting the markets. Little that is meaningful has been done about the problem of too-big-to-fail. That another Great Depression was avoided weakened the argument for more radical changes and allowed the banks to regroup.

Similarly, averting the worst allowed money market mutual funds and insurance companies to mobilize the lobbyists. Insurance companies, other than Prudential Financial and the now notorious AIG, were able to avoid being designated as systemically important by the Financial Stability Oversight Council. The credit-rating agencies, legislative handwaving aside, were able to escape significant regulation and reform.

Likewise, although there is now a Volcker Rule to limit proprietary trading by commercial banks, it is riddled with exceptions, given that the banks, spared a 1930s-style crisis, were not inclined to divest their securities business. Transactions in derivative securities have been moved into clearinghouses, but this only concentrates risk rather than removing it. The Europeans, having avoided their own Great Depression, find it hard to overcome the political obstacles to creating a meaningful banking union. They find it hard to agree on conditions under which their emergency rescue fund can lend and their central bank can backstop financial markets. The crisis created a sense of urgency, but not urgency sufficient to overcome these problems.

Thus, the very success with which policy makers limited the damage from the worst financial crisis in eighty years means we are likely to see another such crisis in less than eighty years.

DRAMATIS PERSONAE

Konrad Adenauer chancellor of the Federal Republic of Germany 1949–1963; played a key role in post–World War II European integration.

Nelson W. Aldrich US senator (Republican, Rhode Island) 1881–1911, who chaired the National Monetary Commission (1909–1912) and helped draft a plan that shaped the Federal Reserve Act.

Winthrop Aldrich banker and musician, son of Nelson W. Aldrich. Chairman of Chase National Bank, 1930–1953.

Phil Angelides real estate developer, treasurer of California 1999–2007, and chairman of the Financial Crisis Inquiry Commission 2009–10.

James Anthony banker whose Manley-Anthony chain was involved in Florida land market speculation in the 1920s. Helped finance George Merrick's Coral Gables project.

Adam Applegarth CEO of the British building society-cum-bank Northern Rock 2001–2007. Lost his position with the bank's crisis and nationalization.

Albert Aupetit secretary general of the Bank of France during the inflation of the 1920s, implicated in the episode when the bank breached the statutory ceiling on its note issue.

Vincent Auriol French politician; Socialist Party spokesman for financial issues in the 1920s and 1930s. Represented France at the 1944 International Monetary and Financial Conference at Bretton Woods.

David Axelrod columnist for the *Chicago Tribune*, political consultant, and senior political advisor to President Barack Obama, 2009–2011.

Roger Babson financial theorist and disciple of Sir Isaac Newton. Remembered for his late-1920s forecasts of a stock market crash.

Sheila Bair chair of the US Federal Deposit Insurance Commission 2005–2011, known for advocating regulatory reform to address the problem of "too big to fail."

Arthur Ballantine American attorney and public official. Undersecretary of the Treasury in the Hoover Administration, 1931–1933.

José Manuel Barroso Portuguese politician (Social Democrat), prime minister of Portugal 2002–2004, president of the European Commission 2004–2014.

Bruce Bent cofounder in 1971 of the first money market mutual fund, the Reserve Fund, known as Primary Reserve Fund when it broke the buck in 2008.

Adolph Berle professor of corporate law at Columbia University. Founding member of FDR's Brains Trust who emphasized the need for government to counter the market power of large corporations.

Ben S. Bernanke economist, professor at Stanford and Princeton Universities, student of the history of the Great Depression, and governor (2002–2005) and chair (2006–2014) of the Federal Reserve Board.

Jared Bernstein member of the Obama-Biden transition team, economic advisor to Vice President Joe Biden 2009–2011.

Gerald Lee Bevan financier and poet. Engaged in business dealings with Clarence Hatry in the 1920s. Convicted and incarcerated for having issued fraudulent balance sheets.

Lorenzo Bini Smaghi economist with degrees from Catholic University of Louvain and University of Chicago. Italian government official. Member of the ECB Executive Board, 2005–2011.

Hugo Black US senator (Democrat, Alabama) 1927–1937 and supporter of the New Deal. Known for his advocacy of work sharing and a national minimum wage. Appointed in 1937 to the US Supreme Court, on which he served until 1971.

Tony Blair British politician (Labour Party). Prime minister of the United Kingdom 1997–2007, whose accomplishments included conferring independence on the Bank of England and creating the Financial Services Authority.

Léon Blum French politician. Graduate of the École Normale Supérieure, affiliated with the French Socialist Party, member of the Chamber of Deputies starting in 1929. Prime minister at the time of the 1936 devaluation of the franc.

John Boehner member, US House of Representatives (Republican, Ohio) from 1991. House majority leader 2006–07, House minority leader 2007–2011, and speaker of the House starting in 2011.

Brooksley Born American attorney and public official. Chair of the Commodity Futures Trading Commission, 1996–1999, who famously sparred with Clinton administration officials over regulation of derivatives transactions.

Louis Brandeis associate justice of the US Supreme Court, 1916–1939. Progressive advocate and opponent of monopoly power and business influence whose followers populated the Roosevelt administration starting in 1933.

Willy Brandt German politician. Leader of the Social Democratic Party, German chancellor 1969–1974, and advocate of European integration.

Aristide Briand eleven times French prime minister between 1909 and 1929. His conciliatory approach to reaching a reparations settlement with Germany was unsuccessful.

Joseph A. Broderick American banker and bank examiner. New York State superintendent of banking at the time of the failure of the Bank of United States in 1930. Served on the Board of Governors of the Federal Reserve System 1936–37.

Gordon Brown British politician. Chancellor of the Exchequer in the government of Tony Blair, 1997–2007. Prime minister 2007–2010. Organized the 2009 G20 London summit.

Harry Brown cofounder in 1971 of the first money market mutual fund, the Reserve Fund, known as Primary Reserve Fund when it broke the buck in 2008.

Scott Brown state senator from Massachusetts who won a special election to the US Senate following the 2010 death of Edward Kennedy. First Republican to represent the state in the Senate since 1972.

Heinrich Brüning Center Party (conservative) politician who served in the German Reichstag (parliament) from 1924. Headed the presidential government that sought to achieve austerity by decree starting in 1930.

William Jennings Bryan member, US House of Representatives (Democrat, Nebraska) 1891–1895. Opponent of the gold standard, Democratic Party candidate for the presidency 1896 and 1900, US secretary of state 1913–1915. Florida real estate promoter.

Warren Buffett American businessman-investor. Principal shareholder in Berkshire Hathaway, which made a $5 billion strategic investment in Goldman Sachs at the height of the 2008 financial crisis.

Karl Buresch Austrian politician (Christian-Social Party), Austrian chancellor 1931–32.

George H. W. Bush forty-first president of the United States 1989–1993.

George W. Bush forty-third president of the United States 2001–2009.

William Calder US senator (Republican, New York) 1917–1923. Chaired the Calder Committee, which investigated the post–World War I housing shortage.

Rogers Caldwell Tennessee businessman-banker whose firm and banks were at the center of the 1930 financial crisis.

David Cameron British politician (Conservative Party). Prime minister of the United Kingdom from 2010.

Joseph Cassano chief financial officer and head of AIG Financial Products, whose positions in credit default swaps brought down the insurance giant in 2008.

Gustav Cassel Swedish economist and professor at Stockholm University 1903–1936, who advocated monetary policy geared toward stabilizing the price level.

James Cayne CEO of Bear Stearns 1993–2008. When its two subprime-linked hedge funds collapsed in 2007, he was playing at a bridge tournament in Nashville.

Anton Cermak American politician (Democrat), forty-fourth mayor of Chicago 1931–1933. Gravely wounded in an assassination attempt on President-Elect Roosevelt on February 15, 1933.

Neville Chamberlain British politician (Conservative Party). Chancellor of the Exchequer 1923–24 and 1931–1937, prime minister 1937–1940. As chancellor, known for shrewd financial management, and as prime minister, known for policy of appeasement.

Roy Chapin auto industry pioneer (cofounder of Hudson Motor Car Company). Secretary of commerce in the final months of the Hoover administration, 1932–33.

Walter Chrysler auto industry executive who participated in Billy Durant's investment pools in the 1920s.

Winston Churchill British politician (Conservative Party). Chancellor of the Exchequer 1924–1929, who took the decision to return to the gold standard at the prewar parity in 1925.

William Clinton forty-second president of the United States 1993–2001.

William Comstock American politician (Democrat). Thirty-third governor of Michigan 1933–1935, who declared the 1933 bank holiday.

Calvin Coolidge thirtieth president of the United States 1923–1929.

Charles Coughlin Roman Catholic priest, radio evangelist, first a supporter and then an opponent of FDR.

James Couzens US senator (Republican, Michigan), 1922–1936. Business partner and subsequently rival of auto executive Henry Ford.

Brian Cowen Irish politician (Fianna Fáil Party). Taoiseach (head of government) during the 2008–2011 financial crisis.

Christopher Cox twenty-eighth chairman of the US Securities and Exchange Commission 2005–2008.

James Cox American newspaper publisher and politician (Democrat). Forty-sixth and forty-eighth governor of Ohio 1913–1915, 1917–1921. Member of the US delegation to the 1933 World Economic Conference.

Daniel Crissinger American attorney and banker. Comptroller of the Currency 1921–1923 and then chairman of the Federal Reserve Board 1923–1927.

Bronson Cutting US senator (Republican, New Mexico), 1927–28, 1929–1935. Favored bank nationalization in 1933, and advocated strict regulation of fractional-reserve banking.

Édouard Daladier French politician. Member of the Radical (Liberal-Centrist) Party. Three times French prime minister, including during the Great Depression (January–October 1933 and again in January–February 1934 during the Stavisky Affair).

Alisdair Darling British politician (Labour Party). Chancellor of the Exchequer in the government of Gordon Brown 2007–2010.

Raoul Dautry French businessman-engineer-politician. Director-general of French State Railways. Member of Pierre Laval's Brains Trust when Laval returned to power in 1935.

Charles Dawes Chicago businessman-banker and musician. Led US negotiations over German reparations in 1924, garnering him the Nobel Peace Prize in 1925. Vice president of the United States 1925–1929. Head of the Reconstruction Finance Corporation in 1932. Involved in the emergency rescue of Central Republic Trust ("the Dawes Bank") in 1932.

Jean-Luc Dehaene Belgian politician (Christian Democratic Party). Born in 1940 to Belgian parents in Montpellier, France, to which his family fled ahead of German troops. Advocate of European integration. Prime minister of Belgium 1992–1999, culminating when the euro was created.

Edward DeMarco American economist and public official. Bankruptcy conservator for Fannie Mae and Freddie Mac 2009–2014, in which capacity he opposed policy initiatives to provide homeowners with principal reduction.

François de Wendel   French industrialist. Regent (board member) of the Bank of France, who threatened resignation over falsification of the central bank's balance sheet in 1925.

Jamie Dimon   American banker. Graduate of Tufts and Harvard Universities. Chairman, President, and CEO of JPMorgan Chase from the mid-2000s. Key player in the 2008 rescue of Bear Stearns.

Christopher Dodd   US senator (Democrat, Connecticut) 1981–2011. Chaired the Senate Banking, Housing, and Urban Affairs Committee when postcrisis financial reform was legislated. Received mortgages on his personal properties from Countrywide Financial.

William Donaldson   twenty-seventh chairman of the US Securities and Exchange Commission, 2003–2005, on whose watch little derivatives regulation took place.

William Donovan   attorney and intelligence officer. Head of the US Office of Strategic Services during World War II, when he collaborated with Cornelius Vander Starr of AIG.

Lewis Douglas   American politician. Member of US House of Representatives (Democrat, Arizona) 1927–1933. Director of Bureau of the Budget in the Roosevelt administration, in which capacity he was an advocate of the gold standard and fiscal responsibility.

Gaston Doumergue   French politician. Member of the Radical (Liberal-Centrist) party, prime minister 1913–14 and 1934, when his conservative unity government failed to make headway on the Great Depression.

Mario Draghi   Italian economist and public official. Employee of Goldman Sachs and the Italian Treasury. Governor of the Bank of Italy from 2006. President of the European Central Bank from 2011.

David Drumm   CEO of Anglo-Irish Bank at the time of its rescue; stepped down in December 2008. Filed for bankruptcy in 2010.

Billy Durant   auto industry pioneer. President of General Motors 1916–1920. Stock market speculator and organizer of investor pools in the 1920s.

Marriner Eccles   businessman-banker who helped draft the 1935 Banking Act. Chairman of the Federal Reserve Board 1934–1948.

Dwight Eisenhower   served under General Douglas MacArthur when US troops were used to clear the Bonus Army of unemployed veterans from Anacostia in 1932. Thirty-fourth president of the United States, 1953–1961.

Rahm Emanuel American politician (Democrat). Political advisor and White House chief of staff to President Barack Obama 2009–10. Mayor of Chicago from 2011.

Otto Ender Austrian politician (Christian Socialist). Chancellor of Austria 1930–31 during the Creditanstalt crisis.

Eugene Fama economist, Nobel laureate (2013), and University of Chicago professor. Father of the efficient-markets view of finance.

Andrew Fenwick scion of British department store family. Non-executive director of Northern Rock in 2008.

Joschka Fischer German politician (Green Party) active in the 1960s student movement. Vice chancellor and foreign minister of Germany 1998–2005. Advocate of European integration and critic of Chancellor Angela Merkel's handling of the crisis.

Irving Fisher economist, Yale University professor, and informal advisor to FDR. Known for his theory of debt deflation and "permanently high plateau" characterization of the stock market in 1929.

Richard Fisher American financier, consultant, and government official. President of the Federal Reserve Bank of Dallas from 2005, known for outspoken anti-inflationary views.

Seán FitzPatrick Irish banker-businessman who served as CEO and then chairman of Anglo-Irish Bank 1996–2008. Resigned in late 2008 amid allegations of hidden loans to his personal accounts.

Henry Flagler American industrialist, property developer, and founder of Standard Oil Company. Developed the Florida East Coast Railway and promoted the cities of Miami and Palm Beach at the turn of the twentieth century.

Pierre-Étienne Flandin conservative French politician (Democratic Republican Alliance). Prime minister (1934–35) of a government that failed to effectively counter the Great Depression.

Edsel Ford son of Henry Ford. President of Ford Motor Co. 1919–1943. Director and majority investor in the Union Guardian Group of banks, which failed following refusal of Reconstruction Finance Corporation assistance in 1933.

Henry Ford auto industry pioneer with stakes in Detroit-area financial institutions that failed in 1933.

Barney Frank outspoken member of the US House of Representatives (Democrat, Massachusetts), 1981–2013. Cosponsor of the Dodd-Frank Wall Street Reform and Consumer Protection Act of 2010.

Felix Frankfurter disciple of Supreme Court Justice Louis Brandeis. Liberal-progressive professor at Harvard Law School, whose students went on to direct FDR's New Deal. Associate justice of the US Supreme Court 1939–1962.

Milton Friedman economist, University of Chicago professor, Nobel laureate (1976). Known for his stable money growth rule and *Monetary History of the United States*, coauthored with Anna Schwartz.

A. P. Frierson banker and president of the Knoxville Clearing House Association at the time of the 1930 banking crisis.

Eigo Fukai Japanese businessman-banker. Aide to Korekiyo Takahashi when the latter arranged Japan's 1904–05 war loan. Deputy governor (1928–1935) and governor (1935–1937) of the Bank of Japan. Japanese delegate to the 1933 World Economic Conference.

Richard Fuld American businessman-banker. Served as CEO and then chairman of Lehman Brothers from 1994 to its demise in 2008.

Timothy Geithner career civil servant who served as deputy assistant, senior deputy assistant, and assistant secretary of treasury for international affairs in the Clinton administration, working with Robert Rubin and Lawrence Summers. President of the Federal Reserve Bank of New York 2003–2009. Seventy-fifth secretary of the Treasury 2009–2013.

Gary Gensler American banker and public official. Goldman Sachs partner. Undersecretary and assistant secretary of treasury in the Clinton administration 1999–2001. Eleventh chairman of the US Commodity Futures Trading Commission 2009–2014.

John Gialdini associate of Clarence Hatry, involved in the fraudulent activities surrounding Hatry's attempt to acquire United Steel Companies in 1929. Arrested, tried, and convicted in Italy.

Claude-Joseph Gignoux French economist and newspaper editor. Member of Pierre Laval's Brains Trust when Laval returned to power in 1935.

S. Parker Gilbert American lawyer, banker, and politician. Appointed agent-general for reparations in 1924, succeeding Owen Young. Associate of J. P. Morgan after the position of agent-general was abolished in 1930.

Hannes Hólmsteinn Gissurarson political scientist, University of Iceland professor, and member of Mont Pelerin Society. Fisheries specialist who advocated transforming Iceland into a financial center.

Carter Glass secretary of the treasury under Woodrow Wilson 1918–1920. US senator (Democrat, Virginia) 1920–1946. Chairman of the Appropriations

Committee 1933–1946 and cosponsor of the Glass-Steagall Act liberalizing the gold standard (1932), and the Glass-Steagall Act separating commercial and investment banking (1933).

Phil Gramm American economist and politician. US senator (Republican, Texas) 1982–2002. As chairman of the Senate Committee on Banking, Housing, and Urban Affairs, cosponsored the Gramm-Leach-Bliley Act of 1999, which removed the last remaining elements of Glass-Steagall.

Hank Greenberg head of American International Group from 1962 to 2005, when he resigned amid charges of fraudulent business practices, later dropped. Went on to sue the US government over the terms of the 2008 AIG bailout and its treatment of shareholders.

Alan Greenspan economist and government official. Chairman of the Board of Governors of the Federal Reserve System 1987–2005.

Ragnar Grímsson Icelandic politician (People's Alliance). President of Iceland from 1996.

Ricardo Gualino Italian industrialist and financier. Made his fortune in the rayon industry after World War I. Associated with the French banker Albert Oustric, whose affairs collapsed in 1930.

Geir Haarde Icelandic politician (Independence Party). Prime minister 2006–2009. Convicted of one count of gross negligence for not holding cabinet meetings during the 2008 crisis.

Peter Haig-Thomas partner of English financial speculators Gerald Lee Bevin and Clarence Hatry. Rowed for Cambridge in 1902 and became rowing coach at Cambridge and Oxford.

Mohammed Bin Kalifa Bin Hamad Al Thani sixth son of former emir of Qatar. Captain of the country's equestrian team. Involved in controversial private share transactions with Iceland's Kaupthing (in Icelandic: Kaupþing) Bank in 2008.

Osachi Hamaguchi Japanese politician (Minseitō Party). Prime minister 1929–1931 of a government that returned Japan to the gold standard and followed orthodox economic policies.

George Harrison Second governor of the Federal Reserve Bank of New York 1928–1941, succeeding Benjamin Strong.

Clarence Hatry English businessman-investor whose holdings collapsed in 1929.

Rudolph Havenstein German attorney and government official. President of the Reichsbank during the hyperinflation of 1922–23.

Willis Hawley   member of the US House of Representatives (Republican, Oregon), 1907–1933. Cosponsored the Smoot-Hawley Tariff bill in 1929–30.

Ralph Hawtrey   British economist, trade cycle theorist, and government official. Served in a succession of posts in H. M. Treasury from 1904 to 1945.

Eli Heckscher   Swedish economist and economic historian. Professor at the Stockholm School of Economics 1909–1945. Known for his contributions to the theory of international trade.

Édouard Herriot   French politician. Member of the Radical (Liberal-Centrist) Party, associated with the so-called Cartel des Gauches. Three times prime minister 1924–25, 1926, and 1932–33.

Adolph Hitler   chancellor of Germany 1933–1945.

Herbert Hoover   thirty-first president of the United States 1929–1933.

Harry Hopkins   executive director of New York State's Temporary Emergency Relief Administration under Governor Franklin Roosevelt. An architect of the New Deal, he supervised the Works Progress Administration, among other programs. FDR's personal emissary to Winston Churchill and Josef Stalin during World War II.

Henry Hollis Horton   American politician (Democrat). Governor of Tennessee 1927–1933. Caught up in the scandal surrounding the collapse of Caldwell & Co. and failure of the Bank of Tennessee in 1930. Did not run for reelection in 1932.

Cordell Hull   US politician and government official (Democrat). Secretary of state in the Roosevelt Administration 1933–1944. Advocate of free trade and the gold standard. Head of US delegation to the 1933 World Economic Conference.

Bruno Iksil   known as the London Whale for his positions as a trader in the London office of JPMorgan Chase, resulting in $2 billion in losses in 2012.

Junnosuke Inoue   Japanese businessman-banker who served as governor of the Bank of Japan 1919–1923 and 1927–28. Assassinated in 1932 in the "League of Blood" incident.

Samuel Insull   British-born businessman who rose from Thomas Edison's personal assistant to controlling the electricity supply of Greater Chicago. Bankruptcy of his companies precipitated the collapse of Central Republic Trust (the "Dawes Bank") in 1932.

Tsuyoshi Inukai   Japanese politician (Seiyūkai Party), prime minister 1931–32. Among his acts was appointing Korekiyo Takahashi as finance minister.

Assassinated by junior naval officers in the May 15, 1932, incident launched by the remnants of the "League of Blood."

Jesse Jones son of a Tennessee tobacco farmer, who rose from managing a lumberyard to create a banking, newspaper, and real estate development empire. Appointed board member (1932) and chairman (1933) of the Reconstruction Finance Corporation. Close advisor to FDR.

Konstantinos Karamanlis Greek politician (New Democracy Party). Prime minister 2004–2009. The large budget deficits that precipitated the Greek crisis occurred on his watch.

Ted Kaufman US senator (Democrat, Delaware), appointed to fill the seat vacated by Vice President Joe Biden in 2009. Critic of "too big to fail" and financial market manipulation. Did not run for office in 2010.

Enda Kenny Irish politician (Fine Gael Party). Taoiseach (head of government) starting in 2011.

John Maynard Keynes British economist, public figure, sometime civil servant. Influential for advocacy of deficit spending in a slump.

Mervyn King British economist. Following a variety of academic posts, served as chief economist, director, deputy governor, and governor (2003–2013) of the Bank of England.

Helmut Kohl German politician (German Democratic Union). Chancellor of Germany 1982–1998. Proponent of European integration and the euro as a quid pro quo for German reunification.

Donald Kohn economist. Longtime staff member at the Federal Reserve Board. Member of the board of governors starting in 2002 and vice chair 2006–2010.

David Komansky CEO of Merrill Lynch 1996–2002. Lobbied to eliminate the Glass-Steagall Act in the 1990s.

Ivar Kreuger Swedish business magnate who secured safety-match monopolies in return for government financing. Collapse of his empire in 1931 threatened the stability of the Swedish banking system. Died in 1932 under mysterious circumstances.

Paul Krugman economist, Nobel laureate (2008), professor at Princeton University at the time of the financial crisis. Advocate of bank nationalization in 2009.

Robert La Follette, Jr. US senator (Republican, Wisconsin) 1925–1947. Advocate of bank nationalization in 1933. Supporter of New Deal legislation.

Jeffrey Lacker economist. President of the Federal Reserve Bank of Richmond from 2004. Known for anti-inflationary views.

Christine Lagarde French antitrust lawyer, business consultant, and public official. Finance minister in the government of Nicolas Sarkozy 2007–2011. Managing director of the International Monetary Fund, succeeding Dominique Strauss-Kahn, from 2011.

Thomas Lamont American banker. Partner in J. P. Morgan & Co. from 1911. Member of the American delegation to the 1919 Paris Peace Conference. Influenced foreign financial diplomacy in the 1920s and 1930s as advisor to Presidents Wilson, Hoover, and Roosevelt.

Alf Landon American politician (Republican). Twenty-sixth governor of Kansas, 1933–1937. Republican nominee for the presidency in 1936, a race he lost to FDR.

Pierre Laval French politician (Independent) and newspaper owner. Four times prime minister 1931–32, 1935–36, 1940, 1942–1944. Issued decree laws in pursuit of austerity in the Depression. Tried and executed for collaboration after World War II.

Luke Lea American politician and newspaper publisher. US senator (Democrat, Tennessee), 1911–1917. Founder and editor of the *Nashville Tennessean*. Convicted for his role in the 1930 collapse of Caldwell & Co. and its associated banks.

Herbert Lehman American banker and politician (Democrat). Partner in Lehman Brothers 1908–1929. Forty-fifth governor of the State of New York 1933–1942, in which capacity he declared the state's 1933 bank holiday.

Carl Levin US senator (Democrat, Michigan) from 1979. Cochair of the Levin-Coburn US Senate Subcommittee, which investigated the 2008–09 financial crisis.

Ken Lewis CEO, president and chairman of Bank of America 2001–2009, during whose tenure the bank purchased Countrywide Financial and Merrill Lynch and sought emergency government assistance.

Edward Liddy CEO of Allstate Insurance 1994–1999 and president until 2005. Member of the board of Goldman Sachs. Chairman and CEO of American International Group 2008–09.

Maurice Lippens chairman of the Belgian-based financial conglomerate Fortis 1990–2008. On his watch the bank aggressively pursued acquisitions and invested in subprime-linked securities.

David Lloyd George British politician (Liberal). Prime minister 1918–1922. Represented Britain at the 1919 Versailles Peace Conference. Resisted France's reparations demands as excessive but was also criticized by Keynes for his anti-German stance.

David Loeb real estate developer and insurance professional who cofounded Countrywide Financial, for which he served as president and CEO 1969–2000.

Huey Long American politician. Fortieth governor of Louisiana from 1928 to 1932 and US senator (Democrat, Louisiana) from 1932 until his assassination in 1935. Populist firebrand who criticized the banks, favored wealth redistribution, and threatened to run against FDR in the forthcoming 1936 presidential campaign.

Hans Luther German politician. Reich minister of food and agriculture 1922–1925. Briefly chancellor in 1925–26. President of the Reichsbank 1930–1933, both preceded and succeeded by Hjalmar Schacht.

Douglas MacArthur American soldier-statesman who exceeded his orders when clearing the Bonus Army of World War I veterans from Anacostia in 1932.

Ramsay MacDonald British politician (Labour). Prime minister in the first Labour government (1929), second Labour government (1929–1931), and National government (1931–1935). His second Labour government grappled ineffectually with the Depression and lost most of its parliamentary seats to the Conservatives in the 1931 general election.

Bernard Madoff American businessman-financier who defrauded his investors in the boom period preceding the Great Recession. Arrested in December 2008. Pleaded guilty to eleven federal felonies in March 2009 and sentenced to 150 years in prison.

Wesley Manley operated Bankers Trust Company of Atlanta and the Anthony-Manley chain of more than sixty banks in Florida and Georgia. Implicated in the Florida land boom of the mid-1920s. Helped to finance George Merrick's Coral Gables project.

Guido Mantega Brazilian economist and politician (Workers Party). Finance minister from 2006. Complained starting in 2011 about the spillovers to his country of the Federal Reserve's quantitative easing and zero interest rate policy.

Bernard Marcus son of Joseph Marcus. Succeeded to the presidency of the Bank of United States in 1928, making him briefly the youngest bank president in the country.

Joseph Marcus American businessman-banker. Immigrated to the United States at the age of seventeen and worked in the apparel industry. Founded the Public Bank in 1906 and the Bank of United States in 1913.

John Wellborn Martin American politician (Democrat). Mayor of Jacksonville 1917–1923 and governor of Florida 1925–1929. Energetic real estate developer and promoter.

Árni Mathiessen Icelandic politician (Independence Party) with a background in veterinarian science and fish pathology. Minister of Fisheries 1999–2005 and prime minister 2005–2009 during the financial crisis.

George May British businessman and public servant. Lifetime employee of the Prudential Assurance Company, from which he retired in 1931. Chaired the Committee on National Expenditure that reported in 1931 on the need for budgetary economies.

John McCain US senator (Republican, Arizona) since 1987. Republican nominee for the presidency in 2008, a race he lost to Barack Obama.

James McDougal founding governor of the Federal Reserve Bank of Chicago, a position he held until 1934. Previously banker and bank examiner. Clashed with the New York Fed over interest rate and gold policies.

William McKinley twenty-fifth president of the United States 1897–1901.

Andrew Mellon banker, businessman, industrialist, and by the early 1920s one of the richest persons in the United States. Secretary of the treasury under Presidents Harding, Coolidge, and Hoover, 1921–1932. Known for policies of austerity and philosophy of liquidationism.

Angela Merkel German politician (Christian Democratic Union). Chancellor of Germany from 2005 and at the height of the euro crisis.

George Merrick son of Congregationalist minister and plantation owner. Florida real estate promoter in the 1920s. Developer of Coral Gables.

Robert Merton economist, MIT and Harvard professor, Nobel laureate (1997), and pioneer in the pricing of options and derivatives.

Eugene Meyer American businessman-financier. Head of the War Finance Corporation in World War I, chairman of the Federal Reserve Board, and head of the Reconstruction Finance Corporation 1930–1933. Went on to purchase the *Washington Post* and serve as first president of the World Bank.

Adolph Miller economist; professor at Cornell, Chicago, and Berkeley; and founding member of the Federal Reserve Board, on which he served until 1936.

Charles Miller American attorney and banker. President of the Reconstruction Finance Corporation in 1932, at the time of the RFC's loan to Central Republic.

Ogden Mills American financier and public official. Undersecretary of the treasury in the Coolidge and Hoover administrations 1927–1932 and treasury secretary under Hoover (1932–33). Fervent critic of the New Deal.

Charles Mitchell American banker. President and then chairman of National City Bank from 1921 until his resignation amid tax-evasion charges in 1933.

Addison Mizner society architect who pioneered Mediterranean and Spanish Colonial Revival styles in the 1920s. His Boca Raton, Florida, development went bankrupt in 1926.

Raymond Moley academician, professor of law at Columbia University, advisor to FDR. Claimed to have originated many of the ideas behind the New Deal.

Émile Moreau governor of the Bank of France 1926–1930. His policies were criticized for absorbing gold inflows and imparting a deflationary bias to the interwar world economy.

Clemént Moret French economist and civil servant. Deputy governor (1929–30) and governor of the Bank of France (1930–1935), who followed orthodox gold standard policies.

Jack Morgan American banker. Son of John Pierpont Morgan. Led J. P. Morgan and Co. following his father's death in 1913.

John Pierpont Morgan American financier-industrialist. His firm was known as J. P. Morgan & Co. from 1895. Played an important role in organizing the bankers' coalition that ended the 1907 financial crisis.

Henry Morgenthau American attorney and businessman. Friend and Hudson Valley neighbor of Franklin Roosevelt. Fifty-second secretary of the treasury 1934–1945.

Bubbi Morthens Icelandic pop singer who took large losses on his investments in Glitnir Bank in the 2008 crisis.

Angelo Mozilo American banker-businessman. Rose from modest roots to head Countrywide Financial, a leading US mortgage lender. Resigned in 2008 amid subprime-related losses. Accused of insider trading by the Securities and Exchange Commission. Reached a $67.5 million settlement in 2010.

Benito Mussolini Italian journalist, politician, and prime minister 1922–1943.

Michael Noonan Irish politician (Fine Gael Party). Minister of finance from 2011, in which capacity he sought to renegotiate the government's guarantee of bank obligations.

Montagu Norman   British banker. Governor of the Bank of England 1920–1944.

George Norris   governor of the Federal Reserve Bank of Philadelphia 1920–1936. Previously served as a director of the bank and as commissioner of the Federal Farm Loan Board.

Barack Obama   forty-fourth president of the United States from 2009.

David Obey   American politician. Member of US House of Representatives (Democrat, Wisconsin) 1969–2011. Chair of the House Appropriations Committee when the Obama stimulus package was passed.

Davið Oddsson   Icelandic politician (Independence Party) and member of the group of libertarian thinkers who gained office in the early 1990s. Long-serving prime minister 1991–2004. Governor of the Central Bank of Iceland 2005–2009.

Bertil Ohlin   Swedish economist, professor at the Stockholm School of Economics 1929–1965. Known for debates with Keynes over German reparations, contributions to the theory of international trade, and advocacy of deficit spending in the Depression.

Peter Orszag   economist in the Clinton White House (1995–1998) and President Obama's director of office of management and budget (2009–10), where he was a voice for fiscal consolidation. Left the Obama administration for Citigroup.

Stefan Ortseifen   CEO of IKB (the Bank for German Industry Obligations) 2004–2007. Dismissed in July 2007 over the bank's subprime-related losses. Indicted in 2009 and found guilty of market manipulation in 2010, making him the first German to be convicted on subprime-related charges.

George Osborne   British politician (Conservative Party). Graduate of University of Oxford with a degree in modern history. Chancellor of the Exchequer in the coalition government of David Cameron from 2010.

Albert Oustric   French businessman-financier who made his fortune from stock flotations, mergers, and acquisitions in the 1920s. Failure of his Banque Adam brought down the French government and led to his conviction for fraud and embezzlement.

George Papaconstantinou   Greek economist with degrees from New York University and the London School of Economics. Finance minister in the government of George Papandreou 2009–2011.

George Papandreou   Greek politician (Panhellenic Socialist Movement, or PASOK). Prime minister 2009–2011 who inherited the Greek debt crisis.

George Patton   served under General Douglas MacArthur when US troops were used to clear the Bonus Army of unemployed veterans from Anacostia in 1932. Commanded the Third and Seventh US Armies during World War II.

Ron Paul   American politician. Member of US House of Representatives (Republican, Texas) 1997–2013. Libertarian spokesperson and author. Critic of the Federal Reserve System.

Henry Paulet   English landowner, soldier, and sportsman. Sixteenth Marquess of Winchester, who became embroiled in the Hatry Scandal in 1929. Declared bankruptcy in 1930 and lived out his life in Monte Carlo.

Henry Paulson   American financier and public official. CEO of Goldman Sachs 1999–2006, where he worked since 1974. Seventy-fourth US secretary of the treasury in the administration of George W. Bush 2006–2009.

John Paulson   merger and acquisitions specialist at Bear Stearns who went on to found a hedge fund specializing in distressed debt. Famously placed big bets against the US housing market starting in 2006.

Ferdinand Pecora   American attorney and jurist. Chief assistant district attorney for New York 1922–1929. Chief counsel to the US Senate Committee on Banking and Currency, which investigated Wall Street practices in 1933.

Peter Peterson   secretary of commerce under President Richard Nixon, 1972–73. Chairman and CEO of Lehman Brothers 1973–1984, and cofounder of the Blackstone private equity group. Campaigner and political contributor to the cause of budget balance.

Harvey Pitt   twenty-sixth chairman of the US Securities and Exchange Commission, 2001–2003. The Enron derivatives scandal occurred on his watch.

Key Pittman   US senator (Democrat, Nevada) 1913–1940. As chairman of the Committee on Foreign Relations, he was a member of the US delegation to the 1933 World Economic Conference.

Raymond Poincaré   French politician (Democratic Republican Alliance). Three times prime minister 1912–13, 1922–1924, 1926–1929, among whose accomplishments was the 1926 stabilization of the franc.

Karl Polanyi   economist and economic historian of Hungarian origin who taught in the UK and United States. His *The Great Transformation* (1944) made the case for a managed capitalism reflecting social and cultural values.

Charles Ponzi   Italian-American financier and Florida property promoter, notorious in the 1920s for his pyramid (or Ponzi) schemes.

William Potter   president of Guaranty Trust Company of New York, who sought to mobilize popular and financial support for the stock market following the Great Crash in 1929.

Charles Prince CEO (from 2003) and chairman (from 2006) of Citigroup, succeeding Sanford Weill. Resigned in November 2007 amid the firm's subprime-related losses.

Romano Prodi Italian academician, economist, and politician. Prime minister 1996–1998 and 2006–2008. President of the European Commission 1999–2004.

Josef Pröll Austrian politician (Austrian People's Party). Vice chancellor and finance minister 2008–2011.

Seward Prosser president and chairman of Bankers Trust Company of New York, who sought to marshal sentiment and financial support for the stock market following the Great Crash of 1929.

Baudouin Prot French banker and civil servant. CEO of BNP Paribas from 2003, including in 2009, when the losses of the firm's two subprime-heavy hedge funds were announced.

George Provopoulos Greek economist. Professor at the University of Athens. Governor of the Bank of Greece 2008–2014.

Franklin Delano Raines American banker-financier and public official. Worked in the Nixon and Carter White Houses. General partner in the investment firm Lazard Frères 1980–1991. Directed US Office of Management and Budget 1996–1998. CEO of Fannie Mae 1999–2004. Resigned in 2004 amid alleged accounting irregularities.

Mariano Rajoy Spanish politician (People's Party). Prime minister of Spain from late 2011.

Basil Ramsey president of the Knoxville-based Holston-Union National Bank and Holston Trust Company, implicated in the 1930 banking crisis. Indicted for using state highway funds to pay off other debts.

Sam Rayburn American politician. Member of US House of Representatives (Democrat, Texas) 1913–1961. Three times speaker of the house 1940–1947, 1949–1953, 1955–1961.

Ronald Reagan fortieth president of the United States 1981–1989.

John Reed chairman and CEO of Citigroup at the time of its merger with Travelers Group in 1998.

Olli Rehn Finnish politician (Centre Party). European commissioner for economic and monetary affairs 2010–2014.

Paul Reynaud French lawyer, statistician, finance minister. As member of the Chamber of Deputies, was a voice for currency devaluation and reflation in 1934.

David Ricardo   British political economist 1772–1823. Financial speculator, economic theorist, and Member of Parliament.

Matthew Ridley   journalist, libertarian philosopher, and popular science writer who chaired the board of Northern Rock in 2008.

Charles Rist   French economist, professor of economics and law in Montpellier and Paris, known for his writings on gold and deflation. Deputy governor of the Bank of France from 1926, who attended the Long Island meeting of central bankers in 1927.

Georges Robineau   attorney, journalist, and bank inspector. Childhood friend of Raymond Poincaré. Governor of the Bank of France 1920–1926.

James Harvey Rogers   economist, professor at Yale University, and monetary advisor to FDR. Critic of the gold standard and advocate of controlled inflation.

Will Rogers   American humorist and social commentator. Engaged in a nationwide lecture tour, much of it traveling by air, in the 1920s.

Christina Romer   economist; professor at the University of California, Berkeley; student of the Great Depression; chair of President Barack Obama's Council of Economic Advisors 2009–10.

Mitt Romney   American businessman and politician (Republican). Nominee for the presidency in 2012, a race he lost to Barack Obama.

Franklin Delano Roosevelt   thirty-second president of the United States 1933–1945.

Nouriel Roubini   economist and professor at New York University, who pointed to the possibility of a dollar crash before the subprime crisis and Great Recession.

Robert Rubin   Goldman Sachs partner. Director of the National Economic Council (1993–1995) and secretary of the treasury (1995–1999) in the Clinton administration. Left the administration to join the board of Citigroup in 1999.

Jacques Rueff   French economist and Bank of France official. Free market advocate and member of the Mont Pelerin Society. Proponent of the gold standard and European integration.

Paul Ryan   American politician. Graduate of Miami University of Ohio, where he majored in economics and political science. Member of the US House of Representatives (Republican, Wisconsin) from 1999. Ranking member of the House Budget Committee from 2007 and chairman from 2011.

Frederic Sackett American attorney and businessman. US senator (Republican, Kentucky) 1925–1930 and US ambassador to Germany 1930–1933.

Paul Samuelson economist, professor at MIT, Nobel laureate (1970), and economic and financial theorist.

Nicolas Sarkozy French politician. Leader of the French Union for a Popular Movement (UMP). President of France 2007–2012.

Robert Schmidt German politician (Social Democrat), journalist, and piano maker who served as economics minister in 1921–22.

Eric Schneiderman American attorney and public official. Sixty-fifth attorney general of New York starting in 2011, in which capacity he sued JPMorgan Chase over securities fraudulently sold to investors by the Bear Stearns units it acquired in 2008.

Gerhard Schröder German politician (Social Democrat). Chancellor of Germany 1998–2005. Known for his colorful youth and labor market reforms.

Alan Schwartz last chairman and CEO of Bear Stearns, a firm where he worked since 1976.

Anna Schwartz economist. Coauthor with Milton Friedman of *Monetary History of the United States*, which powerfully shaped modern views of the Great Depression.

Robert Shiller economist, professor at Yale University, Nobel laureate (2013), and historian of property and financial markets. Famously pointed to the possible existence of a housing bubble before 2007.

Allen Sinai economist with Data Resources 1971–1983, Lehman Brothers 1983–1996, and Decision Economics (which he founded) from 1996.

Saul Singer Russian-American garment worker; president of the Cloak, Suit, and Shirt Manufacturers' Protective Association; entrepreneur and real estate developer. Executive vice president of Bank of United States, which failed in the banking crisis of 1930.

Alfred P. Sloan electrical engineer and business executive who led General Motors from 1923 to his retirement as chairman in 1956.

Reed Smoot US senator (Republican, Utah) 1903–1933. Cosponsored what became the Smoot-Hawley Tariff Act of 1930. Defeated for reelection in 1932.

Gene Sperling attorney, Democratic Party operative, public official. Director of the National Economic Council under President Bill Clinton 1996–2001 and President Barack Obama 2011–2014. Helped negotiate the Gramm-Leach-Bliley Act abolishing the Glass-Steagall Act in 1999.

Eliot Spitzer attorney, public official, and political commentator. New York State attorney general 1999–2006, who used the 1921 Martin Act to pursue financial-industry investigations.

Jürgen Stark German economist. Member of the Executive Board of the European Central Bank 2006–2011. Resigned over opposition to the ECB's crisis-management policies.

Cornelius Vander Starr founder of American Asiatic Underwriters, the firm that became AIG.

Henry Steagall member of US House of Representatives (Democrat, Alabama) 1915–1943. Chairman of the House Banking Committee and cosponsor of the two Glass-Steagall Acts that relaxed gold standard collateral requirements (1932) and separated commercial banking from investment banking (1933).

Joseph Stiglitz economist, professor at Columbia University, and Nobel laureate (2001). Advocate of bank nationalization in 2009.

Henry Stimson American attorney and public official. Secretary of state in the administration of Herbert Hoover 1929–1933. Secretary of war during World Wars I and II.

Hugo Stinnes German businessman-industrialist with interests in the Rhineland and Westphalia, newspaper publisher, and politician. Elected to the Reichstag in 1920, in which he served as a voice for German industry.

Dominique Strauss-Kahn French economist, lawyer, and politician (Socialist Party). Professor of economics at Sciences-Po and Minister of Economy and Finance in the government of Lionel Jospin 1997–1999. Managing director of the International Monetary Fund 2007–2011, until his resignation amid allegations of sexual assault.

Benjamin Strong vice president of Bankers Trust Company of New York at the time of the 1907 financial crisis. Involved in drafting the Aldrich Plan, which helped to shape the Federal Reserve System. Founding governor of the Federal Reserve Bank of New York, an office he held until his death in 1928.

Lawrence Summers economist. Professor and president of Harvard University. Deputy secretary (1995–1999) and secretary (1999–2001) of the treasury in the Clinton administration (1995–1999). Director of the National Economic Council in the Obama Administration (2009–10).

David Swenson economist, graduate of Yale University and manager of the university's endowment. Pioneer of alternative investment strategies.

Korekiyo Takahashi   Japanese official who arranged the loans that financed Japan's 1904–05 war with Russia. Five times finance minister, including in 1931 following Japan's departure from the gold standard, when he pursued aggressively expansionary policies.

Jean-Claude Tannery   governor of the Bank of France 1935–36. Removed owing to his association with policies of deflation when the government of Léon Blum took office in 1936.

André Tardieu   French newspaper editor and politician (Center-Right Democratic-Republican Alliance). Three times prime minister 1929–30, 1930, and 1932. His 1930 government was brought down by the Oustric banking scandal.

Frederick Winslow Taylor   American mechanical engineer who pioneered scientific-management practices in the late nineteenth and early twentieth centuries.

John Taylor   economist, professor at Stanford University, official in the George W. Bush administration 2001–2005. Known for his Taylor Rule for interest rate setting by central banks.

Margaret Thatcher   British politician (Conservative Party). As prime minister 1979–1990, famous for her free-market orientation and policies of financial deregulation.

Elmer Thomas   US senator (Democrat, Oklahoma) 1927–1951. Advocate of silver coinage and reflation during the Great Depression. His Thomas Amendment to the bill that became the Agricultural Adjustment Act of 1933 empowered the president to reduce the gold content of the dollar by up to 50 percent.

Patrick Toomey   American politician. Currency trader for Chemical Bank and Morgan, Grenfell & Co. Member of US House of Representatives (Republican, Pennsylvania) 1999–2005 and US Senate (from 2011). Member of the twelve-person "Supercommittee" on Deficit Reduction appointed in 2011.

Fabrice Tourre   Goldman Sachs trader involved in the Abacus deal. Sued for securities fraud by the Securities and Exchange Commission in 2010.

Melvyn Traylor   president of the First National Trust and Savings Bank of Chicago at the time of the Central Republic Trust crisis of 1932. Member of the US delegation to the 1930 conference establishing the Bank for International Settlements.

Jean-Claude Trichet   French civil servant and European Union official. Governor of the Bank of France (1993–2003) and president of the European Central Bank (2003–2011).

Harry Truman   thirty-third president of the United States 1945–1953.

Rexford Tugwell agricultural economist, professor at Columbia University, and founding member of FDR's Brains Trust. Advocate of economic planning. Involved in New Deal initiatives such as the Agricultural Adjustment Administration.

Arthur Vandenberg US senator (Republican, Michigan) 1928–1951. Steadfast opponent of the New Deal.

Frank Vanderlip American banker and public official. Assistant secretary of the treasury 1897–1901, when he helped negotiate a $200 million loan to the federal government from National City Bank. Vice president and president of National City Bank, precursor of Citibank, 1909–1919. Involved in drafting the Aldrich Plan, which shaped the Federal Reserve System.

Chris Van Hollen member, House of Representatives (Democrat, Maryland), since 2003. From 2010 ranking Democratic member of the House Budget Committee. Member of the twelve-person "Supercommittee" on Deficit Reduction appointed in 2011.

Herman Verwilst Belgian economist, banker, and politician. Interim CEO of Fortis, the Belgian-based financial conglomerate, in 2008.

Gérard Vissering Dutch banker. Head of De Nederlandsche Bank (the Dutch Central Bank), 1912–1931. Blamed for the losses incurred by the central bank as a result of sterling's depreciation, leading to his resignation.

Paul Volcker American public servant. Chairman of the Federal Reserve Board 1979–1987, who opposed weakening the Glass-Steagall Act. His proposal to limit proprietary trading by banks was embraced by President Obama following the 2008–09 financial crisis.

Paul von Hindenburg German soldier-statesman. President of Germany 1925–1934, who appointed Hitler to the chancellorship in 1933.

Robert Wagner US senator (Democrat, New York) 1927–1949. Supporter of New Deal and advocate of labor rights.

Henry A. Wallace farmer, hybrid seed developer, and FDR's first secretary of agriculture (1933–1940). Went on to serve as vice president (1941–1945) and commerce secretary (1945–46) before running as Progressive Party candidate for president in 1948.

James Warburg American banker. Son of Paul Warburg. Financial advisor to FDR. Member of the US delegation to the 1933 World Economic Conference. Eventually a vocal opponent of the New Deal.

Paul Warburg German-American financier. Involved in drafting the Aldrich Plan, which helped to shape the Federal Reserve Act. Member and then vice governor of the Federal Reserve Board 1914–1918.

Elizabeth Warren Harvard University professor of law, crusader for consumer financial rights, US senator (Democrat, Massachusetts) from 2013.

George Warren agricultural economist, professor at Cornell University, and advisor to New York State Governor Franklin Roosevelt. Advocated policies to raise the commodity price level by increasing the price of gold at the outset of the Roosevelt Administration.

Sanford Weill American banker-financier. CEO of Travelers Group and then Citicorp from 1995 to 2003. Helped to engineer the merger of Citigroup and Travelers Insurance Group. Tireless advocate of removing the last vestiges of the Glass-Steagall Act.

Knut Wicksell Swedish economist, professor of law and economics at Lund University 1889–1926, and advisor to the Swedish government. Argued that price stability should be privileged over exchange rate stability.

Albert Wiggin American banker. President of Chase National Bank from 1911 and chairman from 1918. Pecora Commission hearings revealed that he short-sold his shares in the bank in 1929.

Robert Willumstad Citigroup executive who worked with Sanford Weill to engineer Citigroup-Travelers Insurance merger in 1998. Chairman (from 2006) and CEO (from June 2008) of American International Group. His resignation was a condition of the AIG rescue.

M. L. Wilson agricultural economist, professor at Montana State College, then assistant and undersecretary of agriculture 1937–1940. Known for his allotment plan to limit agricultural production in the 1920s.

Woodrow Wilson twenty-eighth president of the United States 1913–1921.

William Woodin businessman-industrialist, musician, and coin collector. Director of the Federal Reserve Bank of New York 1927–1932. Associated with Republican Party but contributor to Franklin Roosevelt's 1932 presidential campaign. Secretary of the Treasury 1933.

Janet Yellen American economist; professor at the University of California, Berkeley; and vice chair (2010–2014) and chair (from 2014) of the Federal Reserve Board.

Owen D. Young American attorney and businessman. Chairman of General Electric Corp., involved in the Dawes and Young Plan restructurings of German reparations in 1924 and 1929, director and then chairman of the Federal Reserve Bank of New York 1923–1940.

ACKNOWLEDGMENTS

THE FIRST TIME I lectured at UC Berkeley on the Great Depression was on October 19, 1987. As those whose memories extend back that far will recall, this was before the World Wide Web. Since it was my first semester at Cal, the morning was spent fine-tuning the lecture, or more precisely the overheads, which focused on the Great Crash of 1929. As we exited the classroom, my new colleague and co-instructor Jan deVries commented, "Nice lecture. Did you hear that the Dow Jones fell by 508 points today?" At 1987 metrics, that was 23 percent, making it the largest one-day decline in stock market history, a record that still stands (one hesitates to write). October 28, 1929, one of the subjects of my lecture, now came in as a distant second, at 13 percent.

What followed—quick and ample provision of liquidity by a Federal Reserve headed by a brand-new chairman named Alan Greenspan—succeeded in averting a serious recession, and indeed prevented an economic slowdown of any magnitude. This appeared to confirm a central tenet of my lecture, namely that anything remotely resembling the Great Depression was no longer possible thanks to the lessons drawn from that earlier historical episode by the likes of Chairman Greenspan. Nor was anything resembling the Great Depression possible owing to other changes to the economy in the course of the twentieth century, such as the shift from relatively volatile manufacturing industry to a stabler service sector, the growth of government and its automatic fiscal stabilizers, and of course advances in financial management.

The Great Recession of 2008–09 is an overdue reminder that this conventional wisdom, taught to generations of students, was both right and wrong. It was right in the sense that central bankers had indeed learned lessons from history about how to respond to financial distress, enabling them to prevent a recession following the stock market crash in 1987. But it was wrong in that other changes to the economy had not, in fact, removed the risk of Great Depression–like event, whose causes entailed much more than the ups and downs of the stock market. It overlooked how financial markets and institutions responded to earlier changes in financial regulation. It neglected how investors adapted to the long period of economic stability engineered by, among others, that selfsame Alan Greenspan. It paid no heed to the possibility that, emergency injections of liquidity into financial markets notwithstanding, policy makers might take other steps that heightened the risk of a catastrophic economic and financial event. Most important, it neglected the primacy of politics, overlooking the tendency to take key decisions on the basis of political considerations rather than economic logic—a lesson of the Great Depression that, no doubt, will now be better remembered. The experience of the intervening period convinced us, collectively, that the Great Depression should be thought of as history. Recent experience is a reminder that this history is very much alive.

It is also a history that, again for better or worse, I have been writing for many years. The treatment here differs from that in my 1992 book by focusing equally on the United States and Europe, the advanced economies on which the Great Depression and even more the recent crisis centered, whereas that earlier book concentrated mainly on Europe. It differs by highlighting individuals as well as institutions as carriers of ideas and makers of policy. It differs most obviously by emphasizing the parallels, and where appropriate the differences, between 1929–1933 and 2008–09, and by explaining how distilled wisdom about the Great Depression shaped perceptions and responses to the Great Recession, and, equally, how the experience of the Great Recession will reshape how we think about the Great Depression.

Producing a book is a collective effort, as every author knows, and I am deeply grateful to all those who contributed to the production of this one. My thinking owes much to the Berkeley colleagues with whom I have co-taught that graduate class in economic history in the course of many years: Jan deVries, Christina Romer, and Brad DeLong. It owes much to colleagues with whom I have written on aspects of the Great Depression: Olivier Accominotti, Muge Adalet, Miguel Almuna, Michael Bordo, Alec Cairncross, Marc Flandreau, Richard Grossman, Tim Hatton, Doug Irwin, Kris Mitchener, Kevin O'Rourke, Richard Portes, Gisela Rua, Jeffrey Sachs, Peter Temin, and Charles Wyplosz. Certain of these collaborations go back more than thirty-five years, while others are so recent as to be not yet published. Some of these authors have gone on to bigger and better things, while others remain stuck, as I do, in the Great Depression. All of them have profoundly influenced my thinking.

For comments on portions of the manuscript and help with sources, I am grateful to Alan Blinder, Paul Blustein, Sigrun Davíðsdóttir, Sebastian Edwards, Price Fishback, Mariko Hatase, Hilmar Hilmarsson, Philip Lane, Ashoka Mody, Kenneth Mouré, Kevin O'Rourke, Jonathan Portes, Richard Portes, Jonathan Rose, Kenneth Snowden, Shinji Takagi, and Eugene White. If the Great Depression and the 2008–09 crisis had a positive aspect, it was in creating this dedicated band of scholars preoccupied by the two periods and the questions they raise. In Berkeley, Erik Johnson provided indispensable help by checking names, dates, facts, and figures and, most important, challenging my interpretations; all remaining problems, to be clear, are mine, not his or anyone else's. My editors promised me an exceptional copy editor, and in Thomas Finnegan they delivered. Again at Berkeley, the invaluable Cheryl Applewood helped further with editing while keeping my office running and my sanity more or less intact.

I have benefited greatly from substantive and stylistic guidance from my unparalleled editor at Oxford University Press, Dave McBride, and my equally unparalleled agent, Andrew Wylie. This is not the first time the three of us have worked together, nor, hopefully, will it be the last.

This one, too, is for Michelle.

Berkeley
April 2014

NOTES

Introduction

1. The Basel Accord was negotiated by the Basel Committee on Banking Supervision. Made up of representatives of the central banks and financial regulators of leading countries, its secretariat is housed at the Bank for International Settlements in Basel, Switzerland. The first accord, "Basel I," dated from 1988, the second, "Basel II," from 2004.

2. This concern was reinforced by the terminology, which encouraged the notion that morality or ethics was involved. As Dembe and Boden (2000) explain, the eighteenth-century mathematicians who helped originate the term in fact used "moral" to mean subjective or intuitive, not virtuous or upright.

3. This was the conclusion made famous by Reinhart and Rogoff (2009a).

4. The cuts in question were to be implemented over ten years.

5. In the case of a permanent increase in deficit spending, households reduce their spending one for one. The literature refers to these as models of "Ricardian Equivalence" (in which government deficits and surpluses and private-sector surpluses and deficits are equivalent and offsetting), an idea that goes back to the late eighteenth and early nineteenth century political economist David Ricardo.

6. In a Ricardian model, a permanent increase in government spending will be offset by a commensurate increase in taxes over time and a one-for-one reduction in private spending, as noted above. But a temporary increase in government spending will require a smaller increase in taxes in each period to service and retire the debt and therefore a less-than-one-for-one reduction in private spending when the stimulus takes place.

7. This was the view of the so-called Ordoliberal School, which developed after World War II (Dullien and Guérot 2012).

8. See Reinhart and Rogoff (2009b). Eventually, other studies, like that of the International Monetary Fund, cast doubt on the existence of this threshold (see Pescatori, Sandri, and Simon 2014).

9. See Alesina and Ardagna (2010). The IMF responded with a critique of the generality of these findings as well (IMF 2010).

10. Agreement was then reached in December 2013 to create a single resolution mechanism. But this was again half a loaf: the EU agreed that it would continue to rely on national resolution authorities for an interim period and fully fund its resolution mechanism only after a transition lasting as long as ten years.

Chapter 1

1. The background to the exposé is described by Harris (2010).

2. This time Ponzi attempted to escape by faking suicide and boarding an Italian freighter, on which he worked as a waiter and dishwasher. Unable to resist describing his exploits, he revealed himself and was arrested when the ship docked in New Orleans. Despite appealing to President Calvin Coolidge and Italian Prime Minister Benito Mussolini, Ponzi was extradited to Massachusetts to serve out his term. On release in 1934 he was deported to Italy. Ponzi died in Brazil after moving there to work for a local airline and allegedly becoming involved in a smuggling ring.

3. Klein (2001), p. 89.

4. "And today the dredge is the national emblem of Florida," Rogers (1925, p. 88) went on to conclude.

5. Interest rates plural because each Reserve bank set its own discount rate, subject to the approval of the Federal Reserve Board (more on this below).

6. So Strong testified to the House Committee on Banking and Currency in 1926. U.S. House of Representatives, Committee on Banking and Currency, "Stabilization," Hearings, 69th Congress, 1st Session, on H.R. 7895 (Washington, D.C., 1927), p. 507.

7. Annual Report of the Federal Reserve Board for 1925, pp. 288–89. Or, as Charles Evans Hughes, President Harding's secretary of state, put it, "The prosperity of the United States largely depends on the economic settlements which may be made in Europe." Cited in Pusey (1951), p. 579.

8. The passage quoted is from a memo he wrote in early 1925, cited in Clarke (1967), p. 74.

9. Wells (1933), pp. 85–86. Among the other things Wells got right was the advent of Wikipedia (as one can learn from the entry on *The Shape of Things to Come* on Wikipedia).

10. Strong also teamed up with a syndicate of banks headed by J. P. Morgan & Co. to extend a $300 million line of credit to the Bank of England and the British government. The Federal Reserve provided $200 million to the Bank

of England, while the J. P. Morgan–headed syndicate lent $100 million to the British government.

11. See Moggridge (1969), pp. 71–75.
12. Clarke (1967), pp. 76–77.
13. Norris (1937), pp. 202–3.
14. On Miller and the real-bills doctrine, see Timberlake (2005, 2008) and Wells (2004).
15. Wueschner (1999), p. xiv.
16. Ibid., p. 27.
17. Parks (2006), p. 23.
18. The amendment had the additional effect of exempting state-chartered banks from corporate profit taxes—a provision that further helps to explain how it ended up on the ballot (Vickers 1994).
19. As the boom gained momentum, anxious property developers, perhaps predictably, accepted smaller and smaller down payments.
20. Developers like Carl Fisher providing financing directly to purchasers might on occasion accept a down payment of, say, 25 percent. As time went on, there were further exceptions; see the discussion of building and loan associations below.
21. Redford (1970), p. 151.
22. Simpson (1933), p. 164.
23. The difference between a B&L and a mutual savings bank was that members in a B&L subscribed shares rather than making deposits. Members accumulated shares by making weekly or monthly installment payments equivalent to the amount they expected to require to finance their homes and took turns borrowing; at least this was the principle, if not always the practice (Rose and Snowden 2013).
24. The regulated mortgage lending sector in the 1920s was relatively small: it was made up of mutual savings banks, state commercial banks, and national banks that had been given authority to lend on real estate only as of 1913.
25. Thus, although B&Ls were not subject to runs, they could still be rendered insolvent by widespread defaults on share installment contracts, as happened in the 1930s.
26. In the words of Snowden and James (2001, p. 5), "Many B&Ls were run as part-time businesses out of second-floor offices—most often as appendages of the real estate or insurance business of their managing officer."
27. As the boom developed and banks grew concerned about default risk, building and loans stepped into the breach, offering both first and second mortgages themselves. These paired mortgages were known as split loans, a terminology and practice that would come back to haunt the housing market after an interval of eighty years.
28. Title and mortgage guarantee companies were required by New York State law (New York State being where many of them were headquartered) to hold a reserve fund against this contingency, but the minimum reserve was set as

a share of capital and surplus, not as a share of bond obligations outstanding (White 2013).

29. This is the conclusion of the study of the market by Goetzmann and Newman (2010).

30. The boom in Detroit was yet another reflection of the importance to the decade of the automobile. Again, Florida was not left out; popular magazines like *The Atlantic Monthly* published advertisements from bond houses such as the Filer-Cleveland Co. offering individual investors bonds yielding a coupon of 8 percent, a very high level for the time, backed by first mortgages on income-paying commercial real estate in Miami.

31. The quote is from George (1986), p. 34. Flagler Street was named for Henry Flagler, of Standard Oil fame, who had been a prime mover in building Florida's railways and, not incidentally, extending them to Miami.

32. That many residents were recent arrivals probably helps to account for their failure to make adequate preparations and for the resulting fatalities.

33. The enforceability of these measures is another matter. On the effectiveness of blue-sky laws in this period, see Chapter 16.

34. Sessa (1961), pp. 41–43.

35. These figures are for the period between March and December 1926.

36. Chain banking, in which a single set of owners acquires several banks as a way of circumventing laws prohibiting branch banking, figures importantly in the 1930 banking crisis and therefore in Chapter 8. As described by Vickers (1994), the Manley-Anthony chain had lent heavily not just for Merrick's Coral Gables project but also for the even more ambitious Boca Raton development of the Ponzi-like Addison Mizner. There are indications that the chain was insolvent even before the real estate bust, owing to insider loans to Manley's and Anthony's auto dealerships and other enterprises, but it stayed in business as a result of the forbearance of the regulators, which finally became impossible with the real estate decline. Following the collapse of the property boom, Mizner's development corporation was taken over by the Central Equities Corporation of Chicago, owned by Vice President Charles Dawes and his brothers. Central Equities stripped the development corporation and its principal lender, the Palm Beach National Bank, of their assets before turning them over to the custody of the bankruptcy court. The same Charles Dawes features in the financial rehabilitation of Europe starting in 1924 and the Chicago banking crisis of 1932 (Chapters 3 and 10, respectively).

37. On the policy of direct pressure, see Chapter 3.

Chapter 2

1. Brooks (1969), pp. 65–66.

2. Consistent with this observation, Galbraith (1954), following Allen (1931), dates the inception of the bubble as March 1928.

3. Technically, control of General Motors passed to Pierre du Pont, yet another MIT graduate, but du Pont quickly appointed Sloan as his right-hand man.

4. Sloan's public relations offensive is described by Marchand (1991).

5. For more on the Dawes Plan, see Chapter 3.

6. The protocol finalizing the reparations bill was signed in 1921. This and related figures in the text are based on calculations in Webb (1988).

7. This was the "transfer problem" over whose solution Keynes and Bertil Ohlin jousted in the 1920s (Keynes 1929, Ohlin 1929).

8. Lloyd George (1932), p. 67.

9. Subsequent accounts affirm this impression of Poincaré as "cold, distant, unemotional" (Wright, 1942, p. 24) but portray the man and his policies as less stridently anti-German. One story has it that Lloyd George had only himself to blame for Poincaré's return to power in January 1922, explaining why he was so bitter about the fact. The British prime minister had treated his sitting French counterpart, Aristide Briand, to a round of golf. This evidence that he was on friendly terms with a British leader who favored compromise on reparations was enough for Briand to be recalled to Paris and replaced by Poincaré (Keiger 1997).

10. Specifically, it announced that it would no longer accept the emergency currency known as "Notgeld" that large businesses paid their workers when they experienced shortages of money. It was one of the ironies of the hyperinflation that the central bank could not keep pace with the demand for money, forcing large enterprises to pay their workers in private money. This was the Notgeld that the Reichsbank now refused to discount.

11. Hawtrey (1962), p. 3.

12. This with inflation measured at an annualized rate. Wholesale price inflation, which reflected the sharp drop in the franc exchange rate, rose to a catastrophic 80-plus percent.

13. The French authorities also used the foreign credits to "squeeze the bears," buying francs and pushing up their value in an attempt to inflict losses on speculators who had sold the franc forward. Whether these operations in fact drove the speculators out of the market or merely had psychological implications is uncertain.

14. And in keeping with the affinity for music of interwar politicians (see Charles Dawes and William Woodin, in Chapters 3 and 15 below), he was also a biographer of Beethoven.

15. This is the conclusion of Blancheton (2012) on the basis of his close reading of the archival evidence.

16. Mouré (2002), p. 106.

17. The classic reference in this context is Sargent and Wallace (1981).

18. See Chapter 26.

19. Moreau (1991), p. 225.

20. Smith (1916), pp. 197, 201.

21. Miller (1935), p. 449.

Chapter 3

1. Lewis (1938), p. 336.
2. Britain's wartime denials to the contrary, munitions were indeed present, as described by Mullaly (2009).
3. The Dawes Brothers and their financial endeavors have already made an appearance in connection with the Florida land boom; see Chapter 1.
4. Timmons (1953), p. 218.
5. The knowledge that any further reduction in the burden of reparations overall would automatically elicit calls from the Europeans for a commensurate reduction in the burden of war debts owed the United States further inclined them in this direction.
6. This was the same strategy used by the lead US negotiator, William Rhodes, when defaulted Latin American debts were restructured in the 1980s and 1990s. See Rhodes (2011).
7. Costigliola (1976), p. 595.
8. In addition, private loans under the Dawes Plan were effectively senior to reparations payments. They enjoyed what was known as "transfer protection," or first call on the limited foreign exchange reserves of the Reichsbank. This encouraged foreign investors to buy German bonds and, even more, German policy makers to encourage German corporations and municipalities to issue them, as a way of minimizing actual reparations payments and strengthening their case for renegotiation. See Ritschl (2013).
9. Note that 1926 was a more difficult year for placing foreign bonds in the United States, what with turbulent financial conditions in France and the coal strike in Britain (see Chapter 2).
10. Flandreau, Gaillard, and Panizza (2010) show that the riskiness of a loan and its probability of default were less a function of whether it was underwritten by an investment or commercial bank than of what they refer to as the "prestige" of the institution—that is, how concerned the underwriter was with the maintenance of its reputation, as captured by how long it had been in existence and its capitalization.
11. Winkler (1933), p. 87.
12. Lewis (1938), p. 377.
13. Cited in ibid., p. 380.
14. Many of these dubious practices came to light as a result of the hearings of the Pecora Commission, which sensationally investigated 1920s financial excesses in 1993 (Chapter 16).
15. White (1990b), p. 147.
16. Shades of collateralized debt obligations being repackaged into yet other collateralized obligations in the period leading up to 2008. See Chapter 5.
17. Einzig (1931), p. 53.
18. Costigliola (1976), p. 495.

19. This was one reason Schacht stepped up his conversion of sterling balances into gold, his hope being that doing so might put pressure on the Bank of England to raise interest rates and divert capital flows in its direction.

20. Gilbert's memorandum is reproduced in *Hearings*, p. 25.

21. This raised the number in operation by half.

22. Klein (2001), p. 147.

23. Bank credit had risen by 8 percent in 1927, when loans on stocks and bonds were the most rapidly growing component of lending. Meltzer (2003), p. 228.

24. This is the so-called leverage cycle of which John Geanakoplos, inspired by the recent crisis, has written (2010).

25. This he eventually did six months later (see Chapter 7).

26. Miller (1935), p. 453.

27. In addition, the New York bank's priorities may have also been affected by the fact that George Harrison replaced Benjamin Strong as head of the bank in late 1928. Strong had repeatedly warned that any attempt to rein in stock market speculation by raising rates might damage the economy (Friedman and Schwartz 1963, p. 254 et seq.). But in 1929 he was no longer present to invest this view with his authority.

28. For example, in late 2013 the Reserve Bank of New Zealand, which is both the country's central bank and its macroprudential regulator, imposed a cap on loan-to-value ratios to cool off the stock market. One of the concerns about the effectiveness of the measure was the extent to which nonbank credit would be substituted for bank credit to the mortgage market. See Reserve Bank of New Zealand (2013).

29. Friedman and Schwartz (1963), p. 266, similarly dismiss the policy of direct pressure as a failure, but they are unclear about what the Fed should have done instead, since they too are critical of the impact on the economy of raising interest rates in mid-1929.

Chapter 4

1. Loeb initially provided underwriting services for the partnership from New York but moved to Southern California once the firm took off.

2. This authorization was provided by the Emergency Home Finance Act of 1970.

3. For more on the regulatory response to the financial crisis of the 1930s see Chapter 15.

4. The contemporary perception was that excessive competition for funds on the part of commercial banks had driven up the cost of attracting demand deposits and encouraged the banks to engage in risky investments, contributing to the banking crisis. In addition, Regulation Q was seen as a means of enabling community banks to compete for deposits and lend to their local communities (Gilbert 1986).

5. More on whom below.

6. Weber (2008), p. B5.

7. This occurred starting in 1966.

8. See Reagan's "Remarks on Signing the Garn–St. Germain Depository Institutions Act of 1982" (October 15), http://www.reagan.utexas.edu/archives/speeches/1982/101582b.htm.

9. That the S&L industry had already been plunged into crisis by the combination of high interest rates and soft housing prices gave the commercial banks little relief. Thrifts responded to their distress by gambling for redemption—and plunging even more aggressively into commercial banking activities.

10. These trends are described by Wilmarth (2002).

11. Weill and Kraushaar (2006), p. 364.

12. Weill and Kraushaar (2006), pp. 265–66.

13. The wooden slab is described in Brooker (2010). Weill's mea culpa is reported in the *Wall Street Journal*'s "Heard on the Street" column (July 26, 2012, p. C12). This is not to argue that the abolition of Glass-Steagall caused the financial crisis. But neither can its role be entirely dismissed, as attempted by Sorkin (2012). The point is that the progressive weakening and elimination of the Glass-Steagall restrictions was part, and in turn indicative, of a broader process in whose absence the financial crisis cannot be understood.

14. In the Irish case, this was partly offshore banking: foreign banks funneled their lending to other countries through their Irish subsidiaries in order to take advantage of the favorable tax treatment extended them by the Irish Republic. Be this as it may, the ratio of bank claims to GDP was nearly as high in Belgium, the Netherlands, and a number of other European countries.

15. The Cypriot case is special in that many liabilities were to large extra-EU depositors, notably Russian oligarchs, rather than Northern European banks. But this does not change the fact that Cyprus became the poster child for an overleveraged and undercapitalized banking system.

16. Whether there was actual evidence supporting the contention that large, diversified banks were more efficient and delivered lower-cost services to their customers is a separate issue. Skeptical contemporary analyses included Rhodes (1994), Pilloff (1996), Peristiani (1997), and DeLong (1998).

17. For more on this argument, see Barth, Brumbaugh, and Wilcox (2000).

18. Suarez and Kolodny (2011), p. 79.

19. This is documented by Philippon (2008).

20. As they did in the upswing beginning in 2001, a point documented using individual bank data by Kalemli-Ozcan, Sorensen, and Yesiltas (2012).

21. Ibid., figure 4. See below on the regulatory changes that facilitated these developments.

22. "Realizing those losses" is another way of saying "mark its assets to market." Following the Enron scandal, which came to light in 2001, financial as well as nonfinancial firms were increasingly required, notably under the provisions of the Sarbanes-Oxley Act of 2002, to mark to market.

23. This is the explanation of Gorton and Souleles (2007) for why, in bad times, sponsoring banks bring their SPVs back onto their balance sheets.

24. It was exactly this mechanism that had launched Enron, which relied heavily on SPVs, on its death spiral in 2001. But this did not slow the spread of the practice.

25. Morgenson and Rosner (2001) argue that the answer to this question is capture: that the banks wanted it this way, and the Federal Reserve as regulator did their bidding. The alternative hypothesis is ignorance.

26. See ISDA (2010).

27. For details see Ranciere and Tornell (2009), figure 1. More precisely, their figure compares private domestic nonfinancial-sector mortgage debt with private domestic nonfinancial-sector nonmortgage debt.

28. Data are from Shiller (2006), as updated and available online at http://www.econ.yale.edu/~shiller/data.htm.

29. New home construction responded predictably: starts of single-family units rose nationally from the customary 1.2 million new units per year to more than 1.7 million units in 2005.

Chapter 5

1. Details in this paragraph are from Mian and Sufi (2009).

2. Brian Clarkson, co-chief operating officer of Moody's Investor Service, in charge of global structured finance and US public finance, acknowledged as much in a 2004 internal email: "To put it bluntly, the issuer could take its business elsewhere unless the rating agency provides a higher rating." Quoted in Tabbi (2013). Becker and Milbourn (2011) consider a "natural experiment": the entry of a third rating agency, Fitch, in competition with Moody's and Standard & Poor's. They show that this increased the scope for ratings shopping and resulted in less informative, more inflated ratings.

3. "Watch out / Housing market went softer / Cooling down / Strong market is now much weaker / Subprime is boiling over / Bringing down the house." Even George Merrick (Chapter 1) could have done better.

4. US Department of Justice (2013), pp. 73–74, 78.

5. More arguments to this effect are found in Bolton, Freixas, and Shapiro (2012).

6. Those nonbank lenders were disproportionately the source of subprime loans that subsequently lapsed into default. This is documented by Dagher and Fu (2012).

7. That Countrywide eventually experienced financial difficulties as a result of subprime loans that went bad and became a takeover target for Bank of America did not make its earlier operations any less profitable for Mozilo personally. Legal action, however, did. In 2009 Mozilo was accused by the SEC of insider trading and securities fraud for having talked up the stock—disguising underlying problems with the company—while selling shares. In 2010 he settled with the SEC, agreeing to $67.5 million in fines, $20 million of which was paid by Countrywide as provided for by his employment contract.

8. The report was published by the center in February (Center for Responsible Lending 2008).

9. See Jacobson (2009). In 2012 Jacobson filed suit against Wells Fargo, alleging that the bank had sought retribution by returning her loan payments and foreclosing on her home.

10. Jacobson's affidavit accused Wells Fargo employees of doing the same. The practice evidently changed in late 2006, when the housing and mortgage industry came under closer scrutiny (Morgenson 2007).

11. These margins are described in internal firm documents reported by Morgenson (2007). Washington Mutual, another leader in the subprime business, similarly estimated that subprime loans and option ARMs were six to ten times as profitable as traditional mortgage products (Bair 2012, p. 76).

12. See Federal Reserve Board (2009).

13. Freddie's initial mandate was to create a secondary mortgage market, which in practice meant purchasing mortgages in California, guaranteeing them, and reselling them to banks in other states as a way of circumventing existing restrictions on cross-state banking and thereby accommodating the Golden State's rapid growth.

14. In Angelides (2011).

15. In addition to purchasing securitizations, Fannie and Freddie could purchase mortgages outright. They continued to do so, but at rates that did nothing to change the picture of their declining importance to the mortgage market after 2003.

16. In 2006 the Office of Federal Housing Enterprise Oversight sued Raines to recover a portion of the bonuses he had received that were based on the overstated earnings. Civil charges were filed against Raines and two other former Fannie executives. These were settled in 2008, with Raines and the other executives agreeing to repay a portion of the payments they had received.

17. On a monthly average basis, the Fed funds rate fell from 6.4 percent in December 2000 to 1.8 percent in December 2001.

18. See, for example, Bernanke (2000).

19. The quotation in the text is from Bernanke (2002a).

20. FOMC Meeting Transcript (November 2002), p. 83, http://www.federalreserve. gov/monetarypolicy/files/FOMC20021106meeting.pdf.

21. This was something that Bernanke himself knew perfectly well, having served on the NBER's Business Cycle Dating Committee from mid-2000 until his appointment to the board of governors in 2002.

22. Dokko et al. (2011), figure 3.

23. See Taylor (2007). There are as many ways of operationalizing the Taylor Rule as there are of measuring inflation and the output gap. Taylor's own retrospective estimates generated a larger gap between actual and warranted policy rates than many of the alternatives. Bernanke's own 2010 estimates, using the data available at the time, point to a smaller discrepancy.

24. This being the conclusion of the Taylor article cited in the preceding note.

25. The staff study in question, with the allusion to "housing-specific shocks," was Dokko et al. (2011).

26. A good statement of the view is Kohn (2009).

27. The overall conclusion of empirical analyses of this question was that good policy was mainly responsible for the moderation of inflation, but that good luck had more to do with the moderation of output fluctuations. See Stock and Watson (2003).

28. Figures here are from the Federal Reserve Bank of St. Louis (Federal Reserve Economic Data website).

29. Rates on conventional mortgages fell from 6.3 to 5.6 percent; http://research. stlouisfed.org/fred2/data/GS10.txt.

30. This quoting from Greenspan's rebuttal (2009) to Taylor's indictment that loose Fed policy in 2003–05 had caused the housing bubble.

31. It is not right to put the onus for global imbalances entirely on Asia. As noted above, oil exporters like Saudi Arabia, benefiting from strong Chinese growth and high petroleum prices, also ran large external surpluses and recycled their savings in the US treasury market. Germany similarly ran growing current account surpluses as the period progressed.

32. This according to the economists Nouriel Roubini and Brad Setser in papers circulated in the fall of 2004. Subsequent estimates tended to be smaller but pointed in the same direction. The speech that made the term "global savings glut" famous was Bernanke (2005).

Chapter 6

1. Figures vary, depending on how they are constructed. Those here are based on annual averages of the S&P/Case Shiller National Composite Index (US) and the European Central Bank Index (existing dwellings for both Ireland and Spain).

2. Although Spain, starting out far behind, made a notable effort to catch up starting in 2005.

3. The precedent for the latter was the European Coal and Steel Community, established in 1951, which applied multilateral oversight to Germany's coal and steel industries, and out of which the European Economic Community subsequently grew.

4. Both cited in Szaz (1999), p. 216.

5. The importance of fiscal transfers for the smooth operation of a monetary union goes back to the work of Peter Kenen (1969). The need for banking union to accompany monetary union was perhaps less widely understood, even in the 1990s, given that the cross-border penetration of European banks was still in its early stages. But less widely understood does not mean that the case was unappreciated; see inter alia Eichengreen (1993).

6. Cited in the *Guardian* (January 12), http://www.theguardian.com/world/1999/ jan/13/martinwalker.

7. For a sampling of such arguments from political science, see McKay (1996) and Jones (2002).

8. This between 1994 and 1998, when the decision on founding membership was taken.

9. In addition to the fact that EU policy was made by consensus, the key country for the monetary union, Germany, marginally violated the Maastricht criterion limiting its debt to 60 percent of GDP in 1997 and 1998, when the decision was taken. If the criterion was going to be waived for Germany, even slightly, then it was correspondingly harder to enforce for other countries.

10. See Story, Thomas, and Schwartz (2010) for details.

11. Yields on Irish government bonds had also been higher than those on German *bunds*, although not that much higher, courtesy of the country's Celtic Tiger status.

12. Given how widely these beliefs were embraced by money managers and how quickly interest rates converged across the Eurozone, it is worth recalling the skepticism of economists that market participants would respond in this way. Bishop (1992) anticipated that market participants would strongly differentiate among potential borrowers according to their debt loads and consequent creditworthiness. Buiter, Corsetti, and Roubini (1993) similarly predicted that large default risk premia would continue to distinguish Europe's high-debt countries.

13. The ECB further encouraged the convergence of interest rates by applying the same haircuts, or discounts, to "repos" of the government securities of euro-area countries. That is, it applied an identical discount to the securities of governments when accepting these as collateral in repurchase operations conducted with commercial banks. This in turn encouraged the banks to invest equally in the securities of, say, Greece and Germany because they could be "repoed" at the same price at the ECB, driving the prices of initially cheaper Greek bonds up to the German level. The associated dangers were pointed to early on by Buiter and Sibert (2005). In practice the ECB repoed mainly very-short-term obligations (including ten-year bonds about to mature). Thus, this mechanism cannot be the entire explanation for why there was such strong convergence in the interest rates on the entire spectrum of government bonds.

14. Quantitatively Ireland was less strongly affected, although the qualitative phenomenon was the same.

15. Those reforms increased the incentive to work, and thus for the unions to bargain for relatively modest increases in wage payments, by combining unemployment assistance and welfare payments and placing a cap on the combination.

16. This is documented in Lane and Pels (2012).

17. Be that as it may, these pressures were all part of the same process. Germany may not have competed directly with Southern European countries that specialized in the production of consumer goods, but it ramped up its exports of capital goods to China, whose producers used them to increase their capacity to export consumer goods to Europe. The impact on distressed Southern European producers was the same.

18. The larger the capital inflow, the larger the cumulative increase in real property prices, and the greater the rise in construction activity, as documented by Obstfeld and Rogoff (2010).

19. Here *capital* refers to the sum of tier 1 capital (shareholders' equity) and tier 2 capital (other "equity like" capital such as undisclosed reserves, provisions, hybrid instruments, and subordinated debt).

20. This on the eve of the crisis.

21. Vendor finance being when a company lends money so that the borrower can buy the vendor's products or property.

22. The "banking glut" idea is developed by Shin (2012).

23. See, for example, Saurina (2009).

Chapter 7

1. Curcio (2000), p. 452.

2. Klein (2001), p. 181.

3. *New York Times* (October 6, 1929, p. N11).

4. *New York Times* (October 28, 1929, p. 1).

5. In a letter published on October 26 in the *New York Times*.

6. *Wall Street Journal* (November 23, 1929, p. 2).

7. Klein (2001), p. 209.

8. In both 1926 and 1928, August was the peak month for motor vehicles; 1927 was different, owing to Henry Ford's suspension of production in order to retool for the Model A (see Chapter 1).

9. They put the peak in textiles in July and the peak in paper in September. By their calculations the peak for automobiles and transport equipment actually came earlier, in February. Burns and Mitchell (1946), p. 69.

10. Cited in Friedman and Schwartz (1963), p. 264.

11. Norman was loath to admit as much, for example in his testimony before the Macmillan Committee, to which he testified in March 1930, but his motivation was evident between the lines. Norman's remarks, heavily edited, were published in 1931 (Committee on Finance and Industry 1931).

12. Lee Bevan and Haig-Thomas had the University of Cambridge in common. Haig-Thomas came from a well-to-do family of coal mine owners and was best known for having rowed for Cambridge in 1902. He went on to be a successful if controversial rowing coach first at Cambridge and then at Oxford.

13. Bevan left prison in 1928 and moved to Havana in order to remain beyond the reach of the ever-attentive British press. Among other things, he shared with George Merrick a taste for poetry, publishing ("on commission," that is, through personal subvention) a book of verse in 1929. A recent biography that tells Bevan's story is Vander Weyer (2011).

14. Quoted in *The Economist* (April 5, 1924, p. 733). Jute Industries did not go on to pay a dividend, and its shares performed poorly. It did, however, survive

into the post–World War II years. Not so British Glass Industries. To create it, Hatry amalgamated a large number of firms producing lightbulbs, lamp glass used for scientific and industrial purposes, and crystal tableware. He financed the construction of two large glass factories as a way of forcing smaller firms into the amalgam. Within two years the company was in financial difficulty. By 1926 it had failed and its assets were sold off to a third party. As *The Economist* (September 28, 1929, p. 576) put it after the 1929 scandal, Hatry "was a pioneer of rationalization in its most irrational form."

15. Of "Ricardian equivalence" fame—see the Introduction, note 5.

16. Manley (1976), p. 56.

17. The Bank of United States episode is described in Chapter 8, the failure of Banque Adam in Chapter 9, and the Icelandic crisis in Chapter 14.

18. After two years of hard labor, Hatry was transferred to Maidstone Prison in Kent, where he became prison librarian (succeeding, among others, Bevan in the position). Freed in 1939, he rented an office near Fleet Street and built a thriving business advising booksellers. In the course of World War II, he acquired bookstores, a printing company, a publishing house, and two magazines and soon was bidding for Wyman & Sons, one of Britain's largest bookselling chains. In the end these ventures were unsuccessful as well, and Hatry spent the 1950s operating Hatchards, a well-known London bookshop, and a series of West End coffee bars. The Marquess of Winchester, for his part, was declared bankrupt and spent the rest of his life in Monte Carlo.

19. The total financial "deficiency" was several times greater, reflecting also the intragroup liabilities of Hatry's various companies.

20. *Wall Street Journal* (January 15, 1930), p. 15.

21. Chandler (1990), p. 329.

22. Quoted in Friedman and Schwartz (1963), p. 339. Data on security purchases are from the *Federal Reserve Bulletin*.

23. *New York Times* (October 26, 1929), p. 16.

24. Meltzer (2003), p. 288.

Chapter 8

1. This according to the board of governors' series, adjusted for the season. Subsequent efforts to reconstruct the national income accounts on a quarterly basis (Balke and Gordon 1986) show real GDP as falling at an alarming 20 percent annual rate in the final three months of the year.

2. The 2008–09 crisis similarly featured a sharp fall in global trade and saw dispute over whether the main cause was anticipations of weak final demand or financial disruptions.

3. In the latter case this was due not just to weak demand but also to a record harvest.

4. This was the diagnosis of the clinicians at the *Economist* (May 31, 1930, p. 1205).

5. The board of governors also authorized the New York bank to purchase $50 million of government securities.

6. "The State of Trade at Home and Abroad," *Economist Monthly Supplement* (May 31, 1930, p. 33).

7. In other countries the decline was more limited, but movement was in the same direction. The fall in industrial production December over December was 11 percent in Canada, 8 percent in Sweden, and 7 percent in France. In the UK, where the Board of Trade constructed industrial production figures quarterly, the 1929Q4–1930Q4 decline was 13 percent.

8. "Events abroad" refers to those occurring in Germany, which are considered below.

9. They were falling, in other words, at a 14 percent annual clip. It could be argued that wholesale prices, which were heavily affected by conditions in distressed commodity markets, were not necessarily the best measure of underlying price level trends. But finished goods prices were falling as well, at a 10 percent annual rate.

10. Hamilton (1992), table 7. Cecchetti (1992), using time series on prices and interest rates to construct a forecasting model, similarly concludes that investors looking forward three to six months would have anticipated deflation by late 1930 and also quite possibly already by late 1929. Be that as it may, the members of the board of governors were not accustomed to distinguishing between real and nominal interest rates. Even if futures markets pointed to falling prices, this did not lead them to alter their conclusion that credit was cheap. In practice the governors referred all but exclusively to nominal interest rates. Meltzer (2003), p. 295.

11. Yields on high-grade bonds remained above 4.5 percent. The spread between AAA and Baa bonds widened further, an indication that firms with marginal credit were being rationed out of financial markets.

12. Miller's words are from his appearance before the US House of Representatives Committee on Banking and Currency (1928), http://www.scribd.com/doc/175280593/housta28.

13. Friedman and Schwartz (1963), p. 368.

14. In addition to the fact that the tariff did little to ameliorate farm problems, Hawley was burdened by being a "dry" while his primary opponent was a "wet" in this, the penultimate year of Prohibition.

15. By comparison, the Fordney-McCumber Tariff of 1922 had pushed up rates by thirteen points. Irwin (2011), pp. 105–7.

16. Ibid., p. 140.

17. *New York Times* (November 11, 1929, p. 2).

18. See Archibald and Feldman (1998).

19. As described in Carey (1999).

20. Quoted in Burner (2005), p. 298.

21. *New York Times* (November 22, 1929, p. 1).

22. All this is described by Hamilton (1985).

23. This is the conclusion of Temin (1976) and Wicker (1996), for example.

24. As described by McFerrin (1969), Caldwell included in his bond transactions a depository agreement that provided for maintaining the proceeds of bond sales at the Bank of Tennessee until they were required to meet construction costs.

25. See Chapter 1.

26. Lea was the great-grandson of a two-term congressman and US senator himself from 1911 to 1917. Horton had previously nominated the younger Lea to fill an open US Senate seat, which he declined, finding it more profitable to remain in real estate.

27. This point is documented further by Richardson and Troost (2009) and Jalil (2012).

28. The episode gave rise to an investigation by the Federal Reserve Board, which concluded that four members of the Atlanta party, including the deputy governor, had gotten drunk on the boat. The Atlanta Fed's own investigation concluded, to the contrary, that all members of the party had performed admirably. Ultimately the board's view prevailed, and the deputy governor tendered his resignation. See Gamble (1989), Richardson and Toorst (2009), and Jalil (2012).

29. *New York Times* (November 14, 1930, p. 19).

30. *Washington Post* (November 14, 1930, p. 2).

31. This is an interesting exception to Friedman and Schwartz's observation that the creation of the Federal Reserve System ruled out the earlier practice of suspending cash payments as a way of containing financial crises. As it happened, the Arkansas bank had no choice; it had the bad luck of being in the Federal Reserve District of St. Louis, and the St. Louis Fed was not inclined to help. See Richardson and Troost (2009).

32. *New York Times* (December 20, 1930, p. 1).

33. This according to Joseph H. Zweeres, the state bank examiner who reviewed Bank of United States in the summer of 1929. *New York Times* (June 5, 1932, p. 3).

34. Trescott (1992), pp. 391–92. Early intervention or not, New York State Superintendent of Banking Joseph A. Broderick was subsequently indicted by a grand jury for neglect of duty for not having taken appropriate steps to head off the Bank of United States failure. Eventually he was acquitted.

35. See Chapter 12.

36. This is suggested by Friedman and Schwartz (1963). See, however, O'Brien (1992) on the limitations of their evidence.

37. The condition of the Bank of United States turned out not as bad as feared. The receiver ended up paying creditors 84 cents on the dollar, not terrible by the standards of financial bankruptcy. This reflected the subsequent recovery of the bank's real estate holdings, the last of which were finally liquidated in 1944. Lehman Brothers' receiver should have done so well.

38. See Chapter 14.

Chapter 9

1. Details are from Bonin (1996).

2. A representative compendium of British commentary is Royal Institute of International Affairs (1931).

3. *New York Times* (July 10, 1931, p. 21).

4. The ECB did so by agreeing to buy bonds only on the secondary market, its statute prohibiting it from purchasing new primary issuance, and by buying the bonds only of countries that first agreed to a program with the EU's emergency rescue fund.

5. This refers to capital and reserves as of 1929, according to Adalet (2009), p. 8. Other data in this paragraph are similarly drawn from this paper. The fact that capital ratios did not recover to pre-inflation levels raises the question of why the banks didn't move faster to raise capital. Part of the explanation is that doing so was expensive, and competition among savings banks, mortgage banks, and universal banks caused them all to attempt to economize on costs, including those of capital.

6. At its peak in 1929, cash and balances on reserve at the central bank as a share of deposits was just 3.8 percent, barely half the pre–World War I level.

7. In 1930 an emergency loan was arranged through the good offices of the Boston-based investment bank Lee, Higginson & Co., with the help of the soon-to-be-notorious safety-match magnate Ivar Kreuger, but it was not repeated. Kreuger started as a civil engineer and co-manager of a construction company, Kreuger & Toll Byggnads AB, known for its innovative building techniques. Construction led him into finance and then, reflecting Sweden's timber resources, into production of safety matches. He purchased concessions from governments granting him national monopolies on the production and sale of matches, which he financed by securitizing the expected returns on future concessions. Kreuger's financial pyramid did not withstand the shock of the Great Depression. He was found dead in his flat in Paris in March 1932, triggering the Skandinaviska Kreditaktiebolaget crisis. A recent biography of Kreuger is Partnoy (2009). When Kreuger's empire collapsed in 1932, Lee, Higginson was stuck with the tab and never entirely recovered.

8. See Ferguson and Temin (2003).

9. This is the argument of Borchardt (1991).

10. More than 50 percent of joint-stock bank assets, to be precise. There were also a number of smaller private banks, whose assets are omitted from this calculation.

11. Even more so than in Germany; the Creditanstalt's own capital in 1925 was barely a fifth of the 1913 level, according to the calculations of Teichova (1994).

12. The expectation was not without basis: even before the crisis in the spring of 1931, the Austrian National Bank had set up a system, in conjunction with Rothschilds in London and a handful of other foreign banks, to

surreptitiously funnel low-cost funding to the Creditanstalt to help it manage its Bodencreditanstalt burden (Aguado 2001).

13. Schubert (1991), p. 12.

14. German banks were important creditors of the Creditanstalt and the other Austrian joint-stock banks. In addition, Austrian policy makers had doubted the economic viability of their small country ever since the Empire was dismantled after World War I and saw the customs union with Germany as a potential solution to this problem. They hoped that with completion of the customs union a stronger Germany might be inclined to provide foreign aid. The Germans for their part worried that Austria might instead form a customs union with the countries of southeast Europe that were previously part of its Empire, should Berlin not offer a better deal. On these and other motivations, see Mommsen and Forster (1998) and Orde (1980).

15. Between them, the government, the Austrian National Bank, the Postal Savings Bank, and various other public agencies now owned fully 50 percent of the bank (Schubert 1991, p. 10).

16. The impact on the central bank was even worse than revealed, as the Austrian National Bank, taking a leaf from the French, dressed its books to disguise the extent to which it had financed foreign withdrawals from the Creditanstalt. Aguado (2001), p. 212.

17. Schubert (1991), p. 15.

18. Hodson (1932), p. 211.

19. Schacht (1955), p. 173. Schacht had worked with Goldschmidt on the board of Danatbank and previously on the board of the Nationalbank für Deutschland during and after World War I.

20. This is the argument of Ferguson and Temin (2003) and Pontzen (2009).

21. Brüning himself had encouraged the idea in meetings with the US ambassador, Frederic Sackett. In addition, there was the fact that reparations had been given effective seniority over private debts as a result of the Young Plan (reversing the senior status that private debt enjoyed under the Dawes Plan). Hence the bankers, Thomas Lamont of J. P. Morgan for example, were already lobbying Hoover for a reparations moratorium.

22. On Meyer's involvement with the Reconstruction Finance Corporation, see Chapter 10.

23. Pusey (1974), p. 209.

24. Laval's complaint is in Warner (1968), p. 32; Hoover's response is in Burner (2005), p. 302. After three weeks of not-so-silent protest, the French government grudgingly accepted the moratorium proposal.

25. The most the chancellor was willing to offer was private reassurance that he would not seek funds for a third armored cruiser.

26. The bank was then put in trusteeship to permit orderly liquidation of its assets. Schacht, as onetime partner, was asked to head the committee of trustees but declined.

27. The Lahusen brothers were then arrested on July 17, after the banks reopened, and Nordwalle quickly declared bankruptcy. The de facto freeze on German payments to foreign creditors was officially recognized by the Standstill Agreement, negotiated at a July 20 meeting of officials in London and signed in September.

Chapter 10

1. On docking on his return, the governor reportedly had to wait for the drive back from Liverpool to London to receive a full briefing. His first day back at work was September 28, a week after sterling was devalued.
2. There was not even a symbolic increase in the discount rate after July 30. Previously the rate had been raised twice, once on July 23 and once a week later, each time by a percentage point.
3. Hawtrey (1938), p. 143.
4. In an untimely coincidence, the committee's report was issued in mid-July. See Committee on Finance and Industry (1931), especially appendices I and IV.
5. Accominotti (2012), p. 17. Whether or not this rendered them insolvent would depend on whether they were able eventually to recoup part of what they were owed.
6. In all, it bought some £30 million of bills to provide the markets with liquidity.
7. Investors who took this position ended up making 20 percent in two months. To the extent that they leveraged their bets, they made greater returns still.
8. Sullivan (1936), p. 1.
9. Federal Reserve Bank of New York (1932), p. 13.
10. Excepting the Atlanta and Minneapolis Reserve Banks, which were already maintaining higher rates than other banks in the system.
11. A comprehensive account of these events is Wicker (1996).
12. Friedman and Schwartz (1963), p. 382.
13. On Kreuger, see Chapter 9.
14. These notes were known as clearinghouse certificates because they were accepted by all members of the clearinghouse, the association through which banks settled, or cleared, payments with one another. Their role and the story of the 1907 crisis are described by Bruner and Carr (2007).
15. Barber (1985), p. 227.
16. To this end, the strong banks insisted that the NCC should value collateral at market—that is to say, fire-sale—prices, advance loans only up to 30 percent of that market value, and not accept real estate. Olson (1977), p. 29.
17. See Chapter 19.
18. Hoover had asked for even quicker action but did not take into account the Christmas recess.
19. This Glass-Steagall Act was different from the act of 1933 that separated commercial banking from investment banking (more on which below).

20. Insull was also able to borrow $2 million from the Owen Young–headed General Electric Corporation in 1931. Vickers (2011) provides a conspiratorial account of the Dawes-Young-Insull relationship and the problems of Central Republic, but, conspiracy or not, the close connection between the three men is undeniable.

21. Fifteen percent of its share capital and "surplus" (or unallocated funds), to be precise.

22. Vickers (2011), pp. 56–57.

23. When in October he was charged with embezzlement by a Cook County grand jury, Insull fled Paris for Milan and then leased a small plane in order to travel on to Greece, which conveniently did not have an extradition treaty with the United States. From there he traveled by ship to Istanbul. Although Turkey had not ratified an extradition treaty with the United States either, Turkish officials arrested Insull and turned him over to the US State Department, which returned him to America. Insull avoided conviction on criminal charges but was tied up in civil litigation until his death in 1938.

24. On the Bear Stearns rescue, see Chapter 12.

25. Although only a ten-day period was covered by the list of banks published on August 23, 1932, everyone knew that more publicity was coming, and indeed, subsequent lists were more extensive. All this is described by Butkiewicz (1995).

26. Kennedy (1973), pp. 84–85.

27. The threat is described in the account of the acting comptroller of the currency, Francis Gloyd Awalt (Awalt 1969, p. 352).

28. In a subsequent grand jury investigation of the Union Guardian affair, Couzens was accused of having withdrawn funds just in advance of the bank holiday, motivated by inside information, and contributing to the run. His biographer argues that the allegation was unfounded. Barnard (1958), pp. 277–78.

29. Lumley (2009), p. 85.

Chapter 11

1. Data from the National Association of Realtors' survey of 149 major markets put the peak at 2005Q4. Other home-price indices, from Case-Shiller and Zillow, place the peak a quarter or two later, but the basic story is the same.

2. Their tales are told by Zuckerman (2009) and Lewis (2010).

3. MacDonald and Robinson (2009), pp. 268–69.

4. Selling CDOs backed by mortgages that it had taken onto the balance sheet in prior deals had the further advantage of limiting Goldman's direct exposure to the housing market downturn. In the event, the firm had to work hard to market the resulting securities. The US Senate's Permanent Subcommittee on Investigations (2011) concluded that Goldman had misled investors to whom it marketed these securities by claiming that the firm's own interest in the

securities was aligned with theirs. The Department of Justice disagreed or at least did not have enough evidence for charges, opting in August 2012 not to prosecute Goldman and its employees. Goldman Sachs did, however, pay $550 million to settle a civil suit brought by the Securities and Exchange Commission.

5. Figures in the text refer to the change year over year. Again, precise numbers depend on one's preferred housing price index, but orders of magnitude are the same.

6. See Chapter 4.

7. Bernanke (2007), p. 1.

8. Reuters (2007).

9. Thus the staff analysis of economic trends at the FOMC's January 30–31, 2007, meeting forecast that "restraint from housing will diminish this year and that its contribution to GDP growth will turn slightly positive next year" (Board of Governors 2013, January 30–31, 2007, transcript p. 13). At the FOMC's March meeting several Reserve bank presidents similarly invoked the "contained" language with reference to the further repercussions of housing market weakness, though Charles Plosser of the Federal Reserve Bank of Philadelphia also acknowledged greater uncertainty surrounding that forecast.

10. CNBC Squawk Box (July 1, 2005).

11. See the secretary's remarks to this effect on April 20, 2007, as reported in Zhou (2007).

12. Minutes of the Federal Open Market Committee (March 20–21, 2007), http://www.federalreserve.gov/fomc/minutes/20070321.htm.

13. Bernanke (2002b).

14. See Greenspan (2005).

15. Six years later the liquidators of the two Bear Stearns funds would sue the rating agencies in New York State court for having knowingly issued misleading ratings in return for fee income.

16. As it turned out, the rush for collateral was so disruptive that the creditors, who included Citigroup, JPMorgan Chase, Goldman Sachs, and Bank of America along with Merrill Lynch, found themselves unable to sell many of these assets at any price.

17. It supported the High-Grade Fund only, and not also its twin, the Enhanced Leverage Fund.

18. Just to complete the catalog of names, in 1974, following its merger with Deutsche Industriebank, IKB became IKB Deutsche Industriebank.

19. The definitive account of the Abacus deal is Zuckerman (2009).

20. Among the ironic aspects of the deal was that the leading shareholder in ACA, with three seats on its board, was none other than Bear Stearns, which had injected capital into the troubled firm in 2004.

21. The ACA executive responsible for the deal later testified that she had no knowledge that Paulson was a short-only investor; Financial Crisis Inquiry

Commission (2011), p. 193. The rating agencies were evidently no better at understanding. The Moody's analyst in charge of rating Abacus testified subsequently that he had been unaware of Paulson's involvement. He denied knowing that the program was designed to maximize the likelihood of failure. Whatever the case, Moody's and S&P both assigned an AAA rating to Abacus' super-senior tranche.

22. Quoted in Financial Crisis Inquiry Commission (2011), p. 247.

23. US District Court, Southern District of New York (2010), para. 58 et seq. This is the SEC action referred to in note 4 above. Investors (the likes of King County, Washington) that had lent to Rhinebridge, a second IKB special purpose vehicle, by purchasing its asset-backed commercial paper, rated AAA on the basis of its supposedly high-quality asset backing, did little better; McLean and Nocera (2010), pp. 280–81. ACA subsequently shed some of the credit risk it assumed when issuing guarantees on the Abacus deal through transactions with another European bank, ABN AMRO. But not enough: ACA itself became insolvent when its credit rating was downgraded to CCC in December 2007, forcing it to post additional collateral to back its credit default swaps. It was subsequently restructured under the supervision of the Maryland Insurance Administration. ABN AMRO also suffered losses and was then acquired by a consortium of banks led by Royal Bank of Scotland at the end of 2007.

24. *New York Times* (July 31, 2007, p. B2).

25. In case anyone needed reminding, the two Bear Stearns funds had formally filed for bankruptcy only days prior to the BNP announcement.

26. That said, borrowers generally prefer the interbank market to avoid the stigma of being forced into borrowing from the central bank, which is often taken as a sign of financial problems.

27. This liquidity was provided at the ECB's refinancing rate, the main rate at which it provides credit to banks.

28. The total approaches $2 trillion when one considers commercial paper of all types, making the commercial paper market overall fully double the size of the treasury bill market.

29. If that was not worrisome enough, investors now realized that households having trouble staying current on their mortgage payments might also have trouble staying current on their credit cards and their car and student loans.

30. See Covitz, Liang, and Suarez (2009) and Kacperczyk and Schnabl (2010) for the gory details.

31. And at worst it was destructive, since the provision of insurance on bank deposits gave investors an incentive to shift out of commercial paper into accounts at insured banks.

32. Typically for two years, after which most such borrowers refinanced into a more conventional mortgage. But two years was a lifetime in the financial circumstances of the mid-2000s.

33. The Rock's last securitization was in May, and the next one was not scheduled until September.

34. Lloyds was the consensus candidate at the time.

35. In early September Lloyds indicated that it would require an official back-stop of as much as £30 billion to go through with the transaction, £30 billion being the amount of Northern Rock's funding set to mature by 2009. The problem was that the Bank of England was not in a position to take a liability of that magnitude onto its balance sheet without a government guarantee, and the government could not go ahead without the approval of the European Commission.

36. Irwin (2013), pp. 6–7; House of Commons Treasury Committee (2008), p. 39. The quote that follows is from this second source.

Chapter 12

1. Gorton and Metrick (2012), p. 14. The origins of Reserve Primary Fund are discussed in Chapter 4. I return to its troubles later in this chapter.

2. The AAA or AA rating in question had to be conferred by at least two nationally recognized credit rating agencies. Funds were also prohibited from holding more than 5 percent of their assets in the securities of an individual issuer.

3. See Gorton and Metrick (2012), p. 13, and McCabe (2010), pp. 28–29.

4. See Chapter 9.

5. See, for example, Clarke (1967).

6. Those swaps were initially capped at a relatively modest $24 billion, but they were soon uncapped and extended to additional central banks.

7. The criticism came later, in Paul (2008).

8. See Bullard (2013). Note, however, that the Federal Reserve Board staff's own forecast finally turned negative, acknowledging the reality of the recession, in April after the Bear Stearns crisis.

9. Transcript of FOMC Meeting of August 5, 2008, p. 67. Board of Governors of the Federal Reserve System (2014), p. 67.

10. The quote is again from St. Louis Fed President James Bullard (Board of Governors of the Federal Reserve System 2014, p. 35), although he was far from alone.

11. See the account of New York Fed president Timothy Geithner (2014), pp. 143–44.

12. These quotes and citations are from the transcripts of the FOMC's April 29–30 meeting.

13. Some authors (e.g., Sahm, Shapiro, and Slemrod 2009), moreover, argue that one-half is probably the upper bound for the share of rebate checks spent by households.

14. See Chapter 8.

15. Stephens was a longtime professor of history at the University of California, Berkeley, and dean of its college of arts and sciences. See Stephens (1916).

16. The reference is to seasonally adjusted figures, as appropriate.

17. This refers to the slide by early March—that is, still prior to the rescue of Bear Stearns.

18. Wessel (2009), p. 159.

19. Paulson (2010), pp. 95–96; Financial Crisis Inquiry Commission (2011), p. 283.

20. The market in question is known as the triparty repo market. A repo, or repurchase agreement, is when one party sells a security to another with an agreement to buy it back later. The difference between the lower initial purchase price and higher repurchase price is the interest earned by the initial purchaser for providing liquidity to the seller. In a triparty repo, a custodian stands between the buyer and seller, acting as intermediary between the two. This was the role that JPMorgan Chase played for Bear Stearns.

21. See Fettig (2002).

22. Paulson (2010), pp. 100–104.

23. Eventually, Paulson discovered that Treasury lacked the power to indemnify the Fed without congressional approval and substituted a personal letter for the explicit guarantee. See Geithner (2014), p. 156.

24. Having guaranteed Bear Stearns' trades, JPMorgan was anxious, moreover, to gain control as quickly as possible. It lacked the stomach for an extended battle with angry shareholders.

25. And then there was the fact that JPMorgan Chase had sold substantial amounts of insurance protection against Bear Stearns' bankruptcy. The acquisition of Bear Stearns relieved it of having to pay out on those contracts.

26. JP Morgan Chase (2009), p. 9.

27. The quote is from Reuters (2012).

28. See Chapter 10.

29. The quotation is from Bernanke (2008).

30. Similarly, it helps to explain why Fuld was reluctant to raise new capital, which would dilute existing shareholdings, including his own.

31. Plath is quoted in the *Wall Street Journal*, July 1, 2012, online.wsj.com, updated 3:52 p.m.

32. The details of Bank of America's acquisition of Merrill Lynch are described by Farrell (2010). The immediate result was $22 billion of additional losses to the proud parent, announced in January 2009, which largely precipitated the second bailout of Bank of America, described below.

33. Suskind (2011), p. 43, emphasis in original.

34. Ultimately, Paulson may still have been prepared to offer a demonstration of the pragmatism for which he was known. He may have been willing to contribute to the Bank of America deal, but as an experienced negotiator he was anxious not to overpay. Holding out for the moment was a way of strengthening his bargaining position. But when his chief of staff described his position to the

press as government money over my dead body, the secretary was painted into a corner; Wessel (2009), p. 15. Paulson may have been intellectually flexible and pragmatic, but he couldn't be seen as drawing a line in the sand and immediately stepping over it. In the midst of a crisis, whether the words were his or those of his chief of staff was immaterial.

35. One indication is the transcript of the FOMC meeting in June (Board of Governors 2014, p. 4).

36. Financial Crisis Inquiry Commission (2011), pp. 325–30.

37. Bernanke and Paulson pointed to the need for expanded resolution authority in a meeting with Barney Frank, but there was no willingness on Capitol Hill to take up the issue (Geithner 2014, p. 164).

38. Once Lehman was placed in bankruptcy, Barclays was able to swoop in and purchase its North American investment banking business for a modest $250 million without now also having to absorb the portfolio of toxic securities.

39. Markets in Japan, Hong Kong, and South Korea were closed for holidays.

40. Lehman's UK bankruptcy administrator then unhelpfully responded by freezing the collateral held by the bank's British operation to prevent those funds from leaking out of the country. Eventually, the hedge funds and others that traded through Lehman's London arm got their money back. But not now. They were forced in the meantime to sell other assets to raise liquidity, which created yet more problems for other investors.

Chapter 13

1. Starr continued to run the company into the 1960s. Among other things, he went on to endow the C. V. Starr East Asian Library at the University of California, Berkeley. The most complete account of Starr's adventures is Shelp and Ehrbar (2006). See also Stafford (1999) and Waller (2011).

2. This history is recounted by Tett (2009).

3. See Morgenson (2008), on which this section draws.

4. Boyd (2011), p. 16.

5. US House of Representatives (2009), p. 32.

6. The activities of AIG Financial Products were overseen by European regulators only when they involved the European business of Banque AIG, a French subsidiary of Financial Products. Otherwise the Europeans, in their wisdom, delegated regulation of the holding company to OTS.

7. See Chapter 12.

8. In 2009 the SEC sued the Bents for fraud, alleging they had misled their investors, regulators, and trustees by inadequately informing them of the Fund's difficulties and leading them to believe they intended to inject additional money. In 2012 the younger Bent was found liable on one count of negligence, but he and his father were acquitted of fraud charges in what was widely viewed as a defeat for the SEC.

9. Quoted in Shifrin (2008).

10. This was reported by McCabe, Ciriani, Holscher, and Martin (2012) on the basis of confidential data.

11. The origins and rationale for Regulation Q were described in Chapter 4 and note 4 of that chapter.

12. This was not the first time Treasury had used the ESF in extremis. It had previously used it to provide emergency currency swaps and guarantees to Mexico in 1994–95 during that country's financial crisis (Schwartz 1997). Congress responded by tightening restrictions on its use, preventing it from being applied to financing another foreign rescue. Displeased that the ESF was now being employed without explicit authorization by the legislative branch to rescue the money market industry, Congress would eventually move a second time to further limit the Treasury secretary's latitude in making use of the fund.

13. Bloomberg News eventually resorted to the Freedom of Information Act to obtain data on borrowing under the AMLF, which it then compared with State Street's reported income; see Condon (2011).

14. US House of Representatives (2009), pp. 51, 62.

15. This, recall, was also the precedent that figured in the Bear Stearns rescue, Bear having been the one bank that refused to contribute to the LTCM pool (Chapter 12).

16. It was necessary subsequently to equip the insurer with additional funds, raising the government's stake to 92 percent.

17. The deal was criticized subsequently as not being tough enough in that the infusion of government money allowed AIG to pay off its bank counterparties, the likes of Société Générale, in full. At the same time it was criticized as too tough on the grounds that shareholders were left with only 20 percent of their previous stake in the company. Hank Greenberg filed suit against the government in US District Court for having acted unconstitutionally, expropriating shareholders, notably himself, without due process or just compensation. His suit was dismissed in 2012.

18. On selling its AIG shares and warrants, the government could claim a positive return of $23 billion. Against this must be set losses to the public sector of approximately $18 billion resulting from tax treatment allowing AIG to use its net operating losses to reduce future tax payments.

19. Paulson (2010), p. 323.

20. If four other governors were not available, it was then possible to proceed with the unanimous vote of those present.

Chapter 14

1. See also Chapter 6.

2. More precisely, they could not provide it without help from the Fed.

3. Strictly speaking, Fortis purchased only ABN AMRO's retail businesses in the Benelux countries, but this does nothing to change the point. The other bits were taken over by the Royal Bank of Scotland and Santander Group. The

Royal Bank of Scotland acquired ABN AMRO's wholesale division and Asian operations, while Santander absorbed its Brazilian and Italian businesses.

4. Greywolf eventually sued Fortis over the failure, resulting in a countersuit that detailed $400 million of losses on the deal.

5. For more on the Irish banking crisis, see Chapter 25.

6. The complete list of countries in which customers could open Kaupthing Edge accounts included also the UK, Belgium, Norway, Germany, Finland, Sweden, Austria, and Switzerland.

7. This has been true of domestic and foreign commentators alike: see Lewis (2009), Boyes (2009), and Jónsson (2009).

8. Grímsson (2005), pp. 1, 4.

9. See Dwyer (2011) for details.

10. On this see Chapter 4.

11. This doubling was between September 2007 and March 2008.

12. The transactions described in this paragraph are analyzed by Baldursson and Portes (2013), from where the present details are drawn. The authors effectively argue that all was well at the Icelandic banks until they were sideswiped by the crisis and then the bankers began gambling for redemption. This seems to go too far in dismissing evidence of earlier excesses.

13. Baldursson and Portes (2013), p. 10.

14. Existing equity was written down by 85 percent, giving the government a 75 percent stake (see also below, as well as note 17 to follow).

15. Its downgrade extended to a fourth financial institution, Straumur Burduras Investment Bank.

16. To its credit, the ECB later postponed some additional margin calls on Glitnir and Landsbanki.

17. While this measure was being prepared, Oddsson and Prime Minister Geir Haarde, Oddsson's successor as party leader, decided in a phone call to lend €500 million to Kaupthing. Contrary to the planned €600 million loan to Glitnir, which never was paid out, this loan was. The motive for the Kaupthing loan has never been fully explained. See Sigrún Davíðsdóttir, *The only secret from October 6 2008: a CBI loan of €500m to Kaupthing—updated (again)* http://uti.is/2013/03/the-only-secret-from-october-6-2008-a-cbi-loan-of-e500m-to-kaupthing/.

18. UK deposit insurance then covered the remainder, up to a maximum of £50,000. At the time of Landsbanki's failure some £800 million of deposit liabilities were above the limit. The UK authorities quickly concluded that, to avoid undermining confidence, these should be covered as well. After reimbursing UK and Dutch depositors, authorities in the two countries sought to recover the money from Iceland. Two bills, based on two agreements, were passed in the Icelandic Parliament authorizing the government to guarantee full repayment up to the EU maximum. In both cases, the president subjected those agreements to public referenda, and in both cases they were defeated. In January 2009, the Court of the European Free Trade

Area ruled that the Icelandic government was not obliged to reimburse the two governments. In 2014 the Dutch and British governments, not easily deterred, sued the Icelandic deposit insurance fund, as distinct from the government, in yet another attempt to recover their costs. The quest would seem quixotic, given that the interest and principal sought by the Dutch and British governments approached $9 billion, or nearly 60 percent of Icelandic GDP, and the deposit insurance fund had only $300 million in assets.

19. Quoted in an interview in the *Wall Street Journal* (2008).
20. The individual signs varied, but the message was universally the same.

Chapter 15

1. Oliver and Marion (2010), p. 95.
2. Chicago's crisis was precipitated by a strike by the Association of Real Estate Taxpayers, which slowed collection of property taxes. The association, which had the populist trapping of suffering working-class homeowners, was in fact a collection of large property owners. The city's consequent inability to pay interest on its municipal bonds, many of which were held by local banks, in turn contributed to the banking crisis that is described in Chapter 10. Cermak's response was to jawbone the banks, including Charles Dawes' Central Republic Trust, to buy additional bonds and to ask the RFC to accept them as collateral in return for loans.
3. Counts vary since some states declared holidays more than once, individual banks sometimes self-declared holidays, some holidays were municipal rather than statewide, and other holidays were limited to parts of states.
4. As he stated in a handwritten appeal delivered to FDR by a Secret Service agent during a banquet at the Hotel Astor in New York on February 18. Hoover had previously attempted to contact Roosevelt directly but was told that he was on a fishing trip on Mr. Astor's yacht. Roosevelt later claimed his failure to respond before March 1 was caused by a secretarial error.
5. A useful summary, if one can get past political overtones, is Best (1991). A subtler one is Moley (1966).
6. See Chapter 1. The contrast with 2009–10, when progressives focused on breaking up big banks rather than big manufacturing companies, reflects the fact that banks in 1933, though sometimes big and often suspect, were limited by anti-branching laws. The banks would receive their own Brandeisian comeuppance with the passage of the Glass-Steagall Act.
7. This made it all the more remarkable that the Supreme Court, under Brandeis' leadership, rejected the NIRA as unconstitutional two years later (see below).
8. *New York Times* (December 31, 1933, p. 2). In Keynes' words, "NRA, which is essentially reform and probably impedes recovery, has been put across too hastily, in the false guise of being part of the technique of recovery." In his January 1935 annual message to Congress, FDR retorted, "The attempt to

make a distinction between recovery and reform is a narrowly conceived effort to substitute the appearance of reality for reality itself. When a man is convalescing from illness, wisdom dictates not only cure of the symptoms, but also removal of their cause." Franklin D. Roosevelt, "Annual Message to Congress," January 4, 1935, online in Gerhard Peters and John T. Woolley, The American Presidency Project, http://www.presidency.ucsb.edu/ws/index.php?pid=14890.

9. One may think of this as a pre-Galbraithian expression of the notion of countervailing power as later expressed in Galbraith (1952).

10. Like Barack Obama's first treasury secretary, Woodin served previously on the board of the Federal Reserve Bank of New York. That the Senate Banking Committee subsequently found Woodin's name on a list of J. P. Morgan's preferred customers and showed that he had received preferred stock options, something for which he was criticized by Huey Long, may have hastened his departure (see below), as did FDR's decision to abandon the gold standard. Woodin also shared with that earlier cabinet member, Charles Dawes, a love for music (Chapter 3); his "Franklin D. Roosevelt March" was played at the inauguration. When in the spring of 1933 maintenance of the gold standard became controversial within the administration, he composed a sonnet entitled "Lullaby to Silver."

11. His famous debt-deflation article was Fisher (1933). To address this problem, Fisher offered a compensated dollar, in which the government would raise the dollar price of gold by 1 percent for every 1 percent fall in the price level; this then delivered intellectual cover for the gold-buying program initiated in October. The compensated-dollar plan was inspired by William Jennings Bryan's 1896 presidential campaign, as described in Fisher (1911). Though he did not advise FDR, Fisher collaborated with the Committee for the Nation, a group of bankers and businessmen organized by Frank Vanderlip, former president of National City Bank, that lobbied for stabilizing the price level (Bratter 1941). As consultant to the committee, Warren was exposed to Fisher's ideas.

12. So in effect did a group of economists at the University of Chicago, whose "Chicago Plan" was submitted to Agriculture Secretary Henry Wallace in March. It proposed allowing banks to reopen after the bank holiday under control of the Federal Reserve System, after which they would be converted into "full reserve" or "100 percent reserve" banks permitted to invest only in safe assets. For the post–Great Recession analog, see Kotlikoff (2010). Alter (2010) describes a private dinner at the White House in April 2009 in which Krugman and Stiglitz backed nationalization.

13. The quotation is from FDR's first inaugural address, available at http://www.inaugural.senate.gov/swearing-in/address/address-by-franklin-d-roosevelt-1933.

14. Mills was a Republican but also a Harvard classmate of Roosevelt. Arthur Ballantine—as noted in Chapter 10—was yet another classmate.

15. This had also been recommended to FDR by Rene Leon, an advisor to the House Banking and Currency Committee. Roosevelt then sent Tugwell to

Washington, where he traced the only extant copy of the act to the Accounts and Deposits Division of the Treasury Department. He found that the relevant clause was underlined in red, indicating that Hoover had already considered this option (Hitzik 2011, p. 39).

16. It was seven pages rather than three. House Banking Committee Chair Henry Steagall did the reading. Carter Glass subsequently provided an abridged reading to the Senate, although by the time it took up the bill, multiple copies were made available by the Government Printing Office.

17. See Moley (1966), p. 144; Henry (1960), pp. 347–48.

18. The Treasury wanted the Federal Reserve System to approve the reopened banks, whereas the Federal Reserve wanted Treasury to assume this responsibility. In the end they split the difference: Reserve banks and other regulators provided recommendations and solvent banks were then reopened with certification by the Treasury.

19. *New York Times* (March 14, 1933, p. 1).

20. Moley (1939), p. 155.

21. The banks remained reluctant to ask for government help, recalling the embarrassment they suffered when a list of RFC-supported institutions was published in January. Jones' response to the worry that banks accepting public capital would be singled out was to insist that all banks should apply for RFC assistance. Speaking to the American Bankers Association in Chicago, he warned the bankers to apply for RFC assistance or else. One is reminded of the reluctance of the leading US banks to borrow from the TARP and the do-so-or-else posture adopted by Treasury Secretary Paulson and New York Fed President Geithner. Beginning with Manufacturers Trust, they now did so. By the middle of 1935, the RFC had purchased some $1.3 billion of stock and capital notes in nearly seven thousand banks.

22. Beard and Smith (1940), p. 78.

23. Norris (1937), pp. 232–33.

24. Nadler and Bogen (1933), p. 174; Silber (2009), p. 25.

25. Paul de Grauwe is the main exponent of the view that the explosion of sovereign spreads in Europe in 2011–12 was panic-driven, in parallel with the run on US banks in 1933. See De Grauwe and Ji (2013). OMT is described in Chapter 26.

26. This is the view of Eggertsson (2008).

27. Franklin D. Roosevelt, "Message to Congress on Economies in Government," March 10, 1933, online in Gerhard Peters and John T. Woolley, The American Presidency Project, http://www.presidency.ucsb.edu/ws/index.php?pid=14496.

28. See Chapter 23.

29. The quote from Douglas is from an article on his appointment in the *New York Times* of March 19, 1933, p. SM3. The same Lewis Douglas would declare a month later, when Roosevelt announced his intention of abandoning the gold standard, that this marked the end of Western civilization.

30. Aside from $150 million of incidental revenue from new taxes on beer and wine, which would take some time to accrue.

31. Note the parallel with the 8½ percent cuts under the so-called Sequester in 2013.

32. MacArthur exceeded his orders, President Hoover having instructed him to move the protesters out of Washington, D.C.'s central business district, but no matter. Hoover upbraided MacArthur only privately, and the press blamed the president for the incident.

33. Roosevelt's deficits in fiscal years 1934 and 1936 ended up being larger than Hoover's in 1932 and 1933. But those deficits were larger by only a small margin; the increase in tax receipts as the economy recovered limited their growth. And with Prohibition now history, the excise tax on alcohol added as much as 15 percent to revenues.

34. Franklin D. Roosevelt, "Annual Message to Congress," January 4, 1935, online in Gerhard Peters and John T. Woolley, The American Presidency Project, http://www.presidency.ucsb.edu/ws/index.php?pid=14890.

35. Roosevelt had already vetoed a bill paying out the bonus once. Congress overrode his second veto in January 1936.

36. Economists of a variety of persuasions have reached this conclusion (Brown 1956, Peppers 1973, Romer 1992). Given Professor Romer's subsequent position in the Obama administration, this analysis had some influence in shaping the 2009 stimulus (Chapter 20).

37. *New York Times* (March 6, 1933, p. 1). Woodin was also a collector of gold coins, explaining why, when a month later he was instructed to issue to an executive order requiring gold coin, bullion, and certificates to be handed over to the government, he exempted rare and unusual coins.

38. McKenney (1939), quoted in Leuchtenburg (1968), p. 21.

39. This according to the Federal Reserve Board's index.

40. See Chapter 10.

41. *New York Times* (April 20, 1933, p. 1). The dollar, meanwhile, sank by 11½ percent against the currencies of countries still on gold, reflecting the expectation that US prices were set to rise.

42. Barnard (1958), pp. 272–73.

43. Warburg (1964), p. 128. James Warburg, son of the German-American financier Paul Warburg, sometimes referred to as the father of the Federal Reserve System, was in London as financial advisor to the US delegation.

44. See Chapter 10.

45. See, for example, coverage by BBC News in Schifferes (2009). British Prime Minister Gordon Brown describes in his memoirs (Brown 2010) how his efforts to organize an internationally coordinated response to the Great Recession (the UK chairing the G20 at the time) were informed by the collapse of the 1933 conference. For more, see Chapter 24. H. G. Wells, having found in Montagu Norman one irresistible target for ridicule, found the London Conference to be another,

asking in *The Shape of Things to Come* "How could men appointed as national representatives accept a pooling of national interests? They were indeed fully prepared to revolutionize the world situation and change gathering misery to hope, plenty and order, but only on the impossible condition that they were not to change themselves and that nothing essential to their importance changed" (p. 131).

46. FDR offered Herriot, during the latter's visit to Washington, D.C., an international agreement under whose terms governments would keep their exchange rates stable but reflate in tandem. The French rejected the offer as inflationary and damaging to confidence (Nichols 1951).

47. That this approach complicated cooperation on other matters was unfortunate but unavoidable. Kennedy, following Hoover, argues that Hitler inferred from the collapse of the conference that the United States was not prepared to play a role in Europe, that "the Western powers had. . . little stomach for concerted action in the face of danger," and that he could do pretty much as he pleased without fear of American reprisal (Kennedy 1999, p. 155).

48. Jones (1951), p. 249.

49. Keynes also offered a third option: an agreement with other countries to stabilize exchange rates but extended to include agreement on joint measures to stabilize price levels. This, however, was not practical, what with important players like France still on the gold standard (see below) and given the bad taste left by the failure of the World Economic Conference.

50. On January 15 the administration sent Congress legislation authorizing the president to lower the gold content of the dollar to 50–60 percent of its previous level. On January 16 the Federal Reserve took over responsibility for executing the gold-purchase program from the RFC. On January 30 Congress then gave the president the authority he required. The next day FDR used it to fix the price of gold at $35 an ounce.

51. Some observers have been critical of the tactics and also the strategy, questioning whether devaluing the dollar and pushing up the price of gold could stabilize the price level. (One is reminded of skepticism about the effectiveness of quantitative easing by central banks in response to the Great Recession.) They point to the fact that there was no one-for-one response of commodity prices to changes in the gold-purchase price (see viz. Kennedy 1999). After jumping up in April, commodity prices fell back in late 1933. But standard models suggest that prices move on expectations of future policy rather than on its implementation. They suggest that when commodity prices are flexible while the prices of labor services are sticky, the flexible prices will overshoot initially and give back some of that ground subsequently (Frankel 1986). US evidence from 1933 is consistent with this view (Temin and Wigmore 1990).

52. French prime minister Charles de Gaulle, or more precisely his finance minister Valéry Giscard d'Estaing, coined the phrase in the 1960s when critiquing the dollar's asymmetric role in the post–World War II Bretton Woods System.

1. Wallace did not see these as alternatives; in addition to technical improvements and crop set-asides he advocated monetary measures in response to farm problems (Shapsmeier and Shapsmeier 1968). The specifics of the set-aside program owed much to the "allotment plan" of Professor M. L. Wilson of Montana State College. Wilson was an advocate of incentives to increase efficiency in the 1920s, but in response to the slow pace of efficiency improvement he gravitated toward the allotment scheme (Rowley 1969). Rex Tugwell discovered Wilson during the 1932 campaign, when he was delegated to attend a meeting sponsored by the Giannini Foundation for Agricultural Economics.

2. As we saw in Chapter 1. The same remained the case in the 1930s; see Field (2011).

3. "Message to Congress Recommending Enactment of the National Industrial Recovery Act" (May 17, 1933), online in Gerhard Peters and John T. Woolley, The American Presidency Project, www.presidency.ucsb.edu/ws/index.php?pid=14646.

4. The work in question was Berle and Means (1933).

5. Some historians, invoking the example of Henry Ford and the five-dollar day, suggest that higher wages may have helped by stimulating consumer spending. But it is hard to build a consistent model in which this positive effect of the NIRA outweighed the negative effects. Ford himself was a die-hard opponent of the act.

6. All this is described in more detail in Sumner (1990).

7. See Weinstein (1980); Friedman and Schwartz (1963), p. 495, citing Roose (1954); and Cole and Ohanian (2004).

8. On this, see Wecter (1948).

9. The reference is to Anderson (2000).

10. *Chicago Tribune* (May 29, 1935, p. 12).

11. The act combined railway pensions into a single pooled fund, something the Court rejected on the grounds that some railways had previously contributed more to their pension schemes than others.

12. Thus the court upheld the Fair Labor Standards Act in *United States v. Darby Lumber Co.*, and upheld a Washington State minimum-wage law, reversing a previous decision regarding New York State's minimum wage.

13. The new entity was initially known as the Federal Bank Deposit Insurance Corporation, or FBDIC, but the name was quickly shortened to FDIC. Glass-Steagall also permitted statewide branching except in states where it was expressly prohibited. Previously, only twelve states had permitted statewide branching, four of which passed legislation permitting it in anticipation of Glass-Steagall. Another dozen permitted more limited branching. Glass, his views colored by the experience of the 1920s, concluded that unit banking was

incompatible with financial stability. It is interesting to observe that the perceived threat to stability in 1933 was fragmentation, the opposite of 2010, when concentration and size—too big to fail and too complex to manage—were the overriding problems.

14. *New York Times* (June 16, 1933, p. 14). The campaign continued even after passage. On June 27, at its annual convention at Lake George, New York, the State Bankers' Association condemned the provisions of Glass-Steagall designed to facilitate statewide branching and adopted a resolution urging repeal or modification of the act.

15. The committee had been investigating the stock market crash and surrounding events since April 1932 under two earlier, ineffectual chief counsels before Pecora took over in January 1933.

16. On Paulson, see Chapter 11. The "friends of Angelo" program is described in US House of Representatives (2009).

17. Aldrich was the son of Nelson Aldrich, the Rhode Island senator (1881–1911) who had helped to found the Federal Reserve System.

18. In addition, the big banks lobbying for federal deposit insurance understood that extension of a deposit-insurance guarantee was less likely so long as insured deposits were seen as funding the risky activities of investment banks. Dividing the financial system into "risky" investment banks and relatively "safe" commercial banks was thus a way of strengthening the case for deposit insurance (more on which below).

19. Katznelson (2013), p. 124.

20. Finally, it has been suggested that Glass-Steagall was a Faustian bargain between large and small banks. The large banks got permission to branch, while the small banks, which had long experienced confidence problems owing to their regionally and economically concentrated portfolios, received deposit guarantees. The problem with this story is that, as we saw above, small banks were far from united in favoring deposit insurance. In many cases, the associations representing them were opposed. The heterogeneity of views among small rural banks is similarly emphasized by Keeton (1990).

21. This is ultimately the explanation for the adoption of deposit insurance in Calomiris and White (1994).

22. These measures were known as blue-sky laws, reflecting complaints that dishonest financial promoters had been selling securities "backed by nothing more than the clear blue sky."

23. Subsequently, use of the Martin Act was strengthened. It was invoked by Eliot Spitzer in order to oust AIG CEO Hank Greenberg, and by his successor, Eric Schneiderman, to extract sue JPMorgan for defrauding purchasers of mortgage-related securities from Bear Stearns—the same lawsuits of which Jamie Dimon so bitterly complained (see Chapter 12).

24. Seligman (1982), p. 49.

25. Brandeis (1914), p. 62.

26. Initially that agency was to be the Federal Trade Commission, reflecting the extent to which blue-sky laws were evaded by interstate sales through the mail. Even earlier Samuel Untermeyer, a longtime securities crusader and counsel to the Pujo Committee, the pre–World War I predecessor of the Pecora Commission, recommended vesting this power with the Post Office (the mails being used, as noted above, to circumvent blue-sky laws). Only in 1934 did opinion coalesce around establishing a self-standing agency, the Securities and Exchange Commission.

27. Figures for 2005 and 2010 refer to single-family units; from the National Association of Home Builders.

28. Calder's advocacy of federal aid for housing, which would have resonated with the advocates of the federal government's "affordable housing goals" eighty years later, did not however prevent his being defeated in a reelection bid in 1922.

29. In a further concession to straitened times, they gave borrowers the option of paying interest only for the first three years. In the 1920s, home mortgages typically had a maturity of just five years. Borrowers were required to make just interest payments, with a balloon payment of principal at the end. In some cases, building and loan associations offered share accumulation contracts that amortized over time and ran for ten or twelve years, but these were a minority of mortgages (Fishback, Rose, and Snowden 2013). HOLC mortgages, in contrast, were amortized over the life of the loan, eliminating the need for balloon payments at the end.

30. If appraisals were much lower than the encumbrance, then a principal reduction was offered, but only if the lender agreed to incur a corresponding loss when receiving payment from the HOLC. Rose (2011) shows that these principal reductions occurred in a minority of cases, in which they averaged 8 percent. In practice, appraisals were often inflated in order to encourage lender participation.

31. To qualify for a HOLC loan, borrowers first had to establish that they were capable of fulfilling the terms. In addition, they had to establish that they had been unable to refinance with a private lender. Some borrowers nonetheless fell behind, leading the HOLC to foreclose on 20 percent of its loans. But with home prices falling only modestly in the second half of the 1930s, HOLC loans were effectively overcollateralized, limiting the corporation's losses. Losses were not eliminated entirely: Fishback et al. (2011) report that the HOLC realized an average loss of 33 percent on every foreclosed home it sold.

32. The fact that the share of mortgage debt was greater than the share of mortgages tells us that its work disproportionately benefited middle- and upper-class homeowners.

33. See Courtmanche and Snowden (2011) and Fishback, Flores-Lagunes, Horrace, Kantor, and Treber (2011). A majority of US states adopted moratoria on foreclosures in the 1930s, but such moratoria were temporary; as such they were unlikely to do much to encourage construction.

34. Fishback et al. (2011) consider the earnings paid to the Treasury by the HOLC, the costs to the Treasury of supplying funds to the HOLC, and the increase in the corporation's balance sheet, and conclude that costs were on the order of $100 million. In 1951 dollars, that being the year the HOLC was wound up, $100 million is the equivalent of $1 billion today. The 2009 federal budget, for comparison, was $3.1 trillion.

35. Fishback, Rose, and Snowden (2013) conclude that home prices were 16 percent higher than otherwise in the typical small community as a result of the intervention of the HOLC.

Chapter 17

1. As described in Chapter 2.
2. A good statement of the new monetary framework is Bernanke, Laubach, Mishkin, and Posen (1999).
3. See Chapter 12.
4. The Bank of Taiwan was a Japanese bank with responsibilities for the governance of Taiwan.
5. Policy makers had debated the possibility in 1923 and again in 1927, but other imperatives dominated on both occasions.
6. Inoue, not incidentally, was a former governor of the bank.
7. As described in Chapter 10.
8. The list of banks in the lead in speculating against the yen is from Takahashi's biographer, Smethurst (2007), p. 251.
9. He did so on his first day in office. It then took three days for the Privy Council, which advised the new prime minister, Tsuyoshi Inukai, to validate his decision.
10. For details see Shima (1983).
11. Those other central bankers anticipated that the bank could eventually sell government bonds into the market, using these open market operations to mop up the increase in the money supply. Eventually the central bank did engage in some such sales, although the sales had a hard time keeping pace with the purchases. See Ide (2003).
12. Smethurst (2007), p. 250.
13. See Chapter 15.
14. There is thus some irony in the fact that Takahashi, who opposed the country's overseas military adventures, was ultimately assassinated by military officers (see below). The young Takahashi sought to continue his studies in the United States with the aid of an American businessman who promised to help him with arrangements in California. On arriving, he found that he was essentially an indentured servant forced to work as a houseboy to repay his costs of transportation. One can imagine that this experience nonetheless had positive implications for his English-language skills.
15. Nanto and Takagi (1985), p. 372.

16. After a recession in 1934, the impressive growth of the economy resumed, and continued for the remainder of the 1930s. Figures here are from the Maddison database (http://www.ggdc.net/maddison/maddison-project/home.htm).

17. When it became evident that no such agreement would be forthcoming, he pushed for forming a currency bloc with the Commonwealth and Empire whose common exchange rate would be fixed but adjustable against gold. Howson (1975), pp. 84–85; Morrison (2013), pp. 33–34. Eventually a sterling bloc did form, as members of the Commonwealth and Empire followed sterling down against the dollar and then pegged to the pound at its new lower level.

18. The new chancellor also oversaw the imposition of the Chamberlain family nostrum: a 33 percent across-the-board tariff on imports.

19. Rock (1969), p. 86.

20. Howson (1980), p. 48.

21. These are the figures for the M3 money supply from Capie and Weber (1985).

22. The UK solidified this achievement through a large-scale war debt conversion in 1932, where it converted its earlier high-interest-rate-bearing bonds into new issues bearing a 2 percent rate. What was true of Britain was similarly true of other members of the Commonwealth and sterling area that followed Britain off gold (as described below). Crafts (2013) estimates that this group of countries was able to reduce the real interest rate on its debt from more than 5 percent in the late 1920s to just 2 percent in the early 1930s. The contrast with the policies of the Cameron government starting in 2010 and across the Eurozone (see Chapters 24 and 26)—and the less than fully supportive policies of the ECB—will be obvious.

23. This is a point made by Urban (2009). Ragnar Nurkse (1944), in his classic account of interwar currency experience, similarly comments on the stability of exchange rates within the sterling area and the willingness of governments to sacrifice their monetary autonomy in pursuit of this supposed higher objective.

24. Wicksell first gave a presentation to this effect to the Swedish Economic Association in 1898. See Berg and Jonung (1998) for an account that emphasizes the influence of these economists.

25. On the Kreuger crisis, see Chapter 9. The discount from the 1929 rate against sterling was in fact relatively modest, on the order of 6 percent.

26. This argument is developed by Straumann and Woitek (2009). Similarly, modern scholarship has not been kind to the notion that Swedish policy makers pursued Keynesian fiscal policies before Keynes (as argued by Thomas 1937).

27. Venezuela was the one country that instead floated the exchange rate throughout the period, its currency and economy being buoyed by strong oil exports (McBeth 1983).

28. Argentina, which still relied heavily on the British market for its beef exports, was an exception. It therefore continued to service its debt, pegged the peso to

sterling, and negotiated an agreement to ensure access to the UK market (the Roca-Runciman Treaty, named after the vice president of Argentina and the president of the British Board of Trade). See Diaz-Alejandro (1970).

29. This is part of the explanation for how Latin American countries succeeded in regaining 1929 levels of output as early as 1932–33 (agricultural production being maintained during the Depression), although there is no denying that the policy choices described here also played a role (on these see Campa 1990).

30. Fishlow (1972) is the classic account of import substitution in Latin America in this period.

31. The same was true of the other countries of Central and Eastern Europe that had previously experienced high inflation and now imposed exchange controls. They too remained reluctant to use their newfound monetary room for maneuver to expand their money supplies and counter deflation (Mitchener and Wandschneider 2013).

32. Cited in Ritschl (2000), p. 1. Because spending on the military-industrial complex was capital-intensive, it created even less employment than otherwise. Autobahn construction, being more labor-intensive, was different but made a significant contribution only in 1935.

33. Under Obama, recall for sake of comparison, the deficit of the federal government rose from 3 percent of GDP in 2008 to 10 percent in 2009.

34. Kindleberger (1989), p. 179.

35. Even countries that went off the gold standard resorted to tariffs when recovery proved disappointing. Thus Britain not only devalued but also imposed a general tariff in February 1932 (see above) and negotiated the Ottawa Agreements with the Commonwealth and Empire. Failure of the Bank of England to cut interest rates more quickly and the lag before the British economy reacted go a long way toward explaining this otherwise peculiar response.

36. An introduction to the literature on tariffs and economic performance over the long run is Broadberry and Crafts (2010). Indeed, some see the origins of the contemporary European Union in the trading bloc constructed by Germany in the 1930s and solidified during World War II, this being the controversial conclusion of Wolf and Ritschl (2011).

37. Later, the Third Reich was able to use an intensified version of the system to extract raw materials and industrial resources from the Central and Western European countries that came under its wartime control.

Chapter 18

1. This is the change in real GDP between 1933Q2 and 1937Q2, according to Balke and Gordon (1986), p. 804. Industrial production figures are from Miron and Romer (1990).

2. The figure is 9 percent if individuals on public work relief are counted as employed.

3. Cited in Warren (1996), p. 66.

4. Senator Huey Long, arguably an even stronger populist challenger, was assassinated in September 1935. Coughlin's Union Party eventually nominated as its presidential candidate William Lemke, a nondescript congressman from North Dakota, who ended up drawing only a small fraction of the vote. For more on Coughlin, see Chapter 10.

5. For the evidence on firm behavior see Calomiris and Hubbard (1995). The argument for high-return investment projects is made by Field (2011); see also Chapter 1.

6. Eccles had a hand in a number of other consequential initiatives of this period; for example, his letter to Senator Patton Harrison of Mississippi planted the idea of the undistributed profits tax.

7. Previously, the board could change reserve requirements only after declaring an emergency and with the consent of the president.

8. FDR nominated Eccles in November 1934, in advance of the Banking Act of 1935, but Eccles made FDR's support for the legislation a condition for accepting (Hyman 1976, p. 159). The president then renominated him as chairman of the reorganized board of governors when the Banking Act became effective in February 1936.

9. Eccles (1951), pp. 56–61. Either that or Eccles patterned his account of the events of 1931 after those in the movie.

10. The Gold Reserve Act of 1934, passed once FDR stabilized the price of gold, established a $2 billion Exchange Stabilization Fund using the profits from devaluation and authorized the secretary of the Treasury, acting with the approval of the president, to use it to purchase and sell government securities on the market. It was this power to counter central bank policy that the Fed now sought to override. This was the same ESF that the US Treasury under Henry Paulson used to guarantee accounts at money market mutual funds in September 2008 (Chapter 13).

11. Friedman and Schwartz (1963), p. 526.

12. See Cargill and Mayer (2006). A subsequent study by Park and Van Horn (2013) using disaggregated data reaches the same conclusion.

13. See Calomiris, Mason, and Wheelock (2011).

14. Hyman (1976), p. 216. As Eccles wrote retrospectively, in 1951, "This decision was in the nature of a precautionary measure. It in no way reversed the Board's easy-money and credit policies. . . . That the $1,790,000,000 in excess reserves which was siphoned off merely eliminated what was superfluous to the needs of commerce, industry, and agriculture was shown by subsequent events. Reserves were still so large and so well-spaced that all but a few member banks met the August 15 order either by utilizing their excess reserve balances with the Reserve banks or by drawing upon their excess balances with our correspondent banks. Moreover, the change had no effect on the credit situation." Eccles (1951), p. 290.

15. Standard practice was to pay for the gold purchased by printing gold certificates equal to the value of the purchase and depositing them at the Federal Reserve, where they could be used as bank reserves. Instead, Treasury now kept the certificates in an inactive account where they could not be used to back expansion of credit.

16. The monetary base was fully 10 percent lower in 1937 than would have been the case in the absence of the downturn. See Irwin (2012), on which this discussion draws.

17. From this point it used gold acquired the previous year to finance additional injections of money and credit.

18. For two cases in point see Romer (2009b) and Crafts and Fearon (2010).

19. Earlier the candidate provocatively asserted that he welcomed the hatred of business. The "hatred" comment was in an October 31 speech at Madison Square Garden announcing the Second New Deal (http://docs.fdrlibrary.marist.edu/od2ndst.html). The "economic royalists" phrase was then from his 1937 inaugural address.

20. See Higgs (1997), as channeled by Boudreaux (2011).

21. Higgs (1997), p. 577. The survey in question was conducted in the spring of 1939.

22. Here Higgs (1997, p. 584) is echoing contemporaries like Ogden Mills, who complained in 1936 how "we cannot have a full recovery so long as the Administration seeks to transform America into a collectivist state" (Mills 1936, p. 65).

23. Economists refer to this as the tendency for the term structure of interest rates to steepen (for long-term rates to rise relative to short-term rates) during a recovery and to "invert" (for long rates to fall below the level of short rates) with the approach of a recession.

24. Although employment was also growing, as a percentage of employed workers the increase was proportionally only slightly smaller (8.5 percent versus 15.1 percent). See Mayer (2004), appendix table A1.

25. Sales were then again lower in 1938. The geography is also right, as Hausman shows: the largest proportional fall in manufacturing employment was in the Upper Midwest, and of all states Michigan experienced the single largest decline. Hausman (2012) is the source of this information.

26. As Mouré (1991, p. 197) describes, Reynaud later claimed that his conversion occurred as early as 1933, but there is little evidence to this effect. Mouré also shows that Reynaud's claims that his advocacy of franc devaluation was entirely unprecedented was similarly an exaggeration.

27. Reynaud became a political outcast until vindicated by subsequent events. He would become Edouard Daladier's minister of finance in 1938—that is, following the devaluation that vindicated his views. After refusing to participate in the Vichy government in 1940, Reynaud was arrested, transferred to Germany, and held there, like his countryman Léon Blum, until the conclusion of World War II.

28. In the bank's annual report for 1935.

29. In addition, the Bank of France now paid out mainly gold bars, not coin, where the cost of a bar was 216,000 francs. This prevented small savers from running on its reserve, although there were reports of tradesmen pooling their resources to secure a bar and then cutting it up.

30. Reflecting the existence of this pastoral safety net, France did less than Britain in providing unemployment insurance and public work relief. Indeed it did not even bother to gather comprehensive statistics on the unemployed.

31. This on July 17, 1933. Further channeling FDR, Laval also formed a "Brains Trust" to advise him on economic policies, made up of Raoul Dautry, the director of the state railways; Claude-Joseph Gignoux, editor of *La Journée Industrielle*; and Jacques Rueff, the ultra-orthodox economist who advised every French prime minister from Raymond Poincaré to Charles de Gaulle. The Communist opposition referred to this as the "brain of trusts" (Jackson 1985, p. 105).

32. As translated by Warner (1968), p. 90.

33. Earlier they had signed a "Unity of Action Pact" in order to form a united front against far-right antiparliamentary forces, which gained prominence starting in 1934.

34. In addition, like FDR three years before, Blum and his allies advocated a reduction in the length of the workweek, measures intended to aid suffering farmers by raising agricultural prices, and tax reform designed to increase the progressivity of the tax system.

35. Cited in Lacouture (1982), p. 362.

36. Shamir (1989), pp. 219–22. Emmanuel Mönick, the French financial attaché in London, played an important role in convincing Blum that exchange control would lead France down the "German path," making it difficult to collaborate with other democratic governments.

37. Details are in Roselli (2006).

Chapter 19

1. Between 1929 and 1932 the fall was almost exactly the same in the advanced countries and the world as a whole. Data from the Maddison database (http://www.ggdc.net/maddison/maddison-project/home.htm) show GDP in the advanced countries falling by a cumulative one percentage point less than global GDP between 1929 and 1932. The fall in global GDP between 2008 and 2009 was 0.4 percentage point, according to the April 2014 edition of the IMF's World Economic Outlook database (http://www.imf.org/external/pubs/ft/weo/2014/01/weodata/index.aspx).

2. The WTO dated from 1995. Its influence was reinforced by—some would say that whatever influence it possessed in fact derived from—the growth of multinational companies and global supply chains that gave business a powerful interest in free and open trade.

3. http://blogs.wsj.com/economics/2010/11/15/open-letter-to-ben-bernanke/.

4. See Chapter 26.

5. The Democrats took control of both houses in the 2006 midterm elections but faced a Republican-controlled White House. In addition to securing the White House, they now extended their majorities in the House and Senate.

6. The $20 billion was known as the first-loss tranche; it would compensate the borrowers for their first $20 billion of losses.

7. Starting in 1937 and extending through World War II, the New York rate was then lowered to 1 percent.

8. See Chapter 13.

9. Paulson (2010), p. 323.

10. Wessel (2009), pp. 237–40; Suskind (2011), pp. 122–23; Irwin (2013), p. 157.

11. In addition he received warrants enabling him to purchase a further $5 billion of common stock with a strike price of $115. With the warrants set to expire at the end of 2013, Goldman shares were trading at around $150.

12. Following Buffett's lead, Treasury also demanded warrants to purchase common stock in qualifying banks in an amount equal to 15 percent of the preferred equity infusion. The warrants were designed to give taxpayers a share in the returns if and when the banking system eventually recovered, but no voting rights were to be assigned to the Treasury.

13. Quoted in Zingales (2009), p. 73. Phillip Swagel, Paulson's chief economist, speaks of Treasury's "chronic disorganization" and of a "haphazard policy process within the administration" (Swagel 2009, p. 5).

14. Congress valued the approach in part because it meant that a significant share of mortgage-backed securities held by the banks would end up in the hands of the government, making it easier to restructure the underlying mortgages.

15. Paulson (2010), pp. 406–8.

16. Ibid., p. 413.

17. The government received another $7 billion in preferred shares as its fee for the guarantee, plus warrants as in the earlier round of capital injections.

18. Swagel (2009), p. 3.

19. The government ended up officially with a positive return on its investment (Congressional Budget Office 2009). But see also Barofsky (2012), who questions whether the TARP accounts, and by implication CBO reports based on them, provide a full and proper accounting of the costs incurred by the government.

Chapter 20

1. Suskind (2011), p. 212.

2. See Chapter 15, note 12.

3. In the case of bank loans, the scheme foresaw the Federal Deposit Insurance Corporation as overseeing the part of the program where banks sold bundles of mortgages to the highest bidder.

4. The only difference was that the guarantee was implicit: although Treasury would lend up to 85 percent of the purchase price, the loan would be "nonrecourse," meaning the government would recover only the residual value of the assets.

5. In addition, there was room for discretion when it came to deciding how much additional capital over and above the implied minimum the banks would be required to hold. See Bair (2012), p. 160, for a critical assessment.

6. Or more precisely, just in advance of their release, the key findings having been leaked to the markets.

7. As she put it in a speech at the Brookings Institution delivered during Obama's second month in office, "One crucial lesson from the 1930s is that a small fiscal expansion has only small effects." The research in question is Romer (1992), while the March 2009 speech is Romer (2009a).

8. This in the words of Murray and Kane (2009).

9. Actually, they chose a value from the upper end of the range of estimated multipliers on the grounds that the Fed would take steps to prevent interest rates from rising and crowding out private spending. This in turn had the effect of biasing downward their bottom-line estimate of needed stimulus spending.

10. Geithner (2014), p. 259.

11. CBO used the forecasting models of the Federal Reserve and two economic consulting firms, Macroeconomic Advisors and Global Insight. The office noted how it had "altered the models' usual formulation to reduce the extent to which interest rates respond to increases in output"—in line with evidence of no response of interest rates—which worked to produce larger counterfactual changes than otherwise (Congressional Budget Office 2010, p. 10).

12. Compare Obama's declaration in a radio address ten days before his inauguration that the stimulus would "likely save or create three million to four million jobs." Transcript at http://www.presidency.ucsb.edu/ws/index.php?pid=85391& st=jobs&st1=#axzz1OPNVsvHl. Three to four million jobs is a goodly number in an economy with, at this time, approximately 140 million employed people, both full- and part-time. The unemployment rate for its part was estimated by CBO to be from 0.7 to 1.8 percentage points lower.

13. See Blanchard and Leigh (2013). Their exercise relied on the variation in growth rates, actual and forecast, and forecasts of changes in fiscal policy for European countries.

14. The first study is Feyrer and Sacerdote (2011), while the second is Chodorow-Reich, Feiveson, Liscow, and Woolston (2012). The problem with cross-state comparisons is that states hit hardest by the recession could have received disproportionate amounts of additional federal funding. If they had more scope to then recover from the slump, simple correlations would erroneously credit the stimulus for this bounce-back effect. Feyrer and Sacerdote adjust for this by considering only the portion of matching funds that can be explained by the seniority of the state's House delegation (that is explainable on political as opposed to contemporaneous economic grounds). Chodorow-Reich

et al. consider only the increase in Medicaid assistance that can be explained by the pattern of pre-recession Medicaid spending.

Chapter 21

1. Such statements were known as forward guidance or, more familiarly, as "open mouth operations," to distinguish them from the central bank's conventional open market operations.

2. In Bernanke and Mishkin (1997) and Bernanke, Laubach, Mishkin, and Posen (1999).

3. Others suggested that the Fed should instead target a 5 percent rate of increase of nominal GDP, which would commit it to generating more inflation when growth was weak and less when the economy was growing strongly. But a nominal GDP target might be hard to explain. It would pose challenges for the Fed's communications strategy.

4. Even after 2012, there were questions about the importance that Fed officials attached to these numerical commitments. The 2 percent inflation target was repeatedly undershot. Chairman Bernanke's warning in June 2013 that the central bank might soon start "tapering" its security purchases caused mortgage rates to shoot up and raised doubts about whether the central bank was committed to maintaining its current policies of ease until the economy had strengthened significantly.

5. As reported in the *New York Times* (July 29, 2010). Bullard (2010) describes his views of the danger of deflation.

6. This evaluation of the Fed, clearly, is very different from that of contemporary observers impressed by the rhetoric of officials that they were prepared to do whatever was needed to avoid deflation and initiate a robust recovery (see, e.g., Wessel 2009 and Irwin 2013). Economists like Krippner (2012) have used the term "structure" of interest rates to estimate how expansionary policy was in this period. Although the Fed was incapable of pushing short-term rates below zero, its asset purchases could affect medium- and long-term rates, notably through expectations channels. Krippner relates the term "structure" to other observable economic variables and concludes that the "shadow" Fed funds rate, adjusted for asset purchases, was on the order of –1 percent in early 2009, when a simple Taylor Rule that relates the Fed funds target to the output gap and the rate of inflation suggests it should have been much lower. Using different methods, Wu and Xia (2013) find the same thing. More distance—and more systematic economic analysis—thus suggests that Fed policy was far from being as expansionary as was called for under the circumstances.

7. Mantega had already raised the currency-war flag a week earlier in a speech to an audience of Brazilian industrial leaders and was quick to repeat the phrase subsequently.

8. See Gagnon, Raskin, Remache, and Sack (2010).

9. The yield on ten-year agency debt fell by 156 basis points and that on agency mortgage-backed securities by 113 basis points, according to their estimates. Time series analysis using monthly data spanning the period January 1985 to June 2008, just prior to the financial crisis, confirms their results, although it yields slightly smaller effects, as does a time series study by Canlin and Wei (2012).

10. See Krishnamurthy and Vissing-Jorgensen (2011).

11. At the same time, QE1 and QE2 were complicated policies, so considering just the minutes or hours around the announcement may not be enough time for investors to evaluate them and for the full effects to materialize.

12. The Fed did not purchase corporate bonds directly under the program, but these are relatively close substitutes for mortgage-backed securities.

13. See Yellen (2011).

Chapter 22

1. The story of the auto bailout would take us far afield; telling it here would be a bit like telling the story of the Tennessee Valley Authority. The rationale for the bailout was that, in the distressed financial conditions of 2008–09, Chrysler and General Motors would have been unable to obtain the working capital needed to keep operating. This would have led to their liquidation, causing unnecessary disruption and costing jobs where they might have been saved. That the companies quickly reemerged from bankruptcy reorganization (Chrysler as a subsidiary of FIAT) and returned to profitability supports the rationale. The government lost some $10 billion on the $80 billion bailout loan because its shares in GM, when sold, did not cover its costs. Those losses might have been avoided had the companies been put through bankruptcy earlier (there was a lengthy delay as the companies were caught in the policy vacuum between the Bush and Obama administrations, much as the banks had been caught in the vacuum between the Hoover and Roosevelt administrations). Losses might also have been minimized had the loan to GM been smaller, forcing the company to negotiate a deeper restructuring of its liabilities. See Rattner (2010).

2. See Chapter 16.

3. Including, it should be noted, mortgages on second homes. Prior to 1979, when the new US bankruptcy code went into effect, a number of states had permitted judges to restructure mortgages on principal residences, and in some cases judges could still restructure second mortgages on such homes.

4. Kaiser (2013), pp. 109–10.

5. See, for example, Kuttner (2013), p. 224.

6. Principal reduction was permitted under HAMP, though it was not required, and fewer than 5 percent of mortgage modifications involved reductions of principal. DeMarco, in his capacity as acting director of the Federal Housing

Finance Agency and conservator for Fannie Mae and Freddie Mac, opposed it, as noted above. Thus, many homeowners whose interest payments were reduced still had an incentive to walk away, creating a likelihood of default on the new loans and eventual foreclosure.

7. Recall how the proponents of Glass-Steagall could push through the measure in part because the big banks realized that their securities market franchises had already been destroyed and could not be rebuilt.

8. In Kaufman (2013).

9. This included so-called common equity tier 1 capital in the amount of 4.5 percent and a "capital conservation buffer" of 2.5 percent.

10. Section 165 of Dodd-Frank required the regulators to impose more stringent capital standards on systemically important financial firms, while the Basel Committee on Banking Supervision developed a framework for calibrating capital surcharges for systemically significant banks.

11. Strictly speaking, the tenth member was not a regulator but an independent member with insurance expertise, insurance regulation having traditionally been left to the states (with now-well-known negative consequences).

12. Subsequently, in September 2013, it so designated a third institution, Prudential Financial. But even then it failed to specify what additional capital requirements would be applied to these systemically important institutions.

13. The new entity was to require each agency to submit its methodology for review, and it would deregister any agency whose methods were judged inadequate, although the office did little in the short run to prove its mettle.

14. In addition, it required smaller banks to report the results of their own company-run stress tests.

15. This in turn caused a number of large hedge funds to pay off their outside investors and turn themselves into "home offices," where they would be free of registration requirements.

16. A bill to cap the nondeposit liabilities of individual banks at 2 percent of US GDP was introduced in the Senate by Ted Kaufman, mentioned above, who happily had no plans to run for election in 2010. The bill was voted down by a nearly two-to-one margin. Kaiser (2013, p. 304) concludes that "like the House, the Senate preferred to try to improve the status quo, not toss it out." The UK, after its experience with several large bank failures and taking the advice of the expert commission chaired by Sir John Vickers, went the other way, advancing legislation to ring-fence the investment bank operations of its financial institutions, essentially breaking them up into retail and investment banks.

17. Kaiser (2013), pp. 238–39.

18. Geithner (2014), p. 421, not an entirely disinterested party, describes how Brown insisted on the 3 percent exemption to protect Fidelity and State Street Corp., two prominent financial institutions from his home state, from the effects of the Volcker Rule. Brown received campaign contributions from

MassMutual, State Street, and other financial-services companies in the period when the 3 percent exemption from the proprietary trading ban was being discussed, as detailed by Slack (2010). The revelation played no small role in his subsequent defeat at the hands of Warren in the 2012 general election.

19. US Senate (2013), p. 4.

Chapter 23

1. Sequestration started a few months later, in April 2013.
2. This is based on extrapolating the 1934–1937 trend. Recall that unemployment fell by an average of 2½ percentage points a year over this period. It then rose by roughly 5 percentage points between 1937 and 1938.
3. This point, with the particulars that follow, has been made by Reinhart and Rogoff (2009b) and more fully in Reinhart and Rogoff (2014).
4. The passage is from FDR's campaign address, Pittsburgh, October 1, 1936, available at http://www.presidency.ucsb.edu/ws/?pid=15149.
5. These are emphasized by Thorndike (2008).
6. The details are in Chapter 18.
7. These estimates are by the leading scholar of top incomes, the economist Emmanuel Saez (2013).
8. See Alter (2013), p. 160 and passim.
9. There was also the question of whether a legislative commitment to cut future deficits would be credible, since it could be reversed by a future Congress, in which case it would have even less impact on interest rates.
10. See Sinai, Orszag, and Rubin (2004).
11. Scheiber (2011), p. 150; Romer (2009b).
12. See below, Chapter 24.
13. This position is argued most powerfully by Alter (2013); see his p. 166 and passim.
14. Earlier, in negotiations headed by Vice President Biden, House Republicans pushed for $1.7 trillion in cuts. The administration's counter then became the basis for its final concession and for the agreement.
15. This assessment came in the Fund's 2013 Article IV review of the United States, released at midyear (IMF 2013a). In an analysis published two months earlier, the Congressional Budget Office put the impact in the middle of this range, estimating that fiscal contraction would chop off perhaps 1½ percentage points of US growth in 2013 (CBO 2013).
16. The issue was featured in a box entitled "Economic Effects of Federal Fiscal Policy," starting on page 10 of the report (Federal Reserve Board 2013).
17. The actual tapering began later, in December 2013.
18. See Bernanke (2013).
19. The first quotation is from Lacker (2013), the second from Robb (2013).

1. See Chapter 11. If they were not announced publicly for a few additional weeks, they were already known to the regulators or should have been.

2. The quotes are from the introductory statement by Trichet following the ECB board meeting on December 1, 2005 (ECB 2005).

3. The *Match* interview is available on the ECB's website: http://www.ecb.europa. eu/press/key/date/2005/html/sp051215.en.html.

4. And it indicated it would do so at fixed rates. This was the policy of "fixed rate tenders with full allotment."

5. A classic study of the question is Friedman and Schwartz (1982); the subsequent literature is enormous.

6. Remarks quoted in Brown (2010), p. 121.

7. The broke-the-fall comment is from then–World Bank President Robert Zoellick, but it is cited approvingly in Brown (2010), where the "one-trillion-dollar plan" is the title of chapter 4.

8. See Bradford and Linn (2010).

9. Figures here are from van Riet (2010). His table 4, p. 25, lists fiscal stimulus packages for individual Eurozone countries and also breaks out other components of the fiscal stance (such as revenue shortfalls and the built-in momentum of public expenditure).

10. Goldstein and Woglom (1992) had optimistically advanced this argument, showing how US state and municipal governments with relatively heavy debts were charged higher interest rates when attempting to borrow. In the event, their optimism was disappointed.

11. "Could a country that is a member of the euro zone default? Investors have generally thought not. . . . It is hard to imagine the leading lights of the European Union or the Frankfurt-based European Central Bank would allow a member to undermine the bloc. But a downgrade of Greece's credit rating has set alarm bells ringing in global markets." *New York Times* (December 9, 2009, p. B2). The fact that Dubai Ports World had just announced in November it was facing difficulties that would likely require it to restructure its debts did not help.

12. *New York Times* (December 12, 2009, p. A4).

13. The quotation is from an interview broadcast on the website of the Christian Democratic Union Party, as reported at http://www.telegraph.co.uk/finance/financialcrisis/9408349/Angela-Merkel-unsure-European-project-will-work.html.

14. Thomsen's previous experience was with programs in Serbia and Romania. He had also been involved in negotiating the Fund's program with Iceland. All this reassured the IMF hierarchy more than it did Athens.

15. Quoted in Thomas and Castle (2011).

16. Commerzbank had acquired Dresdner Bank, combining the country's second- and third-largest banks, just days before the failure of Lehman Brothers, in a transaction that could not have been timed worse. Investing in high-yielding Greek debt

then became an attractive way for management to dig itself out of the resulting financial hole—until, that is, the market in Greek bonds went south.

17. This according to estimates by the Bank for International Settlements. The holdings of French banks were not far behind.

18. The reference is to Provopoulos (2012).

19. European Commission (2010), p. 29.

20. The review in question dated from mid-2009. Later it was claimed that IMF staff already recognized Greece was insolvent but watered down the language in response to objections from the Greek authorities. See again Thomas and Castle (2011). This conclusion is hard to reconcile, however, with staff's rosy growth forecasts.

21. Specifically, "large loans" means loans in excess of six times the recipient country's quota subscription to the institution. The Greek loan far exceeded this limit. IMF staff voiced sufficient reservations about the sustainability of Greece's debt that the IMF amended its "exceptional access policy," for loans greater than six times quota, to include cases where there was "a high risk of international spillover effects," thus enabling the Fund's executive board to go ahead.

22. This according to Olli Rehn, EU commissioner for economic and monetary affairs, quoted in Taylor (2013).

23. Quoted in Erlanger and Saltmarsh (2010).

24. IMF (2013b), p. 28. EU officials involved in the decision, from Rehn to Trichet, disputed the implication that it was mainly opposition from the Europeans, as opposed to the Fund, that ruled out restructuring. Suffice it to say there was plenty of blame to go around.

Chapter 25

1. The backlash was especially strong in Germany. The irony here is that it was German—along with French—officials' reluctance to contemplate a restructuring, given the weakness of their banks, that led to the original approach that left the creditors whole. Hence the Deauville declaration anticipated that restructuring would now be mandatory *but only starting in 2013*. It was a classic instance of Augustinian reasoning: "Save me Oh Lord, just not yet." It was also not a distinction that the markets were capable of drawing.

2. An example is his 2012 *Financial Times* article "Europe Must Stay the Austerity Course" (Rehn 2012).

3. This is the estimate of the combined effects of expenditure cuts and tax increases, in conjunction with a fiscal multiplier as high as 1.7 (Blanchard and Leigh 2013, op. cit.).

4. European Commission (2013), p. 9.

5. More precisely, existing home prices quadrupled, while new home prices tripled, suggesting that those newly built homes on the outskirts of existing cities and in the countryside were imperfect substitutes for the existing housing stock.

6. Between 2000 and 2007, real GDP had grown at an average annual rate of 5.7 percent. There may have been a tendency for the figures to overstate the reality insofar as multinational firms preferred to book their profits in Ireland to take advantage of the country's corporate-profit-friendly tax regime. But the growth of Gross National Product, which strips out these international transfers, ran at an impressive annual average of 5.0 percent over the period.

7. IMF (2006), p. 5. Stress tests by the Central Bank of Ireland, conducted in 2007, similarly concluded that even with a sharp decline in house prices and a sharp rise in unemployment, capital would remain adequate at every bank.

8. Donovan and Murphy (2013), p. 70.

9. This according to the Commission of Investigation into the Banking Sector in Ireland (2011), p. 22. Also called the Nyberg Committee, it reported that the top twenty customers, virtually all property developers, accounted for as much as 50 percent of the bank's Irish loan book.

10. This again is according to the Nyberg Committee, op. cit. (2011), p. 32.

11. Lyons and Carey (2011), p. 25.

12. Ibid., p. 98.

13. Donovan and Murphy (2013), p. 187. Quinn's loans were formally called in 2011, leading to a series of court cases and a stay for the defendant in Mountjoy Prison.

14. As Donovan and Murphy note (ibid.), there are no official written records of the critical meeting, forcing investigators to reply on the recollections and oral testimony of participants. There was then pressure in November from the ECB, which controlled provision of liquidity to the Irish banking system, for further extension of the guarantee (although the letter in question from the ECB to the Irish finance minister has not been released). In mid-2013, the Irish Parliament moved to open an investigation into the decision, in the course of which the process leading to the disastrous decision will presumably come to light.

15. To be precise, 31.2 percent. The deficit was 11 percent of GDP net of bank recapitalization costs.

16. The recession started already in 2008, according to the standard business cycle chronology. Discretionary fiscal tightening over 2008–2010 was a cumulative €14.6 billion, or 9.3 percent of 2010 GDP. The four-year plan for 2011–2014 announced in November 2010 and subsequently agreed with the Troika (see below) then involved a further €15 billion of discretionary fiscal tightening.

17. That the amount of the Troika loan closely matched the ultimate cost to the government of the bank bailout was not a coincidence. There was also a €17.5 billion contribution from Ireland itself (from the Treasury and National Pension Reserve).

18. Not so the IMF, which by custom gets paid back first and in full. Thus, Noonan's proposal was reported to have garnered the support of the Fund.

19. Eventually haircuts would be administered to some holders of junior bank bonds, so-called subordinated debt. Some of these were substantial. But the holders of senior unsecured bonds—unlike the Irish taxpayer—escaped.

20. To be fair, the paragraph in question continued: "We recognise that the risks in the short term are tilted to the downside, and, in particular, the headwinds from fiscal consolidation on domestic demand could be larger than anticipated. Over the longer haul also, continued private and public sector balance sheet adjustments, coupled with a weak banking sector, could delay the recovery." See European Commission (2009), para. 3.

21. The net immigration number was lower, but this does not change the point that this was a costly form of adjustment.

22. This as of the end of 2008.

23. An analysis emphasizing these factors is Antras, Segura-Caytuela, and Rodriguez-Rodriguez (2010).

24. The first €4.3 billion was initially provided as a loan, converted into equity when it became apparent that there was no way the bank could pay it back. Eventually Bankia announced that its losses for the 2012 financial year exceeded €21 billion. Its chairman, Rodrigo Rato, IMF managing director prior to Dominique Strauss-Kahn, was among those investigated in connection with charges that the bank had falsified accounts and manipulated share prices.

25. See Oliver Wyman Group (2012), p. 58 et seq.

26. Mario Draghi's pronouncement, less than two months prior to the consultants' report, that the ECB would "do whatever it takes" to hold the euro together, by implicitly promising more support to the market in Spanish government bonds, worked in the same direction. See Chapter 26.

Chapter 26

1. Prices more than doubled between 2000 and 2007, which tells the tale.

2. This according to figures released by the country's Office of National Statistics in March 2014.

3. See Office for Budget Responsibility (2013), p. 55.

4. The recommendation came in the Fund's Article IV report on the British economy (IMF 2012). Data above on the extent of fiscal consolidation in the UK are similarly from this source.

5. Laeven and Valencia (2012) put the total cost at 8.8 percent of GDP, 7.8 percent after recovery of income through, inter alia, asset sales by the government. There was still the possibility of further losses arising from contingent liabilities (such as asset purchases) as well as future recoveries, although these were unlikely to change the picture.

6. Cited in Winch (1969), p. 118.

7. In his Mais Lecture, delivered on the eve of the election, Osborne pointed to the Reinhart and Rogoff (2009b) argument that debt begins to exercise "a large negative impact on long term growth" when it exceeds 90 percent of GDP (Osborne 2010).

8. As a result of these and related measures, public sector net investment was cut sharply under the coalition's budgets, from 3½ percent of GDP in the last year of the Labour government to 2½ percent in 2010–11, 1¾ percent in 2011–12, and barely 1½ percent in 2012–13. And this in a period of unprecedentedly low interest rates, when the government could have been borrowing to invest in the future.

9. Warner (2013), at http://blogs.telegraph.co.uk/finance/jeremywarner/100025496/oh-god-i-cannot-take-any-more-of-the-austerity-debate/.

10. The criminal case later collapsed and the charges were dropped. A civil suit and countersuit then followed, leading to a financial settlement in late 2012 (terms of which were confidential).

11. Quoted in Sirletti (2011).

12. The institute used a very generous interest rate of 9 percent to discount future interest and principal payments, which implied a 21 percent net present value loss for investors. A more reasonable interest rate of, say, 5 percent, like that used by the IMF in its debt sustainability calculations, painted a very different picture. For details see Zettelmeyer, Trebesch, and Gulati (2013).

13. Restructuring required a quorum of votes representing 50 percent of the face value of outstanding bonds, with bondholders representing two-thirds of the face value of the outstanding privately held debt taking part in the vote. Importantly, these requirements applied across all bonds, not individual bond by individual bond.

14. See, for example, the bank's annual report for 2010 (European Central Bank 2011, pp. 20, 92). The central bank also kept interest rates on hold for the entire year.

15. Eventually, in 2013, the ECB released details on what it had purchased under the SMP. The main beneficiary was Italy, whose bonds accounted for almost half the total purchased, followed by Spain and then Greece.

16. For example, it would lengthen the term of lending under the program and supply LTROs with full allotment, meaning it would provide the banks with as much liquidity against collateral as they might require. The problem, of course, was that the banks were not inclined to demand much liquidity from the ECB because they were not much inclined to lend it to the private sector.

17. As, for example, in March 2011, just before the ECB raised interest rates.

18. The ECB then cut interest rates by 50 basis points at the end of 2011, but the damage was done.

19. Thus, on July 24 Patrick Doering, secretary general of the Free Democratic Party, part of Chancellor Merkel's governing coalition, unhelpfully suggested that "it could help to create confidence in markets if Greece were no longer part of the Eurozone"; Deutsche Börse Group (2012).

20. As widely reported, in inter alia *Daily Telegraph* (June 26, 2012), http://www.telegraph.co.uk/finance/financialcrisis/9428894/Debt-crisis-Mario-Draghi pledges-to-do-whatever-it-takes-to-save-euro.html.

21. For the time being, the ECB didn't actually have to do anything. OMT was not activated in the second half of 2012 or in 2013; the promise alone was enough. One is reminded of how simply granting new powers to the Federal Reserve to discount notes, drafts, bills, and acceptances was enough to reassure holders of bank deposits in the 1933 crisis (see Chapter 15).

22. In February 2014 the Constitutional Court issued a somewhat ambiguous ruling questioning certain aspects of OMT, referring the case to the European Court of Justice, and retaining the right to rule further on the constitutionality of the ECB's measures. This did nothing to clear up the confusion.

23. There was also a "two-pack" of further regulations aimed at strengthening the monitoring of the draft budgetary plans of euro-area members and adoption of a "European Semester" to harmonize the timing of budgetary decision making across member states.

24. The limit on the structural deficit was a more generous 1 percent of GDP for countries with debt ratios of less than 60 percent.

25. This had permitted Germany and France to avoid their application when violating the monetary union's budgetary guidelines in 2003–04, an event that did not exactly enhance the credibility of the Stability and Growth Pact going forward.

26. Under that agreement, a €55 billion fund was to be built up through levies on the banks between 2016 and 2026. In the meantime, resolution costs would be borne by levies on the banks themselves, national governments' resources, and ESM loans to those governments, in that order. This arrangement threatened to transfer the difficulties of one bank first to other banks and then to the sovereign. Moreover, the resolution fund would not possess a credit line equivalent to that extended to the FDIC by the US government, raising further questions about the adequacy of its resources. Overall, this was rather less than the necessary banking union, reflecting political realities, and German reservations in particular.

27. This compares the S&P 90 starting in 1929 and the S&P 500 starting in 2007. Similarly, by August 2013 the S&P 500 was again above its 2007 peak, whereas it took the S&P 90 almost three full decades to match the 1929 peak. World equity market indices, compared by Eichengreen and O'Rourke (2010), show the same thing. By early 2010, they had recovered to within 25 percent of April 2008 (Bear Stearns) levels; after 1929, in contrast, they continued to trend downward, hitting a trough in July 1932 at barely 33 percent of June 1929 levels.

Conclusion

1. The references are of course to Friedman and Schwartz (1963), Keynes (1936), and Polanyi (1944).

2. The most influential statement of this alternative was probably Nurkse (1944), cited in Chapter 17 above.

3. To be sure, six full years after the crisis there was Thomas Piketty (2014). But Piketty dismissed the impact of the crisis on inequality as a blip. He devoted just one page (p. 297) to hypothesizing that inequality causing lower- and middle-class incomes in the United States to stagnate encouraged households to take on additional debt in order to support the continued growth of their living standards—debt that heightened the fragility of the financial system. A systematic analysis of the connections between inequality and the crisis remains to be written.

REFERENCES

Accominotti, Olivier. (2012). "London Merchant Banks, the Central European Panic, and the Sterling Crisis of 1931." *Journal of Economic History* 72, 1–43.

Adalet, Muge. (2009). "Were Universal Banks More Vulnerable to Banking Failures? Evidence from the 1931 German Banking Crisis." Working Paper 0911, Economics Research Forum, Tusiad-Koc University (November).

Aguado, Iago Gil. (2001). "The Creditanstalt Crisis of 1931 and the Failure of the Austro-German Customs Union Project." *Historical Journal* 44, 199–221.

Alesina, Alberto, and Silvia Ardagna. (2010). "Large Changes in Fiscal Policy: Taxes Versus Spending." In Jeffrey Brown (ed.), *Tax Policy and the Economy* 24, 35–68.

Allen, Frederick Lewis. (1931). *Only Yesterday: An Informal History of the Nineteen-Twenties.* New York: Harper & Bros.

Alter, Jonathan. (2010). *The Promise: President Obama, Year One.* New York: Simon & Schuster.

Alter, Jonathan. (2013). *The Center Holds: Obama and His Enemies.* New York: Simon & Schuster.

Anderson, William. (2000). "Risk and the National Industrial Recovery Act: An Empirical Evaluation." *Public Choice* 103, 139–61.

Angelides, Phil. (2011). "Fannie, Freddie and the Financial Crisis." *Bloomberg View* (August 3), http://www.bloomberg.com/news/2011-08-04/fannie-freddie-role-in-the-financial-crisis-commentary-by-phil-angelides.html.

Antràs, Pol, Rubén Segura-Cayuela, and Diego Rodriguez-Rodriguez. (2010). "Firms in International Trade (with an Application to Spain)." Unpublished manuscript, Harvard University, Bank of Spain, and University Complutense (December).

Archibald, Robert, and David Feldman. (1998). "Investment During the Great Depression: Uncertainty and the Role of the Smoot Hawley Tariff." *Southern Economic Journal* 64, 857–79.

Awalt, Francis Gloyd. (1969). "Recollections of the Banking Crisis in 1933." *Business History Review* 43, 347–71.

Bair, Sheila. (2012). *Bull by the Horns: Fighting to Save Main Street from Wall Street and Wall Street from Itself.* New York: Free Press.

Baldursson, Fridrik Mar, and Richard Portes. (2013). "Gambling for Resurrection in Iceland: The Rise and Fall of the Banks." CEPR Discussion Paper no. 9664 (September).

Balke, Nathan, and Robert Gordon. (1986). "Historical Data." In Robert Gordon (ed.), *The American Business Cycle: Continuity and Change.* Chicago: University of Chicago Press, 781–850.

Barber, William. (1985). *From New Era to New Deal: Herbert Hoover, the Economists, and American Economic Policy, 1921–1933.* New York: Cambridge University Press.

Barnard, Harry. (1958). *Independent Man: The Life of Senator James Couzens.* New York: Scribner.

Barofsky, Neil. (2012). *Bailout: An Inside Account of How Washington Abandoned Main Street While Rescuing Wall Street.* New York: Free Press.

Barth, James, R. Dan Brumbaugh, Jr., and James Wilcox. (2000). "The Repeal of Glass-Steagall and the Advent of Broad Banking." *Journal of Economic Perspectives* 14, 191–204.

Beard, Charles, and George Smith. (1940). *The Old Deal and the New.* New York: Macmillan.

Becker, Bo, and Todd Milbourn. (2011). "How Did Increased Competition Affect Credit Ratings?" *Journal of Finance and Economics* 101, 493–514.

Berg, Claes, and Lars Jonung. (1998). "Pioneering Price Level Targeting: The Swedish Experience 1931–1937." Seminar Paper no. 642, Institute for International Economic Studies, Stockholm University (July).

Berle, Adolf, and Gardiner Means. (1933). *The Modern Corporation and Private Property.* New York: Macmillan.

Bernanke, Ben. (1983). "Nonmonetary Effects of the Financial Crisis in the Propagation of the Great Depression." *American Economic Review* 73, 257–76.

Bernanke, Ben. (2000). *Essays on the Great Depression.* Princeton: Princeton University Press.

Bernanke, Ben. (2002a). "Deflation: Making Sure 'It' Doesn't Happen Here." Remarks before the National Economists Club, Washington, DC (November 21), http://www.federalreserve.gov/boarddocs/speeches/2002/20021121/default.htm.

Bernanke, Ben. (2002b). "Remarks by Governor Ben S. Bernanke on the occasion of Milton Friedman's Ninetieth Birthday." University of Chicago, Chicago (November 8), http://www.federalreserve.gov/boarddocs/speeches/2002/20021108/default.htm.

Bernanke, Ben. (2005). "The Global Savings Glut and the U.S. Current Account Deficit." Remarks delivered on the occasion of the Homer Jones Lecture, St. Louis (April 14), http://www.federalreserve.gov/boarddocs/speeches/2005/20050414/.

Bernanke, Ben. (2007). "The Economic Outlook." Testimony before the Joint Economic Committee, U.S. Congress, Board of Governors of the Federal Reserve System (March 28), http://www.federalreserve.gov/newsevents/testimony/bernanke20070328a.htm.

Bernanke, Ben. (2008). "U.S. Financial Markets." Testimony of Chairman Ben S. Bernanke before the Committee on Financial Services, U.S. House of Representatives (September 24), http://www.federalreserve.gov/newsevents/testimony/bernanke20080923a1.htm.

Bernanke, Ben. (2013). "Monitoring the Financial System." Speech at the 49th Annual Conference on Bank Structure and Competition, sponsored by Federal Reserve Bank of Chicago, Chicago (May 10), http://www.federalreserve.gov/newsevents/speech/bernanke20130510a.htm.

Bernanke, Ben, Thomas Laubach, Frederic Mishkin, and Adam Posen. (1999). *Inflation Targeting: Lessons from the International Experience.* Princeton: Princeton University Press.

Bernanke, Ben, and Frederic Mishkin. (1997). "Inflation Targeting: A New Framework for Monetary Policy?" *Journal of Economic Perspectives* 11, 97–116.

Best, Gary Dean. (1991). *Pride, Prejudice and Politics: Roosevelt vs. Recovery 1933–1938.* Westport, CT: Praeger.

Bishop, Graham. (1992). "The EC's Public Debt Disease: Discipline with Credit Spreads and Cure with Price Stability." In D. E. Fair and Christian Boissieu (eds.), *Fiscal Policy, Taxation and the Financial System in an Increasingly Integrated Europe.* Dordrecht: Kluwer, 207–34.

Blanchard, Olivier, and Daniel Leigh. (2013). "Growth Forecast Errors and Fiscal Multipliers." *American Economic Review* 103, 117–20.

Blancheton, Bertrand. (2012). "The False Balance Sheets of the Bank of France and the Origins of the Franc Crisis, 1924–26." *Accounting History Review* 22, 1–22.

Board of Governors of the Federal Reserve System. (2013). "FOMC: Transcripts and Other Historical Materials, 2007." Washington, DC: Board of Governors of the Federal Reserve System, http://www.federalreserve.gov/monetarypolicy/fomchistorical2007.htm.

Board of Governors of the Federal Reserve System. (2014). "FOMC: Transcripts and Other Historical Materials, 2008." Washington, DC: Board of Governors of the Federal Reserve System, http://www.federalreserve.gov/monetarypolicy/fomchistorical2008.htm.

Bolton, Patrick, Xavier Freixas, and Joel Shapiro. (2012). "The Credit Ratings Game." *Journal of Finance* 67, 85–112.

Bonin, Hubert. (1996). "Oustric, un financier prédateur (1914–1930)." *Revue historique* 295, 429–48.

Borchardt, Knut. (1991). *Perspectives on Modern German Economic History and Policy.* Cambridge: Cambridge University Press.

Boudreaux, Donald. (2011). "Becoming More Certain About the Role of Regime Uncertainty." *CATO Unbound* (December 20), http://www.

cato-unbound.org/2011/12/20/donald-j-boudreaux/becoming-more-certain-ab
out-the-role-of-regime-uncertainty/.

Boyd, Roddy. (2011). *Fatal Risk: A Cautionary Tale of AIG's Corporate Suicide*. New York:
Wiley.

Boyes, Roger. (2009). *Meltdown Iceland: Lessons on the World Financial Crisis from a
Small Bankrupt Island*. New York: Bloomsbury USA.

Bradford, Colin, and Johannes Linn. (2010). "The April 2009 London G-20 Summit
in Retrospect." *Brookings Institution Opinion* (April 5), http://www.brookings.edu/
research/opinions/2010/04/05-g20-summit-linn.

Brandeis, Louis. (1914). *Other People's Money—and How the Bankers Use It*.
New York: Frederick A. Stokes.

Bratter, Herbert. (1941). "The Committee for the Nation: A Case History in
Monetary Propaganda." *Journal of Political Economy* 49, 531–53.

Broadberry, Stephen, and Nicholas Crafts. (2010). "Openness, Protectionism and
Britain's Productivity Performance over the Long Run." Working Paper no. 36,
Centre for Competitive Advantage in the Global Economy, University of
Warwick (December).

Brooker, Katrina. (2010). "Citi's Founder, Alone with His Regrets." *New York Times*
(January 2), http://www.nytimes.com/2010/01/03/business/economy/03weill.
html?pagewanted=all.

Brooks, John. (1969). *Once in Golconda: A True Drama of Wall Street, 1920–1938*.
New York: Allworth Press.

Brown, E. Cary. (1956). "Fiscal Policy in the 'Thirties: A Reappraisal." *American
Economic Review* 46, 857–79.

Brown, Gordon. (2010). *Beyond the Crash: Overcoming the First Crisis of Globalization*.
New York: Free Press.

Bruner, Robert, and Sean Carr. (2007). *The Panic of 1907: Lessons Learned from the
Market's Perfect Storm*. New York: Wiley.

Buiter, Willem, Giancarlo Corsetti, and Nouriel Roubini. (1993). "Excessive
Deficits: Sense and Nonsense in the Treaty of Maastricht." *Economic Policy* 8,
57–100.

Buiter, Willem, and Anne Sibert. (2005). "How the Eurosystem's Treatment of
Collateral in Its Open Market Operations Weakens Fiscal Discipline in the
Eurozone (and What to Do About It)." CEPR Discussion Paper no. 5387.
London: Center for Economic Policy Research.

Bullard, James. (2010). "Seven Faces of 'The Peril'." *Federal Reserve Bank of St. Louis
Review* (September–October), 339–52.

Bullard, James. (2013). "The Notorious Summer of 2008." Presentation to the
University of Arkansas Quarterly Business Analysis Luncheon, Rogers,
(November 21), http://research.stlouisfed.org/econ/bullard/pdf/Bullard_
NWArkansas_2013November21_Final.pdf.

Burner, David. (2005). *Herbert Hoover: A Public Life*. Newtown, CT: American
Political Biography Press.

Burns, Arthur, and Wesley Mitchell. (1946). *Measuring Business Cycles*. Cambridge, MA: National Bureau of Economic Research.

Butkiewicz, James. (1995). "The Impact of a Lender of Last Resort During the Great Depression: The Case of the Reconstruction Finance Corporation." *Explorations in Economic History* 32, 197–216.

Calomiris, Charles, and R. Glenn Hubbard. (1995). "Internal Finance and Investment: Evidence from the Undistributed Profits Tax of 1936–1937." *Journal of Business* 68, 443–82.

Calomiris, Charles, Joseph Mason, and David Wheelock. (2011). "Did Doubling Reserve Requirements Cause the Recession of 1937–1938? A Microeconomic Approach." Working Paper 2011–002. St. Louis: Federal Reserve Bank of St. Louis (January).

Calomiris, Charles, and Eugene White. (1994). "The Origins of Federal Deposit Insurance." In Claudia Goldin and Gary Libecap (eds.), *The Regulated Economy: A Historical Approach to Political Economy*. Chicago: University of Chicago Press, 145–88.

Campa, José. (1990). "Exchange Rates and Economic Recovery in the 1930s: An Extension to Latin America." *Journal of Economic History* 50, 667–82.

Canlin, Li, and Min Wei. (2012). "Term Structure Modeling with Supply Factors and the Federal Reserve's Large Scale Asset Purchase Programs." Finance and Economics Discussion Series 2012–37. Washington, DC: Board of Governors of the Federal Reserve System (May), http://www.federalreserve.gov/pubs/feds/2012/201237/201237abs.html.

Capie, Forrest, and Alan Weber. (1985). *A Monetary History of the United Kingdom 1870–1982*. London: Allen & Unwin.

Carey, Kevin. (1999). "Investigating a Debt Channel for the Smoot-Hawley Tariff: Evidence from the Sovereign Bond Market." *Journal of Economic History* 59, 748–61.

Cargill, Thomas, and Thomas Mayer. (2006). "The Effect of Changes in Reserve Requirements During the 1930s: The Evidence from Nonmember Banks." *Journal of Economic History* 66, 417–32.

Cecchetti, Stephen. (1992). "Prices During the Great Depression: Was the Deflation of 1930–1932 Really Unanticipated?" *American Economic Review* 82, 141–56.

Center for Responsible Lending. (2008). "Unfair and Unsafe: How Countrywide's Irresponsible Practices Have Harmed Borrowers and Shareholders." CRL Issue Paper. Durham, NC: Center for Responsible Lending (February 7), http://www.responsiblelending.org/mortgage-lending/research-analysis/unfair-and-unsafe-countrywide-white-paper.pdf.

Chandler, Alfred. (1990). *Scale and Scope: The Dynamics of Industrial Capitalism*. Cambridge: Belknap Press for Harvard University Press.

Chodorow-Reich, Gabriel, Laura Feiveson, Zachary Liscow, and William Gui Woolston. (2012). "Does State Fiscal Relief During Recessions Increase Employment? Evidence from the American Recovery and Reinvestment Act." *American Economic Journal: Economic Policy* 4, 118–45.

Clarke, Stephen O. (1967). *Central Bank Cooperation, 1924–1931*. New York: Federal Reserve Bank of New York.

Cole, Harold, and Lee Ohanian. (2004). "New Deal Policies and the Persistence of the Great Depression: A General Equilibrium Analysis." *Journal of Political Economy* 112, 779–816.

Commission of Investigation into the Banking Sector in Ireland. (2011). "Misjudging Risk: Causes of the Systemic Banking Crisis in Ireland." Dublin: Commission of Investigation into the Banking Sector in Ireland, Dept. of Finance (March).

Committee on Finance and Industry (Macmillan Committee). (1931). *Report of Committee on Finance and Industry (Cmd. 3897)*. London: Her Majesty's Stationery Office.

Condon, Christopher. (2011). "Fed Made State Street Profitable as Money-Fund Middleman in '08." *Bloomberg News* (August 23), http://www. bloomberg.com/news/2011-08-23/fed-made-state-street-profitable-as-money-fund-middleman-in-08.html.

Congressional Budget Office. (2010). "Estimated Impact of the American Recovery and Reinvestment Act on Employment and Economic Output from April 2010 Through June 2010." Publication no. 21671. Washington, DC: Congressional Budget Office (August 24), http://www.cbo.gov/publication/21671.

Congressional Budget Office. (2013). "The Budget and Economic Outlook: Fiscal Years 2013 to 2023." Washington, DC: CBO (February 5), http://www.cbo.gov/ publication/43907.

Costigliola, Frank. (1976). "The United States and the Reconstruction of Germany in the 1920s." *Business History Review* 50, 477–502.

Courtemanche, Charles, and Kenneth Snowden. (2011). "Repairing a Mortgage Crisis: HOLC Lending and Its Impact on Local Housing Markets." *Journal of Economic History* 71, 307–37.

Covitz, Daniel, Nellie Liang, and Gustavo Suarez. (2009). "The Anatomy of a Financial Crisis: The Evolution of Panic-Driven Runs in the Asset-Backed Commercial Paper Market." *Proceedings*, Federal Reserve Bank of San Francisco (January).

Crafts, Nicholas. (2013). "The Eurozone: If Only It Were the 1930s." *Vox* (December 13), http://www.voxeu.org/article/eurozone-if-only-it-were-1930s.

Crafts, Nicholas, and Peter Fearon. (2010). "A Recession to Remember: Lessons from the US, 1937–1938." *Vox* (November 23), http://www.voxeu.org/article/ recession-remember-lessons-us-1937-1938.

Curcio, Vincent. (2000). *Chrysler: The Life and Times of an Automotive Genius*. New York: Oxford University Press.

Dagher, Jihad, and Ning Fu. (2012). "What Fuels the Booms Drives the Busts: Regulation and the Mortgage Crisis." Working Paper no. 11/215. Washington, DC: IMF (September).

De Grauwe, Paul, and Yuemei Ji. (2013). "Panic-Driven Austerity in the Eurozone and Its Implications." *Vox* (February 21), http://www.voxeu.org/article/panic-driven-austerity-eurozone-and-its-implications.

DeLong, Gayle. (1998). "Domestic and International Bank Mergers: The Gains from Focusing Versus Diversifying." Unpublished manuscript, Stern School of Business, New York University.

Dembe, Allard, and Leslie Boden. (2000). "Moral Hazard: A Question of Morality?" *New Solutions* 10, 257–79.

Deutsche Börse Group. (2012). "Germany: Senior Coalition Member Argues for Greek Euro Exit" (July 24), https://mninews.marketnews.com/content/update-germanysenior-coal-member-argues-greek-euro-exit.

Diaz-Alejandro, Carlos. (1970). *Essays on the Economic History of the Argentine Republic.* New Haven: Yale University Press.

Dokko, Jane, Brian Doyle, Michael Kiley, Jinill Kim, Shane Sherlund, Jae Sim, and Skander van den Heuvel. (2011). "Monetary Policy and the Housing Bubble." *Economic Policy* 26, 237–87.

Donovan, Donal, and Antoin Murphy. (2013). *The Fall of the Celtic Tiger.* Oxford: Oxford University Press.

Dullien, Sebastian, and Ulrike Guérot. (2012). "The Long Shadow of Ordoliberalism: Germany's Approach to the Euro Crisis." European Council on Foreign Relations Policy Brief 49 (February).

Dwyer, Gerald. (2011). "Economic Effects of Banking Crises: A Bit of Evidence from Iceland and Ireland." Center for Financial Innovation and Stability, Federal Reserve Bank of Atlanta (March).

Eccles, Marriner. (1951). *Beckoning Frontiers.* New York: Knopf.

Eggertsson, Gauti. (2008). "Great Expectations and the End of the Depression." *American Economic Review* 98, 1476–1516.

Eichengreen, Barry. (1993). "European Monetary Unification." *Journal of Economic Literature* 31, 1321–57.

Eichengreen, Barry, and Kevin O'Rourke. (2010). "A Tale of Two Depressions: What Do the New Data Tell Us?" *Vox* (March 8), http://www.voxeu.org/article/tale-two-depressions-what-do-new-data-tell-us-february-2010-update.

Einzig, Paul. (1931). *The Fight for Financial Supremacy.* London: Kegan Paul, Trench, Trüber.

Erlanger, Steven, and Matthew Saltmarsh. (2010). "Greek Debt Crisis Raises Doubts About the European Union." *New York Times* (March 7), http://www.nytimes.com/2010/05/08/world/europe/08europe.html.

European Central Bank. (2005). "Introductory Statement with Q&A" (December 1), http://www.ecb.europa.eu/press/pressconf/2005/html/is051201.en.html.

European Central Bank. (Various years). *Annual Report.* Frankfurt: European Central Bank.

European Commission. (2009). "Memorandum of Understanding Between the European Commission and Ireland." Brussels: European Commission (December 16).

European Commission. (2010). "The Economic Adjustment Programme for Greece." Occasional Paper 61. Brussels: Directorate-General for Economic and Financial Affairs (May).

European Commission. (2013). "Public Opinion in the European Union: First Results." *Standard Eurobarometer* 79 (spring 2013). Brussels: European Commission, http://ec.europa.eu/public_opinion/archives/eb/eb79/eb79_first_en.pdf.

Farrell, Greg. (2010). *Crash of the Titans: Greed, Hubris, the Fall of Merrill Lynch, and the Near-Collapse of Bank of America.* New York: Crown Business.

Federal Reserve Bank of New York. (1932). *Seventeenth Annual Report of the Federal Reserve Bank of New York for the Year Ended December 31, 1931.* New York: Federal Reserve Bank of New York.

Federal Reserve Board. (2002). "FOMC Meeting Transcript," http://www.federalreserve.gov/monetarypolicy/fomchistorical2002.htm.

Federal Reserve Board. (2009). "Press Release: Release Date July 23, 2009," http://www.federalreserve.gov/newsevents/press/bcreg/20090723a.htm.

Federal Reserve Board. (2013). *Monetary Policy Report.* Washington, DC: Board of Governors of the Federal Reserve System (July 17), http://www.federalreserve.gov/monetarypolicy/files/20130717_mprfullreport.pdf.

Ferguson, Thomas, and Peter Temin. (2003). "Made in Germany: The German Currency Crisis of 1931." *Research in Economic History* 21, 1–53.

Fettig, David. (2002). "Lender of More Than Last Resort: Recalling Section 13(b) and the Years When the Federal Reserve Opened Its Discount Window to Businesses." *The Region.* Federal Reserve Bank of Minneapolis (December), 15–47.

Feyrer, James, and Bruce Sacerdote. (2011). "Did the Stimulus Stimulate? Real Time Estimates of the Effects of the American Recovery and Reinvestment Act." NBER Working Paper no. 16759 (February).

Field, Alexander. (2011). *A Great Leap Forward: 1930s Depression and U.S. Economic Growth.* New Haven: Yale University Press.

Financial Crisis Inquiry Commission. (2011). *The Financial Crisis Inquiry Report.* Washington, DC: Government Printing Office (January).

Fishback, Price, Alfonso Flores-Lagunes, William Horrace, Shawn Kantor, and Jaret Treber. (2011). "The Influence of the Home Owners' Loan Corporation on Housing Markets During the 1930s." *Review of Financial Studies* 24, 1782–1813.

Fishback, Price, Jonathan Rose, and Kenneth Snowden. (2013). *Well Worth Saving: How the New Deal Safeguarded Homeownership.* Chicago: University of Chicago Press.

Fisher, Irving. (1911). *The Purchasing Power of Money: Its Determination and Relation to Credit, Interest and Crises.* New York: Macmillan.

Fisher, Irving. (1933). "The Debt-Deflation Theory of Great Depressions." *Econometrica* 1, 337–57.

Fishlow, Albert. (1972). "Origins and Consequences of Import Substitution in Brazil." In Luis Eugenio di Marco (ed.), *International Economics and Development, Essays in Honor of Raúl Prebisch.* New York: Academic Press, 311–65.

Flandreau, Marc, Norbert Gaillard, and Ugo Panizza. (2010). "Conflicts of Interest, Reputation, and the Interwar Debt Crisis: Banksters or Bad Luck?" CEPR Working Paper no. 7705 (February).

Frankel, Jeffrey. (1986). "Expectations and Commodity Price Dynamics: The Overshooting Model." *American Journal of Agricultural Economics* 68, 344–48.

Friedman, Milton, and Anna J. Schwartz. (1963). *A Monetary History of the United States, 1867–1960.* Princeton: Princeton University Press for the National Bureau of Economic Research.

Friedman, Milton, and Anna J. Schwartz. (1982). *Monetary Trends in the United States and United Kingdom: Their Relation to Income, Prices, and Interest Rates, 1867–1975.* Chicago: University of Chicago Press for the National Bureau of Economic Research.

Gagnon, Joseph, Matthew Raskin, Julie Remache, and Brian Sack. (2010). "Large-Scale Asset Purchases by the Federal Reserve: Did They Work?" Staff Report no. 441. New York: Federal Reserve Bank of New York (March).

Galbraith, John Kenneth. (1952). *American Capitalism: The Concept of Countervailing Power.* Boston: Houghton Mifflin.

Galbraith, John Kenneth. (1954). *The Great Crash, 1929.* New York: Penguin.

Gamble, Richard. (1989). A History of the Federal Reserve Bank of Atlanta, 1914–1989. Atlanta: Federal Reserve Bank of Atlanta, http://www.frbatlanta.org/pubs/atlantafedhistory/.

Geanakoplos, John. (2010). "The Leverage Cycle." *NBER Macroeconomics Annual* 24, 1–65.

Geithner, Timothy. (2014). *Stress Test: Reflections on Financial Crises.* New York: Crown.

George, Paul. (1986). "Brokers, Binders and Builders: Greater Miami's Boom of the Mid-1920s." *Florida Historical Quarterly* 65, 27–51.

Gilbert, R. Alton. (1986). "Requiem for Regulation Q: What It Did and Why It Passed Away." *Federal Reserve Bank of St. Louis Review* (February), 22–37.

Goetzmann, William, and Frank Newman. (2010). "Securitization in the 1920s." NBER Working Paper no. 15650 (January).

Goldstein, Morris, and Geoffrey Woglom. (1992). "Market-Based Fiscal Discipline in Monetary Unions: Evidence from the U.S. Municipal Bond Market." In Matthew Canzoneri, Vittorio Grilli, and Paul Masson (eds.), *Establishing a Central Bank: Issues in Europe and Lessons from the US.* New York: Cambridge University Press, 228–70.

Gorton, Gary, and Andrew Metrick. (2012). "Getting Up to Speed on the Financial Crisis: A One-Weekend Reader's Guide." NBER Working Paper no. 17778 (January).

Gorton, Gary, and Nicholas Souleles. (2007). "Special Purpose Vehicles and Securitization." In Mark Carey and Rene Stulz (eds.), *The Risks of Financial Institutions.* Chicago: University of Chicago Press, 549–97.

Greenspan, Alan. (2005). "Economic Flexibility." Remarks by Chairman Alan Greenspan before the National Italian American Foundation, Washington, DC (October 12), http://www.federalreserve.gov/boarddocs/speeches/2005/20051012/.

Greenspan, Alan. (2009). "The Fed Didn't Cause the Housing Bubble." *Wall Street Journal* (March 11), http://online.wsj.com/article/SB123672965066989281.html.

Grímsson, Ólafur Ragnar. (2005). "How to Succeed in Modern Business: Lessons from the Icelandic Voyage." Speech by the President of Iceland at the Walbrook Club, London (May 3).

Hamilton, David. (1985). "The Causes of the Banking Panic of 1930: Another View." *Journal of Southern History* 51, 581–608.

Hamilton, James. (1992). "Was the Deflation During the Great Depression Anticipated? Evidence from the Commodity Futures Market." *American Economic Review* 82, 157–78.

Harris, Roy. (2010). *Pulitzer's Gold: Behind the Prize for Public Service Journalism.* Columbia: University of Missouri Press.

Hausman, Joshua. (2012). "What Was Bad for GM Was Bad for America: The Automobile Industry and the 1937–38 Recession." Unpublished manuscript, University of California, Berkeley.

Hawtrey, Ralph. (1938). *A Century of Bank Rate.* London: Longmans, Green.

Hawtrey, Ralph. (1962). *The Art of Central Banking.* London: Cass.

Henry, Laurin. (1960). *Presidential Transitions.* Washington, DC: Brookings Institution.

Higgs, Robert. (1997). "Regime Uncertainty: Why the Great Depression Lasted So Long and Why Prosperity Resumed After the War." *Independent Review* 1, 561–90.

Hitzik, Michael. (2011). *The New Deal.* New York: Simon & Schuster.

Hodson, H. V. (1932). "Nemesis: the Financial Outcome of the Postwar Years." In Arnold Toynbee (ed.), *Survey of International Affairs, 1931.* London: Oxford University Press, 161–242.

House of Commons Treasury Committee. (2008). "The Run on the Rock." Fifth Report of Session 2007–8, Vol. 1, HC56–1 (January 26).

Howson, Susan. (1975). *Domestic Monetary Management in Britain, 1919–38.* Cambridge: Cambridge University Press.

Howson, Susan. (1980). "Sterling's Managed Float: The Operations of the Exchange Equalisation Account, 1932–39." *Princeton Studies in International Finance* no. 46, International Finance Section, Department of Economics, Princeton University (November).

Hyman, Sidney. (1976). *Marriner S. Eccles: Private Entrepreneur and Public Servant.* Stanford: Stanford University Graduate School of Business Press.

Ide, Eisaku. (2003). "Policy Debates on Public Finance Between the Ministry of Finance and the Bank of Japan from 1930 to 1936." *Monetary and Economic Studies.* Tokyo: Bank of Japan (December), 87–104.

International Monetary Fund. (2006). "Ireland: Financial System Stability Assessment Update." IMF Country Report no. 06/292 (August).

International Monetary Fund. (2010). "Will It Hurt? Macroeconomic Effects of Fiscal Consolidation." *World Economic Outlook* (October), 93–124.

International Monetary Fund. (2012). "United Kingdom: 2012 Article IV Consultation." IMF Country Report no. 12/190. Washington, DC: IMF (July).

International Monetary Fund. (2013a). "United States: 2013 Article IV Consultation." IMF Country Report no. 13/236. Washington, DC: IMF (July).

International Monetary Fund. (2013b). "Greece: Ex Post Evaluation of Exceptional Access Under the 2010 Stand-By Arrangement." IMF Country Report no. 13/156 (June).

International Swaps and Derivatives Association. (2010). "ISDA Market Survey." New York: ISDA, http://www.ISDA.org/statistics/pdf/ISDA-Market-Survey-annual-data.pdf.

Irwin, Douglas. (2011). *Peddling Protectionism: Smoot-Hawley and the Great Depression.* Princeton: Princeton University Press.

Irwin, Douglas. (2012). "Gold Sterilization and the Recession of 1937–38." *Financial History Review* 19, 249–67.

Irwin, Neil. (2013). *The Alchemists: Three Central Bankers and a World on Fire.* New York: Penguin Press.

Jacobson, Elizabeth. (2009). "I Have a Dream House." *Harper's Magazine* (September), 21–24.

Jackson, Julian. (1985). *The Politics of Depression in France 1932–1936.* Cambridge: Cambridge University Press.

Jalil, Andrew. (2012). "Monetary Intervention Really Did Mitigate Banking Panics During the Great Depression: Evidence Along the Atlanta Federal Reserve District Border." Unpublished manuscript, Occidental College (July).

Jones, Erik. (2002). *The Politics of Economic and Monetary Union: Integration and Idiosyncrasy.* New York: Rowman and Littlefield.

Jones, Jesse. (1951). *Fifty Billion Dollars: My Thirteen Years with the RFC (1932–1945).* New York: Macmillan.

Jónsson, Asgeir. (2009). *Why Iceland? How One of the World's Smallest Countries Became the Meltdown's Biggest Casualty.* New York: McGraw-Hill.

JPMorgan Chase. (2009). "Letter to Shareholders." New York: JPMorgan Chase (March 23), http://files.shareholder.com/downloads/ONE/3173954532x0x36244 0/1ce6e503-25c6-4b7b-8c2e-8cb1df167411/2009AR_Letter_to_shareholders.pdf.

Kacperczyk, Marcin, and Philipp Schnabl. (2010). "When Safe Proved Risky: Commercial Paper During the Financial Crisis of 2007–2009." *Journal of Economic Perspectives* 24, 29–50.

Kaiser, Robert. (2013). *Act of Congress: How America's Essential Institution Works, and How It Doesn't.* New York: Knopf.

Kalemli-Ozcan, Sebnem, Bent Sorensen, and Sevcan Yesiltas. (2012). "Leverage Across Firms, Banks and Countries." *Journal of International Economics* 88, 284–98.

Katznelson, Ira. (2013). *Fear Itself: The New Deal and the Origins of Our Time.* New York: Liveright.

Kaufman, Ted. (2013). "Happy Birthday to Dodd-Frank, a Law That Isn't Working." *Wilmington News Journal* (July 20), http://www.delawareonline.com/article/ 20130721/OPINION1805/307210017/Ted-Kaufman-Happy-birthday-Dodd-Frank-law-isn-t-working.

Keeton, William. (1990). "Small and Large Bank Views of Deposit Insurance: Today vs. the 1930s." *Federal Reserve Bank of Kansas City Economic Review* 75 (September–October), 23–35.

Keiger, J.F.V. (1997). *Raymond Poincaré.* New York: Cambridge University Press.

Kenen, Peter. (1969). "The Theory of Optimum Currency Areas: An Eclectic View." In Robert Mundell and Alexander Swoboda (eds.), *Monetary Problems of the International Economy*. Chicago: University of Chicago Press, 41–60.

Kennedy, David. (1999). *Freedom from Fear: The American People in Depression and War, 1929–1945*. New York: Oxford University Press.

Kennedy, Susan Eastabrook. (1973). *The Banking Crisis of 1933*. Lexington: University Press of Kentucky.

Keynes, John Maynard. (1919). *The Economic Consequences of the Peace*. London: Macmillan.

Keynes, John Maynard. (1923). *A Tract on Monetary Reform*. London: Macmillan.

Keynes, John Maynard. (1929). "The German Transfer Problem." *Economic Journal* 39, 1–7.

Keynes, John Maynard. (1936). *The General Theory of Employment, Interest and Money*. London: Macmillan.

Kindleberger, Charles. (1989). "Commercial Policy Between the Wars." In Peter Matthias and Sydney Pollard (eds.), *The Cambridge Economic History of Europe VIII: The Industrial Economies: The Development of Economic and Social Policies*. Cambridge: Cambridge University Press, 161–196.

Klein, Maury. (2001). *Rainbow's End: The Crash of 1929*. New York: Oxford University Press.

Kohn, Donald. (2009). "Monetary Policy and Asset Prices Revisited." *Cato Journal* 29, 31–44.

Kotlikoff, Laurence. (2010). *Jimmy Stewart Is Dead: Ending the World's Ongoing Financial Plague with Limited Purpose Banking*. New York: Wiley.

Krippner, Leo. (2012). "Yield Curve Modeling and Monetary Policy in Zero Lower Bound Environments." Unpublished manuscript, Reserve Bank of New Zealand (October).

Krishnamurthy, Arvind, and Annette Vissing-Jorgensen. (2011). "The Effects of Quantitative Easing on Interest Rates: Channels and Implications for Policy." *Brookings Papers on Economic Activity* (Fall), 215–65.

Kuttner, Robert. (2013). *Debtor's Prison: The Politics of Austerity Versus Possibility*. New York: Knopf.

Lacker, Jeffrey. (2013). "Economic Outlook, May 2013." Speech to the Risk Management Association, Richmond Chapter, Richmond, VA (May 3), http://www.richmondfed.org/press_room/speeches/president_jeff_lacker/2013/lacker_speech_20130503.cfm.

Lacouture, Jean. (1982). *Léon Blum*. Teaneck, NJ: Holmes & Meier.

Laeven, Luc, and Fabian Valencia. (2012). "Resolution of Banking Crises: The Good, the Bad, and the Ugly." Unpublished manuscript, IMF (August), http://www.imf.org/external/np/seminars/eng/2012/fincrises/pdf/ch13.pdf.

Lane, Philip, and Barbara Pels. (2012). "Current Account Imbalances in Europe." CEPR Discussion Paper 8958 (May).

Leuchtenburg, William (ed.). (1968). *The New Deal: A Documentary History*. Columbia: University of South Carolina Press.

Lewis, Cleona. (1938). *America's Stake in Foreign Investments*. Washington, DC: Brookings Institution.

Lewis, Michael. (2009). "Wall Street on the Tundra." *Vanity Fair* (April), Issue 584, 140–77.

Lewis, Michael. (2010). *The Big Short: Inside the Doomsday Machine*. New York: Norton.

Lloyd George, David. (1932). *The Truth About Reparations and War Debts*. London: William Heinemann.

Lumley, Darwyn. (2009). *Breaking the Banks in Motor City: The Auto Industry, the 1933 Detroit Banking Crisis and the Start of the New Deal*. Jefferson, NC: McFarland.

Lyons, Tom, and Brian Carey. (2011). *The FitzPatrick Tapes: The Rise and Fall of One Man, One Bank and One Country*. Dublin: Penguin Ireland.

Manley, P. S. (1976). "Clarence Hatry." *Abacus* 12, 49–60.

Marchand, David. (1991). "The Corporation Nobody Knew: Bruce Barton, Alfred Sloan, and the Founding of the General Motors 'Family.'" *Business History Review* 65, 825–75.

Mayer, Gerald. (2004). "Union Membership Trends in the United States." Congressional Research Service Federal Publication no. 8-31-2004. Washington, DC: Congressional Research Service (August).

McBeth, Brian. (1983). *Juan Vicente Gómez and the Oil Companies in Venezuela, 1908–1935*. Cambridge: Cambridge University Press.

McCabe, Patrick. (2010). "The Cross Section of Money Market Fund Risks and Financial Crises." Finance and Economics Discussion Series no. 2010–51. Washington, DC: Board of Governors of the Federal Reserve System (September).

McCabe, Patrick, Marco Piriani, Michael Holscher, and Antoine Martin. (2012). "The Minimum Balance at Risk: A Proposal to Mitigate the Systemic Risks Posed by Money Market Funds." Staff Report no. 564. New York: Federal Reserve Bank of New York (July).

McFerrin, John. (1969). *Caldwell and Company: A Southern Financial Empire*. Nashville: Vanderbilt University Press.

MacDonald, Lawrence, and Patrick Robinson. (2009). *A Colossal Failure of Common Sense: The Inside Story of the Collapse of Lehman Brothers*. New York: Crown Business.

McKay, David. (1996). *Rush to Union: Understanding the European Federal Bargain*. Oxford: Clarendon Press.

McKenney, Ruth. (1939). *Industrial Valley*. New York: Harcourt, Brace.

McLean, Bethany, and Joe Nocera. (2010). *All the Devils Are Here: The Hidden History of the Financial Crisis*. New York: Portfolio.

Meltzer, Allan. (2003). *A History of the Federal Reserve, Volume 1: 1913–1951*. Chicago: University of Chicago Press.

Merrick, George. (1920). *Song of the Wind on a Southern Shore and Other Poems of Florida*. Boston: Four Seas.

Mian, Atif, and Amir Sufi. (2009). "The Consequences of Mortgage Credit Expansion: Evidence from the U.S. Mortgage Default Crisis." *Quarterly Journal of Economics* 124, 1449–96.

Miller, A. C. (1935). "Responsibility for Federal Reserve Policies 1927–29." *American Economic Review* 25, 442–57.

Mills, Ogden. (1936). *Liberalism Fights On.* New York: Macmillan.

Miron, Jeffrey, and Christina Romer. (1990). "A New Monthly Index of Industrial Production, 1884–1940." *Journal of Economic History* 50, 321–37.

Mitchener, Kris, and Kirsten Wandschneider. (2013). "Capital Controls and Recovery from the Financial Crisis of the 1930s." CAGE Working Paper no. 132, Department of Economics, University of Warwick (June).

Moggridge, Donald. (1969). *The Return to Gold, 1925: The Formulation of Economic Policy and Its Critics.* Cambridge: Cambridge University Press.

Moley, Raymond. (1939). *After Seven Years.* New York: Harper & Brothers.

Moley, Raymond. (1966). *The First New Deal.* New York: Harcourt, Brace & World.

Mommsen, Hans, and Elborg Forster. (1998). *The Rise and Fall of Weimar Democracy.* Chapel Hill: University of North Carolina Press.

Moreau, Emile. (1991). *The Golden Franc: Memoirs of a Governor of the Bank of France: The Stabilization of the Franc, 1926–1928.* Translated by Stephen D. Stoller and Trevor C. Roberts. Boulder: Westview Press.

Morgenson, Gretchen. (2007). "Inside the Countrywide Lending Spree." *New York Times* (August 26), Section 3, p. 1.

Morgenson, Gretchen. (2008). "Behind Insurer's Crisis, Blind Eye to a Web of Risk." *New York Times* (September 28), A1.

Morgenson, Gretchen, and Joshua Rosner. (2011). *Reckless Endangerment: How Outsized Ambition, Greed and Corruption Led to Economic Armageddon.* New York: Times Books.

Morrison, James. (2013). "Shocking Intellectual Austerity: The Role of Ideas in the Demise of the Gold Standard in Britain." Unpublished manuscript, Politics Department, Princeton University (March).

Mouré, Kenneth. (1991). *Managing the Franc Poincaré: Economic Understanding and Political Constraint in French Monetary Policy, 1928–1938.* Cambridge: Cambridge University Press.

Mouré, Kenneth. (2002). "The Bank of France and the Gold Standard." In Marc Flandreau, Carl-Ludwig Holtfrerich, and Harold James (eds.), *International Financial History in the Twentieth Century: System and Anarchy.* Cambridge: Cambridge University Press, pp. 98–124.

Mullaly, Erin. (2009). "Lusitania's Secret Cargo." *Archaeology* 62 (January/February), http://archive.archaeology.org/0901/trenches/lusitania.html.

Murray, Shailagh, and Paul Kane. (2009). "Congress Passes Stimulus Package." *Washington Post* (February 14), http://www.washingtonpost.com/wp-dyn/content/article/2009/02/13/AR2009021301596.html?sid=ST2009021302017.

Nadler, Marcus, and Jules Bogen. (1933). *The Banking Crisis: The End of an Epoch.* New York: Dodd, Mead.

Nanto, Dick, and Shinji Takagi. (1985). "Korekiyo Takahashi and Japan's Recovery from the Great Depression." *American Economic Association Papers and Proceedings* 75, 369–74.

Nichols, Jeanette. (1951). "Roosevelt's Monetary Diplomacy in 1933." *American Historical Review* 56, 295–317.

Norris, George. (1937). *Ended Episodes.* Philadelphia: Winston.

Nurkse, Ragnar. (1944). *International Currency Experience.* Geneva: League of Nations.

O'Brien, Anthony Patrick. (1992). "The Failure of the Bank of United States: A Defense of Joseph Lucia." *Journal of Money, Credit and Banking* 24, 374–84.

Obstfeld, Maurice, and Kenneth Rogoff. (2010). "Global Imbalances and the Financial Crisis: Products of Common Causes." In Reuven Glick and Mark Spiegel (eds.), *Asia and the Global Financial Crisis.* San Francisco: Federal Reserve Bank of San Francisco, 131–72.

Office for Budget Responsibility. (2013). *Forecast Evaluation Report.* London: Stationery Office.

Ohlin, Bertil. (1929). "The Reparation Problem: A Discussion." *Economic Journal* 39, 172–82.

Oliver, Willard, and Nancy Marion. (2010). *Killing the President: Assassinations, Attempts and Rumored Attempts on U.S. Commanders-in-Chief.* Santa Barbara, CA: ABC-Clio LLC.

Oliver Wyman Group. (2012). "Asset Quality Review and Bottom-Up Stress Test Exercise." (28 September). Madrid: Oliver Wyman.

Olson, James Stuart. (1977). *Herbert Hoover and the Reconstruction Finance Corporation, 1931–1933.* Ames: Iowa State University Press.

Orde, Anne. (1980). "The Origins of the German-Austrian Customs Union Affair of 1931." *Central European History* 13, 34–59.

Osborne, George. (2010). "A New Economic Model." In Forrest Capie and Geoffrey Wood (eds.), *Policy Makers on Policy: The Mais Lectures.* Oxon, UK: Routledge, 209–20.

Park, Haelim, and Patrick Van Horn. (2013). "Did the Reserve Requirement Increases of 1936–1937 Reduce Bank Lending? Evidence from a Natural Experiment." Unpublished manuscript, U.S. Department of Treasury and Southwestern University (September).

Parks, Arva Moore. (2006). *George Merrick's Coral Gables.* Miami: Ponce Circle Development.

Partnoy, Frank. (2009). *The Match King.* New York: Public Affairs Books.

Paul, Ron. (2012). "A Fistful of Euros." *Texas Straight Talk,* http://paul.house.gov/index.php?option=com_content&task=view&id=1957&Itemid=69, accessed April 2, 2013.

Paulson, Henry. (2010). *On the Brink: Inside the Race to Stop the Collapse of the Global Financial System.* New York: Business Plus.

Peppers, Larry. (1973). "Full Employment Surplus Analysis and Structural Change: The 1930s." *Explorations in Economic History* 10, 197–210.

Peristiani, Stavros. (1997). "Do Mergers Improve the X-Efficiency and Scale Efficiency of U.S. Banks? Evidence from the 1980s." *Journal of Money, Credit and Banking* 29, 326–37.

Pescatori, Andrea, Damiano Sandri, and John Simon. (2014). "Debt and Growth: Is There a Magic Threshold?" IMF Working Paper no. WP14/34 (February).

Philippon, Thomas. (2008). "The Evolution of the Financial Industry from 1860 to the Present: Theory and Evidence." Unpublished manuscript, New York University (November).

Piketty, Thomas. (2014). *Capital in the Twenty-First Century.* Cambridge: Belknap Press.

Pilloff, Steven. (1996). "Performance Changes and Shareholder Wealth Creation Associated with Mergers of Publicly Traded Banking Institutions." *Journal of Money, Credit and Banking* 28, 294–310.

Polanyi, Karl. (1944). *The Great Transformation.* New York: Farrar & Rinehart.

Pontzen, Martin. (2009). "Banking Crisis in Germany and the First Step Towards Recovery." Paper presented to Fourth Conference of the Southeast Europe Monetary History Network, Belgrade (March 27).

Provopoulos, George. (2012). "Timely Greek Lessons on the Eurozone Crisis." *Financial Times* (January 23), http://www.ft.com/intl/cms/s/0/1930489c-45c2-11e1-93f1-00144feabdco.html#axzz31u5JbE5H.

Pusey, Merlo. (1951). *Charles Evans Hughes.* New York: Macmillan.

Pusey, Merlo. (1974). *Eugene Meyer.* New York: Knopf.

Ranciere, Romain, and Aaron Tornell. (2009). "Systemic Risk Taking and the U.S. Financial Crisis." Unpublished manuscript, International Monetary Fund and UCLA (September).

Rattner, Steven. (2010). *Overhaul: An Insider's Account of the Obama Administration's Emergency Rescue of the Auto Industry.* New York: Houghton Mifflin Harcourt.

Redford, Polly. (1970). *Billion-Dollar Sandbar.* New York: Dutton.

Rehn, Olli. (2012). "Europe Must Stay the Austerity Course." *Financial Times* (December 10), http://www.ft.com/intl/cms/s/0/35b77c12-42d6-11e2-a3d2-00144feabdco.html#axzz31u5JbE5H.

Reinhart, Carmen, and Kenneth Rogoff. (2009a). *This Time Is Different: Eight Centuries of Financial Folly.* Princeton: Princeton University Press.

Reinhart, Carmen, and Kenneth Rogoff. (2009b). "The Aftermath of Financial Crises." *American Economic Association Papers and Proceedings* 99, 466–72.

Reinhart, Carmen, and Kenneth Rogoff. (2014). "Recovery from Financial Crises: Evidence from 100 Episodes." NBER Working Paper no. 19823 (January).

Reserve Bank of New Zealand. (2013). *Financial Stability Report.* Wellington: Reserve Bank of New Zealand (November).

Reuters. (2007). "Treasury's Paulson—Subprime Woes Likely Contained." Reuters (April 20), http://uk.reuters.com/article/2007/04/20/usa-subprime-paulson-idUKWBT00686520070420.

Reuters. (2012). "JPMorgan Chase's Bear Stearns Buy Lost Bank $10 Billion, CEO Jamie Dimon Says." Reuters (October 10), http://www.huffingtonpost.com/2012/10/10/jpmorgan-chase-bear-stearns-buy_n_1955285.html.

Rhodes, Stephen. (1994). "A Summary of Merger Performance Studies in Banking, 1980–1993." *Staff Studies* 167. Washington, DC: Federal Reserve Board (July).

Rhodes, William. (2011). *Banker to the World: Leadership Lessons from the Front Lines of Global Finance.* New York: McGraw-Hill.

Richardson, Gary, and William Troost. (2009). "Monetary Intervention Mitigated Banking Panics During the Great Depression: Quasi-Experimental Evidence from the Federal Reserve District Border in Mississippi, 1929 to 1933." *Journal of Political Economy* 117, 1031–73.

Ridley, Matt. (1993). *The Red Queen: Sex and the Evolution of Human Nature.* New York: Harper Perennial.

Ritschl, Albrecht. (2000). "Deficit Spending in the Nazi Recovery, 1933–1938: A Critical Reassessment." Working Paper no. 68, Institute for Empirical Research in Economics, University of Zurich (December).

Ritschl, Albrecht. (2013). "Reparations, Deficits and Debt Default: The Great Depression in Germany." In Nicholas Crafts and Peter Fearon (eds.), *The Great Depression of the 1930s: Lessons for Today.* Oxford: Oxford University Press, 110–39.

Robb, Greg. (2013). "Fed's Fisher Sharpens Attack on QE: Central Bank May Be 'Pushing on a String.'" *MarketWatch* (June 4), http://www.marketwatch.com/story/feds-fisher-sharpens-attack-on-qe-2013-06-04.

Rock, William. (1969). *Neville Chamberlain.* New York: Twayne.

Rogers, Will. (1925). "Carl Took Florida from the Alligators and Gave It to the Indianians." In James Smallwood and Steven Graegert (eds.), *Will Rogers' Weekly Letters, Vol. 2: The Coolidge Years 1925–1927.* Stillwater: Oklahoma State University Press, 86–89, http://www.willrogers.com/papers/weekly/WA-Vol-2.pdf.

Romer, Christina. (1992). "What Ended the Great Depression?" *Journal of Economic History* 52, 757–84.

Romer, Christina. (2009a). "Lessons from the Great Depression for Economic Recovery in 2009." Presented at the Brookings Institution, Washington, DC (March 9), http://www.brookings.edu/~/media/events/2009/3/09%20lessons/0309_lessons_romer.pdf.

Romer, Christina. (2009b). "The Lessons of 1937." *The Economist* (June 18), http://www.economist.com/node/13856176.

Roose, Kenneth. (1954). *The Economics of Recession and Revival.* New Haven: Yale University Press.

Rose, Jonathan. (2011). "The Incredible HOLC? Mortgage Relief During the Great Depression." *Journal of Money, Credit and Banking* 43, 1073–1107.

Rose, Jonathan, and Kenneth Snowden. (2013). "The New Deal and the Origins of the Modern American Real Estate Loan Contract." *Explorations in Economic History* 50, 548–66.

Roselli, Alessandro. (2006). *Italy and Albania: Financial Relations in the Fascist Period*. London: Tauris.

Rowley, William. (1969). "M. L. Wilson: 'Believer' in the Domestic Allotment." *Agricultural History* 43, 277–88.

Royal Institute of International Affairs. (1931). *The International Gold Problem*. London: Royal Institute of International Affairs.

Saez, Emmanuel. (2013). "Striking It Richer: The Evolution of Top Incomes in the United States (Updated with 2012 Estimates)." Unpublished manuscript, University of California, Berkeley (September 3), http://elsa.berkeley.edu/~saez/saez-UStopincomes-2012.pdf.

Sahm, Claudia, Matthew Shapiro, and Joel Slemrod. (2009). "Household Response to the 2008 Tax Rebate: Survey Evidence and Aggregate Implications." NBER Working Paper no. 15421 (October).

Sargent, Thomas, and Neil Wallace. (1981). "Some Unpleasant Monetarist Arithmetic." *Federal Reserve Bank of Minneapolis Quarterly Review* 5 (Fall), 1–17.

Saurina, Jesus. (2009). "Dynamic Provisioning: The Experience of Spain," Note no. 7, Financial and Private Sector Development Vice Presidency. Washington, DC: World Bank (July).

Schacht, Hjalmar. (1955). *My First Seventy-Six Years: The Autobiography of Hjalmar Schacht*. Translated by Diana Pyke. London: Allan Wingate.

Scheiber, Noam. (2011). *The Escape Artists: How Obama's Team Fumbled the Recovery*. New York: Simon & Schuster.

Schifferes, Steve. (2009). "Lesson for G20 from 1933 London Summit." *BBC News* (March 23), http://news.bbc.co.uk/2/hi/business/7954532.stm.

Schubert, Aurel. (1991). *The Credit-Anstalt Crisis of 1931*. Cambridge: Cambridge University Press.

Schwartz, Anna. (1997). "From Obscurity to Notoriety: A Biography of the Exchange Stabilization Fund." *Journal of Money, Credit and Banking* 29, 135–53.

Seligman, Joel. (1982). *The Transformation of Wall Street: A History of the Securities and Exchange Commission and Modern Corporate Finance*. Boston: Houghton Mifflin.

Sessa, Frank. (1961). "Anti-Florida Propaganda and Counter Measures During the 1920s." *Tequesta* 21, 41–51.

Shamir, Haim. (1989). *Economic Crisis and French Foreign Policy, 1930–1946*. Leiden and New York: Brill Academic.

Shapsmeier, Edward, and Frederick Shapsmeier. (1968). *Henry A. Wallace of Iowa: The Agrarian Years 1910–1940*. Ames: Iowa State University Press.

Shelp, Ronald, and Al Ehrbar. (2006). *Fallen Giant: The Amazing Story of Hank Greenberg and the History of AIG*. Hoboken, NJ: Wiley.

Shifrin, Matt. (2008). "Hell Bent Innovator." *Forbes* (September 22), http://www.forbes.com/2008/09/22/reserve-primary-bent-pf-ii-in_ms_0922money_inl.html.

Shiller, Robert. (2006). *Irrational Exuberance*, 2nd ed. Princeton: Princeton University Press.

Shima, Kinzo. (1983). "Iwayuru Takagashi Zaisei Nitsuite." *Kinyu Kenkyo* 2, 83–194 [in Japanese].

Shin, Hyun Song. (2012). "Global Banking Glut and Loan Risk Premium." Unpublished manuscript, Princeton University (January).

Silber, William. (2009). "Why Did FDR's Bank Holiday Succeed?" *Economic Policy Review* 15, Federal Reserve Bank of New York, 19–30.

Simpson, Herbert. (1933). "Real Estate Speculation and the Depression." *American Economic Review* 23, 163–71.

Sinai, Allen, Peter Orszag, and Robert Rubin. (2004). "Sustained Budget Deficits: Longer-Run U.S. Economic Performance and the Risk of Financial and Fiscal Disarray." Paper presented to an AEA-NAEFA Joint Session, Allied Social Science Associations Annual Meetings (January 5), http://www.brookings.edu/research/papers/2004/01/05budgetdeficit-orszag.

Sirletti, Sonia. (2011). "Greek Debt Restructuring Would Jeopardize Rest of Europe, Bini Smaghi Says." *Bloomberg News* (May 18), http://www.bloomberg.com/news/2011-05-18/greek-debt-restructuring-would-jeopardize-rest-of-europe-bini-smaghi-says.html.

Slack, Donovan. (2010). "Donations Poured in as Brown's Role Grew." *Boston Globe* (December 12), http://www.boston.com/news/nation/articles/2010/12/12/banks_donations_soared_as_brown_negotiated/?page=full.

Smethurst, Richard. (2007). *From Foot Soldier to Finance Minister: Takahashi Korekiyo, Japan's Keynes*. Cambridge, MA: Harvard University Press for the Harvard University Asia Center.

Smith, H. D. (1916). "Recent Domestic Architecture from the Designs of John Russell Pope." *The Brickbuilder* 25, 189–201.

Snowden, Kenneth, and Joshua James. (2001). "The Federalization of Building & Loans, 1927–1940: The North Carolina Experience." Unpublished manuscript, University of North Carolina, Greensboro.

Sorkin, Andrew Ross. (2012). "Reinstating an Old Rule Is Not a Cure for Crisis." *Deal Book, New York Times* (May 21), http://dealbook.nytimes.com/2012/05/21/reinstating-an-old-rule-is-not-a-cure-for-crisis/.

Stafford, David. (1999). *Roosevelt and Churchill: Men of Secrets*. Woodstock and New York: Overlook Press.

Stephens, H. Morse. (1916). "Nationality and History." *American Historical Review* 21, 225–36.

Stock, James, and Mark Watson. (2003). "Has the Business Cycle Changed? Evidence and Explanations." In Federal Reserve Bank of Kansas City, *Monetary Policy and Uncertainty*. Kansas City: Federal Reserve Bank of Kansas City, 9–56.

Story, Louise, Landon Thomas, and Nelson Schwartz. (2010). "Wall St. Helped to Mask Debt Fueling Europe's Crisis." *New York Times* (February 13), http://www.nytimes.com/2010/02/14/business/global/14debt.html?pagewanted=1&_r=0&sq=greece&st=cse&scp=2.

Straumann, Tobias, and Ulrich Woitek. (2009). "A Pioneer in Monetary Policy? Sweden's Price Level Targeting of the 1930s Revisited." *European Review of Economic History* 13, 251–81.

Suarez, Sandra, and Robin Kolodny. (2011). "Paving the Road to 'Too Big to Fail': Business Interests and the Politics of Financial Deregulation in the U.S." *Politics & Society* 39, 74–102.

Sullivan, Lawrence. (1936). *Prelude to Panic: The Story of the Bank Holiday.* Washington, DC: Statesman Press.

Sumner, Scott. (1990). "Price-Level Stability, Price Flexibility, and Fisher's Business Cycle Model." *Cato Journal* 9, 719–27.

Suskind, Ron. (2011). *Confidence Men: Wall Street, Washington, and the Education of a President.* New York: Harper.

Swagel, Phillip. (2009). "The Financial Crisis: An Inside View." *Brookings Papers on Economic Activity* (Spring), 1–63.

Szász, André. (1999). *The Road to European Monetary Union.* London: Macmillan.

Tabbi, Matt. (2013). "The Last Mystery of the Financial Crisis." *Rolling Stone* (June 19), http://www.rollingstone.com/politics/news/the-last-mystery-of-the-financial-crisis-20130619.

Taylor, John. (2007). "Housing and Monetary Policy." In *Proceedings: Housing, Housing Finance and Monetary Policy.* Kansas City: Federal Reserve Bank of Kansas City, 463–76.

Taylor, Paul. (2013). "Troika Has a Patchy Record on Bailouts." *New York Times* (June 10), http://www.nytimes.com/2013/06/11/business/global/troika-has-a-patchy-record-on-bailouts.html?_r=0.

Teichova, Alice. (1994). "Austria." In Manfred Pohl (ed.), *Handbook on the History of European Banks.* Cheltenham: Edward Elgar, 3–46.

Temin, Peter. (1976). *Did Monetary Forces Cause the Great Depression?* New York: Norton.

Temin, Peter, and Barrie Wigmore. (1990). "The End of One Big Deflation." *Explorations in Economic History* 27, 483–502.

Tett, Gillian. (2009). *Fool's Gold: How the Bold Dream of a Small Tribe at J.P. Morgan Was Corrupted by Wall Street Greed and Unleashed a Catastrophe.* New York: Free Press.

Thomas, Brinley. (1937). *Monetary Policy and Crises: A Study of Swedish Experience.* London: George Routledge and Sons.

Thomas, Landon, and Stephen Castle. (2011). "The Denials That Trapped Greece." *New York Times* (November 5), http://www.nytimes.com/2011/11/06/business/global/europes-two-years-of-denials-trapped-greece.html?pagewanted=all.

Thorndike, Joseph. (2008). "FDR's Unlikely Prescription: Tax Hikes for Recovery." *Tax History Project* (December 4), http://www.taxhistory.org/thp/readings.nsf/Art Web/13F0B2FC36593DC28525751A004A3EDC?OpenDocument.

Timberlake, Richard. (2005). "Gold Standards and the Real Bills Doctrine in U.S. Monetary Policy." *Economic Journal Watch* 2, 196–233.

Timberlake, Richard. (2008). "The Federal Reserve's Role in the Great Contraction and the Subprime Crisis." *Cato Journal* 28, 303–12.

Timmons, Bascom. (1953). *Portrait of an American: Charles G. Dawes.* New York: Henry Holt.

Trescott, Paul. (1992). "The Failure of the Bank of United States, 1930: A Rejoinder to Anthony Patrick O'Brien." *Journal of Money, Credit and Banking* 24, 384–99.

U.S. Department of Justice. (2013). "Complaint for Civil Money Penalties: United States of America, Plaintiff v. McGraw-Hill Companies, Inc., and Standard & Poor's Financial Services LLC" (February 4), http://www.justice.gov/iso/opa/resources/849201325104924250796.PDF.

U.S. District Court, Southern District of New York. (2010). "Securities and Exchange Commission, Plaintiff, v. Goldman Sachs & Co. and Fabrice Tourre, Defendants," April 16, http://www.sec.gov/litigation/complaints/2010/comp21489.pdf.

U.S. House of Representatives. (1928). "Stabilization." Hearings before the Committee on Banking and Currency, House of Representatives, Seventieth Congress, First Session on H.R. 11806, http://www.scribd.com/doc/175280593/housta28.

U.S. House of Representatives. (2009). "Friends of Angelo: Countrywide's Systematic and Successful Effort to Buy Influence and Block Reform." Staff Report, 111th Congress, Committee on Oversight and Government Reform (March 19), http://oversight.house.gov/wp-content/uploads/2012/02/20090319FriendsofAngelo.pdf.

U.S. Senate, Permanent Subcommittee on Investigations. (2013). "JPMorgan Chase Whale Trades: A Case History of Derivatives Risks and Abuses." Washington, DC: Permanent Subcommittee on Investigations (March 15).

Urban, Scott. (2009). "The Name of the Rose: Classifying 1930s Exchange-Rate Regimes." Discussion Paper in Economic and Social History no. 76, University of Oxford (April).

Vander Weyer, Martin. (2011). *Fortune's Spear: The Story of the Blue-Blooded Rogue Behind the Most Notorious City Scandal of the 1920s.* London: Elliot and Thompson.

Van Riet, Ad, ed. (2010). "Euro Area Fiscal Policies and the Crisis." Occasional Paper no. 109. Frankfurt: European Central Bank (April).

Vickers, Raymond. (1994). *Panic in Paradise: Florida's Banking Crash of 1926.* Tuscaloosa and London: University of Alabama Press.

Vickers, Raymond. (2011). *Panic in the Loop: Chicago's Banking Crisis of 1932.* New York: Lexington Books.

Wall Street Journal. (2008). "Excerpts: Iceland's Oddsson: 'We Do Not Intend to Pay the Debts of Banks That Have Been a Little Heedless.'" *Wall Street Journal Online* (October 17), http://online.wsj.com/article/SB122418335729241577.html.

Waller, Douglas. (2011). *Wild Bill Donovan: The Spymaster Who Created the OSS and Modern American Espionage.* New York: Free Press.

Warburg, James. (1964). *The Long Road Home: The Autobiography of a Maverick.* New York: Doubleday.

Warner, Geoffrey. (1968). *Pierre Laval and the Eclipse of France 1931–1945.* London: Eyre & Spottiswoode.

Warner, Jeremy. (2013). "Oh God—I Cannot Take Any More of the Austerity Debate." *Daily Telegraph* (September 11), http://blogs.telegraph.co.uk/finance/jeremywarner/100025496/oh-god-i-cannot-take-any-more-of-the-austerity-debate/.

Warren, Donald. (1996). *Radio Priest: Charles Coughlin, the Father of Hate Radio.* New York: Free Press.

Webb, Steven. (1988). "Latin American Debt Today and German Reparations After World War I—A Comparison." *Weltwirtschaftliches Archiv* 124, 745–74.

Weber, Bruce. (2008). "Harry B. R. Brown, Who Opened Money Markets to Masses, Dies at 82." *New York Times* (August 15), B5.

Wecter, Dixon. (1948). *The Age of the Great Depression, 1929–1941.* New York: Macmillan.

Weill, Sandy, and Judah Kraushaar. (2006). *The Real Deal: My Life in Business and Philanthropy.* New York: Warner Business Books.

Weinstein, Michael. (1980). *Recovery and Redistribution Under the NIRA.* Amsterdam: North Holland.

Wells, Donald. (2004). *The Federal Reserve System: A History.* New York: McFarland.

Wells, H. G. (1933). *The Shape of Things to Come.* New York: Macmillan.

Wessel, David. (2009). *In Fed We Trust: Ben Bernanke's War on the Great Panic.* New York: Crown Business.

White, Eugene, ed. (1990a). *Crashes and Panics: The Lessons from History.* New York: Dow Jones Irwin.

White, Eugene. (1990b). "When the Ticker Ran Late: The Stock Market Boom and Crash of 1929." In Eugene White (ed.), *Crashes and Panics: The Lessons from History.* New York: Dow Jones Irwin, 143–87.

White, Eugene. (2013). "Lessons from the Great American Real Estate Boom of the 1920s." Unpublished manuscript, Rutgers University.

Wicker, Elmus. (1966). *Federal Reserve Monetary Policy 1917–1933.* New York: Random House.

Wicker, Elmus. (1996). *The Banking Panics of the Great Depression.* Cambridge: Cambridge University Press.

Wilmarth, Arthur. (2002). "The Transformation of the U.S. Financial Services Industry, 1975–2000: Competition, Consolidation and Increased Risks." *University of Illinois Law Review* 2002, 215–476.

Winch, Donald. (1969). *Economics and Policy: A Historical Study.* New York: Walker.

Winkler, Max. (1933). *Foreign Bonds: An Autopsy.* Philadelphia: Roland Swain.

Wolf, Nikolaus, and Albrecht Ritschl. (2011). "Endogeneity of Currency Areas and Trade Blocs: Evidence from a Natural Experiment." *Kyklos* 64, 291–312.

Wright, Gordon. (1942). *Raymond Poincaré and the French Presidency.* Stanford, CA: Stanford University Press.

Wu, Jing, and Fan Xia. (2013). "Measuring the Macroeconomic Impact of Monetary Policy at the Zero Lower Bound." Unpublished manuscript, Booth School, University of Chicago and University of California, San Diego (November).

Wueschner, Silvano. (1999). *Charting Twentieth-Century Monetary Policy: Herbert Hoover and Benjamin Strong, 1917–1927*. Westport, CT: Greenwood Press.

Yellen, Janet. (2011). "Unconventional Monetary Policy and Central Bank Communications." Speech at the University of Chicago Booth School of Business U.S. Monetary Policy Forum, New York (February 25).

Zettelmeyer, Jeromin, Christoph Trebesch, and Mitu Gulati. (2013). "The Greek Debt Restructuring: An Autopsy." Peterson Institute Working Paper no. 13–8. Washington, DC: Peterson Institute for International Economics (August).

Zhou, Wanfeng. (2007). "Paulson Urges China to Make Yuan More Flexible." *MarketWatch* (April 20), http://www.marketwatch.com/story/treasurys-paulson-urges-china-to-make-yuan-more-flexible.

Zingales, Luigi. (2009). "Comments on Swagel, 'The Financial Crisis: An Inside View'." *Brookings Papers on Economic Activity* (Spring), 68–75.

Zuckerman, Gregory. (2009). *The Greatest Trade Ever: The Behind-the-Scenes Story of How John Paulson Defied Wall Street and Made Financial History*. New York: Broadway Books.

INDEX